BIG IDEAS MATH®
Geometry

Resources by Chapter

- Family Communication Letters

- Start Thinking and Warm Ups

- Practice A and B

- Enrichment and Extension

- Puzzle Time

- Cumulative Review

Erie, Pennsylvania

Contents

About the Resources by Chapter

Family Communication Letters (English and Spanish)

The Family Communication Letters provide a way to quickly communicate to family members how they can help their student with the material of the chapter. They make the mathematics less intimidating and provide suggestions for helping students see mathematical concepts in common activities.

Start Thinking/Warm Up/Cumulative Review Warm Up

Each Start Thinking/Warm Up/Cumulative Review Warm Up includes two options for getting the class started. The Start Thinking questions provide students with an opportunity to discuss thought-provoking questions and analyze real-world situations. The Warm Up questions review prerequisite skills needed for the lesson. The Cumulative Review Warm Up questions review material from earlier lessons or courses.

Practice

The Extra Practice exercises provide additional practice on the key concepts taught in the lesson. There are two levels of practice provided for each lesson: A (basic) and B (average).

Enrichment and Extension

Each Enrichment and Extension extends the lesson and provides a challenging application of the key concepts.

Puzzle Time

Each Puzzle Time provides additional practice in a fun format in which students use their mathematical knowledge to solve a riddle. This format allows students to self-check their work.

Cumulative Review

The Cumulative Review includes exercises covering concepts and skills from the current chapter and previous chapters.

Chapter 1

Name _____ Date _____

Dear Family,

Have you ever needed to measure angles or find an area or a perimeter in everyday life? Sure, we all have! These are the foundations of geometry. In Chapter 1, your student will be learning how to use these building blocks to solve complex problems in the real world. Whether it's simple home remodeling or a full-fledged career in architecture, geometry is one area of mathematics your student will most certainly use again!

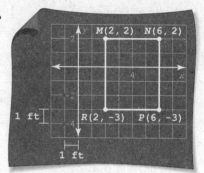

Many careers today require the skills learned in geometry. Contractors work with measurements. Physicists use angles. Architects draw blueprints for houses and buildings. Have you ever discussed with your student what his/her profession might be someday? Now is a great time to start considering how geometry might make them more successful in a future career.

Take some time with your student to talk about what he/she would like to do someday. Record a few ideas, and then spend a few minutes researching how geometry might fit in!

Architect	Architects use measurements, angles, and lengths to draw blueprints.

Discuss the different professions with your student.

- What would be the advantages of good geometry skills for each profession?

- What would be the disadvantages of poor geometry skills for each profession?

Helping your student see the value of learning basic skills of geometry in real life will motivate them to master these concepts with excellence. It may even open up worlds of opportunity for a future career!

Nombre _____ Fecha_____

Capítulo 1 — Nociones básicas de geometría

Estimada familia:

¿Alguna vez han necesitado medir ángulos o hallar un área o un perímetro en la vida cotidiana? ¡Seguro, todos lo hemos necesitado! Estas son las bases de la geometría. En el capítulo 1, su hijo aprenderá cómo usar estos elementos fundamentales para resolver problemas complejos en el mundo real. Ya sea una simple remodelación de una casa o una carrera en arquitectura, ¡la geometría es un área de las matemáticas que sin dudas su hijo volverá a usar!

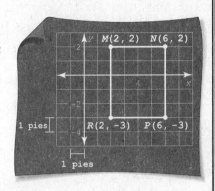

Hoy, muchas carreras exigen las destrezas aprendidas en geometría. Los contratistas trabajan con medidas. Los físicos usan ángulos. Los arquitectos dibujan planos de casas y edificios. ¿Alguna vez han platicado con su hijo cuál podría ser su profesión algún día? Ahora es un momento grandioso para comenzar a considerar cómo la geometría podría hacerlos más exitosos en una futura carrera.

Tómense un tiempo con su hijo para hablar sobre qué le gustaría hacer algún día. ¡Registren algunas ideas y luego dediquen unos minutos a investigar cómo se usaría la geometría!

Arquitecto	Los arquitectos usan medidas, ángulos y longitudes para dibujar planos.

Comenten las diferentes profesiones con su hijo.

- ¿Cuáles serían las ventajas de tener buenas destrezas de geometría para cada profesión?
- ¿Cuáles serían las desventajas de tener malas destrezas de geometría para cada profesión?

Ayudar a su hijo a ver el valor de aprender destrezas básicas de geometría en la vida real lo motivará a dominar estos conceptos con excelencia. ¡Quizás hasta le abra un mundo de oportunidades para una futura carrera!

1.1 Start Thinking

Using dynamic geometry software, connect three lines to make a triangle. Then click and hold on a vertex of the triangle (a vertex is where two lines meet to form a point). Move the vertex left, right, up, and down.

What do you notice about how the angle is changing and how it affects the other angles of the triangle? Explain how this could be useful in explaining why the sum of the angles in any triangle is 180°.

1.1 Warm Up

Name the polygon.

1.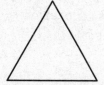

2.

3.

4.

5.

6.

1.1 Cumulative Review Warm Up

Solve for the variable.

1. $\dfrac{25}{8} = \dfrac{200}{b}$

2. $\dfrac{8}{20} = \dfrac{a}{65}$

3. $\dfrac{48}{72} = \dfrac{c}{156}$

4. $\dfrac{3}{36} = \dfrac{p}{60}$

5. $\dfrac{30}{23} = \dfrac{120}{c}$

6. $\dfrac{11}{15} = \dfrac{u}{60}$

1.1 Practice A

In Exercises 1–3, use the diagram.

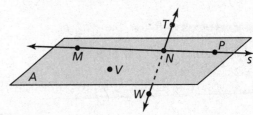

1. Name two points.

2. Name two lines.

3. Name the plane that contains point A, B, and E.

In Exercises 4–7, use the diagram.

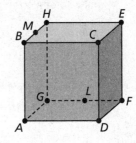

4. Give one other name for $\overleftrightarrow{MN}$.

5. Name three points that are collinear.

6. Name three points that are coplanar.

7. Name a point that is *not* coplanar with points N, P, and T.

In Exercises 8–10, sketch the figure described.

8. plane A and line c intersecting at all points on line c

9. $\overrightarrow{GM}$ and $\overrightarrow{GH}$

10. line $\overleftrightarrow{CD}$ and plane X not intersecting

In Exercises 11–14, use the diagram.

11. Name a point that is coplanar with points A, D, and G.

12. Name the intersection of plane HEG and plane DFE.

13. Name a point that is collinear with BH.

14. Name a point that is *not* coplanar with points C, E, and M.

15. What geometric terms are modeled by the Eiffel Tower?

Name _____ Date _____

1.1 Practice B

In Exercises 1–4, use the diagram.

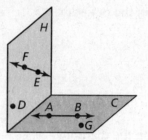

1. Name three points.

2. Name two lines.

3. Name all points in plane H.

4. Name the plane that contains points A, B, and G.

In Exercises 5–8, use the diagram.

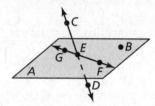

5. Name one pair of opposite rays.

6. Name two points that are collinear with point D.

7. Name the point of intersection of line CD with plane A.

8. Name a point that is *not* coplanar with plane A.

In Exercises 9–11, sketch the figure described.

9. plane A and line $\overleftrightarrow{BC}$ intersecting at point C

10. plane M and plane N *not* intersecting

11. lines a, b, and c intersecting at three points

12. A tripod can be used to level a camera. What geometric figure is modeled by the intersection of a tripod to the ground? Explain.

In Exercises 13 and 14, graph the inequality on a number line. Tell whether the graph is a *segment*, a *ray*, a *point*, or a *line*.

13. $x \geq 2$

14. $-4 < x < 4$

15. What is the maximum number of times two planes can intersect? What is the minimum number of times they can intersect?

1.1 Enrichment and Extension

Points, Lines, and Planes

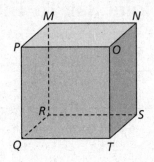

1. Name the three planes that intersect at point P.

2. Name the intersection of plane PQO and plane NMP.

3. Name three lines that intersect at point S.

4. Are points P, M, and Q collinear? Are they coplanar?

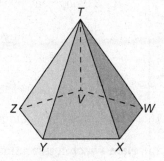

5. Name the intersection of plane XYZ and plane TVW.

6. Name the two planes that intersect at $\overline{XW}$.

7. Name three planes that intersect at point Z.

8. In the figure at right, are there any places where at least four planes intersect? Explain your reasoning.

An equation in two-dimensional space can be written in the standard form $AX + BY = C$. The standard form of a linear equation in three-dimensional space can be written as $AX + BY + CZ = D$, where the point (x, y, z) is a point on the line.

Determine if the given two lines intersect at the given point. Explain your reasoning.

9. $3x + 2y + 4z = 12$
   $x + y + 2z = 6$
   $(0, 4, 1)$

10. $-2x - 4y + z = 8$
    $4x + 2y = -5$
    $(-2, 0, 3)$

1.1 Puzzle Time

What Did The Point Say To The Segment?

A	B	C	D	E	F
G	H	I	J		

Complete each exercise. Find the answer in the answer column. Write the word under the answer in the box containing the exercise letter.

$\overline{AB}$ FOR	
true ANT	
C BECAUSE	
line I'LL	
plane *ABC* A	
ray DOOR	
coplanar HALFWAY	
A IN	

Complete each sentence.

A. Through any two points there is exactly one _____ .

B. Through any three points which are not collinear, there is exactly one _____ .

C. _____ points lie on the same line.

D. _____ points lie on the same plane.

Name each figure shown in the diagram.

E. •
   A

F. •————————•————→
   A   *B*

G. ←———•————————•———→
        A   *B*

H. •————————————•
   A   *B*

I.
   • *A*   *M*
      • *C*
   • *B*

J. $\overrightarrow{AB}$ and $\overrightarrow{AC}$ are opposite rays. True or false?

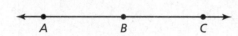

$\overline{AB}$ THE	
BA TEACHER	
collinear YOU	
B CALLED	
false SPLIT	
point LOCKS	
plane MEET	
$\overrightarrow{AB}$ MIDDLE	

1.2 Start Thinking

Measurements of distance are made easy with tools like rulers and measuring tapes. Use a straightedge without measurement units to draw a line on an unlined piece of paper. Then, without using any sort of numbered measuring technique, recreate the line you drew. Use a ruler to compare the two lines.

How could you use a compass to mark half the length of a drawn line segment without ever measuring it?

1.2 Warm Up

Plot the point in the coordinate plane.

1. $A(8, -5)$

2. $B(2, 0)$

3. $C(5, -1)$

4. $D(1, 3)$

5. $E(1, -3)$

6. $F(4, 4)$

7. $G(6, 4)$

8. $H(-3, 1)$

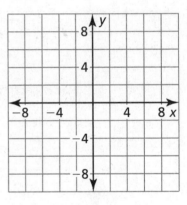

1.2 Cumulative Review Warm Up

Simplify.

1. $\frac{2}{9} + \frac{3}{2}$

2. $4 - 2\frac{1}{4}$

3. $\frac{2}{5} \div \frac{1}{10}$

4. $\frac{3}{9} \times \frac{3}{4}$

5. $\frac{2}{5} \times \frac{10}{5}$

6. $\frac{4}{10} \div \frac{2}{38}$

1.2 Practice A

In Exercises 1 and 2, use a ruler to measure the length of the segment to the nearest eighth of an inch.

1. •————————•

2. •————————————————•

In Exercises 3–5, plot the points in a coordinate plane. Then determine whether $\overline{ST}$ and $\overline{UV}$ are congruent.

3. $S(-1, 2)$, $T(-1, 1)$, $U(3, -5)$, $V(3, -2)$

4. $S(1, -1)$, $T(1, 1)$, $U(3, -4)$, $V(5, -4)$

5. $S(1, 3)$, $T(1, -3)$, $U(3, -2)$, $V(-3, -2)$

In Exercises 6–8, find *KM*.

6.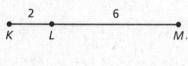

7.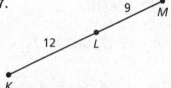

8.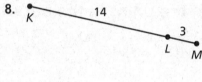

9. Describe and correct the error in finding the length of $\overline{AB}$.

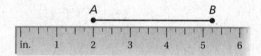

$\boxed{\times \quad |AB| = |1 - 5.25| = 4.25}$

10. A man is 76 inches tall. The length from his head to his shoulders is 14 inches, and the length from his waist to his shoulders is 30 inches. What is the length from his feet to his waist?

In Exercises 11–13, determine whether the statement is true or false. Explain your reasoning.

11. *F* is between *E* and *G*.

12. *C* is between *B* and *D*.

13. *A* is between *B* and *F*.

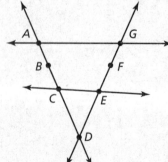

Name_____ Date_____

1.2 Practice B

In Exercises 1 and 2, use a ruler to measure the length of the segment to the nearest eighth of an inch.

1. •————————•   2. •————————————————————•

In Exercises 3 and 4, plot the points in a coordinate plane. Then determine whether $\overline{AB}$ and $\overline{CD}$ are congruent.

3. $A(-7, 1)$, $B(-4, 1)$, $C(3, -5)$, $D(3, -2)$

4. $A(1, -1)$, $B(1, 1)$, $C(3, -4)$, $D(5, -4)$

In Exercises 5–7, find ST.

5.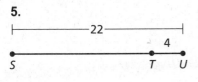

6.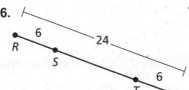

7.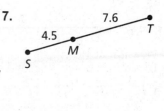

8. The 2014 Winter Olympic Games were held in Sochi, Russia. The distance between Washington, DC and Rome, Italy is about 4480 miles. The distance between Washington, DC and Sochi, Russia is about 5500 miles. What is the distance between Rome, Italy and Sochi, Russia?

In Exercises 9 and 10, point B is between A and C on $\overline{AC}$. Use the information to write an equation in terms of x. Then solve the equation and find AB, BC, and AC.

9. $AB = 13 + 2x$
   $BC = 12$
   $AC = x + 32$

10. $AB = 8x + 5$
    $BC = 5x - 9$
    $AC = 74$

11. You participate in a 150-mile bicycle trip from Madison, Wisconsin to Chicago, Illinois. On the first day, you bike 46.8 miles. On the second day, you bike 51.4 miles. How many miles do you bike on the third day? Which day did you bike the most miles?

Name_____ Date _____

1.2 Enrichment and Extension

Measuring and Constructing Segments

1. In the diagram, $QU = 120$, $SU = 50$, and $RS = ST = TU$. Find the indicated values.

   a. RS **b.** QR

   c. RT **d.** QS

   e. RU **f.** QT

2. You draw a line segment $\overline{AG}$ and state that $\overline{AB} \cong \overline{BC}$, $\overline{CD} \cong \overline{DE} \cong \overline{EF} \cong \overline{FG}$, and $AG = 16$.

   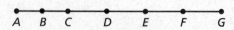

   Your friend then draws a second segment $\overline{HL}$ and states that $\overline{AB} \cong \overline{HI}$, $\overline{CD} \cong \overline{IJ} \cong \overline{JK} \cong \overline{KL}$, and $HL = 11$. Find each indicated measure.

   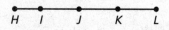

   a. HI **b.** CD **c.** IL

   d. AD **e.** DG **f.** HJ

In Exercises 3–5, use the diagram from Exercise 2 to complete the statement.

3. $\overline{CF} \cong$? 4. $\overline{HJ} \cong$? 5. $\overline{HL} \cong$?

In Exercises 6–8, point **M** is between **L** and **N** on $\overline{LN}$. Use the given information to write an equation in terms of **x**. Solve the equation (disregard any answers that do not make sense in the context of the problem). Then find any missing values.

6. $LM = x^2$

   $MN = x^2 + 9x$

   $LN = 56$

7. $LM = \sqrt{x}$

   $MN = 2\sqrt{x} + 1$

   $LN = 13$

8. $LM = \dfrac{1}{2x} + 3$

   $MN = \dfrac{2}{3}$

   $LN = \dfrac{14}{3} + \dfrac{1}{x}$

Name_____ Date_____

1.2 Puzzle Time

Why Did The Queen Have The King Measure The Rug?

Circle the letter of each correct answer in the boxes below. The circled letters will spell out the answer to the riddle.

Point B is between A and C on $\overline{AC}$. Using the information provided, find the values of x, AB, and BC.

1. $AC = 95, AB = 15x - 10, BC = 5x + 5$

2. $AC = 8x - 16, AB = 3x - 8, BC = 4x$

3. $AC = x - 0.4, AB = x - 4.9, BC = 0.5x$

4. $AC = 38\frac{3}{4}, AB = 6x, BC = 8x + \frac{1}{4}$

5. Line segments that have the same length are called similar segments. True or false?

6. The length of a horizontal segment is the absolute value of the difference of the x-coordinates of the endpoints. Yes or no?

7. Points on a line can be matched with real numbers. Correct or incorrect?

B	A	H	C	E	L	A	U	W	I	A	I	H	N	E	S
no	true	9	19	16	$\frac{1}{2}$	7	1	65	incorrect	5	$\frac{1}{2}$	0.3	6	1.9	30

A	M	G	I	O	F	O	I	D	R	E	U	L	N	E	R
$22\frac{1}{4}$	$11\frac{1}{2}$	4.1	$\frac{1}{2}$	$16\frac{1}{2}$	$\frac{3}{8}$	4.5	5.5	32	8	63	$2\frac{3}{4}$	false	2	yes	correct

Many cities are set up like a coordinate plane with the origin at the center of the city, or where two important streets intersect.

Suppose you have a building located at $(-3, 4)$ and a second building located at $(2, 3)$. How can you find the distance between the two buildings if each unit is the length of a block?

1.3 Warm Up

Find the slope.

1.

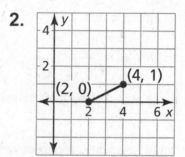

40 ft

20 ft

2.

(2, 0)   (4, 1)

3. $(4, -4), (1, 2)$

4.

x	−5	−1	5	7
y	−3	−1	2	3

1.3 Cumulative Review Warm Up

Find the missing angle measure.

1.

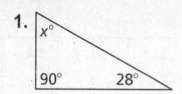

$x°$

$90°$ $28°$

2.

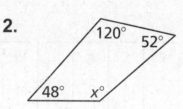

$120°$ $52°$

$48°$ $x°$

3.

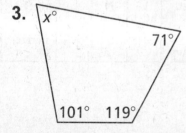

$x°$

$71°$

$101°$ $119°$

4.

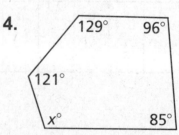

$129°$ $96°$

$121°$

$x°$ $85°$

Name_____ Date_____

1.3 Practice A

In Exercises 1 and 2, identify the segment bisector of $\overline{AB}$. Then find AB.

1.

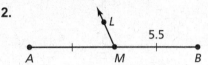

2.

In Exercises 3 and 4, identify the segment bisector of $\overline{ST}$. Then find ST.

3.

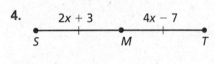

4.

In Exercises 5 and 6, copy the segment and construct a segment bisector by paper folding. Then label the midpoint M.

5.

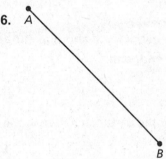

6.

In Exercises 7 and 8, the endpoints of $\overline{JK}$ are given. Find the coordinates of the midpoint M.

7. $J(-3, 2)$ and $K(9, 2)$

8. $J(1, 3)$ and $K(7, 5)$

In Exercises 9 and 10, the midpoint M and one endpoint of $\overline{AB}$ are given. Find the coordinates of the other endpoint.

9. $M(2, 5)$ and $A(2, 3)$

10. $M(-4, -4)$ and $B(-1, -1)$

In Exercises 11 and 12, find the distance between the two points.

11. $Q(5, 6)$ and $P(1, 3)$

12. $G(2, 5)$ and $H(4, -1)$

13. A square has a side length of 4 centimeters. What is the length of the diagonal of the square? What is the length from the corner to the center of the square? Explain.

14. During a soccer game, Player A is 87 feet from the goal but chooses to pass the ball to Player B who is 63 feet away from Player A. How far away is Player B from the goal?

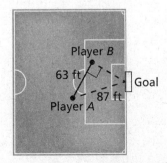

Name _____ Date _____

In Exercises 1 and 2, identify the bisector of $\overline{ST}$. Then find ST.

1.

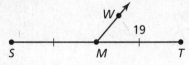

2.

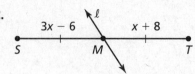

Copy the segment and construct a segment bisector by paper folding. Then label the midpoint *M*.

3.
E _____ F

In Exercises 4 and 5, the endpoints of $\overline{LN}$ are given. Find the coordinates of the midpoint *M*.

4. $L(2, 1)$ and $N(2, 13)$ 5. $L(-6, 0)$ and $N(6, 6)$

In Exercises 6 and 7, the midpoint *M* and one endpoint of $\overline{CD}$ are given. Find the coordinates of the other endpoint.

6. $M(1, 2)$ and $C(-1, 4)$ 7. $M(3, 7)$ and $D(1, 1)$

In Exercises 8 and 9, find the distance between the two points.

8. $A(1, 7)$ and $B(4, 6)$ 9. $G(-1, -5)$ and $H(3, -8)$

10. Your friend draws a square and one diagonal connecting its opposite vertices. Your friend believes that the diagonal is the same length as one side of the square. Do you agree? Explain your reasoning.

11. Is it possible for a segment to have more than one bisector? Explain your reasoning.

12. You walk 2 miles from your house to the park and 4.5 miles from the park to the lake. Then you return home along a straight path from the lake. How many miles do you walk from the lake back to your house? What is the total distance you walk?

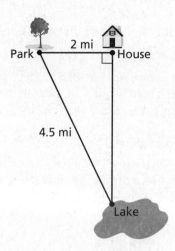

Name_____   Date _____

1.3   Enrichment and Extension

Using the Midpoint and Distance Formulas

1. Use the Midpoint Formula three times to find the three points that divide AB, with endpoints $A(x_1, y_1)$ and $B(x_2, y_2)$, into four equal parts.

2. Given the following endpoints, find the points that divide AB into four equal parts.

    a. $A(-4, 2), B(0, 8)$

    b. $A(-10, 4), B(8, 8)$

3. What number is the midpoint between $13 - \sqrt{27}$ and $13 + \sqrt{27}$? What expression represents the midpoint between $\dfrac{-b - \sqrt{b^2 - 4ac}}{2a}$ and $\dfrac{-b + \sqrt{b^2 - 4ac}}{2a}$?

4. There are two different points on the line $y = -3$ that are exactly 10 units from the point $(4, 3)$. Find the coordinates of the points.

5. Your friend claims that a hexagon with the vertices $A(-2, 1), B(-4, 0),$ $C(-5, -2), D(-4, -4), E(-2, -3),$ and $F(-1, -1)$ is equilateral. Is your friend correct? Explain your reasoning.

In Exercises 6–8, use the information to find the midpoint between points A and B.

In a three-dimensional coordinate system, the midpoint between $A(x_1, y_1, z_1)$ and $B(x_2, y_2, z_2)$ is $\left(\dfrac{x_1 + x_2}{2}, \dfrac{y_1 + y_2}{2}, \dfrac{z_1 + z_2}{2} \right)$.

6. $A(-3, 0, 4)$
    $B(7, 2, 8)$

7. $A(5, 8, -7)$
    $B(-10, 4, 2)$

8. $A(2, 10, 0)$
    $B(5, -1, 3)$

In Exercises 9–11, use the information to find the distance between points A and B.

In a three-dimensional coordinate system, the distance between the two points $A(x_1, y_1, z_1)$ and $B(x_2, y_2, z_2)$ is $AB = \sqrt{(x_2 - x_1)^2 + (y_2 - y_1)^2 + (z_2 - z_1)^2}$.

9. $A(-2, 1, 2)$
    $B(2, -3, 4)$

10. $A(0, 0, -2)$
     $B(-1, 5, 7)$

11. $A(7, 2, -4)$
     $B(5, 8, 3)$

1.3 Puzzle Time

Why Did The Fraction Jump Into Boiling Water?

Write the letter of each answer in the box containing the exercise number.

The endpoints of $\overline{AB}$ are given. Find the coordinates of the midpoint M.

1. $A(-1, 3)$, $B(7, -1)$
2. $A\left(\frac{1}{2}, 4\right)$, $B\left(3, \frac{1}{4}\right)$

3. $A(4.6, -2.2)$, $B(-2.4, 2)$
4. $A(7, 10)$, $B(5, -8)$

5. $A(-15, 10)$, $B(20, 10)$
6. $A(-15, -10)$, $B(15, 15)$

The midpoint M and one endpoint A are given. Find the coordinates of the other endpoint.

7. $A(2, 16)$ and $M(4, 8)$

8. $A(4, -2)$ and $M\left(\frac{1}{2}, 0\right)$

9. $A(-3, -2)$ and $M(2, 6)$

Find the distance between the two points. Round your answer to the nearest tenth.

10. $A(-3, 0)$, $B(2, 0)$
11. $A(0, 3)$, $B(6, 0)$

12. $A(-3, 3)$, $B(3, -3)$
13. $A(-2, -6)$, $B(-2, -2)$

14. $A(2.5, 3.5)$, $B(-4, 0.5)$
15. $A\left(-1\frac{1}{2}, 2\right)$, $B\left(3, -1\frac{1}{2}\right)$

16. $A(-10, -5)$, $B(9, 14)$
17. $A(7, -4)$, $B(1, 6)$

18. $A(3, 14)$, $B(3, 2)$
19. $A(-4, 1)$, $B(4, 1)$

Answers	
D. $M\left(1\frac{3}{4}, 2\frac{1}{8}\right)$	**E.** $B(7, 14)$
A. $M(6, 1)$	**C.** 8
I. 7.6	**D.** $B(6, 0)$
B. $M(0, 2.5)$	**R.** 6.7
I. 5.7	**D.** 4
V. $B(3, 8)$	**N.** $M(3, 1)$
E. 26.9	**T.** $M(2.5, 10)$
U. 5	**K.** 14
E. 7.2	**S.** $M(5, -6)$
T. 12	**N.** 9.2
E. $M(1.1, -0.1)$	**T.** 11.7
W. $B(-3, 2)$	**O.** 8.5
M. 5.3	

15	17		8	4	1	18	9	7		5	12		6	16		11	3	13	10	19	14	2

1.4 Start Thinking

A polygon with three sides is called a *triangle*. The prefix *tri-* means three. One object with the prefix *tri-* is a tripod. Tripods have three legs and are often used to stabilize video cameras.

Find the prefix for *quadrilateral*, *pentagon*, and *hexagon*. Then research one word using each prefix. State what each word means and provide a sentence explaining the usage of the word.

1.4 Warm Up

Find the perimeter and area of the polygon.

1.

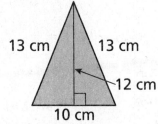

13 cm   13 cm
12 cm
10 cm

2.

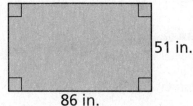

51 in.
86 in.

3.

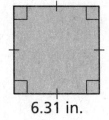

6.31 in.

4.

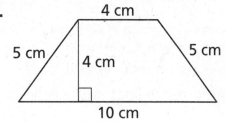

4 cm
5 cm   5 cm
4 cm
10 cm

1.4 Cumulative Review Warm Up

Find the perimeter of the figure.

1.

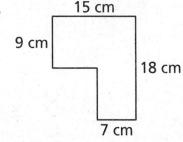

15 cm
9 cm
18 cm
7 cm

2.

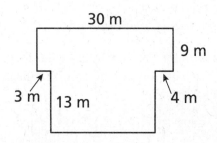

30 m
9 m
3 m   13 m   4 m

Name _____ Date _____

In Exercises 1 and 2, classify the polygon by the number of sides. Tell whether it is *concave* or *convex*.

1.

2.

3. Find the perimeter of quadrilateral *PQRS* with the vertices $P(2, 4)$, $Q(2, 3)$, $R(-2, -2)$, and $S(-2, 3)$.

In Exercises 4 and 5, find the area of the polygon with the given vertices.

4. $T(0, -2)$, $U(3, 5)$, $V(-3, 5)$

5. $A(-3, 3)$, $B(-3, -1)$, $C(4, -1)$, $D(4, 3)$

In Exercises 6–10, use the diagram.

6. Find the perimeter of square *ADEF*.

7. Find the perimeter of $\triangle BCD$.

8. Find the area of square *ADEF*.

9. Find the area of $\triangle ACD$.

10. Find the area of pentagon *ACDEF*.

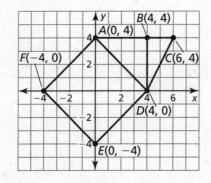

11. A rectangle has vertices $(1, 4)$, $(3, 4)$, and $(3, -3)$. Find the remaining vertex of the rectangle. What is the area of the rectangle?

12. You are installing a fence around your yard. In the figure, your yard is rectangle *ABCD*. Each unit in the coordinate plane represents 10 feet.

    a. What is the perimeter of your entire yard?

    b. You consider only installing a fence around your backyard represented by rectangle *ABEF*. What is the perimeter of your backyard?

    c. The cost of fencing is $50 for each 6-foot section. How much do you save by only installing a fence in the backyard?

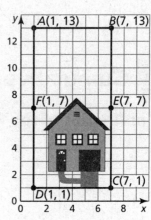

Name_____ Date _____

1.4 Practice B

In Exercises 1 and 2, classify the polygon by the number of sides. Tell whether it is *convex* or *concave*.

1.

2.

3. Find the perimeter of quadrilateral *ABCD* with vertices $A(-2, -2)$, $B(-1, 3)$, $C(5, 3)$, and $D(4, -2)$.

In Exercises 4 and 5, find the area of the polygon with the given vertices.

4. $P(1, 1)$, $Q(-2, 1)$, $R(-1, -4)$

5. $A(3, 7)$, $B(5, 7)$, $C(3, -7)$, $D(5, -7)$

In Exercises 6–10, use the diagram.

6. Find the perimeter of $\triangle ABC$.

7. Find the perimeter of quadrilateral *ACDE*.

8. Find the area of $\triangle ABC$.

9. Find the area of quadrilateral *ACDE*.

10. Find the area of pentagon *ABCDF*.

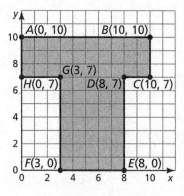

11. You are buying tile for your bathroom floor and baseboards for your bathroom walls. In the figure, the entire polygon represents the layout of the floor. Each unit in the coordinate plane represents 1 foot.

    a. Find the area of the floor.

    b. Find the perimeter of the floor.

    c. The cost of the baseboard is $2 per foot. The cost of the tile is $2.50 per square foot. Find the total cost to buy tile and baseboards for your bathroom.

12. You and your friend go for a walk around town. You walk 0.8 mile east and then 1.5 miles south. You then return to where you started. How far do you travel during your entire walk?

Name _____ Date _____

Finding Area in a Coordinate Plane

1. Find the area of the triangle created by the intersecting lines below.

    $y = -2x + 15$

    $y = -\frac{1}{2}x + 3$

    $y = x + 3$

2. Given the following intersecting lines, find an equation of a third vertical line which intersects the others to create a triangle with an area of 27 square units.

    $y = 3$

    $y = \frac{3}{2}x$

3. Given the graph of $y = \sin(x)$ on the interval $0 \le x \le \pi$, complete the following.

    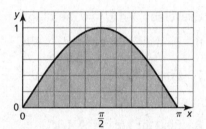

    a. Determine the area of each square unit on the graph. Round to the nearest thousandth.

    b. Approximately how many squares make up the shaded region?

    c. Approximate the area under the curve of $y = \sin(x)$ on $0 \le x \le \pi$.

4. Approximate the area under the curve $y = \cos(x)$ on the interval $0 \le x \le \dfrac{\pi}{2}$.

    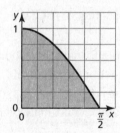

Name_____ Date_____

1.4 Puzzle Time

Why Was The Geometry Book So Sad? It Had ...

Circle the letter of each correct answer in the boxes below. The circled letters will spell out the answer to the riddle.

Indicate the number of sides of the polygon.

1. nonagon　　　　**2.** hexagon　　　　**3.** decagon　　　　**4.** quadrilateral

Find the perimeter, in units, of the polygon with the given vertices. Round to the nearest tenth.

5. $A(8, 0)$, $B(-3, 2)$, $C(10, 2)$ 　　　　**6.** $A(4, -3)$, $B(7, 10)$, $C(-8, 2)$

7. $A(-5, 5)$, $B(5, -5)$, $C(-5, -5)$ 　　　　**8.** $A(4, -3)$, $B(7, 10)$, $C(-8, 2)$, $D(-1, -5)$

9. $A(-4, -8)$, $B(4, -8)$, $C(4, 0)$, $D(0, 3)$, $E(-4, 0)$

Find the area, in square units, of the polygon with the given vertices. Round to the nearest tenth.

10. $A(0, 8)$, $B(6, 5)$, $C(-3, 2)$ 　　　　**11.** $A(-5, 0)$, $B(0, 10)$, $C(5, 0)$

12. $A(7, 0)$, $B(-4, 0)$, $C(-4, 11)$ 　　　　**13.** $A(-5, 5)$, $B(3, -2)$, $C(-4, -10)$, $D(-12, -3)$

14. $A(-4, 0)$, $B(1, 4)$, $C(5, -1)$, $D(0, -5)$ 　　　　**15.** $A(0, -3)$, $B(0, 4)$, $C(10, 4)$, $D(10, -3)$

T	I	E	O	H	O	A	U	M	F	Q	A	H	G	O	J
4	33.4	8	43.3	65.4	70	111	51	45.6	26.2	44.3	34.1	23	5	73	27.1

G	M	D	Z	N	Y	P	I	R	O	B	I	L	E	M	S
10.5	17	38.6	$\frac{1}{2}$	27.0	113	10	115	6	22.5	34.0	48.2	41	60.5	50	9

1.5 Start Thinking

Angle measures are classified into four separate categories: acute $(0° < x < 90°)$, right $(90°)$, obtuse $(90° < x < 180°)$, and straight $(180°)$.

Explain how you can use the definition of a right angle to determine whether an unknown angle measure is acute or obtuse.

1.5 Warm Up

Solve the equation to find the value of the variable.

1. $x° + 40° = 110°$

2. $r° - 44° = 135°$

3. $n° - 19° = 125°$

4. $y° - 55° = 35°$

5. $2t° + 10° = 140°$

6. $2w° - 65° = 175°$

1.5 Cumulative Review Warm Up

Find the value of the variable.

1.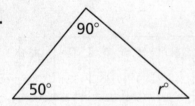

2.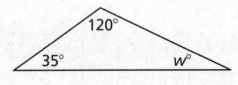

3.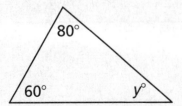

4.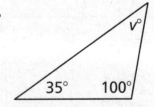

1.5 Practice A

1. Write three names for the angle.

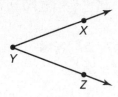

2. Name three different angles in the diagram.

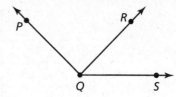

3. Find the angle measure of ∠COA. Then classify the angle.

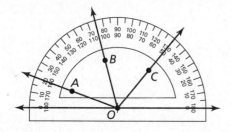

In Exercises 4–7, *m∠ADG* = 92° and *m∠DAG* = 44°.

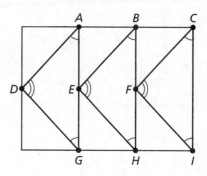

4. Identify the angles congruent to ∠ADG.

5. Identify the angles congruent to ∠DAG.

6. Find *m∠CFI*.

7. Find *m∠EHB*.

In Exercises 8 and 9, find the indicated angle measure.

8. Find *m∠BAD*.

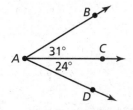

9. Find *x*.

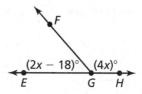

10. In the Ferris wheel, the measure of ∠EFG is 11.25° and the measure of ∠BAF is 70°.

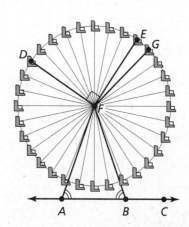

a. Name an example of each of the four types of angles according to their measures in the diagram.

b. How many angles are congruent to ∠EFG?

c. What is the measure of ∠ABF?

d. What is the measure of ∠CBF?

Name_____ Date _____

In Exercises 1–4, find the angle measure. Then classify the angle.

1. $m\angle AOB$

2. $m\angle COD$

3. $m\angle BOD$

4. $m\angle AOD$

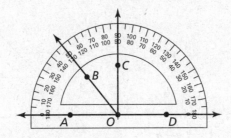

In Exercises 5–8, find the indicated angle measure.

5. $m\angle EFG = 130°$. Find $m\angle HFG$.

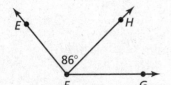

6. $m\angle PRS = 98°$. Find $m\angle QRS$.

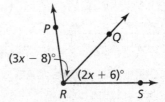

7. $m\angle JNM = 103°$. Find $m\angle JNK$.

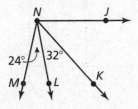

8. Find $m\angle WXZ$.

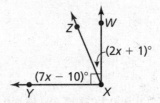

9. Your friend claims it is possible for a straight angle to consist of three acute angles. Is your friend correct? Explain your reasoning.

10. In the suspension bridge, $m\angle AEC = 90°$, $m\angle CAD = 29°$, $m\angle ADE = 61°$, and $\overrightarrow{AD}$ bisects $\angle CAE$.

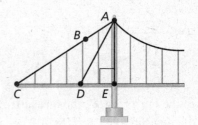

   a. Name an example of an acute angle, right angle, and straight angle according to their angle measures.

   b. Which angle is congruent to $\angle CAD$?

   c. What is the measure of $\angle CAE$?

   d. What is the measure of $\angle CDA$?

1.5 Enrichment and Extension

Measuring and Constructing Angles

1. Let $(2x - 12)°$ represent the measure of an acute angle. What are the possible values of x?

2. Point G lies in the interior of $\angle DEF$. The ratio of $\angle GEF$ to $\angle GED$ is 3 to 5, and $m\angle DEF = 64°$. Find $m\angle DEG$ and $m\angle FEG$.

3. Point O lies in the interior of $\angle MNP$. If $m\angle MNO = x^2 + 10x$, $m\angle ONP = x^2 - 2x$, and $m\angle MNP = 3x^2 + 12$, find the value of x. Then find $m\angle ONP$. (*Hint:* Disregard any answers that do not make sense in the context of the exercise.)

4. Point M lies in the interior of $\angle GEO$. If $m\angle GEM = \frac{2}{3}x$, $m\angle MEO = \frac{1}{4}x$, and $m\angle GEO = \frac{11}{x}$, find the value of x.

5. Angles A and B are complementary, and $m\angle A$ is 8 times greater than $m\angle B$. Find the measure of the angle that forms a linear pair with $\angle A$.

6. Ray SU bisects $\angle RST$. If $m\angle RSU = 2x + 2.5y$, $m\angle UST = -4x + 5y$, and $m\angle RST = 80°$, find the values of x and y.

7. Draw a sketch using the given information.

   D is in the interior of $\angle BAE$. $m\angle BAC = 130°$

   E is in the interior of $\angle DAF$. $m\angle EAC = 90°$

   F is in the interior of $\angle EAC$. $m\angle BAD = m\angle EAF = m\angle FAC$

In Exercises 8–13, use the information from Exercise 7 to find the angle measurement.

8. Find $m\angle FAC$.

9. Find $m\angle BAD$.

10. Find $m\angle FAB$.

11. Find $m\angle DAE$.

12. Find $m\angle FAD$.

13. Find $m\angle BAE$.

1.5 Puzzle Time

Why Shouldn't You Tell A Pigeon A Secret? Because It …

Write the letter of each answer in the box containing the exercise number.

Use the diagram to identify an angle with the given classification.

1. right angle

2. obtuse angle

3. straight angle

4. acute angle

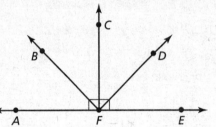

Use the diagram to solve for the angle measurement, given that ∠BAE = 59°.

5. ∠BAC

6. ∠CAD

7. ∠DAE

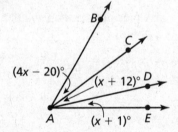

Use the diagram to solve for the angle measurement, given that ∠BAE = 130°.

8. ∠BAC

9. ∠CAD

10. ∠DAE

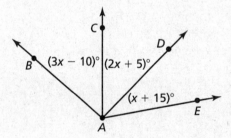

Answers	
I.	23°
H.	40°
A.	∠AFC
D.	20°
S.	35°
C.	12°
O.	17°
R.	∠AFD
U.	70°
I.	45°
P.	11°
R.	24°
T.	37°
A.	∠AFB
M.	27°
E.	∠AFE
U.	75°
R.	50°

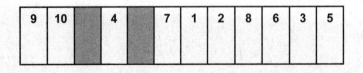

9	10		4		7	1	2	8	6	3	5

1.6 Start Thinking

In Section 1.5, you learned that a straight angle is an angle with a measure of 180°. Imagine the straight angle you are measuring is the x-axis of a coordinate plane and the origin is the center of the angle. If you "pull down" the negative x-axis side so that it is in Quadrant III, how could you find the measure of the angle going counterclockwise?

1.6 Warm Up

Solve.

1. $4x - 0 = 12$

2. $7 = -11c - 4$

3. $11 = -19x - 8$

4. $7 = 5n + 5 - 4n$

5. $3x + 2 + 8 = 2x - 5$

6. $x + 5 + 6x + 17 = x - 2$

1.6 Cumulative Review Warm Up

Write the sentence as an equation and solve.

1. The difference between a number and 14 is 8.

2. Twice the difference between 5 times a number and 6 is 18.

3. Fourteen is 7 times the difference between a number and 2.

4. Four consecutive odd integers such that 2 times the last integer is 5 more than the sum of the first 3 integers.

1.6   Practice A

In Exercises 1–3, use the figures.

1. Name a pair of adjacent complementary angles.

2. Name a pair of nonadjacent complementary angles.

3. Name a pair of nonadjacent supplementary angles.

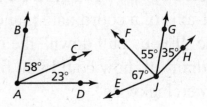

In Exercises 4 and 5, find the angle measure.

4. $\angle 1$ is a complement of $\angle 2$, and $m\angle 2 = 36°$. Find $m\angle 1$.

5. $\angle 3$ is a supplement of $\angle 4$, and $m\angle 4 = 75°$. Find $m\angle 3$.

In Exercises 6 and 7, find the measure of each angle.

6. $\angle WXY$ and $\angle YXZ$ are supplementary angles, $m\angle WXY = (6x + 59)°$, and $m\angle YXZ = (3x - 14)°$.

7. $\angle ABC$ and $\angle CBD$ are complementary angles, $m\angle ABC = (3x + 6)°$, and $m\angle CBD = (4x - 14)°$.

In Exercises 8–10, use the figure.

8. Identify the linear pairs that include $\angle 5$.

9. Are $\angle 3$ and $\angle 5$ vertical angles? Explain your reasoning.

10. Are $\angle 2$ and $\angle 4$ vertical angles? Explain your reasoning.

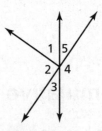

In Exercises 11–13, write and solve an algebraic equation to find the measure of each angle based on the given description.

11. Two angles form a linear pair. The measure of one angle is $24°$ more than the measure of the other angle.

12. The measure of an angle is three times the measurement of its complement.

13. The measure of one angle is 15 less than half the measurement of its supplement.

14. The figure shows the design on an outdoor fence.

   a. Name a pair of adjacent supplementary angles.

   b. Name a pair of nonadjacent supplementary angles.

   c. Identify the linear pairs that include $\angle 5$.

   d. Find $m\angle 3$. Explain your reasoning.

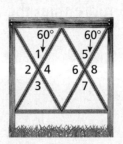

Name_____ Date_____

In Exercises 1–3, use the figures.

1. Name a pair of adjacent complementary angles.

2. Name a pair of nonadjacent complementary angles.

3. Name a pair of nonadjacent supplementary angles.

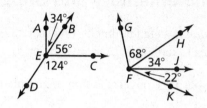

In Exercises 4 and 5, find the angle measure.

4. $\angle 1$ is a complement of $\angle 2$, and $m\angle 2 = 71°$. Find $m\angle 1$.

5. $\angle 3$ is a supplement of $\angle 4$, and $m\angle 4 = 26.7°$. Find $m\angle 3$.

In Exercises 6 and 7, find the measure of each angle.

6. $\angle ABC$ and $\angle CBD$ are supplementary angles, $m\angle ABC = 7x°$ and $m\angle CBD = 8x°$.

7. $\angle WXY$ and $\angle YXZ$ are complementary angles, $m\angle WXY = (2x + 5)°$, and $m\angle YXZ = (8x - 5)°$.

In Exercises 8–11, use the figure.

8. Identify the linear pair(s) that include $\angle 2$.

9. Identify the linear pair(s) that include $\angle 8$.

10. Are $\angle 6$ and $\angle 8$ vertical angles? Explain your reasoning.

11. Are $\angle 7$ and $\angle 9$ vertical angles? Explain your reasoning.

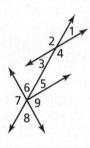

In Exercises 12–14, write and solve an algebraic equation to find the measure of each angle based on the given description.

12. The measure of an angle is 9 more than twice its complement.

13. Two angles form a linear pair. The measure of one angle is four times the measure of the other angle.

14. Two angles form a linear pair. The measure of one angle is 51° more than $\frac{1}{2}$ the measure of the other angle.

In Exercises 15 and 16, tell whether the statement is *always*, *sometimes*, or *never* true. Explain your reasoning.

15. The sum of the measures of a linear pair of angles is 90°.

16. The sum of the measures of a pair of vertical angles is 180°.

Name _____ Date _____

1.6 Enrichment and Extension

Complementary and Supplementary Angles

A *radian* is a standard unit of measure used to measure angles. The conversion from degrees to radians is $180° = \pi$ radians.

Example 1: Convert the sum of complementary and supplementary angles into radians.

Solution: $90° \cdot \dfrac{\pi \text{ radians}}{180°} = \dfrac{\pi}{2}$ radians   Complementary angles sum to $\dfrac{\pi}{2}$ radians.

$180° \cdot \dfrac{\pi \text{ radians}}{180°} = \pi$ radians   Supplementary angles sum to π radians.

Example 2: Determine if the two angles are *complementary*, *supplementary*, or *neither*: $\dfrac{3\pi}{8}$ and $\dfrac{\pi}{4}$

Solution: $\dfrac{\pi}{4} \cdot \left(\dfrac{2}{2}\right) = \dfrac{2\pi}{8}$ Multiply by an identity to get the LCD.

$\dfrac{2\pi}{8} + \dfrac{3\pi}{8} = \dfrac{5\pi}{8}$ Add the two measurements.

The sum of $\dfrac{5\pi}{8}$ does not equal $\dfrac{\pi}{2}$ or π, so the final answer is *neither*.

Determine if the two angles are *complementary*, *supplementary*, or *neither*.

1. $\dfrac{3\pi}{7}, \dfrac{4\pi}{7}$ 2. $\dfrac{\pi}{4}, \dfrac{\pi}{4}$ 3. $\dfrac{5\pi}{18}, \dfrac{5\pi}{9}$

4. $\dfrac{\pi}{8}, \dfrac{7\pi}{8}$ 5. $\dfrac{\pi}{3}, \dfrac{\pi}{4}$ 6. $\dfrac{6\pi}{15}, \dfrac{\pi}{10}$

If possible, find the angle complementary and supplementary to the given angle.

7. $\dfrac{12\pi}{15}$ 8. $\dfrac{23\pi}{42}$ 9. $\dfrac{3\pi}{17}$

10. $\dfrac{2\pi}{5}$ 11. $\dfrac{17\pi}{42}$ 12. $\dfrac{7\pi}{8}$

Name_____ Date _____

1.6 Puzzle Time

Why Did The Student Eat His Math Exam?

A	B	C	D	E	F
G	H	I	J		

Complete each exercise. Find the answer in the answer column. Write the word under the answer in the box containing the exercise letter.

152° NOTES	
58° KEYS	
41° BECAUSE	
61° THE	
126° PIECE	
134° DOOR	
78° WAS	
54° A	
50° CAKE	
82° THE	

Find the angle measure.

A. $\angle 1$ is a complement of $\angle 2$ and $m\angle 1 = 49°$. Find $m\angle 2$.

B. $\angle 3$ is a supplement of $\angle 4$ and $m\angle 3 = 119°$. Find $m\angle 4$.

C. $\angle 5$ and $\angle 6$ are vertical angles and $m\angle 5 = 33°$. Find $m\angle 6$.

D. $\angle 7$ and $\angle 8$ are linear angles and $m\angle 7$ is 4 times that of $m\angle 8$. Find $m\angle 8$.

E. $\angle 1$ is a supplement of $\angle 2$ and $m\angle 2 = 31°$. Find $m\angle 1$.

F. $\angle 3$ is a complement of $\angle 4$ and $m\angle 3 = 12°$. Find $m\angle 4$.

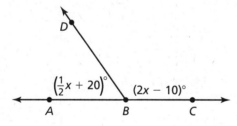

G. Find $m\angle ABD$.

H. Find $m\angle DBC$.

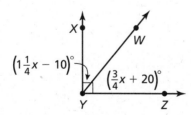

I. Find $m\angle XYW$.

J. Find $m\angle WYZ$.

36° SAID	
34° SAME	
40° OF	
92° CALLED	
65° GOT	
33° TEACHER	
48° SHE	
63° ARE	
149° IT	
173° HER	

Name _____ Date _____

Cumulative Review

In Exercises 1–18, simplify the expression.

1. $|-4 + 5|$ 2. $|2 - 8|$ 3. $|-11 + 9|$

4. $|13 - (-3)|$ 5. $|13 + (-7)|$ 6. $|-6 - 19|$

7. $|9 - 5|$ 8. $|-8 + 5|$ 9. $|4 + (-17)|$

10. $|20 - (-7)|$ 11. $|-11 - 14|$ 12. $|-15 - 2|$

13. $|4 - 7|$ 14. $|-1 - (-5)|$ 15. $|6 + (-18)|$

16. $|12 - (-2) + 8|$ 17. $|-7 + (-4) + 9|$ 18. $|-6 - 12 + 16|$

In Exercises 19–46, simplify.

19. $\dfrac{16 - 4}{3}$ 20. $\dfrac{9 - 11}{2}$ 21. $\dfrac{18 + (-14)}{4}$ 22. $\dfrac{-28 + 16}{2}$

23. $\dfrac{5 - (-13)}{3}$ 24. $\dfrac{-9 + (-9)}{3}$ 25. $\dfrac{15 - 3}{4}$ 26. $\dfrac{-11 - 5}{4}$

27. $\dfrac{7 + 8}{5}$ 28. $\dfrac{-12 - (-17)}{5}$ 29. $\dfrac{32 - (-13)}{5}$ 30. $\dfrac{-31 - 11}{6}$

31. $\dfrac{17 + 7}{6}$ 32. $\dfrac{33 + 15}{6}$ 33. $\dfrac{27 + 22}{7}$ 34. $\dfrac{7 + 25}{8}$

35. $\sqrt{12 + 4}$ 36. $\sqrt{18 + 7}$ 37. $\sqrt{39 + 10}$ 38. $\sqrt{51 + 13}$

39. $\sqrt{9 + 7}$ 40. $\sqrt{11 + 25}$ 41. $\sqrt{15 - (-1)}$ 42. $\sqrt{5 - (-4)}$

43. $\sqrt{73 - 9}$ 44. $\sqrt{14 - 5}$ 45. $\sqrt{36 - 11}$ 46. $\sqrt{42 - 6}$

In Exercises 47–62, solve the equation.

47. $x + 51 = 62$ 48. $x + 26 = -19$ 49. $45 + x = 13$ 50. $27 + x = -12$

51. $x - 14 = 2$ 52. $x - 35 = 68$ 53. $x - 41 = -25$ 54. $x - 28 = -60$

55. $6x = 30$ 56. $-4x = 32$ 57. $7x = -56$ 58. $-11x = -121$

59. $\dfrac{x}{2} = 15$ 60. $\dfrac{x}{-6} = 47$ 61. $\dfrac{x}{-4} = -16$ 62. $\dfrac{x}{13} = -8$

Chapter 1 **Cumulative Review** (continued)

In Exercises 63–71, find the perimeter and area of the figure.

63.

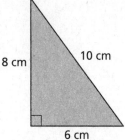

8 cm   10 cm

6 cm

64.

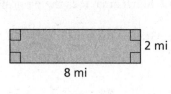

2 mi

8 mi

65.

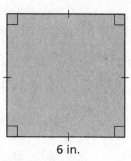

6 in.

66.

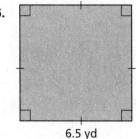

6.5 yd

67.

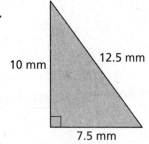

10 mm   12.5 mm

7.5 mm

68.

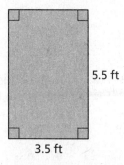

5.5 ft

3.5 ft

69.

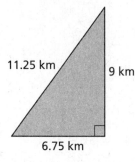

11.25 km   9 km

6.75 km

70.

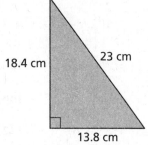

18.4 cm   23 cm

13.8 cm

71.

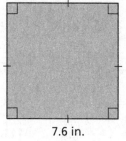

7.6 in.

72. You are planning to frame a picture. The frame goes around the outer edges of the picture, so you need to calculate the perimeter to determine how much material you need. The picture is rectangular and has side lengths of 11 inches and 15 inches. How much material do you need for the frame?

73. You want to cover the top of your desk at home with a decorative cloth, but you need to know how much cloth to purchase. To determine how much cloth you need, you must calculate the area of the top of the desk, which is in the shape of a rectangle. The desktop has measurements of 62 inches and 48 inches. How many square inches of cloth do you need to purchase to make your decorative cloth desk top cover?

74. You are going to tile the bottom of a swimming pool. You need to know how much tile is needed, so you must calculate the area of the base of the pool. The swimming pool is rectangular, and measures 28 feet by 36 feet. How much tile do you need?

Name _____ Date _____

75. You and your friend are going to paint your garage door. Paint is sold by coverage area, so you need to calculate the area of the garage door. The door is rectangular and measures 10 feet by 16 feet. How much area does the paint need to cover?

In Exercises 76–91, solve the inequality. Graph the solution.

76. $a + 7 \geq 15$ **77.** $b + 13 > 12$ **78.** $c + 8 < -11$ **79.** $d + 9 \leq -5$

80. $f - 8 > 19$ **81.** $g - 12 \leq 23$ **82.** $h - 7 \geq -15$ **83.** $j - 3 < 1$

84. $4k < 48$ **85.** $-6m > 36$ **86.** $7n \geq -28$ **87.** $-5p \leq -45$

88. $-\dfrac{s}{3} \leq 7$ **89.** $\dfrac{t}{2} \geq -11$ **90.** $\dfrac{u}{4} > 13$ **91.** $\dfrac{v}{-6} < -10$

In Exercises 92–115, solve the equation.

92. $\dfrac{2x + 5}{3} = -7$ **93.** $\dfrac{5x + 6}{3} = -3$ **94.** $\dfrac{-3x + 1}{4} = 10$ **95.** $2x + 4 = 16$

96. $-3x + 4 = -23$ **97.** $6 - 7x = 48$ **98.** $5x + 18 = -22$ **99.** $6 + 8x = 22$

100. $17 - 2x = 23$ **101.** $\dfrac{x}{4} + 9 = -6$ **102.** $-\dfrac{x}{3} - 5 = 7$ **103.** $\dfrac{x}{4} + 1 = -3$

104. $3x + 6 = 2x - 7$ **105.** $5x + 11 = 7x - 15$ **106.** $-3x + 4 = 7x - 26$

107. $4x + 5 = -17 - 7x$ **108.** $3 - 2x = -17 + 18x$ **109.** $6x - 12 = 3x + 9$

110. $5 - 6x = 14 + 3x$ **111.** $7 - 4x = 25 - 6x$ **112.** $-7x + 45 = 3x + 35$

113. $3x - 41 = -4x + 15$ **114.** $-2x + 29 = -x - 19$ **115.** $-9x + 13 = -5x - 15$

In Exercises 116–119, plot the points in a coordinate plane. Then determine whether $\overline{AB}$ and $\overline{CD}$ are congruent.

116. $A(-2, 3), B(3, 3), C(2, 2), D(2, -3)$ **117.** $A(-4, 3), B(1, 3), C(-1, 2), D(-1, -1)$

118. $A(-2, -1), B(-2, 4), C(-3, 5), D(3, 5)$ **119.** $A(-2, -2), B(2, -2), C(1, -1), D(1, 3)$

120. Find AC.

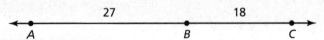

121. Find DF.

Chapter 1 **Cumulative Review** (continued)

122. Find *NP*.

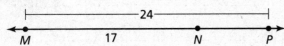

123. Point *M* is the midpoint of $\overline{ST}$. Find the length of $\overline{SM}$.

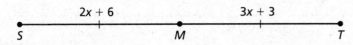

In Exercises 124 and 125, the endpoints of $\overline{CD}$ are given. Find the coordinate of the midpoint *M*.

124. $C(-2, 6)$ and $D(5, 8)$ **125.** $C(-8, 3)$ and $D(5, -2)$

In Exercises 126 and 127, the midpoint *M* and one endpoint of $\overline{GH}$ are given. Find the coordinates of the other endpoint.

126. $M(2, 5)$ and $G(1, 3)$ **127.** $M(-1, -4)$ and $G(-5, -7)$

In Exercises 128–137, use the Distance Formula to find the distance between the two points.

128. $A(6, 6)$ and $B(-1, 9)$ **129.** $C(-9, -1)$ and $D(7, 3)$

130. $E(5, -5)$ and $F(1, -6)$ **131.** $G(-5, 3)$ and $H(2, -8)$

132. $J(-3, -4)$ and $K(0, -6)$ **133.** $L(2, -9)$ and $M(-4, 5)$

134. $N(11, -8)$ and $P(-6, 7)$ **135.** $R(0, 6)$ and $S(-9, 0)$

136. $T(-3, -4)$ and $V(8, 5)$ **137.** $W(-5, -5)$ and $Z(0, -3)$

138. Given that $\angle ABC$ is a right angle, find $m\angle ABD$ and $m\angle DBC$.

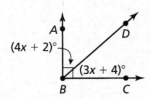

139. Given that $\angle LMN$ is a straight angle, find $m\angle LMP$ and $m\angle PMN$.

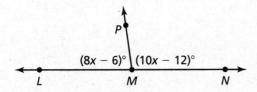

Chapter 2

Name_____ Date _____

Dear Family,

"If you use our age-defying cream, you will look years younger!" "If you buy this product, you will have more energy!" Marketing strategies like these use the logic and reasoning of consumers to persuade them to buy a product. In this chapter, your student will learn various types of logic and reasoning skills (inductive, deductive, and algebraic), and how they can be used to achieve specific results. Your student will also work with postulates and theorems to write proofs about geometric properties.

Today, your student can practice using logic and reasoning skills to sell a product (of their choice/or imagination) to consumers. They will have to think logically, and explain why anyone would want to purchase this product. Discuss these questions with your student:

- Can you think of or make up a product you would like to sell to consumers? (Sample Response: car wax)

- Using logic, what kind of "results" from using this product would persuade a consumer to buy this product? (Sample Response: a really shiny car)

Take time with your student to make a storyboard for your own commercial, using reasoning and logic to persuade consumers to buy your product.

1. Choose a product to sell that will achieve a specific result for consumers. Pick a company name and a product name, and come up with some catchy slogans that will assist in your marketing technique. (Sample Response: "Take your shine to the max—with Eddie's Car Wax!")

2. Brainstorm different techniques that you think will be most useful in selling your product. Will you use humor? fear? data?

3. Write out your storyboard. Will you have characters? What will they do and say?

4. Finally, use a comic strip to show what your commercial will look like. Draw your characters doing and saying things in each slide, using the logic in steps one and two to create a desirable product.

When we sharpen our logic and reasoning skills, it not only helps us understand the geometric world, but the world we live in as well!

Nombre _____ Fecha _____

Razonamiento y demostraciones

Estimada familia:

"¡Si usa nuestra crema antienvejecimiento, ilucirá más joven!". "¡Si compra este producto, itendrá más energía!". Las estrategias de mercado como estas usan la lógica y el razonamiento de los consumidores para persuadirlos a comprar un producto. En este capítulo, su hijo aprenderá varios tipos de destrezas de lógica y razonamiento (inductiva, deductiva y algebraica) y cómo pueden usarse para lograr resultados específicos. Su hijo también trabajará con postulados y teoremas para escribir demostraciones sobre las propiedades geométricas.

Hoy, su hijo puede practicar usando destrezas de lógica y razonamiento para vender un producto (que elijan o imaginen) a los consumidores. Tendrán que pensar con lógica y explicar por qué una persona querría comprar este producto. Comenten estas preguntas con su hijo:

- ¿Se les ocurre o pueden inventar un producto que les gustaría vender a los consumidores? (Respuesta de muestra: cera para carros)

- Según la lógica, ¿qué clase de "resultados" por el uso de este producto persuadirían a un consumidor a comprar este producto? (Respuesta de muestra: un carro muy brilloso)

Con su hijo, tómense un rato para crear un buen guión gráfico para su propio comercial, usando el razonamiento y la lógica para persuadir a los consumidores de comprar su producto.

1. Elijan un producto para vender que logrará un resultado específico para los consumidores. Elijan el nombre para la compañía y para el producto y piensen algunos eslóganes pegadizos que ayudarán en su técnica de mercado. (Respuesta de muestra: "¡Que su carro brille al máximo con la cera para carros de Pablo!")

2. Propongan diferentes técnicas que creen que serán las más útiles para vender su producto. ¿Usarán humor? ¿Miedo? ¿Datos?

3. Escriban el guión gráfico. ¿Tendrán personajes? ¿Qué harán y dirán ellos?

4. Finalmente, usen una historieta para mostrar cómo será su comercial. Dibujen a los personajes haciendo y diciendo cosas en cada diapositiva, usen la lógica en los pasos uno y dos para crear un producto deseable.

Cuando afilamos nuestras destrezas de lógica y razonamiento, no solo nos ayudan a comprender el mundo geométrico, ¡sino también el mundo en que vivimos!

2.1 Start Thinking

The statement "If you are able to open the door, then the door is unlocked" is always true.

Write a statement you know to be true in the same "if-then" form. Support your statement with as many reasons as you can think of to show it is true.

2.1 Warm Up

Complete the statement.

1. A _____ has six sides.

2. If two lines form a _____ angle, they are perpendicular.

3. Two angles that form a right angle are _____ angles.

4. A _____ angle has measure of 180°.

2.1 Cumulative Review Warm Up

The endpoints of $\overline{CD}$ are given. Find the coordinates of the midpoint M.

1. $C(4, -6)$ and $D(8, 8)$

2. $C(-3, 6)$ and $D(1, -4)$

3. $C(-1, -1)$ and $D(5, 8)$

4. $C(-7, -7)$ and $D(-3, 9)$

2.1 Practice A

In Exercises 1 and 2, copy the conditional statement. Underline the hypothesis and circle the conclusion.

1. If you like the ocean, then you are a good swimmer.

2. If it is raining outside, then it is cold.

In Exercises 3 and 4, rewrite the conditional statement in if-then form.

3. All children must attend school.

4. Congruent angles have equal angle measures.

5. Let p be "an animal is a puppy" and let q be "it is a dog." Write each statement in words. Then decide whether it is true or false.

   a. the conditional statement $p \rightarrow q$

   b. the converse $q \rightarrow p$

   c. the inverse $\sim p \rightarrow \sim q$

   d. the contrapositive $\sim q \rightarrow \sim p$

In Exercises 6 and 7, decide whether the statement about the diagram is true. Explain your answer using the definitions you have learned.

6. $\angle 1 + \angle 2 = 90°$

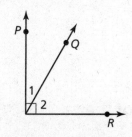

7. $\overline{AD} \cong \overline{DB}$

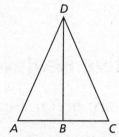

8. Rewrite the definition of the term as a biconditional statement: Obtuse angles are angles with measures greater than $90°$ and less than $180°$.

9. Rewrite the statements as a single biconditional statement: If two angles are supplementary, then the sum of their angle measures is $180°$. If the sum of two angles is $180°$, then they are supplementary angles.

10. If the negation of a statement is true, does that mean that the original statement is automatically false? Explain your reasoning.

11. Write a conditional statement that is false but has a true inverse.

2.1 Practice B

In Exercises 1 and 2, copy the conditional statement. Underline the hypothesis and circle the conclusion.

1. If you like to eat, then you are a good cook.

2. If an animal is a bear, then it is a mammal.

3. Let p be "a tree is an oak tree" and let q be "it is a deciduous tree." Write each statement in words. Then decide whether it is true or false.

   a. the conditional statement $p \rightarrow q$

   b. the converse $q \rightarrow p$

   c. the inverse $\sim p \rightarrow \sim q$

   d. the contrapositive $\sim q \rightarrow \sim p$

In Exercises 4 and 5, decide whether the statement about the diagram is true. Explain your answer using the definitions you have learned.

4. $\angle ACB$ and $\angle DCE$ are vertical angles.

5. $\overline{KL} \perp \overline{LM}$

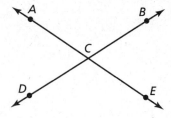
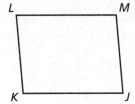

6. Rewrite the two statements as a single biconditional statement: A rectangle is a quadrilateral that has all perpendicular sides. If all sides of a quadrilateral are perpendicular, then it is a rectangle.

7. Your friend claims that only true conditional statements have a true contrapositive. Is your friend correct? Explain your reasoning.

8. Rewrite the conditional statement in if-then form: $3x + 2 = 23$, because $x = 7$.

9. Write a series of if-then statements that allow you to find the measure of each angle, given that $\angle ILH = 38°$. Use the definitions of supplementary and complementary angles that you have learned so far.

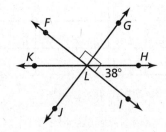

Name _____ Date _____

2.1 Enrichment and Extension

Logical Operators

The logical operator utilized in Lesson 2.1 to form a truth table is *logical implication*, in which a false value is produced when the *hypothesis* is true and the *conclusion* is false.

Another logical operator we can use to create a truth table is called *logical conjunction*, in which a true value is produced when both the *hypothesis* and *conclusion* are true. The symbol used in these tables is denoted as "∧."

Example: Construct a truth table using logical conjunction.

p	q	p ∧ q
T	T	T
T	F	F
F	T	F
F	F	F

In *logical disjunction,* a true value is produced if the *hypothesis* or the *conclusion* is true. The symbol in these tables is denoted as "∨."

p	q	p ∨ q
T	T	T
T	F	T
F	T	T
F	F	F

Complete the table below.

p	q	p ∨ q	~p	~q	~p ∧ ~q	~p ∨ ~q	(~p ∨ ~q) ∧ ~p	(~p ∧ ~q) ∨ ~q
T	T	T						
T	F	T						
F	T	T						
F	F	F						

Name_____ Date _____

2.1 Puzzle Time

What Is Smarter Than A Talking Bird?

Write the letter of each answer in the box containing the exercise number.

Complete the sentence.

1. A conditional statement, symbolized by $p \rightarrow q$, can be written as an "if-then" statement in which p is the _____.

2. A conditional statement, symbolized by $p \rightarrow q$, can be written as an "if-then" statement in which q is the _____.

3. You can determine the conditions under which a conditional statement is true by using a _____.

4. A conditional statement of "If p, then q" is expressed symbolically as _____.

5. A conditional statement that is expressed as "If q, then p" is called the _____.

6. If p = "you are a baseball player" and q = "you are an athlete," the following statement "If you are *not* a baseball player, then you are *not* an athlete" would be called a(n) _____.

7. A _____ statement is a statement that contains the phrase "if and only if."

8. If both p and q of the converse are negated, it is called a _____.

Use this statement. "If (a) you are a vegan, then (b) you eat vegetables" to answer the question.

9. What part is the hypothesis? (a) or (b)

10. Part (a) is the conclusion? yes or no

Complete the sentence.

11. The negation of "math is not fun" would be "_____."

12. "If and only if a polygon has three sides, it is a triangle" is a biconditional statement. True or false?

Answers

G. (a)

E. no

H. conditional

A. yes

E. $p \rightarrow q$

T. triconditional

I. biconditional

O. false

L. hypothesis

A. contrapositive

N. math is fun

Y. postulate

P. inverse

R. truth value

O. introversion

B. true

L. converse

E. conclusion

M. math is boring

S. truth table

Y. (b)

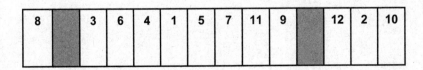

Geometry 45
Resources by Chapter

2.2 Start Thinking

Consider the following statements:

Statement 1 – "If the stove is on, then it is hot."

Statement 2 – "If the stove is hot, then you can cook."

Is the statement "If the stove is on, then you can cook" true?

Write two related statements as above. Write a third statement using the beginning of your first statement and the ending of your second statement. Note if it is true or false.

2.2 Warm Up

Find the common difference of the arithmetic sequence. Find the next two terms.

1. 0.09, 0.15, 0.21, …

2. 3.36, 1.14, −1.08, …

3. 8, 3, −2, …

4. 2.4, 2.9, 3.4, …

5. 2, 4, 6, …

6. 16, 9, 2, …

2.2 Cumulative Review Warm Up

Find the area of the polygon with the given vertices.

1. $G(4, 1)$, $H(4, -2)$, $J(-1, -2)$

2. $N(0, 0)$, $P(3, 0)$, $Q(3, -3)$, $R(0, -1)$

3. $K(-3, 4)$, $L(0, 4)$, $M(0, 0)$, $N(-3, 0)$

4. $P(-4, 4)$, $Q(2, 4)$, $R(2, 0)$, $S(-4, 0)$

2.2 Practice A

In Exercises 1 and 2, describe the pattern. Then write or draw the next two numbers or letters.

1. 2, 5, 11, 23, 47, …

2. A, Z, B, Y, C, …

In Exercises 3 and 4, make and test a conjecture about the given quantity.

3. the difference of any two even integers

4. the product of three negative numbers

5. An angle bisector always creates two acute angles. Find a counterexample to show that the conjecture is false.

In Exercises 6 and 7, use the Law of Detachment to determine what you can conclude from the given information, if possible.

6. If you go swimming, then you will get wet. You went swimming.

7. Two congruent angles have the same angle measure. $m\angle 1 = m\angle 2$

In Exercises 8 and 9, use the Law of Syllogism to write a new conditional statement that follows from the pair of true statements, if possible.

8. If you study, then you will pass the exam. If you pass the exam, then you will pass the class.

9. If a straight angle is bisected, then each angle is 90°. If an angle is 90°, then it is a right angle.

10. If $|x| = x$, then x is positive. The value of x is 3, so $|3| = 3$. State the law of logic that is illustrated.

In Exercises 11 and 12, decide whether inductive reasoning or deductive reasoning is used to reach the conclusion. Explain your reasoning.

11. This weekend, the sun was shining and it did not rain. So, the next time the sun is shining, you know it will not rain.

12. The product of two even integers is always even. Because 92 and 14 are even numbers, the product is even.

13. The three tallest peaks in the Rocky Mountains are 4401 meters, 4398 meters, and 4396 meters. The three tallest peaks in the Appalachian Mountains are 2037 meters, 2026 meters, and 2025 meters. Make a conjecture that compares the Rocky Mountains to the Appalachian Mountains.

14. Use deductive reasoning to write a formula for the perimeter P of a regular polygon with n sides, where each side is s.

Name _____ Date _____

In Exercises 1 and 2, describe the pattern. Then write or draw the next two numbers, letters, or figures.

1. A, 26, B, 25, C, 24, ...

2.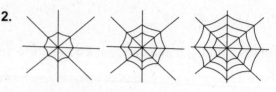

In Exercises 3 and 4, make and test a conjecture about the given quantity.

3. the sum of two absolute values

4. the product of a number and its square

5. Vertical angles are always complementary. Find a counterexample to show that the conjecture is false.

In Exercises 6 and 7, use the Law of Detachment to determine what you can conclude from the given information, if possible.

6. If you eat a healthy breakfast, then you will not be hungry until lunchtime. You are not hungry until lunchtime.

7. Adjacent angles share one common ray. $\angle AOB$ and $\angle DOB$ are adjacent angles.

In Exercises 8 and 9, use the Law of Syllogism to write a new conditional statement that follows from the pair of true statements, if possible.

8. If a polygon has three sides, then it is a triangle. If triangle has two congruent sides, then it is an isosceles triangle.

9. If it is Tuesday, then you mow the grass. If you mow the grass, then you water the flowers.

In Exercises 10 and 11, decide whether inductive reasoning or deductive reasoning is used to reach the conclusion. Explain your reasoning.

10. All mammals have hair. Cats are mammals. So, all cats have hair.

11. Each time you go to school you walk. You went to school today, so you walked.

12. Is it possible to have a series of true conditional statements that lead to a false conclusion? Explain.

13. The table shows the cost per pound of several varieties of organic and nonorganic produce at your local grocery store. What conjecture can you make about the relation between the cost of organic produce and the cost of nonorganic produce? Explain your reasoning.

	Organic	Nonorganic
Bananas	$0.49	$0.29
Carrots	$1.19	$0.89
Strawberries	$3.99	$2.99

2.2 Enrichment and Extension

Inductive Reasoning & Iteration

A common technique that utilizes *inductive reasoning* to find new patterns is called *iteration*. Iteration, simply put, means to repeat the process.

1. Suppose someone picks a number from 1 to 100. You get to guess the number, and the person will tell you if you're too high or too low. What is the maximum number of guesses you will ever need? Using a *binary search*, you can put the possible answers into two equal (or nearly equal) parts, discard the half that does not include what you're looking for, and then repeat the process. Try picking a middle number or the average to start. So, $\frac{100 + 1}{2} = 50.5$, so, 50 would be a good starting number. If it is too high, use 1 and 50 and repeat the process. If it is too low, use 51 and 100 to repeat the process. Find the largest number of guesses required to find a number from 1 to 100.

2. Start with a line segment. Then, on each side, erase the middle third and add two segments the same length. Iterate this with each segment onto the new figure: erase the middle third and add two new segments of the same size. This is called a *fractal*.

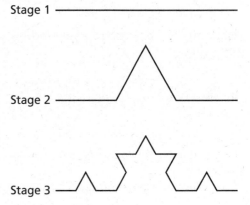

Stage 1

Stage 2

Stage 3

   Now, pretend the initial segment has a length of 1 foot. Find the total length of the shape for the first several stages. If we represent the first stage as $n = 1$, find an expression that models the pattern of the length at a given stage.

3. Below is an image called *Sierpinski's Carpet*. It begins with a blank white square with side lengths of 1 foot. Then it is divided into 9 equal smaller squares with the middle square shaded. Find the fraction of the unshaded area in the first several stages. If we represent the first stage as $n = 1$, find an expression that models the pattern of the shaded area at a given stage.

Stage 1:

Stage 2:

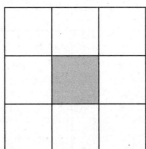

Stage 3:

Puzzle Time

Which Garden Insects Are Always Polite?

Circle the letter of each correct answer in the boxes below. The circled letters will spell out the answer to the riddle.

Complete the sentence.

1. A _____ is an unproven statement that is based on observations.

2. _____ uses facts, definitions, accepted properties, and the laws of logic to form a logical argument.

3. You use _____ when you find a pattern in specific cases and then write a conjecture for the general case.

4. A _____ is a specific case for which the conjecture is false.

State the law of logic represented. (A) Law of Syllogism (B) Law of Detachment (C) neither

5. If you exercise every day, then you will be a better athlete. You exercise every day. So, you will be a better athlete.

6. If you play baseball, then you play a sport. If you play a sport, then you are an athlete. You play baseball, so you are an athlete.

Find the counterexample that makes the conjecture false.

7. $\dfrac{N}{N} = 1$

8. All prime numbers are odd.

L	A	I	F	A	N	D	N
counter-example	$N = 0$	false term	0	C	proposal	conjecture	examples
Y	**H**	**I**	**S**	**B**	**U**	**G**	**S**
inductive reasoning	15	real world	$N = -\dfrac{1}{2}$	A	deductive reasoning	B	2

2.3 Start Thinking

You obtain a blueprint of your home. Only the walls are marked, making an outline of the general shape of the living space.

Make a list of at least five additional labels you would want on the drawing.

2.3 Warm Up

Find the angle measure.

1. $\angle 1$ is a supplement of $\angle 2$ and $m\angle 1 = 32°$. Find $m\angle 2$.

2. $\angle 3$ is a supplement of $\angle 4$ and $m\angle 3 = 155°$. Find $m\angle 4$.

3. $\angle 5$ is a complement of $\angle 6$ and $m\angle 5 = 59°$. Find $m\angle 6$.

4. $\angle 7$ is a complement of $\angle 8$ and $m\angle 7 = 18°$. Find $m\angle 8$.

2.3 Cumulative Review Warm Up

$\overrightarrow{BD}$ bisects $\angle ABC$. Find $m\angle ABD$ and $m\angle CBD$.

1.

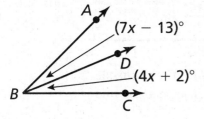

2.

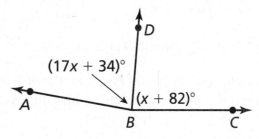

3.

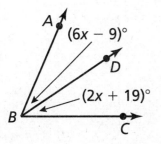

4.

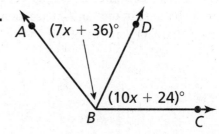

Name _____ Date _____

2.3 Practice A

In Exercises 1–6, use the diagram to write an example of the postulate.

1. Two Point Postulate (Postulate 2.1)

2. Line-Point Postulate (Postulate 2.2)

3. Line Intersection Postulate (Postulate 2.3)

4. Three Point Postulate (Postulate 2.4)

5. Plane-Point Postulate (Postulate 2.5)

6. Plane-Line Postulate (Postulate 2.6)

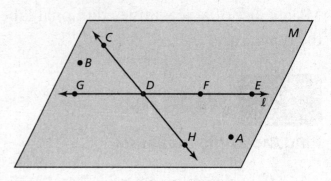

In Exercises 7–9, sketch a diagram of the description.

7. $\overleftrightarrow{GH}$ intersecting $\overleftrightarrow{XY}$ at point A in plane Q

8. $\overline{ST}$ bisected by $\overleftrightarrow{UV}$ at point V in plane R

9. plane C and plane D that intersect at $\overleftrightarrow{AB}$ and point E on plane C

In Exercises 10–14, use the diagram to determine whether you can assume the statement.

10. Planes L and K intersect at $\overleftrightarrow{PS}$.

11. Points U, M, and O are coplanar.

12. $\angle QOP$ is a right angle.

13. $\overleftrightarrow{MQ}$ is in plane L.

14. $\overleftrightarrow{PS}$ and $\overleftrightarrow{MQ}$ intersect at point O.

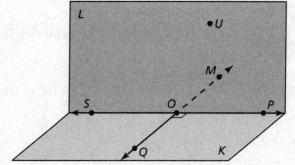

15. Rewrite the Three Point Postulate (Postulate 2.4) in if-then form. Then write the converse, inverse, and contrapositive. Indicate whether these statements are true or false.

16. Your friend claims that if three lines intersect each other, then there are two points of intersection because of the Line Intersection Postulate (Postulate 2.3). Is your friend correct? Explain your reasoning.

2.3 Practice B

In Exercises 1–6, use the diagram to write an example of the postulate.

1. Two Point Postulate (Postulate 2.1)

2. Line-Point Postulate (Postulate 2.2)

3. Line Intersection Postulate (Postulate 2.3)

4. Three Point Postulate (Postulate 2.4)

5. Plane-Line Postulate (Postulate 2.6)

6. Plane Intersection Postulate (Postulate 2.7)

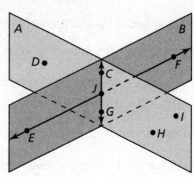

In Exercises 7 and 8, sketch a diagram of the description.

7. $\overleftrightarrow{AB}$, $\overleftrightarrow{CD}$, and $\overleftrightarrow{BD}$ that intersect at exactly two points

8. planes S and T intersecting at a right angle, $\overline{AB}$ on plane S and plane T, and point C is the midpoint of $\overline{AB}$

In Exercises 9–12, use the diagram to determine whether you can assume the statement.

9. Planes W and V intersect at $\overleftrightarrow{TU}$.

10. Points T, U, and R are coplanar.

11. $\angle TZX$ and $\angle UZY$ are vertical angles.

12. $\overleftrightarrow{TU}$ lies in plane W.

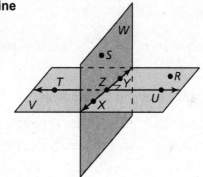

13. The Plane Intersection Postulate (Postulate 2.7) is written in if-then form. Write the converse, inverse, and contrapositive and state which ones are true.

14. Is it possible for three planes to intersect along the same line? Explain your reasoning.

15. Your friend claims that if the Plane-Line Postulate (Postulate 2.6) is true, then all lines that pass through a point in a plane must also be in that same plane. Is your friend correct? Explain your reasoning.

16. $\overleftrightarrow{AB}$ and $\overleftrightarrow{CD}$ lie in plane Z. If $\overleftrightarrow{EF}$ bisects either $\overline{AB}$ or $\overline{CD}$, does $\overleftrightarrow{EF}$ lie in plane Z? If $\overleftrightarrow{EF}$ bisects both $\overline{AB}$ and $\overline{CD}$, does $\overleftrightarrow{EF}$ lie in plane Z? Explain your reasoning.

Name _____ Date _____

Postulates & Diagrams

In Exercises 1–5, let *m* and *n* be two lines that intersect at point *X*.

1. Make a conjecture about the number of planes that contain both lines *m* and *n*.

2. Which postulate allows you to state that there is a point *Y*, distinct from *X*, on line *m*, and a point *Z*, distinct from *X*, on line *n*? Explain your reasoning.

3. Which postulate guarantees that point *Y* is not on line *n*? Explain your reasoning.

4. Which postulates allows you to conclude that there is exactly one plane *P* that contains points *X, Y,* and *Z*? Explain your reasoning.

5. Which postulate guarantees that lines *m* and *n* are contained in plane *P*? Explain your reasoning.

In Exercises 6–8, construct a diagram using the information.

6. Line *a*, line *b*, and line *c* are coplanar, but do not intersect.

7. Point *C* lies in plane *M*. Line *r* intersects line *s* at point *D*. Point *C*, line *r*, and line *s* are not coplanar.

8. Plane *A* and plane *B* intersect at line *s*. Plane *C* intersects plane *A* and plane *B*, but does not contain *s*.

In Exercises 9–12, use the following information.

Plane *P* contains points *A, C, D, E,* and *X*. Plane *Q* contains points *B, C, F,* and *X*. $\overrightarrow{CX}$ and $\overrightarrow{AE}$ intersect at point *X*. $\overrightarrow{BF}$ and $\overrightarrow{AE}$ intersect at point *X*. Point *D* is between points *E* and *C*.

9. Draw a diagram using the given information.

10. Where do planes *Q* and *P* intersect? Explain your reasoning.

11. Are points *D, E,* and *X* collinear? Explain your reasoning.

12. Can you assume that the line between points *D* and *B* lies in plane *Q*? Explain your reasoning.

Name_____ Date_____

2.3 Puzzle Time

Why Do Geese Fly South Every Year?

A	B	C	D	E	F
G	H	I			

Complete each exercise. Find the answer in the answer column. Write the word under the answer in the box containing the exercise letter.

4
GEESE
P
VACATION
3
IT
0
MEET
Q
WALK
6
THE

Match the item that makes the statement correct.

A. If two lines intersect,

B. Through any three noncollinear points

C. If two points lie in a plane,

D. If two planes intersect,

E. Through any two points,

F. A plane contains at least

G. A line contains at least

1. then their intersection is a line.

2. two points.

3. there exists exactly one plane.

4. three noncollinear points.

5. then their intersection is exactly one point.

6. there exists exactly one line.

7. then the line containing them lies in the plane.

7
WOULD
$\overline{AB}$
COLD
5
BECAUSE
1
TAKE
2
FOREVER
$\overline{AB}$
TO

Identify the correct answer using the diagram.

H. The intersection of planes Q and P.

I. What plane is defined by points A, B, and C?

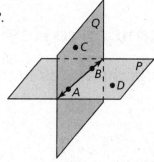

When solving equations, steps are typically done in the opposite order of the order of operations. For example, you need to "undo" subtraction before multiplication to solve $3x - 2 = 4$.

Describe one instance in which you must multiply or divide before undoing addition or subtraction. Create an example to illustrate.

2.4 **Warm Up**

State the mistake made in solving the equation. Rewrite the solution so it is correct.

1. $f - 23 = -17$

    $f - 23 - 23 = -17 - 23$

    $f = -40$

2. $8r = 4$

    $\dfrac{8r}{-8} = \dfrac{4}{-8}$

    $r = -\dfrac{1}{2}$

3. $\dfrac{4}{7}m = 22$

    $\left(\dfrac{7}{4}\right)\dfrac{4}{7}m = \left(\dfrac{4}{7}\right)22$

    $m = \dfrac{88}{7}$

4. $-\dfrac{n}{6} = 3$

    $\dfrac{6}{1} \bullet \left(-\dfrac{n}{6}\right) = 6 \bullet 3$

    $n = 18$

2.4 **Cumulative Review Warm Up**

Write three different angles in the diagram.

1.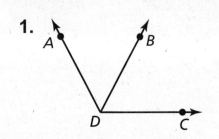

2.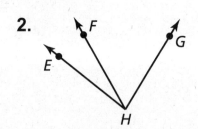

Name_____ Date_____

2.4 Practice A

In Exercises 1–3, solve the equation. Justify each step.

1. $3x + 4 = 31$

2. $3(2x + 1) = 15$

3. $\frac{1}{2}(16x - 8) = 2(x + 16)$

In Exercises 4–6, solve the equation for the given variable. Justify each step.

4. $p = 2v;\ v$

5. $V = \pi r^2 h;\ h$

6. $S = \pi rs + \pi r^2;\ s$

In Exercises 7 and 8, name the property of equality that the statement illustrates.

7. If $x = y$, then $-2x = -2y$.

8. If $m\angle A = m\angle B$ and $m\angle B = 42°$, then $m\angle A = 42°$.

In Exercises 9–11, use the property to copy and complete the statement.

9. Addition Property of Equality: If $m\angle J = 30°$, then $m\angle J + m\angle K =$ _____.

10. Reflexive Property of Equality: $GH =$ _____

11. Distributive Property: If $3(x + 7) = 30$, then _____ + _____ = 30.

12. The formula for the surface area of a rectangular prism is given by the equation $A = 2\ell w + 2\ell h + 2hw$, where ℓ is the length, w is the width, and h is the height. Solve the formula for w and justify each step. Then find the width of the prism if the total surface area is 52 square inches, the length is 2 inches, and the height is 4 inches.

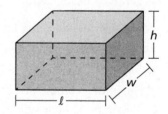

13. In the diagram, $AB = 3$ and $BC = 5$. Find the perimeter of the hexagon. Justify your answer using the properties of equality.

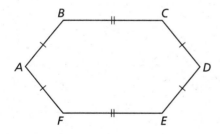

Name _____ Date _____

2.4 Practice B

In Exercises 1 and 2, solve the equation. Justify each step.

1. $3(x - 4) + 3 = x - 2$

2. $-1(x + 5) = 3\big[x + (2x - 1)\big]$

In Exercises 3 and 4, solve the equation for the given variable. Justify each step.

3. $I = \frac{1}{2}mr^2$; m

4. $E = \frac{1}{2}mv^2 + 9.8mh$; h

In Exercises 5 and 6, name the properties of equality that the statement illustrates.

5. If $x = y$, then $2x - 6 = 2y - 6$.

6. If $m\angle A = m\angle B$ and $m\angle B = 42°$, then $m\angle A + 10 = 52°$.

In Exercises 7 and 8, use the property to copy and complete the statement.

7. Multiplication Property of Equality: If $m\angle J = 30°$, then $2m\angle J = $ _____ .

8. Transitive Property: If $3x + y = 7$ and $7 = 5x - 2y$, then _____ .

9. The formula for the volume V of a triangular prism is given by the equation $V = \frac{1}{2}bh\ell$, where b is the base of the triangle, h is the height of the triangle, and ℓ is the length of the prism. Solve the formula for b. Justify each step. Then find the base of a prism with a volume of 128 cubic meters, a height of 8 meters, and a length of 4 meters.

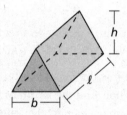

10. In the diagram, $m\angle ACB = 25°$ and $\overleftrightarrow{CE}$ bisects $\angle DCF$. Explain how to find $m\angle DCE$.

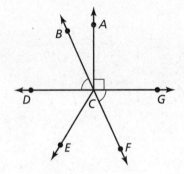

Name_____ Date_____

2.4 Enrichment and Extension

Algebraic Reasoning

In Exercises 1 and 2, solve for the indicated variable. Justify each step.

1. Solve for a: $S = \dfrac{n}{2}\big[2a + (n-1)d\big]$

2. Solve for r: $V = \dfrac{1}{3}\pi h^2(3r - h)$

3. Write a justification for each step of the mathematical induction proof, which proves that $10^n - 1$ is divisible by 9.

   a. $10^k - 1 = 9r$ **a.** _____

   b. $10^k = 9r + 1$ **b.** _____

   c. $10(10^k) = 10(9r + 1)$ **c.** _____

   d. $10^{k+1} = 10(9r + 1)$ **d.** _____

   e. $10^{k+1} = 90r + 10$ **e.** _____

   f. $10^{k+1} - 1 = 90r + 9$ **f.** _____

   g. $10^{k+1} - 1 = 9(10r + 1)$ **g.** _____

4. Suppose you receive a raise at work. Your current wage (in dollars per hour) is represented by c, the percent increase (as a decimal) in your wage is represented by r, and your new wage (in dollars per hour) is represented by n.

   a. Use the given information to write a pay raise formula that you can use to calculate your new wage n.

   b. Solve the formula from part (a) for r and write a reason for each step.

   c. Use the result for part (b) to find your percent increase if your current wage is $10.50 and your new wage will be $10.71.

   d. Suppose your co-worker receives a 4% pay raise and her new wage is $10.24. Find your co-worker's old wage. Explain the steps you used to find your answer.

Puzzle Time

How Can You Share Five Apples With Seven Friends?

Write the letter of each answer in the box containing the exercise number.

Identify the algebraic properties of equality that are represented.

1. If $a = b$, then $a \bullet c = b \bullet c$, $c \neq 0$.

2. If $a = b$, then $a - c = b - c$.

3. If $a = b$, then a can be substituted for b (or b for a) in any equation or expression.

4. If $a = b$, then $\dfrac{a}{c} = \dfrac{b}{c}$, $c \neq 0$.

5. If $a = b$, then $a + c = b + c$.

6. sum: $a(b + c) = ab + ac$,

    difference: $a(b - c) = ab - ac$

7. If $a = b$ and $b = c$, then $a = c$. If $AB = CD$ and $CD = EF$, then $AB = EF$. If $m\angle A = m\angle B$ and $m\angle B = m\angle C$, then $m\angle A = m\angle C$.

8. If $a = b$, then $b = a$. If $AB = CD$, then $CD = AB$. If $m\angle A = m\angle B$, then $m\angle B = m\angle A$.

9. $a = a$, $AB = AB$, $m\angle A = m\angle A$

Answers	
E. Subtraction	R. C
I. Inverse	P. Multiplication
Q. I	A. Addition
M. Substitution	D. Converse
F. G	A. Division
E. Distributive	B. Transformation
V. H	E. Transitive
A. Symmetric	P. D
M. Reverse	C. Reflexive
L. B	O. Algebraic
S. A	U. E
K. F	

Match the property of equality to the statement it illustrates.
(A) Reflexive, (B) Subtraction, (C) Distributive, (D) Multiplication,
(E) Transitive, (F) Symmetric, (G) Division, (H) Addition, (I) Substitution

10. If $x = y$, then $6x = 6y$.

11. If $AB = BC$, then $AB - 2 = BC - 2$.

12. $m\angle A = m\angle A$ 13. If $AB = CD$ and $CD = 6$, then $AB = 6$.

14. If $a = b$, then $b = a$.

3	5	14	2		4	1	10	11	6	12	8	13	9	7

Start Thinking

Draw a rectangle and then draw one diagonal of the rectangle. The formula for the area of a triangle is $A = \frac{1}{2}bh$, where b represents the base and h represents the height of the triangle. The formula for the area of any quadrilateral is $A = bh$.

Use the information above to explain why the formula for the area of a triangle is related to the area of a rectangle.

2.5 Warm Up

Find the complement and the supplement of the angle measure.

1. 59°   2. 20°   3. 53°

4. 22.6°   5. 28°   6. 74°

2.5 Cumulative Review Warm Up

Use the figure.

1. Name a pair of adjacent complementary angles.

2. Find $m\angle AEC$.

3. Find $m\angle AED$.

4. Find $m\angle BED$.

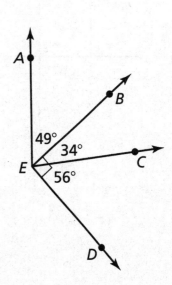

2.5　Practice A

In Exercises 1 and 2, name the property that the statement illustrates.

1. If $\overline{PQ} \cong \overline{RS}$, then $\overline{RS} \cong \overline{PQ}$.

2. $\angle A \cong \angle A$

In Exercises 3 and 4, write a two-column proof for this property.

3. Symmetric Property of Angle Congruence

4. Reflexive Property of Segment Congruence

In Exercises 5 and 6, write a two-column proof.

5. Given $\overrightarrow{BF}$ bisects $\angle AFC$ and $\angle CFD \cong \angle BFC$. Prove $\angle AFB \cong \angle CFD$.

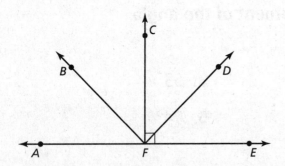

6. Given $\overline{AG}$ bisects $\overline{CD}$, $\overline{IJ}$ bisects $\overline{CE}$, and $\overline{BH}$ bisects $\overline{ED}$. Prove $\overline{KE} \cong \overline{FD}$.

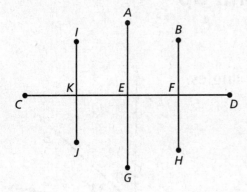

2.5 Practice B

In Exercises 1 and 2, write a two-column proof for this property.

1. Symmetric Property of Segment Congruence

2. Transitive Property of Angle Congruence

In Exercises 3–5, write a two-column proof.

3. Given E bisects $\overline{AI}$, $\overline{BC}$ bisects $\overline{AE}$, and $\overline{FH}$ bisects $\overline{EI}$. Prove $\overline{AD} \cong \overline{EG}$.

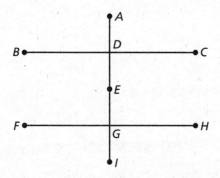

4. Given $m\angle KMN = 28°$ and $m\angle PTS = 118°$. Prove $\angle JMK \cong \angle STR$.

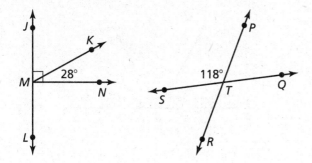

5. Given $\angle ADC \cong \angle BDE$. Prove $\angle ADE \cong \angle BDC$.

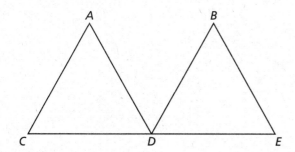

2.5 Enrichment and Extension

Proving Statements About Segments and Angles

In Exercises 1–3, suppose point *T* is the midpoint of $\overline{RS}$ and point *W* is the midpoint of $\overline{RT}$. If $\overline{TS}$ has length $TS = z$, find the following expressions and write a two-column proof justifying your answer.

1. *RT* in terms of *z*

2. *RS* in terms of *z*

3. *RW* in terms of *z*

4. Suppose *M* is the midpoint of $\overline{AB}$, *P* is the midpoint of $\overline{AM}$, and *Q* is the midpoint of $\overline{PM}$. If *a* and *b* are the coordinates of points *A* and *B* on a number line, find the coordinates of points *P* and *Q* in terms of *a* and *b*.

5. Solve for *x* and *y* using the given information.

   a. Given: $\overline{LM} \cong \overline{MN}, \overline{NO} \cong \overline{MN},$

   $LM = 12$

   b. Given: $\angle ABD \cong \angle CBE, \angle DBE \cong \angle CBE,$

   $m\angle DBE = 60°$

   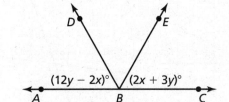

6. Write a two-column proof.

   Given: $m\angle ZYQ = 45°$

   $m\angle ZQP = 45°$

   Prove: $\angle ZQR \cong \angle XYQ$

   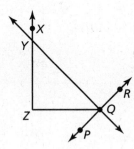

Name_____ Date_____

2.5 Puzzle Time

Which Month Has Twenty-Eight Days?

Circle the letter of each correct answer in the boxes below. The circled letters will spell out the answer to the riddle.

Complete each sentence with the correct answer.

1. A _____ has numbered statements and corresponding reasons that show an argument in a logical order.

2. A _____ is a statement that can be proven.

3. A _____ is a logical argument that uses deductive reasoning to show that a statement is true.

Name the property that is illustrated. (A) Addition, (B) Transitive, (C) Inverse, (D) Symmetric, (E) Distributive, (F) Reflexive, (G) Multiplication

4. If $\angle G \cong \angle H$, then $\angle H \cong \angle G$.   5. If $AB = CD$ and $CD = XY$, then $AB = XY$.

6. $\angle A \cong \angle A$

Complete the proof using the correct reason. (1) Congruent segments, (2) Given, (3) Congruent angles, (4) Symmetric, (5) Reflexive

Given: $\overline{AB} \cong \overline{CD}$ Prove: $\overline{CD} \cong \overline{AB}$

STATEMENTS	REASONS
$\overline{AB} \cong \overline{CD}$	7. _____
$AB = CD$	8. _____
$CD = AB$	9. _____
$\overline{CD} \cong \overline{AB}$	Definition of congruent segments

R	T	K	N	H	F	E	M	Y	B
E	1	0	A	two-column proof	inductive	proof	list	B	3
G	**A**	**U**	**L**	**P**	**L**	**I**	**L**	**D**	**O**
C	4	G	F	deductive	5	$\frac{1}{4}$	theorem	2	D

Start Thinking

As you learned in Section 1.5, there are four types of angles: acute, obtuse, right, and straight.

Make a flowchart that can be used to classify any angle between $0°$ and $180°$. Give one other example of a math concept where a flowchart may prove useful.

2.6 **Warm Up**

Solve.

1. $9x + 6 = 10x - 3$

2. $6y = 5y + 35$

3. $9x + 5 = 5(x - 3)$

4. $17y + 18 = 15y$

5. $14x - 44 = 20x - 2$

6. $7x - 1 = 13x + 41$

2.6 **Cumulative Review Warm Up**

Sketch the figure described.

1. Plane N and line ℓ intersecting at one point

2. $\overrightarrow{CD}$ and $\overrightarrow{CE}$

3. Plane P and $\overrightarrow{QF}$ intersecting at point F

4. Plane C and plane D not intersecting

5. Plane L and segment $\overline{MN}$ intersecting at all points on segment $\overline{MN}$

6. $\overline{MN}$ and $\overrightarrow{PQ}$

Name_____ Date_____

2.6 Practice A

In Exercises 1 and 2, identify the pairs of congruent angles in the figures. Explain how you know they are congruent.

1.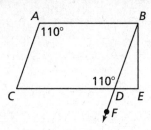

2.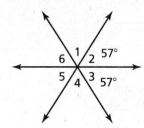

In Exercises 3 and 4, find the values of *x* and *y*.

3.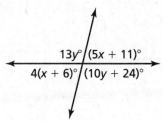

4.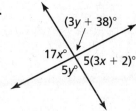

5. Copy and complete the two-column proof.
   Then write a paragraph proof.

   Given: $\angle 1$ and $\angle 2$ are supplementary.

   $\angle 1$ and $\angle 3$ are supplementary.

   Prove: $\angle 2 \cong \angle 3$

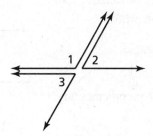

STATEMENTS	REASONS
1. $\angle 1$ and $\angle 2$ are supplementary. $\angle 1$ and $\angle 3$ are supplementary.	1. Given
2. $m\angle 1 + m\angle 2 = 180°$ $m\angle 1 + m\angle 3 = 180°$	2. _____
3. _____	3. Transitive Property
4. $m\angle 2 = m\angle 3$	4. _____
5. _____	5. Definition of congruent angles

2.6 Practice B

In Exercises 1 and 2, identify the pairs of congruent angles in the figures. Explain how you know they are congruent.

1.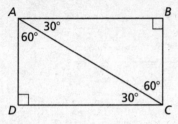

2.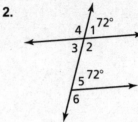

In Exercises 3 and 4, find the values of x and y.

3.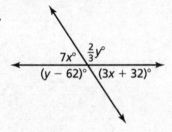

4.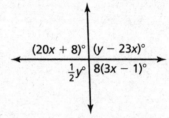

5. Copy and complete the flowchart proof.
   Then write a paragraph proof.

   Given: ∠1 is a right angle.

   ∠5 is a right angle.

   ∠5 and ∠8 are supplementary.

   Prove: ∠3 ≅ ∠8

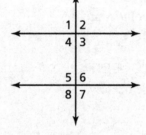

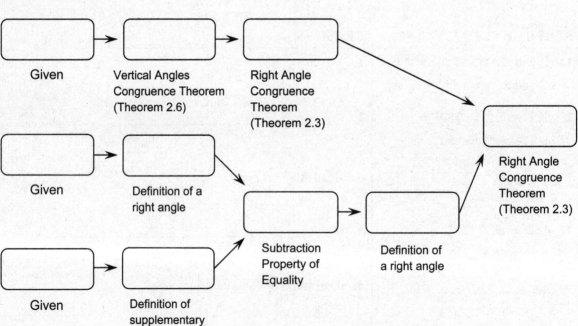

2.6 Enrichment and Extension

Proving Geometric Relationships

In Exercises 1–6, use the information below.

Two lines that are not perpendicular intersect such that $\angle 1$ and $\angle 2$ are a linear pair, $\angle 1$ and $\angle 4$ are a linear pair, and $\angle 1$ and $\angle 3$ are vertical angles. Tell whether the statement is true or false.

1. $\angle 1 \cong \angle 2$ **2.** $\angle 1 \cong \angle 3$ **3.** $\angle 1 \cong \angle 4$

4. $\angle 3 \cong \angle 2$ **5.** $\angle 2 \cong \angle 4$ **6.** $m\angle 3 + m\angle 4 = 180°$

In Exercises 7–9, refer to the diagram to write a two-column proof.

7. Given: $\overline{AB} \perp \overline{BD}, \overline{ED} \perp \overline{BD}, \angle ABC \cong \angle EDC$

    Prove: $\angle CBD \cong \angle CDB$

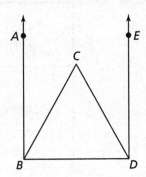

8. Given: $m\angle WYZ = m\angle TWZ = 45°$

    Prove: $\angle SWZ \cong \angle XYW$

9. Given: The hexagon is regular.

    Prove: $m\angle 1 + m\angle 2 = 180°$

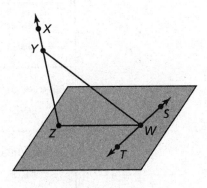

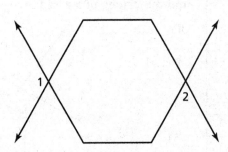

2.6 Puzzle Time

How Can You Make Sure To Start A Fire With Two Sticks?

A	B	C	D	E	F
G	H				

Complete each exercise. Find the answer in the answer column. Write the word under the answer in the box containing the exercise letter.

77° WOOD	
20 AND	
congruent MAKE	
113° THEM	
23° HOT	
80 TREE	
40 A	
vertical OF	

Complete these sentences.

A. All right angles are _____ .

B. _____ angles form a straight line.

C. If two angles form a _____ , then they are supplementary.

D. When two lines intersect, the _____ angles are congruent.

Determine the measure of ∠2 and ∠3 given that m∠1 = 67°.

E. m∠2 =

F. m∠3 =

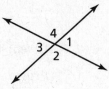

Find the values of x and y.

G. x =

H. y =

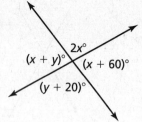

67° IS	
congruence RUB	
60 MATCH	
transitive THE	
supplementary SURE	
inverse USE	
linear pair ONE	
horizontal ARE	

Chapter 2 — Cumulative Review

In Exercises 1–3, find the pattern. Draw the next two figures in the sequence.

1.

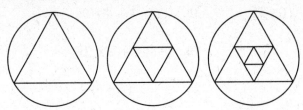

2.

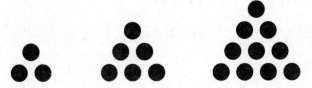

3.

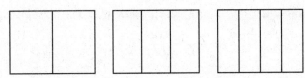

In Exercises 4–11, find the pattern. Write the next two numbers.

4. 2, 4, 6, 8, …

5. 1, 4, 7, 10, …

6. 4, 17, 30, 43, …

7. 7, 16, 25, 34, …

8. $2, 3, \frac{9}{2}, \frac{27}{4}, \dots$

9. $3, \frac{9}{4}, \frac{27}{16}, \frac{81}{64}, \dots$

10. 1, 3, 6, 10, …

11. 2, 5, 9, 14, …

12. A rectangular fence measures 26 feet by 18 feet.

    a. Find the perimeter of the fence.

    b. Find the area of the fence.

13. A square table has an area of 2916 square inches.

    a. Find the side length.

    b. Find the perimeter of the fence.

Chapter 2 Cumulative Review (continued)

In Exercises 14–28, evaluate the expression.

14. $3 + 8 \cdot 10 - 4$

15. $(96 \div 3) \div (1 + 7)$

16. $-1 + 8 - 4 \cdot 9$

17. $(8 \cdot 3) \div (2 + 10) - 7$

18. $7 + 20 \div 5$

19. $(-8)(8 + 6 \cdot 2)$

20. $12 - 8^2 + 30$

21. $-7 + 4 \cdot 9$

22. $9^2 - 3(4 \cdot 5) + 23$

23. $9 + 21(3 - 7)$

24. $19 + 23 - 7(4)$

25. $11(-4) - 8 \cdot 2$

26. $27 \div 3 + 4 - 7 + 9 \cdot 2$

27. $4 + 21 \div 7 \div 3$

28. $6 \cdot 3 \div 2 - 5 + 7$

In Exercises 29–43, simplify the expression.

29. $2s + 16 - 9s$

30. $9c + 18c - 19$

31. $9 + 6g + g$

32. $4 - 7x - 9x + 3$

33. $9 - m + 6m - 4$

34. $4 + 7r + 3r - 1$

35. $(7 + 6j) - 7$

36. $-4a - 6(7 - 5a)$

37. $7(f - 5) + 12$

38. $8 + 6(y - 3)$

39. $-2(b - 2) - 6$

40. $3 + 8(k - 1)$

41. $3w - 2(w + 1)$

42. $7g + 2(3 - 2g)$

43. $(3 - 4p) + 5p$

In Exercises 44–55, solve the equation.

44. $b + 8 = 13$

45. $7m = 49$

46. $k - 2 = 17$

47. $\dfrac{p}{5} = 3$

48. $-4a = 16$

49. $x - 12 = -9$

50. $\dfrac{r}{2} = -11$

51. $6 + h = 15$

52. $\dfrac{w}{6} = 7$

53. $4 + t = -18$

54. $c - 8 = -11$

55. $8e = -56$

56. A school lunch costs $1.85.

   a. How many lunches can you buy with $10?

   b. How many lunches can you buy with $20?

   c. How much does it cost for 15 school lunches?

   d. A normal school week is five days. How much does it cost to purchase a school lunch for an entire school week?

   e. You can purchase a "monthly" lunch ticket, which is 20 days. How much does it cost to purchase a "monthly" lunch ticket?

Chapter 2 **Cumulative Review** (continued)

57. You begin to do push-ups every day after school. You begin with five push-ups and increase your workout by one push-up each day.

    a. How many push-ups do you complete on day three?

    b. How many push-ups do you complete on day five?

    c. When will you complete 12 push-ups?

    d. When will you complete 15 push-ups?

In Exercises 58–69, evaluate.

58. 4^3

59. $(-4)^3$

60. 2^5

61. 5^2

62. -3^2

63. $(-3)^2$

64. 4^2

65. -4^2

66. $(-4)^2$

67. 10^2

68. 100^3

69. $(-2)^5$

In Exercises 70–93, evaluate.

70. $\sqrt{45}$

71. $\sqrt{24}$

72. $\sqrt{125}$

73. $\sqrt{28}$

74. $\sqrt{48}$

75. $\sqrt{32}$

76. $\sqrt{50}$

77. $\sqrt{150}$

78. $\sqrt{160}$

79. $\sqrt{200}$

80. $\sqrt{192}$

81. $\sqrt{72}$

82. $\sqrt{108}$

83. $\sqrt{75}$

84. $\sqrt{147}$

85. $\sqrt{20}$

86. $\sqrt{\dfrac{4}{9}}$

87. $\sqrt{\dfrac{9}{49}}$

88. $\sqrt{\dfrac{36}{81}}$

89. $\sqrt{\dfrac{25}{36}}$

90. $\dfrac{2}{\sqrt{5}}$

91. $\dfrac{1}{\sqrt{3}}$

92. $\dfrac{4}{\sqrt{7}}$

93. $\dfrac{3}{\sqrt{6}}$

In Exercises 94–111, solve the equation.

94. $2x - 4 = 10$

95. $5 + 3x = -4$

96. $6 - 2x = -12$

97. $-5 - 6x = 31$

98. $12x - 9 = 15$

99. $7x - 4 = 5x + 6$

100. $\dfrac{1}{3}x - 5 = -7$

101. $\dfrac{x}{4} + 1 = 9$

102. $12 = \dfrac{x}{7} + 10$

103. $7 - 2x = -x + 9$

104. $3x - 9 = 12 - 4x$

105. $8 - 2x = -22 + 8x$

106. $4 + 3x = -21 - 2x$

107. $-x + 1 = 8x - 17$

108. $5 - 2x = 9x - 28$

109. $14x - 6 = 10x + 22$

110. $4 - 3x = 15 + 8x$

111. $2x - 16 = -5x + 33$

Chapter 2 Cumulative Review (continued)

112. Write the negation of each statement.

    a. The chair is wood.   **b.** The rug is *not* brown.

113. Write the negation of each statement.

    a. The photograph is *not* in color.   **b.** Your homework is finished.

114. Write the negation of each statement.

    a. It is cold outside.   **b.** The bicycle is *not* green.

In Exercises 115–126, simplify the expression.

115. $(x + 4)^2$ **116.** $(x - 2)^2$ **117.** $(x - 3)^2$ **118.** $(x - 1)^2$

119. $(x + 9)^2$ **120.** $(x - 13)^2$ **121.** $(2x + 4)^2$ **122.** $(3x - 1)^2$

123. $(5x + 6)^2$ **124.** $(5x - 1)^2$ **125.** $(3x + 8)^2$ **126.** $(2x - 4)^2$

In Exercises 127–138, factor the trinomial.

127. $x^2 - 5x - 14$ **128.** $x^2 - x - 132$ **129.** $x^2 - 3x - 28$

130. $x^2 - 8x + 15$ **131.** $x^2 - 5x + 6$ **132.** $x^2 - 5x - 36$

133. $x^2 - 1$ **134.** $x^2 - 9$ **135.** $x^2 - 25$

136. $2x^2 + 5x - 12$ **137.** $3x^2 - 26x + 35$ **138.** $5x^2 + 22x + 8$

In Exercises 139–150, solve the equation.

139. $x^2 + 11x + 24 = 0$ **140.** $x^2 + 4x - 12 = 0$ **141.** $x^2 + 11x - 12 = 0$

142. $x^2 + 17x + 72 = 0$ **143.** $x^2 + x - 20 = 0$ **144.** $x^2 + 17x + 70 = 0$

145. $x^2 + 2x - 3 = 0$ **146.** $x^2 + 3x - 10 = 0$ **147.** $x^2 + 10x - 11 = 0$

148. $2x^2 - 7x - 15 = 0$ **149.** $5x^2 - 11x - 12 = 0$ **150.** $6x^2 - 19x - 7 = 0$

151. You text at a rate of 35 words per minute. Your friend texts at a rate of 42 words per minute.

    a. How much faster does your friend text?

    b. How many words can you text in 2.5 minutes?

    c. How many words can your friend text in 2.5 minutes?

    d. How many more words can your friend text in 2.5 minutes?

Chapter 3

Chapter 3 Parallel and Perpendicular Lines

Dear Family,

Parallel and perpendicular lines are used in building bridges all over the world. Your student may not notice, but every bridge they see or cross is made up of these two types of lines.

With your student, look up the following images on the internet.

Pratt Bridge

Pennsylvania Bridge

Parker Bridge

Notice how these bridges are structurally different and have different ways of supporting transportation. Take time to discuss parallel and perpendicular lines that make up the bridge structure or support system.

- Where are parallel lines present in each of the bridges?
- Where are perpendicular lines present in each of the bridges?

Take a trip to a few bridges in your area. Although these bridges may be simpler in design, parallel and perpendicular lines are most likely present. Take pictures of the bridges you see to bring home with you.

Using the images that you found on the internet and the photographs that you took, come up with a creative design for a new bridge. Make use of parallel and perpendicular lines in the structure and support system. Use the space below to draw a diagram. Be sure to label at least one pair each of parallel and perpendicular lines.

Be creative!

Nombre _____ Fecha_____

Rectas paralelas y perpendiculares

Capítulo 3

Estimada familia:

Las rectas paralelas y perpendiculares se usan para construir puentes en todo el mundo. Su hijo tal vez no lo note, pero cada puente que ve o cruza está formado por estas dos clases de rectas.

Con su hijo, busquen las siguientes imágenes en Internet.

Puente Pratt

Puente de Pensilvania

Puente Parker

Observen cómo estos puentes tienen distintas estructuras y diferentes maneras de soportar el transporte. Tómense un tiempo para hablar sobre las rectas paralelas y perpendiculares que forman la estructura del puente o el sistema de soporte.

- ¿Dónde están las rectas paralelas en cada uno de los puentes?
- ¿Dónde están las rectas perpendiculares en cada uno de los puentes?

Vayan de ver algunos puentes de su zona. Aunque estos puentes tengan un diseño más simple, es muy probable que las rectas paralelas y perpendiculares estén presentes. Tomen fotografías de los puentes que vean para llevarse a casa.

Con las imágenes que encontraron en Internet y las fotografías que tomaron, piensen en un diseño creativo para un puente nuevo. Usen rectas paralelas y perpendiculares en la estructura y en el sistema de soporte. Usen el siguiente espacio para dibujar un diagrama. Asegúrense de rotular, al menos, un par de rectas paralelas y perpendiculares.

¡Sean creativos!

3.1 Start Thinking

Sketch two perpendicular lines that intersect at point A. Plot one point on each line that is not A. Call these points B and C. Connect B and C to make $\overline{BC}$. What type of figure do points A, B, and C make? Could you ever plot points B and C to make a perpendicular segment to either original line? A parallel segment? Explain your reasoning.

3.1 Warm Up

Use the diagram.

1. What is another name for $\overrightarrow{BD}$?

2. What is another name for $\overline{EG}$?

3. What is another name for $\overleftrightarrow{CH}$?

4. Name all segments with endpoint B.

5. Name one pair of opposite rays.

6. Name a point on $\overrightarrow{AC}$.

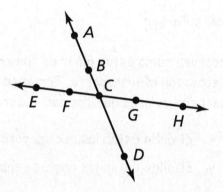

3.1 Cumulative Review Warm Up

The midpoint M and one endpoint of $\overline{JK}$ are given. Find the coordinates of the other endpoint.

1. $M(5, 2)$ and $J(6, -7)$

2. $M(-14, -5)$ and $K(-1, 8)$

3. $M(9, -1)$ and $J(-3, 0)$

3.1 Practice A

In Exercises 1–4, use the diagram.

1. Name a pair of parallel lines.

2. Name a pair of perpendicular lines.

3. Is $\overrightarrow{AB} \parallel \overleftrightarrow{BC}$? Explain.

4. Is $\overleftrightarrow{BD} \perp \overleftrightarrow{CD}$? Explain.

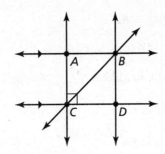

In Exercises 5–8, identify all pairs of angles of the given type.

5. alternate interior

6. alternate exterior

7. corresponding

8. consecutive interior

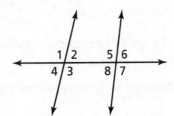

9. Is it possible to draw three lines in two planes such that all three lines are skew? Explain your reasoning.

10. How many pairs of consecutive interior angles do you have when two horizontal lines are intersected by a transversal? How many pairs of consecutive interior angles do you have when three horizontal lines are intersected by a transversal? How many pairs of consecutive interior angles do you have when *n* horizontal lines are intersected by a transversal?

11. The given markings show how the railroad ties on a railroad track are related to each other.

    a. Name two pairs of parallel lines.

    b. Name two pairs of perpendicular lines.

    c. Name all pairs of consecutive interior angles.

    d. Name all pairs of corresponding angles.

    e. Name all pairs of alternate interior angles.

    f. Name all pairs of alternate exterior angles.

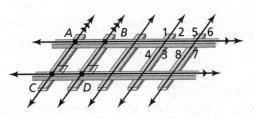

3.1 Practice B

In Exercises 1–6, use the diagram.

1. Name a pair of parallel lines.

2. Name a pair of perpendicular lines.

3. Name a pair of skew lines.

4. Name a pair of parallel planes.

5. Is line *f* parallel to line *g*? Explain.

6. Is line *e* perpendicular to line *g*? Explain.

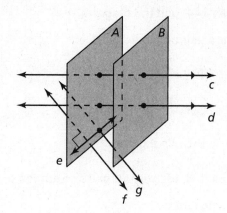

In Exercises 7–11, classify the angle pair as *corresponding, alternate interior, alternate exterior,* or *consecutive interior* angles.

7. ∠4 and ∠9

8. ∠1 and ∠9

9. ∠1 and ∠12

10. ∠6 and ∠11

11. ∠4 and ∠7

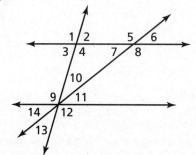

12. Two planes are parallel and each plane contains a line. Are the two lines skew? Explain your reasoning.

13. Use the figure to decide whether the statement is true or false. Explain your reasoning.

   a. The line containing the sidewalk and the line containing the center of the road are parallel to each other.

   b. The line containing the center of the road is skew to the line containing the crosswalk.

   c. The plane containing a stop sign is perpendicular to the plane containing the ground.

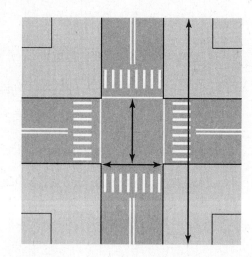

3.1 Enrichment and Extension

Pairs of Lines and Angles

1. If two parallel planes are cut by a third plane, are the lines of intersection parallel? Explain your reasoning and include a drawing.

2. Draw line a parallel to line b. Draw line c parallel to line b. What relationship appears to exist between lines a and c? Make a conjecture about two lines that are parallel to the same line.

3. Draw line ℓ perpendicular to a line m. Draw a line n perpendicular to line m. What relationship appears to exist between line ℓ and line n? Make a conjecture about two lines that are perpendicular to the same line.

In Exercises 4 and 5, draw the figure described.

4. Lines ℓ and m are skew, lines ℓ and n are skew, and lines m and n are parallel.

5. Line ℓ is parallel to plane A, plane A is parallel to plane B, and line ℓ is not parallel to plane B.

6. List all possible answers for each.

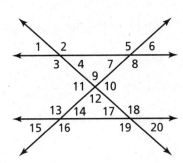

   a. $\angle 1$ and _____ are corresponding angles.

   b. $\angle 13$ and _____ are corresponding angles.

   c. $\angle 14$ and _____ are consective interior angles.

   d. $\angle 4$ and _____ are consective interior angles.

   e. $\angle 7$ and _____ are alternate interior angles.

   f. $\angle 17$ and _____ are alternate interior angles.

   g. $\angle 6$ and _____ are alterior exterior angles.

   h. $\angle 18$ and _____ are alternate exterior angles.

Name _____ Date _____

 3.1 Puzzle Time

What Has A Foot On Each End And One In The Middle?

Write the letter of each answer in the box containing the exercise number.

Fill in the blank.

1. Two lines are _____ if and only if they are both vertical lines or they both have the same slope.

2. Two lines are _____ if and only if one is vertical and the other is horizontal or the slopes of the lines are negative reciprocals of each other.

3. Two lines are _____ if and only if their equations are equivalent.

4. Two lines are _____ lines when they do not intersect and are not coplanar.

5. A(n) _____ is a line that intersects two or more coplanar lines at different points.

Identify the type of the pairs of angles.

6. ∠3 and ∠5

7. ∠1 and ∠8

8. ∠2 and ∠6

9. ∠1 and ∠4

10. ∠4 and ∠5

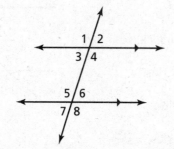

Answers
G. unskew
K. coincident
H. conditional
C. alternate exterior angles
I. transversal
T. angular
U. straight
S. skew
L. horizontal
R. perpendicular
N. lined angles
T. vertical angles
P. inverse angles
A. parallel
D. consecutive interior angles
B. revolving angles
L. converse angles
Y. alternate interior angles
M. intersecting angles
A. corresponding angles

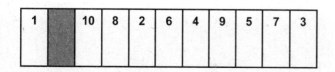

1		10	8	2	6	4	9	5	7	3

Start Thinking

Suppose you are given parallel lines ℓ and m, as well as line t, which intersects lines ℓ and m.

Sketch the lines and label angles 1 through 8 created by the intersections. What is the least number of angle measures you need to be given to figure out all eight angle measures? Explain.

3.2 **Warm Up**

Find the angle measure.

1. $(3x + 22)° = (10x - 6)°$

2. $(7x - 46)° = (9x - 64)°$

3. $(15x + 12)° = (19x - 24)°$

4. $(15x + 8)° = (21x - 10)°$

5. $(16x - 42)° = (9x + 14)°$

6. $(11x + 18)° = (14x)°$

3.2 **Cumulative Review Warm Up**

Sketch a diagram of the description.

1. plane R and line ℓ intersecting plane R at a $45°$ angle

2. $\overline{AB}$ in plane R bisected by point C, with point D also on $\overline{AB}$

3. $\overline{AB}$ in plane R with ray $\overrightarrow{CD}$ such that point C is on $\overline{AB}$

4. planes R and S with line $\overleftrightarrow{XY}$ intersecting each plane

Name_____ Date _____

3.2 Practice A

In Exercises 1 and 2, find *m*∠1 and *m*∠2. Tell which theorem you used in each case.

1.

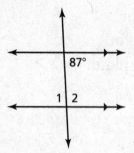

2.

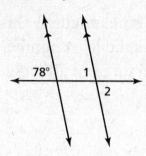

In Exercises 3 and 4, find the value of *x*. Show your steps.

3.

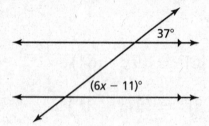

4.

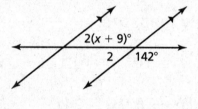

In Exercises 5 and 6, find *m*∠1, *m*∠2, and *m*∠3. Explain your reasoning.

5.

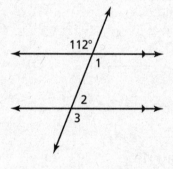

6.

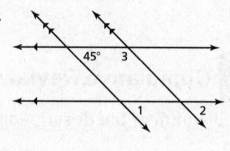

7. Prove the Corresponding Angles Theorem (Thm. 3.1).

8. Prove that if ∠1 ≅ ∠2, then ∠2 ≅ ∠3. What is *m*∠1? Explain.

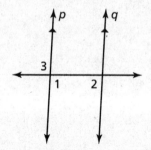

Name_____ Date_____

3.2 Practice B

In Exercises 1 and 2, find $m\angle 1$ **and** $m\angle 2$**. Tell which theorem you used in each case.**

1.

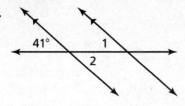

41°

2.

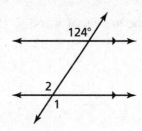

124°

In Exercises 3 and 4, find the value of x**. Show your steps.**

3.

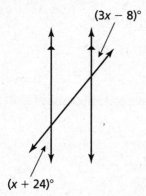

$(3x - 8)°$

$(x + 24)°$

4.

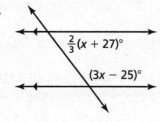

$\frac{2}{3}(x + 27)°$

$(3x - 25)°$

In Exercises 5 and 6, find $m\angle 1$**,** $m\angle 2$**, and** $m\angle 3$**. Explain your reasoning.**

5.

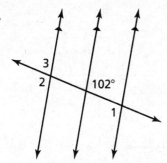

102°

6.

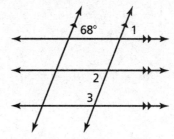

68°

7. The figure shows a two-dimensional representation of a bird made out of origami paper. Find $m\angle 1$ and $m\angle 2$. Explain your reasoning.

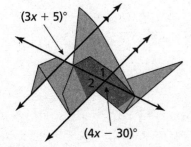

$(3x + 5)°$

$(4x - 30)°$

8. The figure shows three pairs of parallel lines. Which angles are congruent to $\angle 1$? Tell which theorem you used in each case.

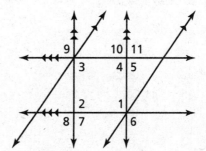

Name _____ Date _____

3.2 Enrichment and Extension

Parallel Lines and Transversals

In Exercises 1 and 2, find the values of *x* and *y*.

1.

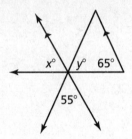

2.

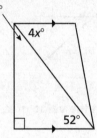

3. Draw a four-sided figure in which $\overline{AB} \parallel \overline{DC}$ and $\overline{AD} \parallel \overline{BC}$. Prove $\angle A \cong \angle C$.

In Exercises 4 and 5, find the measures of all angles in the diagram.

4. Given: $\ell \parallel m$, $m\angle 1 = 35°$, and $m\angle 12 = 111°$

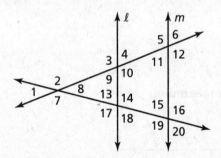

5. Given: $a \parallel b$, $c \parallel d$, $e \parallel f$, $m\angle 7 = 24°$, and $m\angle 20 = 80°$

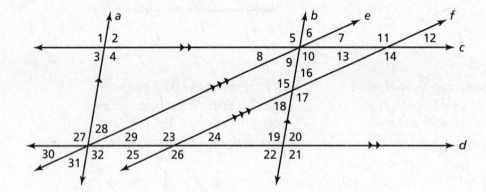

3.2 Puzzle Time

What Did The Acorn Say When It Grew Up?

Circle the letter of each correct answer in the boxes below. The circled letters will spell out the answer to the riddle.

Complete the sentence.

1. If two parallel lines are cut by a transversal, then the pairs of consecutive interior angles are _____.

2. If two parallel lines are cut by a transversal, then the pairs of alternate interior angles are _____.

Using the properties of parallel lines, find the angle measure.

3. $m\angle 2 = 74°$; Find $m\angle 1$.

4. $m\angle 2 = 74°$; Find $m\angle 3$.

5. $m\angle 1 = 114°$; Find $m\angle 8$.

6. $m\angle 4 = 56°$; Find $m\angle 6$.

7. $m\angle 1 = 84°$; Find $m\angle 7$.

8. $m\angle 8 = 116°$; Find $m\angle 2$.

G	E	I	F	O	A	E	M
64°	124°	116°	66°	106°	transitive	complementary	congruent
T	**E**	**I**	**T**	**R**	**Y**	**M**	**E**
84°	74°	34°	96°	114°	supplementary	56°	116°

You are designing a new shopping mall. The mall will be surrounded by four walkways. The north and south walkways are parallel, as are the east and west walkways. The southwest and northeast corners are 60° angles.

Sketch the mall and its walkways. What are the angles of the other two corners? The mall's walkways are running parallel with streets on all four sides. Add these streets to your sketch. What angles do the centers of the intersecting streets create? Explain your reasoning.

3.3 Warm Up

Find the values of x and y.

1.
$(6y + 36)°$
$(-3x + 102)°$ $(7x + 2)°$
$9y°$

2.
$(40y + 20)°$
$8x°$ $(2x + 30°)$
$(60y - 40)°$

3.3 Cumulative Review Warm Up

Use the property to copy and complete the statement.

1. Symmetric Property of Equality:

   If $m\angle 1 = m\angle 2$, then _____.

2. Addition Property of Equality:

   If $EF = GH$, then $EF + HJ = $ _____.

3. Multiplication Property of Equality:

   If $EF = GH$, then $4 \bullet EF = $ _____.

Name_____ Date _____

In Exercises 1 and 2, find the value of *x* that makes *s* ∥ *t*. Explain your reasoning.

1.

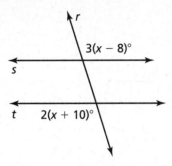

$3(x - 8)°$

$2(x + 10)°$

2.

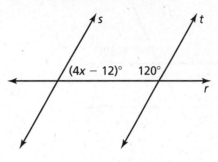

$(4x - 12)°$ $120°$

In Exercises 3 and 4, decide whether there is enough information to prove that
p ∥ *q*. If so, state the theorem you would use.

3.

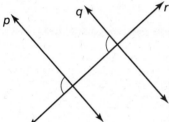

4.

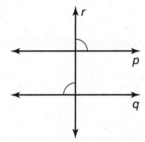

5. Describe and correct the error
in the reasoning.

   Conclusion: *m* ∥ *n*

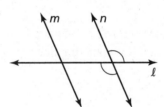

6. **Given:** ∠1 and ∠2 are supplementary

   Prove: *p* ∥ *q*

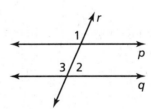

7. The angles formed between the braces and the wings
of a biplane are shown in the figure. Are the top and
bottom wings of a biplane parallel? Explain your
reasoning.

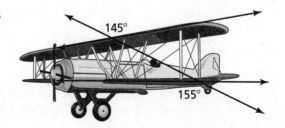

145°

155°

Name _____ Date _____

3.3 Practice B

In Exercises 1 and 2, find the value of x that makes s ∥ t. Explain your reasoning.

1.

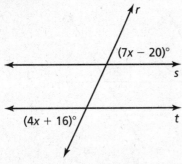

$(7x - 20)°$

$(4x + 16)°$

2.

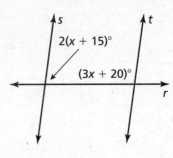

$2(x + 15)°$

$(3x + 20)°$

In Exercises 3 and 4, decide whether there is enough information to prove that p ∥ q. If so, state the theorem you would use.

3.

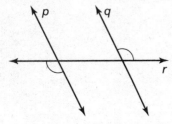

4.

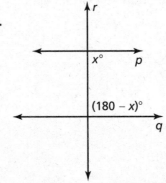

$x°$

$(180 - x)°$

5. The map of the United States shows the lines of latitude and longitude. The lines of latitude run horizontally and the lines of longitude run vertically.

   a. Are the lines of latitude parallel? Explain.

   b. Are the lines of longitude parallel? Explain.

6. Use the diagram to answer the following.

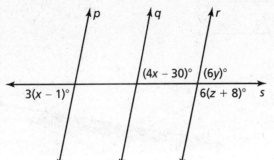

$(4x - 30)°$ $(6y)°$

$3(x - 1)°$ $6(z + 8)°$ s

7. **Given:** $\angle 1 \cong \angle 2$ and $\angle 2 \cong \angle 3$

   Prove: $\angle 1 \cong \angle 4$

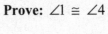

   a. Find the values of x, y, and z that makes p ∥ q and q ∥ r. Explain your reasoning.

   b. Is p ∥ r? Explain your reasoning.

3.3 Enrichment and Extension

Proofs with Parallel Lines

1. $\overline{AB}$ is parallel to $\overline{DE}$, $m\angle w = 135°$, and $m\angle z = 147°$. Find $m\angle BCD$.

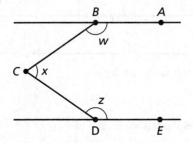

2. $\overline{AC}$ is parallel to $\overline{FG}$. $\overline{BD}$ is the bisector of $\angle CBE$ and $\overline{DE}$ is the bisector of $\angle BEG$. Write a two-column proof that shows $m\angle BDE = 90°$.

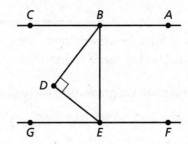

3. Point R is not in plane ABC.

   a. How many lines through R are perpendicular to plane ABC?

   b. How many lines through R are parallel to plane ABC?

   c. How many planes through R are parallel to plane ABC?

4. In the diagram to the right, $e \parallel d$, $g \parallel f$, and $a \parallel b \parallel c$. Find the following.

   a. $m\angle 1$

   b. $m\angle 2$

   c. $m\angle 3$

   d. $m\angle 4$

   e. $m\angle 5$

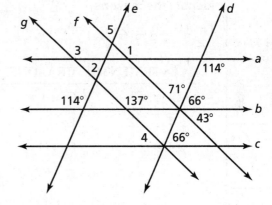

5. Write a two-column proof.

   Given: $\overrightarrow{CA} \parallel \overrightarrow{ED}$, $m\angle FED = m\angle GCA = 45°$

   Prove: $\overrightarrow{EF} \parallel \overrightarrow{CG}$

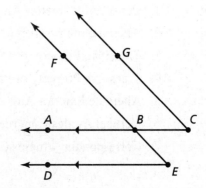

Name _____ Date _____

3.3 Puzzle Time

Why Did The Boy Throw His Clock Out The Window?

A	B	C	D	E	F

G	

Complete each exercise. Find the answer in the answer column. Write the word under the answer in the box containing the exercise letter.

11 TO
13 PLANE
77 BREAK
6 SEE
4 AN
5 BIRD
70 THE
12 HE

Using the diagram, find the value of x that makes r parallel to s.

A. $m\angle 1 = 30°$ and $m\angle 7 = (2x + 10)°$

B. $m\angle 4 = 135°$ and $m\angle 5 = (4x - 3)°$

C. $m\angle 2 = 124°$ and $m\angle 6 = (4x + 4)°$

D. $m\angle 3 = 24°$ and $m\angle 5 = (2x + 2)°$

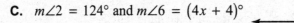
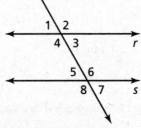

Use the diagram to complete the proof. Use the chart to identify the reasons.

Given: $\angle 2 \cong \angle 8$ **Prove:** $r \parallel s$

STATEMENTS	REASONS
$\angle 2 \cong \angle 8$	Given
$\angle 4 \cong \angle 2$	E.
$\angle 4 \cong \angle 8$	F.
$r \parallel s$	G.

1. Consecutive Interior Angles Converse (Theorem 3.8)
2. Alternate Interior Angles Converse (Theorem 3.6)
3. Transitive Property of Congruence
4. Transitive Property of Parallel Lines (Theorem 3.9)
5. Alternate Exterior Angles Converse (Theorem 3.7)
6. Vertical Angles Congruence Theorem (Theorem 2.6)
7. Corresponding Angles Converse (Theorem 3.5)

7 FLY
3 TIME
30 WANTED
1 TAKE
2 FOREVER
10 BECAUSE
$34\frac{1}{2}$ SOUND
9 HOLD

3.4 Start Thinking

A construction worker building a house uses many tools to ensure the foundation, walls, floors, and ceilings are all "square."

One tool frequently used is a level. A level indicates whether a surface is horizontal (parallel) or vertical (perpendicular) to another surface. Research two more tools a construction worker uses related to perpendicular lines and explain how the tools are used.

3.4 Warm Up

Find the indicated measurement.

1. the height of a triangle with base 30 centimeters and area 375 square centimeters

2. the base of a triangle with height 3 centimeters and area 49.5 square centimeters

3. the area of a triangle with base 33 centimeters and height 29 centimeters

4. the length of a rectangle with width 24 centimeters and area 1104 square centimeters

5. the width of a rectangle with length 7 centimeters and area 49 square centimeters

3.4 Cumulative Review Warm Up

Write a two-column proof for the property.

1. Symmetric Property of Segment Congruence

2. Reflexive Property of Angle Congruence

3.4 Practice A

1. Find the distance from point P to $\overleftrightarrow{AB}$.

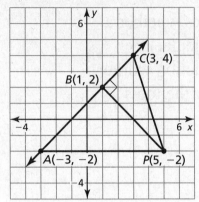

2. Trace line m and point P. Then use a compass and a straightedge to construct a line perpendicular to line m through point P.

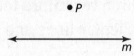

In Exercises 3 and 4, determine which lines, if any, must be parallel. Explain your reasoning.

3.

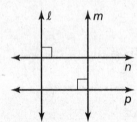

4.

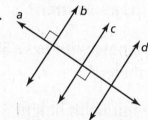

5. **Given:** $\angle 1 \cong \angle 2$, $f \perp h$
   and $f \parallel g$

   Prove: $e \parallel g$

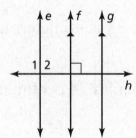

6. Your friend claims that there is only one line that can be drawn perpendicular to $\overline{PQ}$. Is your friend correct? Explain your reasoning.

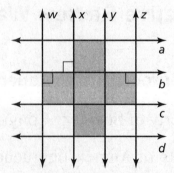

7. Determine which lines must be parallel. Explain your reasoning.

3.4 Practice B

1. Find the distance from point P to $\overrightarrow{QS}$.

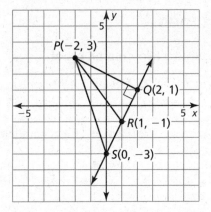

In Exercises 2 and 3, determine which lines, if any, must be parallel. Explain your reasoning.

2.

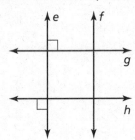

3.

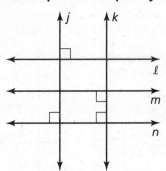

4. Your friend claims that you have enough information to determine that all of the vertical panels are parallel to each other. Is your friend correct? Explain your reasoning.

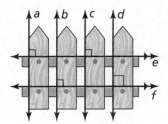

5. **Given:** $\angle 1 \cong \angle 2$, $c \parallel d$, and $b \perp d$

   Prove: $a \parallel b$

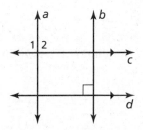

6. Find all the unknown angle measures in the diagram. Justify your answer for each angle measure.

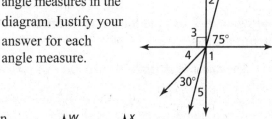

7. You extend the sides of a regular octagon as shown in the figure. You are given that $w \perp y$ and $y \parallel z$.

   Do you have enough information to conclude that $x \perp z$? Explain.

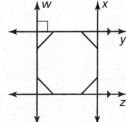

Name _____ Date _____

3.4 Enrichment and Extension

Proofs with Perpendicular Lines

In Exercises 1–4, refer to the diagram to write a two-column proof.

1. Given: $\overline{AC} \perp \overline{BC}$; $\angle 3$ is complementary to $\angle 1$.

Prove: $\angle 3 \cong \angle 2$

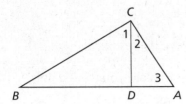

2. Given: $\overrightarrow{AB}$ bisects $\angle DAC$; $\overrightarrow{CB}$ bisects $\angle ECA$; $m\angle 2 = 45°$; $m\angle 3 = 45°$

Prove: $\overleftrightarrow{AD}$ is parallel to $\overleftrightarrow{CE}$.

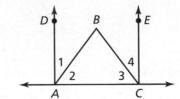

3. Given: $m \perp n$; $\angle 3$ and $\angle 4$ are complementary.

Prove: $\angle 5 \cong \angle 6$

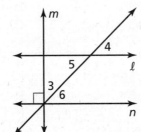

4. Given: $j \perp \ell$; $\angle 1 \cong \angle 3$

Prove: $k \perp m$

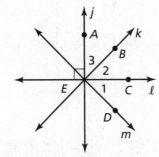

In Exercises 5–8, use the following information to find the distance between the point and the line.

The distance d between the point (x_1, y_1) and the line $Ax + By = C$ is

$$d = \frac{|Ax_1 + By_1 - C|}{\sqrt{A^2 + B^2}}.$$

5. $(3, 6)$; $3x + 4y = -2$

6. $(-2, 1)$; $x - y = 2$

7. $(8, 6)$; $-3x + 5y = -2$

8. $(5, -2)$; $2x + 3y = 1$

Name_____ Date _____

3.4 Puzzle Time

What Snake Is The Best Mathematician?

Write the letter of each answer in the box containing the exercise number.

Complete the sentence.

1. The distance from a point to a line is the length of the _____ segment from the point to the line.

2. If two lines intersect to form a(n) _____ of congruent angles, then the lines are perpendicular.

3. In a plane, if a transversal is perpendicular to one of two _____ lines, then it is perpendicular to the other line.

4. In a(n) _____ , if two lines are perpendicular to the same line, then they are parallel to each other.

Indicate the distance of the segment using the given information. Round to the nearest tenth.

5. Find AX. $A(-4, 5)$, $X(1, -2)$

6. Find CX. $C(6, -4)$, $X(1, -2)$

7. Find DX. $D(-7, 3)$, $X(3, 4)$

8. Find BX. $B(5, 2)$, $X(3, 4)$

Answers
R. 5.4
D. perpendicular
I. vertical pair
P. longest segment
A. plane
A. 9.8
M. straight
D. 11.6
E. linear pair
A. graph
E. 1.9
H. 8.6
V. 5.3
D. 10.0
A. 3.6
T. parallel
M. 4.5
E. 2.8

3	5	8		4	1	7	2	6

3.5 Start Thinking

In a coordinate plane, graph the lines $y = x - 3$ and $y = x + 2$. Do the lines intersect? If so, at what point?

Graph the line $y = -x + 5$ in the same coordinate plane. At what points does this line intersect $y = x - 3$ and $y = x + 2$? How can you describe the angles created by the intersections?

3.5 Warm Up

Graph the line in a coordinate plane.

1. $y = 6x$

2. $y = 4x + 2$

3. $y = x - 3$

4. $y = x + 2$

5. $y = \frac{2}{3}x - 2$

6. $y = -\frac{4}{3}x + 3$

3.5 Cumulative Review Warm Up

Name the property of equality the statement illustrates.

1. If $x = y$, then $2x = 2y$.

2. If $BN = NC$, then $BN - 6 = NC - 6$.

3. $z = z$

4. $m\angle A = m\angle A$

5. If $m\angle D = 38°$ and $m\angle E = 38°$, then $m\angle E = m\angle D$.

6. If $FG = JK$, then $JK = FG$.

3.5 Practice A

In Exercises 1 and 2, find the coordinates of point *P* along the directed line segment *ST* so that *SP* to *PT* is the given ratio.

1. $S(6, 4)$, $T(-4, -8)$; 1 to 3

2. $S(-6, 7)$, $T(9, 25)$; 2 to 3

In Exercises 3 and 4, tell whether the lines through the given points are *parallel*, *perpendicular*, or *neither*. Justify your answer.

3. Line 1: $(2, 3)$, $(4, 12)$

Line 2: $(5, 10)$, $(14, 8)$

4. Line 1: $(-6, -10)$, $(4, -2)$

Line 2: $(-8, -6)$, $(0, 4)$

In Exercises 5 and 6, write an equation of the line passing through point *P* that is parallel to the given line.

5. $P(-1, 3)$, $y = 4x - 7$

6. $P(2, -3)$, $y = -6x + 10$

In Exercises 7 and 8, write an equation of the line passing through point *P* that is perpendicular to the given line.

7. $P(6, 10)$, $y = -3x + 13$

8. $P(0, -8)$, $y = -\frac{1}{3}x - 10$

In Exercises 9 and 10, find the distance from point *Q* to the given line.

9. $Q(2, 6)$, $y = -x + 4$

10. $Q(-10, -4)$, $5x - y = 6$

11. A line through $(3, 5)$ and $(k, 12)$ is perpendicular to a line through $(0, 7)$ and $(2, 10)$. Find the value of *k* that makes the above statement true.

12. Your friend claims that if a line has a slope that is less than 1, then any line perpendicular to it must have a positive slope. Is your friend correct? Explain your reasoning.

13. You and your friend are playing a game of checkers. There are only two pieces left on the board. Find the coordinates of point *P* along the line segment connecting the black and white checkers so that the ratio of the distance between the black checker and *P* to *P* and the white checker is 2 to 1.

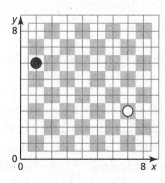

Name _____ Date _____

3.5 Practice B

In Exercises 1 and 2, find the coordinates of point *Q* along the directed line segment *LM* so that *LQ* to *QM* is the given ratio.

1. $L(-1, -2)$, $M(3, 6)$; 5 to 3

2. $L(2, 7)$, $M(-1, 1)$; 2 to 1

3. Tell whether the lines through the given points are *parallel, perpendicular,* or *neither.* Justify your answer.

   Line 1: $(2.5, -2)$, $(9.5, 12)$ Line 2: $(-4, -2)$, $(8, -4)$

4. Write an equation of the line passing through point $P(-1, -4)$ that is parallel to $y = -6x + 8$.

5. Write an equation of the line passing through point $P(-1, 3)$ that is perpendicular to $y = 4x - 7$.

In Exercises 6 and 7, find the distance from point *P* to the given line.

6. $P(4, 8)$, $6 = y + 2x$

7. $P(-2, 1)$, $y = \frac{1}{4}x - 3$

8. A line through $(-1, b)$ and $(c, 8)$ is parallel to a line through $(-6, 3)$ and $(0, 12)$. Find values of b and c that make the above statement true.

9. The graph shows three lines. The slope of line ℓ_1 is m_1, where $-1 \le m_1 < 0$.

   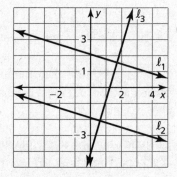

   a. Lines ℓ_1 and ℓ_2 are parallel. What do you know about the slope of line ℓ_2?

   b. Lines ℓ_1 and ℓ_3 are perpendicular. What do you know about the slope of line ℓ_3?

   c. What is the relationship between ℓ_2 and ℓ_3? Justify your answer.

10. Two lines are perpendicular. Is it possible for the lines to have the same *y*-intercept? Justify your answer.

11. The diagram shows a map of a playground. The water fountain lies directly between the swings and the slide. The distance from the swings to the water fountain is one-third the distance from the water fountain to the slide. What point on the graph represents the water fountain?

    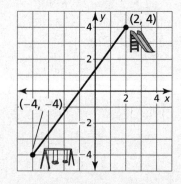

3.5 Enrichment and Extension

Equations of Parallel and Perpendicular Lines

1. Write the equation of the perpendicular bisector for the line segment defined between points $A(2, 5)$ and $B(-6, -1)$.

2. Find the values of a and b in $ax + by = 90$ such that the equation is perpendicular to $-20x + 12y = 36$ and has the same y-intercept.

3. Consider the linear equation $y = 3.62(x - 1.35) + 2.74$.

   a. What is the slope of this line?

   b. What is the value of y when $x = 1.35$?

   c. Find an equation for the line through $(4.23, -2.58)$ that is parallel to this line.

   d. Find an equation for the line through $(4.23, -2.58)$ that is perpendicular to this line.

4. What is the slope of the line $ax + by = c$? Find an equation for the line through the origin that is parallel to the line $ax + by = c$. Find an equation for the line through the origin that is perpendicular to the line $ax + by = c$.

5. A line passes through the points $(k + 10, -2k - 1)$ and $(2, 9)$ and has a y-intercept of 10. Find the value of k and the equation of the line.

6. A line passes through the points $(3k, 6k - 5)$ and $(-1, -7)$ and has a y-intercept of -5. Find the value of k and the equation of the line.

7. Consider the two linear equations $ax + by = c$ and $dx + ey = f$.

   a. Under what conditions will the graphs of the two equations intersect at one point?

   b. Under what conditions will the graphs of the two equations be parallel?

8. Point F is located at $(0, 4)$.

   a. Find coordinates of three points that are equidistant from F and the x-axis.

   b. If possible, write the equations of the lines that are parallel or perpendicular to the line $x = 0$ and pass through the coordinates from part (a).

   c. Consider $G(0, y)$. Find the coordinates of three points that are equidistant from G and the x-axis.

Name _____ Date _____

3.5 Puzzle Time

How Do You Make Seven Even?

Circle the letter of each correct answer in the boxes below. The circled letters will spell out the answer to the riddle.

Complete the sentence.

1. A(n) _____ line segment $\overline{AB}$ is a segment that represents moving from point A to point B.

2. In a coordinate plane, two nonvertical lines are parallel if and only if they have the _____.

3. In a coordinate plane, two nonvertical lines are perpendicular if and only if the product of their _____.

Tell whether the lines through the given points are (1) parallel, (2) perpendicular, (3) neutral, (4) directed, (5) indirective, (6) none of these.

4. Line 1: $(-7, -3)$, $(1, 4)$; Line 2: $(-6, 6)$, $(1, -2)$

5. Line 1: $(-4, -2)$, $(4, 5)$; Line 2: $(-2, 3)$, $(2, -3)$

6. Line 1: $(0, 4)$, $(-6, 0)$; Line 2: $(3, 2)$, $(-3, -2)$

Find the distance from point A to the given line. Round to the nearest tenth.

7. $A(-4, 4)$, $y = 0.8x - 0.4$

8. $A(-3, -3)$, $y = 0.5x + 6.5$

R	D	N	R	P	O	M	A
5	2	6.4	slopes is -1	slopes is $-\dfrac{1}{2}$	5.9	straight	3
P	**T**	**L**	**H**	**L**	**I**	**E**	**S**
7.2	1	6.7	same slope	slopes is 0	4	directed	6

Name_____ Date_____

In Exercises 1–8, evaluate the expression.

1. $7 + 8 - 5 \cdot 3$

2. $14 - 8 \cdot 2 - 7 + 18 \div 2$

3. $(5 - 6)^2 + 3 \cdot 4$

4. $2 \cdot 7(5 - 2) - 4 \div 2$

5. $-(3 + 4)^2 - 5 + 7^2$

6. $15 - 2(5 - 3) + 11^2$

7. $(3 + 5) \div 2 - 4 + 5 \cdot 5$

8. $(-4 + 9)^2 - 1 + 15 \div 3$

In Exercises 9–17, evaluate the expression for the given value of y.

9. $y(y + 4); y = 2$

10. $-y(y - 3); y = -1$

11. $y(8 - y); y = -6$

12. $y^2 - 5y + 3; y = 5$

13. $2y^2 - 4y - 1; y = -3$

14. $-3y^2 + y - 6; y = -4$

15. $(y + 4)(y - 3); y = 2$

16. $(7 - y)(y + 1); y = 9$

17. $(y + 7)(y - 7); y = -5$

In Exercises 18–33, find the reciprocal.

18. 4

19. -6

20. -9

21. 3

22. $\frac{1}{4}$

23. $-\frac{1}{5}$

24. $\frac{1}{7}$

25. $-\frac{1}{9}$

26. $-\frac{4}{7}$

27. $\frac{2}{5}$

28. $\frac{3}{5}$

29. $-\frac{2}{9}$

30. $\frac{5}{2}$

31. $\frac{8}{7}$

32. $-\frac{2}{3}$

33. $-\frac{3}{5}$

34. It starts to snow at 9 A.M. It snows at a rate of 1 inch per hour for the first 2 hours, and then increases to a rate of 1.5 inches per hour for the next 4 hours until the snow stops.

   a. What time does the rate of snowfall change?

   b. How much does it snow from 9 A.M. to 2 P.M.?

   c. At what time does it stop snowing?

35. Newspaper Company A charges $515 per year for home delivery of its newspaper.

   a. How much does the company charge per month?

   b. How much does the company charge per week?

   c. How much does the company charge per day?

Chapter 3 **Cumulative Review** (continued)

In Exercises 36–51, solve the equation. Check your solution.

36. $x - 7 = 9$

37. $x + 4 = 12$

38. $3x = -18$

39. $\dfrac{x}{5} = -7$

40. $2x + 9 = 7$

41. $\dfrac{x}{4} - 3 = -1$

42. $3(x - 5) + 8 = 20$

43. $\dfrac{1}{5}(x - 1) + 8 = -2$

44. $-2(x + 1) - 9 = 11$

45. $4x + 5 = 3x - 7$

46. $7 + 12x = 10x - 15$

47. $-2x + 4 = 3x - 11$

48. $4(x + 5) + 12 = -2(x - 7)$

49. $2(x + 12) - 4 = 7(x + 5) - 10$

50. $-7(x + 11) + 3 = 2(x - 4) - 12$

51. $-2(x - 9) + 4 = 6(x - 4) + 6$

In Exercises 52–63, identify the slope and the *y*-intercept of the line.

52. $y = 3x - 4$

53. $y = -4x + 5$

54. $y = \dfrac{3}{4}x - 7$

55. $y = -\dfrac{5}{6}x + 3$

56. $y = x + 5$

57. $y = -x + 3$

58. $-y = x + 1$

59. $-y = 2x - 9$

60. $3x + y = 8$

61. $2x - y = 5$

62. $-\dfrac{5}{7}x + y = 8$

63. $\dfrac{2}{3}x + y = -4$

64. Goldfish require a tank of at least 10 gallons to live comfortably. Write an expression to show the minimum size tank needed for *x* fish.

65. The national average for emergency responders to arrive on scene is 8 minutes. Company A's average response time is 5 minutes, and Company B's average response time is 5.5 minutes.

   a. Write an equation to represent the time difference (in minutes) of Company A compared to the national average.

   b. Write an equation to represent the time difference (in minutes) of Company B compared to the national average.

   c. How much faster is each company compared to the national average?

Chapter 3 Cumulative Review (continued)

In Exercises 66–77, use the Distance Formula to find the distance between the two points. Round your answer to the nearest tenth.

66. $(14, -3)$ and $(6, 2)$

67. $(8, -4)$ and $(7, 3)$

68. $(-11, -4)$ and $(9, 0)$

69. $(2, -11)$ and $(4, -1)$

70. $(-9, 3)$ and $(4, -7)$

71. $(10, 3)$ and $(-5, -2)$

72. $(12, 10)$ and $(9, -6)$

73. $(7, 6)$ and $(13, 9)$

74. $(6, -14)$ and $(-3, 2)$

75. $(7, -4)$ and $(10, 8)$

76. $(-12, 1)$ and $(-7, 7)$

77. $(10, 3)$ and $(8, -6)$

In Exercises 78–89, the endpoints of a line are given. Find the coordinates of the midpoint.

78. $(-1, 4)$ and $(-3, 7)$

79. $(4, 6)$ and $(12, -8)$

80. $(0, 3)$ and $(-7, -5)$

81. $(4, 3)$ and $(1, 5)$

82. $(6, 9)$ and $(-11, 10)$

83. $(-12, 4)$ and $(6, -3)$

84. $(2, 8)$ and $(9, -12)$

85. $(3, 5)$ and $(-4, 9)$

86. $(-7, 8)$ and $(-4, -5)$

87. $(11, 9)$ and $(-12, -12)$

88. $(-3, 10)$ and $(6, -11)$

89. $(-4, -7)$ and $(3, 8)$

90. An amusement park charges $215 for a season pass or $45 per visit.

    a. You want to visit the amusement park three times. Should you pay for a season pass, or should you pay for each individual visit?

    b. You want to visit the amusement park four times. Should you pay for a season pass, or should you pay for each individual visit?

    c. When is it more beneficial to buy the season pass rather than pay for each individual visit?

91. It costs $4.95 just to place an order through Shopping Company A. There is also a $0.95 charge per pound for your order.

    a. How much does it cost to order something that weighs 3 pounds?

    b. How much does it cost to order something that weighs 5 pounds?

    c. Your order was $11.60. How much did your order weigh?

Chapter 3 **Cumulative Review** (continued)

In Exercises 92–106, write the equation for the line that passes through the given point and has the given slope.

92. $(5, 7)$, $m = 2$

93. $(-13, 12)$, $m = -3$

94. $(1, 6)$, $m = \frac{1}{2}$

95. $(-10, 2)$, $m = \frac{1}{5}$

96. $(-8, 4)$, $m = -\frac{1}{4}$

97. $(-12, -3)$, $m = 8$

98. $(6, 5)$, $m = -4$

99. $(-2, 1)$, $m = -\frac{2}{5}$

100. $(-3, -12)$, $m = \frac{1}{3}$

101. $(-10, 8)$, $m -\frac{1}{2}$

102. $(9, -9)$, $m = \frac{1}{9}$

103. $(3, -4)$, $m = -2$

104. $(-6, 4)$, $m = 3$

105. $(-1, -7)$, $m = 0$

106. $(-9, 6)$, $m = -\frac{1}{3}$

In Exercises 107–112, use the diagram to determine the value of x.

107.

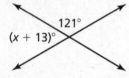

121°
$(x + 13)°$

108.

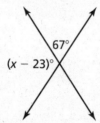

67°
$(x - 23)°$

109.

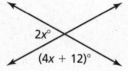

$2x°$
$(4x + 12)°$

110.

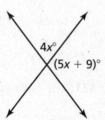

$4x°$
$(5x + 9)°$

111.

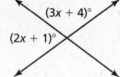

$(3x + 4)°$
$(2x + 1)°$

112.

$(3x - 2)°$
$(5x + 14)°$

Chapter 4

Chapter 4 Transformations

Dear Family,

Where do transformations occur in real life? Do they occur often? Your child may have a difficult time recognizing transformations in objects he or she encounters every day, but real-life transformations are more common than you think.

You and your child can work together to recognize everyday transformations in your neighborhood. For instance, the traffic signs below show different types of transformations.

Two-Way Traffic

Duck Crossing

Railroad Crossing

Roundabout

- What types of transformations are shown in the signs?
- Are the figures in the signs congruent? Are they similar?

Take a walk in your neighborhood with your child and have him or her jot down or sketch any figures he or she thinks are possible transformations. Use the Internet or flip through a magazine to help identify company logos that may contain transformations. Some real-life transformations can be found quickly and easily, such as sliding open a window.

- Describe the types of transformations that your figures represent.
- Are the shapes that make up your figures congruent? Are they similar? How do you know?
- Do your figures represent more than one transformation?
- Discuss whether a figure has any lines of symmetry or whether a logo has rotational symmetry. For example, a logo at a gas station may have rotational symmetry.

Does your child like to play video games? Have him or her create a logo for a fictional video game company that uses one or more transformations.

Be creative!

Capítulo 4 Transformaciones

Estimada familia:

¿Dónde ocurren las transformaciones en la vida real? ¿Se ocurren con frecuencia? A su hijo quizás le cueste reconocer las transformaciones en objetos que ve todos los días, pero las transformaciones en la vida real son más comunes que lo que creen.

Usted y su hijo pueden trabajar juntos para reconocer transformaciones cotidianas en su vecindario. Por ejemplo, las siguientes señales de tránsito muestran diferentes tipos de transformaciones.

Tránsito de dos vías   **Cruce de patos**   **Cruce de ferrocarril**   **Rotonda**

- ¿Qué clases de transformaciones se muestran en las señales?

- ¿Las figuras en las señales son congruentes? ¿Son semejantes?

Con su hijo, salgan a caminar por el vecindario y pídale que anote o dibuje cualquier figura que crea que es una posible transformación. Usen Internet o una revista como ayuda para identificar logos de compañías que puedan contener transformaciones. Algunas transformaciones de la vida real pueden hallarse rápida y fácilmente, tal como una traslación al abrir una ventana.

- Describan los tipos de transformaciones que representan sus figuras.

- ¿Las formas que componen sus figuras son congruentes? ¿Son semejantes? ¿Cómo lo saben?

- ¿Sus figuras representan más de una transformación?

- Comenten si una figura tiene algún eje de simetría o si un logo tiene simetría rotacional. Por ejemplo, un logo en una estación de gasolina podría tener simetría rotacional.

¿A su hijo le gusta jugar videojuegos? Pídale que cree un logo para una compañía de videojuegos ficticia que tenga una o más transformaciones.

¡Sean creativos!

4.1 Start Thinking

Plot $\triangle ABC$ with coordinates $A(-2, 2)$, $B(-4, -2)$, $C(-1, -1)$, and $\triangle A'B'C'$ with coordinates $A'(-2, 0)$, $B'(-4, -4)$, $C'(-1, -3)$ in a coordinate plane. Describe how to get from $\triangle ABC$ to $\triangle A'B'C'$. Compare the ordered pairs for each triangle visually. Explain how to use the ordered pairs for this exercise.

4.1 Warm Up

Translate point _P_. State the coordinates of _P'_.

1. $P(-4, 4)$; 2 units down, 2 units right

2. $P(-3, -2)$; 3 units right, 3 units up

3. $P(2, 2)$; 2 units down, 2 units right

4. $P(-1, 4)$; 3 units left, 1 unit up

5. $P(2, -1)$; 1 unit up, 4 units right

6. $P(6, 0)$; 4 units up, 2 units left

4.1 Cumulative Review Warm Up

Prove the theorem.

1. Alternate Interior Angles Theorem (Theorem 3.2)

2. Alternate Exterior Angles Theorem (Theorem 3.3)

Name_____ Date_____

4.1 Practice A

1. Name the vector and write its component form.

2. The vertices of △ABC are $A(2, 3)$, $B(-1, 2)$, and $C(0, 1)$. Translate △ABC using the vector $\langle 1, -4 \rangle$. Graph △ABC and its image.

3. Find the component form of the vector that translates $A(3, -2)$ to $A'(-1, 4)$.

4. Write a rule for the translation of △RST to △R'S'T'.

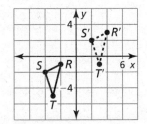

In Exercises 5 and 6, use the translation $(x, y) \rightarrow (x + 1, y - 3)$ to find the image of the given point.

5. $Q(5, 9)$

6. $M(-3, -8)$

In Exercises 7 and 8, graph △CDE with vertices $C(-1, 3)$, $D(0, -2)$, and $E(1, 1)$ and its image after the given translation or composition.

7. **Translation:** $(x, y) \rightarrow (x - 3, y + 1)$

8. **Translation:** $(x, y) \rightarrow (x + 10, y - 8)$
   Translation: $(x, y) \rightarrow (x - 7, y + 15)$

9. You want to plot the collinear points $A(-2, 3)$, $A'(x, y)$, and $A''(3, 7)$ on the same coordinate plane. Do you have enough information to find the values of x and y? Explain your reasoning.

10. You are using the map shown to navigate through the city. You decide to walk to the Post Office from your current location at the Community Center. Describe the translation that you will follow. If each grid on the map is 0.05 mile, how far will you travel?

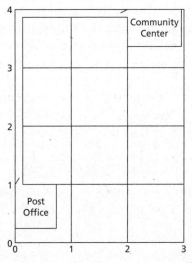

4.1 Practice B

1. The vertices of $\triangle FGH$ are $F(-2, -6)$, $G(3, 0)$, and $H(1, -4)$. Translate $\triangle FGH$ using the vector $\langle -2, 7 \rangle$. Graph $\triangle FGH$ and its image.

2. Find the component form of the vector that translates $A(-4, 8)$ to $A'(7, -9)$.

3. Write a rule for the translation of $\triangle ABC$ to $\triangle A'B'C'$.

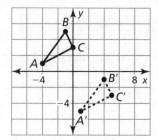

In Exercises 4 and 5, use the translation $(x, y) \rightarrow (x - 4, y + 3)$ to find the image of the given point.

4. $G(-2, 4)$

5. $H(-10, 5)$

6. Graph $\triangle JKL$ with vertices $J(-2, 8)$, $K(1, -3)$, and $L(5, 4)$ and its image after the composition.

   Translation: $(x, y) \rightarrow (x + 6, y - 1)$
   Translation: $(x, y) \rightarrow (x - 1, y - 7)$

7. Is the transformation given by $(x, y) \rightarrow (2x + 2, y + 1)$ a translation? Explain your reasoning.

8. A popular kid's game has 15 tiles and 1 open space. The goal of the game is to rearrange the tiles to put them in order (from least to greatest, starting at the upper left-hand corner and going across each row). Use the figure to write the transformation(s) that describe the path of where the 8 tile is currently, and where it must be by the end of the game. Can this same translation be used to describe the path of all the tiles?

8	2	3	7
5	6	4	14
1	9		13
11	15	10	12

9. Graph any triangle and translate it in any direction. Draw translation vectors for each vertex of the triangle. Is there a geometric relationship between all the translation vectors? Explain why this makes sense in terms of the slope of the line.

10. Point $P(4, -2)$ undergoes a translation given by $(x, y) \rightarrow (x + 3, x - a)$, followed by another translation $(x, y) \rightarrow (x - b, x + 7)$ to produce the image of $P''(-5, 8)$. Find the values of a and b and point P'.

Name_____ Date_____

4.1   Enrichment and Extension

Properties of Vectors

A two-dimensional vector $\vec{V} = \langle a, b \rangle$ in standard position with its tail at $(0, 0)$ has a horizontal component a and a vertical component b. The *magnitude* is the length of the line segment, given by $\left| \vec{V} \right| = \sqrt{a^2 + b^2}$.

Note: a and b may also be denoted by V_1 and V_2.

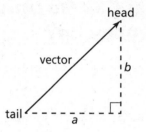

1. Find the magnitude of each vector.

    a. $\langle 5, -3 \rangle$

    b. $\langle -3, 0 \rangle$

    c. head at $(0, 4)$ and tail at $(-3, 2)$

2. Let $\vec{U} = \langle a, b \rangle$ and $\vec{V} = \langle c, d \rangle$ denote vectors in a plane. Write a vector that represents $\vec{U} + \vec{V}$.

3. Let $\vec{U} = \langle 2, -3 \rangle$ and $\vec{V} = \langle -6, 4 \rangle$. Write a vector that represents each of the following.

    a. $\vec{U} + \vec{V}$ **b.** $3\vec{U}$ **c.** $\vec{V} - \vec{U}$ **d.** $2\vec{U} + \vec{V}$

You are familiar with coordinates and vectors in the x-y coordinate plane, but in three dimensions, there are two other coordinate planes. There is the x-z plane and the y-z planc. Using the diagram, determine in which plane(s) $(x$-y, x-z, y-$z)$ each of the following points is located.

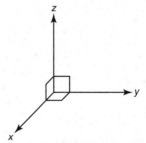

4. $(3, 5, 0)$ 5. $(2, 0, 5)$

6. $(0, -3, 4)$ 7. $(0, 3, 0)$

So, the magnitude of a vector $\vec{V} = \langle V_1, V_2, V_3 \rangle$ in three dimensions is given by $\left| \vec{V} \right| = \sqrt{V_1^2 + V_2^2 + V_3^2}$.

8. Let $\vec{U} = \langle 1, 4, 0 \rangle$ and $\vec{V} = \langle 5, 2, -3 \rangle$. Find the following.

    a. $\left| \vec{U} \right|$ **b.** $\left| \vec{V} \right|$

Name _____ Date _____

4.1 Puzzle Time

What Can Go Up The Chimney Down, But Not Down The Chimney Up?

Write the letter of each answer in the box containing the exercise number.

Complete the following questions.

1. What is another name for the original figure?

2. A translation is a _____ ?

3. A _____ is a quantity that has both direction and magnitude, or size.

Find the coordinates of the preimage.

4. $(x, y) \rightarrow (x + 3, y - 5)$ with endpoints $A'(3, 3)$ and $B'(-2, 4)$

5. $(x, y) \rightarrow (x - 1, y + 3)$ with endpoints $A'(-2, 0)$ and $B'(5, -4)$

Find the rule for the translation of the coordinates.

6. $A(3, -4) \rightarrow A'(1, -8)$
   $B(4, 6) \rightarrow B'(2, 2)$

7. $A(-6, -4) \rightarrow A'(-2, -2)$
   $B(2, 5) \rightarrow B'(6, 7)$

The vector $\langle -3, 2 \rangle$ describes the translations
$A(-1, x) \rightarrow A'(-4y, 1)$ and $B(2z - 1, 1) \rightarrow B'(3, 3)$.

8. Find the value of x.

9. Find the value of y.

10. Find the value of z.

2	7		3	6	4	1	5	8	9	10

Answers

A. $\dfrac{7}{2}$

I. $(x, y) \rightarrow (x + 2, y - 4)$

Y. $A(-3, -6), B(4, -1)$

U. vector

L. $A(6, -2), B(-1, -1)$

N. $(x, y) \rightarrow (x + 4, y + 2)$

V. 1

E. $A(-1, -3), B(6, -7)$

F. 0

B. $A(0, 8), B(-5, 9)$

T. image

M. $(x, y) \rightarrow (x - 2, y - 4)$

G. 2

L. -1

K. flexible motion

R. preimage

L. 1

O. line

A. rigid motion

P. $(x, y) \rightarrow (x - 4, y - 2)$

4.2 Start Thinking

Lay a yardstick at the base of a mirror. Stand at the end of the yardstick so you are 3 feet from the mirror. Is your reflection the same distance from the mirror? Explain why or why not.

Hold up your right hand. Is your reflection holding up its right hand as well? Explain why or why not.

4.2 Warm Up

Reflect point *P*. State the coordinates of *P'*.

1. $P(-5, 3)$; reflection in *y*-axis

2. $P(-4, -3)$; reflection in *y*-axis

3. $P(-1, -5)$; reflection in *y*-axis

4. $P(-1, 1)$; reflection in *x*-axis

5. $P(4, 6)$; reflection in *x*-axis

6. $P(5, 1)$; reflection in *x*-axis

4.2 Cumulative Review Warm Up

Classify the angle.

1. $59°$ 2. $90°$ 3. $153°$

4. $97°$ 5. $29°$ 6. $180°$

Name _____ Date _____

4.2 Practice A

In Exercises 1–3, graph △ABC and its image after a reflection in the given line.

1. $A(0, 2)$, $B(1, -3)$, $C(2, 4)$; x-axis

2. $A(-2, -4)$, $B(6, 2)$, $C(3, -5)$; y-axis

3. $A(4, -1)$, $B(3, 8)$, $C(-1, 1)$; $y = -2$

In Exercises 4 and 5, graph the polygon and its image after a reflection in the given line.

4. $y = -x$

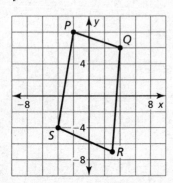

5. $y = x$

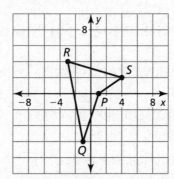

In Exercises 6 and 7, graph △JKL with vertices J(2, 3), K(-2, 1), and L(-1, 5) and its image after the glide reflection.

6. **Translation:** $(x, y) \rightarrow (x - 1, y)$
    Reflection: in the x-axis

7. **Translation:** $(x, y) \rightarrow (x + 2, y - 3)$
    Reflection: in the line $x = -2$

In Exercises 8 and 9, determine the number of lines of symmetry for the figure.

8.

9.

10. Find point W on the y-axis so that $VW + XW$ is a minimum given $V(2, 3)$ and $X(-2, -1)$.

11. A line $y = 3x - 5$ is reflected in $x = a$ so that the image is given by $y = 1 - 3x$. What is the value of a?

12. Your friend claims that it is not possible to have a glide reflection if you have two translations followed by one reflection. Is your friend correct? Explain your reasoning.

Name_____ Date_____

In Exercises 1 and 2, graph △CDE and its image after a reflection in the given line.

1. $C(3, 4)$, $D(2, -1)$, $E(0, -5)$; y-axis

2. $C(1, 6)$, $D(12, 2)$, $E(7, -8)$; $x = 8$

In Exercises 3 and 4, graph the polygon and its image after a reflection in the given line.

3. x-axis

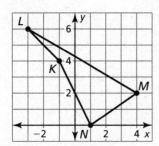

4. $y = -1$

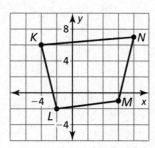

In Exercises 5 and 6, graph △ABC with vertices A(−1, 4), B(2, −1), and C(4, 3) and its image after the glide reflection.

5. **Translation:** $(x, y) \rightarrow (x + 2, y - 1)$
   Reflection: in the line $y = x$

6. **Translation:** $(x, y) \rightarrow (x - 3, y + 1)$
   Reflection: in the line $y = -x$

7. Determine the number of lines of symmetry for the figure.

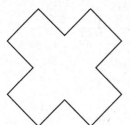

8. Find point P on the x-axis so that $AP + BP$ is a minimum.

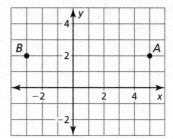

9. Is it possible to perform two reflections of an object so that the final image is identical to the original image? If so, give an example. If not, explain your reasoning.

10. A triangle undergoes a glide reflection. Is it possible for the sides of the triangle to change length during this process? Explain your reasoning.

11. Your friend claims that it is not possible to have a glide reflection if you have one translation followed by two reflections. Is your friend correct? Explain your reasoning.

Name _____ Date _____

Reflections

1. Reflect points F and G in the y-axis. Name the coordinates and connect the points to form a polygon. Give the most specific name for the polygon.

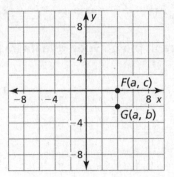

2. Reflect points F and G in the x-axis. Name the coordinates.

3. Reflect the points A and B in the line $y = x$. Connect the points to form a polygon. Give the most specific name for the polygon.

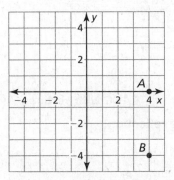

4. Reflect the points A and B in the line $y = -x$. Connect the points to form a polygon. Give the most specific name for the polygon.

The vertices of $\triangle ABC$ are $A(-4, 4)$, $B(0, 7)$, and $C(-1, 3)$. Reflect $\triangle ABC$ in line 1 to obtain $\triangle A'B'C'$. Then reflect $\triangle A'B'C'$ in line 2 to obtain $\triangle A''B''C''$. Graph triangles $\triangle A'B'C'$ and $\triangle A''B''C''$.

5. Line 1: $y = 4$; Line 2: $x = -1$

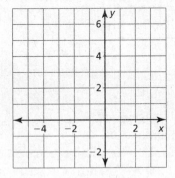

6. Line 1: $x = -3$; Line 2: $y = 5$

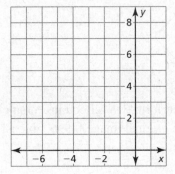

Name_____ Date _____

4.2 Puzzle Time

What Type Of Dance Does A Geometry Teacher Like?

Circle the letter of each correct answer in the boxes below. The circled letters will spell out the answer to the riddle.

Complete the sentence.

1. A _____ is a transformation that uses a line like a mirror to reflect the figure.

2. If (a, b) is reflected in the x-axis, then its image is the point _____.

3. If (a, b) is reflected in the line $y = x$, then its image is the point _____.

4. A _____ reflection is a transformation involving a translation followed by a reflection.

5. A figure in the plane has line _____ when the figure can be mapped onto itself by a reflection in a line.

How many lines of symmetry does the figure have?

6.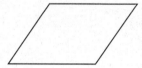

7.

8.

Identify the vertices of the image created after the reflection in the given line.

9. $A(3, 4), B(5, 2)$; $y = x$

10. $A(6, -3), B(-2, 4)$; x-axis

11. $A(-2, -1), B(3, 9)$; $y = -x$

H	S	K	L	Q	U	W	I	A	R	E
9	(b, a)	16	7	0	symmetry	slider	$A'(1, -2),$ $B'(3, -9)$	2	5	$A'(6, 3),$ $B'(-2, -4)$
G	**I**	**D**	**F**	**O**	**A**	**D**	**N**	**E**	**C**	**E**
$A'(3, -4),$ $B'(5, -2)$	$(-b, -a)$	$(a, -b)$	6	4.5	reflection	rotation	$A'(1, 2),$ $B'(-9, -3)$	$\frac{1}{2}$	$A'(4, 3),$ $B'(2, 5)$	glide

4.3 Start Thinking

On a computer with a word processor, use 18-point Arial font to type the capital letters of the alphabet, putting a space between each letter.

Which letter is symmetric when you rotate the paper 90 degrees? Which letters are symmetric when you rotate the paper 180 degrees? Are any letters not symmetric when you rotate the paper 360 degrees?

4.3 Warm Up

Rotate point P counterclockwise about the origin by the given angle. State the coordinates of P'.

1. $P(4, 2)$; $90°$
2. $P(3, 0)$; $90°$
3. $P(6, 0)$; $180°$
4. $P(2, 6)$; $180°$
5. $P(-2, 0)$; $270°$
6. $P(4, 0)$; $270°$

4.3 Cumulative Review Warm Up

State the name of the property.

1. For any segment AB, $\overline{AB} \cong \overline{AB}$.
2. If $\angle A \cong \angle B$, then $\angle B \cong \angle A$.

Name_____ Date_____

4.3 Practice A

1. Trace the polygon and point P. Then draw a $60°$ rotation of the polygon about point P.

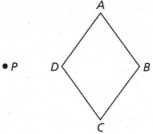

2. Graph the polygon and its image after a $270°$ rotation about the origin.

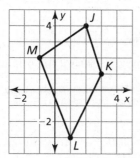

In Exercises 3 and 4, graph $\triangle RST$ **with vertices** $R(2, 3)$, $S(-2, 1)$, **and** $T(-1, 5)$ **and its image after the composition.**

3. **Translation:** $(x, y) \rightarrow (x - 2, y - 1)$
   Rotation: $90°$ about the origin

4. **Reflection:** in the line $x = y$
   Rotation: $180°$ about the origin

In Exercises 5 and 6, determine whether the figure has rotational symmetry. If so, describe any rotations that map the figure onto itself.

5.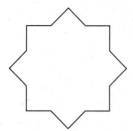

6.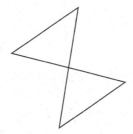

7. Draw $\overline{AB}$ with points $A(2, 0)$ and $B(0, 2)$. Rotate the segment $90°$ counterclockwise about point A. Then rotate the two segments $180°$ about the origin. What geometric figure did you create using the original segment and its images?

8. List the uppercase letters of the alphabet that have rotational symmetry, and state the angle of the symmetry.

Name _____ Date _____

1. Graph the polygon and its image after a 90° rotation about the origin.

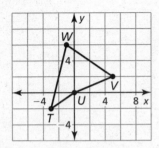

In Exercises 2 and 3, graph △CDE with vertices C(−1, −3), D(4, 2), and E(−5, −1) and its image after the composition.

2. **Rotation:** 180° about the origin

   Translation: $(x, y) \rightarrow (x + 3, y + 1)$

3. **Reflection:** in the line $x = y$

   Rotation: 270° about the origin

In Exercises 4 and 5, determine whether the figure has rotational symmetry. If so, describe any rotations that map the figure onto itself.

4.

5.

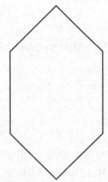

6. Is it possible to have an object that does not have 360° of rotational symmetry? Explain your reasoning.

7. A figure that is rotated 60° is mapped back onto itself. Does the figure have rotational symmetry? Explain. How many times can you rotate the figure before it is back where it started?

8. Your friend claims that he can do a series of translations on any geometric object and get the same result as a rotation. Is your friend correct?

9. Your friend claims that she can do a series of reflections on any geometric object and get the same result as a rotation. Is your friend correct?

10. List the digits from 0−9 that have rotational symmetry, and state the angle of the symmetry.

Name_____ Date _____

4.3 Enrichment and Extension

Rotations

In Exercises 1–4, rotate the line the given number of degrees about the given point. Write the equation of the image.

1. $y = \dfrac{3}{2}x - 3$; $90°$; x-intercept

2. $y = -x + 8$; $180°$; x-intercept

3. $3x + 2y = 6$; $90°$; y-intercept

4. $y = 2x + 5$; $180°$; y-intercept

5. In the diagram, A' and B' are the images of A and B after a $90°$ rotation about point P.

a. Find the coordinates of A'.

b. Find the coordinates of B'.

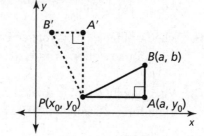

c. The point $(-6, 1)$ is rotated $90°$ about $(2, 1)$. What are the coordinates of the image point?

d. The point $(2, -5)$ is rotated $90°$ about $(-3, 7)$. What are the coordinates of the image of the point?

6. The endpoints of $\overline{FG}$ are $F(1, 2)$ and $G(3, 4)$. Graph $\overline{F'G'}$ and $\overline{F''G''}$ after the given rotations.

a. **Rotation:** $90°$ about the origin; **Rotation:** $180°$ about $(0, 4)$

b. **Rotation:** $270°$ about the origin; **Rotation:** $90°$ about $(-2, 0)$

Name _____ Date _____

4.3 Puzzle Time

What Did One Parallel Line Say To The Other Parallel Line?

A	B	C	D	E	F
G					

Complete each exercise. Find the answer in the answer column. Write the word under the answer in the box containing the exercise letter.

(1,1) MEET	
symmetric AND	
rotation WHAT	
(a, b) DOWN	
(3, −5) SKINNY	
(3, −4) NEVER	
(b, −a) WE	

Complete the sentence.

A. A _____ is a transformation in which a figure is turned about a fixed point.

B. When a point (a, b) is rotated counterclockwise about the origin for a rotation of 90°, $(a, b) \rightarrow ($ ____ $)$.

C. When a point (a, b) is rotated counterclockwise about the origin for a rotation of 180°, $(a, b) \rightarrow ($ ____ $)$.

D. When a point (a, b) is rotated counterclockwise about the origin for a rotation of 270°, $(a, b) \rightarrow ($ ____ $)$.

Triangle ABC has vertices A(−3, 5), B(4, 3), and C(−1, 1).

Find the vertex of the image after a 270° rotation about the origin.

E. A'

F. B'

G. C'

(−a, −a) STRAIGHT	
(−a, −b) SHAME	
(5, 3) WILL	
(−1, −1) NAMED	
(−b, a) A	
(0, 0) DEEP	
(3, 4) LONG	

4.4 Start Thinking

Find at least two objects in each of the following categories: circle, square, triangle, and rectangle (nonsquare). Use a table to compare each object of the same category in the following ways: Are all angle measures the same? Is each shape exactly the same? Are the objects the same size?

4.4 Warm Up

Plot and connect the points in a coordinate plane to make a polygon. Name the polygon.

1. $A(-3, 2), B(-2, 1), C(3, 3)$

2. $E(1, 2), F(3, 1), G(-1, -3), H(-3, -2)$

3. $J(3, 3), K(3, -3), L(-3, -3), M(-3, 3)$

4. $P(2, -2), Q(4, -2), R(5, -4), S(2, -4)$

4.4 Cumulative Review Warm Up

Find the coordinates of point *P* along the directed line segment *AB* so that *AP* to *PB* is the given ratio.

1. $A(4, -3), B(9, -1)$; 2 to 3

2. $A(-1, -5), B(7, 0)$; 4 to 1

3. $A(-1, -4), B(2, 5)$; 3 to 1

4. $A(-2, 1), B(6, -5)$; 3 to 5

Name _____ Date _____

4.4 Practice A

In Exercises 1 and 2, identify any congruent figures in the coordinate plane. Explain.

1.

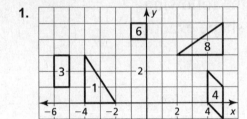

2.

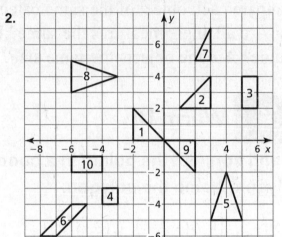

In Exercises 3 and 4, describe a congruence transformation that maps $\triangle ABC$ to $\triangle A'B'C'$.

3.

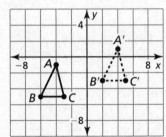

4.

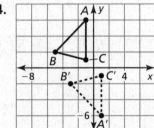

In Exercises 5 and 6, determine whether the polygons with the given vertices are congruent. Use transformations to explain your reasoning.

5. $A(5, 2), B(2, 2), C(2, 7)$ and $S(-4, -5), T(-1, -5), U(-1, 0)$

6. $E(6, -2), F(10, -2), G(10, -8), H(6, -8)$ and $W(4, 8), X(4, 10), Y(8, 10), Z(8, 8)$

7. In the figure, $a \parallel b$, $\triangle CDE$ is reflected in line a, and $\triangle C'D'E'$ is reflected in line b. List three pairs of segments that are parallel to each other. Then determine whether any segments are congruent to $\overline{EE''}$.

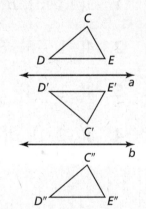

In Exercises 8 and 9, find the measure of the acute or right angle formed by intersecting lines so that P can be mapped to P'' using two reflections.

8. A rotation of $28°$ maps P to P''.

9. The rotation $(x, y) \rightarrow (-y, x)$ maps P to P''.

Name_____ Date _____

1. Identify any congruent figures in the coordinate plane. Explain.

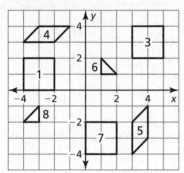

2. Determine whether the polygons with the vertices $A(0, 6)$, $B(8, 6)$, $C(6, 2)$, $D(2, 2)$ and $P(-3, -4)$, $Q(-7, -4)$, $R(-1, -8)$, $S(-5, -8)$ are congruent. Use transformations to explain your reasoning.

In Exercises 3–5, $\triangle JKL$ is reflected in line a, and $\triangle J'K'L'$ is reflected in line b.

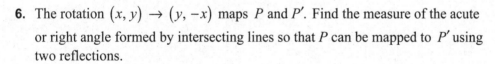

3. $\overline{JK}$ is perpendicular to line a and has a length of 3 units, and vertex K is 1 unit from line a. Find the distance $\overline{JJ'}$.

4. Find the angle of rotation that maps $\triangle JKL$ onto $\triangle J''K''L''$.

5. Is $\overline{JK}$ parallel to $\overline{J''K''}$? Explain your reasoning.

6. The rotation $(x, y) \rightarrow (y, -x)$ maps P and P'. Find the measure of the acute or right angle formed by intersecting lines so that P can be mapped to P' using two reflections.

7. Is it *always, sometimes,* or *never* true that the composition of two reflections results in the same image as a translation? Explain your reasoning.

8. $\triangle A$ is reflected in line s to form $\triangle A'$ and then reflected in line t to form $\triangle A''$. Draw line t and intermediate $\triangle A'$ to complete the figure that represents these transformations.

9. Your friend claims that if you have a series of many parallel lines, reflecting a figure in two of the lines will produce the same result as reflecting the image in four or six of the lines. Is your friend correct? Explain your reasoning.

Name _____ Date _____

4.4 Enrichment and Extension

Matrix Addition and Translation

A *matrix* is a rectangular arrangement of numbers in rows and columns. (The plural of matrix is matrices.) Each number in a matrix is called an *element*. The *dimensions* of a matrix are the numbers of rows and columns. The matrix to the right has three rows and four columns, so the dimensions of the matrix are 3 x 4, read "three by four."

$$\begin{bmatrix} 5 & 4 & 4 & 9 \\ -3 & 5 & 2 & 6 \\ 3 & -7 & 8 & 7 \end{bmatrix}$$

You can represent a figure in the coordinate plane using a matrix with two rows. The first row has the *x*-coordinates of the vertices. The second row has the corresponding *y*-coordinates. Each column represents a vertex, so the number of columns depends on the number of vertices of the figure.

Example: Write a matrix to represent point *D*.

Solution: $\begin{bmatrix} 1 \\ 3 \end{bmatrix}$ The *x*-coordinate is 1 and the *y*-coordinate is 3.

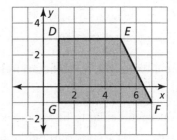

1. Write a matrix to represent point *F*.

2. Write a polygon matrix for *DEFG*.

To add or subtract matrices, you add or subtract corresponding elements, and the resulting matrix must have the same dimensions.

Perform the operation.

3. $\begin{bmatrix} 5 & -3 \\ 6 & -6 \end{bmatrix} + \begin{bmatrix} 1 & 2 \\ 3 & -4 \end{bmatrix}$

4. $\begin{bmatrix} 6 & 8 & 5 \\ 4 & 9 & -1 \end{bmatrix} - \begin{bmatrix} 1 & -7 & 0 \\ 4 & -2 & 3 \end{bmatrix}$

In Exercises 5–8, use the diagram.

5. Write a polygon matrix for $\triangle ABC$.

6. Write a matrix that, when added to the polygon matrix for $\triangle ABC$, translates the coordinates 1 unit left and 3 units up. This matrix is called a *translation matrix*.

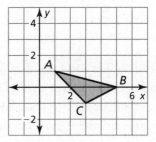

7. Add the translation matrix from Exercise 6 to the polygon matrix *ABC*. The result is called an *image matrix*, which represents the sum of a translation matrix and the matrix of a preimage.

8. Graph a congruent triangle of $\triangle ABC$ translated 1 unit left and 3 units up. Label the triangle $A'B'C'$. What do you notice about the resulting coordinates?

Name _____ Date _____

4.4 Puzzle Time

What Geometric Figure Is Like A Lost Parrot?

Write the letter of each answer in the box containing the exercise number.

1. Complete the sentence. Two geometric figures are _____ figures if and only if there is a rigid motion or a composition of rigid motions that maps one of the figures onto the other.

2. Congruent figures have the same size and shape. True or false?

3. Are three equilateral triangles with respective sides of 3 centimeters, 4 centimeters, and 4 inches congruent? Yes or no?

4. A figure is reflected in line k, and the image is then reflected in line m. The measure of the acute angle formed between lines k and m is $42°$. What is the angle of rotation?

Given △ABC with vertices $A(2, 3)$, $B(4, 3)$, and $C(4, -5)$, and the translation $(x, y) \rightarrow (x + 2, y - 1)$, find the vertex of the image.

5. A'

6. B'

7. C'

8. Complete the sentence. The polygons with vertices $A(0, 7)$, $B(0, 4)$, $C(5, 4)$, $D(5, 7)$ and $E(7, 3)$, $F(7, 0)$, $G(12, 0)$, $H(12, 3)$ _____ congruent.

Answers
R. are not
I. constructed
N. $(6, -6)$
M. yes
A. are
B. $(2, 6)$
G. $(4, 2)$
L. 84
P. no
E. 48
O. true
X. $(2, 4)$
Y. congruent
O. $(6, 2)$
U. $(-6, 6)$

8		3	6	4	1	5	2	7

Shine a flashlight at a wall 6 feet away in a dimly lit room. Measure the diameter of the circle of light created on the wall. Move the flashlight 3 feet away from the wall and measure the new diameter. Move the flashlight 1.5 feet away from the wall and measure the diameter.

Is there a pattern? Explain what happens to the diameter of the circle of light as the flashlight is moved closer to the wall.

4.5 Warm Up

Use the graph to find the indicated length.

1. Find the length of $\overline{BC}$.

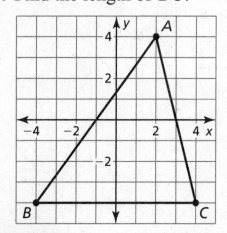

2. Find the length of $\overline{DE}$.

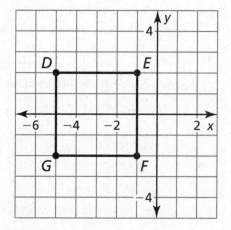

4.5 Cumulative Review Warm Up

Plot the points in a coordinate plane. Then determine whether $\overline{AB}$ and $\overline{CD}$ are congruent.

1. $A(-3, 4)$, $B(-3, 7)$, $C(3, -4)$, $D(3, -1)$

2. $A(7, -2)$, $B(2, -2)$, $C(3, -4)$, $D(5, -4)$

3. $A(9, 2)$, $B(0, 2)$, $C(6, 9)$, $D(6, 2)$

4. $A(7, -9)$, $B(7, 0)$, $C(8, -3)$, $D(-1, -3)$

Name_____ Date_____

4.5 Practice A

In Exercises 1 and 2, find the scale factor of the dilation. Then tell whether the dilation is a *reduction* or an *enlargement*.

1.

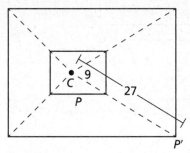

2.

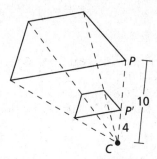

In Exercises 3–5, copy the diagram. Then use a compass and straightedge to construct a dilation of quadrilateral *ABCD* with the given center and scale factor *k*.

3. Center B, $k = 3$

4. Center P, $k = \frac{1}{2}$

5. Center C, $k = 75\%$

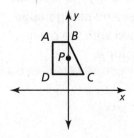

In Exercises 6 and 7, graph the polygon and its image after a dilation with a scale factor *k*.

6. $P(1, 2)$, $Q(2, 2)$, $R(4, -2)$, $S(-1, -3)$; $k = 2$

7. $A(-4, 4)$, $B(-2, 6)$, $C(1, -1)$, $D(-2, -4)$; $k = -75\%$

8. A standard piece of paper is 8.5 inches by 11 inches. A piece of legal-size paper is 8.5 inches by 14 inches. By what scale factor *k* would you need to dilate the standard paper so that you could fit two pages on a single piece of legal paper?

9. The old film-style cameras created photos that were best printed at 3.5 inches by 5 inches. Today's new digital cameras create photos that are best printed at 4 inches by 6 inches. Neither size picture will scale perfectly to fit in an 11-inch by 14-inch frame. Which type of camera will you minimize the loss of the edges of your picture?

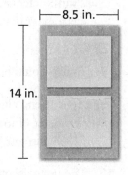

10. Your friend claims that if you dilate a rectangle by a certain scale factor, then the area of the object also increases or decreases by the same amount. Is your friend correct? Explain your reasoning.

11. Would it make sense to state "A dilation has a scale factor of 1?" Explain your reasoning.

4.5 Practice B

In Exercises 1 and 2, find the scale factor of the dilation. Then tell whether the dilation is a *reduction* or an *enlargement*.

1.

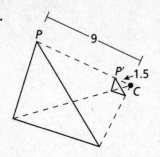

2.

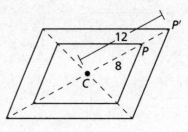

In Exercises 3 and 4, copy the diagram. Then use a compass and straightedge to construct a dilation with the given center and scale factor k.

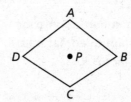

3. Center B, $k = 2$

4. Center P, $k = 75\%$

In Exercises 5 and 6, graph the polygon and its image after a dilation with a scale factor k.

5. $J(-3, 4)$, $K(2, 1)$, $L(3, -2)$, $M(-5, -4)$; $k = 50\%$

6. $V(1, 1)$, $W(-1, 0)$, $X(-4, 2)$, $Y(-3, 4)$, $Z(0, 3)$; $k = -3$

7. You look up at the sky at night and see the moon. It looks like it is about 2 millimeters across. If you then look at the moon through a telescope that has a magnification of 40 times, how big will it look to you through the telescope?

8. What would it mean for an object to be dilated with a scale factor of $k = 0$?

9. Your friend claims that if you dilate a rectangle by a certain scale factor, then the perimeter of the object also increases or decreases by the same factor. Is your friend correct? Explain your reasoning.

10. The image shows an object that has been dilated with an unknown scale factor. Use the given measures to determine the scale factor and solve for the value of x.

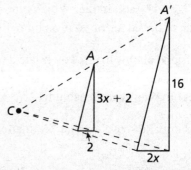

Name_____ Date_____

4.5 Enrichment and Extension

Perimeter, Area, and Dilation

Points $A(0, 0)$, $B(0, 2)$, $C(4, 0)$, and $D(4, 2)$ form a rectangle on the x-y coordinate plane.

1. Plot points A, B, C, and D in a coordinate plane. Find the length, width, perimeter, and area of the rectangle, and then fill in the first row in the chart below.

	Length	Width	Perimeter	Area
1. Points A, B, C, and D				
2. Points A', B', C', and D'				
3. Points D, E, F, and G				

Points A, B, C, and D are transformed under the operation $(x, y) \rightarrow (2x, 2y)$ to generate points A', B', C', and D'. Plot the new rectangle. Then find the new length, width, perimeter, and area, and fill in the second row in the chart above.

Points A', B', C', and D' are transformed under the operation $(x, y) \rightarrow (2x, 2y)$ to generate the points D, E, F, and G. Plot the new rectangle. Then find the new length, width, perimeter, and area, and fill in the last row in the chart above.

2. How does the transformation $(x, y) \rightarrow (2x, 2y)$ affect the length and width? perimeter? area?

3. A right triangle has vertices $A(0, 0)$, $B(10, 0)$, and $C(10, 24)$. How will the perimeter and area of the triangle change under the transformation $(x, y) \rightarrow (4x, 4y)$?

4. Write a general rule for the change in perimeter and area under the transformation $(x, y) \rightarrow a(x, y)$ or $(x, y) \rightarrow (ax, ay)$.

5. Rectangle $RSTU$ is defined by vertices $R(0, 0)$, $S(3, 0)$, $T(3, 5)$, and $U(0, 5)$. Write the transformation notation for $RSTU \rightarrow R'S'T'U'$ if the image has an area of 60 square units.

6. A microscope increases the side lengths of objects eight times. Calculate how big the area of a square will appear that has a side length of 0.6 millimeter.

Name _____ Date _____

4.5 Puzzle Time

What Side Of A House Gets The Most Rain?

Circle the letter of each correct answer in the boxes below. The circled letters will spell out the answer to the riddle.

Complete the sentence or solve the problem.

1. A _____ is a transformation in which a figure is enlarged or reduced with respect to a fixed point C, called the *center*, and a scale factor k, which is the ratio of the lengths of the corresponding sides of the image and the preimage.

2. When the scale factor $k > 1$, a dilation is a(n) _____.

3. When $0 < k < 1$, a dilation is a(n) _____.

4. When a transformation changes the shape or size of a figure, the transformation is _____.

5. You want to reduce a picture that is 10 inches by 12 inches to a picture that is 2.5 inches by 3 inches. What is the scale factor k?

6. A magnifying glass shows the image of an object that is 10 times the object's actual size. Determine the length of the image of the object if the actual length of the object is 8 millimeters.

7. A magnifying glass shows the image of an object that is 6 times the object's actual size. Determine the actual length of the object if the image is 120 millimeters.

Find the coordinates of the vertices after a dilation centered at the origin with scale factor $k = -\frac{1}{3}$.

8. $A(3, 6)$ 9. $B(3, 3)$ 10. $C(9, 0)$

R	T	K	L	Q	H	E	M	A	O
$(-3, -6)$	80 mm	$(-9, 0)$	40	expansion	dilation	$(-1, -1)$	alteration	shrink	reduction
G	**I**	**U**	**T**	**P**	**S**	**I**	**N**	**D**	**E**
8	4	$(-3, 0)$	20 mm	$(1, 1)$	enlargement	$\frac{1}{4}$	rigid	$(-1, -2)$	nonrigid

In a coordinate plane, draw any two squares. Label one *ABCD* and the other *EFGH*. Write down the coordinates for each vertex. Using transformations and/or dilations, explain how to find square *EFGH* beginning with square *ABCD*.

4.6 **Warm Up**

Solve. Round to the nearest tenth, if necessary.

1. $\dfrac{n}{17} = \dfrac{14}{25}$

2. $\dfrac{w}{12} = \dfrac{3}{2}$

3. $\dfrac{x}{5} = \dfrac{31}{35}$

4. $\dfrac{13}{2} = \dfrac{y}{19}$

5. $\dfrac{9}{3} = \dfrac{c}{4}$

6. $\dfrac{2}{1} = \dfrac{n}{17}$

4.6 **Cumulative Review Warm Up**

Decide whether inductive reasoning or deductive reasoning is used to reach the conclusion. Explain.

1. Each time you go to the store, you spend money. So, the next time you go to the store, you will spend money.

2. Irrational numbers cannot be written as fractions. Rational numbers can be written as fractions. So, 2 is a rational number.

3. All women are human. The first lady is a woman, so the first lady is human.

4.6 Practice A

In Exercises 1 and 2, graph △PQR with vertices P(−1, 5), Q(−4, 3), and R(−2, 1) and its image after the similarity transformation.

1. **Rotation:** 180° about the origin

   Dilation: $(x, y) \rightarrow (2x, 2y)$

2. **Dilation:** $(x, y) \rightarrow \left(\frac{1}{2}x, \frac{1}{2}y\right)$

   Reflection: in the x-axis

3. Describe a similarity transformation that maps the black preimage onto the dashed image.

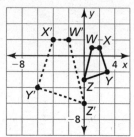

In Exercises 4 and 5, determine whether the polygons with the given vertices are similar. Use transformations to explain your reasoning.

4. $A(-2, 5)$, $B(-2, 2)$, $C(-1, 2)$ and $D(3, 3)$, $E(3, 1)$, $F(2, 1)$

5. $J(-5, -3)$, $K(-3, -1)$, $L(-3, -5)$, $M(-5, -5)$ and $T(3, 3)$, $U(4, 3)$, $V(4, 2)$, $W(3, 1)$

6. Prove that the figures are similar.

   Given Equilateral △GHI with side length a, equilateral △PQR with side length b

   Prove △GHI is similar to △PQR.

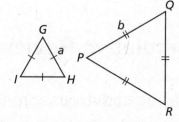

7. Your friend claims you can use a similarity transformation to turn a square into a rectangle. Is your friend correct? Explain your answer.

8. Is the composition of a dilation and a translation commutative? In other words, do you obtain the same image regardless of the order in which the transformations are performed? Justify your answer.

9. The image shown is known as a *Sierpinski triangle*. It is a common mathematical construct in the area of fractals. What can you say about the similarity transformations used to create the white triangles in this image?

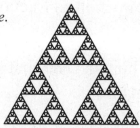

Name_____   Date_____

4.6   Practice B

In Exercises 1 and 2, graph △CDE with vertices C(1, 3), D(5, 3), and E(2, 1) and its image after the similarity transformation.

1. **Translation:** $(x, y) \to (x - 5, y - 2)$

   Dilation: $(x, y) \to (-0.5x, -0.5y)$

2. **Reflection:** in the x-axis

   Dilation: $(x, y) \to (2x, 2y)$

3. Describe a similarity transformation that maps the black preimage onto the dashed image.

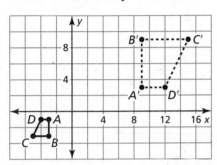

In Exercises 4 and 5, determine whether the polygons with the given vertices are similar. Use transformations to explain your reasoning.

4. $A(-4, 0)$, $B(-4, -2)$, $C(-2, -1)$ and $D(4, 6)$, $E(4, 2)$, $F(8, 2)$

5. $W(0, -1)$, $X(-5, -1)$, $Y(-3, 2)$, $Z(-1, 2)$ and $K(0, -1)$, $L(5, 2)$, $M(3, 4)$, $N(1, 4)$

6. Prove that the figures are similar.

   Given: $\angle ABE \cong \angle DBC$,
   $\overline{AE} \parallel \overline{CD}$

   Prove: △ABE is similar to △DBC.

   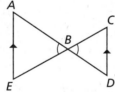

7. Is it possible to draw two circles that are not similar? Explain your reasoning.

8. The image shows what text often looks like when viewed through a magnifying glass. Does this represent a similarity transformation? Explain your reasoning.

9. Your friend draws a sketch of triangles in his notebook like the one shown here. He then claims there are the same number of congruent triangles and similar triangles. Is your friend correct? Explain.

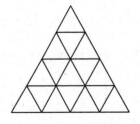

4.6 Enrichment and Extension

Similarity Through the Origin

If a figure is scaled by a factor of *k* about the origin, then the area of the new, similar image changes by a factor of k^2.

Example: A triangle has an area of 10 square units. A new triangle is mapped using $(x, y) \rightarrow (5x, 5y)$. Find the area of the new triangle.

Solution: If the new triangle is dilated by a factor of 5, then $k = 5$, and the new area will increase by a factor of $5^2 = 25$. So, the new area will be $10 \cdot 25 = 250$ square units.

1. A dilated pentagon has an area of 60 square units after being mapped using $(x, y) \rightarrow (2x, 2y)$. What was the original area?

2. In the diagram, square *ABCD* has been enlarged through the origin by a factor of *k*. The resulting image is *EFGH*. What is the value of *k*?

3. Calculate the area of *ABCD*.

4. Calculate the area of *EFGH*.

5. By what factor has the area of *EFGH* increased compared with *ABCD*?

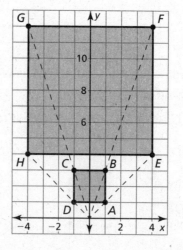

6. In the diagram, Circle A is an enlargement of Circle B by a factor of *k*. The ratio of the area of Circle A to the area of Circle B is 9. The equations of the circles are as follows.

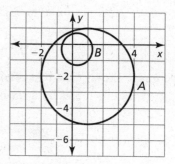

    Circle A: $(x - 1)^2 + (y + 2)^2 = t^2$, where $(1, -2)$ is the center of Circle A and *t* is the length of the radius.

    Circle B: $(x - a)^2 + (y - b) = r^2$, where (a, b) is the center of Circle B and *r* is the length of the radius.

    a. What are the values of *k, a,* and *b*?

    b. What is the relationship between *r* and *t*?

Name_____ Date_____

4.6 Puzzle Time

Why Did The Students Do Multiplication Problems On The Floor?

A	B	C	D	E	F
G	H				

Complete each exercise. Find the answer in the answer column. Write the word under the answer in the box containing the exercise letter.

false NOT	
not similar AND	
not maintain BECAUSE	
nay TO	
always TABLES	
transitional FLOOR	
true CUSTODIAN	
similarity TOLD	

Complete the sentence.

A. Two figures are _____ figures when they have the same shape but not necessarily the same size.

B. _____ transformations preserve length and angle measure.

C. _____ transformations preserve angle measure only.

Determine whether the following are congruent.

D. $A(5, 6)$, $B(3, 3)$, $C(7, 0)$, $D(9, 3)$ and
$R(0, 3)$, $S(-2, 0)$, $T(2, -3)$, $U(4, 0)$
Yes or no?

E. $A(4, 4)$, $B(7, 2)$, $C(5, -2)$, $D(1, 2)$ and
$R(-8, -8)$, $S(14, -4)$, $T(-10, 4)$, $U(2, -4)$
True or false?

F. $A(3, 6)$, $B(6, 3)$, $C(-3, 3)$ and
$R(-1, -2)$, $S(-2, -1)$, $T(1, -1)$
Yea or nay?

Answer the question.

G. If a triangle is transformed by a dilation with a scale factor of -1, will it maintain congruency or not maintain congruency?

H. Do similarity transformations preserve angle measure always or not always?

dilation STAY	
congruence TEACHER	
not always CLASS	
yes THEM	
yea GOT	
maintain USE	
no BAD	
similar THE	

Name_____ Date _____

In Exercises 1–12, simplify the expression.

1. $5x + 3 - 7$

2. $11 + 20x - 13x$

3. $12x + 15 - 8x$

4. $-9(x + 11)$

5. $4(x - 2)$

6. $-6(x - 6)$

7. $3(x + 4) - 12$

8. $6(x - 1) + 3x$

9. $-2(x - 3) - x$

10. $-(x + 15) + 8(3)$

11. $5(x - 14) - 9(2)$

12. $10(-5 + 2x) + 6(-4)$

In Exercises 13–28, solve the equation. Check your solution.

13. $-20 + x = 12$

14. $x + 16 = 6$

15. $x - 4 = -16$

16. $x - 3 = 20$

17. $\dfrac{x}{6} = 5$

18. $-12x = 96$

19. $\dfrac{x}{-8} = 12$

20. $-9x = -72$

21. $6x - 7 = 11$

22. $\dfrac{-x}{11} = 2$

23. $2 - 10x = 42$

24. $5(x + 1) = -10$

25. $3(14 + x) = -18$

26. $2(-1 + 12x) = 46$

27. $8(-7x + 6) = 496$

28. $-3(x + 1) = 33$

29. You buy two types of fish at the local market. You need 1.5 pounds of tilapia and 1 pound of cod. Tilapia costs $3.88 per pound and cod costs $3.53 per pound.

   a. How much is your fish purchase?

   b. You give the cashier $20. How much change do you receive?

30. You are making juice from concentrate. The directions on the packaging say to mix 1 can of juice with 3 cans of water. A can is 12 fluid ounces.

   a. How many fluid ounces is the prepared juice?

   b. How many cups is the prepared juice (remember that 8 fluid ounces = 1 cup)?

   c. How many pints is the prepared juice (remember that 2 cups = 1 pint)?

   d. How many quarts is the prepared juice (remember that 4 cups = 1 quart)?

Name_____ Date_____

In Exercises 31–34, tell whether the two figures are similar.

31.

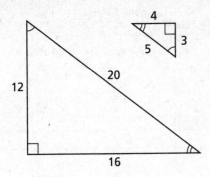

32.

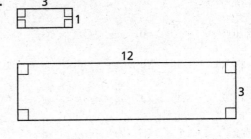

33.

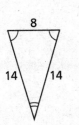

34.

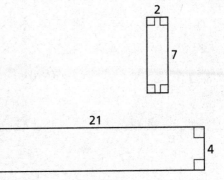

35. You want to decorate around the top of a jar with ribbon. The length around the jar is 18 inches.

   a. How many feet of ribbon do you need?

   b. The ribbon costs $4.80 per yard. How much does it cost per foot?

   c. According to how much ribbon you need, how much will it cost?

36. You and your brother plan to fix a broken window in the garage door. The window measures 1 foot by 1.5 feet.

   a. What are the window measurements in inches?

   b. What is the area of the window in square inches?

   c. The price of glass is $0.03 per square inch. How much will the glass cost for the window?

   d. You pay with a $20 bill. How much change do you receive?

Chapter 4

Cumulative Review (continued)

In Exercises 37–46, use the diagram to find the angle measure.

37. $m\angle AOC$ 38. $m\angle AOD$

39. $m\angle BOE$ 40. $m\angle AOE$

41. $m\angle COD$ 42. $m\angle EOD$

43. $m\angle COE$ 44. $m\angle AOB$

45. $m\angle COB$ 46. $m\angle BOD$

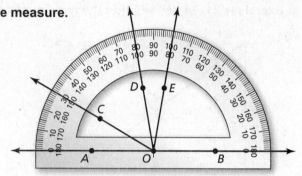

In Exercises 47–52, find the area of the triangle.

47.

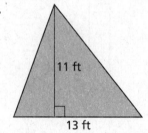

11 ft

13 ft

48.

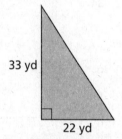

33 yd

22 yd

49.

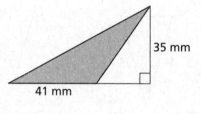

35 mm

41 mm

50.

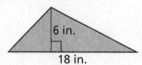

16 cm

5 cm

51.

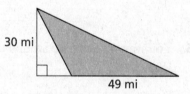

6 in.

18 in.

52.

30 mi

49 mi

53. The length and width of a tissue box are 4.5 inches, and the height is 5 inches. What is the volume of the tissue box?

54. The length of a cereal box is $7\frac{5}{8}$ inches, the width is $2\frac{3}{4}$ inches, and the height is 11 inches. What is the volume of the cereal box?

55. A local discount warehouse store is running a special on family-size cans of soup. The cost for 12 family-size cans of soup is $45.

   a. How much is one can of soup?

   b. Each family-size can of soup is 50 ounces. What is the price of soup per ounce? Round your answer to the nearest cent.

Chapter 4 Cumulative Review (continued)

In Exercises 56–67, write an equation of the line that passes through the given point and has the given slope.

56. $(-11, 9)$; $m = -3$ **57.** $(3, 5)$; $m = 4$ **58.** $(-10, 12)$; $m = \frac{1}{2}$

59. $(-1, -6)$; $m = -5$ **60.** $(4, -10)$; $m = \frac{1}{4}$ **61.** $(-9, -3)$; $m = -\frac{2}{3}$

62. $(12, 8)$; $m = \frac{1}{2}$ **63.** $(-8, -5)$; $m = \frac{3}{8}$ **64.** $(-7, 2)$; $m = \frac{5}{7}$

65. $(-4, -12)$; $m = -\frac{1}{4}$ **66.** $(-5, 7)$; $m = -1$ **67.** $(9, 0)$; $m = \frac{1}{3}$

In Exercises 68–73, write an equation of the line passing through point P that is parallel to the given line.

68. $P(3, 4)$; $y = 3x - 4$ **69.** $P(0, 7)$; $y = -\frac{1}{2}(x + 6)$

70. $P(-2, 5)$; $y = -\frac{1}{2}x + 6$ **71.** $P(2, 0)$; $y = 4x - 7$

72. $P(-3, 1)$; $y = -\frac{1}{3}x$ **73.** $P(-4, -8)$; $3x + y = -12$

In Exercises 74–79, write an equation of the line passing through point P that is perpendicular to the given line.

74. $P(4, 4)$; $y = -4x + 7$ **75.** $P(-2, -8)$; $y = \frac{1}{2}x + 6$

76. $P(4, -3)$; $y = -\frac{1}{4}x + 2$ **77.** $P(-5, 1)$; $y = -5x - 1$

78. $P(0, -5)$; $x = 4$ **79.** $P(2, -6)$; $2y - 4x = 10$

In Exercises 80–87, the vertices of $\triangle ABC$ are $A(1, 3)$, $B(-2, 6)$, $C(0, -4)$. Find the coordinates of the vertices of the image after the translation.

80. $(x, y) \rightarrow (x + 4, y - 3)$ **81.** $(x, y) \rightarrow (x + 2, y + 3)$

82. $(x, y) \rightarrow (x, y + 1)$ **83.** $(x, y) \rightarrow (x + 6, y - 1)$

84. $(x, y) \rightarrow (x + 1, y)$ **85.** $(x, y) \rightarrow (x + 3, y - 5)$

86. $(x, y) \rightarrow (x + 4, y + 5)$ **87.** $(x, y) \rightarrow (x - 3, y + 4)$

Chapter 5

Chapter 5 Congruent Triangles

Dear Family,

We often group objects into two categories: shape and size. Similar figures have the same shape but can be drastically different in size. This can include buildings, cars, and even people.

- Can you think of specific items that have the same shape but are different in size?

Congruent figures have not only the same shape but also the same size. Determining whether two figures are congruent can be tricky because, many times, we cannot move the objects side by side. We have to be more creative in our approach.

Take time with your student to cut out each of the following figures and check to see if they match exactly. If they do, they are congruent. If they don't match but have the same shape, they are similar.

- Which figures are similar?
- Which figures are congruent?

Determining whether figures are similar or congruent can be fun and will lead you to more success in your mathematical future.

Good luck!

Nombre _____ Fecha _____

Estimada familia:

A menudo, agrupamos objetos en dos categorías: forma y tamaño. Las figuras semejantes tienen la misma forma, pero pueden variar drásticamente en tamaño. Esto puede incluir edificios, carros e incluso personas.

- ¿Se les ocurren objetos específicos que tengan la misma forma pero sean de diferentes tamaños?

Las figuras congruentes no solo tienen la misma forma sino que también el mismo tamaño. Determinar si dos figuras son congruentes puede ser complicado porque, muchas veces, no podemos mover los objetos uno al lado del otro. Tenemos que usar un método más creativo.

Tómense un rato con su hijo para recortar cada una de las siguientes figuras y verificar si coinciden exactamente. Si lo hacen, son congruentes. Si no coinciden, pero tienen la misma forma, son semejantes.

- ¿Cuáles figuras son semejantes?

- ¿Cuáles figuras son congruentes?

Determinar si las figuras son semejantes o congruentes puede ser divertido y los llevará a tener más éxito en su futuro matemático.

¡Buena suerte!

5.1 Start Thinking

If $m\angle A = 120°$, what is $m\angle B$? Explain. If $m\angle D = 40°$, what is $m\angle E$? Is your reasoning the same? If the sum of $m\angle B$, $m\angle C$, and $m\angle D$ is 180°, what is $m\angle C$?

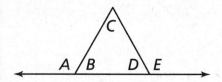

5.1 Warm Up

Find the measurement.

1. $m\angle 1$ 2. $m\angle 2$

3. $m\angle 3$ 4. $m\angle 4$

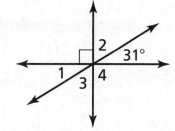

5.1 Cumulative Review Warm Up

Find the value of *x* that makes *m* ∥ *n*.

1.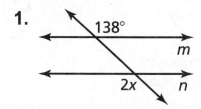

2.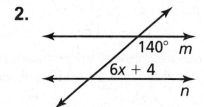

3.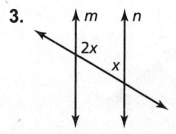

4.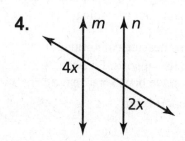

5.1 Practice A

In Exercises 1 and 2, classify the triangle by its sides and by measuring its angles.

1.
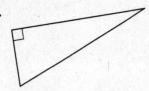

2.

In Exercises 3 and 4, classify △QRS by its sides. Then determine whether it is a right triangle.

3. $Q(2, 2)$, $R(1, -2)$, $S(-4, -4)$

4. $Q(-1, 3)$, $R(3, 2)$, $S(-2, -1)$

In Exercises 5–8, find the value of x.

5.
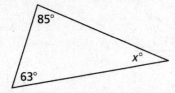

6.
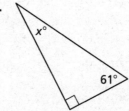

7.
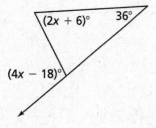

8.
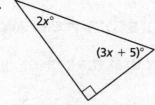

9. The measure of one acute angle of a right triangle is 12 more than 3 times the measure of the other acute angle. Find the measure of each acute angle of the right triangle.

10. Your friend claims that the measure of an exterior angle of a triangle can never be acute because it is the sum of the two nonadjacent angles of the triangle. Is your friend correct? Explain your reasoning.

11. The figure shows the measures of various angles of a roof and its supports. Find the measure of ∠1, the angle between an eave and a horizontal support beam.

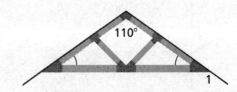

Name_____ Date _____

In Exercises 1 and 2, classify the triangle by its sides and by measuring its angles.

1.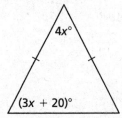

2. $J(1, 2), K(-4, 0), L(-2, 5)$

In Exercises 3–5, find the value of x.

3.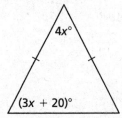

4.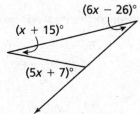

5.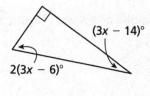

6. $\triangle ABC$ is equilateral, $m\angle A = (6x + 18)°$, and $m\angle B = (3x + 2y)°$. Solve for x and y.

7. The figure shows three exterior angles of $\triangle ABC$. Show that $m\angle 1 + m\angle 2 + m\angle 3 = 360°$.

    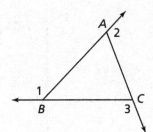

8. In the figure, solve for x and y.

    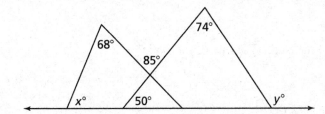

9. Is it possible for a triangle to have angle measures in an extended ratio of $1 : 4 : 7$? If so, find the three angle measures. If not, explain why it is not possible.

10. Your friend says that an exterior angle can never be complementary to any of the interior angles in a triangle. Is your friend correct? Explain your reasoning.

11. In $\triangle ABC$ and $\triangle RST$, $\angle A \cong \angle R$ and $\angle B \cong \angle S$. What can you say about $\angle C$ and $\angle T$? Explain.

5.1 Enrichment and Extension

Angles of Triangles

1. The measures of the angles of a triangle are $\left(9\sqrt{2x+17}\right)°$, $\left(9\sqrt{x}\right)°$, and $\left(12\sqrt{x}+33\right)°$. Find the measure of each angle. Classify the triangle by its angles.

Find the values of x and y. Round your answer to the nearest tenth, if necessary.

2.

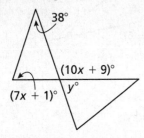

3.

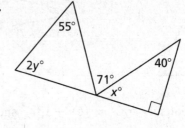

4.

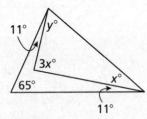

5.

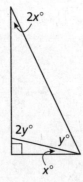

6. Find the measure of angle A in terms of the measure(s) of one or more of the other angles.

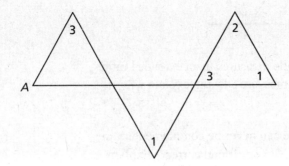

Name_____ Date_____

5.1 Puzzle Time

Did You Hear About The Race Between The Lettuce And The Tomato?

A	B	C	D	E	F
G	H	I	J	K	L

Complete each exercise. Find the answer in the answer column. Write the word under the answer in the box containing the exercise letter.

bilateral SAUCE	
scalene WAS	
100° TO	
acute AND	
equiangular A	
80° THE	
inverse ROLL	
skew SALAD	
exterior TOMATO	
opposite KNIFE	
obtuse "HEAD"	
109° "KETCHUP"	

Identify the type of triangle by its sides.

A. has two congruent sides

B. has three congruent sides

C. has no congruent sides

Identify the type of triangle by its angles.

D. has three congruent angles   **E.** has one obtuse angle

F. has three acute angles   **G.** has one right angle

Complete the statement.

H. The measure of a(n) _____ angle of a triangle is equal to the sum of the measures of the two nonadjacent interior angles.

I. The acute angles of a right triangle are _____.

J. The sum of the measures of the _____ angles of a triangle is 180°.

Solve.

K. Two angles in a triangle measure 36° and 64°. Find the measure of the exterior angle opposite the two angles.

L. The measures of two angles of a triangle are 54° and 17°. Find the measure of the third angle.

right THE	
octagon TURTLE	
71° RABBIT	
equal AND	
equilateral LETTUCE	
complementary WAS	
supplementary RED	
triangular WIN	
isosceles THE	
cute FAST	
interior TRYING	

5.2 Start Thinking

Use a ruler and a protractor to measure the side lengths and angles of each triangle. What are the corresponding sides and angles? Describe how to get △DEF from △ABC.

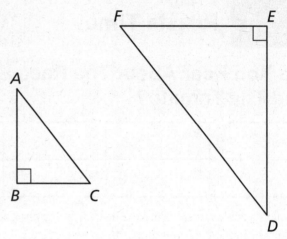

5.2 Warm Up

The triangles are similar. Use proportions to find x.

1.

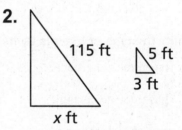

x m [   ]
75 m

18 m [   ]
150 m

2.

115 ft   5 ft

3 ft

x ft

5.2 Cumulative Review Warm Up

1. Graph $\overline{XY}$ with endpoints $X(-2, 0)$ and $Y(5, -6)$ and its image after the transformations.

   Translation: $(x, y) \rightarrow (x, y - 3)$

   Rotation: $90°$ counterclockwise about the origin

5.2 Practice A

1. In the figure, $ABCD \cong EFGH$. Identify all pairs of congruent corresponding parts. Then write another congruence statement for the polygons.

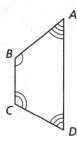
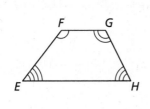

2. In the figure, $\triangle LMN \cong \triangle RST$. Find the values of x and y.

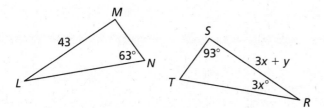

3. Show that the two quadrilaterals are congruent.

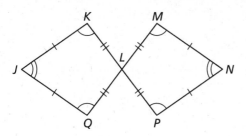

4. Find $m\angle T$. Explain your reasoning.

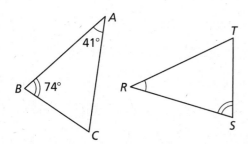

5. The congruence statements $\triangle ABC \cong \triangle DEF$, $\triangle ABC \cong \triangle EFD$, and $\triangle ABC \cong \triangle FDE$ are all valid. What must be true about $\triangle ABC$ and $\triangle DEF$?

5.2 **Practice B**

1. In the figure, $ABCDE \cong HIJFG$. Identify all pairs of congruent corresponding parts. Then complete the congruence statement: $ABCDE \cong G$ _____.

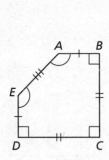 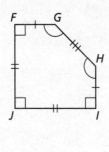

2. Find the values of x, y, and z.

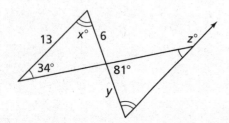

3. Show that the two triangles are congruent.

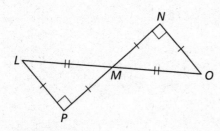

4. In the figure, $RSTU \cong UVQR$. Find the values of x and y and $m\angle RST$.
   Explain your reasoning.

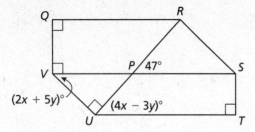

5. Draw a rectangle and label it $ABCD$. Draw diagonal $\overline{AC}$. Are the two triangles formed congruent? Explain.

5.2 Enrichment and Extension

Congruent Polygons

In Exercises 1 and 2, use the diagram to complete a two-column proof.

1. **Given:** $\angle ABD \cong \angle CDB$, $\angle ADB \cong \angle CBD$, $\overline{AD} \cong \overline{BC}$, and $\overline{AB} \cong \overline{DC}$

   Prove: $\triangle ABD \cong \triangle CDB$

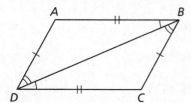

2. **Given:** $\overline{AB} \parallel \overline{DC}$, $\overline{AB} \cong \overline{DC}$, E is the midpoint of $\overline{AC}$ and $\overline{BD}$.

   Prove: $\triangle AEB \cong \triangle CED$

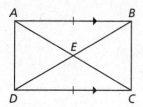

3. In the diagram below, $\triangle ADB \cong \triangle CDA \cong \triangle CDB$.

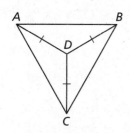

   a. Is $\triangle ABC$ equilateral? Explain your reasoning.

   b. The sum of the measures of $\angle ADB$, $\angle CDA$, and $\angle CDB$ is $360°$. Find $m\angle BDC$.

   c. Find $m\angle DBC$ and $m\angle DCB$.

   d. Explain why the angle measures in part (c) are equal.

   e. Explain why $\triangle ABC$ is equiangular.

Name _____ Date _____

5.2 Puzzle Time

What Did The Grouchy Baker Make?

Write the letter of each answer in the box containing the exercise number.

Complete the statement.

1. A rigid motion maps each part of a figure to a(n) _____ part of its image.

2. If two angles of one triangle are congruent to two angles of another triangle, then the _____ angles are also congruent.

Identify the congruent corresponding part, given that △TSR and △ABC are congruent.

3. $\overline{SR} \cong$ ___

4. $\angle C \cong$ ___

5. $\overline{BC} \cong$ ___

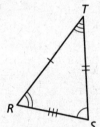

Complete the exercise using the diagram above, given that △TSR and △ABC are congruent.

6. $m\angle R = 19°$, $m\angle B = 56°$; find $m\angle T$.

7. $m\angle R = 19°$, $m\angle B = 56°$; find $m\angle S$.

8. $m\angle R = 19°$, $m\angle B = 56°$; find $m\angle C$.

9. $BC = 11$, $TR = 20$; find RS.

Answers

K. $\overline{SR}$

H. 65

N. 17°

A. $\overline{BC}$

D. second

T. 115°

C. $\angle R$

O. congruent

M. 29

C. corresponding

N. 15

Y. 32

E. third

R. 56°

O. 79°

B. 105°

S. 19°

A. 11

4	7	3	6		1	9	5	2	8

Start Thinking

Connect the points to make $\triangle ABC$. Plot D and E in Quadrant II so that $\overline{AB} \cong \overline{AD}$, $\overline{BC} \cong \overline{DE}$, and $\angle ABC \cong \angle ADE$. Connect the points to make $\triangle ADE$. Is $\triangle ABC \cong \triangle ADE$? If so, is there any other information needed to prove the congruence? Why or why not?

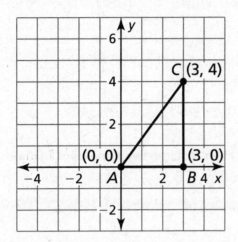

5.3 **Warm Up**

Name the diagonal segment in the figure.

1.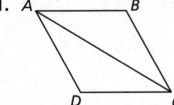

2.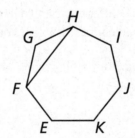

5.3 **Cumulative Review Warm Up**

Use the diagram.

1. What is another name for $\overline{DE}$?

2. What is another name for $\overline{CE}$?

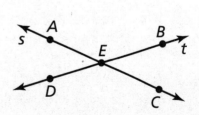

Name_____ Date _____

5.3 Practice A

In Exercises 1 and 2, decide whether enough information is given to prove that the triangles are congruent using the SAS Congruence Theorem (Theorem 5.5). Explain.

1.

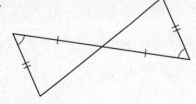

2.

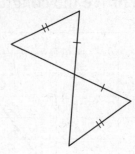

In Exercises 3 and 4, use the given information to name two congruent triangles. Explain your reasoning.

3.

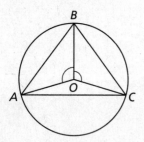

4.

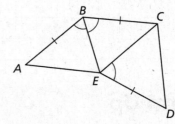

5. Your friend claims that the SAS Congruence Theorem (Theorem 5.5) will apply to a triangle and its image after the triangle has been translated, reflected, rotated, and dilated. Is your friend correct? Explain your reasoning.

6. **Given:** $\angle ABD$ and $\angle CBD$ are right angles and $\overline{BD}$ bisects $\overline{AC}$.

   Prove: $\triangle ABD \cong \triangle CBD$

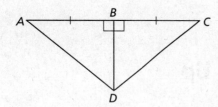

5.3 Practice B

In Exercises 1 and 2, decide whether enough information is given to prove that the triangles are congruent using the SAS Congruence Theorem (Theorem 5.5). Explain.

1.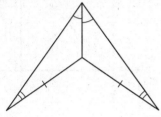

2.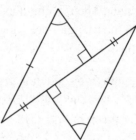

In Exercises 3 and 4, identify three congruent triangles and explain how to show that they are congruent.

3. *P* is the center of the circle.

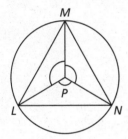

4. Three squares border equiangular and equilateral △*RST*.

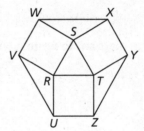

5. Use the information given in the figure to find the values of *x* and *y*.

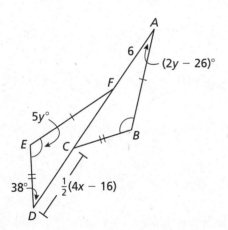

6. **Given:** $\overline{EB} \cong \overline{EC}$, △*AED* is equilateral and equiangular.

   Prove: △*ACD* ≅ △*DBA*

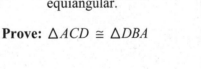
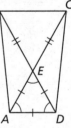

5.3 Enrichment and Extension

Proving Triangle Congruence by SAS

1. Describe how to show that $\triangle PMO \cong \triangle PMN$ using the SSS Congruence Postulate. Then, without using a protractor, find a way to show that the triangles are congruent using the SAS Congruence Postulate.

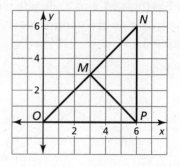

2. Determine whether enough information is given to prove that $\triangle GHI \cong \triangle JKL$. If there is enough information, state which congruence postulate or theorem you used.

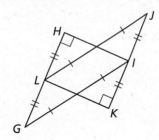

In Exercises 3 and 4, use the diagram to write a two-column proof.

3. **Given:** $\overline{AC} \perp \overline{DB}$, D is the midpoint of $\overline{AC}$.

   Prove: $\triangle ABD \cong \triangle CBD$

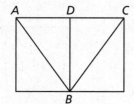

4. **Given:** $DE = BF$, $AE = CF$, $\overline{AE} \perp \overline{DB}$, $\overline{CF} \perp \overline{BD}$.

   Prove: $\triangle AEB \cong \triangle CFD$

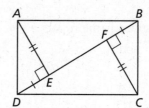

5. In the figure, $\triangle WVX \cong \triangle YZV$. Find the coordinates of X and Y.

5.3 Puzzle Time

What Do You Call A Stubborn Angle?

Circle the letter of each correct answer in the boxes below. The circled letters will spell out the answer to the riddle.

In Exercises 1–6, use the diagram.

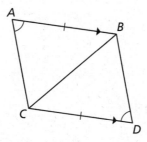

1. Identify the theorem.

   If two sides and the included angle of one triangle are congruent to two sides and the included angle of a second triangle, then the two triangles are congruent.

Identify the parts that are congruent by the given reason in the proof.

STATEMENTS	REASONS
$\overline{AB} \cong \overline{DC}$	Given
$\overline{AB} \parallel \overline{DC}$	Given
2.	Alternate Interior Angles Theorem
3.	Reflexive Property of Congruence
4.	SAS Congruence Theorem

Name the included angle between the pair of sides given.

5. $\overline{AC}$ and $\overline{CB}$

6. $\overline{BC}$ and $\overline{CD}$

T	O	H	B	T	M
$\angle ABC$	$\angle BCD$	$\angle ABC \cong \angle CBD$	$\triangle ABC \cong \triangle DCB$	SAS Congruence	$\triangle ABC \cong \triangle BCD$

U	A	R	M	S	E
$\angle ACB$	$\angle BDC$	$\overline{AC} \cong \overline{BD}$	AAS Congruence	$\angle ABC \cong \angle DCB$	$\overline{BC} \cong \overline{CB}$

In a coordinate plane, draw square *ABCD* with side length
2 units. Draw diagonal $\overline{BD}$ to create △*ABD* and △*CBD*.
Are the two triangles congruent? What is the length of $\overline{BD}$?

Draw square *EFGH* with any side length. Draw a diagonal
to make two triangles. Are these triangles congruent?

5.4 **Warm Up**

Find the missing angle measure.

1.
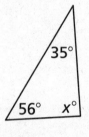

2.
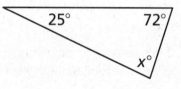

3.
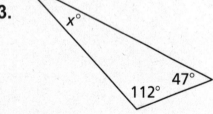

4.
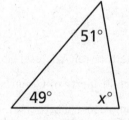

5.4 **Cumulative Review Warm Up**

**Rewrite the definition of the term as a biconditional
statement.**

1. In an isosceles triangle, the legs are of equal length.

2. A tangram is a Chinese puzzle made up of seven pieces.

3. A rectangle is a parallelogram that has four right angles.

5.4 Practice A

In Exercises 1 and 2, find the value of x.

1.

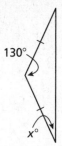

130°

x°

2.

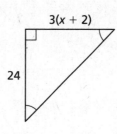

3(x + 2)

24

In Exercises 3 and 4, find the values of x and y.

3.

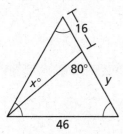

16

80°

x°   y

46

4.

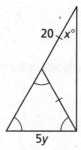

20   x°

5y

5. Explain why △ABC is isosceles.

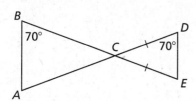

B

70°

C   70°

A   E

D

6. Can an isosceles triangle be an obtuse triangle? Explain.

5.4 Practice B

In Exercises 1 and 2, find the value of x.

1.

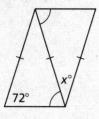

72°
x°

2.

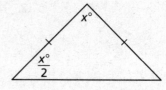

x°
$\frac{x°}{2}$

In Exercises 3 and 4, find the values of x and y.

3.

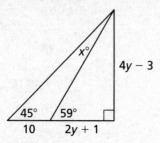

x°
4y − 3
45° 59°
10   2y + 1

4.

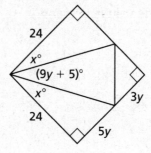

24
x°
(9y + 5)°
x°
24
3y
5y

5. **Given:** ∠CBD ≅ ∠CDB, ∠BAE ≅ ∠DEA

   Prove: $\overline{AD} \cong \overline{EB}$

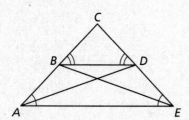

6. **Given:** ∠EBC ≅ ∠ECB, $\overline{AE} \cong \overline{DE}$

   Prove: $\overline{AB} \cong \overline{DC}$

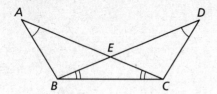

5.4 Enrichment and Extension

Isosceles Triangles

1. In the diagram to the right, $\triangle XYZ$ is isosceles, with $XY = XZ$. What is the value of r in terms of p and q?

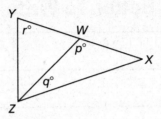

2. In the diagram below, the seven inner triangles in the picture are isosceles. The larger, outer triangle is also isosceles. What is the value of each angle in the picture in terms of a?

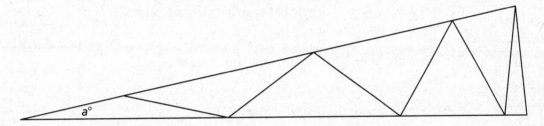

In Exercises 3 and 4, find the values of x and y. Round your answers to the nearest tenth, if necessary.

3.

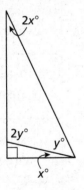

4.

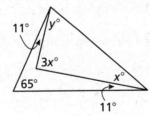

5. Is it possible to partition an arbitrary right triangle into isosceles triangles? Justify your answer.

Name _____ Date _____

5.4 Puzzle Time

Which Hand Is It Better To Write With?

A	B	C	D	E	F
G	H				

Complete each exercise. Find the answer in the answer column. Write the word under the answer in the box containing the exercise letter.

45° FROM	
equiangular WRITE	
perfect RIGHT	
60° A	
bottom FUN	
vertex IT'S	
complementary THE	
13 PEN	

Complete the statement.

A. When an isosceles triangle has exactly two congruent sides, these two sides are the _____.

B. The angle formed by the legs of an isosceles triangle is the _____ angle.

C. The third side of the isosceles triangle is the _____.

D. If two angles of a triangle are congruent, then the sides opposite them are _____.

E. If a triangle is equilateral, then it is _____.

Find the indicated value using the diagram.

F. $XY = 8$, find ZY.

G. $m\angle Y = 60°$, find $m\angle Z$.

H. $YX = 13$, find XZ.

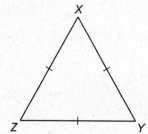

7 LEFT	
congruent TO	
arms WANTED	
8 WITH	
legs NEITHER	
acute WHEN	
base BEST	
15 HOLD	

Use a ruler to construct △*JKL* with *JK* = 1 in., *KL* = 0.5 in., *JL* = 1 in.

What are the angle measurements in △*JKL*? Classify △*JKL*. Construct a new triangle, △*PQR*, with $\overline{JK} \cong \overline{PQ}$, $\overline{KL} \cong \overline{QR}$, $\overline{JL} \cong \overline{PR}$. Are the angles congruent? Do you think it would be possible to create triangles with congruent side lengths but different angles? Why or why not?

5.5 Warm Up

Name the included angle between the pair of sides given.

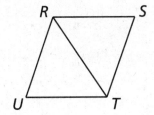

1. $\overline{RU}$ and $\overline{UT}$

2. $\overline{ST}$ and $\overline{TR}$

3. $\overline{TR}$ and $\overline{RS}$

4. $\overline{UT}$ and $\overline{TR}$

5. $\overline{SR}$ and $\overline{RT}$

6. $\overline{RS}$ and $\overline{ST}$

5.5 Cumulative Review Warm Up

Find *m*∠1 and *m*∠2. Tell which theorem you used.

1.

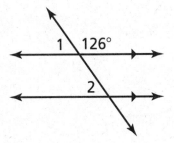

2.

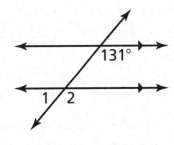

Name _____ Date _____

5.5 Practice A

In Exercises 1–3, decide whether enough information is given to prove that the triangles are congruent using either the SSS Congruence Theorem (Theorem 5.8) or the HL Congruence Theorem (Theorem 5.9). Explain.

1. 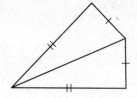 2. 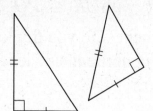 3.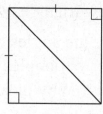

4. **Given:** $\overline{AC}$ bisects $\overline{BD}$, $\overline{AB} \cong \overline{AD}$

   Prove: $\triangle ABC \cong \triangle ADC$

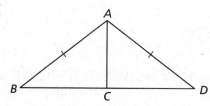

5. **Given:** $\overline{JL} \cong \overline{GF}$, $\overline{KL} \cong \overline{HF}$, $\angle J$ and $\angle G$ are right angles.

   Prove: $\triangle JKL \cong \triangle GHF$

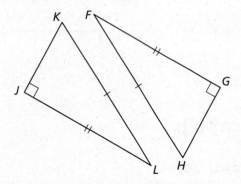

6. The coordinates of two triangles are given by $A(2, 3)$, $B(1, -2)$, $C(4, 5)$ and $F(-2, 2)$, $G(-4, 4)$, $H(-4, -4)$. Use the coordinates to determine whether $\triangle ABC \cong \triangle FGH$.

7. The figure shows a cut gem.

   a. What lengths can you measure to determine whether any two adjacent triangular faces of the gem are congruent?

   b. Assume that all of the triangular faces are congruent. What shape is the outline of the gem when viewed from above?

5.5 Practice B

In Exercises 1–3, decide whether enough information is given to prove that the triangles are congruent. If so, state the theorem you use.

1.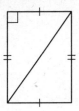

2.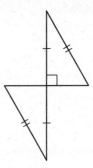

3.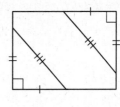

4. Given: $\overline{BC} \cong \overline{ED}$, $\overline{AB} \cong \overline{FE}$, and $\overline{AD} \cong \overline{FC}$

Prove: $\triangle ABD \cong \triangle FEC$

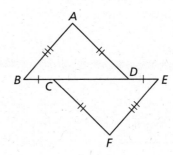

5. Given: $\overline{PS} \cong \overline{RS}$, $\overline{SQ} \perp \overline{PR}$

Prove: $\triangle PSQ \cong \triangle RSQ$

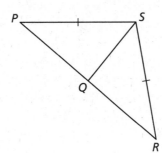

6. Two triangles are formed by the four lines described below. Both triangles share lines a and b. A side of one triangle is contained in line c, and a side of the other triangle is contained in line d. How can you use this information to determine whether the triangles are congruent?

Line a: $y = 3x + 2$

Line b: $y = -\frac{1}{3}x - 1$

Line c: passes through points $(1, 5)$ and $(3, -2)$

Line d: passes through points $(-6, 1)$ and $(-3, -7)$

5.5 Enrichment and Extension

Proving Triangle Congruence by SSS

1. If $\triangle ABC \cong \triangle DEF$, solve for the missing variable.

   a. $A(1, 3)$, $B(4, 1)$, $C(5, 3)$, $D(3, -3)$, $E(6, -5)$, $F(x, -3)$

   b. $A(1, -1)$, $B(-2, 2)$, $C(-3, -4)$, $D(3, 3x - 10)$, $E(6, -1)$, $F(7, 5)$

   c. $A(-3, 0)$, $B(6, 2)$, $C(-1, 9)$, $D(x^2 - 12, -10)$, $E(13, -8)$, $F(6, -1)$

In Exercises 2 and 3, use the diagram to write a two-column proof.

2. **Given:** $\overline{WA} \cong \overline{WT}$; S is the midpoint of $\overline{AT}$.
   Prove: $\angle 1 \cong \angle 2$

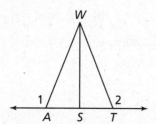

3. **Given:** $\overline{GR} \cong \overline{GT}$, $\overline{RS} \cong \overline{ST}$
   Prove: $\triangle GRS \cong \triangle GST$

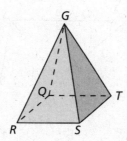

4. Write a paragraph proof showing that if one side of an equilateral triangle is congruent to one side of a second equilateral triangle, then the two triangles are congruent. Include a diagram.

5. In the figure, $\triangle MLN \cong \triangle KLJ$. Find the coordinates of J and K.

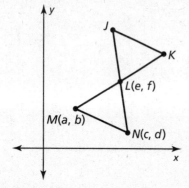

5.5 Puzzle Time

What Did Mozart Become On His Thirteenth Birthday?

Write the letter of each answer in the box containing the exercise number.

Complete the statement.

1. In a right triangle, the sides adjacent to the right angle are the _____.

2. The side opposite the right angle is the _____ of the right triangle.

3. If the hypotenuse and a leg of a right triangle are congruent to the hypotenuse and a leg of a second right triangle, then the two triangles are congruent according to the _____ Theorem.

4. If three sides of one triangle are congruent to three sides of a second triangle, then the two triangles are congruent according to the _____ Theorem.

Solve for the indicated measure.

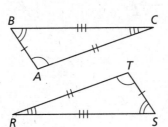

5. $R = 19°$, $\angle B = 56°$, find $m\angle T$.

6. $R = 19°$, $\angle B = 56°$, find $m\angle S$.

7. $R = 19°$, $\angle B = 56°$, find $m\angle C$.

Solve.

8. True or false?
   $\triangle ABC \cong \triangle ZXY$

   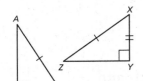

9. Are the two triangles congruent?
   Yes or no?

   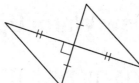

Answers
E. SSS
H. 65°
E. legs
A. SSA
A. yes
T. 115°
C. diagonal
T. hypotenuse
M. AAS
C. arms
G. true
Y. no
E. false
R. 56°
N. HL
A. 105°
E. 19°
A. 91°

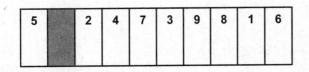

5		2	4	7	3	9	8	1	6

5.6 Start Thinking

Use a straightedge and a protractor to construct $\triangle XYZ$, with $\angle X = 70°$, $\angle Y = 50°$, and $\angle Z = 60°$. Use a ruler to measure the side lengths. Without measuring, construct $\triangle ABC$, with $\angle X \cong \angle A$, $\angle Y \cong \angle B$, and $\angle Z \cong \angle C$. Measure the side lengths of $\triangle ABC$. Is $\triangle XYZ \cong \triangle ABC$? What does this lead you to believe about triangles with the same angle measures?

5.6 Warm Up

Determine which triangle congruence theorem, if any, can be used to prove the triangles are congruent.

1.
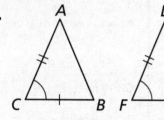

2.
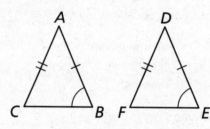

3.
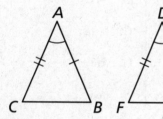

4.
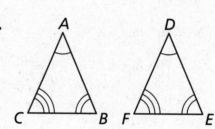

5.6 Cumulative Review Warm Up

1. Graph $\triangle XYZ$, with vertices $X(3, 3)$, $Y(7, -1)$, $Z(8, 1)$, and and its image after the transformations.

   Translation: $(x, y) \rightarrow (x - 13, y - 3)$

   Translation: $(x, y) \rightarrow (x + 6, y + 8)$

5.6   Practice A

In Exercises 1–3, decide whether enough information is given to prove that the triangles are congruent. If so, state the theorem you would use.

1.

2.

3.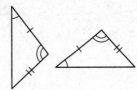

4. **Given:** $\overline{PS} \parallel \overline{RT}$, $\overline{PQ} \cong \overline{TQ}$

   Prove: $\triangle PSQ \cong \triangle TRQ$

   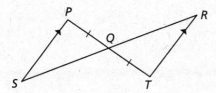

5. **Given:** $\overline{BD}$ bisects $\angle ADC$, $\overline{BD} \perp \overline{AC}$

   Prove: $\triangle ABD \cong \triangle CBD$

   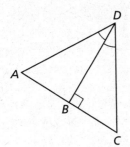

6. Use the information given in the figure and the triangle congruence theorems to determine which pairs of triangles you can prove are congruent. Show your steps. Are there any pairs of triangles that cannot be proven congruent? Explain.

   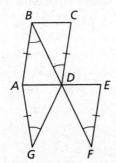

5.6 Practice B

In Exercises 1–3, decide whether enough information is given to prove that the triangles are congruent. If so, state the theorem you would use.

1.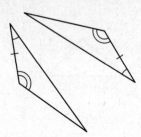

2.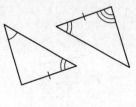

3.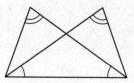

4. **Given:** $\overline{BD}$ bisects $\overline{AE}$, $\angle A \cong \angle E$

   Prove: $\triangle ABC \cong \triangle EDC$

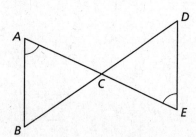

5. **Given:** $\angle I \cong \angle J$, $\overline{IM} \parallel \overline{JN}$ and $\overline{KL} \cong \overline{MN}$

   Prove: $\triangle IKM \cong \triangle JLN$

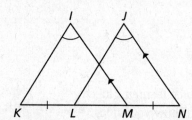

6. Write a paragraph proof to show that opposite sides of a parallelogram are congruent.

   Given: $QRST$ is a parallelogram.

   Prove: $\overline{QR} \cong \overline{TS}$ and $\overline{RS} \cong \overline{QT}$

   $\left(Hint: \text{ Draw } \overline{RT}.\right)$

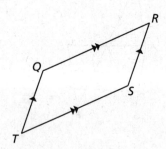

5.6 Enrichment and Extension

Proving Triangle Congruence by ASA and AAS

1. Graph the lines $y = 2x + 5$, $y = 2x - 3$, and $x = 0$. Consider the equation $y = mx + 1$. For what values of m will the graph of the equation form two triangles if added to your graph? For what values of m will those triangles be congruent right triangles? Explain.

2. Graph the lines $-x + y = -1$, $-x + 2y = -1$, $x + 2y = 13$, and $x + y = 7$ in the same coordinate plane. Label the vertices of the two triangles formed by the lines. Prove that the triangles are congruent.

3. Use the graph to prove that $\triangle ABC \cong \triangle CDA$.

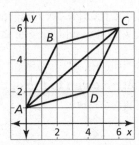

In Exercises 4–6, use the diagram to write a two-column proof.

4. **Given:** $\triangle ABC \cong \triangle ABD$,
   $\angle FCA \cong \angle EDA$

   Prove: $\triangle CAF \cong \triangle DAE$

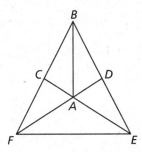

5. **Given:** $\overline{HB} \cong \overline{EB}$, $\angle BHG \cong \angle BEA$,
   $\angle HGJ \cong \angle EAD$, $\angle JGB \cong \angle DAB$

   Prove: $\triangle BHG \cong \triangle BEA$

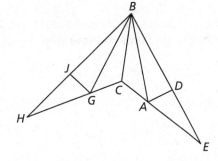

6. **Given:** $\overline{AE} \parallel \overline{BF}$, $\overline{CE} \parallel \overline{DF}$, $\overline{AB} \cong \overline{CD}$

   Prove: $\triangle AEC \cong \triangle BFD$

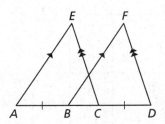

Name_____ Date _____

What Has Two Hands But Can't Clap?

Circle the letter of each correct answer in the boxes below. The circled letters will spell out the answer to the riddle.

Name the correct theorem.

1. If two angles and the included side of one triangle are congruent to two angles and the included side of a second triangle, then the two triangles are congruent.

2. If two angles and a non-included side of one triangle are congruent to two angles and the corresponding non-included side of a second triangle, then the two triangles are congruent.

Using the diagrams, is there enough information given to prove that the triangles are congruent? If so, state the theorem you would use.

3.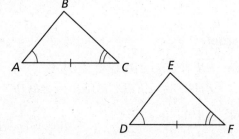

4.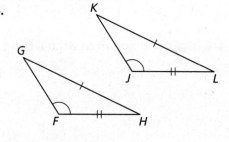

Name the third congruence statement that is needed to prove that
$\triangle ABC \cong \triangle XYZ$ **using the given theorem.**

5. **Given:** $\overline{AC} \cong \overline{XZ}, \angle C \cong \angle Z$,

   Use AAS: ___ $\cong$ ___

6. **Given:** $\overline{AC} \cong \overline{XZ}, \angle C \cong \angle Z$

   Use ASA: ___ $\cong$ ___

A	W	A	L	E	T
$\angle B \cong \angle Y$	ASA	Yes by ASA	Yes by AAS	$\angle C \cong \angle Y$	AAS
C	**I**	**H**	**T**	**E**	**R**
$\angle A \cong \angle X$	Yes by HL	No	SSA	$\angle A \cong \angle Z$	SAS

Find any small triangular-shaped object. Use a ruler and a protractor to measure its side lengths and angle measures.

Use the measurements to construct a congruent triangle. Label the triangle to show its measurements.

5.7 **Warm Up**

Name the property the statement illustrates.

1. If $\overline{RU} \cong \overline{WX}$ and $\overline{WX} \cong \overline{YZ}$, then $\overline{RU} \cong \overline{YZ}$.

2. $\angle A \cong \angle A$

3. If $\angle B \cong \angle C$, then $\angle C \cong \angle B$.

4. $\overline{JK} \cong \overline{JK}$

5. If $\overline{LM} \cong \overline{NP}$, then $\overline{NP} \cong \overline{LM}$.

6. If $\angle Q \cong \angle R$ and $\angle R \cong \angle S$, then $\angle Q \cong \angle S$.

5.7 **Cumulative Review Warm Up**

Write three names for the angles.

1.

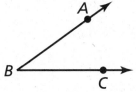

2.

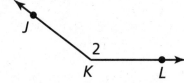

3.

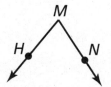

4.

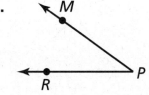

5.7 Practice A

In Exercises 1 and 2, explain how to prove that the statement is true.

1. $\overline{EB} \cong \overline{AC}$

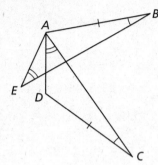

2. $\angle A \cong \angle D$

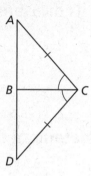

In Exercises 3 and 4, write a plan to prove the given statement.

3. $\overline{PR} \cong \overline{SQ}$

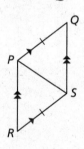

4. $\angle H \cong \angle J$

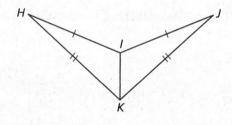

5. Use the figure to explain how to find the distance across the pond indirectly. Then prove that your method works.

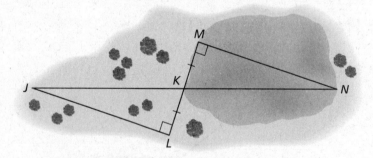

6. Find DE, if possible. Explain your reasoning.

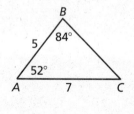

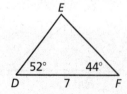

5.7 Practice B

In Exercises 1 and 2, explain how to prove that the statement is true.

1. $\overline{GK} \cong \overline{JK}$

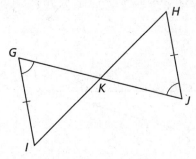

2. $\overline{BA} \cong \overline{CA}$

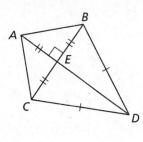

In Exercises 3 and 4, write a plan to prove the given statement.

3. $\overline{DC} \cong \overline{DE}$

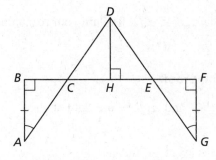

4. $\angle 1 \cong \angle 2$

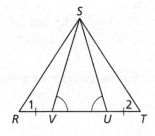

5. You want to know how far it is from point A of the roof you are on to point B of the roof of the building across the street. The buildings are the same height.

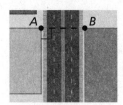

    a. Explain how to use triangles to find AB. Draw a diagram showing the additional points you will use.

    b. Explain how you know your method helps you to find AB.

5.7 Enrichment and Extension

Using Congruent Triangles

In Exercises 1 and 2, for what value(s) of x will the triangles be congruent?

1. $m\angle 3 = x^2$; $m\angle 4 = 7x - 10$

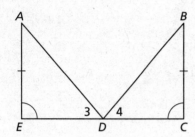

2. $AB = 3x + 4$; $CB = 2 + 2x + 2\sqrt{2x + 1}$

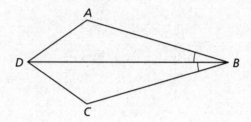

3. Given that $\triangle ABC \cong \triangle DEF$, $m\angle A = 70°$, $m\angle B = 60°$, $m\angle C = 50°$, $m\angle D = (3x + 10)°$, $m\angle E = \left(\dfrac{y}{3} + 20\right)°$, and $m\angle F = (z^2 + 14)°$, find the values of x, y, and z.

4. Use the following vertices of $\triangle ABC$ and $\triangle DEF$ to show that $\angle A \cong \angle D$. Explain your reasoning.
$A(3, 7)$, $B(6, 11)$, $C(11, 13)$, $D(2, -4)$, $E(5, -8)$, $F(10, -10)$

In Exercises 5 and 6, refer to the diagram to write a two-column proof.

5. Given: L is the midpoint of $\overline{JN}$, $\overline{PJ} \cong \overline{QN}$, $\overline{PL} \cong \overline{QL}$, $\angle PKJ$ and $\angle QMN$ are right angles.

Prove: $\angle MQN \cong \angle KPJ$

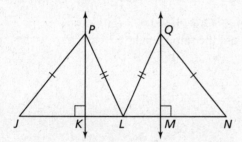

6. Given: $\angle R \cong \angle S$, $\angle 2 \cong \angle 3$

Prove: $\overline{SU} \cong \overline{RU}$

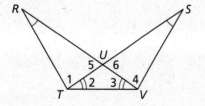

Name_____ Date _____

5.7 Puzzle Time

Why Do Pigs Have Pink Skin?

A	B	C	D	E

Complete each exercise. Find the answer in the answer column. Write the word under the answer in the box containing the exercise letter.

similar **WOLF**	**Complete the statement.**	corresponding parts **IN**
	A. Congruent triangles have congruent _____ parts.	
vertical angles **THEIR**	**B.** When you cannot measure something directly, you can use calculations to discover the length _____.	adjacent angles **HOME**
angular sight **SUN**	**Complete the missing reasons in the proof.**	indirectly **KEEP**
SAS **INSIDES**	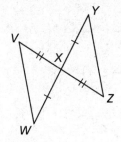	adjacent parts **AND**
ASA **BECAUSE**		corresponding **TO**

STATEMENTS	REASONS
$\overline{VX} \cong \overline{ZX}$	Given
$\overline{WX} \cong \overline{YX}$	Given
$\angle VXW \cong \angle YXZ$	**C.**
$\triangle VXW \cong \triangle ZYX$	**D.**
$\angle V \cong \angle Z$	**E.**

5.8 Start Thinking

Use dynamic geometry software to create any $\triangle ABC$ in a coordinate plane such that the center of the triangle is the origin. Use the software to manipulate the triangle so it has whole-number degree angle measures.

Explain how you can use this triangle and the software to prove that knowing all three angle measures in a triangle is not enough to create a congruent triangle.

5.8 Warm Up

Find the distance between the points with the given coordinates. Round to the nearest tenth, if necessary.

1. $(7, -3), (13, 7)$ **2.** $(-1, -5), (-4, -4)$

3. $(6, -11), (6, 7)$ **4.** $(-3, 0), (4, -2)$

5. $(-15, -8), (-3, -4)$ **6.** $(10, 24), (4, 3)$

5.8 Cumulative Review Warm Up

Use the property to complete the statement.

1. Substitution Property of Equality:

If $CD = 30$, then $CD + EF =$ _____.

2. Multiplication Property of Equality:

If $EF = GH$, then $4 \bullet EF =$ _____.

3. Subtraction Property of Equality:

If $PQ = AB$, then $PQ - JK =$ _____.

Name_____ Date _____

5.8 Practice A

In Exercises 1–4, place the figure in a coordinate plane in a convenient way. Assign coordinates to each vertex. Explain the advantages of your placement.

1. a rectangle 2 units wide and 6 units long

2. an isosceles right triangle with 4-unit legs

3. a rectangle ℓ units long and w units wide

4. an isosceles triangle with base length b and height h

In Exercises 5 and 6, graph the triangle with the given vertices. Find the length and the slope of each side of the triangle. Then find the coordinates of the midpoint of each side. Is the triangle a right triangle? isosceles? Explain. (Assume a and b are positive and $a \neq b$.)

5. $A(0, 0), B(a, 2), C(a, 0)$

6. $J(0, 0), K(0, a), L(b, 0)$

In Exercises 7 and 8, find the coordinates of any unlabeled vertices. Then find the indicated length(s).

7. Find OB.

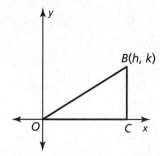

8. Find FD and DE.

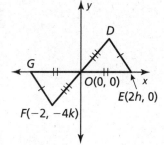

9. Given: Coordinates of vertices of $\triangle ACO$ and $\triangle BDO$

   Prove: $\triangle ACO \cong \triangle BDO$

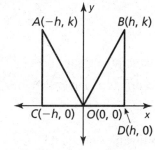

10. Your friend says that a convenient way to draw an equilateral triangle on a coordinate plane is with the base along the x-axis starting at the point $(0, 0)$. Is your friend correct? Explain your reasoning.

11. You are writing a coordinate proof about right triangles with leg lengths in a ratio of 3 to 4. Assign coordinates to represent such a triangle in a coordinate plane in a convenient way, using a shorter leg length of $3a$. Then find the length of the hypotenuse.

5.8 Practice B

In Exercises 1–3, place the figure in a coordinate plane in a convenient way. Assign coordinates to each vertex. Explain the advantages of your placement.

1. a rectangle twice as long as it is wide

2. a right triangle with a leg length of 3 units and a hypotenuse with a positive slope

3. an obtuse scalene triangle

In Exercises 4 and 5, graph the triangle with the given vertices. Find the length and the slope of each side of the triangle. Then find the coordinates of the midpoint of each side. Is the triangle a right triangle? isosceles? Explain.

4. $J(0, 0)$, $K(a, b)$, $L(2a, 0)$

5. $P(0, 0)$, $Q(5a, 0)$, $R(8a, 4a)$

In Exercises 6 and 7, find the coordinates of any unlabeled vertices. Then find the indicated lengths.

6. Find GH and FH.

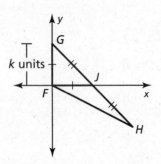

7. Find BC and CD.

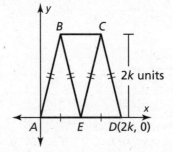

8. The vertices of a quadrilateral are given by the coordinates $W(3, 5)$, $X(5, 0)$, $Y(-3, -4)$, and $Z(-5, 1)$. Is the quadrilateral a parallelogram? a trapezoid? Explain your reasoning.

9. Write a coordinate proof for the following statement.

   Any $\triangle ABC$ formed so that vertex C is on the perpendicular bisector of $\overline{AB}$ is an isosceles triangle.

5.8 Enrichment and Extension

Coordinate Proofs

1. Let $P = (a, b)$, $Q = (0, 0)$, and $R = (-b, a)$, where a and b are positive numbers. Prove that angle PQR is a right angle by introducing two congruent right triangles into your diagram. Verify that the slope of $\overline{QP}$ is the negative reciprocal of the slope of $\overline{QR}$.

2. Prove that quadrilateral $A(1, -2)$, $B(13, 4)$, $C(6, 8)$, and $D(-2, 4)$ is a trapezoid but is *not* an isosceles trapezoid.

3. In the diagram to the right, P is the midpoint of $\overline{OS}$ and Q is the midpoint of $\overline{RS}$.

   a. Find the coordinates of P and Q.

   b. Find the equations of the line segments of $\overline{PR}$ and $\overline{QO}$.

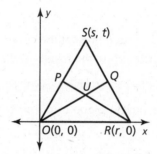

4. In the diagram of trapezoid $TRAP$ below, $\overline{TR} \cong \overline{PA}$, and $D, E, F,$ and G are midpoints of the indicated sides. Prove $DEFG$ is a rhombus.

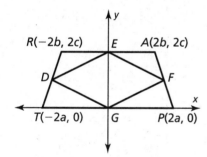

In Exercises 5–8, give all possible coordinates for the desired point, assuming that it lies in the coordinate plane.

5. If $\triangle OAB \cong \triangle OAC$ and $C \neq B$, find C.

6. If $\triangle OAB \cong \triangle ODB$ and $D \neq A$, find D.

7. If $\triangle OAB \cong \triangle AOF$, find F.

8. If $\triangle OAB \cong \triangle BGO$, find G.

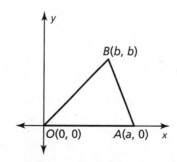

5.8 Puzzle Time

What Do Parachute Jumpers Pack Their Gear In?

Write the letter of each answer in the box containing the exercise number.

Complete the statement.

1. A(n) _____ proof involves placing geometric figures in a coordinate plane.

2. To find the length of a side of a figure, you can use the _____ formula.

3. When you use _____ to represent the coordinates of a figure in a coordinate proof, the results are true for all figures of that type.

Place the figure in a coordinate plane and find the indicated length.

4. A right triangle has leg lengths of 20 and 21 units. Find the length of the hypotenuse.

5. An isosceles triangle has a base length of 126 units and a height of 16 units. Find the length of one of the legs.

6. A rectangle has a length of 80 units and a width of 39 units. Find the length of the diagonal.

7. A square has side length 10 units. Find the approximate length of the diagonal.

Answers
S. 14.1
B. 29
Q. 15.2
I. distance
A. 65
E. 74
G. coordinate
V. 102
E. 28.6
N. slope
A. variables
M. geometric
C. numbers
R. 89

5	2	6		4	3	1	7

Name_____ Date _____

In Exercises 1–20, find the midpoint *M* of the segment with the given endpoints.

1. $G(1, 7)$ and $H(-4, -1)$

2. $N(3, 2)$ and $P(-8, 1)$

3. $B(3, -4)$ and $C(2, 8)$

4. $J(1, 5)$ and $K(3, -5)$

5. $R(8, -1)$ and $S(2, 9)$

6. $E(4, -6)$ and $F(7, 8)$

7. $H(9, 1)$ and $I(-2, -3)$

8. $K(7, 1)$ and $L(-5, -4)$

9. $D(5, 1)$ and $E(4, -3)$

10. $S(3, 1)$ and $T(-3, -2)$

11. $I(-6, 5)$ and $J(4, 1)$

12. $Y(7, -5)$ and $Y(-2, 9)$

13. $V(2, 1)$ and $W(-7, -1)$

14. $C(9, -5)$ and $D(6, -3)$

15. $J(4, -2)$ and $K(-1, -2)$

16. $A(7, 5)$ and $B(8, 4)$

17. $X(-5, -8)$ and $Y(-9, 7)$

18. $P(2, 9)$ and $Q(8, 3)$

19. $W(6, -7)$ and $X(4, 1)$

20. $F(6, -1)$ and $G(-3, 4)$

In Exercises 21–40, find the distance between the two given points. Round your answer to the nearest hundredth.

21. $K(1, 3)$ and $L(-7, 6)$

22. $E(4, 2)$ and $F(-8, 5)$

23. $L(2, 7)$ and $M(-1, -3)$

24. $C(-2, -5)$ and $D(1, 8)$

25. $S(9, 1)$ and $T(5, -5)$

26. $D(-2, 3)$ and $E(4, 1)$

27. $D(-7, -2)$ and $E(8, -1)$

28. $B(9, 0)$ and $C(3, -2)$

29. $A(8, -4)$ and $B(-3, 2)$

30. $J(6, -6)$ and $K(2, -9)$

31. $N(3, -6)$ and $P(3, 1)$

32. $F(1, 2)$ and $G(9, -4)$

33. $B(5, 1)$ and $C(3, -7)$

34. $M(4, 1)$ and $N(8, -4)$

35. $T(9, -3)$ and $U(-2, 5)$

36. $R(1, 2)$ and $S(4, 9)$

37. $P(0, 7)$ and $Q(3, 1)$

38. $K(2, 4)$ and $L(-5, 1)$

39. $U(-3, 2)$ and $V(8, -4)$

40. $H(-9, 8)$ and $I(6, 3)$

Chapter 5 **Cumulative Review** (continued)

41. You are filling a wooden box in the shape of a rectangular prism with potpourri. The box measures 4 inches by 6 inches by 1 inch. What is the volume of the box?

42. You decide to make lasagna for dinner. The baking dish in the shape of a rectangular prism measures 13 inches by 9 inches by 2 inches. What is the volume of the container?

In Exercises 43–50, find *FH*.

43.
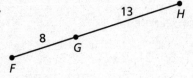

44.
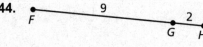

45.
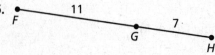

46.
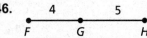

47.
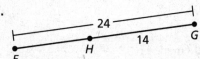

48.
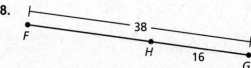

49.
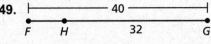

50.
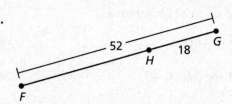

51. You are riding on a ski lift. The lift makes one stop about two-thirds up the mountain and another at the top. The first stop is 5100 feet from the starting point, and the top of the mountain is 7850 feet from the bottom. How far is the first stopping point from the top of the mountain?

52. You are painting the background space for a mural at your school. The dimensions of the mural are 24 feet by 9 feet.

   a. What is the area of the background space?

   b. The paint you plan to use covers 150 square feet per container. How many containers of paint do you need?

   c. Each container of paint costs $15.99. How much will it cost to paint the background space for the mural?

Chapter 5 **Cumulative Review** (continued)

In Exercises 53–58, find the indicated angle measure.

53. Find $m\angle ABC$.

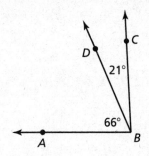

54. Find $m\angle QRS$.

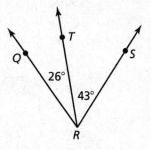

55. $m\angle MNP = 105°$; Find $m\angle MNQ$.

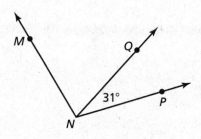

56. $m\angle WXY = 78°$; Find $m\angle WXZ$.

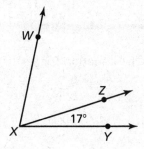

57. $\angle FGH$ is a straight angle. Find $m\angle FGI$.

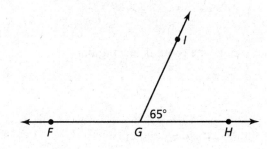

58. $\angle TUV$ is a straight angle. Find $m\angle WUV$.

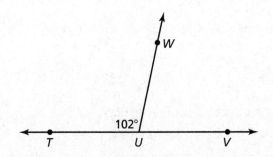

Chapter 5 **Cumulative Review** (continued)

In Exercises 59–82, solve the equation.

59. $x - 14 = 6$

60. $x + 13 = 7$

61. $x - 4 = -9$

62. $3x + 20 = -7$

63. $2x - 14 = 2$

64. $7x - 8 = 20$

65. $12 = -7x - 2$

66. $29 - 4x = 1$

67. $-2x + 3 = -15$

68. $3x + 4 = 5x - 18$

69. $6x - 7 = 3x + 11$

70. $9x + 2 = 7x + 12$

71. $5x - 3 = 7x - 13$

72. $-8x + 4 = -4x - 12$

73. $-3x - 11 = 22 + 8x$

74. $2(x - 4) = 20$

75. $3(4x + 8) = 36$

76. $6(-2x + 11) = -54$

77. $3(x - 4) + 12 = 18$

78. $-2(3x - 8) - 13 = -21$

79. $4 - 3(4x + 6) = 34$

80. $3(x - 6) = 2(x - 12)$

81. $4(x - 7) = 6(x + 6)$

82. $4(x - 5) = 2(4x + 6)$

In Exercises 83–94, solve the equation for y.

83. $3x + y = 9$

84. $-y + 7x = 11$

85. $8x - y = 13$

86. $9x - 3y = 18$

87. $4x + 2y = 12$

88. $5y - 25x = -35$

89. $4y + 0.5x = 12$

90. $-0.5y + 6x = -4$

91. $4y - 0.5x = -32$

92. $\frac{1}{2}x + \frac{1}{4}y = -6$

93. $\frac{3}{4}x - \frac{1}{3}y = 8$

94. $\frac{1}{2}y - 4x = -1$

95. Your family decides to place an area rug in the dining room. The room is rectangular and measures 14 feet by 16 feet.

   a. What is the area of the room?

   b. You want a 1-foot floor border around the entire rug. What are the dimensions of the rug that you want?

   c. What is the area of the rug?

96. You are planting a triangular-shaped garden next to your sidewalk. The garden space is a right triangle with leg lengths of 8 feet and 6 feet.

   a. What is the length of the diagonal of the garden?

   b. You plan to put decorative bricks around the edge of each side of the garden. How much brick do you need?

   c. What is the area of the garden?

Chapter 6

Chapter 6 Relationships Within Triangles

Dear Family,

Did you know that when you slice a pizza or cut a cake to share, you are doing math? These math skills require you to know something about perpendicular bisectors. In this chapter, you will learn about the relationships within a triangle, such as bisectors, altitudes, and midsegments.

Take time with your student and follow the steps below to learn the basics of a few of these terms and concepts.

Directions:

1. Plot the three points $(-6, 2)$, $(7, 8)$, and $(10, 2)$, and connect the points to make a triangle.

2. Plot the two points $(2, 10)$ and $(2, -5)$, and draw a line through these points. Label this a perpendicular bisector.

3. Draw a point at $(2, 2)$ where the bottom of the triangle and the perpendicular bisector intersect. Draw a line segment from $(7, 8)$ to $(2, 2)$. Label this a median.

4. Draw a point at $(7, 2)$ on the bottom side of the triangle. Draw a line segment from $(7, 8)$ to $(7, 2)$. Label this an altitude.

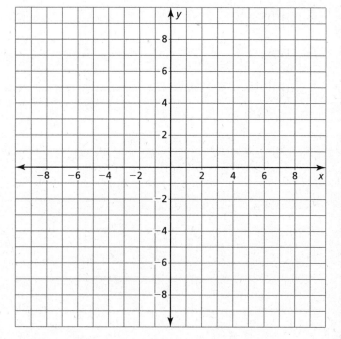

Nice job! Now that you have drawn the complete picture, maybe you can do some extra analyzing on your own.

- What are two features of the perpendicular bisector in relationship to the angle it makes and the line segment it intersects?

- What kind of angle does an altitude make with its opposite side?

Being able to see and use these concepts will not only help you along the way in your math class, it may even help you get an equal size piece of cake as those you are sharing it with!

Relaciones con triángulos

Estimada familia:

¿Sabían que cuando cortan una pizza o un pastel en porciones para compartir, están haciendo cálculos matemáticos? Estas destrezas matemáticas exigen que sepan algo sobre bisectrices perpendiculares. En este capítulo, aprenderán sobre las relaciones dentro de un triángulo, tal como bisectrices, alturas y segmentos medios.

Con su hijo, tómense un tiempo y sigan los siguientes pasos para aprender las nociones básicas de algunos de estos términos y conceptos.

Instrucciones:

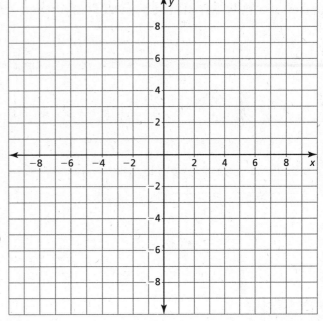

1. Marquen los tres puntos 2 $(-6, 2)$, $(7, 8)$, y $(10, 2)$, y conecten los puntos para formar un triángulo.

2. Marquen los dos puntos $(2, 10)$ y $(2, -5)$, y tracen una recta que pase por estos puntos. Rotúlenla como una bisectriz perpendicular.

3. Dibujen un punto en $(2, 2)$ donde se intersecan la parte inferior del triángulo y la bisectriz perpendicular. Dibujen un segmento de recta desde $(7, 8)$ hasta $(2, 2)$. Rotúlenlo mediana.

4. Dibujen un punto en $(7, 2)$ en la parte inferior del triángulo. Dibujen un segmento de recta desde $(7, 8)$ hasta $(7, 2)$. Rotúlenlo altura.

¡Buen trabajo! Ahora que han formado el dibujo completo, quizás puedan hacer un análisis extra por su cuenta.

- ¿Cuáles son dos características de la bisectriz perpendicular en relación con el ángulo que forma y el segmento de recta que interseca?

- ¿Qué clase de ángulo forma una altura con su lado opuesto?

Lograr ver y usar estos conceptos no solo los ayudará en su clase de matemáticas, ¡también incluso podría ayudarlos a terminar con una porción de pastel igual a las que tienen las personas con quienes lo comparte!

6.1 Start Thinking

A triangular roof truss is to be created according to the diagram. The king post is constructed in the center of the bottom chord. What conclusions can you make about the roof lines as the king post gets longer? What conclusions can you make about the two top chords and the angles they form?

king post

top chord   top chord

bottom chord

6.1 Warm Up

The diagram includes a pair of congruent triangles. Use the congruent triangles to find the value of *x* in the diagram.

1.

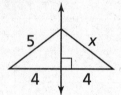

2.

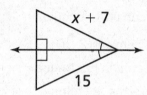

3.

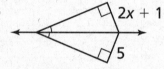

4.

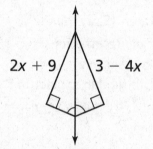

6.1 Cumulative Review Warm Up

Write a proof.

1. **Given:**

    P is the midpoint of $\overline{MN}$ and $\overline{TQ}$.

    Prove:

    $\triangle MQP \cong \triangle NTP$

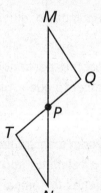

2. **Given:**

    $\overline{AB} \cong \overline{DC}$,
    $\overline{AC} \cong \overline{DB}$

    Prove:

    $\triangle ABC \cong \triangle DCB$

6.1 Practice A

In Exercises 1–3, tell whether the information in the diagram allows you to conclude that point *P* lies on the perpendicular bisector of $\overline{RS}$, or on the angle bisector of ∠*DEF*. Explain your reasoning.

1.
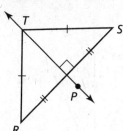

2.
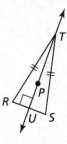

3.
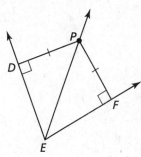

In Exercises 4–7, find the indicated measure. Explain your reasoning.

4. *AD*

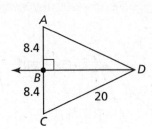

5. *GJ*

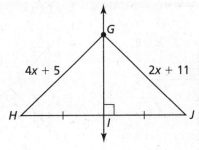

6. *PQ*

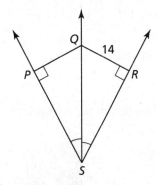

7. *m∠DGF*

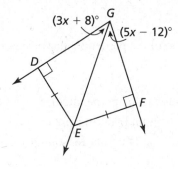

8. Write an equation of the perpendicular bisector of the segment with the endpoints $A(-2, -2)$ and $B(6, 0)$.

9. Explain how you can use the perpendicular bisector of a segment to draw an isosceles triangle.

10. In a right triangle, is it possible for the bisector of the right angle to be the same line as the perpendicular bisector of the hypotenuse? Explain your reasoning. Draw a picture to support your answer.

6.1 Practice B

In Exercises 1–3, tell whether the information in the diagram allows you to conclude that point *P* lies on the perpendicular bisector of $\overline{RS}$, or on the angle bisector of ∠*DEF*. Explain your reasoning.

1.

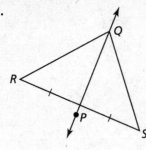

2.

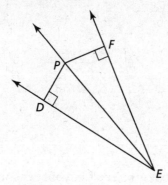

3.

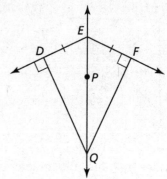

In Exercises 4–6, find the indicated measure. Explain your reasoning.

4. *AC*

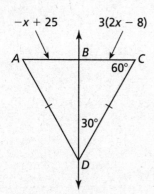

5. *m∠LNM*

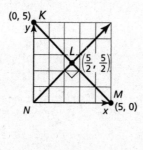

6. *m∠UTW*

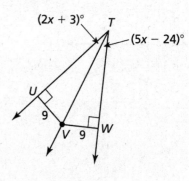

7. Write an equation of the perpendicular bisector of the segment with the endpoints $G(3, 7)$ and $H(-1, -5)$.

8. In the figure, line *m* is the perpendicular bisector of $\overline{PR}$. Is point *Q* on line *m*? Is point *S* on line *m*? Explain your reasoning.

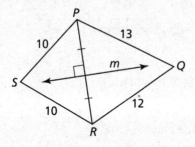

9. You are installing a fountain in the triangular garden pond shown in the figure. You want to place the fountain the same distance from each side of the pond. Describe a way to determine the location of the fountain using angle bisectors.

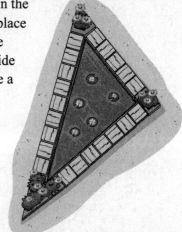

6.1   Enrichment and Extension

Perpendicular Bisectors

1. Given points $A(-2, 7)$ and $B(3, 3)$, find the value of x, such that

$P\left(-\frac{1}{10}x + 3, -1\right)$ is on the perpendicular bisector of $\overline{AB}$.

2. Use the Distance Formula to write an equation that models the points
$P(x, y)$ on the perpendicular bisector of $\overline{AB}$, where $AP = PB$ and the
endpoints of $\overline{AB}$ are $A(-1, 5)$ and $B(5, 2)$. Then simplify the equation
to linear form.

In Exercises 3 and 4, find the values of *x* and *y*.

3.

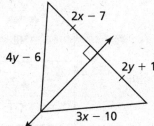

4.

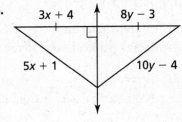

**In Exercises 5 and 6, use the information in the diagram to prove the given
statement.**

5. $\overline{PV}$ is the perpendicular bisector of $\overline{TQ}$
for regular polygon $PQRST$.

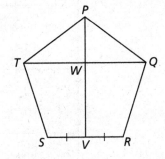

6. $\overline{LP} \cong \overline{NP}$ if $\angle 1 \cong \angle 4$ and $\overline{LQ} \cong \overline{NQ}$.

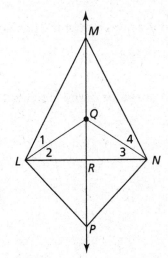

6.1 Puzzle Time

Why Did The Elephant Jump Up And Down?
Because He . . .

A	B	C	D	E	F
G	H				

Complete each exercise. Find the answer in the answer column. Write the word under the answer in the box containing the exercise letter.

construction MOUSE		vertex THE
6 SHAKE		(−3, 7) FOOT
angle MEDICINE		bisector TOOK
correct AND		−3 OF
(6, 10) TO		equidistant HIS
endpoints AND		9 IT
4 RAN		line RED
(−1, 7) TAIL		(1, 1) FORGOT

Complete the sentence.

A. A perpendicular _____ of a line segment is the line that is perpendicular to the segment at its midpoint.

B. A point is _____ from two figures when the point is the same distance from each figure.

C. If a point is on the bisector of an angle, then it is equidistant from the two sides of the _____.

D. In a plane, if a point is on the perpendicular bisector of a segment, then it is equidistant from the _____ of the segment.

Find the midpoint of the line segment given two points.

E. $A(-2, 8)$, $B(4, -6)$ **F.** $X(5, 17)$, $Y(7, 3)$

Find the value of the indicated variable.

G. $CE = 3x + 5$, $DE = 2x + 11$; Find x.

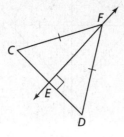

H. $m\angle SBK = (4y - 3)°$,
$m\angle KBW = (2y + 15)°$,
$\overline{SK} \cong \overline{WK}$. Find y.

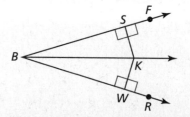

6.2 Start Thinking

A manufacturing company's logo is created with a circle inside an equiangular triangle, as shown in the figure. Extend the line segments coming from each of the vertices so they pass through the circle. What do you notice about these line segments?

6.2 Warm Up

Use a compass and a straightedge to bisect the geometric figure.

1.
A ●———————————● B

2.

3.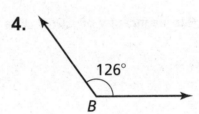

4.

6.2 Cumulative Review Warm Up

Graph the polygon and its image after a reflection in the given line.

1. $y = x$

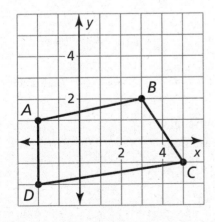

2. $y = 2$

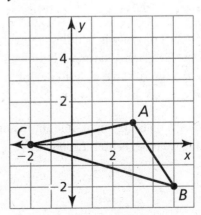

Name _____ Date _____

6.2 Practice A

In Exercises 1–3, the perpendicular bisectors of △*ABC* intersect at point *G*, or the angle bisectors of △*XYZ* intersect at point *P*. Find the indicated measure. Tell which theorem you used.

1. *BG*

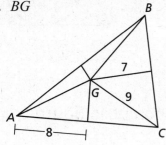

2. *CG*

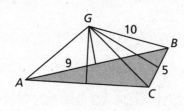

3. *PS*

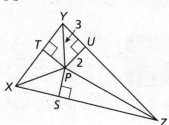

In Exercises 4 and 5, find the coordinates of the circumcenter of the triangle with the given vertices.

4. $J(6, 0)$, $K(0, 0)$, $L(0, 4)$

5. $U(0, 0)$, $V(-4, 0)$, $W(-6, 6)$

In Exercises 6 and 7, *P* is the incenter of △*QRS*. Use the given information to find the indicated measure.

6. $PJ = 4x - 8$, $PL = x + 7$
   Find *PK*.

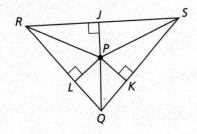

7. $PN = 6x + 2$, $PM = 8x - 14$
   Find *PL*.

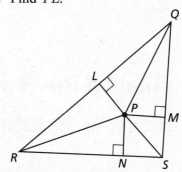

8. Draw an obtuse isosceles triangle. Find the circumcenter *C*. Then construct the circumscribed circle.

9. A cellular phone company is building a tower at an equal distance from three large apartment buildings. Explain how you can use the figure at the right to determine the location of the cell tower.

   Building 2
   •

   Building 1
   •

   Building 3
   •

10. Your friend says that it is impossible for the circumcenter of a triangle to lie outside the triangle. Is your friend correct? Explain your reasoning.

6.2 Practice B

In Exercises 1–3, find the indicated measure. Tell which theorem you used.

1. *PC*

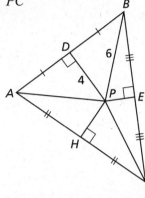

2. *AP*

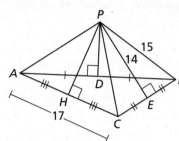

3. *MP*

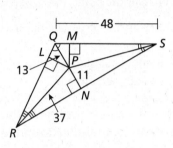

4. Find the coordinates of the circumcenter of the triangle with the vertices $A(4, 12)$, $B(14, 6)$, and $C(-6, 2)$.

In Exercises 5 and 6, use the diagram and the given information to find the indicated measures.

5. $LG = 6x - 14$, $NG = -3x + 22$

Find *MG* and *NG*.

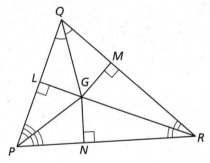

6. $GL = 4x - 2$, $GE = 3x + 2$, $GK = 2x + 8$

Find *GJ* and *GE*.

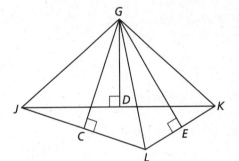

7. You are using a rotary sprinkler to water the triangular lawn.

   a. Explain how to locate the sprinkler the same distance from each side of the triangular lawn.

   b. Explain how to locate the sprinkler the same distance from each vertex of the triangular lawn.

   c. Which is closer to vertex *B*, the *incenter* or the *circumcenter*? Explain your reasoning.

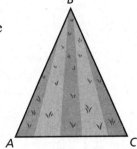

8. Explain when the circumcenter of a triangle lies outside the triangle.

9. In the figure at the right, what value of *x* makes *G* the incenter of $\triangle JKL$?

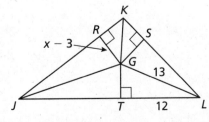

6.2 Enrichment and Extension

Bisectors of Triangles

1. Consider the point $P(-1, 3)$. Find the point Q for which the line $2x + y = 5$ serves as the perpendicular bisector of $\overline{PQ}$.

2. A triangle has sides lengths of 24, 10, and 26 units. What is the radius of the circumscribed circle?

In Exercises 3 and 4, use the following information to find the coordinates of the incenter N of the triangle. Round to the nearest tenth, if necessary.

For $\triangle ABC$, with vertices $A(x_1, y_1)$, $B(x_2, y_2)$, and $C(x_3, y_3)$, the coordinates of the incenter N are given by $N\left(\dfrac{ax_1 + bx_2 + cx_3}{a + b + c}, \dfrac{ay_1 + by_2 + cy_3}{a + b + c} \right)$, where a, b, and c are the lengths of the sides opposite of A, B, and C respectively.

3.

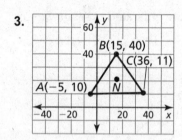

4.

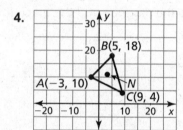

5. Write a two-column proof.

   Given: $\overline{GJ}$ is the perpendicular bisector of $\overline{HK}$.

   Prove: $\angle GHM \cong \angle GKM$

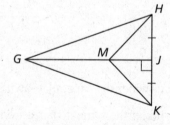

6. Write a paragraph proof.

   Given: $\overline{FC}$ is the perpendicular bisector of $\overline{AB}$.

   $\overline{FE}$ is the perpendicular bisector of $\overline{BD}$.

   Prove: $\overline{AF} \cong \overline{FD}$

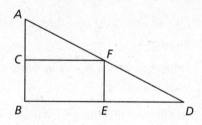

Name_____ Date _____

6.2 Puzzle Time

What Did The Computer Do At Lunchtime? It . . .

Write the letter of each answer in the box containing the exercise number.

Complete the sentence.

1. When three or more lines, rays, or segments intersect in the same point, they are called _____ lines, rays, or segments.

2. The circumcenter of a triangle is _____ from the vertices of the triangle.

3. The angle _____ of a triangle are congruent.

4. The _____ of the triangle is the point of intersection of angle bisectors.

5. The incenter of a triangle always lies _____ the triangle.

Find the indicated measure using the diagram. The perpendicular bisectors are at points D, E, and F. Angle bisectors are at A, B, and C.

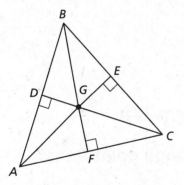

6. $AG = 13$, $BD = 5$; Find GD.

7. $GF = 8$, $GC = 17$; Find AF.

8. G is the incenter, $GD = 4x - 1$, and $GE = 3x + 5$; Find GF.

Answers
H. 12
U. circumcenter
D. inside
T. equiangular
N. measurements
A. concurrent
M. 5
R. outside
E. 15
Y. 23
E. 6
B. bisectors
O. congruent
S. 18
T. equidistant
A. incenter

6	1	5		4		3	8	2	7

Draw a right triangle and construct the three altitudes.
What conclusions can you make about the three altitudes
of your triangle?

6.3 **Warm Up**

**Use a compass and a straightedge to perform the
indicated construction.**

1. Construct a line perpendicular to line *m* through point *P*.

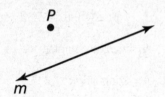

2. Construct a line perpendicular to line ℓ through point *Q*.

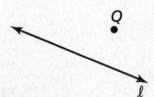

6.3 **Cumulative Review Warm Up**

**Write an equation of the line passing through point *P* that
is perpendicular to the given line.**

1. $P(-2, 4)$, $y = -\frac{2}{3}x + \frac{5}{2}$

2. $P(5, 11)$, $y = 8$

3. $P\left(\frac{3}{4}, -9\right)$, $y = x$

4. $P(1, -7)$, $y = 2x + 3$

5. $P(3, -2)$, $3x - 5y = 4$

6. $P\left(-\frac{1}{2}, -\frac{3}{2}\right)$, $x = -3$

6.3 Practice A

In Exercises 1–4, point *P* is the centroid of △*ABC*. Use the given information to find the indicated measures.

1. *BL* = 12
Find *BP* and *PL*.

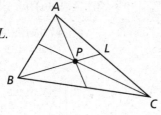

2. *CP* = 16
Find *PL* and *CL*.

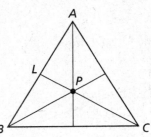

3. *AL* = 27
Find *AP* and *PL*.

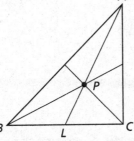

4. *BP* = 102
Find *PL* and *BL*.

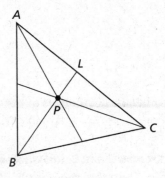

In Exercises 5 and 6, find the coordinates of the centroid of the triangle with the given vertices.

5. *Q*(−2, 6), *R*(4, 0), *S*(10, 6)

6. *U*(3, 3), *V*(5, −1), *W*(−2, 1)

In Exercises 7 and 8, tell whether the orthocenter is *inside*, *on*, or *outside* the triangle. Then find the coordinates of the orthocenter.

7. *J*(1, 3), *K*(−3, 1), *L*(0, 0)

8. *D*(−3, −2), *E*(−2, −2), *F*(1, 2)

9. To transport a triangular table, you remove the legs. You secure the glass top to the frame by looping a string from a hole in each vertex around the opposite side, then pulling it tight and tying it. At what point of concurrency do the three strings intersect? Explain your reasoning.

10. Your friend claims that it is impossible for the centroid and the orthocenter of a triangle to be the same point. Is your friend correct? Explain your reasoning.

6.3 Practice B

In Exercises 1–3, point Q is the centroid of △JKL. Use the given information to find the indicated segment lengths.

1. $AQ = 21$

   Find QL and AL.

2. $JA = 72$

   Find JQ and QA.

3. $KQ = 10$

   Find QA and KA.

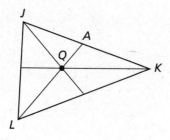
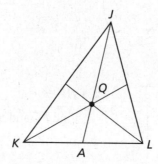
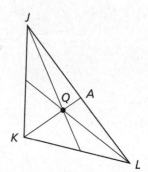

4. Find the coordinates of the centroid of the triangle with the vertices $A(-6, 8)$, $B(-3, 1)$, and $C(0, 3)$.

In Exercises 5 and 6, tell whether the orthocenter is *inside*, *on*, or *outside* the triangle. Then find the coordinates of the orthocenter.

5. $Q(-1, 5)$, $R(4, 3)$, $S(-1, -2)$

6. $L(4, 6)$, $M(-3, 2)$, $N(-2, -6)$

7. Given two vertices and the centroid of a triangle, how many possible locations are there for the third vertex? Explain your reasoning.

8. Given two vertices and the orthocenter of a triangle, how many possible locations are there for the third vertex? Explain your reasoning.

9. The centroid of a triangle is at $(2, -1)$ and vertices at $(3, -5)$ and $(-7, -4)$. Find the third vertex of the triangle.

10. The orthocenter of a triangle is at the origin, and two of the vertices of the triangle are at $(-5, 0)$ and $(3, 4)$. Find the third vertex of the triangle.

11. Your friend claims that it is possible to draw an equilateral triangle for which the circumcenter, incenter, centroid, and orthocenter are not all the same point. Do you agree? Explain your reasoning.

12. Your friend claims that when the median from one vertex of a triangle is the same as the altitude from the same vertex, the median divides the triangle into two congruent triangles. Do you agree? Explain your reasoning.

13. Can the circumcenter and the incenter of an obtuse triangle be the same point? Explain.

6.3 Enrichment and Extension

Medians in Triangles

The location of the centroid N for a triangle in three-dimensional space is calculated by averaging the x-, y-, and z-coordinates of the three points.

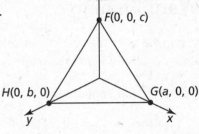

1. If $R(x_1, y_1, z_1)$, $S(x_2, y_2, z_2)$, and $T(x_3, y_3, z_3)$, find the location of the centroid N in $\triangle RST$.

2. Find the centroid N for the triangle in the figure, with vertices on the x-, y-, and z-axes.

3. The midpoint of $\overline{GH}$ is T. Calculate the coordinates of T. Then prove that $FN = 2 \bullet NT$.

In Exercises 4–6, point P is the centroid of $\triangle ABC$. Use the given information to find the value(s) of x.

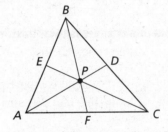

4. $AP = x^2 - 2,\ PD = 2x - 3$

5. $CP = x^2 + 1,\ PE = 4x - 3$

6. $CP = 3x + 5,\ CE = x^2 + 2$

In Exercises 7 and 8, use the following information to find the area of the triangle described.

The formula below can be used to find the area A of a triangle using the measures of the medians m.

$$A = \frac{4}{3}\sqrt{s(s - m_1)(s - m_2)(s - m_3)},\ \text{where } s = \frac{1}{2}(m_1 + m_2 + m_3).$$

7. $m_1 = 19,\ m_2 = 17,\ m_3 = 10$ 8. $m_1 = 1.2,\ m_2 = 3.4,\ m_3 = 4.2$

9. Given the diagram to the right, find the equations of the medians of the triangle. Use M as the median from vertex A to $\overline{BC}$, N as the median from vertex B to $\overline{AC}$, and P as the median from vertex C to $\overline{AB}$. Then find their intersection point.

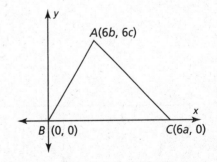

Puzzle Time

What Did The Librarian Use For Bait When She Went Fishing?

Circle the letter of each correct answer in the boxes below. The circled letters will spell out the answer to the riddle.

Complete the sentence.

1. A(n) _____ of a triangle is a segment from a vertex to the midpoint of the opposite side.

2. The lines containing the medians of a triangle are concurrent. The point of concurrency, called the _____, is inside the triangle.

3. The centroid of a triangle is two-thirds of the distance from each vertex to the _____ of the opposite side.

4. A(n) _____ of a triangle is the perpendicular segment from a vertex to the opposite side or to the line that contains the opposite side.

5. The lines containing the altitudes of a triangle are concurrent. This point of concurrency is the _____ of the triangle.

Find the indicated measurement using the diagram as a reference. Point G is the centroid.

6. $FC = 36$; Find GC.

7. $FC = 36$; Find FG.

8. $GF = 9$; Find FC.

9. $GF = 9$; Find GC.

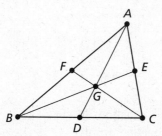

Z	A	R	U	L	B	I	M	O	O
9	27	15	point	congruent	18	straight	3	12	orthocenter

K	G	E	F	W	O	I	S	R	M
centroid	21	center	1	24	median	bisector	0	altitude	midpoint

6.4 Start Thinking

Copy the triangle and construct the midpoint M of $\overline{AB}$.
Then from point M, construct a line segment parallel
to $\overline{BC}$. This line segment should intersect $\overline{AC}$ at a
point N. What is the relationship between the measure
of $\overline{MN}$ and the measure of $\overline{BC}$?

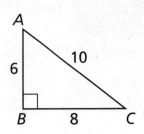

6.4 Warm Up

Use the diagram to determine the following.

1. Find the midpoint of $\overline{XZ}$.

2. Find the midpoint of $\overline{XY}$.

3. Find the measure of $\overline{ZY}$.

4. Find the measure of $\overline{XY}$.

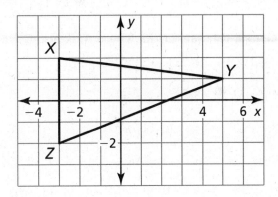

6.4 Cumulative Review Warm Up

Find the measure of the unknown angle(s) in the triangle.

1.

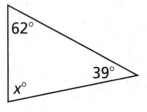

2.

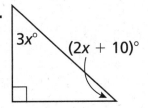

3.

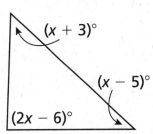

Name _____ Date _____

In Exercises 1–5, use the graph of △ABC.

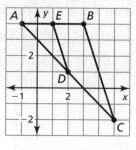

1. In △ABC, show that the midsegment $\overline{ED}$ is parallel to $\overline{BC}$ and that $ED = \frac{1}{2}BC$.

2. Find the coordinates of the endpoints of midsegment $\overline{EF}$, which is opposite $\overline{AC}$.

3. Show that $\overline{EF}$ is parallel to $\overline{AC}$ and that $EF = \frac{1}{2}AC$.

4. State the coordinates of the endpoints of midsegment $\overline{DF}$.

5. Show that $\overline{DF}$ is parallel to $\overline{AB}$ and $DF = \frac{1}{2}AB$.

In Exercises 6–11, use △QRS where A, B, and C are the midpoints of the sides.

6. When $AB = 16$, what is QS?

7. When $SR = 68$, what is CA?

8. When $SR = 46$, what is BR?

9. When $CA = 3x - 1$ and $SR = 5x + 4$, what is CA?

10. When $QS = 6x$ and $CS = 5x - 8$, what is AB?

11. When $QR = 5x + 2$ and $CB = 2x + 5$, what is AR?

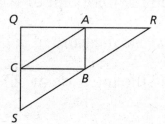

12. Your friend claims that because each midsegment is half as long as the corresponding side of the triangle, the perimeter of the midsegment triangle is half the perimeter of the original triangle. Is your friend correct? Explain your reasoning.

13. A building has the shape of a pyramid with a square base. The midsegment parallel to the ground of each triangular face of the pyramid has a length of 58 feet. Find the length of the base the pyramid.

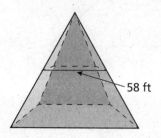

58 ft

6.4 Practice B

In Exercises 1–4, use the graph of △ABC.

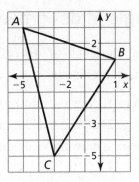

1. Find the coordinates of the midpoint D of $\overline{AB}$, the midpoint E of $\overline{CB}$, and the midpoint F of $\overline{AC}$.

2. Graph the midsegment triangle, $\triangle DEF$.

3. Show that $\overline{FD} \parallel \overline{CB}$, $\overline{FE} \parallel \overline{AB}$, and $\overline{DE} \parallel \overline{AC}$.

4. Show that $FD = \frac{1}{2}CB$, $FE = \frac{1}{2}AB$, and $DE = \frac{1}{2}AC$.

In Exercises 5–8, use △LMN. where U, V, and W are the midpoints of the sides.

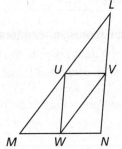

5. When $LV = 9$, what is UW?

6. When $LU = 2(x - 5)$ and $VW = 8 - x$, what is LM?

7. When $NL = 2x(12 + x)$ and $UW = (x + 4)^2$, what is LV?

8. When $UV = 2y + 14$ and $MN = 13 - y$, what is WN?

9. The bottom two steps of a stairwell are shown. Explain how to use the given measures to verify that the bottom step is parallel to the floor.

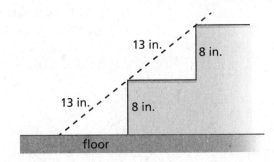

10. Your friend claims that a triangle with side lengths of a, b, and c will have half the area of a triangle with side lengths of $2a$, $2b$, and $2c$. Is your friend correct? Explain your reasoning.

6.4 Enrichment and Extension

The Triangle Midsegment Theorem

1. In $\triangle ABC$, the length of $\overline{AB}$ is 24. In the triangle, a succession of midsegments are formed.

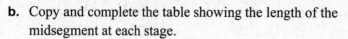

   a. At Stage 1, draw the midsegment of $\triangle ABC$. Label it $\overline{DE}$.
      At Stage 2, draw the midsegment of $\triangle DEC$. Label it $\overline{FG}$.
      At Stage 3, draw the midsegment of $\triangle FGC$. Label it $\overline{HJ}$.

   b. Copy and complete the table showing the length of the midsegment at each stage.

Stage n	0	1	2	3	4	5
Midsegment length	24					

   c. From part (b), let y represent length of the midsegment at Stage n. Construct a scatter plot for the data given in the table. Then find a function that gives the length of the midsegment at Stage n.

   d. Find a function that gives the length of the midsegment at Stage n, if the length of $\overline{AB}$ is w.

2. In $\triangle GHJ$, $K(2, 3)$ is the midpoint of $\overline{GH}$, $L(4, 1)$ is the midpoint of $\overline{HJ}$, and $M(6, 2)$ is the midpoint of $\overline{GJ}$. Find the coordinates of G, H, and J.

3. Find the perimeter and area of $\triangle DEF$, if $\overline{DE}$, $\overline{EF}$, and $\overline{DF}$ are midsegments.

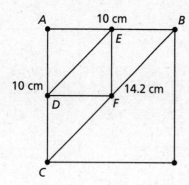

4. Write a paragraph proof.

   Given: $\triangle ABC \cong \triangle DEF$;
   T, U, and V are midpoints of $\triangle ABC$;
   X, Y, and Z are midpoints of $\triangle DEF$.

   Prove: $\triangle TUV \cong \triangle XYZ$

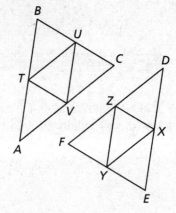

Puzzle Time

What Did The Stamp Say To The Envelope?

A	B	C	D	E	F
G	H				

Complete each exercise. Find the answer in the answer column. Write the word under the answer in the box containing the exercise letter.

12 **AND**	
10.6 **WILL**	
theorem **FAR**	
half **ME**	
5.3 **AGAIN**	
the same **AND**	
8 **WE**	
11 **ARE**	

Complete the sentence.

A. A(n) _____ of a triangle is a segment that connects the midpoints of two sides of the triangle.

B. Every triangle has three midsegments, which form the midsegment _____.

C. The segment connecting the midpoints of two sides of a triangle is parallel to the third side and is _____ as long as that side.

In the diagram, G, H, and J are midpoints of the sides of △DEF. Find the measure of the segment.

D. $\overline{GH}$

E. $\overline{HJ}$

F. $\overline{GJ}$

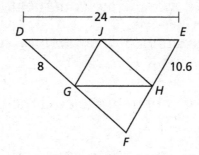

In the diagram, $\overline{HI}$ is a midsegment of △KLM. Find the measure of the segment.

G. $KM = 15$; Find HI.

H. $HI = 22$; Find KM.

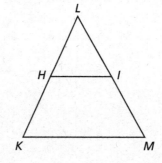

median **THE**	
24 **STAMP**	
44 **PLACES**	
midsegment **STICK**	
16 **POST**	
triangle **WITH**	
7.5 **GO**	
15 **DONE**	

Examine the triangle and determine the largest angle and the longest side. What is the relationship between the largest angle and the longest side in the triangle?

1.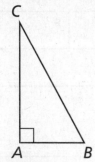

2.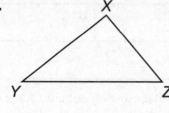

3.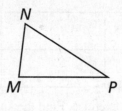

6.5 Warm Up

Complete the phrase with the most logical conclusion.

1. If there is no right angle in a triangle, then…

2. If two lines do not have the same slope, then…

3. If a quadrilateral does not have four right angles, then…

4. If no two angles of a triangle are congruent, then…

5. If the sum of the measures of the interior angles of a polygon is not 180°, then…

6. If a triangle does not contain three congruent angles, then…

6.5 Cumulative Review Warm Up

Find the value of x that makes $m \parallel n$.

1.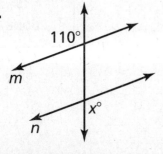

2.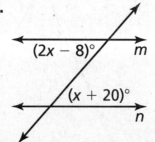

3.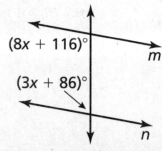

Name_____ Date _____

In Exercises 1 and 2, list the angles of the given triangle from smallest to largest.

1.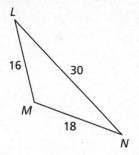

2.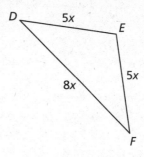

In Exercises 3 and 4, list the sides of the given triangle from shortest to longest.

3.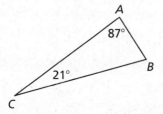

4.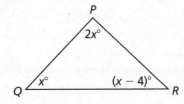

In Exercises 5 and 6, is it possible to construct a triangle with the given side lengths? Explain.

5. 15, 37, 53

6. 9, 16, 8

7. Write an indirect proof that a triangle has at most one obtuse angle.

8. Describe the possible values of x in the figure shown.

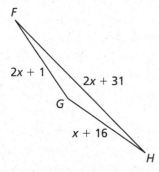

9. List the angles of the given triangle from smallest to largest. Explain your reasoning.

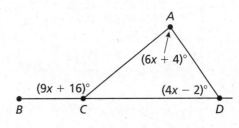

10. The shortest distance between two points is a straight line. Explain this statement in terms of the Triangle Inequality Theorem (Theorem 6.11).

6.5 Practice B

In Exercises 1 and 2, list the angles of the given triangle from smallest to largest.

1.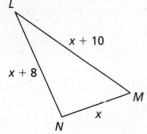

2.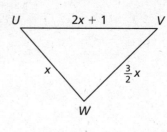

In Exercises 3 and 4, list the sides of the given triangle from shortest to longest.

3.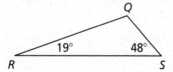

4.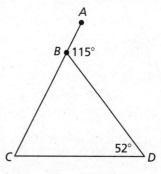

5. Write an indirect proof that a right triangle has exactly two acute angles.

6. Is it possible to construct a triangle with side lengths $5(2x - 6)$, $3x + 80$, and $x^2 + 41$ if $x = 9$? Explain.

7. The figure shows several triangles, with labeled side lengths. Which of the triangles are labeled correctly? Explain.

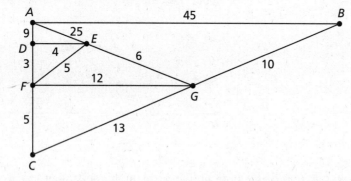

8. Your friend claims that if you are given the three angle measures of a triangle, you can construct a triangle that obeys the Triangle Inequality Theorem (Theorem 6.11), even if you are not given any of the side lengths. Is your friend correct? Explain your reasoning.

Name_____ Date _____

6.5 Enrichment and Extension

Inequalities in One Triangle

In Exercises 1 and 2, list the sides in order from shortest to longest.

1.

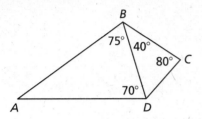

2.

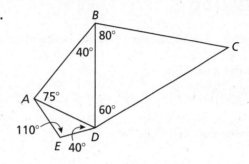

In Exercises 3 and 4, prove the statement.

3. The length of any one median of a triangle is less than half the perimeter of the triangle.

4. The sum of the lengths of the three medians of a triangle is greater than half the perimeter of the triangle.

5. For what combinations of angle measures in an isosceles right triangle are the congruent sides shorter than the base of the triangle? Longer than the base of the triangle?

6. If $m\angle A < m\angle B < m\angle C$, describe the possible values of x.

a.

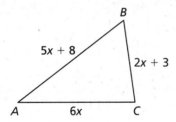

b.

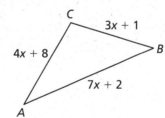

7. Prove that a perpendicular segment is the shortest line segment from a point to a plane.

   Given: $\overline{PC} \perp$ plane M

   Prove: $PD > PC$

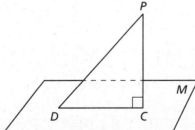

6.5 Puzzle Time

What Do You Get When You Cross A Snake With A Kangaroo?

Write the letter of each answer in the box containing the exercise number.

Complete the sentence.

1. If one side of a triangle is longer than another side, then the angle opposite the _____ side is larger than the angle opposite the other side.

2. If one angle of a triangle is larger than another angle, then the side opposite the _____ angle is longer than the side opposite the other angle.

3. The sum of the lengths of any two sides of a triangle is _____ the length of the third side.

Complete the step for an Indirect Proof.

4. Identify the statement you want to _____.

5. Assume _____ that this statement is false by assuming that its opposite is true.

6. Reason _____ until you reach a contradiction.

7. Point out that the desired conclusion must be true because the _____ proves the temporary assumption false.

Use the diagram.

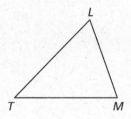

8. $m\angle T = 35°$, $m\angle L = 51°$; Identify the longest side.

9. $m\angle T = 35°$, $m\angle L = 51°$; Identify the shortest side.

Answers
P. $\overline{TL}$
A. permanently
U. longer
T. smaller
J. logically
R. systematically
A. $\overline{LM}$
E. larger
N. $\overline{TM}$
M. greater than
H. equal to
O. contradiction
K. disprove
R. prove
L. truth
P. temporarily
Y. shorter

9		6	1	3	8		4	7	5	2

6.6 Start Thinking

Consider two line segments $\overline{AB}$ and $\overline{BC}$ hinged at point B so that $\angle ABC$ can change in size as shown in the diagram. What happens to the length of $\overline{AC}$ as the angle increases in size? How large can the angle be and still form a triangle? What value is the length of $\overline{AC}$ approaching as the angle increases in size?

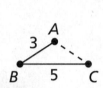 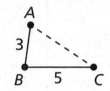 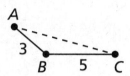

6.6 Warm Up

Determine if you can prove the two triangles are congruent. If they are congruent, explain your reasoning.

1. $\triangle ABE$ and $\triangle DCE$

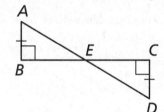

2. $\triangle NOT$ and $\triangle NDT$

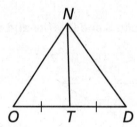

3. $\triangle XYZ$ and $\triangle QRZ$

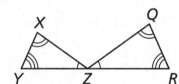

4. $\triangle CDB$ and $\triangle CEA$

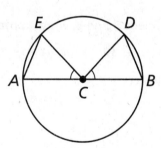

6.6 Cumulative Review Warm Up

Tell whether the black figure is a translation, reflection, rotation, or dilation of the gray figure.

1.

2.

3.

Name _____ Date _____

6.6 Practice A

In Exercises 1–4, copy and complete the statement with <, >, or =. Explain your reasoning.

1. AC _____ DF

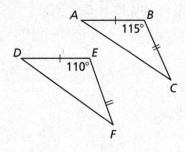

2. $m\angle HGI$ _____ $m\angle IGJ$

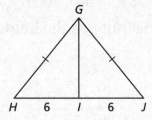

3. $m\angle 1$ _____ $m\angle 2$

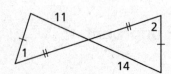

4. KL _____ MN

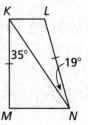

In Exercises 5 and 6, write and solve an inequality for the possible values of x.

5.

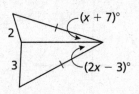

6.

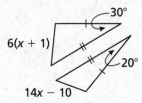

In Exercises 7 and 8, write a proof.

7. Given: $\overline{TV} \cong \overline{UW}$, $TU > VW$

Prove: $m\angle TVU > m\angle WUV$

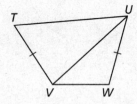

8. Given: $m\angle 1 > m\angle 2$, B is the midpoint of AC.

Prove: $AF > CF$

9. The figure shows two sliding boards. The slide is the same length in each case, but one is steeper than the other. Can you apply the Hinge Theorem (Theorem 6.12) or the Converse of the Hinge Theorem (Theorem 6.13) in this problem? Explain your reasoning.

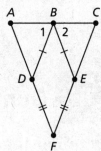
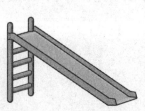

6.6 Practice B

In Exercises 1–4, copy and complete the statement with <, >, or = . Explain your reasoning.

1. BC _____ DE

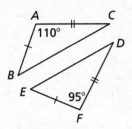

2. JI _____ GH

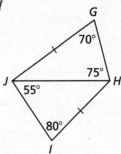

3. $m\angle 1$ _____ $m\angle 2$

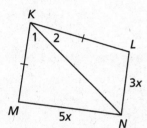

4. $m\angle U$ _____ $m\angle R$

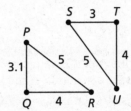

In Exercises 5 and 6, write and solve an inequality for the possible values of x.

5.

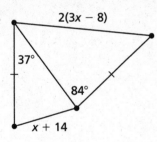

6.

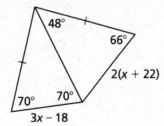

7. Use the figure to write a proof.

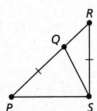

Given: $\overline{PQ} \cong \overline{SR}$

Prove: $m\angle PQS > m\angle RSQ$

8. Two sailboats started at the same location. Sailboat A traveled 5 miles west, then turned 29° toward the north and continued for 8 miles. Sailboat B first went south for 8 miles, then turned 51° toward the east and continued for 5 miles. Which sailboat was farther from the starting point? Explain your reasoning.

9. How are the Hinge Theorem (Theorem 6.12) and the SAS Congruence Theorem (Theorem 5.5) similar? How are they different? Explain your reasoning.

6.6   Enrichment and Extension

Inequalities in Two Triangles

1. In $\triangle DEF$, $\overline{DM}$ is a median. Determine if each statement is *always, sometimes,* or *never* true.

   a. If $m\angle 2 > m\angle 1$, then $ED > FD$.

   b. If $m\angle E > m\angle F$, then $\angle 1$ is obtuse.

   c. If $\angle 2$ is acute, then $m\angle F > m\angle E$.

   d. If $m\angle E < m\angle F$, then $m\angle 1 < m\angle 2$.

   e. If $m\angle 2 > m\angle 1$, then $ED > FD$.

   f. If $m\angle D = 90°$, then $FD > ED$.

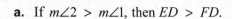

2. *Concentric* circles are circles that have the same center and different radii. The circles in the figure are concentric. The measure of $\angle BAC$ is 93°, and the measure of $\angle DAE$ is 60°. Explain why BC must be greater than DE.

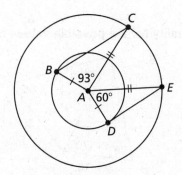

3. In $\triangle PQR$, $\angle SQR \cong \angle SRQ$, $PQ > PR$, $m\angle PSR = (4y + 9)°$, and $m\angle QSP = (6y - 24)°$. Find the range of values for y.

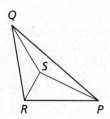

4. Write a two-column proof.

   Given: D is the midpoint of $\overline{BC}$.

   $m\angle ADB = 100°$

   Prove: $m\angle C > m\angle A$

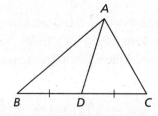

6.6 Puzzle Time

Which Animals Grow Down?

Circle the letter of each correct answer in the boxes below. The circled letters will
spell out the answer to the riddle.

Complete the sentence.

1. If two sides of one triangle are congruent to two sides of another triangle, and
   the included angle of the first is larger than the included angle of the second,
   then the fact that the third side of the first is longer than the third side of the
   second demonstrates the _____ Theorem.

Complete with < or > using the diagram for △POR and △LMK.

2. $\overline{PO} \cong \overline{LM}$, $\overline{OR} \cong \overline{MK}$,

   $KL = 20$, $RP = 14$,

   $m\angle M$ _____ $m\angle O$

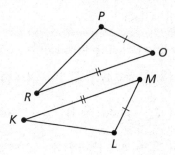

Complete using the diagram.

3. If $IK = IT$ and $m\angle EIT > m\angle EIK$,
   which is longer, $\overline{KE}$ or $\overline{TE}$?

4. If $IT = IK$ and $TE < KE$,
   which is larger, $\angle TIE$ or $\angle KIE$?

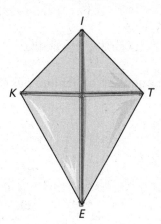

D	F	R	U
>	<	$\overline{KE}$	hinge
O	C	G	K
$\angle TIE$	$\overline{TE}$	ledge	$\angle KIE$

Chapter 6 Cumulative Review

In Exercises 1–8, write the sentence as an inequality.

1. A number c is greater than 9 or less than -3.

2. A number s is more than 2 and less than 11.

3. A number m is at most -7 and more than -10.

4. A number p is fewer than 15 and at least 1.

5. A number j is less than or equal to 6.

6. A number v is greater than 8 and less than 13.

7. A number r is less than 12 and greater than or equal to -5.

8. A number b is no less than 17 or less than 3.

In Exercises 9–23, find the slope of a line passing through the given points.

9. $(1, -11)$ and $(-7, 1)$

10. $(7, 2)$ and $(3, -2)$

11. $(-12, 4)$ and $(-12, 11)$

12. $(1, 6)$ and $(6, -13)$

13. $(5, -1)$ and $(-8, 1)$

14. $(-2, 0)$ and $(-4, 3)$

15. $(0, -3)$ and $(-5, 3)$

16. $(-3, 6)$ and $(1, -9)$

17. $(-4, 4)$ and $(-4, -7)$

18. $(3, -5)$ and $(-4, 4)$

19. $(-6, 12)$ and $(-1, 9)$

20. $(-7, -3)$ and $(-1, 4)$

21. $(2, 15)$ and $(5, 13)$

22. $(7, -8)$ and $(-8, -7)$

23. $(10, 7)$ and $(-14, 8)$

In Exercises 24–31, write an equation of the line passing through point P that is parallel to the given line.

24. $P(-5, 0)$, $y = -2x + 6$

25. $P(4, 2)$, $y = x - 6$

26. $P(3, -1)$, $y = \frac{1}{2}x + 5$

27. $P(-4, 1)$, $y = -\frac{1}{3}x - 7$

28. $P(-6, -1)$, $x = 0$

29. $P(-3, 1)$, $x = 5$

30. $P(-4, -5)$, $-3x + 6y = 2$

31. $P(0, -1)$, $5x + 3y = -6$

32. A local pizza shop charges \$12.50 for a large, one-topping pizza. Each additional topping is \$1.25.

   a. Write an equation for the total cost C of a large pizza with t toppings.

   b. How much does it cost for a three-topping pizza?

   c. How much does it cost for a five-topping pizza?

Chapter 6 **Cumulative Review** (continued)

In Exercises 33–40, write an equation of the line passing through point *P* that is perpendicular to the given line.

33. $P(-3, 5)$, $y = 8x - 1$

34. $P(-9, -6)$, $y = \frac{2}{3}x + 2$

35. $P(-5, 6)$, $x = 3$

36. $P(9, 0)$, $x = -4$

37. $P(0, -7)$, $7x + 4y = 1$

38. $P(4, -8)$, $-9x + 9y = 18$

39. $P(1, -1)$, $8x + 2y = -6$

40. $P(-3, 7)$, $-6x + 9y = -3$

In Exercises 41–46, find the values of *x* and *y*.

41.

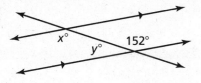

42.

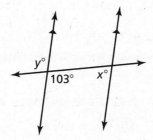

43.

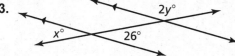

44.

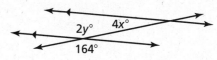

45.

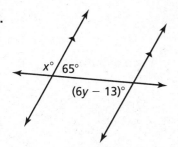

46.

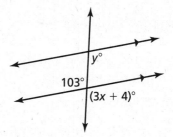

47. $\angle A$ is a vertical angle of a $67°$ angle. $\angle B$ and the $67°$ angle are supplementary.

    a. What is the measure of $\angle A$?

    b. What is the measure of $\angle B$?

48. $\angle M$ is supplementary to a $134°$ angle. $\angle N$ is twice the measure of $\angle M$.

    a. What is the measure of $\angle M$?

    b. What is the measure of $\angle N$?

Chapter 6 **Cumulative Review** (continued)

In Exercises 49–52, use the translation $(x, y) \rightarrow (x + 2, y - 3)$.

49. What is the image of $A(1, 0)$?

50. What is the image of $B(-6, 9)$?

51. What is the preimage of $C'(-3, -9)$?

52. What is the preimage of $D'(-8, 5)$?

In Exercises 53–56, use the translation $(x, y) \rightarrow (x - 4, y + 5)$.

53. What is the image of $A(-1, 3)$?

54. What is the image of $B(7, 4)$?

55. What is the preimage of $C'(-9, 2)$?

56. What is the preimage of $D'(0, 3)$?

In Exercises 57–62, graph △ABC and its image after a reflection in the given line.

57. $A(-8, 6)$, $B(-5, -2)$, $C(0, 9)$; x-axis

58. $A(7, 1)$, $B(-1, -7)$, $C(4, -6)$; y-axis

59. $A(5, 2)$, $B(-4, -3)$, $C(-9, 0)$; x-axis

60. $A(0, 3)$, $B(8, -1)$, $C(-5, 9)$; $x = 2$

61. $A(6, -2)$, $B(6, -6)$, $C(-7, 8)$; $y = -1$

62. $A(1, 3)$, $B(0, -4)$, $C(-3, 8)$; $x = 1$

In Exercises 63–69, graph the polygon and its image after a dilation with scale factor k. Assume the center of dilation is the origin.

63. $D(3, 8)$, $E(0, -4)$, $F(-7, 5)$; $k = 2$

64. $M(-1, 8)$, $N(2, 9)$, $P(-3, -2)$; $k = -2$

65. $S(6, -3)$, $T(2, -8)$, $U(-7, -5)$, $V(-7, 4)$; $k = 4$

66. $J(4, -12)$, $L(8, 16)$, $M(-28, -4)$; $k = 0.25$

67. $W(-4, 0)$, $X(6, -8)$, $Y(0, 4)$, $Z(-4, 6)$; $k = 150\%$

68. $A(8, 12)$, $B(0, 0)$, $C(-16, 4)$; $k = -0.25$

69. $E(-9, 3)$, $F(15, 3)$, $G(12, 0)$, $H(-6, -12)$; $k = -\dfrac{2}{3}$

Chapter 6

Cumulative Review (continued)

In Exercises 70–73, classify the triangle by its sides and by measuring its angles.

70.

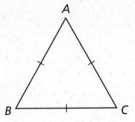

71.

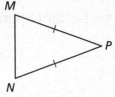

72.

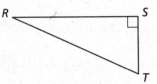

73.

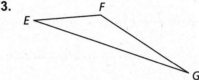

In Exercises 74–77, find $m\angle 1$. Then classify the triangle by its angles.

74.

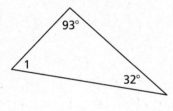

75.

76.

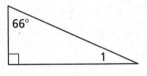

77.

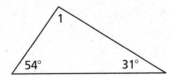

78. A right triangle has angle measures A and $57°$. What is the measure of $\angle A$?

79. An isosceles triangle has angle measures A, B, and $76°$. What are the measures of the base angles A and B?

80. A scalene triangle has angle measures A, $38°$, and $66°$. What is the measure of $\angle A$?

Chapter 7

Name_____ Date _____

Quadrilaterals and Other Polygons

Dear Family,

In this chapter, your student will learn the properties of shapes with four sides, which are also called *quadrilaterals*. The prefix "quad-" means "four" and the term "lateral" means "sides." So, a quadrilateral is a shape with four sides.

One property of quadrilaterals your student will learn about is the relationship between diagonals. Find a square object such as a tabletop. Encourage your student to use measuring tape to find the lengths of the two diagonals of the square object.

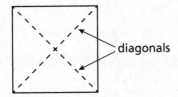

diagonals

- What do you notice about the lengths of the diagonals?

Find other square objects such as a napkin or the jewel case for a CD and repeat the experiment.

- Do the lengths of the diagonals show a general pattern?

Find several rectangular objects and measure the diagonals.

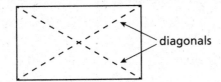

diagonals

- Do the diagonals of rectangles follow the same pattern as the diagonals for squares?

Try to find other objects that have a surface that is a four-sided shape that is not a square or a rectangle. Measure and compare the diagonals.

- Do the patterns you noticed for squares and rectangles appear to extend to other types of quadrilaterals?

Have fun and be creative!

Nombre _____ Fecha _____

Cuadriláteros y otros polígonos

Estimada familia:

En este capítulo, su hijo aprenderá las propiedades de formas con cuatro lados, que también se llaman *cuadriláteros*. El prefijo "cuad-" significa "cuatro" y el término "látero" significa "lados". Entonces, un cuadrilátero es una forma con cuatro lados.

Una propiedad de los cuadriláteros que aprenderá su hijo es la relación entre diagonales. Hallen un objeto cuadrado, tal como el tablero de una mesa. Haga que su hijo use cinta métrica para hallar las longitudes de las dos diagonales del objeto cuadrado.

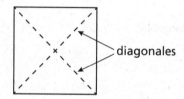
diagonales

- ¿Qué observan sobre las longitudes de las diagonales?

Hallen otros objetos cuadrados, tal como una servilleta o el estuche de un CD y repitan el experimento.

- ¿Las longitudes de las diagonales muestran un patrón en general?

Hallen varios objetos rectangulares y midan las diagonales.

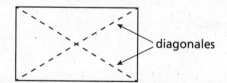
diagonales

- ¿Las diagonales de los rectángulos siguen el mismo patrón que las diagonales de los cuadrados?

Traten de hallar otros objetos que tengan una superficie que sea una forma con cuatro lados que no sea un cuadrado ni un rectángulo. Midan y comparen las diagonales.

- ¿Los patrones que observaron en los cuadrados y rectángulos parecen aplicarse a otros tipos de cuadriláteros?

¡Diviértanse y sean creativos!

7.1 Start Thinking

The polygon in the diagram has been formed by adjoining triangles. Use your knowledge of the sum of the measures of the interior angles of a triangle to determine the sum of the measures of the interior angles of the polygon.

1. Pentagon

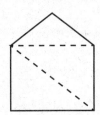

2. Hexagon

3. Heptagon

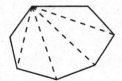

7.1 Warm Up

Find the value of *x* in the diagram.

1.

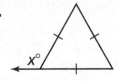

2.

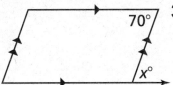

3.

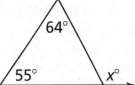

7.1 Cumulative Review Warm Up

Write an equation of the perpendicular bisector of the segment with endpoints *P* and *Q*.

1. $P(-3, -2), Q(5, -2)$

2. $P(5, 0), Q(5, -2)$

3. $P(7, -4), Q(3, 2)$

4. $P(-8, 8), Q(6, 3)$

Name _____ Date _____

7.1 Practice A

1. Find the sum of the measures of the interior angles of a heptagon.

2. The sum of the measures of the interior angles of a convex polygon is 3060°. Classify the polygon by the number of sides.

3. Find the measure of each interior and exterior angle of a regular 30-gon.

In Exercises 4 and 5, find the value of x.

4.
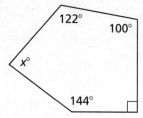

5.
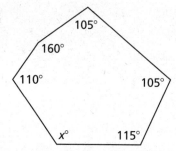

In Exercises 6 and 7, find the measures of ∠X and ∠Y.

6.
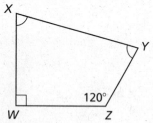

7.
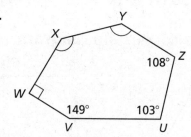

In Exercises 8 and 9, find the value of x.

8.
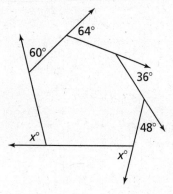

9.
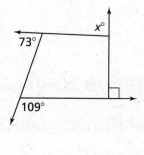

10. A pentagon has three angles that are congruent and two other angles that are supplementary to each other. Find the measure of each of the three congruent angles in the pentagon.

11. You are designing an amusement park ride with cars that will spin in a circle around a center axis, and the cars are located at the vertices of a regular polygon. The sum of the measures of the angles' vertices is 6120°. If each car holds a maximum of four people, what is the maximum number of people who can be on the ride at one time?

Name_____ Date _____

7.1 Practice B

In Exercises 1 and 2, find the value of x.

1.
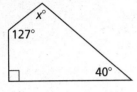

2.
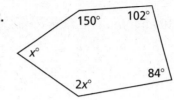

In Exercises 3 and 4, find the measures of ∠X and ∠Y.

3.
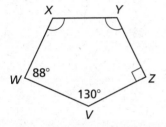

4.
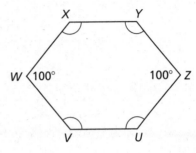

In Exercises 5 and 6, find the value of x.

5.
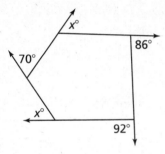

6.
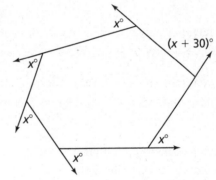

7. Find the measure of each interior angle and each exterior angle of a regular 24-gon.

8. Each exterior angle of a regular polygon has a measure of 18°. Find the number of sides of the regular polygon.

9. A polygon has two pairs of complementary interior angles and three sets of supplementary interior angles. The sum of the remaining interior angles is 1440°. How many sides does the polygon have? Explain.

10. The figure shows interior angle measures of the kite.

   a. Find the sum of the measures of the interior angles of the convex polygon.

   b. Find the value of x.

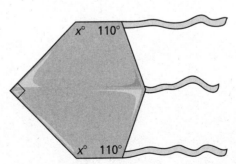

7.1 Enrichment and Extension

Angles of Polygons

In Exercises 1–8, use the figure to find the measure of the angle.

1. ∠A

2. ∠B

3. ∠C

4. ∠D

5. ∠E

6. ∠F

7. ∠G

8. ∠H

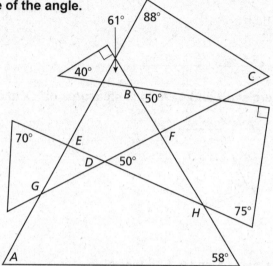

9. In an equiangular polygon, the measure of each exterior angle is 25% of the measure of each interior angle. What is the name of the polygon?

10. *A* and *B* are regular polygons and *A* has two more sides than *B*. The measure of each interior angle of *A* is six degrees greater than the measure of each interior angle of *B*. How many sides does *A* have?

11. The pentagon at the right has been dissected into three triangles with angles labeled as shown. Use the three triangles to prove that the sum of the interior angles of any pentagon is always 540°.

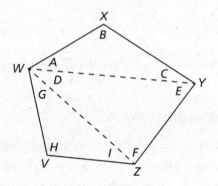

Name_____ Date_____

7.1 Puzzle Time

Why Did The Pioneers Cross The Country In Covered Wagons?

A	B	C	D	E	F
G	H	I	J		

Complete each exercise. Find the answer in the answer column. Write the word under the answer in the box containing the exercise letter.

concurrent **WAS**	
corner **INDIANS**	
exterior **WAIT**	
midsegment **GOLD**	
2520° **A**	
diagonal **DIDN'T**	
acute **HORSE**	
109° **FORTY**	
octagon **TRAIN**	
100° **FOR**	

Complete the sentence.

A. In a polygon, two vertices that are endpoints of the same side are called _____ vertices.

B. A(n) _____ of a polygon is a segment that joins two nonconsecutive vertices.

C. The sum of the measures of the interior angles of a(n) _____ n-gon is $(n - 2) \cdot 180°$.

D. The sum of the measures of the _____ angles of a quadrilateral is 360°.

E. The sum of the measures of the _____ angles of a convex polygon, one angle at each vertex, is 360°.

Find the correct answer to the question for the interior angles of the convex polygon.

F. Two angles of a triangle measure 54° and 17°. Find the measure of the third angle.

G. Find the sum of the measures of the interior angles of a 14-gon.

H. The sum of four angles in a pentagon is 440°. Find the missing angle measure.

I. The sum of three angles in a pentagon is 320°, and the other two angles are $(x + 30)°$ and $(x - 70)°$. Find x.

J. What regular polygon has each interior angle measuring 135°?

interior **TO**
consecutive **THEY**
90° **THE**
non-convex **NOW**
120° **WEATHER**
convex **WANT**
decagon **FIRST**
130° **A**
289° **FOR**
2160° **YEARS**

Start Thinking

A scout is working on a construction project that involves building a 10-foot by 12-foot storage shed. He lays out a footprint of the building on the site using tent stakes and string, as shown in the diagram. The scout is certain of the measure of each side but does not have the proper tools to determine if the angles in each corner are right angles. Can the conclusion be made that the sides are definitely parallel? Consider how the scout could determine if the corner angles are right angles, by just using a tape measure.

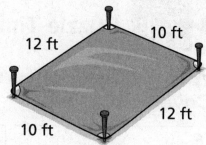

7.2 **Warm Up**

Write a two-column proof.

1. Given: $\overline{MN} \cong \overline{PO}$, $\overline{NO} \cong \overline{MP}$

   Prove: $\triangle PMN \cong \triangle NOP$

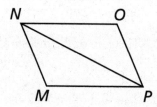

2. Given: $\overline{AB} \cong \overline{CD}$, $\overline{AB} \perp \overline{BD}$,

   $\overline{CD} \perp \overline{BD}$

   Prove: $\overline{AD} \cong \overline{BC}$

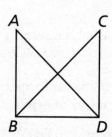

7.2 **Cumulative Review Warm Up**

Solve the equation. Justify each step.

1. $2x - 8 = 5 + 4x$

2. $\frac{1}{2}(3x + 8) = 2x - 3$

3. $\frac{11 - x}{5} = 9 - 7x$

7.2 Practice A

In Exercises 1–4, find the value of each variable in the parallelogram.

1.

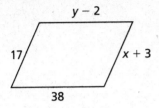

2.

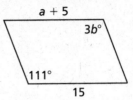

3.

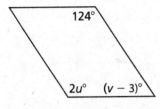

4.

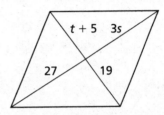

5. Find the coordinates of the intersection of the diagonals of the parallelogram with vertices $(-2, -1)$, $(1, 3)$, $(6, 3)$, and $(3, -1)$.

In Exercises 6 and 7, three vertices of parallelogram *ABCD* are given. Find the remaining vertex.

6. $A(-2, 0)$, $B(-2, -2)$, $D(2, 2)$

7. $A(-1, -3)$, $C(1, 2)$, $D(-1, -2)$

8. The measure of one interior angle of a parallelogram is $30°$ more than two times the measure of another angle. Find the measure of each angle of the parallelogram.

9. Your friend claims that you can prove that two parallelograms are congruent by proving that they have two pairs of congruent opposite angles. Is your friend correct? Explain your reasoning.

10. Use the diagram to write a two-column proof.

    Given: *PQRS* is a parallelogram.

    Prove: $\triangle PQT \cong \triangle RST$

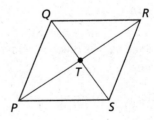

7.2 **Practice B**

In Exercises 1–4, find the value of each variable in the parallelogram.

1.

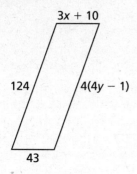

3x + 10

124   4(4y − 1)

43

2.

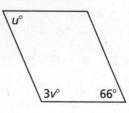

u°

3v°   66°

3.

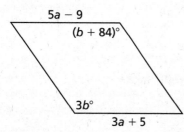

5a − 9

(b + 84)°

3b°

3a + 5

4.

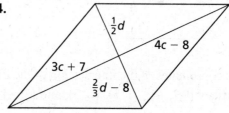

½d

4c − 8

3c + 7

⅔d − 8

5. Find the coordinates of the intersection of the diagonals of the parallelogram with vertices $(-2, -4)$, $(-4, 4)$, $(2, 12)$, and $(4, 4)$.

6. Three vertices of parallelogram $ABCD$ are $A(1, 5)$, $B(1, 1)$, and $D(2, 2)$. Find the coordinates of the remaining vertex.

7. Use the diagram to write a two-column proof.

   Given: $CEHF$ is a parallelogram.
   D bisects $\overline{CE}$ and G bisects $\overline{FH}$.

   Prove: $\triangle CDF \cong \triangle HGE$

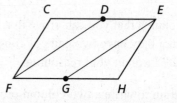

8. State whether each statement is *always, sometimes,* or *never* true for a parallelogram. Explain your reasoning.

   a. The opposite sides are congruent.

   b. All four sides are congruent.

   c. The diagonals are congruent.

   d. The opposite angles are congruent.

   e. The adjacent angles are congruent.

   f. The adjacent angles are complementary.

7.2 Enrichment and Extension

Properties of Parallelograms and Diagonals

The given coordinates represent three vertices of a parallelogram. Write the coordinates of each other point that could be the fourth vertex.

1. $A(-5, -1)$, $B(2, -1)$, $C(-2, -7)$

2. $A(2, 5)$, $B(-1, 2)$, $C(5, 1)$

3. $A(a, b)$, $B(a + 2, b)$, $C(a + 4, b + 3)$

4. $A(a, b)$, $B(a^2, b)$, $C(a^2, b^2)$

A *diagonal* is a line that connects one vertex of a polygon to a nonadjacent vertex. You can see from the picture below the diagonals drawn in a square, pentagon, and hexagon.

  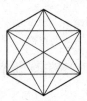

5. Complete the chart to the right to show the number of diagonals in each polygon.

6. Write a formula to find the number of diagonals in any n-gon.

7. How many diagonals does a decagon have? 13-gon?

8. If a polygon has 189 diagonals, how many sides does the polygon have?

Number of sides (n)	Number of diagonals (d)
3	
4	
5	
6	
7	

9. There are six people in a tennis tournament who will play in *round-robin*, in which everyone has to play everyone else.

a. Draw a diagram that would represent this situation.

b. How many games will be played in this tennis tournament?

c. Write a simplified equation for the number of games played in round-robin play with n players.

7.2 Puzzle Time

Where Did Columbus Land When He Found America?

Write the letter of each answer in the box containing the exercise number.

Complete the sentence.

1. A _____ is a quadrilateral with both pairs of opposite sides parallel.

2. If a _____ is a parallelogram, then its opposite sides are congruent.

3. If a quadrilateral is a parallelogram, then its consecutive angles are _____.

4. If a quadrilateral is a parallelogram, then its diagonals _____ each other.

5. If a quadrilateral is a parallelogram, then its opposite angles are _____.

Answers			
T. bisect		**A.** 42°	
D. 40		**E.** parallelogram	
L. acute		**H.** 82°	
M. 17		**O.** supplementary	
C. 98°		**D.** intersect	
E. 108°		**A.** quadrilateral	
H. congruent		**B.** 14	
T. 110°		**R.** triangle	
E. 10		**C.** polygon	
S. complementary			
N. 80			

Use the diagram.

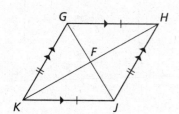

6. $KG = 17$, $KJ = 14$. Find GH.

7. $m\angle GKJ = 86°$, $m\angle GHJ = (x + 6)°$. Find x.

8. $KH = 20$. Find KF.

9. $m\angle HJK = 82°$. Find $m\angle GKJ$.

10. $m\angle HJK = 82°$. Find $m\angle HGK$.

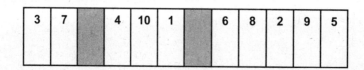

3	7		4	10	1		6	8	2	9	5

Examine the diagram and determine if there appears to be enough information to conclude that the quadrilateral is a parallelogram. If there is not enough information, give an example of additional information that would allow you to prove the quadrilateral is a parallelogram.

1. 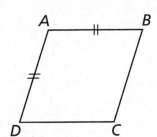   **2.** 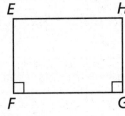   **3.**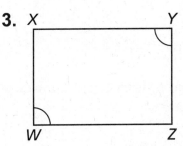

7.3 **Warm Up**

Use the points $A(-2, 5)$, $B(-5, 1)$, $C(3, 2)$, and $D(1, -2)$ to find the indicated slope or measure.

1. Find the slope of $\overline{AB}$.

2. Find the measure of $\overline{AC}$.

3. Find the slope of $\overline{CD}$.

4. Find the measure of $\overline{BD}$.

5. Find the slope of $\overline{AC}$.

6. Find the measure of $\overline{AB}$.

7.3 **Cumulative Review Warm Up**

For the conditional statement, write the converse, the inverse, and the contrapositive. Then determine if each statement is true.

1. If a triangle is right, then it contains two acute angles.

2. If two lines have the same slope, then they are parallel.

3. If there is ice on the road, then I will not go shopping.

Name _____ Date _____

7.3 Practice A

In Exercises 1 and 2, state which theorem you can use to show that the quadrilateral is a parallelogram.

1.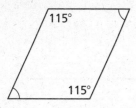

2.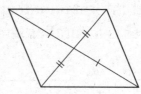

In Exercises 3 and 4, find the value of *x* that makes the quadrilateral a parallelogram.

3.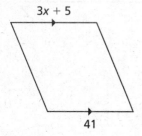

4.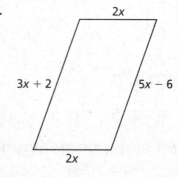

In Exercises 5 and 6, graph the quadrilateral with the given vertices in a coordinate plane. Then show that the quadrilateral is a parallelogram.

5. $A(-4, -2), B(-2, 1), C(4, 1), D(2, -2)$

6. $E(-4, 1), F(-1, 5), G(11, 0), H(8, -4)$

7. Use the diagram to write a two-column proof.

   Given: $\angle A \cong \angle ABE$

   $\overline{AE} \cong \overline{CD}, \overline{BC} \cong \overline{DE}$

   Prove: *BCDE* is a parallelogram.

   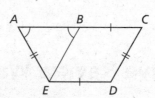

8. In the diagram of the handrail for a staircase shown, $m\angle A = 145°$ and $\overline{AB} \cong \overline{CD}$.

   a. Explain how to show that *ABDC* is a parallelogram.

   b. Describe how to prove that *CDFE* is a parallelogram.

   c. Can you prove that *EFHG* is a parallelogram? Explain.

   d. Find $m\angle ACD$, $m\angle DCE$, $m\angle CEF$, and $m\angle EFD$.

   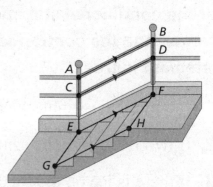

7.3 Practice B

In Exercises 1 and 2, state which theorem you can use to show that the quadrilateral is a parallelogram.

1.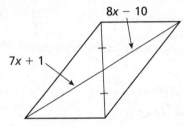

2.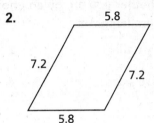

In Exercises 3 and 4, find the value of *x* that makes the quadrilateral a parallelogram.

3.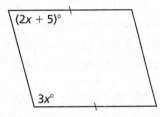
$8x - 10$
$7x + 1$

4.
$(2x + 5)°$
$3x°$

In Exercises 5 and 6, graph the quadrilateral with the given vertices in a coordinate plane. Then show that the quadrilateral is a parallelogram.

5. $W(-3, -1)$, $X(-3, 4)$, $Y(3, 2)$, $Z(3, -3)$

6. $A(-4, 0)$, $B(2, 2)$, $C(5, -1)$, $D(-1, -3)$

7. Use the diagram to write a two-column proof.

Given: $\angle A \cong \angle FDE$

F is the midpoint of $\overline{AD}$.

D is the midpoint of $\overline{CE}$.

Prove: $ABCD$ is a parallelogram.

8. A quadrilateral has two pairs of congruent angles. Can you determine whether the quadrilateral is a parallelogram? Explain your reasoning.

9. An octagon star is shown in the figure on the right.

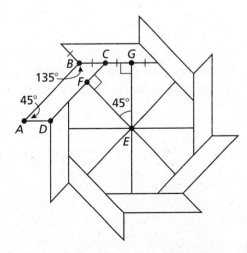

a. Find $m\angle FCG$, $m\angle BCF$, and $m\angle D$.

b. State which theorem you can use to show that the quadrilateral is a parallelogram.

c. The length of $\overline{AB}$ is three times the length of $\overline{AD}$. Write an expression for the perimeter of parallelogram $ABCD$ in terms of the variable *x*.

7.3 Enrichment and Extension

Proving That a Quadrilateral Is a Parallelogram

In Exercises 1–8, decide whether you are given enough information to determine that the quadrilateral is a parallelogram.

1. The opposite sides are parallel.

2. The opposite sides are congruent.

3. Two pairs of consecutive sides are congruent.

4. Two pairs of consecutive angles are congruent.

5. The diagonals are congruent.

6. The diagonals bisect each other.

7. All four sides are congruent.

8. The consecutive angles are supplementary.

9. If two opposite angles of a quadrilateral measure 120° and the measures of the other angles are multiples of 10, what is the probability that the quadrilateral is a parallelogram?

10. The diagonals of quadrilateral $EFGH$ intersect at $D(-1, 4)$. Two vertices of $EFGH$ are $E(2, 7)$ and $F(-3, 5)$. What must be the coordinates of G and H to ensure that $EFGH$ is a parallelogram?

11. In the diagram at the right, $PQRS$ and $QTSU$ are parallelograms. Is $PTRU$ also a parallelogram? Explain why or why not.

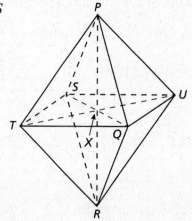

12. Consider the supplementary angle relationships that you need to know to prove that a quadrilateral is a parallelogram. Make a conjecture using the least number of relationships that are necessary.

Name_____ Date _____

Puzzle Time

What Kind Of Ship Can Last Forever?

Circle the letter of each correct answer in the boxes below. The circled letters will spell out the answer to the riddle.

Complete the sentence.

1. If both pairs of opposite sides of a quadrilateral are _____, then the quadrilateral is a parallelogram.

2. If both pairs of opposite angles of a quadrilateral are congruent, then the quadrilateral is a _____.

3. If one _____ of opposite sides of a quadrilateral are congruent and parallel, then the quadrilateral is a parallelogram.

4. If the diagonals of a quadrilateral _____ each other, then the quadrilateral is a parallelogram.

5. A quadrilateral is _____ a parallelogram.

Name the correct theorem number or give the correct value that would make the figure a parallelogram.

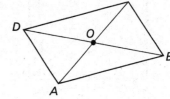

6. Given $m\angle D = 72°$, find $m\angle A$.

7. Given $m\angle A = m\angle C = 89°$, and $m\angle D = m\angle B$, indicate the theorem number that makes it a parallelogram.

8. $DO = 12$, $BO = 12$, $AO = 16$. Find CO.

9. $DC = 4x + 2$, $AB = 5x - 3$, $AD = CB$. Find x.

10. $AD = 2x + 1$, $CB = x + 8$, $DC = AB$. Find x.

F	A	R	O	R	N	I	M	S	E
108°	7.7	always	equal	congruent	side	sometimes	12	72°	parallelogram

I	G	N	F	D	S	H	E	I	P
supplementary	6	pair	intersect	16	7.8	bisect	24	7	5

7.4 Start Thinking

A rhombus and a square are both quadrilaterals with four congruent sides, but a square always contains four right angles. Examine the diagrams below and determine some other distinctive characteristics of the rhombus and the square.

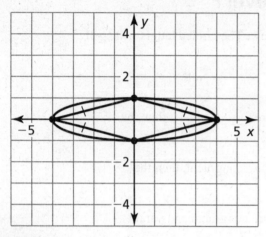 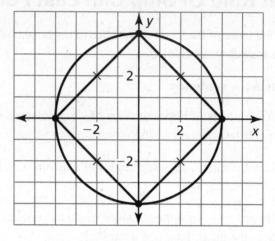

7.4 Warm Up

Use the diagrams to determine the measure of each angle.

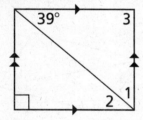 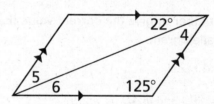

1. $m\angle 1$ 2. $m\angle 2$ 3. $m\angle 3$

4. $m\angle 4$ 5. $m\angle 5$ 6. $m\angle 6$

7.4 Cumulative Review Warm Up

Determine whether the statement is *always*, *sometimes*, or *never* true. Explain your reasoning.

1. An isosceles triangle is a right triangle.

2. A right triangle is a scalene triangle.

3. An equilateral triangle is an equiangular triangle.

4. A right triangle is an equilateral triangle.

7.4 Practice A

In Exercises 1–5, the diagonals of rhombus *ABCD* intersect at *E*. Given that m∠*EAD* = 67°, *CE* = 5, and *DE* = 12, find the indicated measure.

1. m∠*AED*

2. m∠*ADE*

3. m∠*BAE*

4. *AE*

5. *BE*

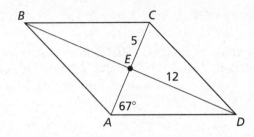

In Exercises 6 and 7, find the lengths of the diagonals of rectangle *JKLM*.

6. $JL = 3x + 4$

   $KM = 4x - 1$

7. $JL = 2x - 6$

   $KM = \frac{3}{2}x + 1$

In Exercises 8 and 9, decide whether quadrilateral *WXYZ* is a rectangle, a rhombus, or a square. Give all names that apply. Explain your reasoning.

8. $W(3, 1), X(3, -2), Y(-5, -2), Z(-5, 1)$

9. $W(4, 1), X(1, 4), Y(-2, 1), Z(1, -2)$

10. Use the figure to write a two-column proof.

    Given: *PSUR* is a rectangle.

    $\overline{PQ} \cong \overline{TU}$

    Prove: $\overline{QS} \cong \overline{RT}$

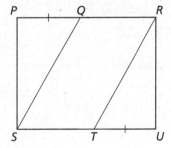

11. In the figure, all sides are congruent and all angles are right angles.

    a. Determine whether the quadrilateral is a rectangle. Explain your reasoning.

    b. Determine whether the quadrilateral is a rhombus. Explain your reasoning.

    c. Determine whether the quadrilateral is a square. Explain your reasoning.

    d. Find m∠*AEB*.

    e. Find m∠*EAD*.

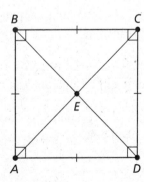

7.4 Practice B

In Exercises 1 and 2, decide whether quadrilateral *JKLM* is a rectangle, a rhombus, or a square. Give all names that apply. Explain your reasoning.

1. $J(3, 5)$, $K(7, 6)$, $L(6, 2)$, $M(2, 1)$

2. $J(-4, -1)$, $K(-1, 5)$, $L(5, 2)$, $M(2, -4)$

In Exercises 3–7, the diagonals of rhombus *ABCD* intersect at *M*. Given that $m\angle MAB = 53°$, $MB = 16$, and $AM = 12$, find the indicated measure.

3. $m\angle AMD$

4. $m\angle ADM$

5. $m\angle ACD$

6. DM

7. AC

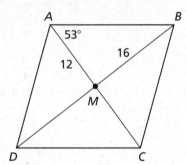

8. Find the point of intersection of the diagonals of the rhombus with vertices $(-1, 2)$, $(3, 4)$, $(5, 8)$, and $(1, 6)$.

9. Use the figure to write a two-column proof.

   Given: *WXYZ* is a parallelogram.

   $\angle XWY \cong \angle XYW$

   Prove: *WXYZ* is a rhombus.

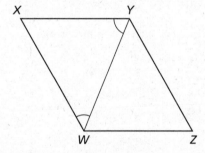

10. Your friend claims that you can transform every rhombus into a square using a similarity transformation. Is your friend correct? Explain your reasoning.

11. A quadrilateral has four congruent angles. Is the quadrilateral a parallelogram? Explain your reasoning.

12. A quadrilateral has two consecutive right angles. If the quadrilateral is not a rectangle, can it still be a parallelogram? Explain your reasoning.

13. Will a diagonal of a rectangle ever divide the rectangle into two isosceles triangles? Explain your reasoning.

Name_____ Date_____

7.4 Enrichment and Extension

Properties of Special Parallelograms

In Exercises 1–3, determine whether the quadrilateral can be a parallelogram. If not, write *impossible*. Explain.

1. The diagonals are congruent, but the quadrilateral has no right angles.

2. Each diagonal is 3 centimeters long and the two opposite sides are 2 centimeters long.

3. Two opposite angles are right angles, but the quadrilateral is not a rectangle.

In Exercises 4–7, use the information given in the diagram to solve for the missing variable.

4. Find the value of w.

5. Find the value of x.

6. Find the value of y.

7. Find the value of z.

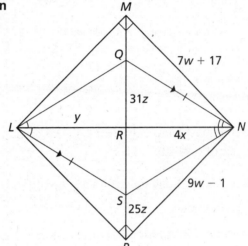

8. In $LMNP$ shown at the right, $m\angle MLN = 32°$, $m\angle NLP = (x^2)°$, $m\angle MNP = 12x°$, and $\angle MNP$ is an acute angle. Find $m\angle NLP$.

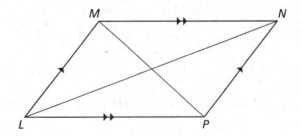

9. Write a coordinate proof of part of Theorem 7.13 (*Hint:* write the vertices in terms of a and b.)

   Given: $DFGH$ is a parallelogram.

   $\overline{DG} \cong \overline{HF}$

   Prove: $DFGH$ is a rectangle.

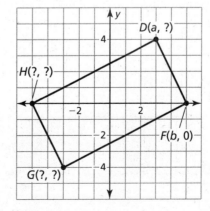

Name _____ Date _____

7.4 Puzzle Time

What Do You Have To Know To Get Top Grades In Geometry?

Write the letter of each answer in the box containing the exercise number.

Complete the sentence.

1. A rhombus is a parallelogram with _____ congruent sides.

2. A rectangle is a parallelogram with four _____ angles.

3. A square is a _____ with four congruent sides and four right angles.

4. A parallelogram is a rhombus if and only if its _____ are perpendicular.

5. A parallelogram is a rhombus if and only if each diagonal _____ a pair of opposite angles.

6. A parallelogram is a rectangle if and only if its diagonals are _____ .

Decide whether each is a *rhombus*, *rectangle*, *square*, *none* of these, or *all* of these.

7. $A(-8, -3), B(-5, 3), C(1, 0), D(-2, -6)$

8. $A(-6, -3), B(-6, -8), C(-2, -5), D(-2, 0)$

9. $A(-7, 1), B(-4, -4), C(2, 2), D(-3, 4)$

Answers	
E. 61	H. diagonals
G. two	A. four
A. square	T. kite
L. parallelogram	T. none
N. 111	O. acute
L. right	D. intersects
G. rhombus	R. rectangle
L. bisects	M. all
E. 26	S. congruent
O. angles	P. 119
I. 5	U. 11
R. perpendicular	

Given rhombus *ABCD*, find the measure of the indicated angle in degrees.

10. $m\angle A = 119°$. Find $m\angle B$.

Find the length of the diagonals of rectangle *QRST* given the following information.

11. $QS = 4x + 6, RT = 6x - 4$

12. $QS = 9x + 12, RT = 11x - 10$

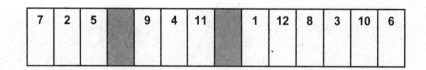

| 7 | 2 | 5 | | 9 | 4 | 11 | | 1 | 12 | 8 | 3 | 10 | 6 |

A kite is to be constructed according to the diagram with $1\frac{1}{4}$ yards of nylon fabric, one 38-inch dowel, and one 24-inch dowel. Describe the construction of the kite in geometric terms. Reference the segments and angles shown in the diagram.

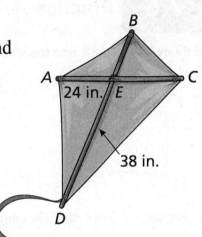

7.5 Warm Up

Use the diagrams to determine the measure of the angle.

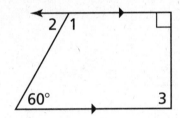

1. $m\angle 1$ **2.** $m\angle 2$ **3.** $m\angle 3$

4. $m\angle 4$ **5.** $m\angle 5$ **6.** $m\angle 6$

7.5 Cumulative Review Warm Up

$\overline{MN}$ **is a midsegment of** $\triangle ABC$**. Find the values of** *x* **and** *y*.

1.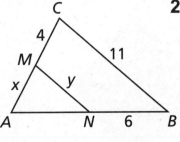

2.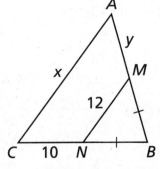

3.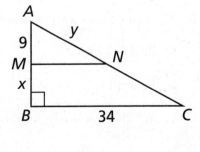

7.5 Practice A

In Exercises 1 and 2, find the value of x.

1.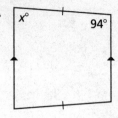

2.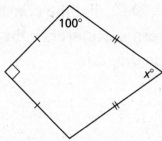

In Exercises 3 and 4, find the length of the midsegment of the trapezoid with the given vertices.

3. $A(0, 3)$, $B(4, 5)$, $C(4, -2)$, $D(0, -2)$

4. $E(-3, 3)$, $F(1, 3)$, $G(3, -3)$, $H(-5, -3)$

In Exercises 5 and 6, give the most specific name for the quadrilateral. Explain your reasoning.

5.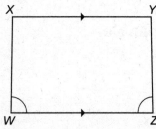

6.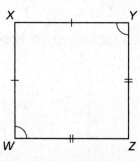

7. Describe and correct the error in finding the most specfice name for the quadrialteral.

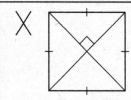

The quadrilateral has two pairs of consecutive congruent sides and the diagonals are perpendicular. So, the quadrilateral is a kite.

8. Use the diagram to write a two-column proof.

Given: $ABCD$ is a parallelogram.

$\overline{AE} \cong \overline{AD}$

Prove: $ABCE$ is an isosceles trapezoid.

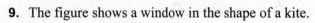

9. The figure shows a window in the shape of a kite.

a. Find $m\angle XVW$.

b. Find $\overline{XY}$.

c. Which angle is congruent to $\angle XYZ$?

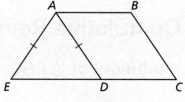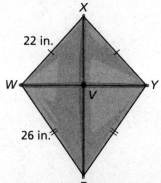

Name_____ Date_____

7.5 Practice B

In Exercises 1 and 2, show that the quadrilateral with the given vertices is a trapezoid. Then decide whether it is isosceles.

1. $T(-1, -2), U(-1, 3), V(3, 4), W(3, -3)$ 2. $P(0, 0), Q(2, 4), R(5, 4), S(5, 0)$

In Exercises 3 and 4, find the value of x.

3.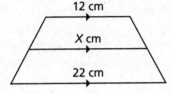

4.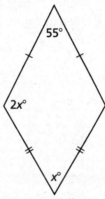

In Exercises 5 and 6, give the most specific name for the quadrilateral. Explain your reasoning.

5.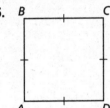

6.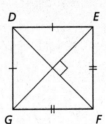

7. Use the diagram to write a two-column proof.

   Given: $VXYZ$ is a kite.
   $\overline{XY} \cong \overline{YZ}, \overline{WX} \cong \overline{UZ}$

   Prove: $\triangle WXV \cong \triangle UZV$

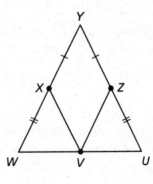

8. Three vertices of a trapezoid are given by $(3, -6), (3, -2),$ and $(6, -8)$. Find the fourth vertex such that the trapezoid is an isosceles trapezoid.

9. Is it possible to have a concave kite? Explain your reasoning.

10. The diagram shows isosceles trapezoid $JKLP$ with base lengths a and b, and height c.

    a. Explain how you know $JKMN$ is a rectangle. Write the area of $JKMN$.

    b. Write the formula for the area of $\triangle JNP$.

    c. Write and simplify the formula for the area of trapezoid $JKLP$.

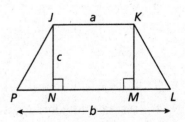

Name _____ Date _____

Properties of Trapezoids and Kites

1. Each square section in an iron railing contains four small kites. The figure shows the dimensions of one kite. What length of iron is needed to outline one small kite? How much iron is needed to outline one complete section, including the square?

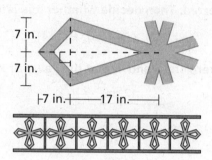

2. Find the value of *a* in the figure to the right so that *PQRS* is isosceles.

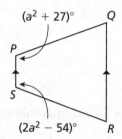

3. The perimeter of an isosceles trapezoid *ABCD* is 27.4 inches. If *BC* = 2(*AB*), find *AD*, *AB*, *BC*, and *CD*.

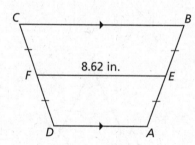

8.62 in.

In Exercises 4 and 5, the given coordinates represent three vertices of an isosceles trapezoid. Write the coordinates of the point that could be the fourth vertex.

4. $(a, b), (a, -b), (a + 3, b)$

5. $(a, b), (a, b - c), (a - c, b - 2c)$

6. One base of a non-isosceles trapezoid has the vertices $(x, y + z)$ and $(x + z, y + 2z)$. A third vertex is the point (x, y). Describe the set of points that could be the fourth vertex.

7. If the coordinates $(0, 0), (2, 5),$ and $(5, 2)$ represent three vertices of a convex kite, describe the coordinates of each point that could be the fourth vertex.

Name_____ Date _____

7.5 Puzzle Time

What Word Is Always Spelled Incorrectly?

Circle the letter of each correct answer in the boxes below. The circled letters will spell out the answer to the riddle.

Complete the sentence.

1. A _____ is a quadrilateral with exactly one pair of parallel sides.

2. The parallel sides of a trapezoid are the _____.

3. Base angles of a trapezoid are two _____ angles whose common side is a base.

4. The nonparallel sides are the _____ of the trapezoid.

5. If the legs of a trapezoid are congruent, then the trapezoid is an _____ trapezoid.

6. A trapezoid is isosceles if and only if its _____ are congruent.

7. The _____ of a trapezoid is parallel to each base and its length is one-half the sum of the lengths of the bases.

8. If a quadrilateral is a _____, then its diagonals are perpendicular.

Find the indicated measurement using quadrilateral ABCD as a reference.

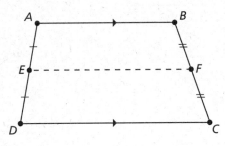

9. $\overline{AD} \cong \overline{BC}$, $m\angle D = 75°$. Find $m\angle A$.

10. $AB = 17$, $DC = 25$. Find EF.

Find the indicated measurement using quadrilateral ABCD as a reference.

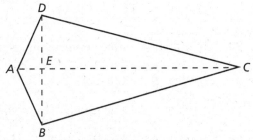

11. $\overline{AD} \cong \overline{AB}$, $\overline{DC} \cong \overline{BC}$, $m\angle A = 130°$, $m\angle C = 30°$.
    Find $m\angle B$.

G	I	N	U	C	N	O	Y	R	R
9	kite	21	point	trapezoid	18	100°	3	105°	consecutive

E	G	C	A	T	O	L	S	T	Y
bases	21	legs	1	midsegment	median	diagonals	0	altitude	isosceles

Chapter 7 Cumulative Review

In Exercises 1–16, solve the equation.

1. $6(x - 2) = 18$

2. $-4(x + 7) = 36$

3. $2(x - 3) = -16$

4. $4(6 - x) = 24$

5. $9(8 - x) = -63$

6. $5(2 + x) = -30$

7. $2(x - 6) + 12 = 32$

8. $8(x + 2) - 12 = -4$

9. $3(x - 10) + 16 = -20$

10. $6(8 - x) + 11 = -1$

11. $-2(9 - x) - 13 = -15$

12. $10(5 - x) - 14 = 16$

13. $4(x + 11) + 2(x + 9) = 44$

14. $3(x - 10) + 8(x + 1) = 11$

15. $-5(x + 2) + 2(x + 12) = 2$

16. $7(x - 1) + 4(x + 6) = -5$

In Exercises 17–22, classify the polygon.

17.
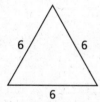

18.
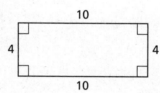

19.
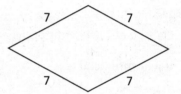

20.
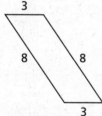

21.
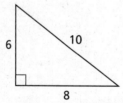

22.
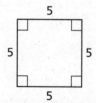

23. The equation for the perimeter of a square can be expressed as $4(x + 2) = 44$.

    a. What is the value of x?

    b. What is the side length of the square?

24. The length of a rectangle is $3x + 4$ and the width is $2x + 7$.

    a. Write an equation for the perimeter P of the rectangle.

    b. The perimeter of the rectangle is 62 feet. What is the value of x?

    c. What are the length and width of the rectangle?

Chapter 7 Cumulative Review (continued)

In Exercises 25–30, tell whether the figure to the right is a *translation*, *reflection*, *rotation*, or *dilation* of the figure to the left.

25.
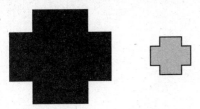

26.

27.

28.
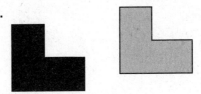

29.

30.
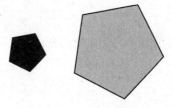

In Exercises 31–33, use the translation $(x, y) \rightarrow (x + 2, y - 5)$.

31. What is the image of $A(-3, 7)$?

32. What is the image of $B(9, 8)$?

33. What is the image of $C(4, -6)$?

In Exercises 34–37, use the translation $(x, y) \rightarrow (x - 4, y + 3)$.

34. What is the image of $A(8, -3)$?

35. What is the image of $B(-12, -1)$?

36. What is the preimage of $C'(-2, 8)$?

37. What is the preimage of $D'(3, 8)$?

Name _____ Date _____

In Exercises 38–41, find the measure of the exterior angle.

38.

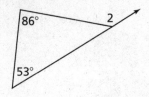

39.

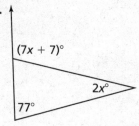

40.

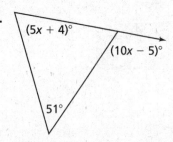

41.

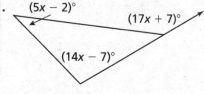

In Exercises 42 and 43, find the values of x and y.

42. $\triangle EFG \cong \triangle JKL$

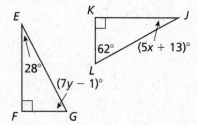

43. $\triangle VWX \cong \triangle QRS$

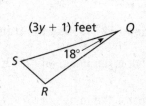

44. A right triangle has interior angles of $6x°$ and $(4x + 10)°$.

   a. What is the value of x?

   b. What is the measure of the $6x°$ angle?

   c. What is the measure of the $(4x + 10)°$ angle?

45. A right triangle has interior angles of $(4x + 1)°$ and $(19x - 3)°$.

   a. What is the value of x?

   b. What is the measure of the $(4x + 1)°$ angle?

   c. What is the measure of the $(19x - 3)°$ angle?

Chapter 7 **Cumulative Review** (continued)

In Exercises 46–53, name the included angle between the pair of sides given.

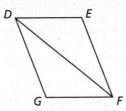

46. $\overline{GD}$ and $\overline{GF}$ **47.** $\overline{EF}$ and $\overline{GF}$ **48.** $\overline{GD}$ and $\overline{FD}$ **49.** $\overline{FE}$ and $\overline{ED}$

50. $\overline{ED}$ and $\overline{FD}$ **51.** $\overline{DF}$ and $\overline{EF}$ **52.** $\overline{ED}$ and $\overline{GD}$ **53.** $\overline{GF}$ and $\overline{DF}$

In Exercises 54–57, find the indicated measure. Explain your reasoning.

54. SV

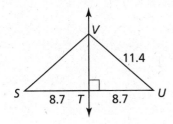

55. GH

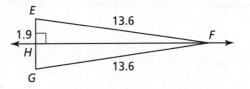

56. KL

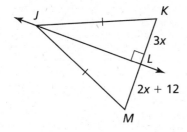

57. AD

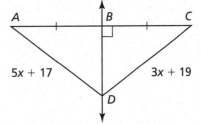

58. A line segment AC is bisected by point B. The length of AB is $8x + 12$ and the length of BC is $6x + 18$.

   a. What is the value of x?

   b. What is the length of $\overline{AB}$?

   c. What is the length of $\overline{AC}$?

Chapter 8

Chapter 8 Similarity

Dear Family,

In this chapter, your student will be learning about figures that have the same shape but different sizes. These figures are called *similar figures*. For instance, the two photos below are similar because all the dimensions of the photo on the left are proportional to all the dimensions of the photo on the right.

24"

6"

4"

16"

Find a flagpole, tree, telephone pole, or another tall, straight object that casts a shadow. You and your shadow form the sides of a triangle that is similar to the flagpole and its shadow. By measuring the length of your shadow and the length of the flagpole's shadow, you can determine the height of the flagpole using your height!

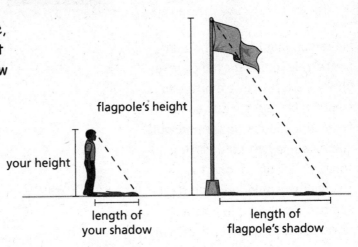

flagpole's height

your height

length of your shadow

length of flagpole's shadow

Have your student measure the length of the flagpole's shadow and the length of your shadow. Explain that using methods in this chapter, your student will be able to use this information to calculate the height of the flagpole or any other tall, straight object that casts a shadow.

Your student should hold on to the measurements as motivation for learning the material in the chapter. The reward will come when your student is able to apply a concept learned in class to a hands-on experience with indirect measurement.

Have fun and be creative!

Capítulo 8 · Semejanza

Estimada familia:

En este capítulo, su hijo aprenderá sobre las figuras que tienen la misma forma, pero diferentes tamaños. Estas figuras se llaman *figuras semejantes*. Por ejemplo, las dos siguientes fotografías son semejantes porque todas las dimensiones de la fotografía de la izquierda son proporcionales con todas las dimensiones de la fotografía de la derecha.

24″

6″

4″

16″

Hallen un mástil, un árbol, un poste telefónico u otro objeto alto y derecho que emita una sombra. Ustedes y sus sombras forman los lados de un triángulo que es semejante al mástil y su sombra. ¡Medir la longitud de sus sombras y la longitud de la sombra del mástil les permite determinar la altura del mástil usando sus alturas!

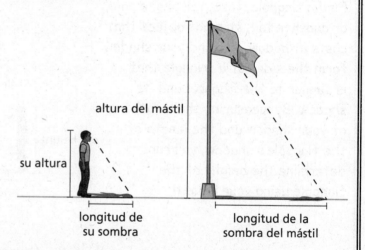

altura del mástil

su altura

longitud de su sombra

longitud de la sombra del mástil

Pidan a su hijo que mida la longitud de la sombra del mástil y la longitud de su sombra. Expliquen que si usa los métodos de este capítulo, su hijo podrá usar esta información para calcular la altura del mástil o cualquier otro objeto alto y derecho que emita una sombra.

Su hijo debería aferrarse a las medidas como motivación para aprender el material de este capítulo. La recompensa llegará cuando su hijo logre usar un concepto aprendido en clase en una experiencia práctica con medición indirecta.

¡Diviértanse y sean creativos

8.1 Start Thinking

A map of the state of Virginia is inserted into a research paper on the Civil War. The clip art is not the correct size, so the student tries to adjust the sizing. Review the diagrams below and discuss how the three are related. Would you say the two resized figures are "similar" to the original?

Original
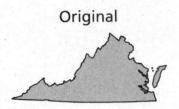

1st Resizing

2nd Resizing

8.1 Warm Up

Solve the proportion.

1. $\dfrac{x}{4} = \dfrac{3}{8}$

2. $\dfrac{12}{x} = \dfrac{3}{5}$

3. $\dfrac{x}{9} = \dfrac{1}{x}$

4. $\dfrac{x + 3}{2} = \dfrac{3}{5}$

5. $\dfrac{4 - x}{12} = \dfrac{3}{-7}$

6. $\dfrac{1}{2x + 1} = \dfrac{x - 3}{9}$

8.1 Cumulative Review Warm Up

Use the diagram to find the measure of the angle.

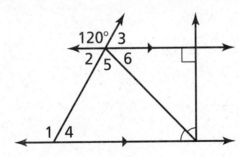

1. $\angle 1$

2. $\angle 2$

3. $\angle 3$

4. $\angle 4$

5. $\angle 5$

6. $\angle 6$

8.1 Practice A

In Exercises 1 and 2, find the scale factor. Then list all pairs of congruent angles and write the ratios of the corresponding side lengths in a statement of proportionality.

1. △LMN ~ △QRS

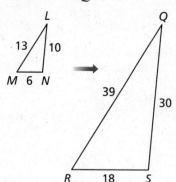

2. ABCD ~ EFGH

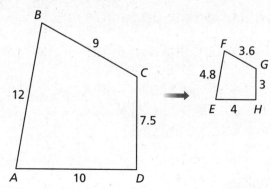

In Exercises 3 and 4, the polygons are similar. Find the value of x.

3.

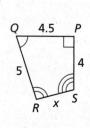
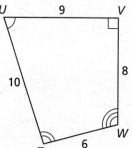

4.

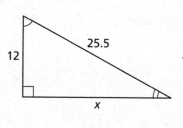

In Exercises 5–11, △ABC ~ △XYZ.

5. Find the scale factor of △ABC to △XYZ.

6. Find m∠X.

7. Find CD.

8. Find the area of △ABC. Then find the area of △XYZ.

9. Find the ratio of the area of △ABC to the area of △XYZ.

10. Find BC and YZ. Explain your reasoning.

11. Find the ratio of the perimeter of △ABC to the perimeter of △XYZ.

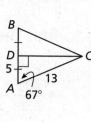
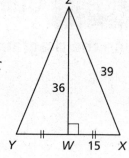

12. You are building a roof on a garage such that the gable of the house is similar to the gable of the garage as shown in the diagram. The area of the gable on the house is 3024 square feet. Find the area of the gable on the garage.

42 ft

House gable

14 ft

Garage gable

Name_____ Date_____

8.1 Practice B

In Exercises 1 and 2, find the scale factor. Then list all pairs of congruent angles and write the ratios of the corresponding side lengths in a statement of proportionality.

1. $\triangle ABC \sim \triangle HIJ$

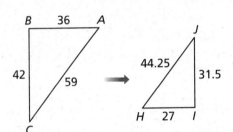

2. $WXYZ \sim STUV$

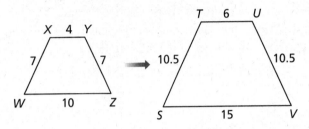

In Exercises 3 and 4, the polygons are similar. Find the value of *x*.

3.

4.

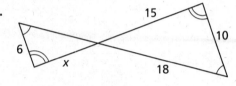

In Exercises 5 and 6, the figures are similar. Find the missing corresponding side length.

5. Figure A has a perimeter of 60 inches and one of the side lengths is 5 inches. Figure B has a perimeter of 84 inches.

6. Figure A has an area of 4928 square feet and one of the side lengths is 88 feet. Figure B has an area of 77 square feet.

7. In the diagram, $\triangle ABC \sim \triangle ADE$.

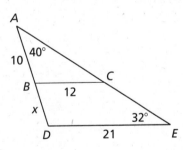

a. Find the scale factor from $\triangle ABC$ to $\triangle ADE$.

b. Find the value of *x*.

c. Find $m\angle ABC$.

d. The perimeter of $\triangle ABC$ is about 42.4 units. Find the perimeter of the $\triangle ADE$.

e. The area of $\triangle ABC$ is about 71.75 square units. Find the area of the $\triangle ADE$.

f. Is $\overline{BC} \parallel \overline{DE}$? Explain your reasoning.

Name_____ Date _____

Rep-Tiles and Rep-*n* Tiles

A figure is called a *rep-tile* if copies of the figure fit together to form a larger similar figure. The figures below are examples of rep-tiles, where four equal figures fit together to form a larger similar figure. Notice the larger square and the four equal squares inside it. Likewise, the equilateral triangle has four equilateral triangles inside of it. The inner figures are all similar to the outer figures.

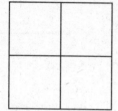
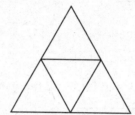

Because these two figures each have four replicas within the larger figure, they are classified more specifically as a rep-4 tile.

1. Draw four smaller, congruent figures inside the trapezoid below. The figures must be similar to the original figure.

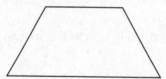

Create a rep-9 tile, or a rep-tile of nine congruent figures similar to the original figure.

2.

3.

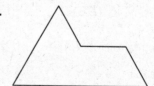

Name_____ Date_____

8.1 Puzzle Time

What Did One Elevator Say To The Other Elevator?

A	B	C	D	E	F
G	H	I			

Complete each exercise. Find the answer in the answer column. Write the word under the answer in the box containing the exercise letter.

Complete the sentence.

120 MOUSE	
square AM	
side UP	
40 SOMETHING	
equal I	
36 AND	
corresponding THINK	
100 WITH	
similar GOING	

A. A similarity transformation preserves _____ measure.

B. A similarity transformation also enlarges or reduces side lengths by a _____ factor k.

C. If two polygons are similar, then the ratio of any two _____ lengths in the polygons is equal to the scale factor of the similar polygons.

D. If two polygons are similar, then the ratio of their perimeters is _____ to the ratios of their corresponding side lengths.

E. If two polygons are similar, then the ratio of their areas is equal to the _____ of the ratios of their corresponding side lengths.

Triangles XYZ and PQR are similar. Find the indicated value.

F. $p = 15$, $q = 21$, $r = 9$, $x = 20$, $z = 12$; Find y.

G. What is k, the scale factor for Exercise F?

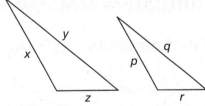

Polygons DEFG and PQRS are similar. Find the indicated value.

H. The perimeter of the smaller polygon is 60 inches, and the ratio of the side lengths is $\frac{3}{5}$. Find the perimeter of the larger polygon.

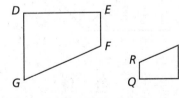

I. The perimeter of the larger polygon is 280 inches, and the ratio of the side lengths is $\frac{1}{7}$. Find the perimeter of the smaller polygon.

28 COMING	
areas AIR	
21 WRONG	
$\frac{3}{4}$ DOWN	
equal HIGH	
scale I	
70 RED	
$\frac{1}{4}$ FAST	
angle HEY	

8.2 Start Thinking

The diagram shows the layout for a quilting triangle. If you know the measure of ∠*A* is 30°, what conclusions can you make about the other angles in the design?

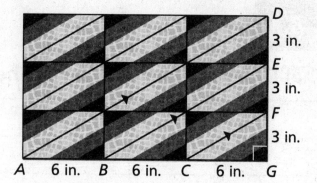

8.2 Warm Up

Find the value of x.

1.   **2.**   **3.**   **4.**

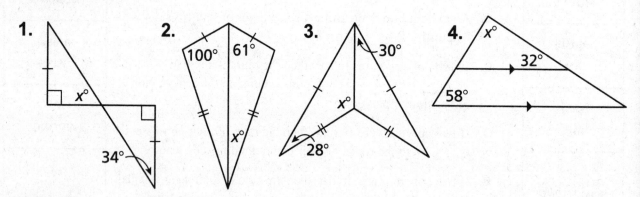

8.2 Cumulative Review Warm Up

Find the indicated measure in □ *JKLM*.

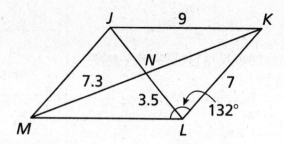

1. *ML*   **2.** *MJ*   **3.** *JN*

4. *MK*   **5.** *m∠MJK*   **6.** *m∠LMJ*

Name_____ Date_____

In Exercises 1 and 2, determine whether the triangles are similar. If they are, write a similarity statement. Explain your reasoning.

1.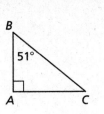

2.

In Exercises 3 and 4, show that the two triangles are similar.

3. △*ABD* and △*ACE*

4. △*WXZ* and △*ZXY*

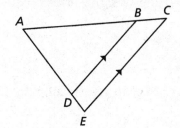

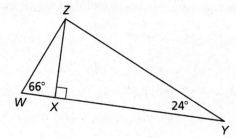

5. In the diagram, △*ABC* ~ △*EDC*.

   a. Is $\overline{AB} \parallel \overline{DE}$? Explain your reasoning.

   b. Show that △*ACD* ~ △*ECB*.

   c. Find *m∠CAD*.

   d. Find *ED*.

   e. Find *AD*. Explain your reasoning.

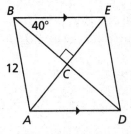

In Exercises 6 and 7, is it possible for △*ABC* and △*XYZ* to be similar? Explain your reasoning.

  6. *m∠A* = 43°, *m∠B* = 61°, *m∠Y* = 61°, and *m∠Z* = 74°

  7. ∠*A* and ∠*X* are right angles and ∠*B* ≅ ∠*Z*.

  8. Use the figure to write a two-column proof.

     Given: ∠*Q* ≅ ∠*T*

     Prove: $\overline{PQ} \parallel \overline{ST}$

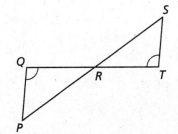

Name_____ Date _____

8.2 Practice B

In Exercises 1 and 2, determine whether the triangles are similar. If they are, write a similarity statement. Explain your reasoning.

1.

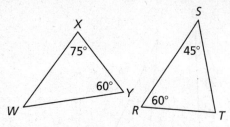

2.

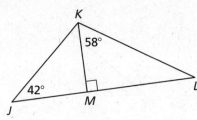

In Exercises 3 and 4, show that the two triangles are similar.

3. △ECG and △EDF

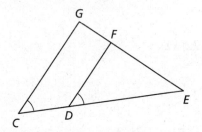

4. △XWY and △ZYW

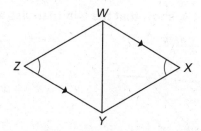

In Exercises 5 and 6, is it possible for △**ABC** and △**XYZ** to be similar? Explain your reasoning.

5. $\angle A$ and $\angle X$ are supplementary and $\angle B$ and $\angle Z$ are complementary.

6. $m\angle A = 75°$ and $m\angle Z = 105°$

7. Your friend claims that if you know three angles of one quadrilateral are congruent to three angles of another quadrilateral, then the two quadrilaterals are similar. Is your friend correct? Explain your reasoning.

8. The height of the Empire State Building is 1250 feet tall. Your friend, who is 6 feet 3 inches tall, is standing nearby and casts a shadow that is 33 inches long. What is the length of the shadow of the Empire State Building?

9. Use the figure to write a two-column proof.

   Given: $\angle ABC$ and $\angle BDC$ are right angles.

   Prove: $\angle A \cong \angle CBD$

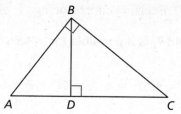

10. Use the figure to write a two-column proof.

    Given: $\overline{YZ} \cong \overline{YV}$

    $\overline{XY} \cong \overline{WY}$

    Prove: △$XYW \sim$ △VYZ

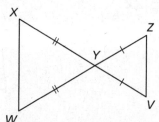

8.2 Enrichment and Extension

Proving Triangle Similarity by AA

In Exercises 1–6, use the diagram to find two pairs of coordinates for the points that satisfy the similarity statement.

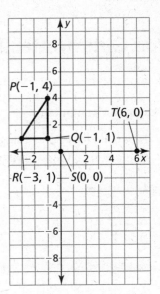

1. Given △PQR ~ △STU, find the coordinates of U.

2. Given △PQR ~ △VST, find the coordinates of V.

3. Given △PQR ~ △SWT, find the coordinates of W.

4. Given △PQR ~ △TSX, find the coordinates of X.

5. Given △PQR ~ △YTS, find the coordinates of Y.

6. Given △PQR ~ △TZS, find the coordinates of Z.

7. If $PT = x$, $PQ = 3x$, and $SR = \dfrac{8}{x}$, find PS in terms of x.

   Explain your reasoning.

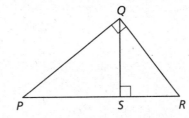

In Exercises 8 and 9, use the diagram and the information given to complete a two-column proof.

8. **Given:** ∠PQR is a right angle.

   $\overline{QS}$ is the altitude of △PQR drawn from the right angle.

   Prove: △PSQ ~ △QSR

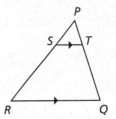

9. **Given:** $\overline{AC} \parallel \overline{GE}$

   $\overline{BG} \parallel \overline{CF}$

   Prove: △ABH ~ △EFD

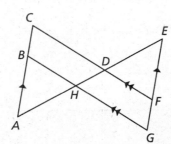

8.2 Puzzle Time

What Gets Wetter The More It Dries?

Write the letter of each answer in the box containing the exercise number.

Complete the sentence.

1. If two angles of one triangle are congruent to two angles of another triangle, then the two triangles are _____.

Use the diagram.

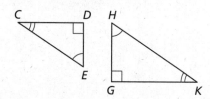

2. If $m\angle C = 36°$, then $m\angle H = 54°$. True or false?

3. $\triangle EDC \sim \triangle$_____

4. If $m\angle E = 73°$, find $m\angle K$.

Use the diagram.

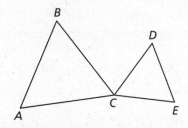

5. $m\angle A = 42°$, $m\angle D = 95°$, $m\angle E = 42°$, $\angle B \cong \angle D$; Find $m\angle ACB$.

6. $m\angle A = m\angle E = m\angle ACB = m\angle ECD = 59°$; Find $m\angle D$.

Answers
K. 73°
L. 17°
U. false
T. 62°
A. congruent
M. right angle
W. similar
E. 43°
I. *EDC*
O. true
D. 42°
A. *HGK*
B. *KGH*

3		6	2	1	5	4

8.3 Start Thinking

A carpentry class is working on a project for the local childcare centers. The students are making wooden trees to go with the centers' train sets. They work from a sample that was cut from a three-inch tall triangular block of wood. The goal is to make more trees, proportional to the sample, but larger. Use the diagrams below to determine the lengths of the sides x and y of the triangles for trees made from four-inch and five-inch blocks of wood.

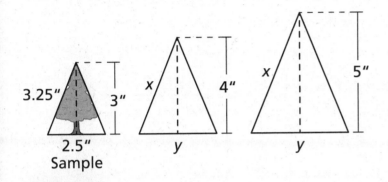

8.3 Warm Up

Use the diagram to copy and complete the statement.

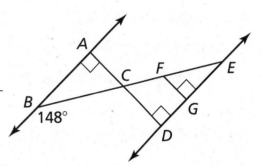

1. $\triangle ABC \sim$ _____
2. $\triangle FEG \sim$ _____
3. $m\angle ACB =$ _____
4. $m\angle FEG =$ _____
5. $m\angle ACE =$ _____
6. $\overline{AD} \parallel$ _____

8.3 Cumulative Review Warm Up

Write an equation of the line passing through point *P* that is perpendicular to the given line.

1. $P(0, -3)$, $y = -5x$

2. $P(4, 0)$, $y = 9x + 8$

3. $P(-2, 4)$, $2x - 3y = -8$

4. $P\left(-\frac{2}{3}, 1\right)$, $y - 8 = -\frac{5}{2}(x + 3)$

Name_____   Date _____

8.3   Practice A

1. Determine whether $\triangle ABC$ or $\triangle DEF$ is similar to $\triangle XYZ$.

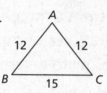 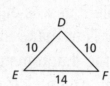 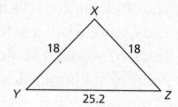

In Exercises 2 and 3, find the value of *x* that makes $\triangle PQR \sim \triangle JKL$.

2.

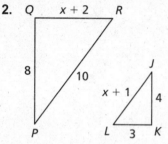

3.

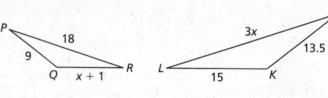

4. Verify that $\triangle TUV \sim \triangle XYZ$. Find the scale factor of $\triangle TUV$ to $\triangle XYZ$.

$\triangle TUV: TU = 15, UV = 21, TV = 18$ $\triangle XYZ: XY = 35, YZ = 49, XZ = 42$

In Exercises 5 and 6, show that the triangles are similar and write a similarity statement. Explain your reasoning.

5.

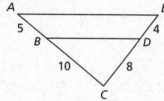

6.

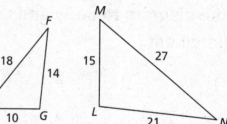

In Exercises 7–11, use the diagram to copy and complete the statement.

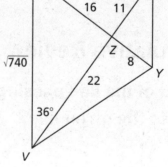

7. $\triangle VWZ \sim$ _____

8. $m\angle VZY =$ _____

9. $m\angle VWY =$ _____

10. $m\angle WXY =$ _____

11. $XY =$ _____

12. In the figure for Exercises 7–11, is $\triangle WXZ \sim \triangle YVZ$? Explain your reasoning.

13. Use the figure to write a two-column proof.

Given: $\dfrac{PR}{QR} = \dfrac{TR}{SR}$ **Prove:** $\overline{QS} \parallel \overline{PT}$

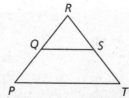

Name_____ Date_____

8.3 Practice B

In Exercises 1 and 2, find the value of x that makes △ABC ~ △RST.

1.
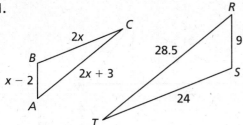

2.
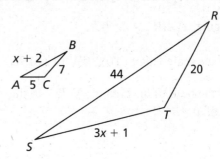

3   Verify that △JKL ~ △PQR. Find the scale factor of △JKL to △PQR.

△JKL: JK = 15, KL = 30, JL = 25   △PQR: PQ = 12, QR = 24, PR = 20

In Exercises 4 and 5, show that the triangles are similar and write a similarity statement. Explain your reasoning.

4.
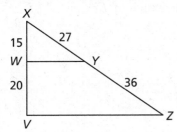

5.
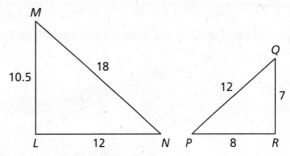

6. △ABC has side lengths 42, 21, and 35 units. The shortest side of a triangle similar to △ABC is 9 units long. Find the other lengths of the triangle.

7. Use the figure to find the values of x, y, and z that makes △DEF ~ △GHF.

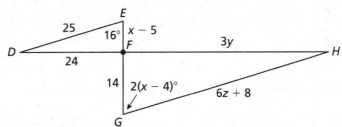

Use the figure to write a two-column proof

8. **Given:** $\dfrac{AC}{DF} = \dfrac{AB}{DE}$ **Prove:** $\angle B \cong \angle E$

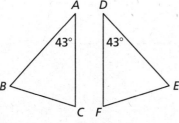

9. **Given:** $LN = 2x$
    $MN = 2y$
    $NP = x$
    $NQ = y$
    Prove: $\triangle MLN \sim \triangle PQN$

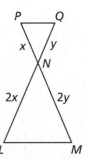

8.3 Enrichment and Extension

Proving Triangles Similar by SSS and SAS

1. In the figure, $\triangle ABC \sim \triangle VWX$.

   a. Find the scale factor of $\triangle VWX$ to $\triangle ABC$.

   b. Find the ratio of the area of $\triangle VWX$ to the area of $\triangle ABC$.

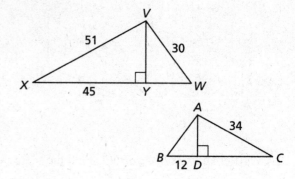

2. Given $\triangle DEF \sim \triangle GHI$, $m\angle D = 50°$, $m\angle G = (2x + 5y)°$, $m\angle I = (5x + y)°$, and that $m\angle E = (102 - x)°$, find $m\angle I$.

3. A portion of a water slide in an amusement park is shown. Find the length of $\overline{EF}$, if the posts and $\overline{EF}$ form a right angle with the ground

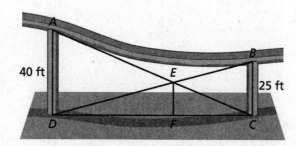

4. A streetlight is mounted at the top of a 15-foot pole. A 6-foot man walks away from the pole along a straight path. How long is his shadow when he is 40 feet from the pole?

5. Use the information and the diagram to prove the statement.

   Given: $\overline{AH} \parallel \overline{CF}$ and $\overline{CA} \parallel \overline{FH}$

   Prove: $\triangle BKD \sim \triangle GKJ$

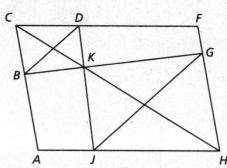

Name_____ Date_____

8.3 Puzzle Time

What Speaks Every Language?

Circle the letter of each correct answer in the boxes below. The circled letters will spell out the answer to the riddle.

Complete the sentence.

1. If the corresponding side lengths of two triangles are _____, then the triangles are similar.

2. If an angle of one triangle is congruent to an angle of a second triangle and the lengths of the sides including these angles are proportional, then the triangles are _____.

3. If two nonvertical lines are _____, then they have the same slope.

4. If two _____ lines are perpendicular, then the product of their slopes is −1.

Name the triangle that is not similar.

5.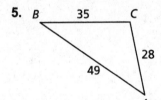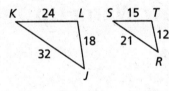

6.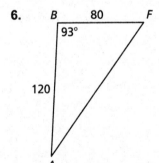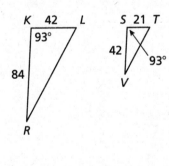

T	A	H	I	N	K	E
△ABC	proportional	concurrent	△VST	parallel	△RKL	△ABF
R	**S**	**C**	**O**	**H**	**O**	**B**
congruent	perpendicular	similar	equal	△JKL	nonvertical	△RST

In the diagram, $\overrightarrow{BE} \parallel \overrightarrow{CD}$ and $\overrightarrow{BE}$ bisects $\angle ABD$. Examine the diagram and make conclusions regarding congruent angles, congruent segments, similar triangles, and proportionality.

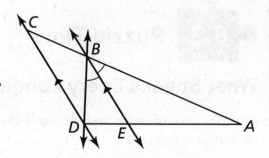

8.4 **Warm Up**

Solve the proportion.

1. $\dfrac{x-1}{3} = \dfrac{2x}{5}$

2. $\dfrac{2x+3}{3x} = \dfrac{4}{9}$

3. $\dfrac{2x}{x+3} = \dfrac{3x}{x-3}$

4. $\dfrac{x}{2x+1} = \dfrac{5}{4-x}$

5. $\dfrac{2}{1-x} = \dfrac{x-8}{x+1}$

6. $\dfrac{x}{2x-6} = \dfrac{2}{x-4}$

8.4 **Cumulative Review Warm Up**

Prove the triangles are congruent.

1. **Given:** $\overline{AC} \cong \overline{AB}$, $\overline{AD} \cong \overline{AE}$ **Prove:** $\triangle ADB \cong \triangle AEC$

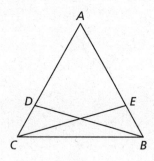

2. **Given:** $\overline{MR} \perp \overline{KP}$, $\overline{KO} \perp \overline{PM}$

    $\angle RKM \cong \angle OMK$

    Prove: $\triangle RKM \cong \triangle OMK$

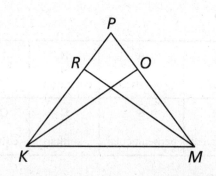

Name_____ Date _____

8.4   Practice A

In Exercises 1 and 2, find the length of $\overline{AB}$.

1.

2.

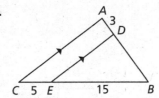

In Exercises 3 and 4, determine whether $\overline{QR} \parallel \overline{ST}$.

3.

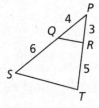

4.

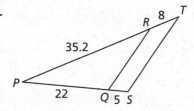

In Exercises 5 and 6, find the length of the indicated line segment.

5. $\overline{DF}$

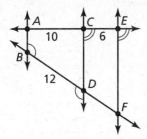

6. $\overline{HJ}$

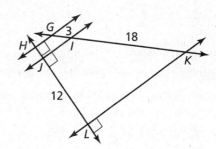

In Exercises 7 and 8, find the value of the variable.

7.

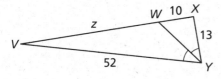

8.

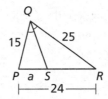

9. The diagram shows the skyline of a city. Find the distance between point E and point F for which $\overline{BE} \parallel \overline{CF}$. Explain your reasoning.

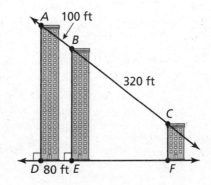

Name _____ Date _____

8.4 Practice B

In Exercises 1 and 2, find the length of the indicated line segment.

1. $\overline{XY}$

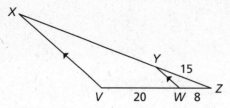

2. $\overline{PR}$

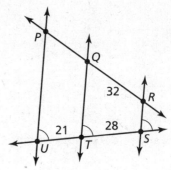

In Exercises 3 and 4, find the value of the variable.

3.

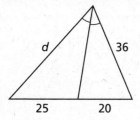

4.

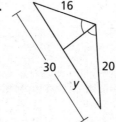

5. The figure shows parallelogram $ABCD$, where E and F are the midpoints of $\overline{BC}$ and $\overline{AD}$ respectively. Your friend claims that $\overline{EF}$ is parallel to $\overline{AB}$ and $\overline{CD}$ by the Three Parallel Lines Theorem (Theorem 8.8). Is your friend correct? Explain your reasoning.

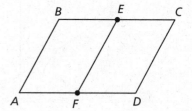

6. The figure shows a triangle such that the length of $\overline{LP}$ is nine less than twice the length of $\overline{PN}$. Do you have enough information to find LP and PN? Explain your reasoning. If so, find LP and PN.

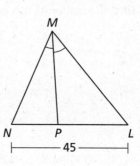

7. Use the diagram to write a two-column proof.

   Given: $\overline{WY}$ bisects $\angle XYZ$.

   $\overline{YW}$ bisects $\angle XWZ$.

   $YZ \cong WZ$

   Prove: $WXYZ$ is a kite.

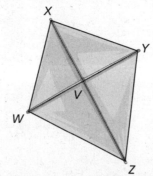

8.4 Enrichment and Extension

Proportionality Theorems

Use the diagram to find the value of each variable.

1.
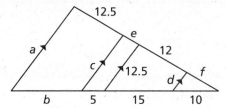

2.
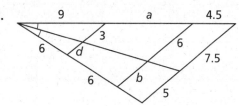

3. You take a picture of a painting at an art gallery. The painting is above eye level, and you frame the painting so the top and bottom match with the top and bottom of your view finder. Your camera's auto-focus feature focuses at the height of the angle bisector shown in the diagram. How far from the bottom of the painting is the focus?

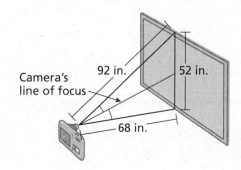

4. In the diagram, $\overline{WX} \parallel \overline{YZ}$ and $\overline{XV} \parallel \overline{ZS}$.

   a. Find the value of x.

   b. Find the value of y.

   c. Find the perimeter of $\triangle ZQS$.

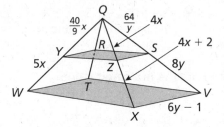

5. In $\triangle ABC$, altitude $\overline{BE}$ is extended so that EG equals the measure of altitude $\overline{CF}$. A line through G and parallel to $\overline{AC}$ meets $\overline{BA}$ at H. Prove that $AH = AC$.

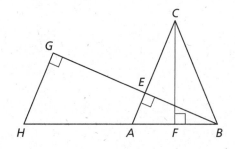

8.4 Puzzle Time

What Part Of A Car Is The Laziest?

A	B	C	D	E	F

G	

Complete each exercise. Find the answer in the answer column. Write the word under the answer in the box containing the exercise letter.

6 STOP	
perpendicular BRAKES	
parallel THE	
two SIT	
sides WHEELS	
16 TIRED	
3 AND	

Complete the sentence.

A. If a line _____ to one side of a triangle intersects the other two sides, then it divides the two sides proportionally.

B. If a line divides two _____ of a triangle proportionally, then it is parallel to the third side.

C. If _____ parallel lines intersect two transversals, then they divide the transversals proportionally.

D. If a(n) _____ bisects an angle of a triangle, then it divides the opposite side into segments whose lengths are proportional to the lengths of the other two sides.

Find the indicated value.

E. Find x.

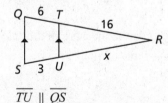

$$\overline{TU} \parallel \overline{QS}$$

F. Find c.

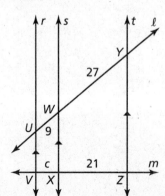

G. Find y.

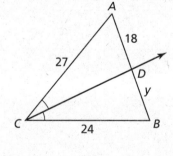

8 ARE	
line LINES	
7 ALWAYS	
angles REST	
ray THEY	
36 RUN	
three BECAUSE	

Name_____ Date_____

Cumulative Review

In Exercises 1–12, tell whether the ratios form a proportion.

1. $\dfrac{66}{48}, \dfrac{11}{6}$

2. $\dfrac{2}{3}, \dfrac{6}{9}$

3. $\dfrac{39}{15}, \dfrac{13}{5}$

4. $\dfrac{81}{73}, \dfrac{9}{7}$

5. $\dfrac{13}{24}, \dfrac{26}{35}$

6. $\dfrac{6}{19}, \dfrac{18}{57}$

7. $\dfrac{48}{24}, \dfrac{12}{6}$

8. $\dfrac{12}{10}, \dfrac{30}{25}$

9. $\dfrac{86}{98}, \dfrac{43}{47}$

10. $\dfrac{27}{63}, \dfrac{9}{12}$

11. $\dfrac{4}{25}, \dfrac{14}{85}$

12. $\dfrac{40}{62}, \dfrac{96}{155}$

In Exercises 13–27, solve the equation.

13. $x^2 = 36$

14. $x^2 = 144$

15. $x^2 = 9$

16. $x^2 + 7 = 23$

17. $x^2 + 11 = 75$

18. $x^2 + 18 = 67$

19. $x^2 - 23 = 98$

20. $x^2 - 3 = 33$

21. $x^2 - 28 = 141$

22. $5x^2 - 15 = 110$

23. $3x^2 + 18 = 210$

24. $4x^2 - 30 = 166$

25. $6x^2 - 13 = 41$

26. $2x^2 + 8 = 136$

27. $7x^2 - 41 = 526$

In Exercises 28–42, find the midpoint M of the segment with the given endpoints.

28. $J(-10, 8)$ and $K(5, -4)$

29. $C(0, 8)$ and $D(-9, -9)$

30. $T(12, 3)$ and $U(6, -11)$

31. $W(5, 0)$ and $X(5, 9)$

32. $D(10, 1)$ and $E(-2, -3)$

33. $N(-8, -12)$ and $P(7, 7)$

34. $B(6, 0)$ and $C(12, 6)$

35. $H(2, 1)$ and $J(9, 6)$

36. $R(-6, 9)$ and $S(9, -4)$

37. $K(-5, -11)$ and $L(-8, 6)$

38. $M(-3, 10)$ and $N(-2, 7)$

39. $E(10, 4)$ and $F(0, -2)$

40. $G(-5, -5)$ and $H(12, -7)$

41. $S(11, 6)$ and $T(-4, 7)$

42. $Y(-4, -9)$ and $Z(-6, 3)$

In Exercises 43–57, find the distance between the two points.

43. $W(1, -8)$ and $X(-9, 1)$

44. $L(-10, 6)$ and $M(3, -1)$

45. $G(11, 6)$ and $H(5, 11)$

46. $P(-7, 12)$ and $Q(1, -9)$

47. $S(6, 1)$ and $T(-3, -3)$

48. $C(-5, 3)$ and $D(2, -7)$

49. $B(11, 11)$ and $C(-3, 12)$

50. $F(12, 4)$ and $G(-2, -9)$

51. $M(-2, 10)$ and $N(-7, -12)$

52. $J(11, 10)$ and $K(7, 7)$

53. $D(10, 10)$ and $E(-1, -12)$

54. $K(5, -6)$ and $L(-8, 10)$

55. $R(9, 0)$ and $S(-1, -4)$

56. $N(-4, 0)$ and $P(10, -12)$

57. $T(0, 9)$ and $U(-12, -4)$

Chapter 8

Cumulative Review (continued)

In Exercises 58–64, use the diagram.

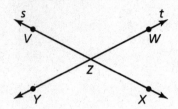

58. What is another name for $\overline{VX}$?

59. What is another name for $\overline{WY}$?

60. What is another name for ray $\overrightarrow{YW}$?

61. What is another name for ray $\overrightarrow{XV}$?

62. Name all rays with endpoint Z.

63. Name two pairs of opposite rays.

64. Name one pair of rays that are not opposite rays.

In Exercises 65–68, identify the segment bisector of $\overline{RS}$. Then find RS.

65.

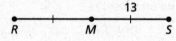

66.

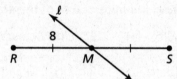

67.

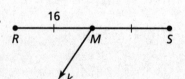

68.

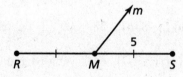

Chapter 8 **Cumulative Review** (continued)

In Exercises 69–72, identify the segment bisector of $\overline{JK}$. Then find *JK*.

69.

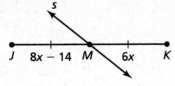

70.

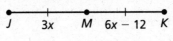

71.

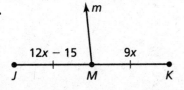

72.

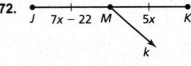

In Exercises 73–79, copy and complete the statement. State which theorem you used.

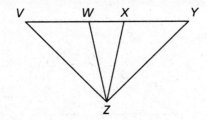

73. If $\overline{WZ} \cong \overline{XZ}$, then $\angle$____ $\cong \angle$____.

74. If $\overline{XZ} \cong \overline{XY}$, then $\angle$____ $\cong \angle$____.

75. If $\angle V \cong \angle WZV$, then ____ $\cong$ ____.

76. If $\overline{ZV} \cong \overline{ZY}$, then $\angle$____ $\cong \angle$____.

77. If $\angle ZWX \cong \angle ZXW$, then ____ $\cong$ ____.

78. If $\angle XZY \cong \angle Y$, then ____ $\cong$ ____.

79. If $\angle V \cong \angle Y$, then ____ $\cong$ ____.

Chapter 8 Cumulative Review (continued)

In Exercises 80–85, $\overline{DE}$ is a midsegment of $\triangle ABC$. Find the value of x.

80.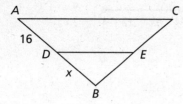

81.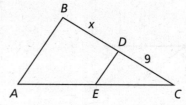

82.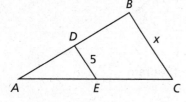

83.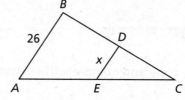

84.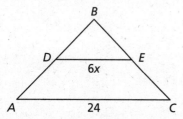

85.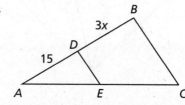

In Exercises 86 and 87, list the sides of the triangle from shortest to longest.

86.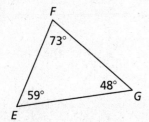

87.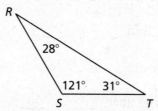

Chapter 9

Name _____ Date _____

Chapter 9
Right Triangles and Trigonometry

Dear Family,

In this chapter, your student will learn about triangles and trigonometry. Trigonometry has a rich history of applications in fields such as surveying, navigation, and astronomy. For instance, in the 19th century, India conducted the Great Trigonometric Survey, using trigonometry to measure the heights of mountains in the Himalayas.

Trigonometry can be used to measure the heights of tall objects, such as buildings and trees, without using a 60-foot-long roll of measuring tape and a cherry picker.

Find a tall tree and ask your student to look at the top of the tree. Tell your student that it is possible to estimate the height of the tree using only the distance that you are standing from the tree and the angle at which you are looking up at the tree.

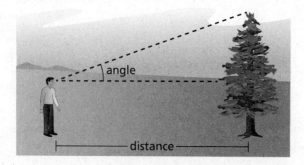

This angle can be measured using special tools, or you can make a rough estimate by considering how far you have to tilt your head to see the top of the tree. If your head is tilted halfway between looking straight forward and looking straight up, that is about 45° angle.

Have your student estimate the angle to the top of the tree and measure the distance to the tree. Your student can hold onto these measurements as motivation.

Explain that at the end of the chapter, it will be possible to use those two measurements to estimate how tall the tree is!

Have fun and stay motivated!

Nombre _____ Fecha_____

Estimada familia:

En este capítulo, su hijo aprenderá sobre triángulos y trigonometría. La trigonometría tiene una amplia historia de usos en campos tal como la agrimensura, la navegación y la astronomía. Por ejemplo, en el siglo XIX, la India llevó a cabo el Gran Proyecto de Topografía Trigonométrica, donde se usó la trigonometría para medir la altura de las montañas del Himalaya.

La trigonometría puede usarse para medir las alturas de objetos altos, tal como edificios y árboles, sin usar un rollo de cinta métrica de 60 pies de largo y una grúa.

Hallen un árbol y pidan a su hijo que mire la cima del árbol. Expliquen a su hijo que es posible estimar la altura del árbol usando solamente la distancia a la que están del árbol y el ángulo en el cual miran el árbol.

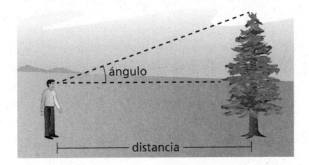

Este ángulo puede medirse usando herramientas especiales o pueden hacer una estimación aproximada si consideran cuánto tienen que inclinar la cabeza para ver la cima del árbol. Si inclinan la cabeza a mitad de camino entre mirar hacia adelante y mirar hacia arriba, es un ángulo de aproximadamente 45°.

Pidan a su hijo que estime el ángulo hasta la cima del árbol y que mida la distancia hasta el árbol. Su hijo puede aferrarse a estas mediciones como motivación.

Expliquen que cuando terminen el capítulo, ¡será posible usar estas dos mediciones para estimar la altura del árbol!

¡Diviértanse y manténganse motivados!

Draw and cut out a figure as shown in Diagram A with two connected squares. What is the area of the figure? Add segments to your figure to create two triangles as shown in Diagram B.

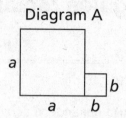

Diagram A

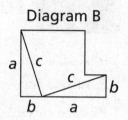

Diagram B

Cut along the hypotenuse c of each triangle so that the figure is now in three separate pieces. Reassemble the three pieces to create a square. What is the area of the square? How do your results relate to the Pythagorean Theorem?

9.1 **Warm Up**

Solve the equation.

1. $4^2 + 3^2 = x^2$

2. $13^2 + x^2 = 25^2$

3. $\left(\frac{5}{2}\right)^2 - x^2 = \left(\frac{1}{3}\right)^2$

4. $\left(9\sqrt{3}\right)^2 - x^2 = 2^2$

5. $\left(\sqrt{5}\right)^2 + x^2 = 12^2$

6. $\left(5\sqrt{10}\right)^2 - \left(\sqrt{2}\right)^2 = x^2$

9.1 **Cumulative Review Warm Up**

Find the perimeter of the polygon with the given vertices.

1. $X(-2, 1)$, $Y(4, 1)$, $Z(-2, -4)$

2. $P(3, 5)$, $Q(3, 4)$, $R(-1, 4)$, $S(-1, 5)$

3. $A(-4, 7)$, $B(3, 5)$, $C(0, 1)$

4. $T(3, 6)$, $U(-4, 6)$, $V(-1, 2)$, $W(6, 2)$

9.1 Practice A

In Exercises 1–6, find the value of *x*. Then tell whether the side lengths form a Pythagorean triple.

1.

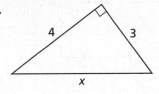

2.

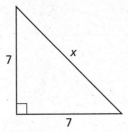

3.

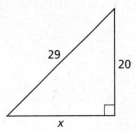

4.

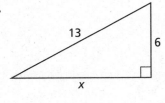

5.

6.

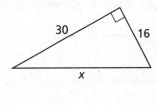

In Exercises 7 and 8, tell whether the triangle is a right triangle.

7.

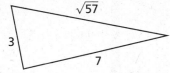

8.

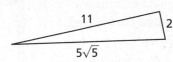

In Exercises 9–12, verify that the segment lengths form a triangle. Is the triangle *acute*, *right*, or *obtuse*?

9. 5, 12, and 13

10. 5, 7, and 8

11. 2, 10, and 11

12. $\sqrt{8}$, 4, and 6

13. A ski lift forms a right triangle, as shown. Use the Pythagorean Theorem (Theorem 9.1) to approximate the horizontal distance traveled by a person riding the ski lift. Round your answer to the nearest whole foot.

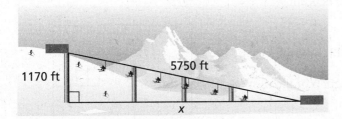

Name _____ Date _____

9.1 Practice B

In Exercises 1–3, find the value of *x*. Then tell whether the side lengths form a Pythagorean triple.

1.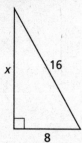

2.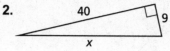

3.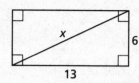

In Exercises 4 and 5, tell whether the triangle is a right triangle.

4.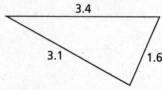

5.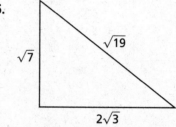

6. You construct a picture frame with a diagonal piece attached to the back for support, as shown. Can you tell from the dimensions whether the corners of the frame are right angles? Explain.

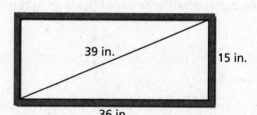

In Exercises 7–9, verify that the segment lengths form a triangle. Is the triangle *acute*, *right*, or *obtuse*?

7. 14, 48, and 50

8. 7.1, 13.3, and 19.5

9. $\sqrt{67}$, 4, and 9

10. A triangle has side lengths of 12 feet and 18 feet. Your friend claims that the third side must be greater than 6 feet. Is your friend correct? Explain.

11. The diagram shows the design of a house roof. Each side of the roof is 24 feet long, as shown. Use the Pythagorean Theorem (Theorem 9.1) to answer each question.

    a. What is the approximate width *w* of the house?

    b. What is the approximate height *h* of the roof above the ceiling?

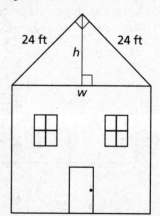

9.1 Enrichment and Extension

Pythagorean Theorem

In Exercises 1 and 2, use the diagram.

1. The dimensions of a rectangular piece of paper $ABCD$ are $AB = 10$ and $BC = 9$. It is folded so that corner D is matched with a point F on edge $\overline{BC}$. Given that $DE = 6$, find EF, EC, and FC.

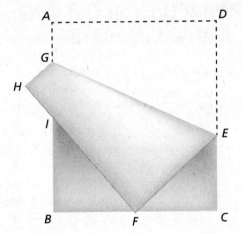

2. The lengths of $\overline{EF}$, $\overline{EC}$, and $\overline{FC}$ are all functions of length DE. The area of $\triangle EFC$ is also a function of DE. Using $DE = x$, write formulas for these four functions.

3. Find all values of k so that $(-1, 2)$, $(-10, 5)$, and $(-4, k)$ are the vertices of a right triangle.

4. Suppose the numbers a, b, and c form a Pythagorean triple. Is each of the following also always a Pythagorean triple? Explain.

   a. $a + 1, b + 1, c + 1$ b. $2a, 2b, 2c$

   c. a^2, b^2, c^2 d. $\sqrt{a}, \sqrt{b}, \sqrt{c}$

5. If $RHOM$ is a rhombus, find the value of x.

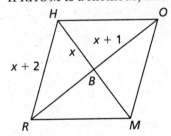

6. A pencil box in the shape of a rectangular prism measures 16 centimeters by 12 centimeters by 8 centimeters. Find the length of the longest pencil that would fit inside the box.

7. A cube-shaped bead has a length, width, and height of 2 centimeters. A hole is drilled through the bead diagonally from one corner to the opposite corner that is farthest away from it. How many of these beads must be strung together to form a length of about 5 feet? (1 in. ≈ 2.54 cm)

9.1 Puzzle Time

What Do You Get When You Cross A Computer With A Lifeguard?

Write the letter of each answer in the box containing the exercise number.

Complete the sentence.

1. In a(n) _____ triangle, the square of the length of the hypotenuse is equal to the sum of the squares of the lengths of the legs.

2. A(n) _____ triple is a set of three positive integers, a, b, and c, that satisfy the equation $c^2 = a^2 + b^2$.

3. If the square of the length of the _____ side of a triangle is equal to the sum of the squares of the lengths of the other two sides, then the triangle is a right triangle.

4. For any $\triangle ABC$, where c is the length of the longest side, if $c^2 < a^2 + b^2$, then $\triangle ABC$ is _____.

5. For any $\triangle ABC$, where c is the _____ of the longest side, if $c^2 > a^2 + b^2$, then $\triangle ABC$ is obtuse.

Find the value of x.

6. $a = 20$, $b = 99$; Find x.

7. $a = 60$, $b = 91$; Find x.

Answers	
V. 1	**B.** obtuse
S. acute	**S.** 2
N. length	**I.** angle
E. 101	**H.** special
R. right	**K.** null
U. $\sqrt{101}$	**A.** 40
M. 113	**E.** 109
O. shortest	**C.** 28
C. 36	**R.** longest
A. Pythagorean	
T. 98	**E.** 3

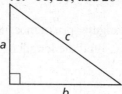

Classify the triangle as (1) acute, (2) obtuse, or (3) right, based on the given side lengths.

8. 20, 21, and 29   9. 15, 19, and 24   10. 11, 23, and 26

Find the indicated value.

11. $a = x$, $b = 45$, $c = 53$; Find x.

12. $a = 9$, $b = x$, $c = 41$; Find x.

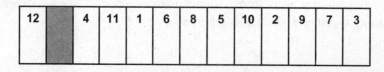

12		4	11	1	6	8	5	10	2	9	7	3

9.2 Start Thinking

Draw an equilateral triangle and label the sides 2*s*. Draw a perpendicular bisector from a vertex of the equilateral triangle to create two congruent right triangles. Find each side length of the right triangles in terms of *s*. Is it possible for the side lengths to form a Pythagorean triple? Explain.

9.2 Warm Up

Solve the equation. Write your answer in simplest form.

1. $8 = x\sqrt{2}$

2. $1.5 = x\sqrt{3}$

3. $2x = 8\sqrt{7}$

4. $5\sqrt{2} = \sqrt{3}x$

5. $\frac{9}{2} = x\sqrt{3}$

6. $8.4 = \sqrt{2}x$

9.2 Cumulative Review Warm Up

Given that the polygons are similar, find the value of *x*.

1.

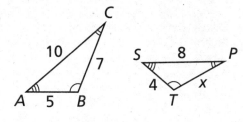

2.

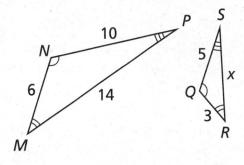

3.

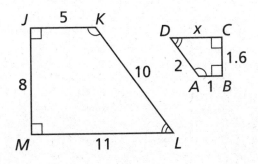

4.

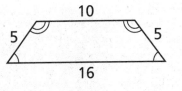

Name _____ Date _____

9.2 Practice A

In Exercises 1–3, find the value of x. Write your answer in simplest form.

1.

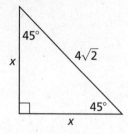

2.

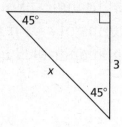

3.

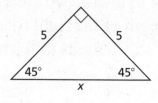

In Exercises 4–6, find the values of x and y. Write your answers in simplest form.

4.

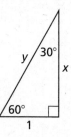

5.

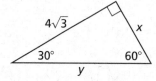

6.

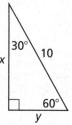

In Exercises 7 and 8, find the area of the figure. Round decimal answers to the nearest tenth.

7.

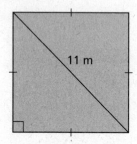

8.

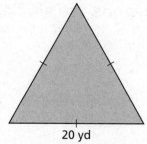

9. A 12-foot ladder is leaning up against a wall, as shown. How high does the ladder reach up the wall when x is 30°? 45°? 60°? Round decimal answers to the nearest tenth, if necessary.

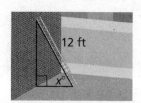

9.2 Practice B

In Exercises 1 and 2, copy and complete the table. Write your answers in simplest form.

1.

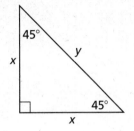

x	5		$\sqrt{2}$	
y		$4\sqrt{2}$		24

2.

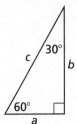

a	11			
b		9		$5\sqrt{3}$
c			16	

3. The side lengths of a triangle are given. Determine whether each triangle is a *45°-45°-90° triangle*, a *30°-60°-90° triangle*, or *neither*.

    a. $5, 10, 5\sqrt{3}$ **b.** $7, 7, 7\sqrt{3}$ **c.** $6, 6, 6\sqrt{2}$

In Exercises 4–6, find the values of the variables. Write your answers in simplest form.

4.

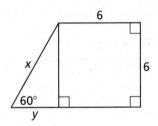

5.

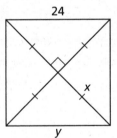

6.

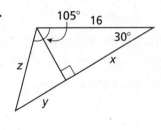

7. You build a two-person tent, as shown. How many square feet of material is needed to make the tent, assuming the tent has a floor?

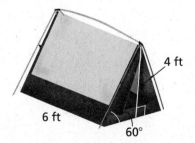

9.2 Enrichment and Extension

Special Right Triangles

1. Find the values of *s, v, w, x, y,* and *z.*

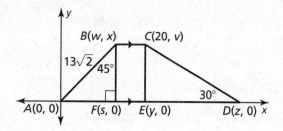

2. *ABCD* is a rectangle. *AB* = 1, and $\overline{BE}$ and $\overline{BD}$ trisect ∠*ABC*. What is the perimeter of △*BED*?

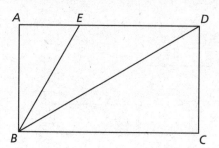

3. The circumference of a circle *J* is 14π. What is the value of *x*?

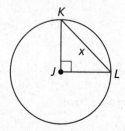

4. The area of semicircle *D* is 18π. What is the perimeter of △*ABC*?

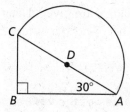

5. A circle with radius $\sqrt{2}$ is centered at the origin in a coordinate plane. How many points *P*(*x, y*) can be found on the circle, such that *x* and *y* are integers? Find the coordinates of the points.

6. In the diagram below, *YZ* = 4. Find the side lengths of △*VWX*, a 15°-75°-90° triangle. Round decimal answers to the nearest hundredth.

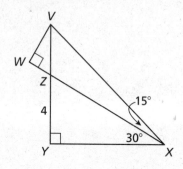

7. In the diagram below, *CD* = $\sqrt{3}$. Find the side lengths of △*BCD*, a 15°-75°-90° triangle. Round decimal answers to the nearest hundredth, when necessary.

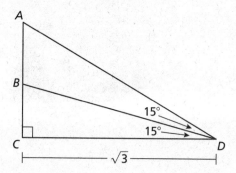

Name_____ Date_____

Puzzle Time

What Is Always In Its House, No Matter Where It Goes?

Circle the letter of each correct answer in the boxes below. The circled letters will spell out the answer to the riddle.

Complete the sentence.

1. In a 45°-45°-90° triangle, the hypotenuse is _____ times as long as each leg.

2. A 45°-45°-90° triangle is a(n) _____ right triangle that can be formed by cutting a square in half.

3. In a 30°-60°-90° triangle, the hypotenuse is twice as long as the shorter leg, and the longer leg is _____ times as long as the shorter leg.

Find the value of *x*. Write your answer in simplest radical form.

4.

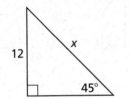

5.

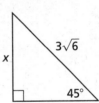

6.

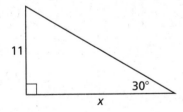

7.

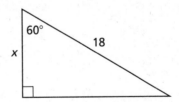

A	L	A	T	E	U	R
$12\sqrt{2}$	$18\sqrt{3}$	3	$\sqrt{2}$	acute	9	$3\sqrt{3}$
T	L	O	V	E	N	Y
$11\sqrt{3}$	$\sqrt{3}$	4	$12\sqrt{3}$	isosceles	2	$11\sqrt{2}$

9.3 Start Thinking

In the diagram below, $\overline{CD}$ is an altitude to the hypotenuse of $\triangle ABC$.

1. **Prove:** $\triangle ABC \sim \triangle ACD$

2. **Prove:** $\triangle ABC \sim \triangle CBD$

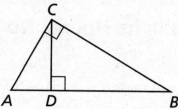

3. Use the information from the two proofs to make a conclusion about the two smaller triangles in the diagram.

9.3 Warm Up

Given that the triangles are similar, find the missing side length.

1.

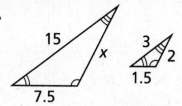

2.

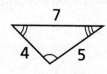

3.

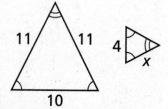

4.

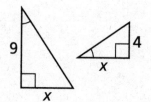

9.3 Cumulative Review Warm Up

Use the diagram to find $m\angle 1$ and $m\angle 2$.

1.

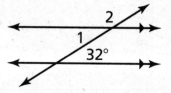

2.

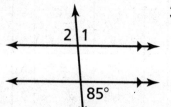

3.

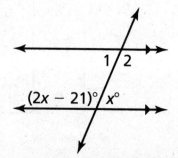

9.3 Practice A

In Exercises 1 and 2, identify the similar triangles.

1.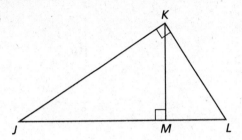

2.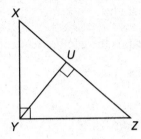

In Exercises 3–5, find the value of x.

3.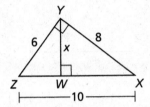

4.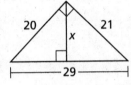

5.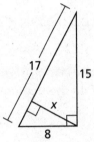

In Exercises 6–8, find the geometric mean of the two numbers.

6. 3 and 12

7. 4 and 14

8. 10 and 24

In Exercises 9–11, find the value of x.

9.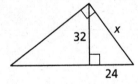

10.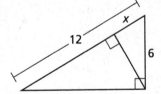

11.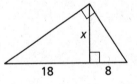

12. You are designing a diamond-shaped kite. You know that $AB = 38.4$ centimeters, $BC = 72$ centimeters, and $AC = 81.6$ centimeters. You want to use a straight crossbar $\overline{BD}$. About how long should it be?

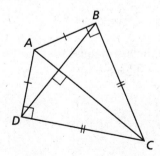

Name_____ Date _____

In Exercises 1–3, use the diagram.

1. Identify the similar triangles.

2. Which segment's length is the geometric mean of AB and DB?

3. Find CD, AD, and AC.

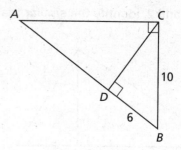

In Exercises 4–6, find the value of x.

4.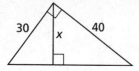

5.

6.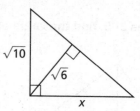

In Exercises 7–9, find the geometric mean of the two numbers.

7. 12 and 24

8. 16 and 25

9. $\frac{1}{2}$ and 40

In Exercises 10–12, find the value(s) of the variable(s).

10.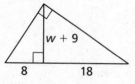

11.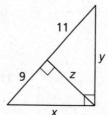

12.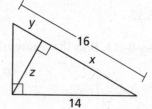

13. You build a cornhole game. The game is constructed from a sheet of plywood supported by two boards. The two boards form a right angle and their lengths are 12 inches and 46.5 inches.

    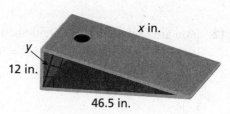

    a. Find the length x of the plywood to the nearest inch.

    b. You put in a support that is altitude y to the hypotenuse of the right triangle. What is the length of the support? Round your answer to the nearest tenth.

    c. Where does the support attach to the plywood? Explain.

9.3 Enrichment and Extension

Geometric Mean

1. In right triangle RST, altitude $\overline{SU}$ is drawn to the hypotenuse $\overline{RT}$, $RS = 8$, and the ratio of RU to UT is 1 to 3. What is the length of $\overline{RT}$?

2. In right triangle ABC, altitude $\overline{BD}$ is drawn to hypotenuse $\overline{AC}$. If $AD = 5$ and $BC = 2\sqrt{21}$, find the length of $\overline{DC}$, $\overline{BD}$, and $\overline{AB}$.

3. The *harmonic mean* of a and b is $\dfrac{2ab}{a+b}$. The Greek mathematician Pythagoras found that three equally taut strings on stringed instruments will sound harmonious if the length of the middle string is equal to the harmonic mean of the lengths of the shortest and longest string.

   a. Find the harmonic mean of 10 and 15.

   b. Find the harmonic mean of 6 and 14.

   c. Will equally taut strings whose lengths have the ratio of $4 : 6 : 12$ sound harmonious? Explain your reasoning.

4. In polygon $PQRS$ at the right, $PQ = PS$ and $QR = SR$. Find PR and QS.

In Exercises 5 and 6, the vertices of △ABC are given. Use the point-slope formula to find the coordinates of a point D such that $\overline{CD}$ is the altitude to the hypotenuse.

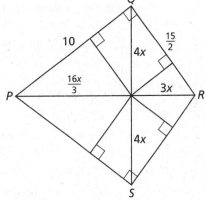

5. $A(-1, 1)$, $B(1, -1)$, $C(1, 1)$

6. $A(2, 0)$, $B(-2, 8)$, $C(2, 8)$

7. Square $ABCD$ in the diagram at the right has side lengths of 1, and the midpoints of its sides are labeled P, Q, R, and S. Find the length of a side of the shaded square.

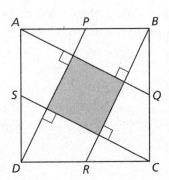

Name _____ Date _____

9.3 Puzzle Time

Why Did The Forest Ranger Change Jobs?

A	B	C	D	E	F
G	H	I			

Complete each exercise. Find the answer in the answer column. Write the word under the answer in the box containing the exercise letter.

26.5 **LEAF**	
bisector **WAS**	
geometric **HE**	
9.1 **TIME**	
15.5 **TO**	
△CDB **WANTED**	
18.8 **FOREST**	
7.1 **OVER**	
27.6 **END**	

Complete the sentence.

A. If the _____ is drawn to the hypotenuse of a right triangle, then the two triangles formed are similar to the original triangle and to each other.

B. In a right triangle, the altitude from the right angle to the hypotenuse divides the hypotenuse into two segments. The length of the altitude is the _____ mean of the lengths of the two segments.

C. Identify the smallest similar triangle using the diagram for $\triangle ABC$.

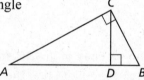

Find x. Round your answer to the nearest tenth.

D. $AC = 63$, $AB = 16$, $CB = 65$

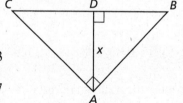

E. $AC = 12$, $AB = 5$, $CB = 13$

F. $AC = 15$, $AB = 8$, $CB = 17$

Find the geometric mean of the two numbers. Round your answer to the nearest tenth.

G. 15 and 24

H. 18 and 30

I. 20 and 35

length **THE**	
23.2 **NEW**	
△BCD **GRASS**	
altitude **BECAUSE**	
16.5 **GREENER**	
23.1 **WITH**	
4.6 **TURN**	
5.4 **TREE**	
19.0 **A**	

9.4 Start Thinking

Use a ruler and a protractor to draw three right triangles as shown in the diagrams below. Make one hypotenuse exactly 3 inches, one exactly 4 inches, and the other exactly 5 inches. Use a ruler to find the measures of the remaining sides of each triangle. Determine the value of each of the ratios below. Compare the ratios and make a conjecture about them in general, for any 30°-60°-90° triangle.

1. $\dfrac{y_1}{x_1}$　　　　**2.** $\dfrac{y_2}{x_2}$　　　　**3.** $\dfrac{y_3}{x_3}$

　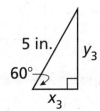

9.4 Warm Up

Find the measure of the missing leg in the right triangle, and then calculate the ratio $\dfrac{y_1}{x_1}$.

1.
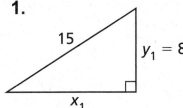

2.
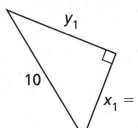

3.
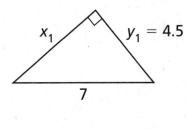

9.4 Cumulative Review Warm Up

Draw a segment with the given length. Construct the point that divides the segment into the given ratio.

1. 4 in.; 2 to 3　　　**2.** 7 cm; 1 to 4　　　**3.** 12 cm; 3 to 5

Name _____ Date _____

9.4 Practice A

1. Find the tangents of the acute angles in the right triangle. Write each answer as a fraction and as a decimal rounded to four decimal places.

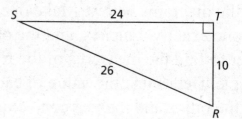

2. Describe and correct the error in writing the statement of the tangent ratio for the given figure.

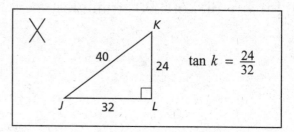

In Exercises 3–8, find the value of *x*. Round your answer to the nearest tenth.

3.

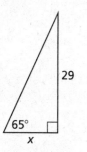

4.

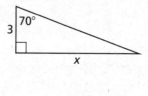

5.

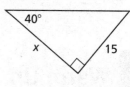

6.

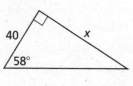

7.

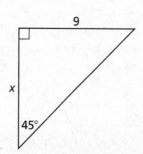

8.

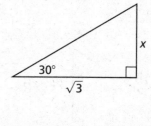

9. You are measuring the height of a water slide. You stand 58 meters from the base of the slide. You measure the angle of elevation from the ground to the top of the water slide to be 13°. Find the height *h* of the slide to the nearest meter.

Name_____ Date _____

In Exercises 1 and 2, find the tangents of the acute angles in the right triangle.
Write each answer as a fraction and as a decimal rounded to four decimal places.

1.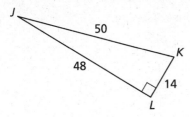

2.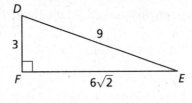

3. Draw and label the sides and angles of a triangle for which the tangents of the
acute angles are equal to 1.

In Exercises 4–6, find the value(s) of the variable(s). Round your answer(s) to the
nearest tenth.

4.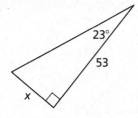

5.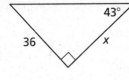

6.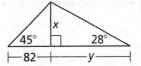

7. A surveyor is standing 30 feet from the base of a tall building. The surveyor
measures the angle of elevation from the ground to the top of the building to
be 65°. Find the height h of the building to the nearest foot.

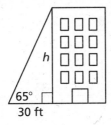

8. In the diagram, $\overline{RQ} \perp \overline{PQ}$, $m\angle QPS = 32°$, $m\angle RPS = 24°$, and $PQ = 14$.
Find RS to the nearest tenth of a unit.

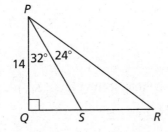

9.4 Enrichment and Extension

The Tangent Ratio

1. Quadrilateral *ABCD* is a rhombus. Given that $AC = 10$ and $BD = 16$, find all side lengths and angle measures in the figure below. Explain your reasoning.

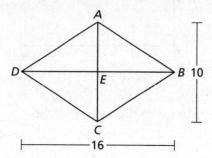

In Exercises 2–4, use the diagram.

2. Write an equation for $\tan x°$ and an equation for $\tan(90° - x°)$ in terms of a, b, and c.

3. How are the expressions in Exercise 2 related?

4. For what value of x is the relationship in Exercise 3 between the tangent of an angle and the tangent of the angle's complement true? Explain.

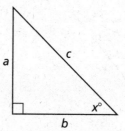

5. What is the perimeter of an equilateral triangle with an altitude of 15 inches? Round your answer to the nearest hundredth.

6. In the diagram at the right, $AC = 42$. What is *AD*? Round your answer to the nearest tenth.

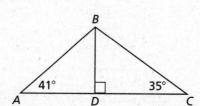

7. Explain how you can use the special right triangle below to show that $\tan a° + \tan b° \neq \tan(a° + b°)$.

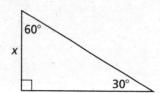

8. Find the measure of the acute angle formed by the intersecting lines $3x + 2y = 12$ and $x - 2y = -2$, to the nearest tenth of a degree.

Name_____ Date_____

9.4 Puzzle Time

What Exam Does An Exterminator Have To Take?

Write the letter of each answer in the box containing the exercise number.

Complete the sentence.

1. A(n) _____ of the lengths of two sides in a right triangle is called a trigonometric ratio.

2. The tangent ratio is a(n) _____ for acute angles that involves the lengths of the legs of a right triangle.

3. The angle that an upward line of sight makes with a line drawn horizontally is called the angle of _____.

4. The _____ is the ratio of the leg opposite a given angle to the leg adjacent to the given angle in a right triangle.

Use the diagram. Round your answer to the nearest tenth.

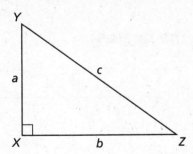

5. $a = 10$, $b = 15$, $c = 5\sqrt{13}$; Find the tangent of $\angle Z$.

6. $a = 10$, $b = 15$, $c = 5\sqrt{13}$; Find the tangent of $\angle Y$.

7. $a = 18$, $m\angle Y = 42°$; Find b.

8. $b = 22$, $m\angle Z = 30°$; Find a.

9. $b = 28$, $m\angle Y = 64°$; Find a.

Answers

O. geometric ratio

T. tangent

A. 0.7

N. side

P. ratio

T. hypotenuse

S. 13.7

H. 1.1

E. 0.1

S. trigonometric ratio

E. 1.5

R. 1.6

T. elevation

U. 22

T. 16.2

B. 28

S. depression

E. 12.7

5		1	8	2	3		7	6	9	4

9.5 Start Thinking

In Lesson 9.4, we discussed the tangent ratio which involves the two legs of a right triangle. In this lesson, we will discuss the sine and cosine ratios, which are trigonometric ratios for acute angles that involve the lengths of a leg and the hypotenuse of a right triangle. Consider what you know about the length of the hypotenuse of any right triangle. If we define the ratios as shown below, what conclusions can you make about the values of the sine and cosine of an acute angle in a right triangle?

$$\text{Sine of an acute angle} = \frac{\text{length of side opposite angle}}{\text{length of hypotenuse}}$$

$$\text{Cosine of an acute angle} = \frac{\text{length of side adjacent to angle}}{\text{length of hypotenuse}}$$

9.5 Warm Up

Find the value of x. Round your answer to the nearest tenth.

1.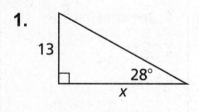

2.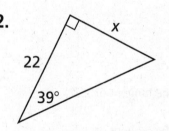

3.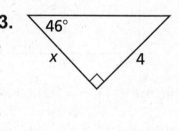

9.5 Cumulative Review Warm Up

Find the coordinates of the circumcenter of the triangle with the given vertices.

1. $A(4, 2), B(8, 5), C(8, 2)$

2. $M(3, 0), N(-2, 6), P(1, -4)$

3. $F(3, -2), D(0, 0), R(8, -4)$

4. $X(10, -3), Y(2, 7), Z(-2, -5)$

9.5 Practice A

In Exercises 1 and 2, find sin *J*, sin *K*, cos *J*, and cos *K*. Write each answer as a fraction and as a decimal rounded to four places.

1.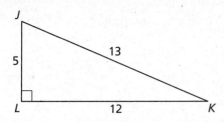

2.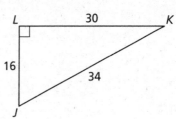

In Exercises 3–6, write the expression in terms of sine or cosine.

3. sin 22°   **4.** cos 56°   **5.** cos 15°   **6.** sin 37°

In Exercises 7–9, find the value of each variable using sine and cosine. Round your answers to the nearest tenth.

7. 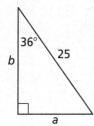   **8.** 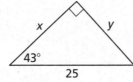   **9.**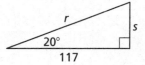

10. Which statement *cannot* be true? Explain.

  A. sin *A* = 0.5   **B.** sin *A* = 1.2654

  C. sin *A* = 0.9962   **D.** sin *A* = $\frac{3}{4}$

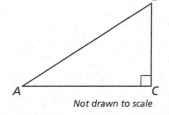

11. The angle of depression is 11° from the bottom of a boat to a deep sea diver at a depth of 120 feet. Find the distance *x* the diver must swim up to the boat to the nearest foot.

Name _____ Date _____

9.5 Practice B

In Exercises 1 and 2, find sin *R*, sin *S*, cos *R*, and cos *S*. Write each answer as a fraction and as a decimal rounded to four places.

1.
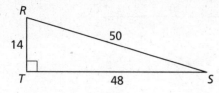

2.
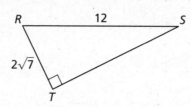

In Exercises 3–5, write the expression in terms of sine and/or cosine.

3. $\sin 7°$

4. $\cos 31°$

5. $\tan 60°$

In Exercises 6–8, find the value of each variable using sine and cosine. Round your answers to the nearest tenth.

6.
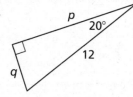

7.
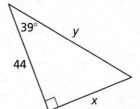

8.
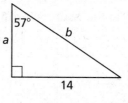

9. Find the perimeter of the figure shown. Round your answer to the nearest centimeter.

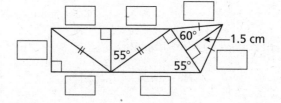

10. You use an extension ladder to repair a chimney that is 33 feet tall. The length of the extension ladder ranges in one-foot increments from its minimum length to its maximum length. For safety reasons, you should always use an angle of about 75.5° between the ground and your ladder.

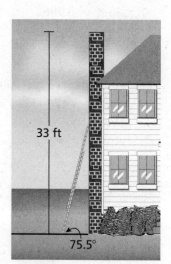

33 ft

75.5°

   a. Your smallest extension ladder has maximum length of 17 feet. How high does this ladder safely reach on the chimney? Round your answer to the nearest tenth of a foot.

   b. You place the ladder 3 feet from the base of the chimney. How many feet long should the ladder be? Round your answer to the nearest foot.

   c. To reach the top of the chimney, you need a ladder that reaches 30 feet high. How many feet long should the ladder be? Round your answer to the nearest foot.

Name_____ Date _____

The Sine and Cosine Ratios

In Exercises 1 and 2, find the missing variable(s). Round your answers to the nearest thousandths.

1.

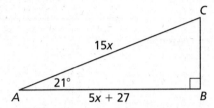

2.

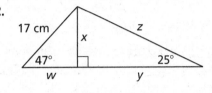

3. In right $\triangle RTX$, $\sin R = \frac{5}{13}$. If the hypotenuse of the triangle is 117 units, what is the triangle's perimeter?

4. Find the perimeter of the isosceles trapezoid. Round your answer to the nearest tenth.

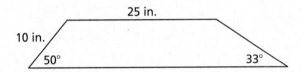

5. In right $\triangle ABC$, $m\angle B = 90°$ and $m\angle A = 30°$. What is the ratio of the longest leg to the hypotenuse?

In Exercises 6 and 7, use the diagram at the right.

6. Write an expression for $(\sin a°)^2 + (\cos a°)^2$ in terms of x, y, and z. Then use the Pythagorean Theorem (Theorem 9.1) to simplify the expression.

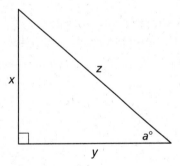

7. Suppose $\sin a° = 0.6$. What is the value of $\cos a°$?

9.5 Puzzle Time

What Is A Computer Virus?

Write the letter of each answer in the box containing the exercise number.

Complete the sentence.

1. The _____ and cosine ratios are trigonometric ratios for acute angles that involve the lengths of a leg and the hypotenuse of a right triangle.

2. The sine of an angle is equal to the _____ of its complement.

3. The cosine of an angle is equal to the sine of its _____.

4. The angle that a downward line of sight makes with a horizontal line is called the angle of _____.

Write the sine in terms of cosine.

5. $\sin 48°$ 6. $\sin 78°$ 7. $\sin 25°$

Write the cosine in terms of sine.

8. $\cos 36°$ 9. $\cos 15°$ 10. $\cos 71°$

Find the indicated value using the diagram. Round to four decimal places.

11. $a = 17$, $b = 15$, $c = 8$; Find the sine of angle X.

12. $a = 26$, $b = 10$, $c = 24$; Find the cosine of angle Z.

13. $a = 25$, $b = 24$, $c = 7$; Find the cosine of angle X.

14. $a = 15$, $b = 9$, $c = 12$; Find the sine of angle Z.

15. $a = 22$, $m\angle Z = 41°$; Find b.

16. $a = 22$, $m\angle Z = 41°$; Find c.

Answers	
L. $\sin 54°$	**M.** 14.4333
A. tangent	**M.** $\cos 48°$
N. cosine	**T.** sine
E. $\sin 19°$	**A.** $\sin 75°$
L. $\cos 12°$	**I.** 0.8000
A. 0.8824	**S.** 0.8213
S. $\cos 65°$	**S.** $\cos 42°$
O. elevation	**N.** supplement
L. 0.3846	**N.** depression
U. $\cos 35°$	**R.** 0.2800
V. $\sin 13°$	
I. complement	**E.** 16.6036
D. 0.6554	**G.** 12.7998

9		1	10	13	16	14	4	11	6		3	12	8	2	15	7	5

9.6 Start Thinking

Use the triangles shown in the diagram and the definitions
of sin θ, cos θ, and tan θ to determine the value of θ.

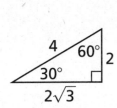

1. $\sin \theta = \dfrac{2\sqrt{3}}{4}$

2. $\cos \theta = \dfrac{3}{3\sqrt{2}}$

3. $\tan \theta = \dfrac{2}{2\sqrt{3}}$

4. $\sin \theta = \dfrac{1}{2}$

5. $\cos \theta = \dfrac{1}{2}$

6. $\tan \theta = 1$

9.6 Warm Up

Find the value of *x*. Then find the value of sin θ, cos θ,
and tan θ for the triangle.

1.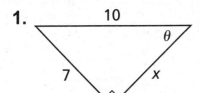

2.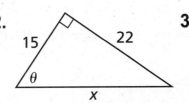

3.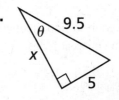

9.6 Cumulative Review Warm Up

Decide whether you can use the given information to
prove $\triangle ABC \cong \triangle XYZ$. Explain your reasoning.

1. $\angle A \cong \angle X$, $\angle Z \cong \angle C$, $\overline{BC} \cong \overline{YZ}$

2. $\angle Y \cong \angle B$, $\angle A \cong \angle X$, $\angle Z \cong \angle C$

3. $\overline{CA} \perp \overline{AB}$, $\overline{ZX} \perp \overline{XY}$, $\overline{CB} \cong \overline{ZY}$, $\overline{YX} \cong \overline{BA}$

9.6 Practice A

In Exercises 1–3, determine which of the two acute angles has the given trigonometric ratio.

1. The sine of the angle is $\frac{8}{17}$.

2. The cosine of the angle is $\frac{15}{17}$.

3. The tangent of the angle is $\frac{15}{8}$.

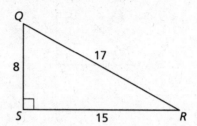

In Exercises 4–6, let $\angle B$ be an acute angle. Use a calculator to approximate the measure of $\angle B$ to the nearest tenth of a degree.

4. $\sin B = 0.64$

5. $\cos B = 0.12$

6. $\tan B = 2.18$

In Exercises 7–9, solve the right triangle. Round decimal answers to the nearest tenth.

7.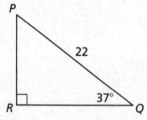

8.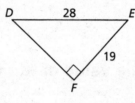

9.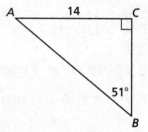

10. Use the diagram to find the distance across the suspension bridge. Round your answer to the nearest foot.

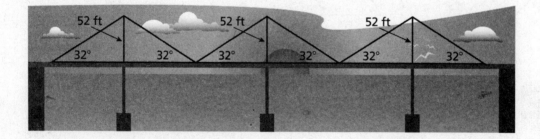

11. Use the diagram to find the acute angle formed by Washington Boulevard and Willow Way. Round your answer to the nearest tenth.

9.6 Practice B

In Exercises 1 and 2, determine which of the two acute angles has the given trigonometric ratio.

1. The cosine of the angle is $\dfrac{3}{4}$.

2. The tangent of the angle is $\dfrac{3\sqrt{7}}{7}$.

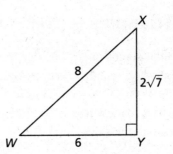

In Exercises 3–5, let ∠H be an acute angle. Use a calculator to approximate the measure of ∠H to the nearest tenth of a degree.

3. $\sin H = 0.41$

4. $\cos H = 0.05$

5. $\tan H = 5.18$

In Exercises 6–8, solve the right triangle. Round decimal answers to the nearest tenth.

6.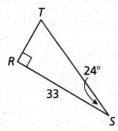

7.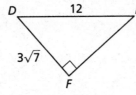

8.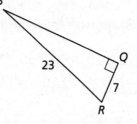

9. You are in a hot air balloon that is 600 feet above the ground. You can see two people. The angles of depression to person B and to person C are $30°$ and $20°$, respectively.

   a. How far is person B from the point on the ground below the hot air balloon?

   b. How far is person C from the point on the ground below the hot air balloon?

   c. How far apart are the two people?

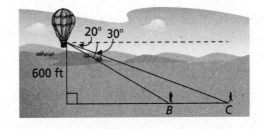

10. On a *typographic map,* the contour lines show changes in elevation of the land. You and a friend are hiking on Kasatochi Island.

    a. Find the difference in elevation (in miles) between you and your friend.

    b. Use a ruler to find the horizontal distance (in miles) between you and your friend.

    c. What is the angle of elevation from you to your friend?

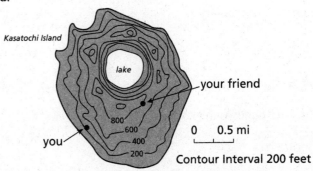

9.6 Enrichment and Extension

Solving Right Triangles

1. A vertical stone pillar stands on a slope that makes a 22° angle with the horizontal. At a time of the day when the angle of elevation of the sun is 62°, the stone pillar casts a shadow that is 20.5 meters long as measured along the slope.

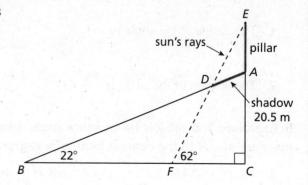

a. Find $m\angle DEA$.

b. Find $m\angle EDA$.

c. Find $m\angle DAE$.

Aside from the trigonometric functions, sine, cosine, and tangent, we can also use the functions *cosecant*, *secant,* and *cotangent* when describing the ratios of sides in a right triangle. The functions are defined as:

Cosecant, denoted as $\csc \theta = \dfrac{1}{\sin \theta} = \dfrac{\text{hyp}}{\text{opp}}$

Secant, denoted as $\sec \theta = \dfrac{1}{\cos \theta} = \dfrac{\text{hyp}}{\text{adj}}$

Cotangent, denoted as $\cot \theta = \dfrac{1}{\tan \theta} = \dfrac{\text{adj}}{\text{opp}}$

In Exercises 2–4, write the following trigonometric ratios for the triangle to the right.

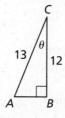

2. $\csc \theta$

3. $\sec \theta$

4. $\cot \theta$

In Exercises 5–7, find the measure of the acute angle. Round to the nearest tenth, if necessary.

5. $\csc \theta = 2$ 6. $\sec \theta = \dfrac{7}{5}$ 7. $\cot \theta = \dfrac{15}{4}$

8. In right triangle RST, $\angle S$ is the right angle, and $\sec T = \dfrac{14}{5}$. Find $m\angle R$.

Round your answer to the nearest tenth.

Name_____ Date _____

9.6 Puzzle Time

What Is The Worst Thing To Make In Pottery Class?

Circle the letter of each correct answer in the boxes below. The circled letters will spell out the answer to the riddle.

Complete the following.

1. The inverses of the trigonometric ratios sine, cosine, and tangent permit you to find the measurement of an angle. True or false?

2. To solve a right _____ means to find the measures of all of its sides and angles.

3. You can solve a right triangle when you know either of the following: (1) two side lengths; (2) one side length and the measure of one acute angle. Yes or no?

Determine which of the two acute angles has the given trigonometric ratio.

4. The cosine of the angle is $\frac{8}{13}$.

5. The sine of the angle is $\frac{8}{13}$.

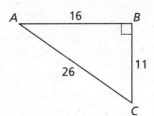

Let ∠A, ∠B, and ∠C be acute angles. Use a calculator to approximate the measures of the indicated angle to the nearest tenth of a degree.

6. $m\angle B = \tan^{-1} 0.52$

7. $m\angle A = \sin^{-1} 0.38$

8. $m\angle C = \cos^{-1} 0.74$

S	H	M	U	S	I	N	S
no	∠B	triangle	27.7	false	22.3	angle	∠A
T	**N**	**A**	**K**	**R**	**E**	**S**	**E**
27.5	33.5	42.3	true	22.6	yes	∠C	42.4

9.7 Start Thinking

Use the triangle in the diagram to find the value of each ratio. How do the three ratios relate? Do you think this relationship would be the same if the triangle was not a right triangle?

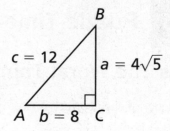

1. $\dfrac{a}{\sin A}$

2. $\dfrac{b}{\sin B}$

3. $\dfrac{c}{\sin C}$

9.7 Warm Up

Solve the proportion. Round your answer to the nearest tenth.

1. $\dfrac{a}{\sin 28°} = \dfrac{21}{\sin 65°}$

2. $\dfrac{15}{\sin 40°} = \dfrac{c}{\sin 94°}$

3. $\dfrac{b}{\sin 9°} = \dfrac{63}{\sin 105°}$

4. $\dfrac{54}{\sin B} = \dfrac{61}{\sin 73°}$

5. $\dfrac{16}{\sin 81°} = \dfrac{15}{\sin A}$

6. $\dfrac{110}{\sin C} = \dfrac{85}{\sin 36°}$

9.7 Cumulative Review Warm Up

Find the measures of $\angle X$ and $\angle Z$.

1.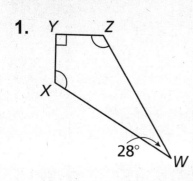

2.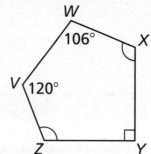

3.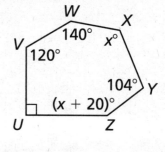

Name_____ Date_____

9.7 Practice A

In Exercises 1–3, use a calculator to find the trigonometric ratio. Round your answer to four decimal places.

1. $\cos 115°$

2. $\tan 95°$

3. $\sin 148°$

In Exercises 4 and 5, find the area of the triangle. Round your answer to the nearest tenth.

4.

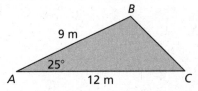

5.

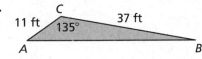

6. Place each triangle case into one of the three categories according to the first step in solving the triangle.

Law of Sines	Law of Cosines	Neither

AAA   AAS   ASA   SSS   SSA   SAS

In Exercises 7–12, solve the triangle. Round decimal answers to the nearest tenth.

7.

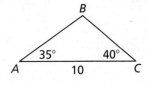

8.

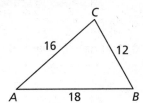

9.

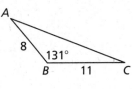

10.

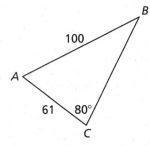

11.

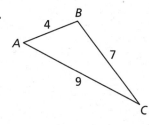

12.

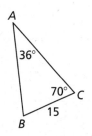

13. Determine the measure of angle A in the design of the streetlamp shown in the diagram.

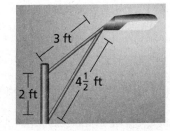

Name_____ Date _____

9.7 Practice B

In Exercises 1–3, use a calculator to find the trigonometric ratio. Round your answer to four decimal places.

1. tan 133°

2. cos 128°

3. sin 91°

In Exercises 4 and 5, find the area of the triangle. Round your answer to the nearest tenth.

4.
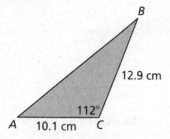

5.
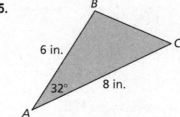

6. A parking lot has the shape of a parallelogram, as shown. Explain how you can find the area of the parking lot without using right triangles. Then find the area of the parking lot.

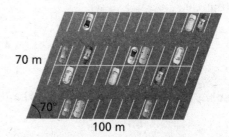

In Exercises 7–12, solve the triangle. Round decimal answers to the nearest tenth.

7.
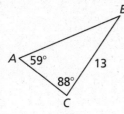

8.
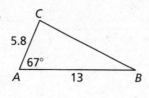

9.
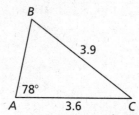

10.
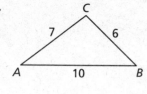

11.
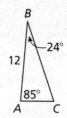

12.
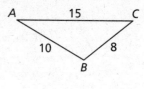

13. A bike frame has a top tube length of 20.75 inches, a seat tube length of 8.9 inches, and a seat tube angle of 71°.

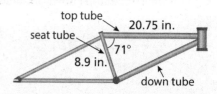

  a. Find the approximate length of the down tube.

  b. Find the angle between the seat tube and down tube.

Name_____ Date_____

Law of Tangents

In addition to the Law of Sines and the Law of Cosines, there is another formula, the *Law of Tangents*, that can be used to solve the missing sides and angles of a triangle.

The Law of Tangents can be written as

$$\frac{a+b}{a-b} = \frac{\tan\dfrac{A+B}{2}}{\tan\dfrac{A-B}{2}} \quad \text{or} \quad \frac{a-b}{a+b} = \frac{\tan\dfrac{A-B}{2}}{\tan\dfrac{A+B}{2}},$$

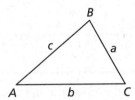

where a and b are arbitrary sides and A and B are arbitrary angles.

Example: Solve the triangle to the right using the Law of Tangents.

Solution: Because $A + B + C = 180°$,

$$A + B = 180° - C = 180° - 96° = 84°,$$

$$\text{so, } \frac{A+B}{2} = 42°.$$

$$\frac{a-b}{a+b} = \frac{\tan\dfrac{A-B}{2}}{\tan\dfrac{A+B}{2}} = \frac{5-3}{5+3} = \frac{\tan\dfrac{A-B}{2}}{\tan 42°} \qquad \text{Substitution}$$

$$\frac{2}{8}\tan 42° = \tan\frac{A-B}{2} \qquad \text{Multiply each side by } \tan 42°.$$

$$0.2251 = \tan\frac{A-B}{2} \qquad \text{Simplify.}$$

$$12.7° = \frac{A-B}{2} \qquad \text{Take the inverse of each side.}$$

$$25.4° = A - B \qquad \text{Multiply each side by 2.}$$

Using the equations $A - B = 25.4°$ and $A + B = 84°$, and solving the systems of equations, you have $A = 54.7°$ and $B = 29.3°$. You can find the remaining side c by using the Law of Sines: $\dfrac{c}{\sin C} = \dfrac{a}{\sin A} \rightarrow c = \dfrac{a \sin C}{\sin A} = \dfrac{5 \sin 96°}{\sin 54.7°} \approx 6.09.$

In Exercise 1–3, use the Law of Tangents to solve the triangle. Round your answer to the nearest tenth.

1. In $\triangle ABC$, a is 52, b is 28, and $m\angle C = 80°$.

2. In $\triangle ABC$, c is 14, b is 9, and $m\angle A = 62°$.

3. In $\triangle ABC$, c is 20, b is 13, and $m\angle A = 66°$.

9.7 **Puzzle Time**

Why Should You Always Walk A Mile In People's Shoes Before You Criticize Them?

A	B	C	D	E	F
G	H	I	J	K	L

Complete each exercise. Find the answer in the answer column. Write the word under the answer in the box containing the exercise letter.

0.8391 FEET	
−0.8391 A	
false SOCKS	
included YOU'LL	
−0.1763 TO	
cotangent AND	
16.8 SHOES	
8.9 ROAD	
true BECAUSE	
0.9063 AND	
129.6 END	
173.7 HAVE	

Complete the sentence.

A. If $\triangle ABC$ has sides of length a, b, and c, then the following are true: $a^2 = b^2 + c^2 - 2bc \cos A$, $b^2 = a^2 + c^2 - 2ac \cos B$, and $c^2 = a^2 + b^2 - 2ab \cos C$. True or false?

B. The Law of _____ can be used to solve triangles when two sides and the included angle are known, or when all three sides are known.

C. The area of any triangle is given by one-half the product of the lengths of two sides times the sine of their _____ angle.

D. The Law of _____ can be used to solve triangles when two angles and the length of any side are known, or when the lengths of two sides and an angle opposite one of the two sides are known.

Find the trigonometric ratio. Round your answer to four decimal places.

E. tan 140°   **F.** sin 170°   **G.** cos 135°   **H.** sin 115°

Find the area of the triangle in square units. Round your answer to the nearest tenth.

I. $x = 21$, $z = 18$, $m\angle R = 44°$

J. $x = 26$, $y = 15$, $m\angle S = 63°$

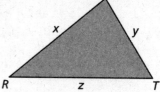

Solve for the indicated measure. Round decimal answers to the nearest tenth.

K. $x = 11$, $y = 14$, $m\angle A = 40°$; Find z.

L. $x = 15$, $y = 24$, $m\angle C = 98°$; Find z.

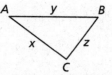

−0.4226 THE	
14.9 SO	
sines BE	
0.1736 MILE	
opposite PATH	
9.0 THEIR	
cosines THEN	
−0.7071 AWAY	
tangent HURT	
131.3 YOU'LL	
174.0 NICE	

Chapter 9 Cumulative Review

In Exercises 1–18, simplify the expression.

1. $\sqrt{108}$

2. $\sqrt{288}$

3. $\sqrt{243}$

4. $\sqrt{1440}$

5. $\sqrt{405}$

6. $\sqrt{448}$

7. $\sqrt{50}$

8. $\sqrt{112}$

9. $\sqrt{45}$

10. $\dfrac{9}{\sqrt{5}}$

11. $\dfrac{4}{\sqrt{7}}$

12. $\dfrac{7}{\sqrt{3}}$

13. $\dfrac{5}{\sqrt{11}}$

14. $\dfrac{11}{\sqrt{2}}$

15. $\dfrac{8}{\sqrt{3}}$

16. $\dfrac{2}{\sqrt{6}}$

17. $\dfrac{9}{\sqrt{3}}$

18. $\dfrac{9}{\sqrt{11}}$

In Exercises 19–30, solve the equation for x.

19. $10 = \dfrac{x}{8}$

20. $5 = \dfrac{x}{3}$

21. $16 = \dfrac{x}{7}$

22. $11 = \dfrac{x}{5}$

23. $13 = \dfrac{x}{8}$

24. $11 = \dfrac{x}{17}$

25. $3 = \dfrac{27}{x}$

26. $11 = \dfrac{22}{x}$

27. $9 = \dfrac{54}{x}$

28. $20 = \dfrac{100}{x}$

29. $6 = \dfrac{69}{x}$

30. $8 = \dfrac{58}{x}$

In Exercises 31–45, solve the proportion.

31. $\dfrac{x}{16} = \dfrac{10}{5}$

32. $\dfrac{11}{x} = \dfrac{14}{154}$

33. $\dfrac{14}{x} = \dfrac{8}{12}$

34. $\dfrac{x}{6} = \dfrac{20}{15}$

35. $\dfrac{22}{2} = \dfrac{x}{6}$

36. $\dfrac{10}{x} = \dfrac{2}{39}$

37. $\dfrac{15}{18} = \dfrac{5}{x}$

38. $\dfrac{14}{x} = \dfrac{3}{27}$

39. $\dfrac{x}{4} = \dfrac{25}{8}$

40. $\dfrac{x + 1}{4} = \dfrac{56}{32}$

41. $\dfrac{x + 3}{5} = \dfrac{49}{35}$

42. $\dfrac{x - 4}{8} = \dfrac{3}{24}$

43. $\dfrac{2x + 7}{4} = \dfrac{91}{28}$

44. $\dfrac{3x - 5}{9} = \dfrac{80}{45}$

45. $\dfrac{13}{4x - 6} = \dfrac{117}{18}$

Chapter 9

Cumulative Review (continued)

In Exercises 46–51, find the radius and diameter of the circle.

46.

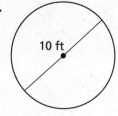

10 ft

47.

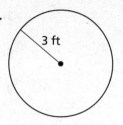

3 ft

48.

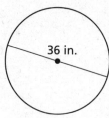

36 in.

49.

17 ft

50.

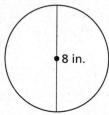

8 in.

51.

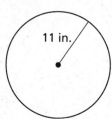

11 in.

In Exercises 52–57, find the value of x.

52.

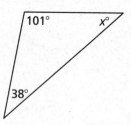

101° $x°$
38°

53.

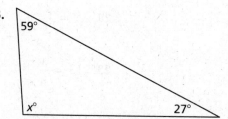

59° $x°$ 27°

54.

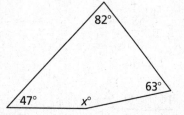

82°   63°   47° $x°$

55.

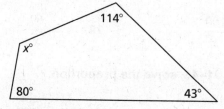

114° $x°$ 80°   43°

56.

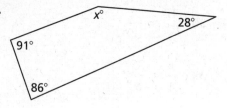

$x°$ 28°   91°   86°

57.

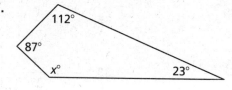

112°   87° $x°$ 23°

Chapter 9 Cumulative Review (continued)

In Exercises 58–61, classify the triangle by its sides and angles.

58.

59.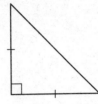

60.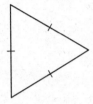

61.

In Exercises 62–65, find the value of each variable in the parallelogram.

62.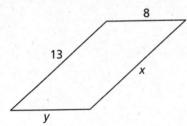

63.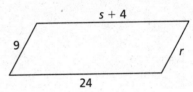

64.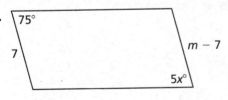

65.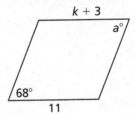

66. A piece of artwork has an equilateral triangle drawn on it. The side lengths are 10 inches, $2x$ inches, and $5y$ inches.

   a. What is the value of x?

   b. What is the value of y?

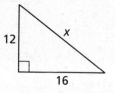

Cumulative Review (continued)

Chapter 9

In Exercises 67–72, find the value of x.

67.

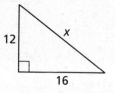

12
x
16

68.

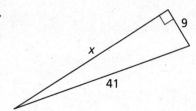

9
x
41

69.

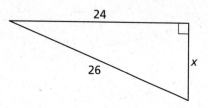

24
26
x

70.

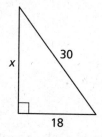

30
x
18

71.

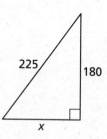

225
180
x

72.

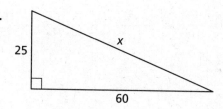

25
x
60

In Exercises 73 and 74, find the value of x. Write your answer in simplest form.

73.

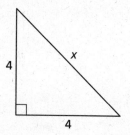

4
x
4

74.

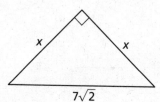

x   x
$7\sqrt{2}$

75. A mirror is in the shape of an isosceles right triangle and has leg lengths of 6 inches.

    a. What is the length of the hypotenuse?

    b. What is the perimeter of the mirror? Leave your answer including the radical.

    c. Approximate the length from part (b) to the nearest tenth.

Chapter 10

Name_____ Date _____

Dear Family,

In this chapter, your student will be learning about the relationships between lines, segments, and angles in circles. Gather these materials to investigate the relationship between the radius of a circle and a line that touches the circle at only one point:

- two toothpicks

- a circular disc (for example, a CD or a DVD)

To perform this experiment, lay the disc on a flat surface. Lay a toothpick on the disc so that one end lies at the center and the other end lies on the edge. Lay the other toothpick so that it only touches the disc at the point where the first toothpick touches the edge, as shown below.

- What angle do the toothpicks appear to make?

If you have a protractor available, measure the angle to confirm your answer. Keep one end of the first toothpick at the center of the disc and rotate the other end to another point on the edge of the disc. Lay the second toothpick using the same directions as before.

- Do the toothpicks make the same angle?

Repeat this experiment several times.

- What does your experiment suggest about the angle between the radius of a circle and a line that touches the circle at only one point?

Have fun experimenting!

Capítulo 10 Círculos

Estimada familia:

En este capítulo, su hijo aprenderá sobre las relaciones entre rectas, segmentos y ángulos en los círculos. Reúnan estos materiales para investigar la relación entre el radio de un círculo y una recta que toca el círculo en solo un punto:

- dos palillos de dientes
- a un disco circular (por ejemplo, un CD o un DVD)

Para llevar a cabo este experimento, coloquen el disco sobre una superficie plana. Coloquen un palillo de dientes sobre el disco de manera que un extremo quede en el centro y el otro extremo esté en el borde. Coloquen el otro palillo de manera que solo toque el disco en el punto donde el primer palillo toca el borde, como se muestra.

- ¿Qué ángulo parecen formar los palillos de dientes?

Si tienen un transportador, midan el ángulo para confirmar la respuesta. Mantengan un extremo del primer palillo en el centro del disco y roten el otro extremo hasta otro punto en el borde del disco. Coloquen el segundo palillo usando las mismas instrucciones que antes.

- ¿Los palillos forman el mismo ángulo?

Repitan este experimento varias veces.

- ¿Qué sugiere su experimento sobre el ángulo entre el radio de un círculo y una recta que toca el círculo en solo un punto?

¡Diviértanse experimentando!

10.1 Start Thinking

On a piece of graph paper, draw a circle that has a radius of 5 and center at $(0, 0)$.

1. Draw the segment that connects the points $(3, 4)$ and $(-4, -3)$ on the circle. Is this segment a diameter? Explain your answer.

2. Draw the segment that connects the point $(3, -4)$ with the origin. What is the name of this segment? Explain your answer.

3. Is it possible to draw a line that intersects the circle only once? Is it possible to draw a line that intersects the circle more than twice? If so, add an example of these lines to your drawing.

10.1 Warm Up

Find the value of *r*.

1.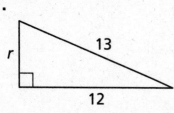

2.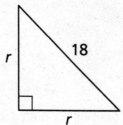

3.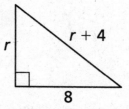

10.1 Cumulative Review Warm Up

Determine if the segment lengths form a triangle. If so, is the triangle acute, obtuse, or right?

1. 3, 7, and 9

2. 14, 7, and 20

3. $\frac{9}{2}$, 6, and $\frac{15}{2}$

4. $\frac{11}{5}$, $\frac{7}{2}$, and $\frac{19}{5}$

5. 4, 4, and 6

6. 10, 20, and 30

Name_____ Date_____

10.1 Practice A

In Exercises 1–5, use the diagram.

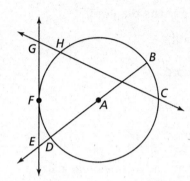

1. Name the circle.

2. Name two radii.

3. Name two chords.

4. Name a secant.

5. Name a tangent.

In Exercises 6 and 7, tell whether $\overline{AB}$ is tangent to $\odot C$. Explain your reasoning.

6.

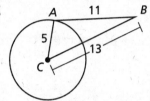

7.

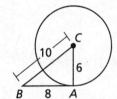

In Exercises 8 and 9, point B is a point of tangency. Find the radius r of $\odot C$.

8.

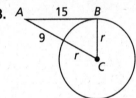

9.

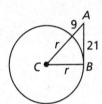

In Exercises 10 and 11, points B and D are points of tangency. Find the value(s) of x.

10.

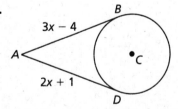

11.

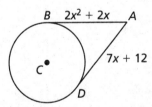

12. Construct $\odot C$ with a 1-inch radius and a point A outside of $\odot C$. Then construct a line tangent to $\odot C$ that passes through A.

13. Two sidewalks are tangent to a circular park centered at P, as shown.

    a. What is the length of sidewalk $\overline{AB}$? Explain.

    b. What is the diameter of the park?

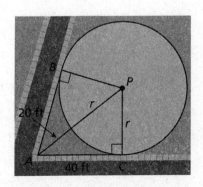

Name _____ Date _____

10.1 Practice B

In Exercises 1–5, use the diagram.

1. Name two radii.

2. Name two chords.

3. Name a diameter.

4. Name a secant.

5. Name a tangent and a point of tangency.

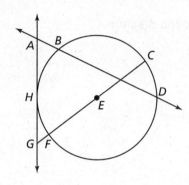

In Exercises 6 and 7, tell whether $\overline{AB}$ is tangent to $\odot C$. Explain your reasoning.

6.

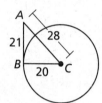

7.

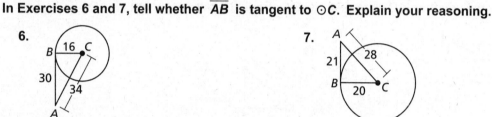

In Exercises 8 and 9, point B is a point of tangency. Find the radius r of $\odot C$.

8.

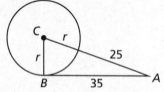

9.

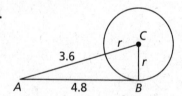

In Exercises 10 and 11, points B and D are points of tangency. Find the value(s) of x.

10.

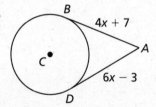

11.

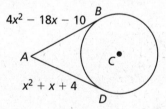

12. When will two circles have no common tangents? Justify your answer.

13. During a basketball game, you want to pass the ball to either Player A or Player B. You estimate that Player B is about 15 feet from you, as shown.

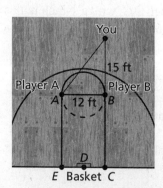

   a. How far away from you is Player A?

   b. How can you prove that Player A and Player B are the same distance from the basket?

10.1   Enrichment and Extension

Lines and Segments That Intersect Circles

1. In the figure, $\overline{AB}$ is tangent to circle C. Find the length of $\overline{DB}$.

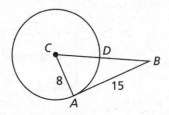

2. In the figure, $OB = 13$ and $\overline{AB}$ is tangent to circle O, whose diameter $\overline{AC}$ has
    a length of 18. Find BC.

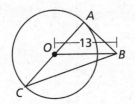

3. In the figure, $OC = 10$, $m\angle ABC = 54°$, and $\overline{BA}$ and $\overline{BC}$ are tangents
    to circle O. Find BC.

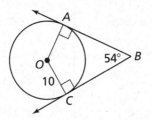

4. Write a paragraph proof for the following.

    Given: Circle G and circle H

          $\overline{IM}$ and $\overline{JL}$ are common tangents.

    Prove: $\overline{IM} \cong \overline{JL}$

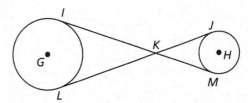

10.1 Puzzle Time

Why Did The Scientists Stay At The Math Teacher's House?

Write the letter of each answer in the box containing the exercise number.

Complete the sentence.

1. Coplanar circles that intersect in one point are called _____ circles.

2. A chord is a segment whose _____ are on a circle.

3. A diameter is a(n) _____ that contains the center of the circle.

4. A(n) _____ is a line that intersects a circle in two points.

5. A tangent is a line in the plane of a circle that intersects the circle in exactly one point, the point of _____.

6. Coplanar circles that have a common center are called _____ circles.

7. A line or segment that is tangent to two coplanar circles is called a(n) _____ tangent.

8. In a plane, a line is tangent to a circle if and only if the line is _____ to a radius of the circle at its endpoint on the circle.

9. Tangent segments from a common external point are _____.

Find the indicated answers using the diagram.

10. Given $x = 28$, $y = 45$, and $z = 53$, is $\overline{AB}$ tangent to circle C? Yes or no?

11. Find the radius y of circle C, given that $x = 12$ and $z = y + 8$.

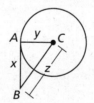

B and D are points of tangency. Find the value of x using the diagram.

12. $j = 3x + 1$, $k = 4x - 5$

13. $j = x^2 - 2x + 3$, $k = 4x - 6$

14. $j = 8x + 5$, $k = 4x + 6$

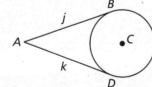

Answers	
G. yes	
B. connected	
A. lines	**I.** chord
E. common	**C.** radius
P. perpendicular	
M. cotangent	
S. tangent	**L.** urgency
E. 0.25	**H.** secant
U. consistent	**R.** 5
T. 0.5	
N. endpoints	
A. no	
W. congruent	
S. unique	**R.** parallel
A. tangency	
V. concentric	
N. 8	**R.** 2
I. 3	**M.** negative
S. 6	**D.** 7

4	14			9	5	12			1	7	11	6	13	2	10			8	3

10.2 Start Thinking

As the minute hand on a clock makes one complete revolution, we say that it has rotated 360°. What amount of time corresponds to this 360° rotation? Use this information to determine the angle the minute hand on a clock creates for the following amounts of time.

1. 30 minutes

2. 45 minutes

3. 10 minutes

4. 9 minutes

5. 48 minutes

6. 52 minutes

10.2 Warm Up

Determine the value of x for the circle graph. Pay close attention to the units.

1.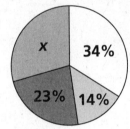

2.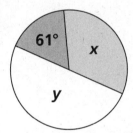

3.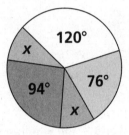

10.2 Cumulative Review Warm Up

Find the value of x that makes the quadrilateral a parallelogram.

1.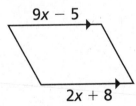

2.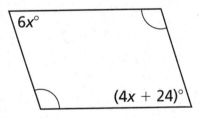

3.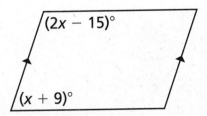

4.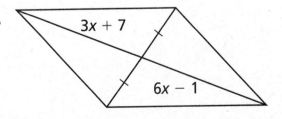

10.2 Practice A

In Exercises 1–4, identify the given arc as a *major arc*, *minor arc*, or *semicircle*. Then find the measure of the arc.

1. $\overset{\frown}{NM}$

2. $\overset{\frown}{JLM}$

3. $\overset{\frown}{NLK}$

4. $\overset{\frown}{LMN}$

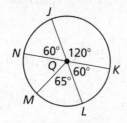

5. A recent survey asked high school girls to name the sport they like to watch the most. The results are shown in the circle graph. Find each indicated measure.

   a. $m\overset{\frown}{FG}$

   b. $m\overset{\frown}{EGB}$

   c. $m\overset{\frown}{DB}$

   d. $m\overset{\frown}{ACE}$

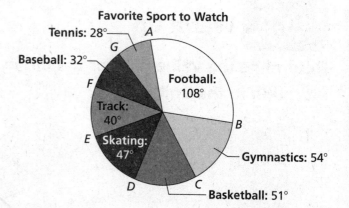

Favorite Sport to Watch

Tennis: 28°
Baseball: 32°
Football: 108°
Track: 40°
Skating: 47°
Gymnastics: 54°
Basketball: 51°

In Exercises 6 and 7, tell whether the given arcs are congruent. Explain why or why not.

6. $\overset{\frown}{EF}$ and $\overset{\frown}{GH}$

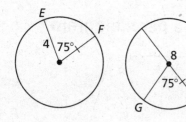

7. $\overset{\frown}{STV}$ and $\overset{\frown}{UVT}$

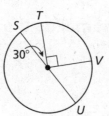

8. Each wheel shown is divided into congruent sections. Find the measure of each arc.

   a.

   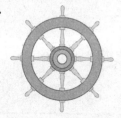

   b.

Name_____ Date _____

 Practice B

10.2

In Exercises 1–4, identify the given arc as a *major arc*, *minor arc*, or *semicircle*.
Then find the measure of the arc of ⊙*U* if $\overline{SQ}$ and $\overline{PR}$ are diameters.

1. $\overset{\frown}{QRS}$

2. $\overset{\frown}{TS}$

3. $\overset{\frown}{TPS}$

4. $\overset{\frown}{PQ}$

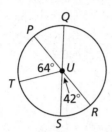

In Exercises 5–7, tell whether the given arcs are congruent. Explain why or why not.

5. $\overset{\frown}{AC}$ and $\overset{\frown}{BD}$

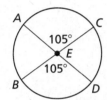

6. $\overset{\frown}{NM}$ and $\overset{\frown}{OP}$

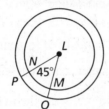

7. $\overset{\frown}{AB}$ and $\overset{\frown}{CD}$

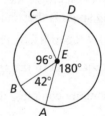

8. The spokes on a bicycle wheel divide
the wheel into congruent sections.
What is the measure of each arc in
this circle?

9. Find the measure of each arc.

a. $\overset{\frown}{AC}$

b. $\overset{\frown}{DAB}$

10. A water sprinkler covers the area shown in the figure. It moves
through the covered area at a rate of about 5° per second.

a. What is the measure of the arc covered by the sprinkler?

b. When the sprinkler starts at the far left position, how long
will it take for the sprinkler to reach the far right position?

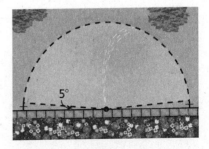

10.2 Enrichment and Extension

Finding Arc Measures

1. A company builds metal stands for bicycle wheels. A new design calls for a V-shaped stand that will hold wheels with a 13-inch radius. The sides of the stand form a 70° angle To the nearest tenth of an inch, what should the length of the side of the V-shaped stand be so that it is tangent to the wheel?

2. In the figure to the right, the diameter of circle O is 28 centimeters. The chord $\overline{AB}$ intercepts an arc whose measure is 86°. What is the length of $\overline{AB}$?

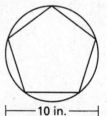

3. Your friend is wrapping 1 meter of twine around a spool with a 2-centimeter diameter. The spool is thin and accommodates only one wrap of twine before the twine stacks on top of itself. The twine has a diameter of $\frac{1}{2}$ centimeter, which increases the diameter of the spool by 1 centimeter with each wrap.

   a. Find how many complete times your friend will wrap the twine around the spool.

   b. Find the percentage of a complete circle that the last wrapping of the twine will make. Round your answer to the nearest tenth.

4. A regular pentagon is inscribed in a circle with 10-inch diameter. From the center of the circle, construct five congruent triangles.

   a. Find the measure of each central angle formed by the triangles.

   b. Using trigonometry, find the length of one side of the pentagon.

   c. Find the perimeter of the pentagon.

   d. Find the area of the pentagon.

   e. Devise a formula that can be used to find the area A of a regular n-gon given the diameter d of its circumscribed circle.

In Exercises 5–7, C is the center of the circle. Find the value of x.

5.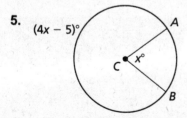

6.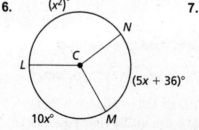

7.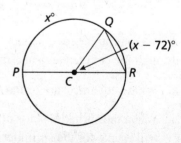

Name_____ Date_____

10.2 Puzzle Time

What Fruit Is Always In A Bad Mood?

Circle the letter of each correct answer in the boxes below. The circled letters will spell out the answer to the riddle.

Complete the sentence.

1. A(n) _____ angle of a circle is an angle whose vertex is the center of the circle.

2. The measure of a(n) _____ arc is the measure of its central angle.

3. The measure of a(n) _____ arc is the difference of 360° and the measure of the related minor arc.

4. The measure of an arc formed by two adjacent arcs is the _____ of the measures of the two arcs.

5. Two circles are congruent circles if and only if they have the same _____.

6. All circles are _____.

7. Two arcs are similar arcs if and only if they have the same _____.

Use the diagram.

8. Name the gray minor arc.

9. Name the black major arc.

10. $m\angle ACB = 72°$; Find the measure of $\overset{\frown}{ADB}$.

Use the diagram to find the measure of the arc.

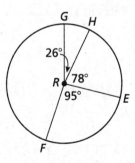

11. $\overset{\frown}{GHE}$

12. $\overset{\frown}{GFE}$

T	A	H	E	C	R	M	E	A	N	P	B
$\overset{\frown}{AB}$	concentric	central	256°	104°	288°	center point	360°	sum	108°	$\overset{\frown}{ABD}$	$\overset{\frown}{ADB}$
O	A	P	T	A	P	I	L	O	S	E	R
$\overset{\frown}{AD}$	measure	similar	congruent	single	major	difference	radius	large	199°	minor	$\overset{\frown}{AC}$

10.3 Start Thinking

Determine if the statement is always true, sometimes true, or never true. Explain your reasoning.

1. A chord is a diameter.

2. A diameter is a chord.

3. A chord and a radius have the same measure.

4. A chord is longer than a diameter.

10.3 Warm Up

Find the value of *x* given that *C* is the center of the circle and that the circle has a diameter of 12.

1.
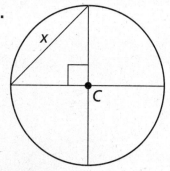

2.
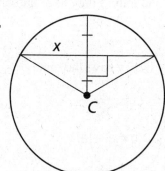

3.
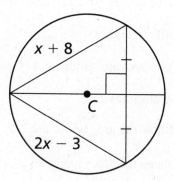

10.3 Cumulative Review Warm Up

Write a proof.

1. **Given:** *B* is the midpoint of $\overline{EC}$ and $\overline{DA}$.

   Prove: $\triangle AEB \cong \triangle DCB$

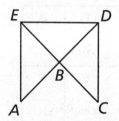

2. **Given:** $\angle BDE \cong \angle BED$
   $\angle A \cong \angle C$

   Prove: $\triangle AED \cong \triangle CDE$

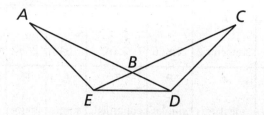

Name_____ Date_____

In Exercises 1 and 2, use the diagram of ⊙T.

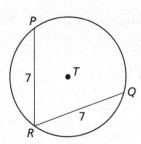

1. If $m\widehat{PQ} = 130°$, find $m\widehat{RQ}$.

2. If $m\widehat{PR} = 100°$, find $m\widehat{PQ}$.

In Exercises 3–5, find the value of x.

3.

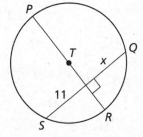

4.

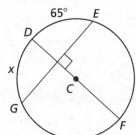

5.

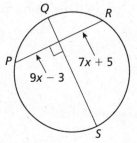

6. Determine whether $\overline{AB}$ is a diameter of each circle. Explain your reasoning.

a.

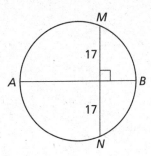

b.

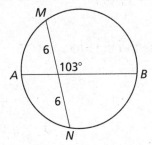

In Exercises 7–9, use the diagram to find the given length. In the diagram, QR = ST = 12.

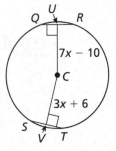

7. CU

8. UR

9. the radius of ⊙C

10. In the diagram of ⊙R, which congruence relation is *not* necessarily true?

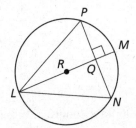

   A. $\overline{PQ} \cong \overline{QN}$ **B.** $\overline{NL} \cong \overline{LP}$

   C. $\widehat{MN} \cong \widehat{MP}$ **D.** $\widehat{PN} \cong \widehat{PL}$

Name _____ Date _____

10.3 Practice B

In Exercises 1–4, use the diagram of ⊙C.

1. Explain why $\overset{\frown}{AD} \cong \overset{\frown}{BE}$.

2. Find the value of x.

3. Find $m\overset{\frown}{AD}$ and $m\overset{\frown}{BE}$.

4. Find $m\overset{\frown}{BD}$.

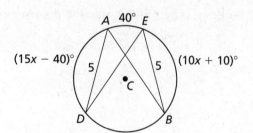

In Exercises 5–7, find the value of x.

5.

6.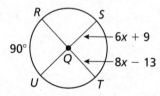

7.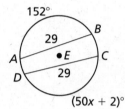

8. Determine whether $\overline{AB}$ is a diameter of the circle. Explain your reasoning.

In Exercises 9 and 10, find the radius of ⊙C.

9.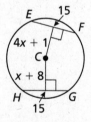

10.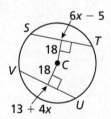

11. Copy and complete the proof.

    Given: $\overline{PQ}$ is a diameter of ⊙U.

    $\overset{\frown}{PT} \cong \overset{\frown}{QS}$

    Prove: $\triangle PUT \cong \triangle QUS$

    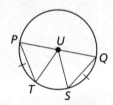

STATEMENTS	REASONS
1. $\overline{PQ}$ is a diameter of ⊙U.	1. _____
2. _____	2. Congruent Corresponding Chords Theorem (Thm. 10.6)
3. $\overline{UP} \cong \overline{UQ} \cong \overline{UT} \cong \overline{US}$	3. _____
4. $\triangle PUT \cong \triangle QUS$	4. _____

12. Briefly explain what other congruence theorem you could use to prove that $\triangle PUT \cong \triangle QUS$ in Exercise 11.

10.3 Enrichment and Extension

Using Chords of Circles

In Exercises 1–6, give the degree measure of the arc intercepted by the chord described. Round to the nearest tenth, if necessary.

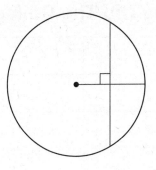

1. a chord congruent to the radius

2. a chord one-third the length of the radius

3. a chord congruent to the segment from the center to the chord

4. a chord twice the length of the segment from the center to the chord

5. a chord one-fourth the length of the circumference

6. a chord with length $\frac{1}{\pi}$ times the length of the circumference

7. $\overline{PQ}$ is a chord of a circle with center O. $\overline{OA}$ intersects $\overline{PQ}$ at R.
   If $PR = 1.5$ and the measure of $\overparen{PQ} = 80°$, is PQ necessarily 3?
   Is the measure of $\overparen{PA}$ 40°? If not, sketch a counterexample.

8. $\overline{AB}$ is the diameter of circle O, as shown. P is a point such that
   $PA = 9$ and $PB = 25$. Find the length of the shortest chord
   through point P.

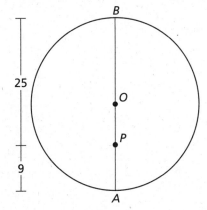

10.3 Puzzle Time

Why Did The College Give A Baby Ghost A Scholarship?

A	B	C	D	E	F
G	H	I	J		

Complete each exercise. Find the answer in the answer column. Write the word under
the answer in the box containing the exercise letter.

Complete the sentence.

A. A(n) _____ is a segment with endpoints on a circle.

B. In the same circle, or in congruent circles, two minor arcs are congruent if and only if their _____ chords are congruent.

C. If a diameter of a circle is perpendicular to a chord, then the diameter _____ the chord and its arc.

D. If one chord of a circle is a(n) _____ bisector of another chord, then the first chord is a diameter.

E. In the same circle, or in congruent circles, two chords are congruent if and only if they are _____ from the center.

F. A diameter divides a circle into two congruent _____.

Find the measure of the given arc or chord in ⊙C.

G. $\overset{\frown}{AB}$

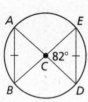

H. $\overline{UV}$

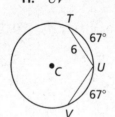

I. $\overline{QR}$

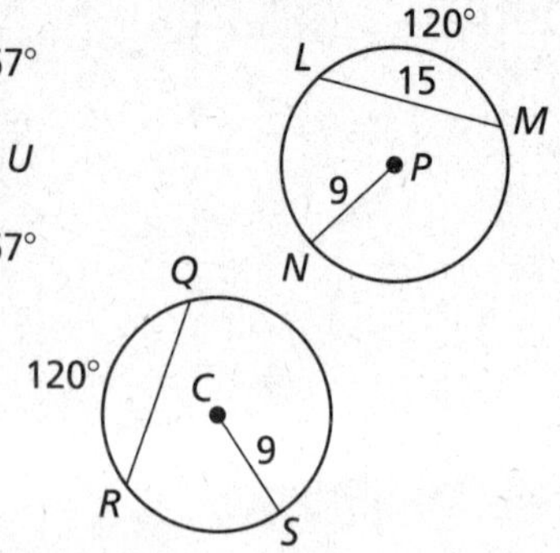

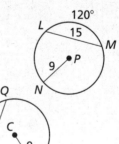

Find the value of x.

J.

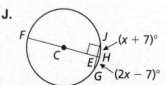

Answer column (left):

| equidistant SCHOOL |
| intersects FOR |
| 98° ALL |
| chord BECAUSE |
| 12 ARE |
| 6 A |
| straight EVERYONE |
| perpendicular THE |
| circles GHOSTS |
| similar IS |

Answer column (right):

| semicircles TO |
| at EVEN |
| 14 SPIRIT |
| 7.5 WELCOME |
| corresponding IT |
| secant COLLEGE |
| bisects WANTED |
| 7 GROW UP |
| 82° HAVE |
| 15 LITTLE |

10.4 Start Thinking

Consider $\odot M$ shown in the diagram. How are $m\angle BMC$ and $m\overset{\frown}{BC}$ related? How are $m\angle A$ and $m\angle B$ related? Explain your answer. Use this information to make a conclusion about the relationship between $m\overset{\frown}{BC}$ and $m\angle A$.

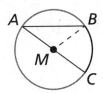

10.4 Warm Up

Find the measure of each angle in the polygon.

1.

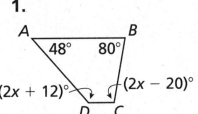

2.

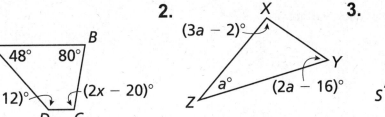

3.

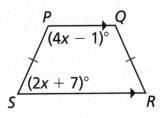

10.4 Cumulative Review Warm Up

Find the area of the geometric figure. Round your answer to the nearest tenth, when necessary.

1.

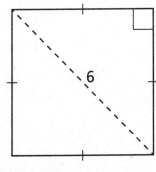

2.

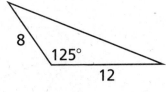

3.

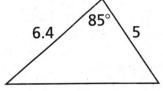

10.4 Practice A

In Exercises 1–3, find the indicated measure.

1. $m\angle K$

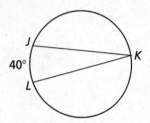

2. $m\widehat{DF}$

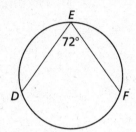

3. $m\widehat{ST}$

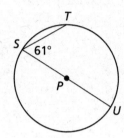

4. In the diagram shown, which statement is true? Explain.

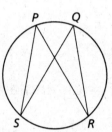

   A. $\angle SPR \cong \angle PSQ$ **B.** $\angle RQS \cong \angle RPS$

   C. $\angle RPS \cong \angle PRQ$ **D.** $\angle PRQ \cong \angle SQR$

In Exercises 5–7, find the value of each variable.

5.

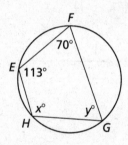

6.

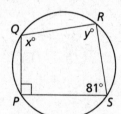

7.

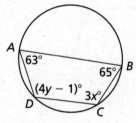

8. Describe and correct the error in finding $m\angle B$.

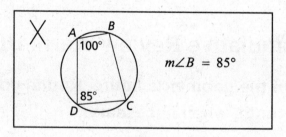

9. You make a design using a pencil and a circular wheel, as shown.

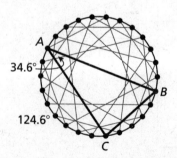

   a. Find $m\angle ABC$.

   b. Find $m\angle ACB$.

   c. What type of triangle is $\triangle ABC$? Explain.

10.4 Practice B

In Exercises 1–8, find the measure of the indicated arc or angle in ⊙P given $m\widehat{LM} = 84°$ and $m\widehat{KN} = 116°$.

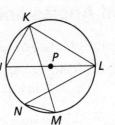

1. $m\angle JKL$

2. $m\angle MKL$

3. $m\angle KMN$

4. $m\angle JKM$

5. $m\angle KLN$

6. $m\angle LNM$

7. $m\widehat{MJ}$

8. $m\widehat{LKJ}$

In Exercises 9–11, find the value of each variable.

9.

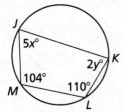

10.

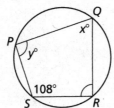

11.

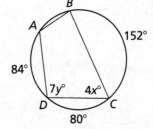

12. Copy and complete the proof.

   Given: ⊙P

   Prove: $\triangle AED \sim \triangle BEC$

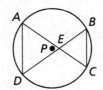

STATEMENTS	REASONS
1. ⊙P	1. Given
2. _____	2. Vertical Angles Congruence Theorem (Thm. 2.6)
3. $\angle CAD \cong \angle DBC$	3. _____
4. $\triangle AED \sim \triangle BEC$	4. _____

13. Your friend claims that the angles $\angle ADB$ and $\angle BCA$ could be used in Step 3 of Exercise 12. Is your friend correct? Explain your reasoning.

14. Determine whether $\overline{AB}$ is a diameter of the circle. Explain your reasoning.

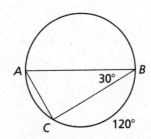

Name _____ Date _____

10.4 Enrichment and Extension

Inscribed Angles and Polygons

1. Triangles *EFH* and *FGH* are inscribed in circle *T* with $\overset{\frown}{EH} \cong \overset{\frown}{EF}$. Find the measure of each numbered angle if $m\angle 2 = 3a + 2$ and $m\angle 3 = 12a - 2$.

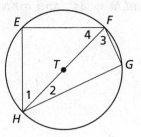

2. A regular 13-gon is inscribed in a circle. Find the measure of each arc intercepted by the sides of the polygon. Round your answer to the nearest hundredth of a degree.

In Exercises 3 and 4, find the measure of the numbered angles in the figure.

3.

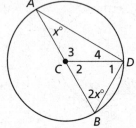

4.

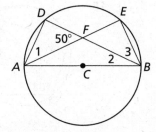

In Exercises 5 and 6, use the figure below, which shows a pentagon inscribed in circle *O*. Assume $\overline{AB} \cong \overline{BC} \cong \overline{CD}$ and $m\angle ABC = 132°$.

5. Find $m\angle AEB$.

6. Find $m\angle COD$.

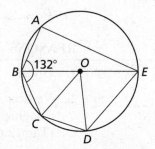

7. A puzzle in the form of a quadrilateral is inscribed in a circle. The vertices of the quadrilateral divide the circle into four arcs in a ratio of 1 : 2 : 5 : 4. Find the angle measures of the quadrilateral.

10.4 Puzzle Time

How Did The Lettuce Get An A On The Test?

Write the letter of each answer in the box containing the exercise number.

Complete the sentence.

1. A(n) _____ angle is an angle whose vertex is on a circle and whose sides contain chords of the circle.

2. An arc that lies between two lines, rays, or segments is called a(n) _____ arc.

3. If the endpoints of a chord or arc lie on the sides of an inscribed angle, the chord or arc is said to _____ the angle.

4. The measure of an inscribed angle is _____ the measure of its intercepted arc.

5. If two inscribed angles of a circle intercept the same arc, then the angles are _____.

6. A polygon is an inscribed polygon when all of its _____ lie on a circle.

7. The circle that contains the vertices of a polygon is a(n) _____ circle.

8. If a right triangle is inscribed in a circle, then the hypotenuse is a(n) _____ of the circle.

9. A quadrilateral can be inscribed in a circle if and only if its opposite angles are _____.

Find the indicated measure using the diagram.

10. $m\overset{\frown}{FG} = 98°$, $m\overset{\frown}{GD} = 142°$; Find $m\angle G$.

11. $m\angle G = 78°$; Find $m\overset{\frown}{FD}$.

Find the indicated measure using the diagram.

12. $x° = $

13. $y° = $

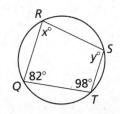

Answers	
I. inscribed	**A.** 89°
A. intercepted	**S.** subtend
H. complementary	
R. 71°	**D.** $\frac{1}{2}$
T. congruent	**M.** upset
E. vertices	**P.** 39°
U. circumscribed	**N.** sides
I. diameter	**N.** inclined
H. supplementary	
E. concentric	
D. 60°	**S.** 156°
K. acute	**N.** twice
E. 82°	**B.** 41°
T. 98°	**L.** radius
O. encircle	

8	13		7	3	6	4		1	5	11		9	12	2	10

Consider two unique chords inside the same circle. Discuss some
of the ways the two chords can be drawn within the circle. Include
a diagram for each of your possibilities. Use your diagrams to
make conclusions about the arcs that are formed by the chords.

10.5 **Warm Up**

Find the indicated measure.

1. $m\overset{\frown}{BC}$

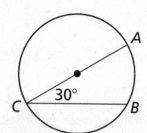

2. $m\angle P$

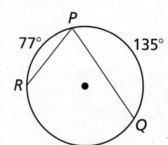

3. $m\overset{\frown}{EH}$

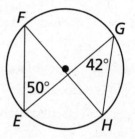

10.5 **Cumulative Review Warm Up**

Determine the number of lines of symmetry for the figure.

1.

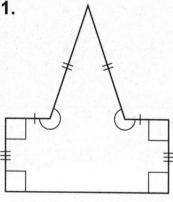

2.

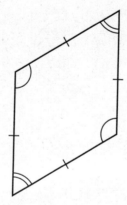

3.

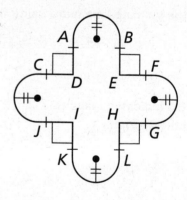

Name_____ Date_____

10.5 Practice A

In Exercises 1–3, line _t_ is tangent to the circle. Find the indicated measure.

1. $m\widehat{AB}$

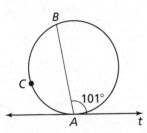

2. $m\widehat{FH}$

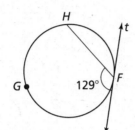

3. $m\angle 1$

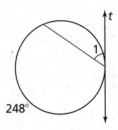

In Exercises 4–7, find the value of _x_.

4.

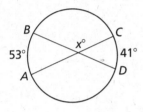

5.

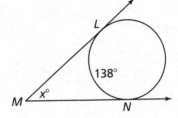

6.

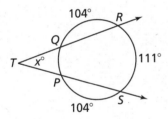

7.

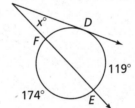

8. Describe and correct the error in finding the angle measure.

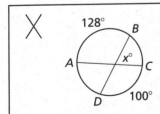

$$m\angle X = \tfrac{1}{2}(128° + 100°)$$
$$= 114°$$

9. Parallel light rays enter the eye and are bent by the lens to converge at a single point on the retina called the *focal point*. When a person is farsighted, the rays converge behind the retina, as shown in the diagram. When $m\widehat{XY} = 52°$ and $m\widehat{WZ} = 10°$, find the measure of angle *F*.

Focal Point of a Farsighted Eye

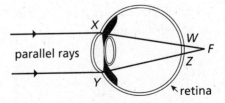

10.5 Practice B

In Exercises 1–6, use the diagram to find the measure of the angle.

1. $m\angle CAF$

2. $m\angle AFB$

3. $m\angle CEF$

4. $m\angle CFB$

5. $m\angle DCF$

6. $m\angle BCD$

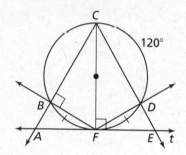

7. In the diagram, ℓ is tangent to the circle at P. Which relationship is *not* true? Explain.

   A. $m\angle 1 = 110°$ B. $m\angle 2 = 70°$

   C. $m\angle 3 = 80°$ D. $m\angle 4 = 90°$

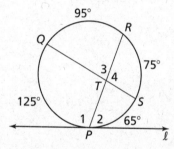

In Exercises 8–10, find the value of x.

8.
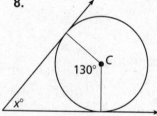

9.
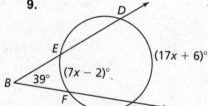

10.
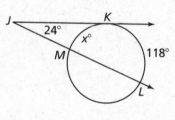

11. In the diagram, the circle is inscribed in $\triangle PQR$.

   a. Find $m\widehat{EF}$.

   b. Find $m\widehat{FG}$.

   c. Find $m\widehat{GE}$.

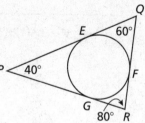

12. A plane at point U is flying at an altitude of 7 miles above Earth. What is the measure of arc TV that represents the part of Earth you can see from the airplane? The radius of Earth is about 4000 miles.

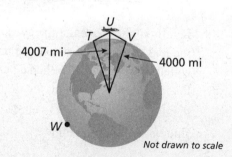

Not drawn to scale

10.5 Enrichment and Extension

Angle Relationships in Circles

1. In the figure, $m\angle P = 16°$ and $m\overset{\frown}{CO} = 96°$. Find each indicated measurement.

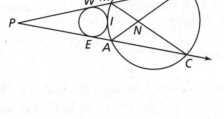

   a. $m\overset{\frown}{WE}$

   b. $m\overset{\frown}{WIE}$

   c. $m\angle OAC$

   d. $m\angle MOA$

   e. $m\overset{\frown}{AM}$

   f. $m\angle CNO$

A regulation pocket billiard ball is a perfect sphere with a diameter 2.25 inches. At the start of a game of pocket billiards, the 15 balls must be arranged in five rows in a triangular rack, as shown.

2. The figure depicts just two rows of billiards in a rack. Use the figure to find each of the following.

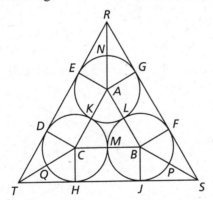

   a. $m\overset{\frown}{KL}$

   b. $m\angle ERG$

   c. ED

   d. AE

   e. ER

   f. TR

3. Write a paragraph proof.

   Given: $\overset{\frown}{RS} \cong \overset{\frown}{TU}$, $\overset{\frown}{RU} \cong \overset{\frown}{ST}$

   Prove: Q is the center of the circle.

Name _____ Date _____

10.5 Puzzle Time

What Do You Call More Than One L?

Circle the letter of each correct answer in the boxes below. The circled letters will spell out the answer to the riddle.

Complete the sentence.

1. If a tangent and a chord intersect at a point on a circle, then the measure of each angle formed is _____ the measure of its intercepted arc.

2. If two chords intersect _____ a circle, then the measure of each angle is one half the *sum* of the measures of the arcs intercepted by the angle and its vertical angle.

3. A circumscribed angle is an angle whose sides are _____ to a circle.

4. The measure of a circumscribed angle is equal to 180° minus the measure of the _____ angle that intercepts the same arc.

Line *k* is tangent to the circle. Find the indicated measure.

5. $m\widehat{AB} = 150°$; Find $m\angle 1$.

6. $m\angle 2 = 112°$; Find $m\angle 1$.

7. $m\angle 2 = 142°$; Find $m\widehat{BCA}$.

Find the indicated measure.

8. $m\widehat{AB} = 50°$, $m\widehat{DC} = 170°$; Find $m\angle 1$.

9. $m\angle 2 = 132°$; Find $m\angle 1$.

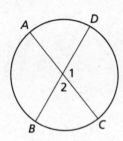

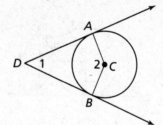

A	E	P	Y	A	R	A	E	S
inside	96°	$\frac{1}{2}$	twice	68°	110°	284°	obtuse	300°
M	**L**	**F**	**I**	**L**	**E**	**N**	**L**	**R**
115°	tangent	55°	secant	48°	central	outside	75°	66°

10.6 Start Thinking

Draw a diagram similar to the one shown to the right with a 10-centimeter diameter circle, a point P outside the circle, and four rays passing through the circle. Label the points of intersection as shown. Use a ruler to find the measures of the following segments. What relationship exists between each pair of measurements?

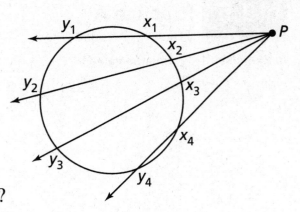

1. $\overline{PX_1}, \overline{PY_1}$ **2.** $\overline{PX_2}, \overline{PY_2}$ **3.** $\overline{PX_3}, \overline{PY_3}$ **4.** $\overline{PX_4}, \overline{PY_4}$

10.6 Warm Up

Solve the equation.

1. $4(7 + 4) = 2(x + 6)$

2. $x(x + 5) = (x + 1)(x + 2)$

3. $2x(5) = (2x + 3)(x + 1)$

4. $(x + 2)(x + 5) = 2x(x + 2)$

5. $(x + 4)(x + 2) = 2x(x - 3)$

6. $(2x - 1)(x + 5) = (x + 1)(x + 2)$

10.6 Cumulative Review Warm Up

Find the value of the variable.

1.
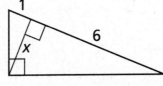

2.
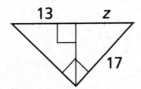

3.
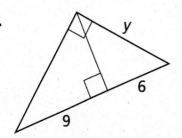

Name _____ Date _____

10.6 Practice A

In Exercises 1–12, find the value of x.

1.
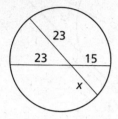
23
23   15
x

2.
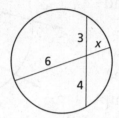
3 x
6
4

3.
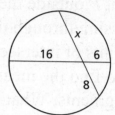
x
16   6
8

4.
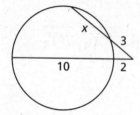
x
3
10   2

5.
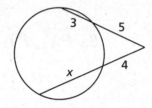
3   5
x   4

6.
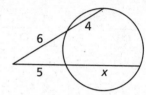
4
6
5   x

7.
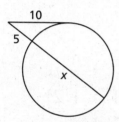
10
5
x

8.
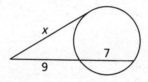
x
7
9

9.
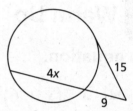
4x   15
9

10.
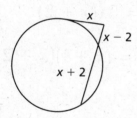
x
x − 2
x + 2

11.
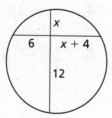
x
6   x + 4
12

12.
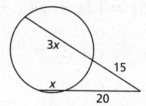
3x
15
x
20

13. The Xs show the positions of two basketball
teammates relative to the circular "key" on a
basketball court. The player outside the key
passes the ball to the player on the key.
What is the length of the pass?

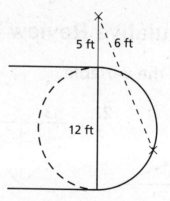
5 ft   6 ft
12 ft

10.6 Practice B

In Exercises 1–9, find the value of x.

1.

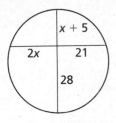

x + 5

2x   21

28

2.

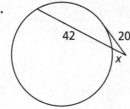

42   20

x

3.

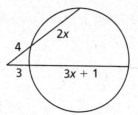

2x

4

3   3x + 1

4.

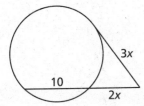

3x

10

2x

5.

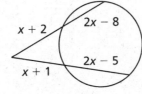

x + 2   2x − 8

2x − 5

x + 1

6.

3x − 3

2x

x + 6

x

7.

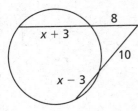

8

x + 3

10

x − 3

8.

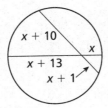

x + 10

x

x + 13

x + 1

9.

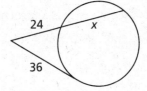

24   x

36

10. A large industrial winch is shown.
There are 15 inches of cable hanging
free off of the spool and the distance
from the end of the cable to the spool
is 8 inches. What is the diameter of
the spool?

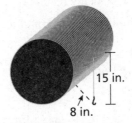

15 in.

8 in.

11. The diagram shows a cross-section of a
large storm drain pipe with a small amount
of standing water. The distance across the
surface of the water is 48 inches and the
water is 4.25 inches deep at its deepest
point. What is the diameter of the storm
drain pipe?

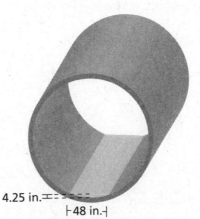

4.25 in.

⊢48 in.⊣

10.6 Enrichment and Extension

Segment Relationships

In Exercises 1 and 2, find the indicated measurement(s).

1. AC and BD

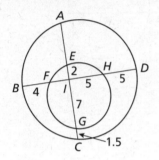

2. PY

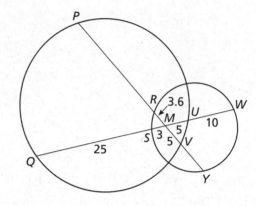

3. In the diagram, $\overline{EF}$ is a tangent segment, $m\widehat{AD} = 140°$, $m\widehat{AB} = 20°$, $m\angle EFD = 60°$, $AC = 6$, $AB = 3$, and $DC = 10$.

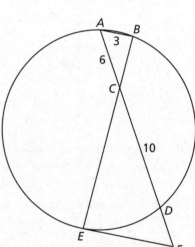

a. Find $m\angle CAB$.

b. Show that $\triangle ABC \sim \triangle FEC$.

c. Let $EF = y$ and $DF = x$. Use the results of part (b) to write a proportion involving x and y. Solve for y.

d. Use a theorem from this section to write another equation involving x and y.

e. Use the results of parts (c) and (d) to solve for x and y.

f. Find CE. Explain your reasoning.

4. Write a paragraph proof for the following.

Given: $\overline{QT}$ is tangent to both circles at T.

Prove: $OP \cdot OQ = OR \cdot OS$.

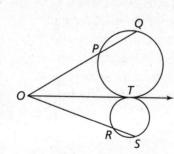

Name_____ Date_____

10.6 Puzzle Time

Why Won't The Circles Invite The Ellipses Over For Dinner?

A	B	C	D	E	F
G	H	I			

Complete each exercise. Find the answer in the answer column. Write the word under the answer in the box containing the exercise letter.

Complete the sentence.

A. When two chords intersect in the _____ of a circle, each chord is divided into two segments that are called segments of the chord.

B. A tangent segment is a segment that is tangent to a circle at a(n) _____.

C. A(n) _____ segment is a segment that contains a chord of a circle and has exactly one endpoint outside the circle.

D. The part of a secant segment that is outside the circle is called a(n) _____ segment.

Find the value of x.

E.

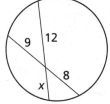

F.

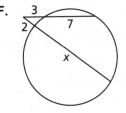

G.

H.

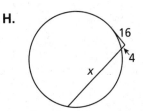

I.

15 ROUND	endpoint THE
2 COMPLEX	16 EAT
interior BECAUSE	3 ALWAYS
8 LUNCH	13 ECCENTRIC
6 TOO	exterior SNOB
60 THE	4 CIRCLES
side SQUARE	secant ELLIPSES
cotangent FOOD	center NICE
external ARE	10 FOR

The standard form of the equation of a circle centered at $(0, 0)$ is $x^2 + y^2 = r^2$, where r is the radius. Find the equation of the circle shown. Graph the circle $x^2 + y^2 = 9$.

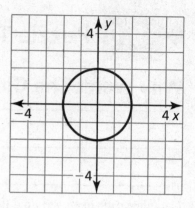

10.7 **Warm Up**

Find the measure of $\overline{PQ}$ and its midpoint.

1. $P = (2, 8)$
$Q = (-2, 8)$

2. $P = (0, -5)$
$Q = (7, -7)$

3. $P = (-4, -3)$
$Q = (-6, 11)$

4. $P = \left(\frac{1}{2}, -3\right)$
$Q = \left(-\frac{5}{2}, \frac{3}{2}\right)$

10.7 **Cumulative Review Warm Up**

Find the measure of the arc.

1. $\overset{\frown}{AB}$

2. $\overset{\frown}{CD}$

3. $\overset{\frown}{DE}$

4. $\overset{\frown}{BCD}$

5. $\overset{\frown}{AED}$

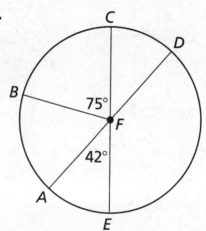

Name_____ Date _____

10.7 Practice A

In Exercises 1–4, write the standard equation of the circle with the given center and radius.

1.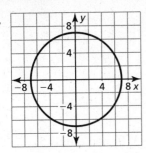

2.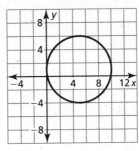

3. a circle with center $(0, 0)$ and radius 8

4. a circle with center $(0, -5)$ and radius 2

In Exercises 5 and 6, use the given information to write the standard equation of the circle.

5. The center is $(0, 0)$, and a point on the circle is $(3, -4)$.

6. The center is $(3, -2)$, and a point on the circle is $(23, 19)$.

In Exercises 7–9, match each graph with its equation.

7.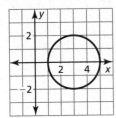

8.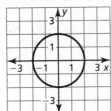

9.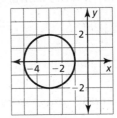

A. $x^2 + y^2 = 4$

B. $(x - 3)^2 + y^2 = 4$

C. $(x + 3)^2 + y^2 = 4$

10. The equation of a circle is $x^2 + y^2 - 6y + 9 = 4$. Find the center and radius of the circle. Then graph the circle.

11. Prove or disprove that the point $(-3, 3)$ lies on the circle centered at the origin with radius 4.

12. You are using a math software program to design a pattern for an Olympic flag. In addition to the dimensions shown in the diagram, the distance between the outer edges any two adjacent rings in the same row is 3 inches.

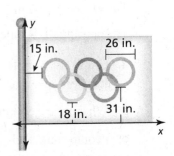

  a. Use the given dimensions to write equations representing the outer circles of the five rings. Use inches as units in a coordinate plane with the lower left corner of the flag on the origin.

  b. Each ring is 3 inches thick. Explain how you can adjust the equations of the outer circles to write equations representing the inner circles.

10.7 Practice B

In Exercises 1–4, write the standard equation of the circle with the given center and radius.

1.
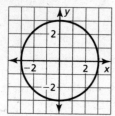

2.
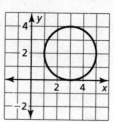

3. a circle with center $(4, -7)$ and radius 4

4. a circle with center $(-3, 0)$ and radius 5

In Exercises 5–7, use the given information to write the standard equation of the circle.

5. The center is $(0, 0)$, and a point on the circle is $(1, 0)$.

6. The center is $(4, -1)$, and a point on the circle is $(-1, -1)$.

7. The center is $(2, 4)$, and a point on the circle is $(-3, 16)$.

In Exercises 8–11, find the center and radius of the circle. Then graph the circle.

8. $x^2 + y^2 = 100$

9. $(x - 2)^2 + (y - 9)^2 = 4$

10. $x^2 + y^2 + 4y + 4 = 36$

11. $x^2 - 2x + 5 + y^2 = 8$

In Exercises 12 and 13, prove or disprove the statement.

12. The point $(-3, 4)$ lies on the circle centered at the origin with radius 5.

13. The point $\left(2, \sqrt{3}\right)$ lies on the circle centered at the origin and containing the point $(-3, 0)$.

14. After an earthquake, you are given seismograph readings from three locations where the coordinates are miles.

   The epicenter is 5 miles away from $A(2, 1)$.

   The epicenter is 6 miles away from $B(-2, -2)$.

   The epicenter is 4 miles away from $(-6, 4)$.

   a. Graph three circles in one coordinate plane to represent the possible epicenter locations determined by each of the seismograph readings.

   b. What are the coordinates of the epicenter?

   c. People could feel the earthquake up to 9 miles from the epicenter. Could a person at $(4, -5)$ feel it? Explain.

10.7 Enrichment and Extension

Circles in the Coordinate Plane

1. The x- and y-axis are tangent to a circle with radius 3 units. Write a standard equation of the circle.

2. A town wants to add a grocery store that is equidistant from the farthest houses in the community. Planners use a grid system to model the locations of the three houses as $C(4, 3)$, $D(2, -7)$, and $E(-2, -3)$. Determine the ideal location for the grocery store, and write an equation of the circle that models the situation.

3. Find the standard equation of the circle with its center on the y-axis that is tangent to $y = -2$ and $y = -17$.

4. Find the standard equation of the circle that has a diameter of 15 units and has a center at the intersection of $y = x + 7$ and $y = 2x - 5$.

5. Circle C_1 has equation $(x + 2)^2 + (y + 4)^2 = 64$, and circle C_2 has equation $(x - h)^2 + (y - 1)^2 = 81$. The distance between the centers of circles C_1 and C_2 is 13.

   a. Find all possible values of h.

   b. If a segment connecting the centers of the circles is drawn, let A be the intersection of the segment and circle C_1, and let B be the intersection of the segment and circle C_2. Find AB.

   c. For each possible value of h, find the standard equations of the circles that are concentric with circle C_1 and tangent to circle C_2.

The equation of a sphere is an extension of the equation of a circle. The standard equation of a sphere with center (i, j, k) and radius r units is

$$(x - i)^2 + (y - j)^2 + (z - k)^2 = r^2.$$

6. Write an equation for each sphere described.

   a. center $(-5, 0, 4)$ and radius 11

   b. center $(10, -6, 2)$ and point $(10, -1, 10)$ on the sphere

   c. diameter with endpoints $(-8, 1, -7)$ and $(6, 3, -1)$

10.7 Puzzle Time

What Should You Do When It Rains?

Write the letter of each answer in the box containing the exercise number.

Write the standard equation of the circle.

1. center $(5, 2)$ and radius 4

2. center $(-3, -4)$ and radius 3

3. The center is $(0, 0)$, and a point on the circle is $(0, 8)$.

4. The center is $(2, 3)$, and a point on the circle is $(6, 0)$.

Find the center and radius of the circle.

5. $x^2 + y^2 = 81$

6. $(x + 4)^2 + (y - 3)^2 = 64$

7. The point $(-4, 3)$ lies on a circle centered at the origin that contains the point $(3, 4)$. True or false?

Use the Black Box readings from locations *A*, *B*, and *C* to find the epicenter of the box.

- The epicenter is 3 miles away from $A(0, 0)$.

- The epicenter is 3 miles away from $B(3, 3)$.

- The epicenter is 3 miles away from $C(-3, 3)$.

8. What is the epicenter of the Black Box?

Answers

C. $(x + 3)^2 + (y + 4)^2 = 9$

M. $x^2 + y^2 = 8$

B. $(x - 2)^2 + (y + 3)^2 = 25$

C. $x^2 + y^2 = 64$

E. $(x - 2)^2 + (y - 3)^2 = 25$

G. $(x + 5)^2 + (y + 2)^2 = 16$

D. center $= (0, 0), r = 9$

L. center $= (4, -3), r = 8$

N. center $= (-4, 3), r = 8$

K. false   **I.** true

U. $(x + 4)^2 + (y + 3)^2 = 9$

O. $(0, 3)$

R. center $= (1, 1), r = 3$

I. $(x - 5)^2 + (y - 2)^2 = 16$

S. $(3, 0)$

3	8	1	6	2	7	5	4

Chapter 10 Cumulative Review

In Exercises 1–12, find the product.

1. $(x - 3)(x - 7)$

2. $(j + 1)(j + 3)$

3. $(c + 12)(c - 8)$

4. $(m - 10)(m - 2)$

5. $(y + 11)(y + 10)$

6. $(s + 6)(s + 5)$

7. $(5q + 3)(q - 4)$

8. $(6p + 1)(2p - 7)$

9. $(-2f + 7)(f + 12)$

10. $(6b - 2)(9b - 3)$

11. $(3g - 2)(-5g + 12)$

12. $(7k - 7)(3k + 8)$

In Exercises 13–28, solve the equation.

13. $x^2 - x - 72 = 0$

14. $x^2 - 22x + 120 = 0$

15. $x^2 - 18x + 72 = 0$

16. $x^2 + x - 42 = 0$

17. $x^2 - 8x + 7 = 0$

18. $x^2 - 4x - 32 = 0$

19. $x^2 - x - 110 = 0$

20. $x^2 - 13x + 36 = 0$

21. $x^2 + 10x = -9$

22. $x^2 - 7x = 8$

23. $x^2 + 2x = 8$

24. $x^2 + 13x = -40$

25. $x^2 = -7x - 6$

26. $x^2 = 6x + 16$

27. $x = -x^2 + 56$

28. $3x + 28 = x^2$

In Exercises 29–38, solve the equation.

29. $5x = 215$

30. $\frac{1}{3}x = 34$

31. $\frac{1}{4}x = 28$

32. $6x = 108$

33. $7x = 182$

34. $\frac{1}{4}x = 21$

35. $\frac{1}{7}x = 19$

36. $3x = 78$

37. $152 = 8x$

38. $\frac{1}{5}x = 255$

Chapter 10 **Cumulative Review** (continued)

In Exercises 39–46, find *FH*.

39.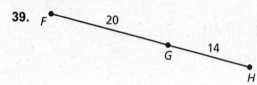

40.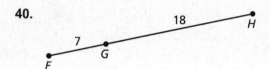

41.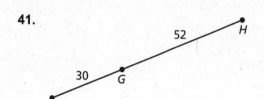

42.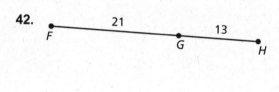

43.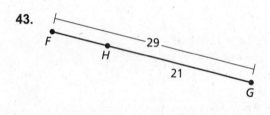

44.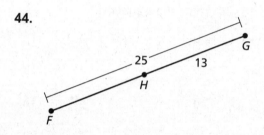

45.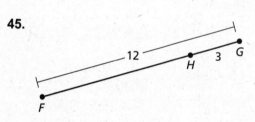

46.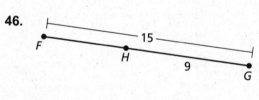

47. Point *S* is between points *R* and *T* on $\overline{RT}$. *RS* = 7 and *ST* = 11. What is the length of $\overline{RT}$?

48. Point *S* is between points *R* and *T* on $\overline{RT}$. *RS* = *x* + 3 and *ST* = *x* + 8.

   a. Write an expression to represent the length of $\overline{RT}$.

   b. The value of *x* is 3. What is the length of $\overline{RS}$?

   c. The value of *x* is 3. What is the length of $\overline{ST}$?

   d. The value of *x* is 3. What is the length of $\overline{RT}$?

Chapter 10 **Cumulative Review** (continued)

In Exercises 49–56, the endpoints of $\overline{CD}$ are given. Find the coordinates of the midpoint *M*.

49. $C(-2, -1)$ and $D(-4, -5)$

50. $C(5, 1)$ and $D(-9, 10)$

51. $C(10, -8)$ and $D(-12, 7)$

52. $C(-8, 11)$ and $D(-7, -4)$

53. $C(-5, 1)$ and $D(-8, -8)$

54. $C(2, -5)$ and $D(9, -7)$

55. $C(3, 0)$ and $D(-8, 9)$

56. $C(-7, 3)$ and $D(2, -4)$

In Exercises 57–64, find the distance between the two points.

57. $A(-12, 12)$ and $B(1, -12)$

58. $C(5, -12)$ and $D(9, -2)$

59. $E(-1, 11)$ and $F(12, 3)$

60. $G(9, 8)$ and $H(-7, -10)$

61. $J(-12, -5)$ and $K(2, 8)$

62. $L(-6, 8)$ and $M(4, 5)$

63. $R(-8, 10)$ and $S(12, -3)$

64. $T(6, -12)$ and $V(-2, -12)$

In Exercises 65 and 66, name three different angles in the diagram.

65.

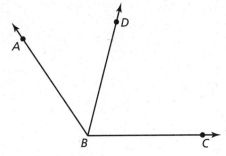

66.

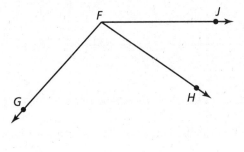

In Exercises 67 and 68, find the indicated angle measure.

67. $m\angle ABC$

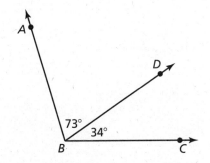

68. $m\angle LMN$

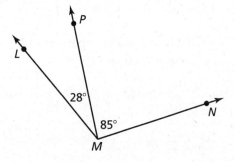

Name _____ Date _____

In Exercises 69–74, find the value of *x*.

69.
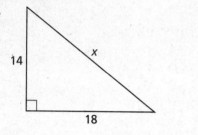

70.
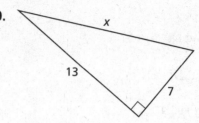

71.
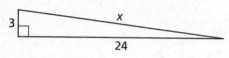

72.
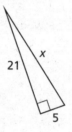

73.
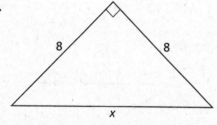

74.
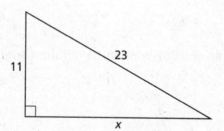

75. A dinner plate is in the shape of an isosceles right triangle. The leg length is 13 inches.

    a. What is the length of the hypotenuse? Round your answer to the nearest tenth.

    b. What is the perimeter of the plate? Round your answer to the nearest tenth.

76. A piece of wall art is comprised of mirrors in the shapes of squares, rectangles, circles, and triangles. One of the triangles is in the shape of a right triangle and has one leg length of 3 inches and another leg length of 7 inches.

    a. What is the length of the hypotenuse of the specified mirror piece? Round your answer to the nearest tenth.

    b. What is the perimeter of the specified mirror piece? Round your answer to the nearest tenth.

Chapter 11

Name _____ Date _____

Dear Family,

In this chapter, your student will apply area and volume to model real-life situations. Area and volume are important concepts because they precisely describe how much space an object occupies. This allows for comparisons, such as comparing the capacity of two pools or bathtubs, and calculations, such as determining the average number of people per square mile in a city.

Find a newspaper and look at the advertisements for houses and apartments with your student. Point out how the advertisements describe the living residence in terms of square footage. Engage your student with these questions.

- Why is it important to know how many square feet are available in a living residence?

- Why would you be more interested in the square footage of a living residence than the volume?

> **Prime Rental!**
> **192 Oak Lane**
> **1800 ft^2**
> 2 bathrooms, 3 bedrooms

In the classifieds, there may be advertisements for storage units. These advertisements may describe the areas or the volumes of the units. Keeping in mind the conversation you just had about living space, follow up with these questions about storage space.

- When would you be more interested in the volume rather than the area of a storage space?

> **Storage Unit**
> **200 ft^3**
> Keep your goods safe!

> **Space Available**
> **8 ft × 8 ft**
> **Rent today!**

- When would you be more interested in the area rather than the volume?

Tie these ideas together by discussing when it is more appropriate to use area and when it is more appropriate to use volume to describe a space. Discuss how important it is to have a precise way to measure and compare available amounts of space.

Challenge your student to come up with another situation where area is better than volume for describing a real-life object and a situation where volume is better.

Have fun and be creative!

Nombre _____ Fecha _____

Estimada familia:

En este capítulo, su hijo usará el área y el volumen para representar situaciones de la vida real. El área y el volumen son conceptos importantes porque describen con precisión cuánto espacio ocupa un objeto. Esto permite hacer comparaciones, tal como comparar la capacidad de dos piscinas o bañeras, y cálculos, tal como determinar el número promedio de personas por milla cuadrada en una ciudad.

Hallen un periódico y busquen casas y departamentos en los avisos con su hijo. Señalen cómo los avisos describen la vivienda en términos de pies cuadrados. Motive a su hijo con estas preguntas.

- ¿Por qué es importante saber cuántos pies cuadrados tiene una vivienda?

- ¿Por qué les interesaría más los pies cuadrados de una vivienda que el volumen?

¡Bienes raíces de primera clase!
Calle Oak 192
8800 pies²
2 baños, 3 habitaciones

En los clasificados, hay muchos avisos para unidades de depósito. Estos avisos pueden describir las áreas o los volúmenes de las unidades. Teniendo en cuenta su conversación sobre el espacio de una vivienda, sigan con estas preguntas sobre el espacio de depósito.

- ¿Cuándo les interesaría más el volumen en lugar del área de un espacio de depósito?

- ¿Cuándo les interesaría más el área que el volumen?

Unidad de almacenamiento
200 pies³
¡Mantenga sus bienes a salvo!

Espacio disponible
8 pies × 8 pies
¡Rente hoy!

Para unir estas ideas, comenten cuándo es más adecuado usar el área y cuándo es más adecuado usar el volumen para describir un espacio. Comenten la importancia de tener una manera precisa de medir y comparar las cantidades de espacio disponibles.

Desafíe a su hijo para que piense en otra situación donde el área sea mejor que el volumen para describir un objeto de la vida real y una situación donde el volumen sea mejor.

¡Diviértanse y sean creativos!

11.1 Start Thinking

The circle in the figure has a diameter of
10 centimeters. What is the circumference
of the circle? Use the circumference to
calculate the length of the arc that would
be created for the given measure of θ.

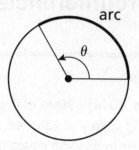
arc

1. $\theta = 180°$ **2.** $\theta = 90°$ **3.** $\theta = 150°$

11.1 Warm Up

**Use the diagram to find the measure of the indicated angle
and the circumference of the circle.**

1. $m\angle BCD$ **2.** $m\angle YMX$ **3.** $m\angle RPQ$

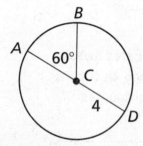
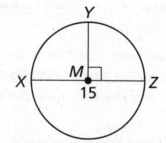
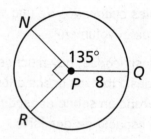

11.1 Cumulative Review Warm Up

Use the diagram to find the indicated measure.

1. $m\widehat{WZY}$ **2.** DE **3.** CQ

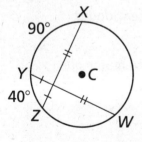
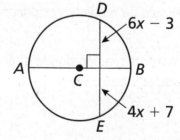
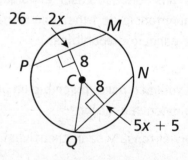

11.1 Practice A

In Exercises 1–4, find the indicated measure.

1. radius of a circle with a circumference of 42π meters

2. circumference of a circle with a radius of 27 feet

3. circumference of a circle with a diameter of 15 inches

4. diameter of a circle with circumference 39 centimeters

5. Maple trees suitable for tapping for syrup should be at least 1.5 feet in diameter. You wrap a rope around a tree trunk, then measure the length of the rope needed to wrap one time around the trunk. This length is 4 feet 2 inches. Explain how you can use this length to determine whether the tree is suitable for tapping.

In Exercises 6–8, find the arc length of $\overarc{AB}$.

6.
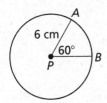

7.
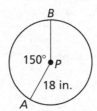

8.
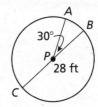

In Exercises 9 and 10, find the perimeter of the region.

9.
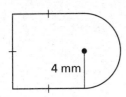

10.
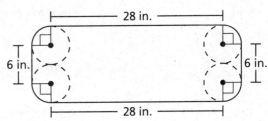

In Exercises 11 and 12, convert the angle measure.

11. Convert $60°$ to radians.

12. Convert $\dfrac{5\pi}{4}$ radians to degrees.

13. A carousel has a diameter of 50 feet. To the nearest foot, how far does a child seated near the outer edge travel when the carousel makes 8 revolutions?

50 ft

Name _____ Date _____

11.1 Practice B

In Exercises 1 and 2, find the indicated measure.

1. exact diameter of a circle with a circumference of 36 meters

2. exact circumference of a circle with a radius of 5.4 feet

3. Find the circumference of a circle inscribed in a square with a side length of 14 centimeters.

In Exercises 4–9, use the diagram of circle _D_ with ∠EDF ≅ ∠FDG to find the indicated measure.

4. $m\overarc{EFG}$

5. $m\overarc{EHG}$

6. arc length of $\overarc{EFG}$

7. arc length of $\overarc{EHG}$

8. $m\overarc{EHF}$

9. arc length of $\overarc{FEG}$

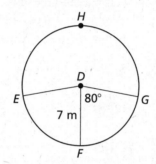

In Exercises 10–12, find the indicated measure.

10. $m\overarc{AB}$

11. circumference of ⊙_F_

12. radius of ⊙_J_

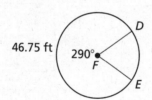

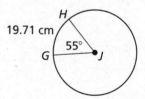

In Exercises 13 and 14, convert the angle measure.

13. Convert 105° to radians.

14. Convert $\dfrac{5\pi}{6}$ radians to degrees.

15. The chain of a bicycle travels along the front and rear sprockets, as shown in the figure. The circumferences of the rear sprocket and the front sprocket are 12 inches and 20 inches, respectively.

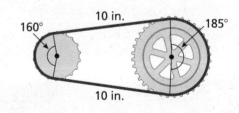

   a. How long is the chain? Round your answer to the nearest tenth.

   b. On a chain, the teeth are spaced in $\frac{1}{2}$-inch intervals.

   About how many teeth are there on this chain?

Name_____ Date _____

Circumference and Arc Length

1. Use the diagram of circle B.

    a. Find the circumference of circle B.

    b. Find the arc length of $\overset{\frown}{AC}$.

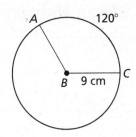

2. Points A and B lie on circle C, as shown. If the length of $\overset{\frown}{AB}$ is 8 units, what is the radius of circle C to the nearest unit?

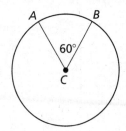

3. Find the circumference of a circle inscribed in a rhombus with diagonals that are 12 centimeters long and 16 centimeters long. (*Hint:* Diagonals of a rhombus are perpendicular and bisect each other.)

Find the perimeter of the region.

4.

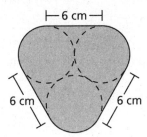

5.

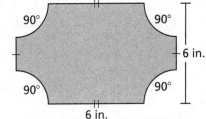

Puzzle Time

Why Did The Stage Manager Put Paste On The Programs?

A	B	C	D	E	F
G	H	I	J		

Complete each exercise. Find the answer in the answer column. Write the word under the answer in the box containing the exercise letter.

area **FACE**	
5π **AFTER**	
$\dfrac{2\pi}{9}$ **TO**	
PICTURE AND	
11.00 **WAS**	
10π **GLUED**	
$\dfrac{\pi}{9}$ **WHEN**	
arc **THE**	
58.27 **SEATS**	
17.51 **WOULD**	

Complete the sentence.

A. A(n) _____ for a three-dimensional figure is a two-dimensional pattern that can be folded to form the three-dimensional figure.

B. The _____ of a circle is the distance around the circle.

C. A(n) _____ length is a portion of the circumference of a circle.

Find the indicated measure, round to the nearest hundredth where appropriate.

D. circumference of a circle with radius 7 inches

E. diameter of a circle with circumference 55 feet

F. exact radius of a circle with a circumference of 34π

G. exact circumference of a circle with a diameter of 10 inches

Convert the angle measure.

H. Convert $40°$ to radians.

I. Convert $\dfrac{3\pi}{8}$ radians to degrees.

Find the perimeter of the shaded region.

J.

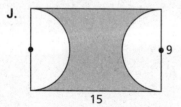

15

9

8.76 **STAGE**	
37.5° **TICKET**	
17 **BE**	
circumference **THAT**	
33.86 **PROGRAM**	
net **SO**	
radius **TASTE**	
43.98 **AUDIENCE**	
67.5° **THEIR**	
34 **STAYING**	

11.2 Start Thinking

The circle in the diagram has a diameter of 14 inches. What is the area of the circle? Use the area of the circle to calculate the area of the sector created by the given measure of θ.

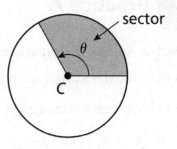

sector

1. $\theta = 180°$ 2. $\theta = 270°$ 3. $\theta = 100°$

11.2 Warm Up

Find the indicated measure.

1. area of a circle with a radius of 9 inches

2. area of a circle with a diameter of 4 feet

3. radius of a circle with an area of 100 square miles

4. diameter of a circle with an area of 42 square meters

5. area of a circle with a circumference of 12π centimeters

11.2 Cumulative Review Warm Up

Find the values of x and y without using a calculator. Write your answers in simplest form.

1.
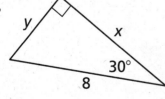

2.
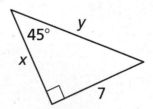

3.
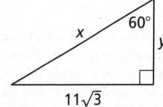

11.2 Practice A

In Exercises 1–4, find the indicated measure.

1. area of a circle with a radius of 6.8 feet

2. area of a circle with a diameter of 19.2 centimeters

3. radius of a circle with an area of 1017.9 square meters

4. diameter of a circle with an area of 707 square inches

5. About 1.2 million people live in a region with a 6-mile radius. Find the population density in people per square mile.

6. A region with a 15-mile diameter has a population density of about 5000 people per square mile. Find the number of people who live in the region.

In Exercises 7–10, find the areas of the sectors formed by ∠JLK.

7.
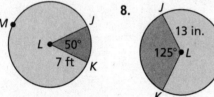

8.

9.

10.
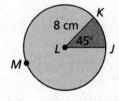

11. Find the area of ⊙H.

12. Find the area of ⊙M.

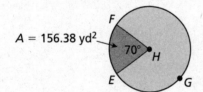

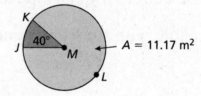

In Exercises 13–15, find the area of the shaded region.

13.
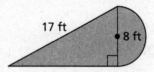

14.
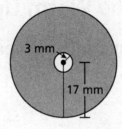

15.
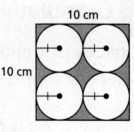

16. The diagram shows the coverage of a security camera outside a building. A new security camera is installed in the same position that doubles the radius of the coverage area. How does this affect the coverage area? Explain.

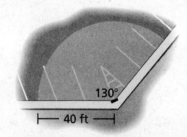

11.2 Practice B

In Exercises 1–4, find the indicated measure.

1. area of a circle with a radius of 6.75 inches

2. area of a circle with a diameter of $\frac{3}{10}$ mile

3. radius of a circle with an area of 63.7 square kilometers

4. diameter of a circle with an area of 1040.62 square yards

5. About 150,000 people live in a circular region with a population density of about 1578 people per square mile. Find the radius of the region.

6. About 1.75 million people live in a circular region with a population density of about 5050 people per square mile. Find the radius of the region.

In Exercises 7–10, find the areas of the sectors formed by $\angle JLK$.

7.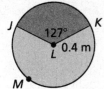

8.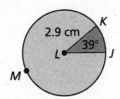

9.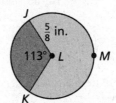

10.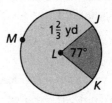

11. Find the radius of $\odot H$.

12. Find the radius of $\odot M$.

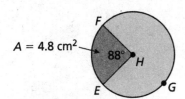

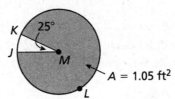

In Exercises 13–15, find the area of the shaded region.

13.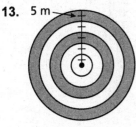

14.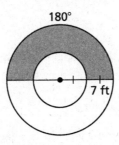

15.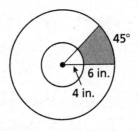

16. A piece of cake is a sector of a cylinder as shown. What is the volume of the piece of cake?

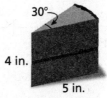

11.2 Enrichment and Extension

Areas of Circles and Sectors

1. A square and a circle intersect so that each side of the square contains a chord of the circle equal in length to the radius of the circle. What is the ratio of the area of the square to the area of the circle?

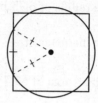

2. If the area of a sector is one-tenth of the area of the circle, what is the central angle of the sector?

3. In the diagram, the larger of the two concentric circles has a radius of 5 meters, and the smaller circle has a radius of 2 meters. What is the area of the shaded region in terms of π?

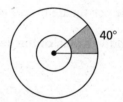

4. Circle O is inscribed in equilateral triangle ABC and tangent to the sides of the triangle. If the area of $\triangle ABC$ is $24\sqrt{3}$ square units, what is the area of circle O?

5. The central angles of a target measure $45°$. The inner circle has a radius of 1 foot, and the outer circle has a radius of 2 feet. Assuming that all arrows hit the target at random, find the following probabilities.

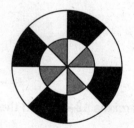

   a. hitting a gray region

   b. hitting a black region

   c. hitting a gray or black region

6. $\triangle ABC$ is formed by joining the centers of three congruent tangent circles. If the radius of each circle is 6 centimeters, find the area of $\triangle ABC$.

7. Consider an arc of a circle with a radius of 3 inches.

   a. Copy and complete the table. Leave your answers in terms of π.

Measure of arc, x	30°	60°	90°	120°	150°	180°
Area of sector, y						

   b. Write an equation that represents the relationship between x and y.

Name_____ Date_____

◣11.2 Puzzle Time

What Driver Goes Around In Circles?

Write the letter of each answer in the box containing the exercise number.

Complete the sentence.

1. A(n) _____ of a circle is the region bounded by two radii of the circle and their intercepted arc.

2. The _____ density of a city, county, or state is a measure of how many people live within a given area.

Find the indicated measurement. Round your answer to the nearest hundredth.

3. area of a circle with radius 3 inches

4. area of a circle with diameter 12 feet

5. radius of a circle with area 42 square feet

6. radius of a circle with area 425 square inches

7. diameter of a circle with area 24.8 square inches

8. diameter of a circle with area 284π square centimeters

9. About 180,000 people live in a region with a 10-mile radius. Find the population density in people per square mile. Round your answer to the nearest hundredth.

Find the area of the indicated sector using the diagram. Round your answer to the nearest hundredth, if necessary.

10. $m\angle Z = 48°$, $ZY = 6$; Find the area in square units of the sector XZY.

11. area of sector $XYZ = 50$, $m\angle Z = 60°$; Find the area in square units of $\odot Z$.

12. $m\angle Z = 55°$, $ZY = 7$; Find the area in square units of the sector XWY.

Answers	
K. 320	**C.** 3.66
H. 5.03	**R.** 572.96
X. 7.32	**W.** sector
S. 23.26	**R.** population
T. section	**D.** 246.88
A. 28.27	**D.** 33.70
M. high	**A.** 18.84
E. 11.63	**R.** triangle
R. 113.10	**L.** 452.16
V. 15.08	**C.** 11.24
E. 130.42	**S.** 5.62
T. 16.85	**I.** 300
W. 120.42	

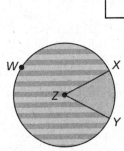

3		7	5	9	12	1	8	4	11	10	6	2

11.3 Start Thinking

Consider the regular polygon shown in the diagram. Discuss how you could determine the area of the polygon.

1. Triangle

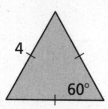

2. Hexagon

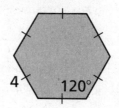

11.3 Warm Up

Find the value of *x* in the right triangle.

1.

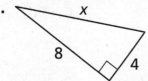

2.

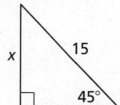

3.

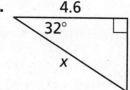

11.3 Cumulative Review Warm Up

Determine if the statement is always true, sometimes true, or never true.

1. Isosceles triangles are similar.

2. The sum of the lengths of two sides of a triangle is greater than the length of the third side.

3. A square is a rhombus.

4. Opposites sides of a kite are parallel.

5. The diagonals of a parallelogram bisect each other.

6. An equilateral polygon is regular.

11.3 Practice A

In Exercises 1–4, find the area of the kite or rhombus.

1.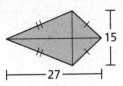

2.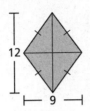

3.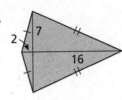

4.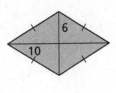

In Exercises 5–8, find the measure of a central angle of a regular polygon with the given number of sides. Round answers to the nearest tenth of a degree, if necessary.

5. 9 sides

6. 16 sides

7. 20 sides

8. 28 sides

In Exercises 9–12, find the given angle measure for regular hexagon *ABCDEF*.

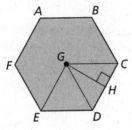

9. $m\angle CGD$

10. $m\angle CGH$

11. $m\angle HCG$

12. $m\angle EGC$

In Exercises 13–17, find the area of the regular polygon.

13.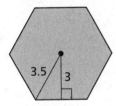

14.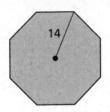

15.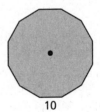

16. a pentagon with an apothem of 7 centimeters

17. a decagon with a radius of 20 meters

18. Use the figure of the gazebo floor.

   a. An arm rail is built around the perimeter of the gazebo. What is the length of the arm rail?

   b. A container of wood sealer covers 200 square feet. How many containers of sealer do you need to cover the entire floor of the gazebo? Explain your reasoning.

Name _____ Date _____

In Exercises 1–4, find the area of the kite or rhombus.

1.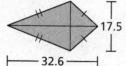
17.5
32.6

2.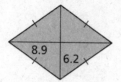
8.9 6.2

3.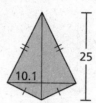
25
10.1

4.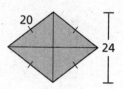
20
24

In Exercises 5–8, find the given angle measure for regular heptagon *ABCDEFG*. Round your answer to the nearest tenth of a degree, if necessary.

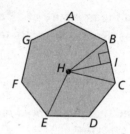

5. $m\angle BHC$

6. $m\angle BHI$

7. $m\angle IBH$

8. $m\angle EHB$

In Exercises 9–11, find the area of the shaded region.

9.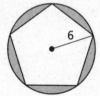
6

10.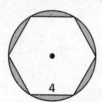
4

11.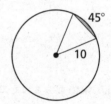
45°
10

12. The area of a kite is 384 square feet. One diagonal is three times as long as the other diagonal. Find the length of each diagonal.

13. The area of a rhombus is 484 square millimeters. One diagonal is one-half as long as the other diagonal. Find the length of each diagonal.

14. You are laying concrete around a gazebo that is a regular octagon with a radius of 8 feet. The concrete will form a circle that extends 15 feet from the vertices of the octagon.

  a. Sketch a diagram that represents this situation.

  b. What is the area of the concrete to the nearest square foot?

15. The perimeter of a regular 11-gon is 16.5 meters. Is this enough information to find the area? If so, find the area and explain your reasoning. If not, explain why not.

Name_____ Date _____

11.3 Enrichment and Extension

Areas of Polygons

1. A circle is inscribed in a rhombus with diagonals of 2 feet and 4 feet. What is the area (in square feet) of the region of the rhombus that is outside the circular region? Round your answer to the nearest tenth.

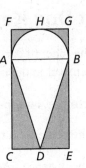

2. A sign has a shape consisting of a semicircle and an isosceles triangle. A rectangular board of wood enclosing the sign measures 2 feet by 4 feet. The shaded regions will be removed. $BE = 3BG$ and $\overline{AB}$ is parallel to $\overline{CE}$. Find the area of the sign itself.

The diagram below shows the first four stages in the construction of the Koch Snowflake.

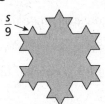
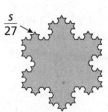

Stage 0   Stage 1   Stage 2   Stage 3

3. What is the area of A_0 of the snowflake at Stage 0 in terms of s?

4. What is the area of each triangle *added* at Stage 1 in terms of s?

5. How many triangles are added at Stage 1? What is the total area A_1 of the snowflake at Stage 1?

6. What is the total area A_2 of the snowflake at stage 2?

7. What is the total area A_3 of the snowflake at stage 3?

After several calculations, it can be shown that a formula for the area of the snowflake at any stage n, where n is greater than 0, is $A_n = \dfrac{\sqrt{3}}{4}s^2 + \dfrac{\sqrt{3}}{12}\left(1 + \dfrac{4}{9} + \dfrac{4^2}{9^2} + \cdots + \dfrac{4^{n-1}}{9^{n-1}}\right)s^2$. The part of the formula

$\left(1 + \dfrac{4}{9} + \dfrac{4^2}{9^2} + \cdots + \dfrac{4^{n-1}}{9^{n-1}}\right)$ is called an infinite geometric series where the ratio between consecutive

terms is $\dfrac{4}{9}$. A formula for finding the sum of an infinite geometric series is $S = \dfrac{a}{1-r}$, where a is the

first time and r is the ratio between terms.

8. Use the formula to find the sum S.

9. What is the area of the Koch Snowflake?

11.3 Puzzle Time

What Dog Keeps The Best Time?

Circle the letter of each correct answer in the boxes below. The circled letters will spell out the answer to the riddle.

Complete the sentence.

1. The center of a regular polygon is the center of its _____ circle.

2. The distance from the center to any side of a regular polygon is called the _____ of the polygon.

3. A(n) _____ angle of a regular polygon is an angle formed by two radii drawn to consecutive vertices of the polygon.

4. The area of a regular n-gon with side length s is one half the product of the apothem and the _____.

5. The area of a rhombus or kite is half the product of the _____.

Find the area. Round your answer to the nearest whole number.

6. $d_1 = 14, d_2 = 7$

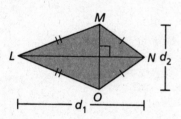

7. $AO = 8, BO = 11$

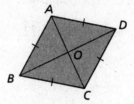

8. $OP = 11, OQ = 5$

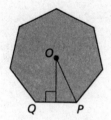

9. $OP = 9, QP = 4$

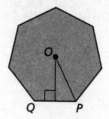

A	P	O	O	W	A	T	D	C
diagonals	right	outside	sides	central	perimeter	343	tangent	49
L	**H**	**E**	**D**	**C**	**O**	**H**	**G**	**O**
88	226	256	apothem	radius	176	98	circumscribed	185

Each of the prisms shown below is a polyhedron. A polyhedron is a solid that is bounded by polygons, called faces. The faces intersect to form segments called edges. When three or more edges intersect, they form a point called a vertex. Count the number of faces F, vertices V, and edges E, for each of the prisms. Then determine the value of the expression $F + V - E$ for each prism. How do the values of F, V, and E relate?

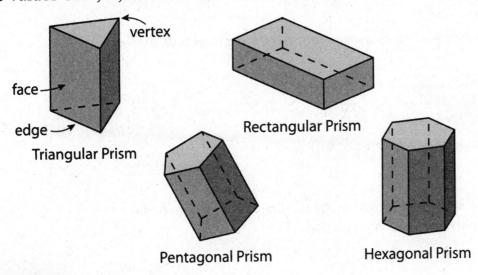

Triangular Prism

Rectangular Prism

Pentagonal Prism

Hexagonal Prism

11.4 **Warm Up**

Determine if the figure is a polygon. If not, explain why.

1. rhombus

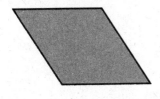

2. circle

3. rectangular solid

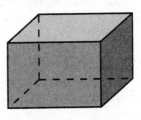

11.4 **Cumulative Review Warm Up**

Find the distance between the two points.

1. $(-3, 1), (5, 1)$ **2.** $(7, -8), (9, -3)$ **3.** $\left(\frac{1}{2}, \frac{2}{3}\right), \left(\frac{5}{2}, -\frac{3}{2}\right)$

11.4 Practice A

In Exercises 1–3, tell whether the solid is a polyhedron. If it is, name the polyhedron.

1.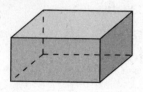

2.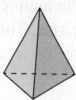

3.

In Exercises 4–6, describe the cross section formed by the intersection of the plane and the solid.

4.

5.

6.

In Exercises 7–9, sketch the solid produced by rotating the figure around the given axis. Then identify and describe the solid.

7.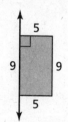

8.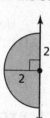

9.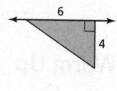

10. Is the block shown a polyhedron? Explain your reasoning.

11. Sketch a cube. Is it possible for a cross section of a cube to be a square? Explain your reasoning. If so, describe or sketch two different ways in which the plane could intersect the solid.

12. Consider the rectangular prism in Exercise 1. The length of the prism is 4 inches, the width is 2 inches, and the height is 2 inches.

    a. What is the perimeter of the cross section?

    b. What is the area of the cross section?

11.4 Practice B

In Exercises 1–3, describe the cross section formed by the intersection of the plane and the solid.

1.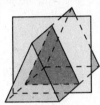

2.

3.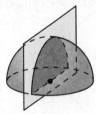

In Exercises 4–6, sketch the solid produced by rotating the figure around the given axis. Then identify and describe the solid.

4.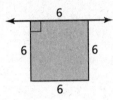

5.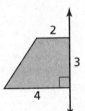

6.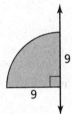

7. Which of the parts shown are polyhedrons? Explain your reasoning.

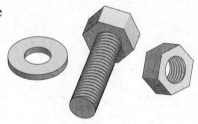

8. Sketch the composite solid produced by rotating the composite figure around the given axis. Then identify and describe the composite solid.

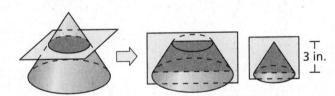

9. A cone with a height of 6 inches and radius of 4 inches is sliced in half by a horizontal plane, creating a circular cross section with a radius of 2 inches. Each piece is then sliced in half by a vertical plane, as shown.

   a. Describe the shape formed by each cross section.

   b. What are the perimeters and areas of the cross sections?

   c. Suppose the horizontal plane is tilted, slicing the original cone as shown at the right. Is the cross section a circle? If it is not, describe how it is different from a circle and sketch the cross section.

11.4 Enrichment and Extension

Three-Dimensional Figures

Draw the solid revolution formed by the shape rotated around the z-axis.

1.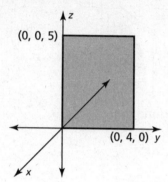

2.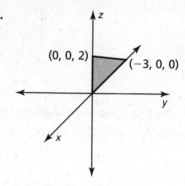

3. If you find the cross section of a solid of revolution in a plane that is perpendicular to the axis of rotation, you will always get the same shape. What is it?

4. The figure to the right is an example of an oblique cylinder. Is this a solid of revolution? Explain your reasoning.

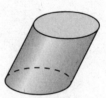

A *double cone* is formed by two cones that share the same vertex. Sketch each cross section formed by a double cone and plane.

5.

6.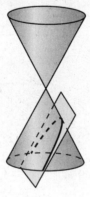

7.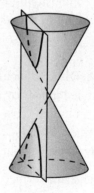

Name_____ Date_____

 **11.4 Puzzle Time**

Why Was Everyone So Tired On April 1st?

A	B	C	D	E	F
G	H	I	J		

Complete each exercise. Find the answer in the answer column. Write the word under the answer in the box containing the exercise letter.

true **MOST**	
cylinder **A**	
Egyptian triangle **BEFORE**	
polyhedron **BECAUSE**	
merging **MIDNIGHT**	
pentagonal prism **DAYS**	
platonic hut **FOR**	
vertex **JUST**	
tritex **OIL**	
triangular prism **OF**	

Complete the sentence.

A. A(n) _____ is a solid that is bounded by polygons called faces.

B. The intersection of a plane and a solid is called a _____ section.

C. An edge of a polyhedron is a line segment formed by the _____ of two faces.

D. A(n) _____ of a polyhedron is a point where three or more edges meet.

E. There are six Platonic solids. True or false?

Identify what solid is produced by rotating the indicated figure around the given axis.

F. a 4-by-4 square on a vertical axis

G. a 3-by-3 right triangle on a vertical axis

Identify the polyhedron.

H.   **I.**   **J.**

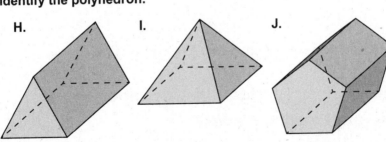

rectangular pyramid **THIRTY-ONE**	
hat box **HOME**	
prism **FOOLS**	
intersection **HAD**	
plain **SLEEP**	
cross **THEY**	
box **AND**	
false **FINISHED**	
cone **MARCH**	
pyramid **THE**	

11.5 Start Thinking

Consider the stack of coins shown in Figure A. What is the volume of the cylinder formed by the stack of coins? The same coins are stacked as shown in Figure B. What is the volume of this new cylinder? Did the height of the stack change? Did the volume change? What conclusion can you make about the volume of a cylinder, right or oblique?

Figure A   **Figure B**

11.5 Warm Up

Find the volume of the solid.

1.

6 cm   8 cm

7 cm

2.

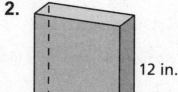

12 in.

10 in.   4 in.

3.

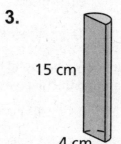

15 cm

4 cm

11.5 Cumulative Review Warm Up

Use a calculator to find the trigonometric ratio. Round your answer to four decimal places.

1. sin 139°   **2.** sin 98°   **3.** tan 165°

4. cos 122°   **5.** cos 173°   **6.** tan 103°

Name_____ Date_____

11.5 Practice A

In Exercises 1 and 2, find the volume of the prism.

1.
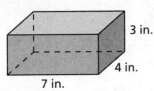
3 in.
4 in.
7 in.

2.
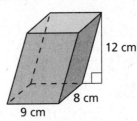
12 cm
8 cm
9 cm

In Exercises 3 and 4, find the volume of the cylinder.

3.
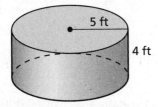
5 ft
4 ft

4.
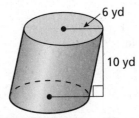
6 yd
10 yd

5. A cylindrical container with a radius of 12 centimeters is filled to a height of 6 centimeters with coconut oil. The density of coconut oil is 0.92 gram per cubic centimeter. What is the mass of the coconut oil to the nearest gram?

In Exercises 6 and 7, find the missing dimension.

6. Volume = 240 m^3

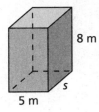
8 m
s
5 m

7. Volume = 1244 in.^{3}

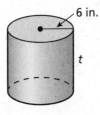
6 in.
t

In Exercises 8 and 9, find the area of the base of the rectangular prism with the given volume and height. Then give a possible length and width.

8. $V = 96$ ft^3, $h = 8$ ft

9. $V = 144$ cm^3, $h = 6$ cm

10. The prisms are similar. Find the volume of Prism B.

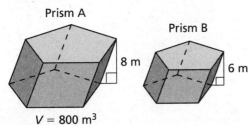
Prism A
Prism B
8 m
6 m
$V = 800$ m^3

11. Find the volume of the composite solid.

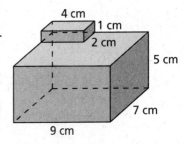
4 cm
1 cm
2 cm
5 cm
7 cm
9 cm

12. A cylindrical swimming pool is approximately 12 feet wide and 4 feet deep. About how many gallons of water does the swimming pool contain? Remember that 1 cubic foot is approximately 7.48 gallons.

Name_____ Date _____

11.5 Practice B

In Exercises 1 and 2, find the volume of the prism.

1.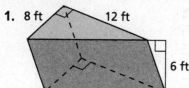
8 ft   12 ft
6 ft

2.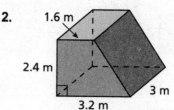
1.6 m
2.4 m
3 m
3.2 m

In Exercises 3 and 4, find the volume of the cylinder.

3.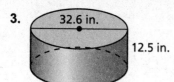
32.6 in.
12.5 in.

4.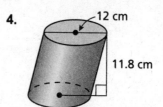
12 cm
11.8 cm

5. A cylindrical container with a radius of 8 centimeters is filled to a height of 10 centimeters with sulfuric acid. The density of sulfuric acid is 1.84 grams per cubic centimeter. What is the mass of the sulfuric acid to the nearest gram?

In Exercises 6 and 7, find the missing dimension.

6. Volume = 120 ft^3

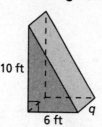
10 ft
6 ft
q

7. Volume = 254.5 m^3

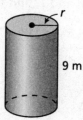
r
9 m

In Exercises 8 and 9, find the area of the base of the rectangular prism with the given volume and height. Then give a possible length and width.

8. $V = 216$ yd^3, $h = 12$ yd

9. $V = 448$ in.^{3}, $h = 14$ in.

10. The cylinders are similar. Find the volume of Cylinder B.

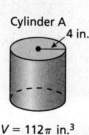
Cylinder A
4 in.
$V = 112\pi$ in.^{3}

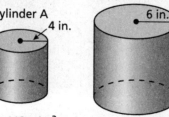
Cylinder B
6 in.

11. Find the volume of the composite solid.

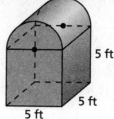
5 ft
5 ft
5 ft

12. An aquarium shaped like a rectangular prism has a length of 24 inches, a width of 12 inches, and a height of 18 inches. You fill the aquarium half full with water. When you submerge a rock in the aquarium, the water level rises 0.5 inch. Find the volume of the rock.

Name_____ Date_____

11.5 Enrichment and Extension

Volumes of Prisms and Cylinders

Find the volume of the three-dimensional figure in terms of x.

1.
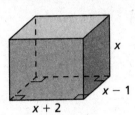

2.
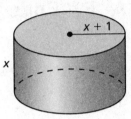

3. A rectangular prism has a volume of 720 cubic centimeters. Its surface area is 484 square centimeters and the edge lengths are consecutive integers. Determine the longest segment that can be drawn to connect two vertices.

4. The volume in cubic units of a cylinder is equal to its surface area in square units. Prove that the radius and height must both be greater than 2.

In Exercises 5 and 6, find the volume of the right prism or right cylinder.

5.
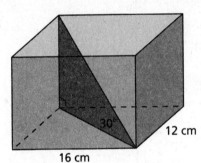

6.
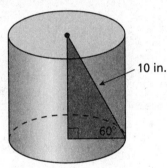

In Exercises 7–9, the figure is a cylinder with an oblique face. The volume V of such a cylinder is given by $V = \dfrac{\pi r^2}{2}(h_1 + h_2)$.

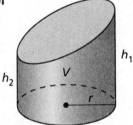

7. Find the volume of a cylinder with an oblique face in which $r = 8$ centimeters, $h_1 = 13$ centimeters, and $h_2 = 10$ centimeters.

8. Find the radius of a cylinder with an oblique face in which $V = 300\pi$ cubic inches, $h_1 = 13$ inches, and $h_2 = 11$ inches.

9. Find h_2 of a cylinder with an oblique face in which $V = 88\pi$ cubic feet, $r = 4$ feet, and $h_1 = 6$ feet.

11.5 Puzzle Time

What Starts With A "P," Ends With An "E," And Has One Million Letters In It?

Write the letter of each answer in the box containing the exercise number.

Complete the sentence.

1. The _____ of a solid is the number of cubic units contained in its interior.

2. _____ Principle states that if two solids have the same height and the same cross-sectional area at every level, then they have the same volume.

3. _____ is the amount of matter that an object has per unit volume.

Find the volume in square feet of the figure. Round your answer to the nearest hundredth.

4.
7 ft
9 ft

5.
9 ft
22 ft

6.
6 ft   20 ft
4 ft

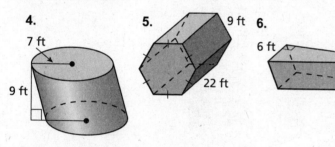

Find the value of the variable.

7.
z m
17 m
$V = 213.52$ m³

8.
u ft
16 ft   6 ft
$V = 2304$ ft³

9.
14 cm
11 cm w cm
$V = 770$ cm³

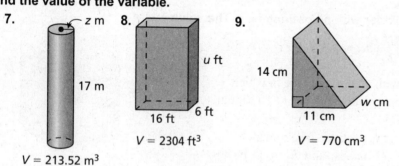

10. An element has a volume of 20.2 cubic centimeters and a mass of 121.2 grams. Find the density (in grams per cubic centimeter).

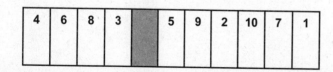

| 4 | 6 | 8 | 3 | | 5 | 9 | 2 | 10 | 7 | 1 |

Answers
E. volume
I. 6
J. area
O. 4629.77
P. Shepherd's
Q. 16
S. 24
T. 5
F. Cavalieri's
C. 2
D. mass
E. 1440
F. 15
O. 240
P. 1385.44
T. density
U. 2202.5
F. 10
G. 2315.82
P. 1384.74

11.6 Start Thinking

The diagrams show a cube and a pyramid. Each has a square base with an area of 25 square inches and a height of 5 inches. How do the volumes of the two figures compare? Explain your answer.

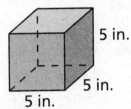

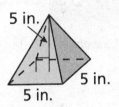

11.6 Warm Up

Find the area of the figure.

1.

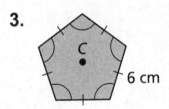

14 in.

30 in.

2.

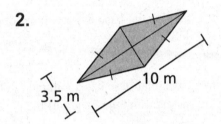

10 m

3.5 m

3.

C

6 cm

11.6 Cumulative Review Warm Up

Use the given information to write the standard equation of the circle.

1. The center is $(2, 5)$, and the measure of the radius is 7 units.

2. The center is $(-3, 9)$, and the measure of the diameter is 6 units.

3. The center is $(8, -4)$, and a point on the circle is $(0, -4)$.

4. The center is $(-11, -3)$, and a point on the circle is $(1, 2)$.

Name_____ Date _____

In Exercises 1–3, find the volume of the pyramid.

1.
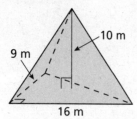
10 m
9 m
16 m

2.
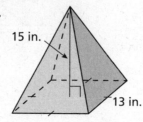
15 in.
13 in.

3.
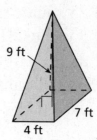
9 ft
7 ft
4 ft

In Exercises 4–6, find the indicated measure.

4. A pyramid with a square base has a volume of 320 cubic centimeters and a height of 15 centimeters. Find the side length of the square base.

5. A pyramid with a rectangular base has a volume of 60 cubic feet and a height of 6 feet. The width of the rectangular base is 4 feet. Find the length of the rectangular base.

6. A pyramid with a triangular base has a volume of 80 cubic meters and a base area of 20 square meters. Find the height of the pyramid.

In Exercises 7 and 8, the pyramids are similar. Find the volume of Pyramid B.

7. Pyramid A
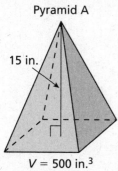
15 in.
$V = 500$ in.^{3}

Pyramid B

6 in.

8. Pyramid A
4 mm
$V = 16$ mm^3

Pyramid B
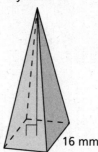
16 mm

In Exercises 9–11, find the volume of the composite solid.

9.
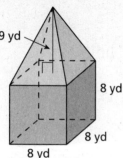
9 yd
8 yd
8 yd
8 yd

10.
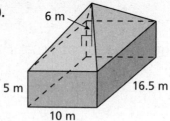
6 m
5 m
10 m
16.5 m

11.
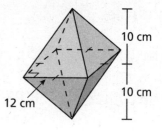
10 cm
10 cm
12 cm

12. The Pyramid Arena in Memphis, Tennessee is about 98 meters tall and has a square base with a side length of about 180 meters. A prism-shaped building has the same square base as the Pyramid Arena. What is the height of the building if it has the same volume as the Pyramid Arena?

Name_____ Date_____

11.6 Practice B

In Exercises 1–3, find the volume of the pyramid.

1.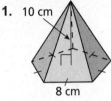
10 cm

8 cm

2.
7 ft

4 ft

3.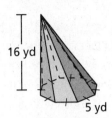
16 yd

5 yd

In Exercises 4 and 5, find the indicated measure.

4. A pyramid with a square base has a volume of 119.07 cubic meters and a height of 9 meters. Find the side length of the square base.

5. A pyramid with a hexagonal base has a volume of about 1082.54 cubic inches and a base area of about 259.81 square inches. Find the height of the pyramid.

In Exercises 6 and 7, the pyramids are similar. Find the volume of Pyramid B.

6.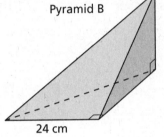

Pyramid A   Pyramid B

10 cm

$V = 160$ cm

24 cm

7.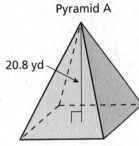

Pyramid A

20.8 yd

$V = 2059.2$ yd^3

Pyramid B

5.2 yd

In Exercises 8–10, find the volume of the composite solid.

8.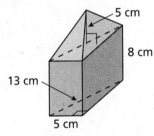
5 cm

8 cm

13 cm

5 cm

9.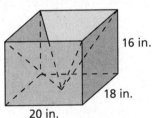
16 in.

18 in.

20 in.

10.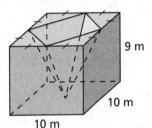
9 m

10 m

10 m

11. The volume of the pyramid shown is $48\sqrt{3}$ cubic meters. Find the value of x.

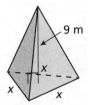
9 m

x

x x

Name _____ Date _____

11.6 Enrichment and Extension

Volumes of Pyramids

1. A right square pyramid has a base with a perimeter of 36 centimeters and a height of 12 centimeters. One-third of the distance from the base, the pyramid is cut by a plane parallel to its base. What is the volume of the top pyramid?

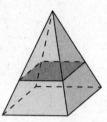

2. A regular octahedron has 8 faces that are equilateral triangles. Find the volume of a regular octahedron with a side length of 10 centimeters.

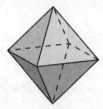

3. A three-dimensional figure in a coordinate space has vertices $A(0, 0, 0)$, $B(8, 0, 0)$, $C(0, 10, 0)$, $D(8, 10, 0)$, and $E(4, 4, 12)$. The height of the figure is EF, where the location of F is $F(4, 4, 0)$. Find the volume of the figure.

4. A three-dimensional figure in a coordinate space has vertices $P(0, 0, 0)$, $N(-10, 0, 0)$, $L(0, -10, 0)$, $M(-10, -10, 0)$, $K(-5, -5, -6)$, and $J(-5, -5, 7)$. What is the formula for finding the volume of the figure? What is the volume?

A *pyramidal frustum* is made by taking off the top half of a pyramid, with a cut parallel to the base. In order to find the volume of a pyramidal frustum, you can use the formula $V = \dfrac{h}{3}\left(A + A' + \sqrt{A \bullet A'}\right)$, where A is the area of the larger base, A' is the area of the smaller base, and h is the height.

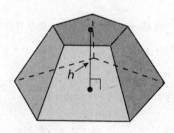

5. Find the volume of the truncated square pyramid whose larger base edge is 24 centimeters, smaller base edge is 14 centimeters, and lateral edge is 13 centimeters.

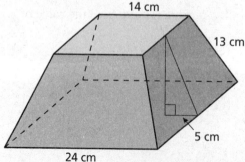

Name_____ Date _____

11.6 Puzzle Time

What Do You Get When It Rains On Your Convertible?

Circle the letter of each correct answer in the boxes below. The circled letters will spell
out the answer to the riddle.

Round your answer to nearest tenth.

1. A pyramid with a square base has a volume of 60 cubic meters and a height of
   2 meters. Find the side length in meters of the square base.

2. A pyramid with a rectangular base has a volume of 180 cubic inches and a height
   of 4 inches. The width of the rectangular base is 6 inches. Find the length in inches
   of the rectangular base.

3. The side lengths of the bases and length of the heights of two similar square pyramids,
   Pyramid A and Pyramid B, have a scale factor k of $\frac{1}{2}$. The smaller pyramid (Pyramid A)

   has a height of 3 units and a volume of 100 cubic units. Find the volume
   in cubic units of Pyramid B.

Find the volume (in cubic inches) of the figure. Round your answer to nearest tenth.

4.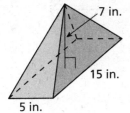

5.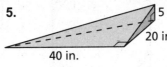

6.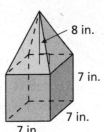

Find the value of the variable. Round your answer to nearest tenth.

7.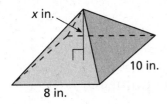

   Volume $= 120$ in.^{3}

8.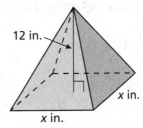

   Volume $= 600$ in.^{3}

A	W	E	C	B	A	T	M
22.5	489.3	30.5	800	130.7	473.7	15	24.4
S	R	P	A	O	M	O	L
4	4.5	175	5.5	9.5	200	12.2	666.7

11.7 Start Thinking

You are making cone-shaped hats for a drama production. The pattern calls for circles with a 20-inch diameter. You are to cut out a sector created by a 60° angle, as shown in the figure. What is the circumference of the circular base of the cone? Use this circumference and the formula $C = 2\pi r$ to find the radius of the circular base of the cone. You want to cover the top of the hat with fabric. What is the surface area that you will cover?

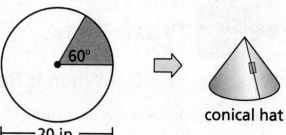

conical hat

11.7 Warm Up

Find the area of the shaded region.

1.

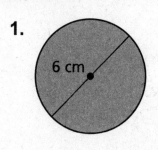

6 cm

2.

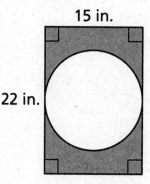

15 in.

22 in.

3.

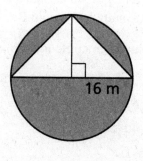

16 m

11.7 Cumulative Review Warm Up

Find an equation of the line.

1. parallel to the line $y = 2x + 3$, passes through the point $(0, -8)$

2. parallel to the line $y = x$, passes through the point $(-2, 7)$

3. perpendicular to the line $y = -5x - 7$, passes through the point $(-1, -3)$

11.7 Practice A

In Exercises 1 and 2, find the surface area of the right cone.

1.

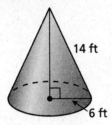

14 ft

6 ft

2.

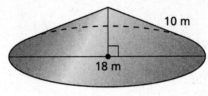

10 m

18 m

In Exercises 3 and 4, find the volume of the cone.

3.

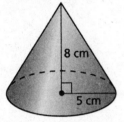

8 cm

5 cm

4.

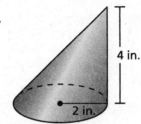

4 in.

2 in.

In Exercises 5 and 6, the cones are similar. Find the volume of Cone B.

5.

Cone A   Cone B

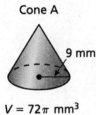 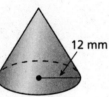

9 mm   12 mm

$V = 72\pi$ mm^3

6.

Cone A   Cone B

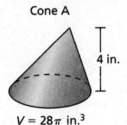

4 in.   2 in.

$V = 28\pi$ in.^{3}

In Exercises 7 and 8, find the volume of the composite solid.

7.

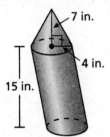

7 in.

4 in.

15 in.

8.

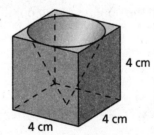

4 cm

4 cm

4 cm

9. A cone has height h and a base with radius r. You want to change the cone so its volume is tripled. What is the new height if you only change the height? What is the new radius if you only change the radius? Explain.

10. A snack stand serves shaved ice in cone-shaped containers and cylindrical containers. Which container gives you more shaved ice for your money? Explain.

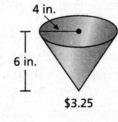

4 in.

6 in.

$3.25

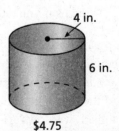

4 in.

6 in.

$4.75

Name _____ Date _____

11.7 Practice B

In Exercises 1 and 2, find the surface area of the right cone.

1.

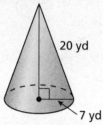

20 yd

7 yd

2.

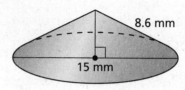

8.6 mm

15 mm

In Exercises 3 and 4, find the volume of the cone.

3.

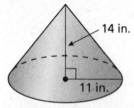

14 in.

11 in.

4.

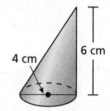

4 cm

6 cm

In Exercises 5 and 6, the cones are similar. Find the volume of Cone B.

5.

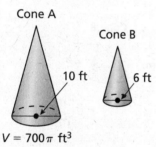

Cone A

Cone B

10 ft

6 ft

$V = 700\pi$ ft^3

6.

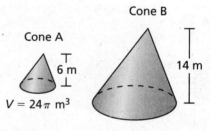

Cone B

Cone A

6 m

14 m

$V = 24\pi$ m^3

In Exercises 7 and 8, find the volume of the composite solid.

7.

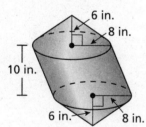

6 in.

8 in.

10 in.

6 in.

8 in.

8.

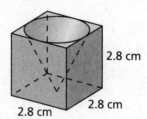

2.8 cm

2.8 cm

2.8 cm

9. A cone has height h and a base with radius r. You want to change the cone so its volume is halved. What is the new height if you only change the height? What is the new radius if you only change the radius? Explain.

10. During a chemistry lab, you use a funnel to pour a solvent into a flask. The radius of the funnel is 4 centimeters and its height is 12 centimeters. You pour the solvent into the funnel at a rate of 60 milliliters per second and the solvent flows out of the funnel at a rate of 40 milliliters per second. How long will it be before the funnel overflows? (Remember that 1 milliliter is equal to 1 cubic centimeter.)

Name_____ Date _____

Surface Area and Volumes of Cones

1. A disk has a radius of 10 meters. A 90° sector is cut away, and a cone is formed.

   a. What is the circumference of the base of the cone?

   b. What is the area of the base of the cone?

   c. What is the volume of the cone?

A cone is inscribed in a regular pyramid with a base edge length of 2 feet and a height of 2 feet. Find the volume of the cone.

2.   3. 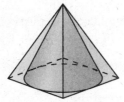   4.

5. Find the volume of the cone to the right.

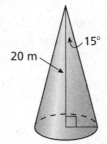

6. How could you change the height of a cone so that its volume would remain the same when its radius was tripled?

The *frustum* of a cone is formed by removing the top of a cone with a cut parallel to the base. In the figure at the right, r is the radius of the top of the frustum, R is the radius of the bottom, h is the height, and ℓ is the slant height.

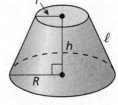

The surface area S of a frustum of a cone in terms of r, R, and ℓ can be written as $S = \pi(r + R)\ell + \pi r^2 + \pi R^2$, or in terms of r, R, and h as

$$S = \pi(r + R)\sqrt{(R - r)^2 + h^2} + \pi r^2 + \pi R^2.$$

7. Find the surface area of the frustum of a cone with $r = 6$ feet, $R = 8$ feet, and $\ell = 13$ feet.

8. Find the surface area of the frustum of a cone with $r = 2.1$ meters, $R = 7.9$ meters, and $h = 12.2$ meters.

11.7 Puzzle Time

Why Do Traffic Lights Never Go Swimming?

A	B	C	D	E	F
G					

Complete each exercise. Use $\pi \approx 3.14$. Find the answer in the answer column. Write the word under the answer in the box containing the exercise letter.

418.7 CHANGE	
lateral BECAUSE	
side THE	
342.5 WET	
575.7 TO	
612.7 WATER	
470.5 TOO	

Complete the sentence.

A. The _____ surface of a cone consists of all segments that connect the vertex with points on the base edge.

B. A right cone has a radius of 2 feet and a slant height of 9 feet. The volume is _____ cubic feet. Round your answer to the nearest tenth.

Find the surface area (in square units) of the cone. Round your answer to the nearest tenth.

C.

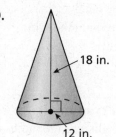

14 in.

6 in.

D.

18 in.

12 in.

E.

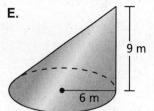

9 m

6 m

F.

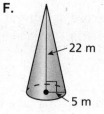

22 m

5 m

G.

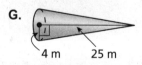

4 m   25 m

16.9 STOP	
339.1 LONG	
417.8 AND	
248.5 GREEN	
36.7 THEY	
525.7 WAIT	
376.8 TAKE	

11.8 Start Thinking

You buy a friend a basketball as a gift. You want to construct a container to put the ball in to disguise it when it is wrapped. You construct the two containers shown in the diagram. Find the surface area of each container. Do the containers have the same surface area as the ball? If not, which container has a surface area that is closer to that of the ball?

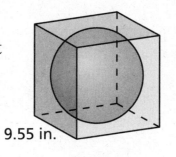

9.55 in.

Cube

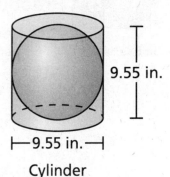

9.55 in.

9.55 in.

Cylinder

11.8 Warm Up

Use the diagram and the given surface area to find the value of x.

1. $S = 1350$ in.^{2}

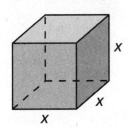

x

x

x

Cube

2. $S = 270$ in.^{2}

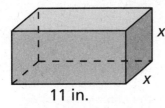

x

x

11 in.

Rectangular solid

3. $S = 78\pi$ in.^{2}

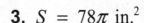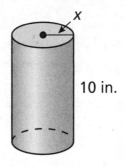

x

10 in.

Cylinder

11.8 Cumulative Review Warm Up

Tell whether the line, ray, or segment is best described as a radius, chord, diameter, secant, or tangent of ⊙C.

1. $\overline{CF}$

2. $\overrightarrow{AB}$

3. $\overline{FB}$

4. $\overline{EF}$

5. $\overleftrightarrow{DF}$

6. $\overline{BC}$

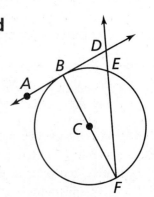

11.8 Practice A

In Exercises 1–3, find the surface area of the sphere.

1.
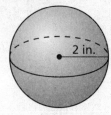
2 in.

2.
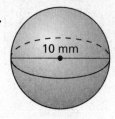
10 mm

3.
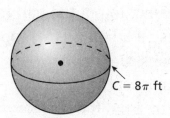
$C = 8\pi$ ft

In Exercises 4 and 5, find the indicated measure.

4. the radius of a sphere with a surface area of 36π square meters

5. the diameter of a sphere with a surface area of 81π square yards

In Exercises 6–8, find the volume of the sphere.

6.
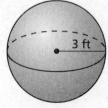
3 ft

7.
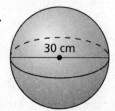
30 cm

8.
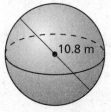
10.8 m

In Exercises 9 and 10, find the volume of the sphere with the given surface area.

9. Surface Area = 4π in.^{2}

10. Surface Area = 676π km^2

In Exercises 11 and 12, find the volume of the composite solid.

11.
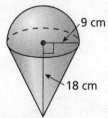
9 cm
18 cm

12.
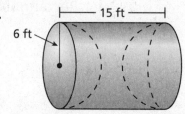
15 ft
6 ft

13. Find the surface area and volume of the solid
produced by rotating the figure at the right
around the given axis.

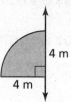
4 m
4 m

14. A sphere is inscribed in a cube with a volume
of 8 cubic yards. What is the surface area of
the sphere? Explain your reasoning.

15. In 2000, the International Table Tennis Federation changed the official diameter of
a table tennis ball from 38 millimeters to 40 millimeters. Without calculating surface
areas and volumes, determine how the surface area and volume of the ball changed.
Explain your reasoning. Find the surface areas and volumes to check your answer.

Name_____ Date _____

11.8 Practice B

In Exercises 1–3, find the surface area of the sphere or hemisphere.

1.
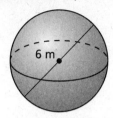
6 m

2.
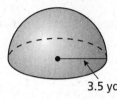
3.5 yd

3.
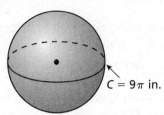
C = 9π in.

In Exercises 4 and 5, find the indicated measure.

4. the radius of a sphere with a surface area of 100π square centimeters

5. the diameter of a sphere with a surface area of 6.25π square inches

In Exercises 6–8, find the volume of the sphere or hemisphere.

6.
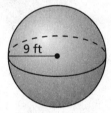
9 ft

7.
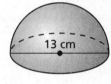
13 cm

8.
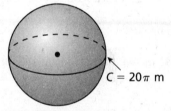
C = 20π m

In Exercises 9 and 10, find the volume of the sphere with the given surface area.

9. Surface Area = 144π ft²

10. Surface Area = π mi²

In Exercises 11 and 12, find the volume of the composite solid.

11.
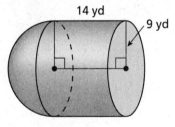
14 yd
9 yd

12.
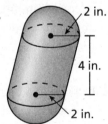
2 in.
4 in.
2 in.

13. The diameter of a spherical balloon shrinks to one-half of its original size. Describe how the surface area and volume of the balloon change.

14. A museum has two spherical cannonballs on display. Each cannonball is made of a type of iron that weighs about 463 pounds per cubic foot.

   a. The diameter of the smaller cannonball is 1 inch less than the diameter of the larger cannonball. Can you determine how much less the smaller cannonball weighs than the larger cannonball? Explain your reasoning.

   b. The smaller cannonball displaces 33.5 cubic inches of water when dropped in a bucket full of water. To the nearest pound, how much less does the smaller cannonball weigh than the larger cannonball?

11.8 Enrichment and Extension

Surfaces Areas and Volumes of Spheres

1. Four balls, each with a radius of 1 inch, fit snugly into a 2-inch by 2-inch by 8-inch box. Is the total volume left over inside the box greater than or less than the volume of a fifth ball? Justify your answer.

2. A vessel is in the shape of a hemisphere mounted on a cylinder of same radius of 8 meters. The height of the cylindrical portion is 4 meters. Determine the approximate capacity of the tank in liters. Round your answer to the nearest liter.

3. The top of a gumball machine is a sphere with a diameter of 18 inches. The machine holds a maximum capacity of 3300 gumballs, which leaves about 43% of the space in the machine empty. Estimate the diameter of each gumball. Round your answer to the nearest tenth.

4. The surface area of a sphere can be used to determine its volume.

   a. Solve the surface area formula of a sphere to obtain an expression for r in terms of S.

   b. Substitute your result from part (a) into the volume formula to find the volume V of a sphere in terms of its surface area S.

   c. Graph the relationship between volume and surface area with S on the horizontal axis and V on the vertical axis. What shape is the graph?

5. A sphere has a radius r. Draw a composite figure made up of a square prism (not a cube) and a square pyramid that has the same volume as the sphere.

6. Find the surface area of the composite figure from Exercise 5.

7. Consider a composite figure made up of a cylinder and a cone that has the same volume as a sphere with radius r. Find the figure's surface area.

11.8 Puzzle Time

What Do Chickens Collect On The Beach?

Circle the letter of each correct answer in the boxes below. The circled letters will spell out the answer to the riddle.

Complete the sentence.

1. A(n) _____ is the set of all points in space equidistant from a given point.

2. A chord of a sphere is a(n) _____ whose endpoints are on the sphere.

3. If a plane contains the center of a sphere, then the intersection is a(n) _____ circle of the sphere.

4. Find the radius (in feet) of a sphere with a surface area of 8π square feet.

5. Find the diameter (in centimeters) of a sphere with a surface area of 156π square centimeters.

Find the volume in cubic feet. Round your answer to the nearest tenth.

6.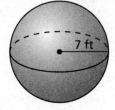
7 ft

7.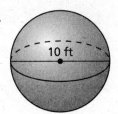
10 ft

8.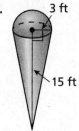
3 ft
15 ft

9. Sphere A is similar to Sphere B. The scale factor of the lengths of the radii of Sphere A to Sphere B is 1 to 4. Sphere A has a radius of 6 units and a volume of 288π cubic units. Find the volume (in cubic units) of Sphere B.

A	M	E	I	G	N	G	S	O
line	718.0	sphere	6.7	1436.8	147	523.6	$18,432\pi$	4365.6

R	H	E	G	L	E	M	L	S
big	great	$2\sqrt{39}$	circle	$\sqrt{2}$	3.4	2304π	197.9	segment

Chapter 11 Cumulative Review

In Exercises 1–6, find the missing dimension.

1. A rectangle has a perimeter of 32 feet and a length of 7 feet. What is the width of the rectangle?

2. A square has a perimeter of 64 centimeters. What is the length of one side of the square?

3. A triangle has a perimeter of 23 inches. One side length is 7 inches, and another side length is 11 inches. What is the length of the third side of the triangle?

4. A rectangle has an area of 126 square kilometers and a length of 7 kilometers. What is the width of the rectangle?

5. A triangle has an area of 77 square meters and a height of 14 meters. What is the length of the base of the triangle?

6. A square has an area of 324 square millimeters. What is the length of the sides of the square?

In Exercises 7–10, the endpoints of $\overline{CD}$ are given. Find the coordinates of the midpoint M.

7. $C(-6, 5)$ and $D(8, -1)$
8. $C(-5, -7)$ and $D(3, 9)$

9. $C(-1, 1)$ and $D(-5, 7)$
10. $C(9, 2)$ and $D(7, -6)$

In Exercises 11–14, the midpoint M and one endpoint of $\overline{GH}$ are given. Find the coordinate of the other endpoint.

11. $M(1, 3)$ and $G(-1, 6)$
12. $M(2, 4)$ and $H(9, 5)$

13. $M(-9, 1)$ and $H(-8, -3)$
14. $M(-7, 8)$ and $G(-8, 8)$

In Exercises 15–20, find the distance between the two points.

15. $A(-2, -4)$ and $B(-3, -4)$
16. $C(10, -9)$ and $D(-9, -4)$

17. $E(-10, 1)$ and $F(1, -5)$
18. $G(-9, -1)$ and $H(-2, -6)$

19. $J(6, 2)$ and $K(-4, -7)$
20. $M(6, 3)$ and $N(6, -3)$

In Exercises 21 and 22, write three names for the angle.

21.
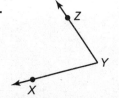

22.
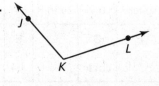

Chapter 11 Cumulative Review (continued)

In Exercises 23–26, describe the pattern. Then write the next two numbers or letters.

23. 2, 4, 6, 8, 10, …

24. −1, 3, −5, 7, −9, …

25. A, D, G, J, M, …

26. B, D, F, H, J, …

In Exercises 27–34, solve the equation.

27. $-6x + 11 = 17$

28. $10x - 2 = 8$

29. $2x + 7 = -x - 11$

30. $-9x + 10 = 2x - 1$

31. $9(x - 1) = 9$

32. $2(10 + 2x) = 32$

33. $-7(x - 3) = 70$

34. $5(-7x - 7) = -70$

In Exercises 35–40, solve the equation for y.

35. $4x + y = -7$

36. $10x - 2y = -4$

37. $-6x + 6y = 48$

38. $5x + \dfrac{1}{2}y = 3$

39. $7x - \dfrac{y}{5} = 10$

40. $\dfrac{2}{3}y - 6x = -4$

In Exercises 41–44, find the values of x and y.

41.

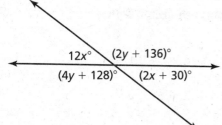

$12x°$ $(2y + 136)°$
$(4y + 128)°$ $(2x + 30)°$

42.

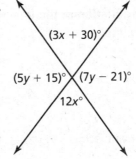

$(3x + 30)°$
$(5y + 15)°$ $(7y - 21)°$
$12x°$

43.

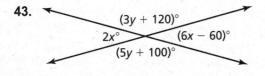

$(3y + 120)°$
$2x°$ $(6x - 60)°$
$(5y + 100)°$

44.

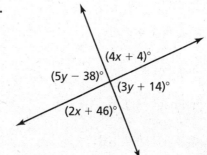

$(4x + 4)°$
$(5y - 38)°$
$(3y + 14)°$
$(2x + 46)°$

Chapter 11 **Cumulative Review** (continued)

In Exercises 45–48, find the value of *x*.

45.

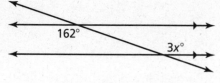

162°
3*x*°

46.

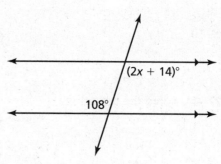

(2*x* + 14)°
108°

47.

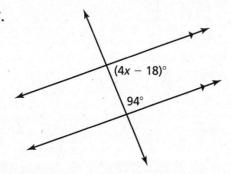

(4*x* − 18)°
94°

48.

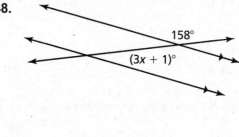

158°
(3*x* + 1)°

In Exercises 49–52, write an equation of the line passing through the point *P* that is parallel to the given line.

49. $P(10, -9), y = 3x + 5$

50. $P(-5, -1), y = -8x + 4$

51. $P(-8, 4), -2y = -8x + 6$

52. $P(-1, 1), 10x + 5y = -25$

In Exercises 53–56, write an equation of the line passing through the point *P* that is perpendicular to the given line.

53. $P(-4, -4), y = -4x - 2$

54. $P(7, -4), y = -x + 10$

55. $P(3, -9), y = \frac{3}{2}x - 7$

56. $P(3, 2), y = \frac{1}{8}x + 9$

In Exercises 57–61, use the translation $(x, y) \rightarrow (x - 1, y + 2)$.

57. What is the image of $A(-8, 0)$?

58. What is the image of $B(7, -5)$?

59. What is the image of $C(-5, 5)$?

60. What is the preimage of $D'(8, 3)$?

61. What is the preimage of $E'(-12, -1)$?

Chapter 11 **Cumulative Review** (continued)

In Exercises 62–66, use △PQR with vertices P(−3, 0), Q(1, 2), and R(5, −2) to determine the vertices of its image after the translation.

62. $(x, y) \rightarrow (x - 7, y + 11)$

63. $(x, y) \rightarrow (x + 8, y - 4)$

64. $(x, y) \rightarrow (x - 10, y - 1)$

65. $(x, y) \rightarrow (x + 2, y - 6)$

66. $(x, y) \rightarrow (x - 6, y - 1)$

In Exercises 67–71, use the vertices of the polygon to determine the vertices of its image after a dilation with scale factor k.

67. $A(9, -7), B(7, 0), C(0, -4); k = 3$

68. $X(-2, -10), Y(0, 11), Z(11, -11); k = 2$

69. $M(-6, 0), N(-12, 9), P(9, 6); k = \frac{1}{3}$

70. $Q(-10, -8), R(0, -12), S(8, 10), T(6, -12); k = \frac{1}{2}$

71. $D(8, 2), E(8, -10), F(7, 4), F(6, 1); k = 4$

72. You are presented with three different shapes.

  a. You have a circle with a radius of 8 inches. Find the circumference of the circle. Round your answer to the nearest tenth.

  b. You have a square with a side length of 14 inches. Find the perimeter of the square.

  c. You have a rectangle with a length of 11 inches and a width of 16 inches. Find the perimeter of the rectangle.

73. You are presented with three different shapes.

  a. You have a circle with a radius of 4 centimeters. Find the area of the circle. Round your answer to the nearest tenth.

  b. You have a square with a side length of 7 centimeters. Find the area of the square.

  c. You have a rectangle with a length of 8 centimeters and a width of 6 centimeters. Find the area of the rectangle.

  d. Which of the three shapes has the largest area?

Chapter 12

Chapter 12 Probability

Dear Family,

What is your favorite game to play as a family? Is this game based on chance, strategy, or both? Some board games use dice, cards, or a spinner to determine how a player must move around the board. Other games involve drawing tiles out of a bag or drawing from a deck of cards. When you play these games, you hope to draw, spin, or roll outcomes that are in your favor. You then use these outcomes and some strategy to try and win the game. In this chapter, you will be using dice, coins, cards, and spinners to study probability. It can be frustrating to play a game when you seem to always draw, spin, or roll outcomes that are not in your favor. Which game involving probabilities do you find to be the most frustrating? Which game do you find to be the most fair?

As a family, complete the table using examples of games you have played.

	Die or Dice (with numbers)	Die or Dice (with letters)	Drawing from a deck of cards	Drawing from a bag	Spinner
Name of game					
Total number of outcomes					
Is the probability of each outcome equally likely?					
Does the game involve chance, strategy, or both?					

The best outcome of game night is having fun together!

Nombre _____ Fecha _____

Capítulo 12 Probabilidad

Estimada familia:

¿Cuál su juego favorito para jugar en familia? ¿Es un juego basado en posibilidad, estrategia o ambas? En algunos juegos de mesa, se usan dados, tarjetas o una rueda giratoria para determinar cómo debe moverse un jugador por el tablero. En otros juegos, se sacan fichas de una bolsa o se saca una tarjeta de un mazo de tarjetas. Cuando juegan a estos juegos, esperan sacar, girar o lanzar resultados que estén a su favor. Luego, usan estos resultados y alguna estrategia para tratar de ganar el juego. En este capítulo, usarán dados, monedas, tarjetas y ruedas giratorias para estudiar la probabilidad. Puede ser frustrante jugar a un juego cuando siempre parecen sacar, girar o lanzar resultados que no los favorecen. ¿Cuál juego donde se usan las probabilidades les parece más frustrante? ¿Cuál juego les parece más justo?

En familia, completen la tabla con ejemplos de juegos que hayan jugado.

	Dado o dados (con números)	Dado o dados (con letras)	Sacar de un mazo de tarjetas	Sacar de una bolsa	Rueda giratoria
Nombre del juego					
Número total de resultados					
¿La probabilidad de cada resultado es igualmente probable?					
¿El juego implica posibilidad, estrategia o ambas?					

¡El mejor resultado de una noche de juego es divertirse juntos!

12.1 Start Thinking

Last season's basketball uniforms were stored in two boxes. One box contains 15 numbered jerseys; the other contains the matching numbered shorts. Your coach tells you to grab a jersey from one box and a pair of shorts from the other box. All 15 players grab a jersey from the first box.

1. You are the first one to reach into the box of shorts. You grab the first pair of shorts you touch. How likely is it that you will grab the number that matches your jersey?

2. Assuming the 15 uniforms are numbered 1 to 15, list all the possible outcomes for your uniform if your jersey is number 11.

12.1 Warm Up

List the possible outcomes for the situation.

1. tossing a coin three times

2. spinning a spinner twice that contains four equally likely colors—blue, red, yellow, and green

3. spinning the spinner mentioned in Exercise 2 followed by tossing a coin

12.1 Cumulative Review Warm Up

Let θ be an acute angle of a right triangle. Evaluate the other five trigonometric functions of θ.

1. $\sin \theta = \dfrac{4}{7}$

2. $\cos \theta = \dfrac{8}{9}$

3. $\tan \theta = \dfrac{5}{4}$

4. $\csc \theta = \dfrac{8}{3}$

5. $\cot \theta = \dfrac{3}{4}$

6. $\sec \theta = \dfrac{9}{5}$

Name _____ Date _____

12.1 Practice A

In Exercises 1 and 2, find the number of possible outcomes in the sample space. Then list the possible outcomes.

1. You flip three coins.

2. A clown has three purple balloons labeled a, b, and c, three yellow balloons labeled a, b, and c, and three turquoise balloons labeled a, b, and c. The clown chooses a balloon at random.

3. Your friend has eight sweatshirts. Three sweatshirts are green, one is white, and four are blue. You forgot your sweatshirt, so your friend is going to bring one for you as well as one for himself. What is the probability that your friend will bring two blue sweatshirts?

4. The estimated percentage student GPA distribution is shown. Find the probability of each event.

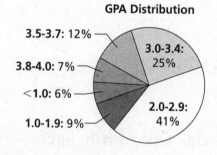

GPA Distribution

3.5-3.7: 12%
3.8-4.0: 7%
<1.0: 6%
1.0-1.9: 9%
3.0-3.4: 25%
2.0-2.9: 41%

   a. A student chosen at random has GPA of at least 3.0.

   b. A student chosen at random has GPA between 1.0 and 2.9, inclusive.

5. A bag contains the same number of each of four different colors of marbles. A marble is drawn, its color is recorded, and then the marble is placed back in the bag. This process is repeated until 40 marbles have been drawn. The table shows the results. For which marble is the experimental probability of drawing the marble the same as the theoretical probability?

Drawing Results			
yellow	red	blue	black
12	10	7	11

12.1 Practice B

In Exercises 1 and 2, find the number of possible outcomes in the sample space. Then list the possible outcomes.

1. You roll a die and draw a token at random from a bag containing three pink tokens and one red token.

2. You draw 3 marbles without replacement from a bag containing two brown marbles and three yellow marbles.

3. When two six-sided dice are rolled, there are 36 possible outcomes.

   a. Find the probability that the sum is 5.

   b. Find the probability that the sum is not 5.

   c. Find the probability that the sum is less than or equal to 5.

   d. Find the probability that the sum is less than 5.

4. A tire is hung from a tree. The outside diameter is 34 inches and the inside diameter is 14 inches. You throw a baseball toward the opening of the tire. Your baseball is equally likely to hit any point on the tire or in the opening of the tire. What is the probability that you will throw the baseball through the opening in the tire?

In Exercises 5–7, tell whether the statement is *always*, *sometimes*, or *never* true. Explain your reasoning.

5. If there are exactly five possible outcomes and all outcomes are equally likely, then the theoretical probability of any of the five outcomes occurring is 0.20.

6. The experimental probability of an event occurring is equal to the theoretical probability of an event occurring.

7. The probability of an event added to the probability of the complement of the event is equal to 1.

8. A manufacturer tests 900 dishwashers and finds that 24 of them are defective. Find the probability that a dishwasher chosen at random has a defect. An apartment building orders 40 of the dishwashers. Predict the number of dishwashers in the apartment with defects.

12.1 Enrichment and Extension

Sample Spaces and Probability

The diagram at right shows a method of graphically recording the results of 12 coin tosses that occur in one-second intervals. The horizontal axis shows time t and the vertical axis shows position s. Beginning at the origin, the graph moves one unit up to record "heads" and one unit down to record "tails."

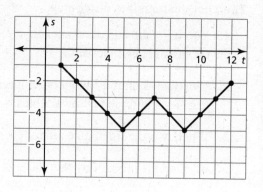

This type of graph is called a *random walk*. Random walks are mathematical formalizations of paths that consist of successions of random steps. Other examples include tracing the path of a molecule as it travels in a liquid or gas, or the price of a fluctuating stock.

1. Using H for "heads" and T for "tails," write the sequence for the random walk shown above.

Graph the random walk for the given coin sequences A, B, and C.

2. A: H, H, H, H, T, T, T, H, T, H, T, T, T, T, H

3. B: T, T, H, T, T, H, H, T, H, T, T, H, H, H, H

4. C: H, H, H, H, T, T, H, T, T, H, H, H, T, T, T

Refer to the graphs of sequences A, B, and C. For each sequence, give the time, if it exists, at which the random walk first returns to position $s = 0$. Then give the amount of time that the random walk spends in the first quadrant.

5. Sequence A 6. Sequence B 7. Sequence C

8. With a partner, toss a coin 20 times to generate a random walk. Generate 5 such walks.

    a. In what percent of your walks do you return to position $s = 0$ during the walk?

    b. What is the average number of tosses to return to position $s = 0$?

9. Give an example of a real-life situation for which a random walk would be an appropriate model. How are these models helpful when analyzing data?

Name_____ Date_____

12.1 Puzzle Time

What Happens When You Throw A Clock In The Air?

Write the letter of each answer in the box containing the exercise number.

Find the number of possible outcomes in the sample space.

1. You roll a die and flip two coins.

2. You draw two marbles without replacement from a bag containing four red marbles, two yellow marbles, and five blue marbles.

3. You flip six coins.

4. A bag contains eight black cards numbered 1 through 8 and six red cards numbered 1 through 6. You choose a card at random.

Find the probability.

5. You draw a number card from a standard deck of cards.

6. When two six-sided dice are rolled, there are 36 possible outcomes. Find the probability that the sum is less than 5.

7. In a classroom of 20 students, 12 students have brown hair, 4 students have blonde hair, 3 students have red hair, and one student has black hair. Find the probability of randomly selecting a blonde haired student from the classroom.

Answers
P. $\dfrac{1}{5}$
T. 24
E. 14
S. $\dfrac{9}{13}$
I. 40
M. 64
U. $\dfrac{1}{6}$

1	2	3	4	5		6	7

Abbey has applied for admittance to her favorite college. Abbey's softball team is playing for the district championship. If they win, they will play for the state championship. Which of the three events (being accepted at her favorite college, winning the district championship, and winning the state championship) are dependent? Which are independent? Explain.

12.2 Warm Up

A group of 128 students was asked to select their favorite high school sport: basketball, football, lacrosse, or baseball. The table shows the results. Use the results to find the probabilities that a student chosen at random from this group would prefer the following.

Survey Results			
basketball	football	lacrosse	baseball
48	35	20	25

1. lacrosse

2. football

3. baseball or basketball

4. football or lacrosse

5. one of the four sports

6. none of the four sports

12.2 Cumulative Review Warm Up

Factor the polynomial completely.

1. $2x^2 - 8$

2. $18x^2 - 3x - 36$

3. $8 - 27x^3$

4. $x^4 - 7x^2 - 18$

5. $5x^7 + 5x^4$

6. $x^4 - 5x^3 - 9x^2 + 45x$

12.2 Practice A

In Exercises 1 and 2, tell whether the events are *independent* or *dependent*. Explain your reasoning.

1. A box contains an assortment of tool items on clearance. You randomly choose a sale item, look at it, and then put it back in the box. Then you randomly choose another sale item.

   Event *A*: You choose a hammer first.

   Event *B*: You choose a pair of pliers second.

2. A cooler contains an assortment of juice boxes. You randomly choose a juice box and drink it. Then you randomly choose another juice box.

   Event *A*: You choose an orange juice box first.

   Event *B*: You choose a grape juice box second.

In Exercises 3 and 4, determine whether the events are independent.

3. You are playing a game that requires rolling a die twice. Use a sample space to determine whether rolling a 2 and then a 6 are independent events.

4. A game show host picks contestants for the next game, from an audience of 150. The host randomly chooses a thirty year old, and then randomly chooses a nineteen year old. Use a sample space to determine whether randomly choosing a thirty year old first and randomly selecting a nineteen year old second are independent events.

5. A hat contains 10 pieces of paper numbered from 1 to 10. Find the probability of each pair of events occurring as described.

   a. You randomly choose the number 1, you replace the number, and then you randomly choose the number 10.

   b. You randomly choose the number 5, you do not replace the number, and then you randomly choose the number 6.

6. The probability that a stock increases in value on a Monday is 60%. When the stock increases in value on Monday, the probability that the stock increases in value on Tuesday is 80%. What is the probability that the stock increases in value on both Monday and Tuesday of a given week?

12.2 Practice B

In Exercises 1 and 2, tell whether the events are *independent* or *dependent*. Explain your reasoning.

1. You and a friend are picking teams for a softball game. You randomly choose a player. Then your friend randomly chooses a player.

   Event *A*: You choose a pitcher.

   Event *B*: Your friend chooses a first baseman.

2. You are making bracelets for party favors. You randomly choose a charm and a piece of leather.

   Event *A*: You choose heart-shaped charm first.

   Event *B*: You choose a brown piece of leather second.

In Exercises 3 and 4, determine whether the events are independent.

3. You are playing a game that requires flipping a coin twice. Use a sample space to determine whether flipping heads and then tails are independent events.

4. A game show host picks contestants for the next game from an audience of 5 females and 4 males. The host randomly chooses a male, and then randomly chooses a male. Use a sample space to determine whether randomly choosing a male first and randomly choosing a male second are independent events.

5. A sack contains the 26 letters of the alphabet, each printed on a separate wooden tile. You randomly draw one letter, and then you randomly draw a second letter. Find the probability of each pair of events.

   a. You replace the first letter before drawing the second letter.

      Event *A*: The first letter drawn is T.

      Event *B*: The second letter drawn is A.

   b. You do not replace the first letter tile before drawing the second letter tile.

      Event *A*: The first letter drawn is P.

      Event *B*: The second letter drawn is S.

6. At a high school football game, 80% of the spectators buy a beverage at the concession stand. Only 20% of the spectators buy both a beverage and a food item. What is the probability that a spectator who buys a beverage also buys a food item?

Name_____ Date_____

12.2 Enrichment and Extension

Independent and Dependent Events

	25 to 34	35 to 54	55 and over	Total
Did not complete high school	5325	9152	16,035	30,512
Completed high school	14,061	24,070	18,320	56,451
1 to 3 years of college	11,659	19,926	9662	41,247
4 or more years of college	10,342	19,878	8005	38,225
Total	41,387	73,026	52,022	166,435

In Exercises 1–4, use your knowledge of probability to analyze the table about years of education completed by age. If a person is chosen at random from this population:

1. What is the probability that the person is in the 25 to 34 age range and in the 55 and over age range?

2. What is the probability that a person is between 25 and 34 years of age and they have completed 1 to 3 years of college?

3. If the person is in the 55 and over age range, what is the probability that they completed 1 to 3 years of college?

4. If the person has completed high school, what is the probability that they are 35 to 54 years old?

5. If a person is vaccinated properly, the probability of his/her getting a certain disease is 0.05. Without a vaccination, the probability of getting the disease is 0.35. Assume that $\frac{1}{3}$ of the population is properly vaccinated.

   a. If a person is selected at random from the population, what is the probability of that person's getting the disease?

   b. If a person gets the disease, what is the probability that he/she was vaccinated?

6. Suppose a test for diagnosing a certain serious disease is successful in detecting the disease in 95% of all persons infected, but that it incorrectly diagnoses 4% of all healthy people as having the serious disease. If it is known that 2% of the population has the serious disease, find the probability that a person selected at random has the serious disease if the test indicates that he or she does.

7. The probability that a football player weighs more than 230 pounds is 0.69, that he is at least 75 inches tall is 0.55, and that he weighs more than 230 pounds and is at least 75 inches tall is 0.43. Find the probability that he is at least 75 inches tall if he weighs more than 230 pounds.

12.2 Puzzle Time

What Do You Put In A Barrel To Make It Lighter?

Write the letter of each answer in the box containing the exercise number.

Tell whether the events are dependent or independent.

1. You roll number cube and select a card from a standard deck of cards.

   Event A: You roll a 3.

   Event B: You select a face card.

2. A bag of marbles contains 3 red marbles, 2 yellow marbles, and 4 blue marbles. You randomly choose a marble, and without replacing it, you randomly choose another marble.

   Event A: You choose a red marble first.

   Event B: You choose a blue marble second.

Find the probability.

3. A container contains 13 almonds, 8 walnuts, and 19 peanuts. You randomly choose one nut and eat it. Then you randomly choose another nut. Find the probability that you choose a walnut on your first pick and an almond on your second pick.

4. The letters M, A, R, B, L, and E are each written on a card and placed into a hat. You randomly choose a card, return it, and then choose another card. Find the probability that you choose a vowel on your first pick and a consonant on your second pick.

5. A bag contains 3 red chips, 4 blue chips, 5 yellow chips, and 3 green chips. You randomly choose a chip, and without replacing it, you randomly choose another chip. Find the probability that you choose a yellow chip on your first pick and a blue chip on your second pick.

Answers
L. $\dfrac{2}{9}$
H. dependent
E. $\dfrac{2}{21}$
O. $\dfrac{1}{15}$
A. independent

1		2	3	4	5

In a survey, 50 students were asked: Do you own a dog or a cat? The Venn diagram shows the results. Use the information in the Venn diagram to complete the two-way table. Discuss which format you prefer for displaying the survey results and why.

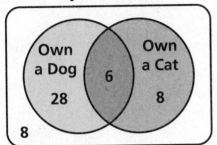

Survey of 50 Students

		Owns a Dog		
		Yes	No	Total
Owns a Cat	Yes			
	No			
	Total			

12.3 **Warm Up**

1. Complete the two-way table.

		Age Started Driving		
		≤ 16	> 16	Total
Gender	Male	28		33
	Female		8	22
	Total			

12.3 **Cumulative Review Warm Up**

Graph the function.

1. $y = \left(\frac{1}{2}\right)^{x-3}$
2. $y = \log_2(x + 1)$
3. $y = -\frac{2}{3}(3)^x$

4. $y = 2 - \log_3 x$
5. $y = 2^{x+4} - 5$
6. $y = -2 + \frac{1}{2}\log_4(x - 3)$

12.3 Practice A

In Exercises 1 and 2, complete the two-way table.

1.

		Ran a Half Marathon		
		Yes	No	Total
Role	Student	12		124
	Teacher	7		
	Total		263	

2.

		Owns Dog		
		Yes	No	Total
Owns Cat	Yes	24	61	
	No	107		
	Total			226

3. In a survey, 112 people feel that the amount of fresh water allowed to empty into the salt water river should be reduced, and 87 people did not feel that the amount of fresh water allowed to empty into the salt water river should be reduced. Of those who feel that the amount of fresh water released should be reduced, 98 people fish the salt water river. Of those that do not feel that the amount of fresh water released should be reduced, 12 people fish the salt water river.

   a. Organize these results in a two-way table. Then find and interpret the marginal frequencies.

   b. Make a two-way table that shows the joint and marginal relative frequencies.

   c. Make a two-way table that shows the conditional relative frequencies for each fish category.

Name_____ Date_____

12.3 Practice B

In Exercises 1 and 2, use the two-way table to create another two-way table that shows the joint and marginal relative frequencies.

1.

		Surfing Style		
		Regular	Advanced	Total
Gender	Male	86	24	110
	Female	77	18	95
	Total	163	42	205

2.

		Fishing License		
		Yes	No	Total
Hunting License	Yes	65	37	102
	No	177	341	518
	Total	242	378	620

3. In a survey, 5 people exercise regularly and 21 people do not. Of those who exercise regularly, 1 person felt tired. Of those that did not exercise regularly, 1 person felt tired.

   a. Organize these results in a two-way table. Then find and interpret the marginal frequencies.

   b. Make a two-way table that shows the joint and marginal relative frequencies.

   c. Make a two-way table that shows the conditional relative frequencies for each exercise category.

12.3 Enrichment and Extension

Two-Way Tables and Probability

The table shows the joint relative frequencies for how many adults and students attended a concert at the local park on Friday night, and whether or not each bought a program for the concert at the concession stand.

Use the table to complete the exercises.

	Yes	No
Adults	0.42	0.31
Students	0.21	0.06

1. Find the marginal relative frequencies for the data. Round your answers to the nearest hundredth, if necessary.

	Yes	No	Total
Adults	0.42	0.31	
Students	0.21	0.06	
Total			

2. Based on this data, use a percentage to express how likely it is that a student at a football game next Friday will not buy a program at the concession stand. Round your answer to the nearest whole percent, if necessary.

3. Based on this data, use a percentage to express how likely it is that an adult at a football game next Friday will buy a program at the concession stand. Round your answer to the nearest whole percent, if necessary.

4. Based on this data, use a percentage to express how likely it is an adult or student at a football game next Friday will buy a program at the concession stand. Round your answer to the nearest whole percent, if necessary.

5. If 35 students did not buy a program at the concession stand, then how many adults and students altogether do the data represent?

12.3 Puzzle Time

How Is A Basketball Player Like A Baby?

Write the letter of each answer in the box containing the exercise number.

Complete the two-way table.

	Response		
	Yes	No	Total
Male	15	**1.**	**2.**
Female	**3.**	**4.**	37
Total	**5.**	42	84

	Choice		
	AWD	4WD	Total
SUV	**6.**	10	**7.**
Van	5	**8.**	12
Total	16	**9.**	**10.**

	Highest Level of Education		
	High School	College	Total
Male	58	**11.**	113
Female	**12.**	94	**13.**
Total	**14.**	**15.**	362

Answers

B. 42

B. 249

Y. 10

L. 213

O. 11

T. 32

T. 21

I. 55

E. 149

H. 7

D. 17

H. 47

R. 33

E. 27

B. 155

1	2	3	4		5	6	7	8		9	10	11	12	13	14	15	16

Use the spinner shown to complete the exercises.

1. What is the sample space if the spinner is spun one time?

2. What is the probability of the spinner stopping on 3?

3. What is the probability of the spinner stopping on a white space?

4. What is the probability of the spinner stopping on a black space or an even number?

5. What is the probability of the spinner stopping on 6 or a white space?

12.4 **Warm Up**

There are three different colors of gumballs in a package, but not the same number of each color. Use the given probabilities of randomly selecting red and blue to find the missing probability if you know there are 24 gumballs in the package.

1. $P(\text{red}) = \frac{5}{24}$, $P(\text{blue}) = \frac{1}{3}$, $P(\text{green}) =$

2. $P(\text{red}) = \frac{1}{6}$, $P(\text{blue}) = \frac{1}{2}$, $P(\text{green or blue}) =$

12.4 **Cumulative Review Warm Up**

Write a rule for the *n*th term of the sequence.

1. 0, 3, 6, 9, 12, ...

2. $\frac{1}{4}, \frac{2}{6}, \frac{3}{8}, \frac{4}{10}, \frac{5}{12}, ...$

3. −2, 4, −8, 16, −32, ...

12.4 Practice A

In Exercises 1 and 2, events *A* and *B* are disjoint. Find *P(A or B)*.

1. $P(A) = 0.4$, $P(B) = 0.2$

2. $P(A) = \frac{1}{3}$, $P(B) = \frac{1}{2}$

3. At the high school swim meet, you and your friend are competing in the 50 Freestyle event. You estimate that there is a 40% chance you will win and a 35% chance your friend will win. What is the probability that you or your friend will win the 50 Freestyle event?

In Exercises 4 and 5, you roll a die. Find *P(A or B)*.

4. **Event *A*:** Roll a 2.

   Event *B*: Roll an odd number.

5. **Event *A*:** Roll an even number.

   Event *B*: Roll a number greater than 3.

6. You bring your cat to the veterinarian for her yearly check-up. The veterinarian tells you that there is a 75% probability that your cat has a kidney disorder or is diabetic, with a 40% chance it has a kidney disorder and a 50% chance it is diabetic. What is the probability that your cat has both a kidney disorder and is diabetic?

7. A game show has three doors. A Grand Prize is behind one of the doors, a Nice Prize is behind one of the doors, and a Dummy Prize is behind one of the doors. You have been watching the show for a while and the table gives your estimates of the probabilities for the given scenarios.

	Door 1	Door 2	Door 3
Grand Prize	0.25	0.45	0.3
Nice Prize	0.4	0.25	0.35
Dummy Prize	0.35	0.3	0.35

   a. Find the probability that you win either the Grand Prize or a Nice Prize if you choose Door 1.

   b. Find the probability that you win either the Grand Prize or a Nice Prize if you choose Door 2.

   c. Find the probability that you win either the Grand Prize or a Nice Prize if you choose Door 3.

   d. Which door should you choose? Explain.

12.4 Practice B

In Exercises 1 and 2, events *A* and *B* are disjoint. Find *P(A or B)*.

1. $P(A) = 0.375$, $P(B) = 0.2$

2. $P(A) = \frac{1}{4}$, $P(B) = \frac{1}{5}$

3. You are performing an experiment to determine how well pineapple plants grow in different soils. Out of the 40 pineapple plants, 16 are planted in sandy soil, 18 are planted in potting soil, and 7 are planted in a mixture of sandy soil and potting soil. What is the probability that a pineapple plant in the experiment is planted in sandy soil or potting soil?

In Exercises 4 and 5, you roll a die. Find *P(A or B)*.

4. **Event *A*:** Roll a prime number.
   Event *B*: Roll a number greater than 2.

5. **Event *A*:** Roll an even number.
   Event *B*: Roll an odd number.

6. An Educational Advisor estimates that there is a 90% probability that a freshman college student will take either a mathematics class or an English class, with an 80% probability that the student will take a mathematics class and a 75% probability that the student will take an English class. What is the probability that a freshman college student will take both a mathematics class and an English class?

7. A test diagnoses a disease correctly 92% of the time when a person has the disease and 80% of the time when the person does not have the disease. Approximately 4% of people in the United States have the disease. Fill in the probabilities along the branches of the probability tree diagram and then determine the probability that a randomly selected person is correctly diagnosed by the test.

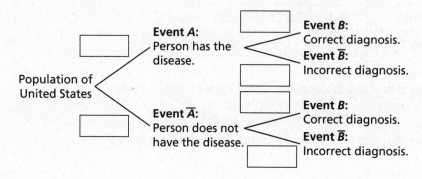

12.4 Enrichment and Extension

Probability of Disjoint and Overlapping Events

Use the formula for overlapping events to complete the exercises.

1. A certain drug causes a skin rash or hair loss in 35% of patients. Twenty-five percent of patients experience only a skin rash, and 5% experience both a skin rash and hair loss. A doctor wants to know the probability that a patient will experience hair loss only.

   a. Using A to represent "experiences a skin rash" and B to represent "experiences hair loss," write a symbolic representation of the problem.

   b. Using the symbolic representation from part (a), find the probability that a patient will experience hair loss only.

2. You and your friend recorded a compact disc together. The CD contained solos and duets. Your friend recorded twice as many duets as solos, and you recorded six more solos than duets. When a CD player selects one of these songs at random, the probability that it will select a duet is 25%. Let s represent the number of solos that your friend recorded.

   a. Write a rational equation to express the probability of randomly selecting a duet in terms of s.

   b. Solve the equation. Then determine the total number of songs recorded.

   c. Find the probability of selecting one of your solos or a duet when a CD player selects one song at random.

3. Police report that 78% of drivers stopped on suspicion of driving under the influence are given a breath test, 36% a blood test, and 22% both tests. What is the probability that a randomly selected driver suspected of driving under the influence is given a blood test or a breath test, but not both?

4. A bag contains 36 marbles, some of which are red and the rest are black. The black and red marbles are either clear or opaque. When a marble is randomly selected from the bag, the probability that it is red is $\frac{1}{4}$, that it is opaque is $\frac{7}{9}$, and that it is red or opaque is $\frac{11}{12}$.

   a. How many marbles are black?

   b. How many marbles are black and opaque?

Name _____ Date _____

12.4 Puzzle Time

What Are A Plumber's Favorite Shoes?

Write the letter of each answer in the box containing the exercise number.

Find the probability.

1. In a group of 25 students at lunch, 10 prefer ketchup on their hamburger, 10 prefer mustard on their hamburger, and 5 like both ketchup and mustard on their hamburger. The rest of the students in the group prefer neither. What is the probability that a student selected from this group will prefer ketchup or mustard on their hamburger?

2. A card is randomly selected from a standard deck of 52 cards. What is the probability that it is a 2 or an 8?

3. In a class of 50 high school juniors, 32 students either play a sport or are in the marching band. There are 22 juniors who play a sport and 16 who are in the marching band. What is the probability that a randomly selected junior plays a sport and is in the marching band?

4. You roll a die. What is the probability that you roll an even number or a 5?

5. You roll a die. What is the probability that you roll an odd number or a factor of 6?

Answers
O. $\dfrac{3}{25}$
L. $\dfrac{2}{13}$
G. $\dfrac{2}{3}$
C. $\dfrac{3}{5}$
S. $\dfrac{5}{6}$

1	2	3	4	5

12.5 Start Thinking

A die is rolled and then two coins are tossed. The possible outcomes are shown in the tree diagram below. How many outcomes are possible? What does each row in the tree diagram represent? What does each branch in the tree diagram represent? Describe two ways of determining the total number of outcomes from the tree diagram.

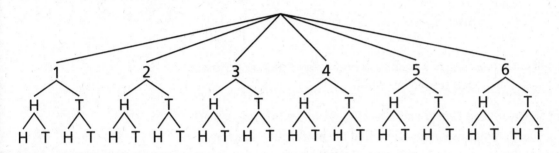

12.5 Warm Up

Count the number of different ways the letters can be arranged.

1. POP   **2.** TAP   **3.** NOON   **4.** KEEP

12.5 Cumulative Review Warm Up

Solve △ABC. Round your answers to four decimal places.

1.

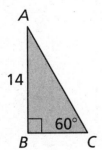

2.

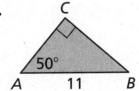

3.

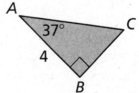

Name _____ Date _____

In Exercises 1–3, find the number of ways that you can arrange (a) all of the letters and (b) 2 of the letters in the given word.

1. HAT   2. PORT   3. CHURN

In Exercises 4–9, evaluate the expression.

4. $_4P_3$ 5. $_6P_2$ 6. $_8P_1$

7. $_5P_4$ 8. $_9P_5$ 9. $_{11}P_0$

10. Fifteen sailboats are racing in a regatta. In how many different ways can three sailboats finish first, second, and third?

11. Your bowling team and your friend's bowling team are in a league with 6 other teams. In tonight's competition, find the probability that your friend's team finishes first and your team finishes second.

In Exercises 12 and 13, count the possible combinations of r letters chosen from the given list.

12. H, I, J, K, L; $r = 3$ 13. U, V, W, X, Y; $r = 2$

In Exercises 14–19, evaluate the expression.

14. $_6C_1$ 15. $_7C_5$ 16. $_8C_8$

17. $_9C_7$ 18. $_{11}C_5$ 19. $_{12}C_2$

20. You and your friends are ordering a 3-topping pizza. The pizzeria offers 8 different pizza toppings. How many combinations of 3 pizza toppings are possible?

In Exercises 21 and 22, tell whether the question can be answered using *permutations* or *combinations*. Explain your reasoning. Then answer the question.

21. On a biology lab exam, there are 8 stations available. You must complete the labs at 6 of the 8 stations. In how many ways can you complete the exam?

22. Your committee is voting on their logo. There are 7 possible logos and you are to rank your top 3 logos. In how many ways can you rank your top 3 logos?

Name_____ Date _____

12.5 Practice B

In Exercises 1–3, find the number of ways that you can arrange (a) all of the letters and (b) 2 of the letters in the given word.

1. SMILE **2.** POLITE **3.** WONDERFUL

In Exercises 4–9, evaluate the expression.

4. $_6P_4$ **5.** $_{12}P_1$ **6.** $_{10}P_7$

7. $_{11}P_0$ **8.** $_{25}P_2$ **9.** $_{20}P_6$

10. You have textbooks for 7 different classes. In how many different ways can you arrange them together on your bookshelf?

11. You make wristbands for Team Spirit Week. Each wristband has a bead containing a letter of the word COLTS. You randomly draw one of the 8 beads from a cup. Find the probability that COLTS is spelled correctly when you draw the beads.

In Exercises 12 and 13, count the possible combinations of *r* letters chosen from the given list.

12. P, Q, R, S, T, U; $r = 2$ **13.** G, H, I, J, K, L; $r = 4$

In Exercises 14–19, evaluate the expression.

14. $_9C_1$ **15.** $_7C_7$ **16.** $_{10}C_4$

17. $_{13}C_7$ **18.** $_{14}C_8$ **19.** $_{25}C_5$

In Exercises 20 and 21, tell whether the question can be answered using *permutations* or *combinations*. Explain your reasoning. Then answer the question.

20. Ninety-five tri-athletes are competing in a triathlon. In how many ways can 3 tri-athletes finish in first, second, and third place?

21. Your band director is choosing 6 seniors to represent your band at the Band Convention. There are 44 seniors in the band. In how many groupings can the band director choose 6 seniors?

12.5 Enrichment and Extension

Permutations and Combinations

As you learned, a *permutation* is an arrangement of objects in a specific order. Sometimes there are also other conditions that must be satisfied. In such cases, you should deal with the special conditions first.

Example: Using the letters in the word *square*, how many 6-letter arrangements with no repetitions are possible if vowels and consonants alternate, beginning with a vowel?

Of the 6 letters in the word, 3 are vowels (u, a, e) and 3 are consonants (s, q, r).

Beginning with a vowel, every other slot is to be filled by a vowel. There are 3 such slots and 3 vowels to be arranged in them.

$$\underline{3} \times \underline{} \times \underline{2} \times \underline{} \times \underline{1} \times \underline{}$$

The remaining 3 slots have 3 consonants to be arranged in them.

$$\underline{3} \times \underline{3} \times \underline{2} \times \underline{2} \times \underline{1} \times \underline{1}$$

Multiply to determine the total number of arrangements.

There are 36 possible arrangements.

The girls Amy, Ann, and Doris and the boys Al, Aaron, Bob, and Roy are in a nursery group. Determine the number of ways the children can be arranged in a line with the following conditions.

1. A girl is always at the head of the line.

2. Roy is always at the head of the line.

3. A child whose name begins with A is always at the head of the line.

4. A child whose name begins with A is always at the head and the rear of the line.

The diamond suit from a standard deck of 52 playing cards is removed from the deck, shuffled, and laid out in a row. Determine the number of possible arrangements.

5. The first card is the ace.

6. The first card is a face card.

Use the digits 0, 1, 2, 3, 4 without repetition. Determine the number of ways to form each arrangement.

7. 3-digit numerals whose values are at least 100.

8. 4-digit numerals whose values are at least 1000 and less than 4000.

9. 4-digit numerals whose values are at least 2000 and less than 3000.

12.5 Puzzle Time

Why Was The Pantry So Good At Telling The Future?

Write the letter of each answer in the box containing the exercise number.

Evaluate the expression.

1. $_3P_1$

2. $_7P_3$

3. $_{10}P_4$

4. $_{21}P_4$

5. $_9P_6$

6. $_{11}P_8$

7. $_{15}P_3$

8. $_6P_6$

9. $_5C_2$

10. $_{30}C_{28}$

11. $_{15}C_9$

12. $_8C_4$

13. $_{19}C_{14}$

14. $_8C_8$

15. $_{44}C_{41}$

16. $_9C_4$

17. $_{28}C_{25}$

18. $_{20}C_{15}$

Answers	
E. 60,480	T. 435
I. 3	K. 5040
W. 6,652,800	O. 15,504
H. 720	A. 10
W. 5005	A. 70
R. 120	T. 210
S. 11,628	I. 1
T. 3276	N. 143,640
N. 13,244	S. 126
W. 2730	E. 3360

19. A row contains five empty desks. How many different ways could five students sit in the desks in the row?

20. Sixteen students are competing in the 100-yard dash. In how many different ways can the students finish first, second, and third?

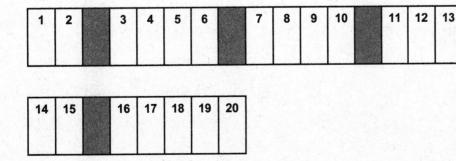

The spinner in the diagram is spun twice. An outcome is identified as the sum of the two spins, so there are seven possible outcomes. Complete the chart to determine the frequency of each outcome. Do you notice a pattern in the chart?

$$\begin{array}{cccccccc} & & 2+1 & & & & & \\ & 1+1 & 1+2 & & & & & \\ \hline 2 & 3 & 4 & 5 & 6 & 7 & 8 \end{array}$$

Sum of the two spins

Frequency

12.6 Warm Up

Evaluate the expression without the use of a calculator.

1. $_4C_2$ **2.** $_7C_1$ **3.** $_5C_0$ **4.** $_9C_4$

5. $_8C_8$ **6.** $_{11}C_{10}$ **7.** $_6C_3$ **8.** $_{10}C_2$

12.6 Cumulative Review Warm Up

Identify the amplitude and the period of the function.

1. $y = 2\cos(3x)$ **2.** $y = 3 - \sin\left(\dfrac{\pi x}{4}\right)$

3. $y = \dfrac{4}{3}\sin(3x - \pi)$ **4.** $y = \cos(x) + 8$

5. $y = \dfrac{1}{2}\sin(x - 4)$ **6.** $y = 3.8\cos(1.5x + 7)$

12.6 Practice A

In Exercises 1 and 2, make a table and draw a histogram showing the probability distribution for the random variable.

1. X = the letter that is spun on a wheel that contains 2 sections labeled "A," five sections labeled "B," and 1 section labeled "C."

2. F = the type of fruit randomly chosen from a bowl that contains three apples, four pears, and four oranges.

In Exercises 3 and 4, use the probability distribution to determine (a) the number that is most likely to be spun on a spinner, and (b) the probability of spinning an even number.

3.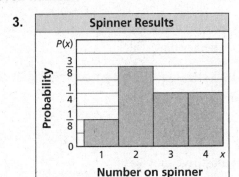

4.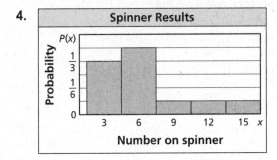

In Exercises 5–7, calculate the probability of flipping a coin 20 times and getting the given number of heads.

5. 2   6. 7   7. 14

8. Describe and correct the error in calculating the probability of rolling a five exactly four times in six rolls of a six-sided number cube.

$$\times \quad P(k = 4) = {}_6C_4 \left(\frac{1}{6}\right)^4 \left(\frac{5}{6}\right)^6 \approx 0.0039$$

12.6 Practice B

In Exercises 1 and 2, make a table and draw a histogram showing the probability distribution for the random variable.

1. $V = 1$ if a randomly chosen letter consists only of line segments (i.e. A, E, F, ...) and 2 otherwise (i.e. B, C, D, G, ...).

2. $X =$ the number of digits in a random perfect square from 1 to 1225.

In Exercises 3–5, calculate the probability of flipping a coin 20 times and getting the given number of heads.

3. 3   4. 15   5. 18

6. According to a survey, 22% of high school students watch at most five movies a month. You ask seven randomly chosen high school students whether they watch at most five movies a month.

   a. Draw a histogram of the binomial distribution for your survey.

   b. What is the most likely outcome of your survey?

   c. What is the probability that at most three people watch at most five movies a month.

7. Describe and correct the error in calculating the probability of rolling a four exactly five times in six rolls of a six-sided number cube.

$$\times \quad P(k = 4) = {}_6C_4\left(\frac{1}{6}\right)^4\left(\frac{5}{6}\right)^{6-4} \approx 0.008$$

8. A cereal company claims that there is a prize in one out of five boxes of cereal.

   a. You purchase 5 boxes of the cereal. You open four of the boxes and do not get a prize. Evaluate the validity of this statement: "The first four boxes did not have a prize, so the next one will probably have a prize."

   b. What is the probability of opening four boxes without a prize and then a box with a prize?

   c. What is the probability of opening all five boxes and not getting a prize?

   d. What is the probability of opening all five boxes and getting five prizes?

Name_____ Date_____

12.6 Enrichment and Extension

Binomial Distributions

You can find the mean and standard deviation of a binomial distribution using the following formulas: Mean: $\mu = np$ and Standard Deviation: $\sigma = \sqrt{np(1 - p)}$.

Sometimes the mean is referred to as the average or expected value when referenced in problems.

Example: Ninety percent of the people who open a checking account at a particular bank keep the account open at least one year. A random sample of 20 new accounts is taken and the bank looks at how many will be kept open for at least one year. What are the expected value and standard deviation of the distribution?

Mean (expected value): $\mu = np = 20 \cdot 0.90 = 18$

Standard Deviation: $\sigma = \sqrt{np(1 - p)} = \sqrt{20 \cdot 0.90 \cdot 0.10} \approx 1.34$

Complete the exercises using your knowledge of the binomial distribution.

1. An Olympic archer is able to hit the bull's-eye 80% of the time. Assume that each shot is independent of the others. If she shoots six arrows, find the following.

   a. The mean and standard deviation of the number of bull's-eyes she may get.

   b. The probability she gets at most four bull's-eyes.

   c. The probability she gets at least four bull's-eyes.

   d. The probability she misses the bull's-eye at least once.

2. It is generally believed that nearsightedness affects about 12% of all children. A school district tests the vision of 169 incoming kindergarten children. How many would you expect to be nearsighted? What is the standard deviation?

3. At a certain college, 6% of all students come from outside the United States. Incoming students are assigned at random to freshman dorms, where students live in residential clusters of 40 freshmen sharing a common lounge area. How many international students would you expect to find in a typical cluster? What is the standard deviation?

4. The degree to which democratic and non-democratic countries attempt to control the news media was examined in the *Journal of Peace Research* (Nov. 1997). Between 1948 and 1996, 80% of all democratic regimes allowed a free press. In contrast, over the same time period, 10% of all non-democratic regimes allowed a free press. In a random sample of 50 democratic regimes, how many would you expect to allow a free press? What is the standard deviation?

12.6 Puzzle Time

What Did The Police Do With The Hamburger?

Write the letter of each answer in the box containing the exercise number.

Use the probability distribution to determine the probability.

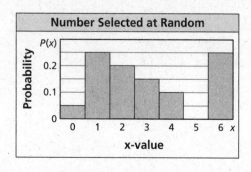

Answers
L. 80%
M. 100%
I. 1.5%
G. 1 or 6
I. 40%
L. 5
E. 25%
R. 60%
D. 75%
H. 0%

1. What is the most likely number to be selected?

2. What is the probability of selecting an even number?

3. What is the probability of selecting a multiple of three?

4. What is the least likely number to be selected?

5. What is the probability of selecting a number other than two?

6. What is the probability of selecting a three or four?

7. What is the probability of selecting a number that is no greater than four?

8. What is the probability of selecting a five?

9. What is the probability of selecting a three, replacing it, then selecting a four?

10. What is the probability of selecting a number that is not less than zero?

1	2	3	4	5	6	7		8	9	10

Chapter 12 Cumulative Review

In Exercises 1–10, write and solve a proportion to answer the question.

1. What percent of 80 is 14?

2. What number is 74% of 78?

3. 25.2 is what percent of 35?

4. What percent of 48 is 9?

5. What number is 45% of 63?

6. 15.68 is what percent of 98?

7. What percent of 120 is 45?

8. What number is 32% of 230?

9. 12.1 is what percent of 55?

10. What percent of 68 is 57.8?

Draw a Venn diagram of the set described.

11. Of the positive numbers less than or equal to 9, set A consists of the factors of 9 and set B consists of all odd numbers.

12. Of the positive numbers less than or equal to 13, set A consists of all odd numbers and set B consists of all prime numbers.

13. Of the positive numbers less than or equal to 36, set A consists of all the multiples of 2 and set B consists of all the multiples of 3.

14. Of all positive numbers less than or equal to 24, set A consists of the factors of 24 and set B consists of all even numbers.

15. Of all positive numbers less than or equal to 36, set A consists of all the multiples of 3 and set B consists of all factors of 36.

16. Of all positive numbers less than or equal to 14, set A consists of all even numbers and set B consists of all factors of 14.

17. Your history test has 55 questions. You get 48 questions correct. What is the percent of correct answers? Round your answer to the nearest tenth of a percent.

18. Your English test has 25 questions. You get 23 questions correct. What is the percent of incorrect answers? Round your answer to the nearest tenth of a percent.

19. Your biology test has 35 questions.

   a. You get 29 questions correct. What is the percent of correct answers? Round your answer to the nearest tenth of a percent.

   b. Your friend gets 31 questions correct. What is the percent of correct answers for your friend? Round your answer to the nearest tenth of a percent.

   c. How much better did your friend do on the test?

Chapter 12 **Cumulative Review** (continued)

In Exercises 20–33, describe the transformation of $f(x) = x^2$ represented by g.
Then graph the function.

20. $g(x) = x^2 - 1$

21. $g(x) = x^2 + 9$

22. $g(x) = x^2 - 5$

23. $g(x) = (x - 3)^2$

24. $g(x) = (x + 6)^2$

25. $g(x) = (x - 4)^2$

26. $g(x) = (x + 9)^2 - 3$

27. $g(x) = (x - 2)^2 - 6$

28. $g(x) = (x + 5)^2 + 8$

29. $g(x) = -x^2$

30. $g(x) = 4x^2$

31. $g(x) = -3x^2$

32. $g(x) = \frac{1}{4}x^2$

33. $g(x) = -\frac{1}{2}x^2$

In Exercises 34–43, determine the vertex and axis of symmetry.

34. $f(x) = (x + 5)^2$

35. $g(x) = (x - 9)^2$

36. $h(x) = x^2 + 4$

37. $f(x) = x^2 - 5$

38. $h(x) = (x + 8)^2 + 1$

39. $g(x) = (x - 3)^2 + 8$

40. $f(x) = -2x^2 + 7$

41. $g(x) = 3(x + 1)^2 - 1$

42. $h(x) = \frac{1}{2}(x - 6)^2 - 7$

43. $g(x) = -2(x - 8)^2 - 6$

In Exercises 44–47, find the value of x.

44. Area of square = 49

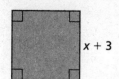

$x + 3$

45. Area of rectangle = 32

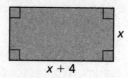

x

$x + 4$

46. Area of circle = 36π

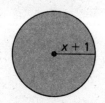

$x + 1$

47. Area of square = 81

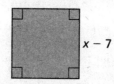

$x - 7$

Chapter 12 Cumulative Review (continued)

In Exercises 48–53, simplify the radical expression.

48. $\sqrt{-144}$

49. $\sqrt{-49}$

50. $5\sqrt{-100}$

51. $-12\sqrt{-121}$

52. $4\sqrt{-500}$

53. $-3\sqrt{-128}$

In Exercises 54–59, add or subtract. Write the answer in standard form.

54. $(8 - 14i) - (9 - 5i)$

55. $(-6 + 6i) + (-3 - 14i)$

56. $(3 + 8i) + (3 + 2i)$

57. $(3 - 14i) - (-5 + 9i)$

58. $(-5 + 6i) + (5 - 8i)$

59. $10 + (18 + 5i) - 11$

In Exercises 60–65, multiply. Write the answer in standard form.

60. $15i(1 + 10i)$

61. $-6i(5 + 8i)$

62. $(6 - 14i)(7 - 6i)$

63. $(2 + 15i)(-11 - 12i)$

64. $(17 - 17i)^2$

65. $(10 + 12i)^2$

In Exercises 66–71, evaluate the expression without using a calculator.

66. $81^{1/4}$

67. $256^{1/4}$

68. $125^{1/3}$

69. $36^{3/2}$

70. $216^{2/3}$

71. $81^{3/4}$

In Exercises 72–77, evaluate the expression using a calculator. Round your answer to two decimal places when appropriate.

72. $9^{1/3}$

73. $28^{-1/4}$

74. $6561^{1/4}$

75. $18^{2/3}$

76. $32,768^{1/5}$

77. $27^{5/3}$

In Exercises 78–83, simplify the expression.

78. $e^4 \cdot e^6$

79. $e^{-2} \cdot e^{10}$

80. $\dfrac{12e^7}{2e^{-2}}$

81. $\dfrac{9e^8}{3e^{-10}}$

82. $\left(4e^{12x}\right)^3$

83. $\left(3e^{-2x}\right)^6$

Chapter 12 Cumulative Review (continued)

In Exercises 84–91, write the first six terms of the sequence.

84. $a_n = n + 7$

85. $f(n) = 4 - n$

86. $a_n = -8 + n$

87. $f(n) = n^3$

88. $a_n = n^3 - 2$

89. $a_n = n^2 - 3$

90. $f(n) = (n - 7)^2$

91. $f(n) = (n + 1)^2$

In Exercises 92–100, find the sum.

92. $\displaystyle\sum_{i=1}^{4} 4i$

93. $\displaystyle\sum_{m=0}^{9} m^2$

94. $\displaystyle\sum_{h=1}^{5} 2h^2$

95. $\displaystyle\sum_{k=4}^{9} (3k + 1)$

96. $\displaystyle\sum_{n=2}^{7} (-4n + 5)$

97. $\displaystyle\sum_{d=3}^{5} \frac{d}{d + 2}$

98. $\displaystyle\sum_{z=7}^{9} \frac{z - 2}{z}$

99. $\displaystyle\sum_{f=8}^{13} 2$

100. $\displaystyle\sum_{f=6}^{12} 3f^2$

101. You want to save $300 for a new bicycle. You begin by saving one penny on the first day. You save an additional penny each day after that. For example, you will save two pennies on the second day, three pennies on the third day, and so on.

    a. How much money will you have saved after 50 days?

    b. Use a series to determine how many days it takes you to save $350.

102. A dance team is arranged in rows on a stage. The first row has three dancers, and each row after the first has one more dancer than the row before it.

    a. Write a rule for the number of dancers in the nth row.

    b. How many dancers are on the stage with six rows?

    c. How many dancers are on the stage with seven rows?

    d. How many more dancers are on stage where there are seven rows, compared to when there are six rows?

Answers

Chapter 1

1.1 Start Thinking

When the vertex of the triangle is moved in any direction, its angle measure also changes. Because all three sides of the triangle are connected, this also affects the other angles; If one angle becomes lesser, the sum of the other angles must become greater, and vice versa. All angles must be in relation to one another so that the sum of their angles always equals the same amount $(180°)$.

1.1 Warm Up

1. triangle   2. pentagon   3. hexagon

4. octagon   5. rhombus   6. decagon

1.1 Cumulative Review Warm Up

1. $b = 64$ 2. $a = 26$ 3. $c = 104$

4. $p = 5$ 5. $c = 92$ 6. $u = 44$

1.1 Practice A

1. *Sample answer:* C, E

2. *Sample answer:* $\overrightarrow{AB}, \overrightarrow{CD}$

3. plane G 4. line s

5. *Sample answer:* N, T, W

6. *Sample answer:* M, N, V

7. V

8.
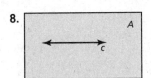

9. *Sample answer:*
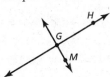

10.

11. *Sample answer:* L 12. $\overleftrightarrow{EF}$

13. M 14. *Sample answer:* A

15. point, line

1.1 Practice B

1. *Sample answer:* A, B, D

2. $\overleftrightarrow{AB}, \overleftrightarrow{EF}$

3. D, E, F 4. plane C

5. *Sample answer:* $\overline{EG}, \overline{EF}$

6. C, E 7. E

8. *Sample answer:* C

9.

10.
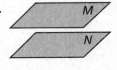

11.
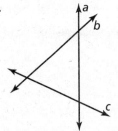

12. plane; Because three points determine a plane, the three feet of a tripod create a plane on the ground.

13.
ray

14.
segment

15. infinite; zero

1.1 Enrichment and Extension

1. *Sample answer:* plane PMR, plane PQO, plane PON

2. $\overline{PO}$ 3. $\overline{ST}, \overline{SR}, \overline{SN}$

4. no; yes   5. $\overline{VW}$

6. plane TXW and plane VWX

7. plane ZVT, plane ZYT, plane ZVW

8. yes; The only place where all planes will meet in the pyramid is at point T.

Answers

9. yes; When substituted into each equation, it is a solution.

10. no; It is not a solution to either equation.

1.1 Puzzle Time

I'LL MEET YOU HALFWAY IN THE MIDDLE FOR A SPLIT

1.2 Start Thinking

Set the compass to be more than half the length of the line segment. Draw a semicircle with the compass. Turn the compass around and do the same from the other side, so that the semicircles intersect above and below the line. Use the straightedge to connect the two intersections. The point where the new line intersects the original line is the midpoint of the original line.

1.2 Warm Up

1–8.

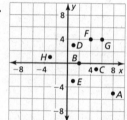

1.2 Cumulative Review Warm Up

1. $\frac{31}{18}$ **2.** $1\frac{3}{4}$ **3.** 4

4. $\frac{1}{4}$ **5.** $\frac{4}{5}$ **6.** $7\frac{3}{5}$

1.2 Practice A

1. $1\frac{1}{4}$ in.   **2.** $2\frac{5}{8}$ in.

3.

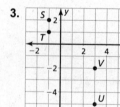

no

4.

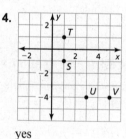

yes

5.

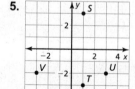

yes

6. 8   **7.** 21   **8.** 17

9. The ruler is lined up at the 2-inch mark; $AB = |2 - 5.25| = 3.25$

10. 32 in.

11. true; F is on $\overline{EG}$ between E and G.

12. true; C is on $\overleftrightarrow{BD}$ between B and D.

13. false; A, B, and F are not collinear.

1.2 Practice B

1. $\frac{7}{8}$ in.   **2.** $2\frac{1}{8}$ in.

3.

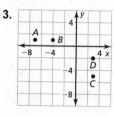

yes

4.

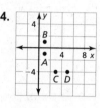

yes

5. 18   **6.** 12   **7.** 12.1

8. about 1020 mi

9. $2x + 25 = x + 32$; $x = 7$; $AB = 27$; $BC = 12$; $AC = 39$

10. $13x - 4 = 74$; $x = 6$; $AB = 53$; $BC = 21$; $AC = 74$

11. 51.8 mi; the third day

1.2 Enrichment and Extension

1. a. 25   **b.** 45   **c.** 50   **d.** 70   **e.** 7   **f.** 95

2. a. 2   **b.** 3   **c.** 9   **d.** 7   **e.** 9   **f.** 5

3. $\overline{DG}$ or $\overline{IL}$ **4.** $\overline{BD}$ **5.** $\overline{BF}$

6. $x^2 + x^2 + 9x = 56$; $x = \frac{7}{2}$; $LM = \frac{49}{4}$; $MN = \frac{175}{4}$

7. $\sqrt{x} + 2\sqrt{x} + 1 = 13$; $x = 16$; $LM = 4$; $MN = 9$

8. $\frac{1}{2x} + 3 + \frac{2}{3} = \frac{14}{3} + \frac{1}{x}$; $x = -\frac{1}{2}$; $LM = 2$;

$LN = \frac{8}{3}$

1.2 Puzzle Time

HE WAS A GOOD RULER

Answers

1.3 Start Thinking

Plot the two points. Draw a right triangle containing those points as vertices, along with a third point. Using the coordinate plane, calculate the side lengths of the legs 5 and 1. Then use the Pythagorean Theorem to find the length of the hypotenuse, $\sqrt{5^2 + 1^2} = \sqrt{26} \approx 5.1$. This is the distance in blocks between the points.

1.3 Warm Up

1. 2 **2.** $\frac{1}{2}$ **3.** -2 **4.** $\frac{1}{2}$

1.3 Cumulative Review Warm Up

1. $x = 62$ **2.** $x = 140$ **3.** $x = 69$ **4.** $x = 109$

1.3 Practice A

1. line d; 30

2. $\overrightarrow{ML}$; 11

3. $\overline{MR}$; 28

4. M; 26

5.
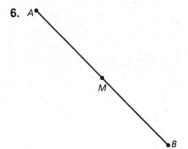

6. A
M
B

7. $(3, 2)$ **8.** $(4, 4)$ **9.** $(2, 7)$

10. $(-7, -7)$ **11.** 5 **12.** about 6.3

13. about 5.7 cm; about 2.8 cm; The center of the square is the segment bisector of the diagonal.

14. 60 ft

1.3 Practice B

1. $\overrightarrow{MW}$; 38

2. line ℓ; 30

3. E M F
Not drawn to scale

4. $(2, 7)$ **5.** $(0, 3)$ **6.** $(3, 0)$

7. $(5, 13)$ **8.** about 3.2 **9.** 5

10. no; If one side of the square is s, then the length of the diagonal is $\sqrt{s^2 + s^2} = \sqrt{2s^2} = s\sqrt{2}$.

11. yes; *Sample answer:* A segment can be bisected by two different lines.

12. about 2 mi; about 10.5 mi

1.3 Enrichment and Extension

1. $\left(\dfrac{3x_1 + x_2}{4}, \dfrac{3y_1 + y_2}{4}\right)$, $\left(\dfrac{x_1 + x_2}{2}, \dfrac{y_1 + y_2}{2}\right)$, $\left(\dfrac{x_1 + 3x_2}{4}, \dfrac{y_1 + 3y_2}{4}\right)$

2. a. $\left(-3, \frac{7}{2}\right), (-2, 5), \left(-1, \frac{13}{2}\right)$

b. $\left(-\frac{11}{2}, 5\right), (-1, 6), \left(\frac{7}{2}, 7\right)$

3. 13; $-b$ **4.** $(12, -3)$ and $(-4, -3)$

5. yes; The distance between each vertex is $\sqrt{5}$.

6. $(2, 1, 6)$ **7.** $\left(-\frac{5}{2}, 6, -\frac{5}{2}\right)$ **8.** $\left(\frac{7}{2}, \frac{9}{2}, \frac{3}{2}\right)$

9. 6 **10.** $\sqrt{107}$ **11.** $\sqrt{89}$

1.3 Puzzle Time

IT WANTED TO BE REDUCED

1.4 Start Thinking

quad-, penta-, hexa-; *Sample answer:* A quadraphonic sound is a form of surround sound involving four speakers. A pentathlon is an athletic competition for individuals consisting of five events. A hexapod is an animal having six feet, typically with three distinct sets of two legs.

1.4 Warm Up

1. $P = 36$ cm, $A = 60$ cm^2

2. $P = 274$ in., $A = 4386$ in.^{2}

3. $P = 25.24$ in., $A = 39.8161$ in.^{2}

4. $P = 24$ cm, $A = 28$ cm^2

1.4 Cumulative Review Warm Up

1. 66 cm **2.** 104 m

Answers

1.4 Practice A

1. quadrilateral; convex   2. hexagon; concave

3. about 16.5 units   4. 21 square units

5. 28 square units   6. about 22.6 units

7. about 10.5 units   8. 32 square units

9. 12 square units   10. 44 square units

11. $(1, -3)$; 14 square units

12. a. 360 ft   b. 240 ft   c. $1000

1.4 Practice B

1. heptagon; convex   2. decagon; concave

3. about 22.2 units   4. 7.5 square units

5. 28 square units   6. about 13.2 units

7. about 24.6 units   8. 6 square units

9. 36 square units   10. 48 square units

11. a. 65 ft^2 b. 40 ft   c. $242.50

12. 4 mi

1.4 Enrichment and Extension

1. 24 square units   2. $x = -4$ or $x = 8$

3. a. about 0.063 square units

   b. about 32 squares

   c. about 2 square units

4. about 1 square unit

1.4 Puzzle Time

TOO MANY PROBLEMS

1.5 Start Thinking

If the angle is larger than a right angle, it is obtuse. If the angle is smaller than a right angle, it is acute.

1.5 Warm Up

1. $x = 70°$ 2. $r = 179°$ 3. $n = 144°$

4. $y = 90°$ 5. $t = 65°$ 6. $w = 120°$

1.5 Cumulative Review Warm Up

1. $r = 40°$ 2. $w = 25°$ 3. $y = 40°$ 4. $v = 45°$

1.5 Practice A

1. $\angle XYZ$, $\angle ZYX$, $\angle Y$

2. $\angle PQR$, $\angle RQS$, $\angle SQP$

3. 110°; obtuse   4. $\angle BEH$, $\angle CFI$

5. $\angle AGD$, $\angle EBH$, $\angle BHE$, $\angle FCI$, $\angle CIF$

6. 92°   7. 44°   8. 55°   9. $x = 33$

10. a. *Sample answer:* $\angle EFG$ is acute, $\angle DFE$ is right, $\angle FBC$ is obtuse, $\angle ABC$ is straight.

    b. 31 angles

    c. 70°

    d. 110°

1.5 Practice B

1. 50°; acute   2. 90°; right

3. 130°; obtuse   4. 180°; straight

5. 44°   6. 46°   7. 47°   8. 23°

9. yes; Because an acute angle is less than 90°, the sum of three acute angles can be equal to 180°.

10. a. *Sample answer:* $\angle ACE$ is acute, $\angle AEC$ is right, $\angle CDE$ is straight.

    b. $\angle DAE$

    c. 58°

    d. 119°

1.5 Enrichment and Extension

1. $6 < x < 51$

2. $m\angle DEG = 40°$, $m\angle FEG = 24°$

3. 6; 24°   4. $2\sqrt{3}$

5. 100°   6. $x = 5, y = 12$

7.

Answers

8. $45°$ **9.** $45°$ **10.** $175°$

11. $95°$ **12.** $140°$ **13.** $140°$

1.5 Puzzle Time

IS A CARRIER

1.6 Start Thinking

The angle formed is now greater than $180°$. So, add the angle formed from the negative x-axis to its position in Quadrant III to $180°$ to get the total angle measure.

1.6 Warm Up

1. $x = 3$ **2.** $c = -1$ **3.** $x = -1$

4. $n = 2$ **5.** $x = -15$ **6.** $x = -4$

1.6 Cumulative Review Warm Up

1. $n - 14 = 8, n = 22$

2. $2(5n - 6) = 18, n = 3$

3. $14 = 7(n - 2), n = 4$

4. $2(x + 6) = \left[x + (x + 2) + (x + 4) \right] + 5, x = 1,$
$x + 2 = 3, x + 4 = 5, x + 6 = 7$

1.6 Practice A

1. $\angle FJG, \angle GJH$ **2.** $\angle CAD, \angle EJF$

3. $\angle BAC, \angle EJG$

4. $54°$ **5.** $105°$

6. $m\angle WXY = 149°, m\angle YXZ = 31°$

7. $m\angle ABC = 48°, m\angle CBD = 42°$

8. $\angle 4$ and $\angle 5$

9. yes; The sides form two pairs of opposite rays.

10. no; The sides do not form two pairs of opposite rays.

11. $x + (x + 24) = 180; 78°$ and $102°$

12. $x + 3x = 90; 22.5°$ and $67.5°$

13. $x + \left(\frac{1}{2}x - 15 \right) = 180; 50°$ and $130°$

14. a. *Sample answer:* $\angle 1, \angle 2$

    b. *Sample answer:* $\angle 2, \angle 5$

    c. $\angle 6$ and $\angle 5, \angle 8$ and $\angle 5$

    d. $60°; \angle 1$ and $\angle 3$ are vertical angles so they have the same angle measure.

1.6 Practice B

1. $\angle AEB$ and $\angle BEC$ **2.** $\angle BEC$ and $\angle HFJ$

3. $\angle CED$ and $\angle HFK$

4. $19°$ **5.** $153.3°$

6. $m\angle ABC = 84°, m\angle CBD = 96°$

7. $m\angle WXY = 23°, m\angle YXZ = 67°$

8. $\angle 1$ and $\angle 2, \angle 3$ and $\angle 2$

9. $\angle 7$ and $\angle 8$

10. yes; The sides form two pairs of opposite rays.

11. no; The sides do not form two pairs of opposite rays.

12. $x + (2x + 9) = 90; 27°$ and $63°$

13 $x + 4x = 180; 36°$ and $144°$

14. $x + \left(\frac{1}{2}x + 51 \right) = 180; 86°$ and $94°$

15. never; The sum of the angle measures of a linear pair is $180°$.

16. sometimes; When the sides of two angles form two pairs of opposite rays that meet at a $90°$ angle, the sum of the angle measures is $180°$.

1.6 Enrichment and Extension

1. supplementary   **2.** complementary

3. neither   **4.** supplementary

5. neither   **6.** complementary

7. complementary: not possible, supplementary: $\frac{1}{5}\pi$

8. complementary: not possible, supplementary: $\frac{19}{42}\pi$

9. complementary: $\frac{11}{34}\pi$, supplementary: $\frac{14}{17}\pi$

10. complementary: $\frac{1}{10}\pi$, supplementary: $\frac{3}{5}\pi$

Answers

11. complementary: $\frac{2}{21}\pi$, supplementary: $\frac{25}{42}\pi$

12. complementary: not possible, supplementary: $\frac{1}{8}\pi$

1.6 Puzzle Time

BECAUSE THE TEACHER SAID IT WAS A PIECE OF CAKE

Cumulative Review

1. 1	**2.** 6	**3.** 2	**4.** 16
5. 6	**6.** 25	**7.** 4	**8.** 3
9. 13	**10.** 27	**11.** 25	**12.** 17
13. 3	**14.** 4	**15.** 12	**16.** 22
17. 2	**18.** 2	**19.** 4	**20.** −1
21. 1	**22.** −6	**23.** 6	**24.** −6
25. 3	**26.** −4	**27.** 3	**28.** 1
29. 9	**30.** −7	**31.** 4	**32.** 8
33. 7	**34.** 4	**35.** 4	**36.** 5
37. 7	**38.** 8	**39.** 4	**40.** 6
41. 4	**42.** 3	**43.** 8	**44.** 3

45. 5   **46.** 6   **47.** $x = 11$

48. $x = -45$ **49.** $x = -32$ **50.** $x = -39$

51. $x = 16$ **52.** $x = 103$ **53.** $x = 16$

54. $x = -32$ **55.** $x = 5$ **56.** $x = -8$

57. $x = -8$ **58.** $x = 11$ **59.** $x = 30$

60. $x = -282$ **61.** $x = 64$ **62.** $x = -104$

63. perimeter = 24 cm, area = 24 cm^2

64. perimeter = 20 mi, area = 16 mi^2

65. perimeter = 24 in., area = 36 in.^{2}

66. perimeter = 26 yd, area = 42.25 yd^2

67. perimeter = 30 mm, area = 37.5 mm^2

68. perimeter = 18 ft, area = 19.25 ft^2

69. perimeter = 27 km, area = 30.375 km^2

70. perimeter = 55.2 cm, area = 126.96 cm^2

71. perimeter = 30.4 in., area = 57.76 in.^{2}

72. 52 in.   **73.** 2976 in.^{2}

74. 1008 ft^2 **75.** 160 ft^2

76. $a \geq 8$

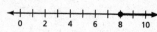

77. $b > -1$

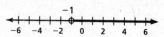

78. $c < -19$

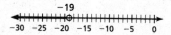

79. $d \leq -14$

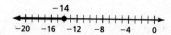

80. $f > 27$

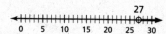

81. $g \leq 35$

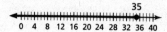

82. $h \geq -8$

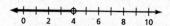

83. $j < 4$

84. $k < 12$

85. $m < -6$

Answers

86. $n \geq -4$

87. $p \geq 9$

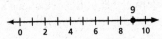

88. $s \geq -21$

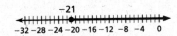

89. $t \geq -22$

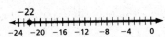

90. $u > 52$

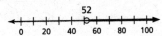

91. $v > 60$

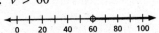

92. $x = -13$ **93.** $x = -3$ **94.** $x = -13$

95. $x = 6$ **96.** $x = 9$ **97.** $x = -6$

98. $x = -8$ **99.** $x = 2$ **100.** $x = -3$

101. $x = -60$ **102.** $x = -36$ **103.** $x = -16$

104. $x = -13$ **105.** $x = 13$ **106.** $x = 3$

107. $x = -2$ **108.** $x = 1$ **109.** $x = 7$

110. $x = -1$ **111.** $x = 9$ **112.** $x = 1$

113. $x = 8$ **114.** $x = 48$ **115.** $x = 7$

116.

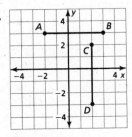

$\overline{AB} \cong \overline{CD}$

117.

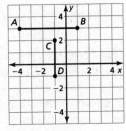

$\overline{AB} \not\cong \overline{CD}$

118.

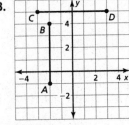

$\overline{AB} \not\cong \overline{CD}$

119.

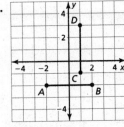

$\overline{AB} \cong \overline{CD}$

120. 45 **121.** 49 **122.** 7

123. 12 **124.** $M\left(\frac{3}{2}, 7\right)$ **125.** $M\left(-\frac{3}{2}, \frac{1}{2}\right)$

126. $H(3, 7)$ **127.** $H(3, -1)$

128. $\sqrt{58}$ **129.** $\sqrt{272}$ or $4\sqrt{17}$

130. $\sqrt{17}$ **131.** $\sqrt{170}$

132. $\sqrt{13}$ **133.** $\sqrt{232}$ or $2\sqrt{58}$

134. $\sqrt{514}$ **135.** $\sqrt{117}$ or $3\sqrt{13}$

136. $\sqrt{202}$ **137.** $\sqrt{29}$

138. $m\angle ABD = 50°, m\angle DBC = 40°$

139. $m\angle LMP = 82°, m\angle PMN = 98°$

Answers

Chapter 2

2.1 Start Thinking

Sample answer: If an animal is a horse, then it is a mammal; If an animal is not a mammal, then it cannot be a horse. Any fact stated in the form of an "if-then" statement could be used, as long as it is factual and leads the reader to believe the original statement as a result.

2.1 Warm Up

1. hexagon
2. right
3. complementary
4. straight

2.1 Cumulative Review Warm Up

1. $(6, 1)$
2. $(-1, 1)$
3. $\left(2, \frac{7}{2}\right)$
4. $(-5, 1)$

2.1 Practice A

1. If <u>you like the ocean</u>, then ⟨you are a good swimmer.⟩

2. If <u>it is raining outside</u>, then ⟨it is cold.⟩

3. If you are a child, then you must attend school.

4. If angles are congruent, then they have equal angle measures.

5. a. conditional: If an animal is a puppy, then it is a dog; true

   b. If an animal is a dog, then it is a puppy; false

   c. If an animal is not a puppy, then it is not a dog; false

   d. If an animal is not a dog, then it is not a puppy; true

6. true; By definition, the sum of two complementary angles is $90°$.

7. false; The sides are not congruent.

8. An angle is obtuse if and only if the angle measure is greater than $90°$ and less than $180°$.

9. Two angles are supplementary if and only if the sum of their angle measures is $180°$.

10. yes; By definition, the negation of a true sentence is false, and the negation of a false sentence is true.

11. *Sample answer:* If two angles are not complementary, then the sum of their angle measures is $180°$.

2.1 Practice B

1. If <u>you like to eat</u>, then ⟨you are a good cook.⟩

2. If <u>an animal is a bear</u>, then it ⟨is a mammal.⟩

3. a. If a tree is an oak tree, then it is a deciduous tree; true

   b. If a tree is a deciduous tree, then it is an oak tree; false

   c. If a tree is not an oak tree, then it is not a deciduous tree; false

   d. If a tree is not a deciduous tree, then it is not an oak tree; true

4. true; Vertical angles share opposite rays.

5. false; The angles of a parallelogram are not always perpendicular.

6. A quadrilateral is a rectangle if and only if it has all perpendicular sides.

7. yes; By definition, true statements always have true contrapositives.

8. If $x = 7$, then $3x + 2 = 23$.

9. If $m\angle ILH = 38°$, then $m\angle GLH = 52°$ because they are complementary angles. If $m\angle ILH = 38°$, then $m\angle FLK = 38°$ because they are vertical angles. If $m\angle GLH = 52°$, then $m\angle KLJ = 52°$ because they are vertical angles.

2.1 Enrichment and Extension

p	q	$p \vee q$	$\sim p$	$\sim q$	$\sim p \wedge \sim q$
T	T	T	F	F	F
T	F	T	F	T	F
F	T	T	T	F	F
F	F	F	T	T	T

$\sim p \vee \sim q$	$(\sim p \vee \sim q) \wedge \sim p$	$(\sim p \wedge \sim q) \vee \sim q$
F	F	F
T	F	T
T	T	F
T	T	T

2.1 Puzzle Time

A SPELLING BEE

Answers

2.2 Start Thinking

yes; *Sample answer:*

Statement 1: "If I can go sledding, then there is snow on the ground."

Statement 2: "If there is snow on the ground, then it is cold outside."

Statement 3: "If I can go sledding, then it is cold outside."; true

2.2 Warm Up

1. 0.06; 0.27, 0.33
2. −2.22; −3.3, −5.52
3. −5; −7, −12
4. 0.5; 3.9, 4.4
5. 2; 8, 10
6. −7; −5, −12

2.2 Cumulative Review Warm Up

1. 7.5 square units
2. 6 square units
3. 12 square units
4. 24 square units

2.2 Practice A

1. The next number is one more than twice the preceding number; 95, 191

2. The list items are letters in alphabetical order followed by letters in reverse alphabetical order; X, D

3. The difference of any two even integers is always even. *Sample answer:* $36 - 16 = 20$

4. The product of three negative numbers is always negative. *Sample answer:* $(-2)(-3)(-5) = -30$

5. The bisector of a straight angle creates two right angles.

6. You got wet.   7. not possible

8. If you study, then you will pass the class.

9. If a straight angle is bisected, then each angle is a right angle.

10. Law of Syllogism

11. inductive reasoning; The conjecture is based on the assumption that the weather pattern will continue.

12. deductive reasoning; The conjecture is based on the fact that $92 \times 14 = 1288$, which is even.

13. The Rocky Mountains are taller than the Appalachian Mountains.

14. $P = ns$

2.2 Practice B

1. The list items are letters in alphabetical order followed by numbers in decreasing numerical order starting with 26; D, 23

2. The pattern is a sequence of spider webs, each web having one more row of webs than the previous web.

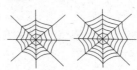

3. The sum of two absolute values is always positive; *Sample answer:* $\left|-3\right| + \left|7\right| = 3 + 7 = 10$

4. The product of a number and its square is the number to the third power; *Sample answer:* $(5)(5)^2 = 5(25) = 125 = 5^3$

5. If the angles are right, obtuse, or any acute angle other than 45°, then they will not be complementary.

6. not possible

7. $\angle AOB$ and $\angle DOB$ share a common ray.

8. not possible

9. If it is Tuesday, then you water the flowers.

10. deductive reasoning; The facts of mammals and laws of logic were used to draw the conclusion.

11. inductive reasoning; The conjecture is based on the assumption that a pattern will continue.

12. no; Based on the Law of Syllogism, a series of true conditional statements will always be true.

13. Using inductive reasoning, you can make the conjecture that organic produce costs more than nonorganic produce because this was true in all of the specific cases listed in the table.

2.2 Enrichment and Extension

1. 7 guesses

2. lengths in ft: Stage 1: 1, Stage 2: $\frac{4}{3}$, Stage 3: $\frac{16}{9}$, Stage 4: $\frac{64}{27}$; The expression that models the pattern of the length at a given stage is $\left(\frac{4}{3}\right)^{n-1}$.

Answers

3. areas in ft^2: Stage 1: 1, Stage 2: $\frac{8}{9}$, Stage 3: $\frac{64}{81}$, Stage 4: $\frac{512}{729}$; The expression that models that pattern of the shaded area at a given stage is $\left(\frac{8}{9}\right)^{n-1}$.

2.2 Puzzle Time

LADY BUGS

2.3 Start Thinking

Sample answer: doors, windows, scale, stairs, water lines

2.3 Warm Up

1. 148° **2.** 25° **3.** 31° **4.** 72°

2.3 Cumulative Review Warm Up

1. $m\angle ABD = 22°$, $m\angle CBD = 22°$

2. $m\angle ABD = 85°$, $m\angle CBD = 85°$

3. $m\angle ABD = 33°$, $m\angle CBD = 33°$

4. $m\angle ABD = 64°$, $m\angle CBD = 64°$

2.3 Practice A

1. *Sample answer:* There is exactly one line through points C and H.

2. *Sample answer:* Line ℓ contains points G and D.

3. *Sample answer:* $\overrightarrow{CH}$ and $\overrightarrow{GE}$ intersect at point D.

4. *Sample answer:* Points B, H, and E are noncollinear and define plane M.

5. *Sample answer:* Plane M contains the noncollinear points B, H, and E.

6. *Sample answer:* Points G and E lie in Plane M so, $\overrightarrow{GE}$ lies in plane M.

7. *Sample answer:*

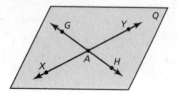

8. *Sample answer:*

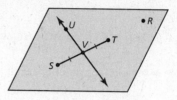

9. *Sample answer:*

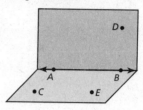

10. yes **11.** no **12.** yes

13. no **14.** yes

15. If three points are noncollinear, then there exists exactly one plane that contains them; converse: If there exists exactly one plane that contains three points, then the three points are noncollinear. inverse: If three points are collinear, then there are multiple planes that contain all three points. contrapositive: If there are multiple planes that contain three points, then the three points are collinear; The converse, inverse, and contrapositive are true.

16. no; Three lines must intersect each other at three points.

2.3 Practice B

1. *Sample answer:* There is exactly one line through points C and G.

2. *Sample answer:* $\overleftrightarrow{EF}$ contains points E and F.

3. *Sample answer:* $\overleftrightarrow{CG}$ and $\overleftrightarrow{EF}$ intersect at point J.

4. *Sample answer:* Plane A contains the noncollinear points D, H, and I.

5. *Sample answer:* Points E and F lie in plane B. So, $\overleftrightarrow{EF}$ lies in plane B.

6. *Sample answer:* Planes A and B intersect at $\overleftrightarrow{CG}$.

7. *Sample answer:*

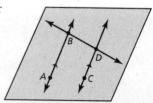

Answers

8. *Sample answer:*

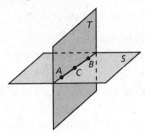

9. no   **10.** yes   **11.** yes   **12.** no

13. converse: If two planes share a line, then the two planes intersect. inverse: If two planes do not intersect, then their intersection is not a line. contrapositive: If the intersection of two planes is not a line, then the two planes do not intersect; The converse, inverse, and contrapositive are true.

14. yes; Because three noncollinear points define a plane, two points on a line define an infinite number of planes.

15. no; The line that passes through a point on a plane does not lie in the plane unless there is another point on the line that is also in the plane.

16. no; yes; Because of the Plane Line Postulate (Post. 2.6), $\overleftrightarrow{EF}$ only lies in plane Z when it contains two points in plane Z.

2.3 Enrichment and Extension

1. There exists exactly one plane that contains both lines m and n.

2. Line-Point Postulate (Post. 2.2); A line contains at least two points.

3. Line Intersection Postulate (Post. 2.3); If two lines intersect, then their intersection is exactly one point.

4. Three Point Postulate (Post. 2.4); Through any three non-collinear points, there exists exactly one plane.

5. Plane-Line Postulate (Post. 2.6); If two points lie in a plane, then the line containing them lies in the plane.

6. 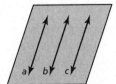   **7.**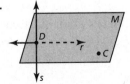

8. 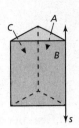   **9.**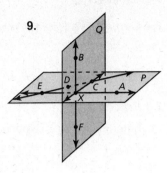

10. $\overleftrightarrow{XC}$; If two planes intersect, their intersection is a line; Plane Intersection Postulate (Post. 2.7).

11. no; Points C, D, E, and X would all be collinear, but line $\overleftrightarrow{EX}$ and $\overleftrightarrow{CX}$ intersect only at point X, so this is impossible.

12. no; This does not follow the Plane-Line Postulate (Post. 2.6) because D lies in plane P but not in plane Q, and B lies in plane Q but not in plane P.

2.3 Puzzle Time

BECAUSE IT WOULD TAKE THE GEESE FOREVER TO WALK

2.4 Start Thinking

Sample answer: One instance when it is necessary is when there is a quotient containing the variable and addition or subtraction in the numerator and a real number in the denominator;

$$\frac{x + 4}{-7} = 20$$

2.4 Warm Up

1. Each side of the equation was subtracted by 23 rather than added; $f - 23 = -17$;
$f - 23 + 23 = -17 + 23$; $f = 6$

2. Each side of the equation was divided by -8, rather than 8; $8r = 4$; $\frac{8r}{8} = \frac{4}{8}$; $r = \frac{1}{2}$

3. The right side of the equation was multiplied by $\frac{4}{7}$ rather than $\frac{7}{4}$; $\frac{4}{7}m = 22$; $\left(\frac{7}{4}\right)\frac{4}{7}m = \left(\frac{7}{4}\right)22$; $m = 38.5$

4. Each side of the equation was multiplied by 6, rather than -6; $-\frac{n}{6} = 3$; $-\frac{6}{1} \bullet \left(-\frac{n}{6}\right) = -6 \bullet 3$; $n = -18$

Answers

2.4 Cumulative Review Warm Up

1. $\angle ADC$, $\angle ADB$, $\angle BDC$

2. $\angle EHG$, $\angle EHF$, $\angle GHF$

2.4 Practice A

1.

Equation	Explanation and Reason
$3x + 4 = 31$	Write the equation; Given
$3x = 27$	Subtract 4 from each side; Subtraction Property of Equality
$x = 9$	Divide each side by 3; Division Property of Equality

2.

Equation	Explanation and Reason
$3(2x + 1) = 15$	Write the equation; Given
$6x + 3 = 15$	Multiply; Distributive Property
$6x = 12$	Subtract 3 from each side; Subtraction Property of Equality
$x = 2$	Divide each side by 6; Division Property of Equality

3.

Equation	Explanation and Reason
$\frac{1}{2}(16x - 8) = 2(x + 16)$	Write the equation; Given
$8x - 4 = 2x + 32$	Multiply; Distributive Property
$6x = 36$	Add 4 to each side and subtract $2x$ from each side; Addition and Subtraction Properties of Equality
$x = 6$	Divide each side by 6; Division Property of Equality

4.

Equation	Explanation and Reason
$p = 2v$	Write the equation; Given
$\frac{p}{2} = v$	Divide each side by 2; Division Property of Equality
$v = \frac{p}{2}$	Rewrite the equation; Symmetric Property of Equality

5.

Equation	Explanation and Reason
$V = \pi r^2 h$	Write the equation; Given
$\frac{V}{\pi r^2} = h$	Divide each side by πr^2; Division Property of Equality
$h = \frac{V}{\pi r^2}$	Rewrite the equation; Symmetric Property of Equality

6.

Equation	Explanation and Reason
$S = \pi rs + \pi r^2$	Write the equation; Given
$S - \pi r^2 = \pi rs$	Subtract πr^2 from each side; Subtraction Property of Equality
$\frac{S - \pi r^2}{\pi r} = s$	Divide each side by πr; Division Property of Equality
$s = \frac{S - \pi r^2}{\pi r}$	Rewrite the equation; Symmetric Property of Equality

7. Multiplication Property of Equality

8. Transitive Property of Equality

9. $30° + m\angle K$ **10.** GH **11.** $3x$; 21

12.

Equation	Explanation and Reason
$A = 2\ell w + 2\ell h + 2hw$	Write the equation; Given
$A - 2\ell h = 2\ell w + 2hw$	Subtract $2\ell h$ from each side; Subtraction Property of Equality
$A - 2\ell h = w(2\ell + 2h)$	Factor w; Distributive Property
$\frac{A - 2\ell h}{2\ell + 2h} = w$	Divide each side by $2\ell + 2h$; Division Property of Equality
$w = \frac{A - 2\ell h}{2\ell + 2h}$	Rewrite the equation; Symmetric Property of Equality

$w = 3$ in.

13. $P = 22$ units; Commutative and Addition Properties of Equality

Answers

2.4 Practice B

1. Equation | Explanation and Reason

Equation	Explanation and Reason
$3(x - 4) + 3 = x - 2$	Write the equation; Given
$3x - 12 + 3 = x - 2$	Multiply; Distributive Property
$2x = 7$	Add 9 to each side and subtract x from each side; Addition and Subtraction Properties of Equality
$x = 3.5$	Divide each side by 2; Division Property of Equality

2. Equation | Explanation and Reason

Equation	Explanation and Reason
$-1(x + 5) = 3\left[x + (2x - 1)\right]$	Write the equation; Given
$-x - 5 = 3(x + 2x - 1)$	Multiply; Distributive Property
$-x - 5 = 3x + 6x - 3$	Multiply; Distributive Property
$-10x = 2$	Add 5 to each side and subtract $9x$ from each side; Addition and Subtraction Properties of Equality
$x = -0.2$	Divide each side by 10; Division Property of Equality

3. Equation | Explanation and Reason

Equation	Explanation and Reason
$I = \frac{1}{2}mr^2$	Write the equation; Given
$2I = mr^2$	Multiply each side by 2; Multiplication Property of Equality
$\frac{2I}{r^2} = m$	Divide each side by r^2; Division Property of Equality
$m = \frac{2I}{r^2}$	Rewrite the equation; Symmetric Property of Equality

4. Equation | Explanation and Reason

Equation	Explanation and Reason
$E = \frac{1}{2}mv^2 + 9.8mh$	Write the equation; Given
$E - \frac{1}{2}mv^2 = 9.8mh$	Subtract $\frac{1}{2}mv^2$ from each side; Subtraction Property of Equality
$\frac{E - \frac{1}{2}mv^2}{9.8m} = h$	Divide each side by 9.8m; Division Property of Equality
$h = \frac{E - \frac{1}{2}mv^2}{9.8m}$	Rewrite the equation; Symmetric Property of Equality

5. Multiplication and Subtraction Properties of Equality

6. Transitive and Addition Properties of Equality

7. $60°$

8. $3x + y = 5x - 2y$

9. Equation | Explanation and Reason

Equation	Explanation and Reason
$V = \frac{1}{2}bh\ell$	Write the equation; Given
$\frac{2V}{h\ell} = b$	Multiply each side by 2 and divide each side by $h\ell$; Multiplication and Division Properties of Equality
$b = \frac{2V}{h\ell}$	Rewrite the equation; Symmetric Property of Equality
$b = 8$ m	

10. *Sample answer:* $m\angle BCD = 65°$ so $m\angle GCF = 65°$ and $m\angle FCD = 115°$, so $m\angle FCE = m\angle DCE = 57.5°$

Answers

2.4 Enrichment and Extension

1.

STATEMENTS	REASONS
1. $S = \dfrac{n}{2}\big[2a + (n-1)d\big]$	1. Given
2. $S \bullet \dfrac{2}{n} = \big[2a + (n-1)d\big]$	2. Multiplication Property of Equality
3. $\dfrac{S2}{n} - (n-1)d = 2a$	3. Subtraction Property of Equality
4. $\dfrac{S}{n} - \dfrac{(n-1)d}{2} = a$	4. Division Property of Equality

2.

STATEMENTS	REASONS
1. $V = \dfrac{1}{3}\pi h^2(3r - h)$	1. Given
2. $3V = \pi h^2(3r - h)$	2. Multiplication Property of Equality
3. $\dfrac{3V}{\pi h^2} = 3r - h$	3. Division Property of Equality
4. $\dfrac{3V}{\pi h^2} + h = 3r$	4. Addition Property of Equality
5. $\dfrac{V}{\pi h^2} + \dfrac{h}{3} = r$	5. Division Property of Equality

3. a. Given

   b. Addition Property of Equality

   c. Multiplication Property of Equality

   d. Simplify.

   e. Distributive Property

   f. Subtraction Property of Equality

   g. Distributive Property

4. a. $n = c(1 + r)$

   b. $n = c(1 + r)$ Given

      $\dfrac{n}{c} = 1 + r$ Division Property of Equality

      $\dfrac{n}{c} - 1 = r$ Subtraction Property of Equality

   c. $r = 2\%$

   d. $c = \dfrac{10.24}{1.04} \approx 9.85$; Solve the formula

   $n = c(1 + r)$, for r to yield $\dfrac{n}{c} - 1 = r$.

   Substitute $n = 10.24$ and $r = 0.04$ into the

   equation to yield $\dfrac{10.24}{c} - 1 = 0.04$. Using the

   Addition Property of Equality, add 1 to each side

   to obtain $\dfrac{10.24}{c} = 1.04$. Next, multiply by c and

   divide by 1.04 to obtain $c = \dfrac{10.24}{1.04} \approx 9.85$.

2.4 Puzzle Time

MAKE APPLESAUCE

2.5 Start Thinking

The formula for the area of a triangle is derived directly from the formula for the area of a rectangle. By drawing a diagonal, the rectangle is now split into two congruent triangles. So, each triangle is half the area of the rectangle, and the formula for the area of a triangle is $A = \frac{1}{2}bh$.

2.5 Warm Up

1. complement: $31°$, supplement: $121°$

2. complement: $70°$, supplement: $160°$

3. complement: $37°$, supplement: $127°$

4. complement: $67.4°$, supplement: $157.4°$

5. complement: $62°$, supplement: $152°$

6. complement: $16°$, supplement: $106°$

2.5 Cumulative Review Warm Up

1. $\angle BEC, \angle DEC$ 2. $83°$

3. $139°$ 4. $90°$

2.5 Practice A

1. Symmetric Property of Segment Congruence

2. Reflexive Property of Angle Congruence

Answers

3.

STATEMENTS	REASONS
1. $\angle A \cong \angle B$	1. Given
2. $m\angle A = m\angle B$	2. Definition of congruent angles
3. $m\angle B = m\angle A$	3. Symmetric Property of Equality
4. $\angle B \cong \angle A$	4. Definition of congruent angles

4.

STATEMENTS	REASONS
1. $AB = AB$	1. Reflexive Property of Equality
2. $\overline{AB} \cong \overline{AB}$	2. Definition of congruent segments

5.

STATEMENTS	REASONS
1. $\overline{BF}$ bisects $\angle AFC$	1. Given
2. $\angle AFB \cong \angle BFC$	2. Definition of angle bisector
3. $\angle CFD \cong \angle BFC$	3. Given
4. $\angle BFC \cong \angle CFD$	4. Symmetric Property of Angle Congruence (Thm. 2.2)
5. $\angle AFB \cong \angle CFD$	5. Transitive Property of Angle Congruence (Thm. 2.2)

6.

STATEMENTS	REASONS
1. $\overline{AG}$ bisects $\overline{CD}$ $\overline{IJ}$ bisects $\overline{CE}$ $\overline{BH}$ bisects $\overline{ED}$	1. Given
2. $CE = ED$ $CK = KE$ $EF = FD$	2. Definition of segment bisector
3. $2KE = CE$ $2FD = ED$	3. Definition of segment bisector
4. $2KE = 2FD$	4. Transitive Property of Equality
5. $KE = FD$	5. Division Property of Equality
6. $\overline{KE} \cong \overline{FD}$	6. Definition of congruent segments

2.5 Practice B

1.

STATEMENTS	REASONS
1. $\overline{AB} \cong \overline{CD}$	1. Given
2. $AB = CD$	2. Definition of congruent segments
3. $CD = AB$	3. Symmetric Property of Equality
4. $\overline{CD} \cong \overline{AB}$	4. Definition of congruent segments

2.

STATEMENTS	REASONS
1. $\angle A \cong \angle B$ $\angle B \cong \angle C$	1. Given
2. $m\angle A = m\angle B$ $m\angle B = m\angle C$	2. Definition of congruent angles
3. $m\angle A = m\angle C$	3. Transitive Property of Equality
4. $\angle A \cong \angle C$	4. Definition of congruent angles

3.

STATEMENTS	REASONS
1. E bisects $\overline{AI}$ $\overline{BC}$ bisects $\overline{AE}$ $\overline{FH}$ bisects $\overline{EI}$	1. Given
2. $\overline{AE} \cong \overline{EI}$ $\overline{AD} \cong \overline{DE}$ $\overline{EG} \cong \overline{GI}$	2. Definition of midpoint
3. $AE = EI$ $AD = DE$ $EG = GI$	3. Definition of congruent segments
4. $AD + AD = AE$ $EG + EG = EI$	4. Segment Addition Postulate (Post. 1.2)
5. $2AD = AE$ $2EG = EI$	5. Properties of Addition
6. $2AD = 2EG$	6. Substitution Property of Equality
7. $AD = EG$	7. Division Property of Equality
8. $\overline{AD} \cong \overline{EG}$	8. Definition of congruent segments

Answers

4.

STATEMENTS	REASONS
1. $m\angle KMN = 28°$	1. Given
2. $m\angle KMN + m\angle JMK$ $= 90°$	2. Definition of complementary angles
3. $28° + m\angle JMK$ $= 90°$	3. Substitution Property of Equality
4. $m\angle JMK = 62°$	4. Subtraction Property of Equality
5. $m\angle PTS = 118°$	5. Given
6. $m\angle PTS + m\angle STR$ $= 180°$	6. Definition of supplementary angles
7. $118° + m\angle STR$ $= 180°$	7. Substitution Property of Equality
8. $m\angle STR = 62°$	8. Subtraction Property of Equality
9. $m\angle JMK = m\angle STR$	9. Transitive Property of Equality
10. $\angle JMK \cong \angle STR$	10. Definition of congruent angles

5.

STATEMENTS	REASONS
1. $\angle ADC \cong \angle BDE$	1. Given
2. $m\angle ADC = m\angle BDE$	2. Definition of congruent angles
3. $m\angle ADC + m\angle ADE$ $= 180°$	3. Definition of supplementary angles
4. $m\angle BDC + m\angle BDE$ $= 180°$	4. Definition of supplementary angles
5. $m\angle ADC + m\angle ADE$ $= m\angle BDC + m\angle BDE$	5. Transitive Property of Equality
6. $m\angle ADC + m\angle ADE$ $= m\angle BDC + m\angle ADC$	6. Substitution Property of Equality
7. $m\angle ADE = m\angle BDC$	7. Subtraction Property of Equality
8. $\angle ADE \cong \angle BDC$	8. Definition of congruent angles

2.5 Enrichment and Extension

1. $RT = z$;

STATEMENTS	REASONS
1. T is the midpoint of $\overline{RS}$.	1. Given
2. $\overline{RT} \cong \overline{TS}$	2. Definition of midpoint
3. $RT = TS$	3. Definition of congruent segments
4. $TS = z$	4. Given
5. $RT = z$	5. Substitution Property of Equality

2. $2z = RS$;

STATEMENTS	REASONS
1. T is the midpoint of $\overline{RS}$.	1. Given
2. $\overline{RT} \cong \overline{TS}$	2. Definition of midpoint
3. $RT = TS$	3. Definition of congruent segments
4. $TS = z$	4. Given
5. $RT = z$	5. Transitive Property
6. $RT + TS = RS$	6. Segment Addition Postulate (Post. 1.2)
7. $z + z = RS$	7. Substitution Property of Equality
8. $2z = RS$	8. Simplify.

Answers

3. $RW = \dfrac{z}{2}$;

STATEMENTS	REASONS
1. T is the midpoint of $\overline{RS}$.	1. Given
2. $\overline{RT} \cong \overline{TS}$	2. Definition of midpoint
3. $RT = TS$	3. Definition of congruent segments
4. $TS = z$	4. Given
5. $RT = z$	5. Transitive Property
6. W is the midpoint of $\overline{RT}$.	6. Given
7. $\overline{RW} \cong \overline{WT}$	7. Definition of midpoint
8. $RW = WT$	8. Definition of congruent segments
9. $RW + WT = RT$	9. Segment Addition Postulate (Post. 1.2)
10. $RW + RW = RT$	10. Substitution Property of Equality
11. $2RW = RT$	11. Simplify.
12. $RW = \dfrac{RT}{2}$	12. Division Property of Equality
13. $RW = \dfrac{z}{2}$	13. Substitution Property of Equality

4. coordinate of point P: $\dfrac{3a + b}{4}$; coordinate of point Q: $\dfrac{5a + 3b}{8}$.

5. a. $x = 10$, $y = 2$

   b. $x = 18$, $y = 8$

6.

STATEMENTS	REASONS
1. $m\angle ZYQ = 45°$	1. Given
2. $m\angle ZQP = 45°$	2. Given
3. $m\angle ZYQ = m\angle ZQP$	3. Substitution Property of Equality
4. $\angle ZYQ \cong \angle ZQP$	4. Definition of congruent angles
5. $m\angle XYQ + m\angle ZYQ = 180°$	5. Definition of linear pair
6. $m\angle ZQP + m\angle ZQR = 180°$	6. Definition of linear pair
7. $m\angle XYQ + m\angle ZYQ = m\angle ZQP + m\angle ZQR$	7. Substitution Property of Equality
8. $m\angle XYQ + m\angle ZQP = m\angle ZQP + m\angle ZQR$	8. Substitution Property of Equality
9. $m\angle XYQ = m\angle ZQR$	9. Subtraction Property of Equality
10. $\angle XYQ \cong \angle ZQR$	10. Definition of congruent angles

2.5 Puzzle Time

THEY ALL DO

2.6 Start Thinking

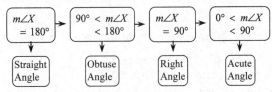

Sample answer: factoring polynomials

2.6 Warm Up

1. $x = 9$ **2.** $y = 35$ **3.** $x = -5$

4. $y = -9$ **5.** $x = -7$ **6.** $x = -7$

Answers

2.6 Cumulative Review Warm Up

1.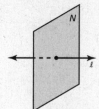

2.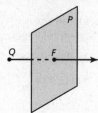

3.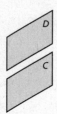

4.

5.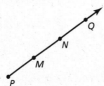

6.

5. STATEMENTS	REASONS
1. ∠1 and ∠2 are supplementary. ∠1 and ∠3 are supplementary.	**1.** Given
2. $m\angle 1 + m\angle 2 = 180°$ $m\angle 1 + m\angle 3 = 180°$	**2.** Definition of supplementary angles
3. $m\angle 1 + m\angle 2$ $= m\angle 1 + m\angle 3$	**3.** Transitive Property of Angle Congruence (Thm. 2.2)
4. $m\angle 2 = m\angle 3$	**4.** Subtraction Property of Equality
5. ∠2 ≅ ∠3	**5.** Definition of congruent angles

Proof: Because ∠1 and ∠2 are supplementary and ∠1 and ∠3 are supplementary, $m\angle 1 + m\angle 2 = 180°$ and $m\angle 1 + m\angle 3 = 180°$ by the definition of supplementary angles. By the Transitive Property of Angle Congruence (Thm. 2.2), $m\angle 1 + m\angle 2 = m\angle 1 + m\angle 3$. By the Subtraction Property of Equality, $m\angle 2 = m\angle 3$. So, ∠2 ≅ ∠3 by the definition of congruent angles.

2.6 Practice A

1. ∠A ≅ ∠BDC, ∠BDC ≅ ∠EDF, ∠A ≅ ∠EDF, ∠CDF ≅ ∠BDE; ∠A ≅ ∠BDC by definition because they have the same measure. ∠BDC ≅ ∠EDF by the Vertical Angles Congruence Theorem (Thm. 2.6). ∠A ≅ ∠EDF by the Transitive Property. ∠CDF ≅ ∠BDE by the Vertical Angles Congruence Theorem (Thm. 2.6).

2. ∠1 ≅ ∠4, ∠2 ≅ ∠5, ∠3 ≅ ∠6, ∠2 ≅ ∠3, ∠2 ≅ ∠6, ∠3 ≅ ∠5, ∠5 ≅ ∠6; ∠1 ≅ ∠4, ∠2 ≅ ∠5, and ∠3 ≅ ∠6 by the Vertical Angles Congruence Theorem (Thm. 2.6). ∠2 ≅ ∠3 by definition because they have the same measure. ∠2 ≅ ∠6 and ∠3 ≅ ∠5 by the Transitive Property of Angle Congruence (Thm. 2.2). ∠5 ≅ ∠6 by substitution.

3. $x = 13, y = 8$

4. $x = 5, y = 19$

2.6 Practice B

1. ∠D ≅ ∠B, ∠DAC ≅ ∠ACB, ∠BAC ≅ ∠ACD, ∠BAD ≅ ∠BCD, ∠D ≅ ∠BAC, ∠B ≅ ∠BAD, ∠D ≅ ∠BCD, and ∠B ≅ ∠BCD; ∠D ≅ ∠B by the Right Angles Congruence Theorem (Thm. 2.3). ∠DAC ≅ ∠ACB and ∠BAC ≅ ∠ACD by definition because they have the same measures. Because $m\angle DAC + m\angle BAC = 90°$ and by the Angle Addition Postulate (Post. 1.4), ∠DAC + ∠BAC ≅ ∠DAB and $m\angle DAB = 90°$. By the same reasoning, $m\angle BCD = 90°$. So, ∠BAD ≅ ∠BCD by the Right Angles Congruence Theorem (Thm. 2.3). ∠D ≅ ∠BAD, ∠B ≅ ∠BAD, ∠D ≅ ∠BCD, and ∠B ≅ ∠BCD by the Transitive Property.

Answers

2. $\angle 1 \cong \angle 3$, $\angle 2 \cong \angle 4$, $\angle 1 \cong \angle 5$, $\angle 2 \cong \angle 6$, $\angle 4 \cong \angle 6$; $\angle 1 \cong \angle 3$, and $\angle 2 \cong \angle 4$ by the Vertical Angles Congruence Theorem (Thm. 2.6). $\angle 1 \cong \angle 5$ by definition because they have the same angle measure. Because $\angle 1$ and $\angle 2$ form a linear pair and $\angle 5$ and $\angle 6$ form a linear pair, $m\angle 1 + m\angle 2 = 180°$ and $m\angle 5 + m\angle 6 = 180°$ by the Linear Pair Postulate (Post. 2.8). So, by the Congruent Supplements Theorem (Thm. 2.4), $\angle 2 \cong \angle 6$. Because $\angle 1$ and $\angle 4$ form a linear pair and $\angle 5$ and $\angle 6$ form a linear pair, $m\angle 1 + m\angle 4 = 180°$ and $m\angle 5 + m\angle 6 = 180°$ by the Linear Pair Postulate (Post. 2.8). So, by the Congruent Supplements Theorem (Thm. 2.4), $\angle 4 \cong \angle 6$.

3. $x = 8$, $y = 186$ **4.** $x = 4$, $y = 184$

5.

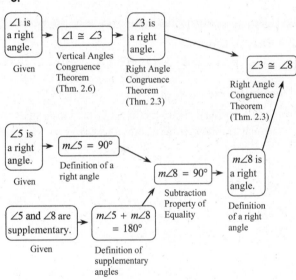

Because $\angle 1$ is a right angle and $\angle 1 \cong \angle 3$ by the Vertical Angles Congruence Theorem (Thm. 2.6), $\angle 1 \cong \angle 3$ by the Right Angle Congruence Theorem (Thm. 2.3). Because $\angle 5$ is a right angle, $m\angle 5 = 90°$. $\angle 5$ and $\angle 8$ are supplementary angles so, $m\angle 5 + m\angle 8 = 180°$ by the definition of supplementary angles. By the Subtraction Property of Equality, $m\angle 8 = 90°$. So, $\angle 8$ is a right angle by the definition of a right angle. Because $\angle 3$ and $\angle 8$ are right angles, $\angle 3 \cong \angle 8$ by the Right Angles Congruence Theorem (Thm. 2.3).

2.6 Enrichment and Extension

1. false   **2.** true   **3.** false

4. false   **5.** true   **6.** true

7.

STATEMENTS	REASONS
1. $\overline{AB} \perp \overline{BD}$ $\overline{ED} \perp \overline{BD}$	1. Given
2. $\angle ABD$ is a right angle. $\angle EDB$ is a right angle.	2. Definition of perpendicular lines
3. $m\angle ABD = 90°$ $m\angle EDB = 90°$	3. Definition of right angle
4. $m\angle ABC + m\angle CBD$ $= 90°$ $m\angle EDC + m\angle CDB$ $= 90°$	4. Angle Addition Postulate (Post. 1.4)
5. $\angle ABC \cong \angle EDC$	5. Given
6. $m\angle ABC = m\angle EDC$	6. Definition of congruent angles
7. $m\angle ABC + m\angle CBD$ $= m\angle EDC + m\angle CDB$	7. Substitution Property of Equality
8. $m\angle EDC + m\angle CBD$ $= m\angle EDC + m\angle CDB$	8. Substitution Property of Equality
9. $m\angle CBD = m\angle CDB$	9. Subtraction Property of Equality
10. $\angle CBD \cong \angle CDB$	10. Definition of congruent angles

Answers

8.

STATEMENTS	REASONS
1. $m\angle WYZ = m\angle TWZ$ $= 45°$	1. Given
2. $\angle TWZ$ and $\angle SWZ$ are a linear pair. $\angle WYZ$ and $\angle XYW$ are a linear pair.	2. Definition of linear pair
3. $\angle TWZ$ and $\angle SWZ$ are supplementary. $\angle WYZ$ and $\angle XYW$ are supplementary.	3. Linear Pair Postulate (Post. 2.8)
4. $m\angle TWZ + m\angle SWZ$ $= 180°$ $m\angle WYZ + m\angle XYW$ $= 180°$	4. Definition of supplementary angles
5. $m\angle TWZ + m\angle SWZ$ $= m\angle WYZ + m\angle XYW$	5. Transitive Property of Equality
6. $45° + m\angle SWZ$ $= 45° + m\angle XYW$	6. Substitution Property of Equality
7. $m\angle SWZ = m\angle XYW$	7. Subtraction Property of Equality
8. $\angle SWZ \cong \angle XYW$	8. Definition of congruent angles

9.

STATEMENTS	REASONS
1. The hexagon is regular.	1. Given
2. All interior angles of the hexagon are congruent.	2. Definition of regular hexagon
3. $\angle 1$ is congruent to an interior angle of the hexagon.	3. Vertical Angles Congruence Theorem (Thm. 2.6)
4. $\angle 2$ is supplementary to an interior angle of the hexagon.	4. Linear Pair Postulate (Post. 2.8)
5. $\angle 2$ is supplementary to $\angle 1$.	5. Substitution
6. $m\angle 1 + m\angle 2 = 180°$	6. Definition of supplementary angles

2.6 Puzzle Time

MAKE SURE ONE OF THEM IS A MATCH

Cumulative Review

1. Each additional figure has an additional inscribed equilateral triangle in the previous triangle.

2. Each additional figure has a bottom row containing one more solid circle than the previous figure.

3. Each additional figure is the same rectangle with one more equal division.

Answers

4. Add 2 starting at 2; 10, 12

5. Add 3 starting at 1; 13, 16

6. Add 13 starting at 4; 56, 69

7. Add 9 starting at 7; 43, 52

8. Multiply by $\frac{3}{2}$ starting at 2; $\frac{81}{8}$, $\frac{243}{16}$

9. Multiply by $\frac{3}{4}$ starting at 3; $\frac{243}{256}$, $\frac{729}{1024}$

10. Increase what you add by 1 each term. Start at 1 and start by adding 2; 15, 21

11. Increase what you add by 1 each term. Start at 2 and start by adding 3; 20, 27

12. a. 88 ft   **b.** 468 ft^2

13. a. 54 in.   **b.** 216 in.

14. 79   **15.** 4   **16.** -29 **17.** -5

18. 11   **19.** -160 **20.** -22 **21.** 29

22. 44   **23.** -75 **24.** 14   **25.** -60

26. 24   **27.** 5   **28.** 11

29. $-7s + 16$ **30.** $27c - 19$ **31.** $7g + 9$

32. $-16x + 7$ **33.** $5m + 5$ **34.** $10r + 3$

35. $6j$ **36.** $26a - 42$ **37.** $7f - 23$

38. $6y - 10$ **39.** $-2b - 2$ **40.** $8k - 5$

41. $w - 2$ **42.** $3g + 6$ **43.** $p + 3$

44. $b = 5$ **45.** $m = 7$ **46.** $k = 19$

47. $p = 15$ **48.** $a = -4$ **49.** $x = 3$

50. $r = -22$ **51.** $h = 9$ **52.** $w = 42$

53. $t = -22$ **54.** $c = -3$ **55.** $e = -7$

56. a. 5 lunches   **b.** 10 lunches   **c.** $27.75
   d. $9.25   **e.** $37

57. a. 7 push-ups   **b.** 9 push-ups   **c.** day 8
   d. day 11

58. 64   **59.** -64 **60.** 32   **61.** 25

62. -9 **63.** 9   **64.** 16   **65.** -16

66. 16   **67.** 100   **68.** 1,000,000

69. -32 **70.** $3\sqrt{5}$ **71.** $2\sqrt{6}$ **72.** $5\sqrt{5}$

73. $2\sqrt{7}$ **74.** $4\sqrt{3}$ **75.** $4\sqrt{2}$ **76.** $5\sqrt{2}$

77. $5\sqrt{6}$ **78.** $4\sqrt{10}$ **79.** $10\sqrt{2}$ **80.** $8\sqrt{3}$

81. $6\sqrt{2}$ **82.** $6\sqrt{3}$ **83.** $5\sqrt{3}$ **84.** $7\sqrt{3}$

85. $2\sqrt{5}$ **86.** $\frac{2}{3}$ **87.** $\frac{3}{7}$ **88.** $\frac{2}{3}$

89. $\frac{5}{6}$ **90.** $\frac{2\sqrt{5}}{5}$ **91.** $\frac{\sqrt{3}}{3}$ **92.** $\frac{4\sqrt{7}}{7}$

93. $\frac{\sqrt{6}}{2}$ **94.** $x = 7$ **95.** $x = -3$

96. $x = 9$ **97.** $x = -6$ **98.** $x = 2$

99. $x = 5$ **100.** $x = -6$ **101.** $x = 32$

102. $x = 14$ **103.** $x = -2$ **104.** $x = 3$

105. $x = 3$ **106.** $x = -5$ **107.** $x = 2$

108. $x = 3$ **109.** $x = 7$ **110.** $x = -1$

111. $x = 7$

112. a. The chair is *not* wood.
   b. The rug is brown.

113. a. The photograph is in color.
   b. Your homework is *not* finished.

114. a. It is *not* cold outside.
   b. The bicycle is green.

115. $x^2 + 8x + 16$ **116.** $x^2 - 4x + 4$

117. $x^2 - 6x + 9$ **118.** $x^2 - 2x + 1$

119. $x^2 + 18x + 81$ **120.** $x^2 - 26x + 169$

121. $4x^2 + 16x + 16$ **122.** $9x^2 - 6x + 1$

123. $25x^2 + 60x + 36$ **124.** $25x^2 - 10x + 1$

125. $9x^2 + 48x + 64$ **126.** $4x^2 - 16x + 16$

Answers

127. $(x + 2)(x - 7)$ **128.** $(x - 12)(x + 11)$

129. $(x - 7)(x + 4)$ **130.** $(x - 5)(x - 3)$

131. $(x - 2)(x - 3)$ **132.** $(x + 4)(x - 9)$

133. $(x + 1)(x - 1)$ **134.** $(x + 3)(x - 3)$

135. $(x + 5)(x - 5)$ **136.** $(2x - 3)(x + 4)$

137. $(3x - 5)(x - 7)$ **138.** $(5x + 2)(x + 4)$

139. $x = -8$ and $x = -3$

140. $x = -6$ and $x = 2$

141. $x = -12$ and $x = 1$

142. $x = -9$ and $x = -8$

143. $x = -5$ and $x = 4$

144. $x = -10$ and $x = -7$

145. $x = -3$ and $x = 1$

146. $x = -5$ and $x = 2$

147. $x = -11$ and $x = 1$

148. $x = -\frac{3}{2}$ and $x = 5$

149. $x = -\frac{4}{5}$ and $x = 3$

150. $x = -\frac{1}{3}$ and $x = \frac{7}{2}$

151. **a.** 7 words per min
    b. 87.5 words
    c. 105 words
    d. 17.5 words

Chapter 3

3.1 Start Thinking

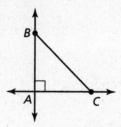

right triangle; no; no; Because points B and C connect perpendicular lines, you cannot plot either point to make a perpendicular segment or a parallel segment.

3.1 Warm Up

1. *Sample answer:* $\overleftrightarrow{BC}$ **2.** $\overleftrightarrow{GE}$

3. $\overline{CG}$ **4.** $\overline{AB}, \overline{BC}, \overline{BD}$

5. *Sample answer:* $\overrightarrow{FE}$ and $\overrightarrow{FG}$

6. *Sample answer:* D

3.1 Cumulative Review Warm Up

1. $K(4, 11)$ **2.** $J(-27, -18)$ **3.** $K(21, -2)$

3.1 Practice A

1. $\overleftrightarrow{AB}$ and $\overleftrightarrow{CD}$ **2.** $\overleftrightarrow{AC}$ and $\overleftrightarrow{CD}$

3. no; $\overleftrightarrow{AB} \parallel \overleftrightarrow{CD}$ and by the Parallel Postulate (Post. 3.1), there is exactly one line parallel to $\overleftrightarrow{AB}$ through point C.

4. no; They are intersecting lines.

5. $\angle 2$ and $\angle 8$, $\angle 3$ and $\angle 5$

6. $\angle 1$ and $\angle 7$, $\angle 4$ and $\angle 6$

7. $\angle 1$ and $\angle 5$, $\angle 2$ and $\angle 6$, $\angle 3$ and $\angle 7$, $\angle 4$ and $\angle 8$

8. $\angle 2$ and $\angle 5$, $\angle 3$ and $\angle 8$

9. no; By definition, skew lines are not coplaner.

10. 2 pairs; 4 pairs; $(2n - 2)$ pairs

11. **a.** $\overleftrightarrow{AB}$ and $\overleftrightarrow{CD}$, $\overleftrightarrow{AC}$ and $\overleftrightarrow{BD}$

    b. $\overleftrightarrow{AC}$ and $\overleftrightarrow{CD}$, $\overleftrightarrow{BD}$ and $\overleftrightarrow{CD}$

    c. $\angle 2$ and $\angle 5$, $\angle 3$ and $\angle 8$

Answers

d. ∠1 and ∠5, ∠2 and ∠6, ∠3 and ∠7, ∠4 and ∠8

e. ∠2 and ∠8, ∠3 and ∠5

f. ∠1 and ∠7, ∠4 and ∠6

3.1 Practice B

1. lines *c* and *d*   **2.** lines *e* and *f*

3. *Sample answer:* lines *c* and *e*

4. planes *A* and *B*

5. no; lines *f* and *g* appear to be coplanar and although they do not intersect, there is not enough information to determine that the lines are parallel.

6. no; lines *e* and *g* appear to be coplanar and intersect at a 90° angle, but there is not enough information to determine that the lines are perpendicular.

7. alternate interior   **8.** corresponding

9. alternate exterior   **10.** corresponding

11. consecutive exterior

12. no; The lines do not intersect, however they could be coplanar to a third plane.

13. a. true; The road and the sidewalk appear to lie in the same plane and they do not intersect.

b. false; The road and the crosswalk appear to intersect.

c. true; A properly installed stop sign intersects the ground at a 90° angle.

3.1 Enrichment and Extension

1. yes; The two lines of intersection are coplanar because they are both in the third plane. The two lines do not intersect because they are in parallel planes. Because they are coplanar and do not intersect, they are parallel.

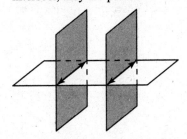

2.

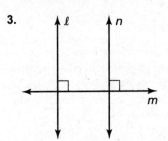

Line *a* appears to be parallel to line *c*; If two lines are parallel to the same line, then they are parallel to each other.

3.

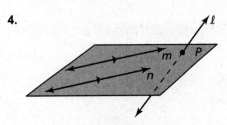

Line *ℓ* seems to be parallel to line *n*; If two lines are perpendicular to the same line, then they are parallel to each other.

4.

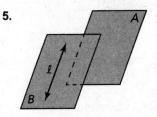

5.

6. a. ∠5, ∠11, ∠17

b. ∠5, ∠9, ∠17

c. ∠8, ∠12, ∠17

d. ∠7, ∠9, ∠18

e. ∠2, ∠10, ∠14

f. ∠4, ∠10, ∠16

g. ∠3, ∠11, ∠15

h. ∠15

3.1 Puzzle Time

A YARDSTICK

Answers

3.2 Start Thinking

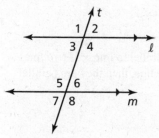

one angle measure; With the measurement of one of the angles, you can use the properties of corresponding angles, alternative interior angles, alternate exterior angles, and consecutive interior angles to find the other seven measurements.

3.2 Warm Up

1. $34°$ **2.** $17°$ **3.** $147°$

4. $53°$ **5.** $86°$ **6.** $84°$

3.2 Cumulative Review Warm Up

1.

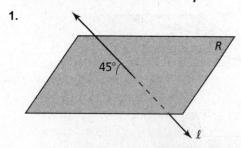

2.

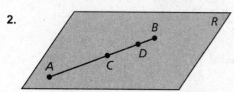

3.

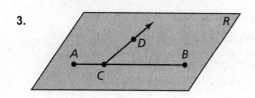

4.

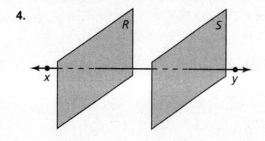

3.2 Practice A

1. $m\angle 1 = 87°, m\angle 2 = 93°; m\angle 1 = 87°$ by the Alternate Interior Angles Theorem (Thm. 3.2). $m\angle 2 = 93°$ by the Consecutive Interior Angles Theorem (Thm. 3.4).

2. $m\angle 1 = 78°, m\angle 2 = 78°; m\angle 1 = 78°$ by the Corresponding Angles Theorem (Thm. 3.1). $m\angle 2 = 78°$ by the Alternate Exterior Angles Theorem (Thm. 3.3).

3. $8; 37° = (6x - 11)°$

$$48 = 6x$$
$$8 = x$$

4. $10;$

$$m\angle 2 + 142° = 180°$$
$$2(x + 9)° + 142° = 180°$$
$$2x + 18 + 142 = 180$$
$$2x + 160 = 180$$
$$2x = 20$$
$$x = 10$$

5. $m\angle 1 = 112°, m\angle 2 = 68°, m\angle 3 = 112°;$ Because the $112°$ angle is a vertical angle to $\angle 1$, by the Vertical Angles Congruence Theorem (Thm. 2.6) they are congruent. Because $\angle 1$ and $\angle 2$ are consecutive interior angles, they are supplementary by the Consecutive Interior Angles Theorem (Thm. 3.4). Because the given $112°$ angle and $\angle 3$ are alternate exterior angles, they are congruent by the Alternate Exterior Angles Theorem (Thm. 3.3).

6. $m\angle 1 = 45°, m\angle 2 = 45°, m\angle 3 = 135°;$ Because the given $45°$ angle is a corresponding angle with $\angle 1$, and $\angle 1$ is a corresponding angle with $\angle 2$, they are all congruent by the Corresponding Angles Theorem (Thm. 3.1). Because the $45°$ angle is a consecutive interior angle with $\angle 3$, they are supplementary by the Consecutive Angles Theorem (Thm. 3.4).

Answers

7.

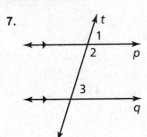

STATEMENTS	REASONS
1. $p \parallel q$	**1.** Given
2. $m\angle 1 + m\angle 2 = 180°$	**2.** Linear Pair Postulate (Post. 2.8)
3. $m\angle 2 + m\angle 3 = 180°$	**3.** Consecutive Interior Angles Theorem (Thm. 3.4)
4. $\angle 1 \cong \angle 3$	**4.** Congruent Supplements Theorem (Thm. 2.4)

8.

STATEMENTS	REASONS
1. $\angle 1 \cong \angle 2$	**1.** Given
2. $\angle 1 \cong \angle 3$	**2.** Vertical Angles Congruence Theorem (Thm. 2.6)
3. $\angle 2 \cong \angle 3$	**3.** Transitive Property of Angle Congruence (Thm. 2.2)

$m\angle 1 = 90°$; Because $\angle 1$ is congruent and supplementary to $\angle 2$, the measure of each angle is 90°.

3.2 Practice B

1. $m\angle 1 = 41°, m\angle 2 = 41°$; $m\angle 1 = 41°$ by the Corresponding Angles Theorem (Thm. 3.1). $m\angle 2 = 41°$ by the Vertical Angles Congruence Theorem (Thm. 2.6).

2. $m\angle 1 = 124°, m\angle 2 = 124°$; $m\angle 1 = 124°$ by the Alternate Exterior Angles Theorem (Thm. 3.3). $m\angle 2 = 124°$ by the Vertical Angles Congruence Theorem (Thm. 2.6).

3. 16; $(x + 24)° = (3x - 8)°$
$$x + 32 = 3x$$
$$32 = 2x$$
$$16 = x$$

4. 51; $\frac{2}{3}(x + 27)° + (3x - 25)° = 180°$
$$\frac{2}{3}x + 18 + 3x - 25 = 180$$
$$\frac{11}{3}x - 7 = 180$$
$$x = 51$$

5. $m\angle 1 = 102°, m\angle 2 = 102°, m\angle 3 = 78°$; Because the given 102° angle is an alternate interior angle with $\angle 1$, they are congruent by the Alternate Interior Angles Congruence Theorem (Thm. 3.2). Because the given 102° angle and $\angle 2$ are alternate exterior angles, they are congruent by the Alternate Exterior Angles Theorem (Thm. 3.3). Because $\angle 2$ and $\angle 3$ are a linear pair, they are supplementary by the Linear Pair Postulate (Post. 2.8).

6. $m\angle 1 = 68°, m\angle 2 = 68°, m\angle 3 = 112°$; Because the given 68° angle and $\angle 1$ are corresponding angles, they are congruent by the Corresponding Angles Theorem (Thm. 3.1). Because $\angle 1$ and $\angle 2$ are alternate exterior angles, they are congruent by the Alternate Exterior Angles Theorem (Thm. 3.3). Because angle $\angle 2$ and $\angle 3$ are consecutive angles, they are supplementary by the Consecutive Interior Angles Theorem (Thm. 3.4).

7. $m\angle 1 = 110°, m\angle 2 = 70°$; Because $(3x + 5)° = (4x - 30)°$, the value of x is 35. So, $(3x + 5)° = 110°$ and $(4x - 30)° = 110°$. By the Corresponding Angles Theorem (Thm. 3.1), $m\angle 1 = 110°$. By the Linear Pair Postulate (Post 2.8), $m\angle 2 = 70°$.

Answers

8. $\angle 3$, $\angle 5$, $\angle 6$, $\angle 7$, $\angle 9$, and $\angle 10$; Because $\angle 1$ and $\angle 3$ are supplementary to $\angle 2$ by the Consecutive Interior Angles Theorem (Thm. 3.4), $\angle 1 \cong \angle 3$ by the Congruent Supplements Theorem (Thm. 2.4). $\angle 1 \cong \angle 5$ and $\angle 1 \cong \angle 7$ by the Alternate Interior Angles Theorem (Thm. 3.3). $\angle 1 \cong \angle 6$ by the Vertical Angles Congruence Theorem (Thm. 2.6). Because $\angle 3 \cong \angle 9$ by the Vertical Angles Congruence Theorem (Thm. 2.6), $\angle 1 \cong \angle 9$ by the Transitive Property of Angle Congruence (Thm. 2.2). Because $\angle 5 \cong \angle 10$ by the Vertical Angles Congruence Theorem (Thm. 2.6), $\angle 1 \cong \angle 10$ by the Transitive Property of Angle Congruence (Thm. 2.2).

3.2 Enrichment and Extension

1. $x = 65$, $y = 60$ 2. $x = 13$, $y = 12$

3.
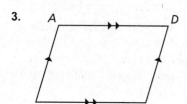

STATEMENTS	REASONS
1. $\overline{AB} \parallel \overline{DC}$, $\overline{AD} \parallel \overline{BC}$	1. Given
2. $\angle A$ and $\angle B$ are supplementary.	2. Consecutive Interior Angles Theorem (Thm. 3.4)
3. $\angle B$ and $\angle C$ are supplementary.	3. Consecutive Interior Angles Theorem (Thm. 3.4)
4. $m\angle A + m\angle B = 180°$	4. Definition of supplementary angles
5. $m\angle B + m\angle C = 180°$	5. Definition of supplementary angles
6. $m\angle A + m\angle B = m\angle B + m\angle C$	6. Substitution
7. $m\angle A = m\angle C$	7. Subtraction Property of Equality
8. $\angle A \cong \angle C$	8. Definition of congruent angles

4. $m\angle 1 = 35°$, $m\angle 2 = 145°$, $m\angle 3 = 111°$, $m\angle 4 = 69°$, $m\angle 5 = 111°$, $m\angle 6 = 69°$, $m\angle 7 = 145°$, $m\angle 8 = 35°$, $m\angle 9 = 69°$, $m\angle 10 = 111°$, $m\angle 11 = 69°$, $m\angle 12 = 111°$, $m\angle 13 = 76°$, $m\angle 14 = 104°$, $m\angle 15 = 76°$, $m\angle 16 = 104°$, $m\angle 17 = 104°$, $m\angle 18 = 76°$, $m\angle 19 = 104°$, $m\angle 20 = 76°$

5. $m\angle 1 = 100°$, $m\angle 2 = 80°$, $m\angle 3 = 80°$, $m\angle 4 = 100°$, $m\angle 5 = 100°$, $m\angle 6 = 56°$, $m\angle 7 = 24°$, $m\angle 8 = 24°$, $m\angle 9 = 56°$, $m\angle 10 = 100°$, $m\angle 11 = 156°$, $m\angle 12 = 24°$, $m\angle 13 = 24°$, $m\angle 14 = 156°$, $m\angle 15 = 124°$, $m\angle 16 = 56°$, $m\angle 17 = 124°$, $m\angle 18 = 56°$, $m\angle 19 = 100°$, $m\angle 20 = 80°$, $m\angle 21 = 100°$, $m\angle 22 = 80°$, $m\angle 23 = 156°$, $m\angle 24 = 24°$, $m\angle 25 = 24°$, $m\angle 26 = 156°$, $m\angle 27 = 100°$, $m\angle 28 = 56°$, $m\angle 29 = 24°$, $m\angle 30 = 24°$, $m\angle 31 = 56°$, $m\angle 32 = 100°$

3.2 Puzzle Time
GEOMETRY

3.3 Start Thinking

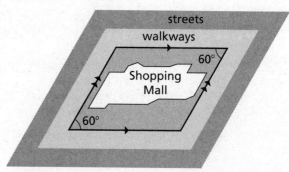

$120°$; $60°$ and $120°$, respectively; The angles are the same as the shopping mall sidewalks because they are parallel to them.

3.3 Warm Up

1. $x = 10$, $y = 12$ 2. $x = 5$, $y = 3$

3.3 Cumulative Review Warm Up

1. $m\angle 2 = m\angle 1$ 2. $GH + HJ$ 3. $4 \cdot GH$

3.3 Practice A

1. $x = 44$; Lines s and t are parallel when the marked alternate exterior angles are congruent.

$$3(x - 8)° = 2(x + 10)°$$
$$3x - 24 = 2x + 20$$
$$x = 44$$

Answers

2. $x = 18$; Lines s and t are parallel when the marked consecutive interior angles are supplementary.

$$(4x - 12)° + 120° = 180°$$
$$4x + 108 = 180$$
$$4x = 72$$
$$x = 18$$

3. yes; Corresponding Angles Converse (Thm. 3.5)

4. no

5. This diagram shows that the vertical angles are congruent, and we do not have enough information to prove that $m \parallel n$.

6.

STATEMENTS	REASONS
1. $\angle 1$ and $\angle 2$ are supplementary.	1. Given
2. $\angle 2$ and $\angle 3$ are supplementary.	2. Linear Pair Postulate (Post 2.8)
3. $\angle 1 \cong \angle 3$	3. Congruent Supplements Theorem (Thm. 2.4)
4. $p \parallel q$	4. Corresponding Angles Converse (Thm. 3.5)

7. no; The labeled angles must be congruent to prove the wings are parallel.

3.3 Practice B

1. $x = 12$; Lines s and t are parallel when the marked alternate exterior angles are congruent.

$$(4x + 16)° = (7x - 20)°$$
$$36 = 3x$$
$$12 = x$$

2. $x = 26$; Lines s and t are parallel when the marked consecutive interior angles are supplementary.

$$2(x + 15)° + (3x + 20)° = 180°$$
$$2x + 30 + 3x + 20 = 180$$
$$5x + 50 = 180$$
$$5x = 130$$
$$x = 26$$

3. yes; Alternate Exterior Angles Converse (Thm. 3.7)

4. yes; Consecutive Interior Angles Converse (Thm. 3.8)

5. a. yes; Lines a and b are parallel by the Alternate Interior Angles Converse (Thm. 3.6). Lines b and c are parallel by the Alternate Exterior Angles Converse Theorem (Thm. 3.7). Line c and d are parallel by the Corresponding Angles Converse (Thm. 3.5). Lines b and c are parallel by the Alternate Exterior Angles Converse (Thm. 3.7). By the Transitive Property of Parallel Lines (Thm. 3.9), all the lines of latitude are parallel.

b. no; There is not enough information to prove that the lines of longitude are parallel.

6. a. $x = 27$, $y = 13$, $z = 9$; Lines p and q are parallel when the marked alternate exterior angles are congruent.

$$3(x - 1)° = (4x - 30)°$$
$$3x - 3 = 4x - 30$$
$$27 = x$$

Lines q and r are parallel when the marked corresponding angles are congruent.

$$(4x - 30)° = (6y)°$$
$$4(27) - 30 = 6y$$
$$78 = 6y$$
$$13 = y$$

The angles $6y°$ and $6(z + 8)°$ form a linear pair, so they are supplementary.

$$6y° + 6(z + 8)° = 180°$$
$$6(13) + 6(z + 8) = 180$$
$$78 + 6z + 48 = 180$$
$$6z = 54$$
$$z = 9$$

b. yes; Because $3(x - 1)° = 78°$ and $6y° = 78°$, lines p and q are parallel by the Alternate Exterior Converse (Thm. 3.7).

Answers

7. STATEMENTS	REASONS
1. $\angle 1 \cong \angle 2$	1. Given
2. $c \parallel d$	2. Alternate Exterior Angles Converse (Thm. 3.7)
3. $\angle 2 \cong \angle 3$	3. Given
4. $a \parallel b$	4. Alternate Interior Angles Converse (Thm. 3.6)
5. $\angle 3 \cong \angle 4$	5. Corresponding Angles Theorem (Thm. 3.1)
6. $\angle 1 \cong \angle 4$	6. Transitive Property of Angle Congruence (Thm. 2.2)

3.3 Enrichment and Extension

1. $78°$

2.

STATEMENTS	REASONS
1. $\overline{AC}$ is parallel to $\overline{FG}$. $\overline{BD}$ is the bisector of $\angle CBE$. $\overline{DE}$ is the bisector of $\angle BEG$.	1. Given
2. $\angle CBE \cong \angle BEF$	2. Alternate Interior Angles Theorem (Thm. 3.2)
3. $m\angle CBE = m\angle BEF$	3. Properties of Angle Congruence (Thm. 2.2)
4. $\angle ABE \cong \angle BEG$	4. Alternate Interior Angles Theorem (Thm. 3.2)
5. $m\angle ABE = m\angle BEG$	5. Properties of Angle Congruence (Thm. 2.2)
6. $\angle CBE + \angle ABE = 180°$	6. Definition of linear pair
7. $\angle CBE + \angle BEG = 180°$	7. Substitution
8. $\frac{1}{2}\angle CBE = \angle DBE$	8. Definition of angle bisector
9. $\frac{1}{2}\angle BEG = \angle BED$	9. Definition of angle bisector
10. $\frac{1}{2}\angle CBE + \frac{1}{2}\angle BEG = \frac{1}{2}(180°)$	10. Multiplication Property of Equality
11. $\frac{1}{2}\angle CBE + \frac{1}{2}\angle BEG = 90°$	11. Simplify
12. $\angle DBE + \angle BED = 90°$	12. Substitution
13. $m\angle DBE + m\angle BED + m\angle EDB = 180°$	13. Property of triangles
14. $180° = 90° + \angle EDB$	14. Substitution
15. $90° = \angle EDB$	15. Subtraction Property of Equality

Answers

3. a. one line

b. an infinite number of lines

c. one plane

4. a. 137°

b. 71°

c. 137°

d. 43°

e. 71°

5.

STATEMENTS	REASONS
1. $\overrightarrow{CA} \parallel \overrightarrow{ED}$ $m\angle FED = 45°$	1. Given
2. $\angle ABE$ and $\angle DEB$ are supplementary	2. Consecutive Interior Angles Theorem (Thm. 3.4)
3. $m\angle ABE + m\angle DEB$ $= 180°$	3. Definition of supplementary angles
4. $m\angle ABE + 45°$ $= 180°$	4. Substitution Property of Equality
5. $m\angle ABE = 135°$	5. Subtraction Property of Equality
6. $m\angle FBC = 135°$	6. Vertical Angles Congruence Theorem (Thm. 2.6)
7. $m\angle GCA = 45°$	7. Given
8. $135° + 45° = 180°$	8. Addition
9. $m\angle FBC + m\angle GCA$ $= 180°$	9. Substitution Property of Equality
10. $\angle FBC$ and $\angle GCA$ are supplementary.	10. Definition of supplementary angles.
11. $\overrightarrow{EF} \parallel \overrightarrow{CG}$	11. Consecutive Interior Angles Converse Theorem (Thm. 3.8)

3.3 Puzzle Time

BECAUSE HE WANTED TO SEE TIME FLY

3.4 Start Thinking

Sample answer: framing square and chalk line; A framing square ensures cuts made with saws are precise. The chalk line helps builders keep a horizontal surface when needed.

3.4 Warm Up

1. 25 cm

2. 33 cm

3. 478.5 cm^2

4. 46 cm

5. 7 cm

3.4 Cumulative Review Warm Up

1. Given $\overline{AB} \cong \overline{CD}$, prove $\overline{CD} \cong \overline{AB}$

STATEMENTS	REASONS
1. $\overline{AB} \cong \overline{CD}$	1. Given
2. $AB = CD$	2. Definition of congruent segments
3. $CD = AB$	3. Symmetric Property of Equality
4. $\overline{CD} \cong \overline{AB}$	4. Definition of congruent segments

2. Given $\angle A$, prove $\angle A \cong \angle A$

STATEMENTS	REASONS
1. $\angle A$	1. Given
2. $m\angle A = m\angle A$	2. Reflexive Property of Angle Measures
3. $\angle A \cong \angle A$	3. Definition of congruent angles

3.4 Practice A

1. about 5.7 units

2.

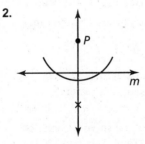

3. none; The only thing that can be concluded from the diagram is that $\ell \perp n$ and $m \perp p$. In order to say that the lines are parallel, you need to know something about the intersections of ℓ and p or m and n.

Answers

4. $b \parallel c$; Because $a \perp b$ and $a \perp c$, lines b and c are parallel by the Lines Perpendicular to a Transversal Theorem (Thm. 3.12).

5.

STATEMENTS	REASONS
1. $\angle 1 \cong \angle 2$	1. Given
2. $e \perp h$	2. Linear Pair Perpendicular Theorem (Thm. 3.10)
3. $e \parallel f$	3. Lines Perpendicular to a Transversal Theorem (Thm. 3.12)
4. $e \parallel g$	4. Transitive Property of Parallel Lines (Thm. 3.9)

6. no; There is only one perpendicular bisector that can be drawn, but there is an infinite number of perpendicular lines.

7. $w \parallel x$, $w \parallel z$, $x \parallel z$; Because $w \perp b$ and $x \perp b$, $w \parallel x$ by the Lines Perpendicular to a Transversal Theorem (Thm. 3.12). Because $w \perp b$ and $z \perp b$, $w \parallel z$ by the Lines Perpendicular to a Transversal Theorem (Thm. 3.12). Because $w \parallel x$ and $w \parallel z$, $x \parallel z$ by the Transitive Property of Parallel Lines Theorem (Thm. 3.9).

3.4 Practice B

1. $2\sqrt{5}$ units

2. $g \parallel h$; Because $e \perp g$ and $e \perp h$, lines g and h are parallel by the Lines Perpendicular to a Transversal Theorem (Thm. 3.12).

3. $\ell \parallel n$, $m \parallel n$, $\ell \parallel m$; Because $j \perp \ell$ and $j \perp n$, lines ℓ and n are parallel by the Lines Perpendicular to a Transversal Theorem (Thm. 3.12). Because $k \perp m$ and $k \perp n$, lines m and n are also parallel by the Lines Perpendicular to a Transversal Theorem (Thm. 3.12). Because $\ell \parallel n$ and $m \parallel n$, lines ℓ and m are parallel by the Transitive Property of Parallel Lines Theorem (Thm. 3.9).

4. yes; Because $e \parallel f$, $a \perp e$ and $c \perp e$, lines a and c are perpendicular to line f by the Perpendicular Transversal Theorem (Thm. 3.11). Because $a \perp f$, $b \perp f$, $c \perp f$, and $d \perp f$, by the Lines Perpendicular to a Transversal Theorem (Thm. 3.12) and the Transitive Property of Parallel Lines (Thm. 3.9), lines a, b, c, and d are all parallel to each other.

5.

STATEMENTS	REASONS
1. $\angle 1 \cong \angle 2$	1. Given
2. $a \perp c$	2. Linear Pair Perpendicular Theorem (Thm. 3.10)
3. $c \parallel d$	3. Given
4. $a \perp d$	4. Perpendicular Transversal Theorem (Thm. 3.9)
5. $b \perp d$	5. Given
6. $a \parallel b$	6. Lines Perpendicular to a Transversal Theorem (Thm. 3.12)

6. $m\angle 1 = 90°$, $m\angle 2 = 15°$, $m\angle 3 = 90°$, $m\angle 4 = 45°$, $m\angle 5 = 15°$; $m\angle 1 = 90°$, because it is vertical angles with a right angle, so it has the same angle measure. $m\angle 2 = 90° - 75° = 15°$, because it is complementary to the $75°$ angle. $m\angle 3 = 90°$, because it is marked as a right angle. $m\angle 4 = 75° - 30° = 45°$, because together with the $30°$ angle, the angles are vertical angles with the $75°$ angle, so the angle measures are equal. $m\angle 5 = 15°$, because it is vertical angles with $\angle 2$, so the angles have the same measure.

7. no; You do not know anything about the relationship between lines x and y or x and z.

Answers

3.4 Enrichment and Extension

1.

STATEMENTS	REASONS
1. $\overline{AC} \perp \overline{BC}$; $\angle 3$ is complementary to $\angle 1$	1. Given
2. $\angle 1$ is complementary to $\angle 2$	2. Definition of perpendicular lines
3. $m\angle 1 + m\angle 2 = 90°$	3. Definition of complementary angles
4. $m\angle 1 + m\angle 3 = 90°$	4. Definition of complementary angles
5. $m\angle 1 + m\angle 2 = m\angle 1 + m\angle 3$	5. Substitution
6. $m\angle 2 = m\angle 3$	6. Substitution Property of Equality
7. $m\angle 3 = m\angle 2$	7. Symmetric Property of Equality
8. $\angle 3 \cong \angle 2$	8. Definition of congruent angles

2.

STATEMENTS	REASONS
1. $\overrightarrow{AB}$ bisects $\angle DAC$; $\overrightarrow{CB}$ bisects $\angle ECA$ $m\angle 2 = 45°$ $m\angle 3 = 45°$	1. Given
2. $m\angle 2 = m\angle 1$	2. Definition of angle bisector
3. $m\angle 1 = 45°$	3. Substitution
4. $m\angle 1 + m\angle 2 = m\angle DAC$	4. Angle addition
5. $45° + 45° = m\angle DAC$	5. Substitution
6. $90° = m\angle DAC$	6. Simplify
7. $\angle DAC$ is a right angle	7. Definition of a right angle
8. $\overrightarrow{DA} \perp \overrightarrow{AC}$	8. Definition of perpendicular lines
9. $m\angle 3 = m\angle 4$	9. Definition of angle bisector
10. $m\angle 4 = 45°$	10. Definition of congruent angles
11. $m\angle 3 + m\angle 4 = m\angle ECA$	11. Angle addition
12. $45° + 45° = m\angle ECA$	12. Substitution
13. $90° = m\angle ECA$	13. Simplify
14. $\angle ECA$ is a right angle.	14. Definition of a right angle
15. $\overrightarrow{EC} \perp \overrightarrow{AC}$	15. Definition of perpendicular lines
16. $\overrightarrow{AD}$ is parallel to $\overrightarrow{CE}$.	16. Lines Perpendicular to a Transversal Theorem (Thm. 3.12)

Answers

3.

STATEMENTS	REASONS
1. $m \perp n$	1. Given
2. $\angle 3$ and $\angle 6$ are complementary.	2. Definition of complementary angles
3. $\angle 3$ and $\angle 4$ are complementary.	3. Given
4. $\angle 4 \cong \angle 6$	4. Congruent Complements Theorem (Thm. 2.5)
5. $\angle 4 \cong \angle 5$	5. Vertical Angles Congruence Theorem (Thm. 2.6)
6. $\angle 5 \cong \angle 6$	6. Transitive Property of Congruence (Thm 2.2)

4.

STATEMENTS	REASONS
1. $j \perp \ell, \angle 1 \cong \angle 3$	1. Given
2. $m\angle 2 + m\angle 3 = 90°$	2. Definition of complementary angles
3. $m\angle 1 = m\angle 3$	3. Definition of congruent angles
4. $m\angle 2 + m\angle 1 = 90°$	4. Substitution
5. $\angle BED$ is a right angle	5. Definition of a right angle
6. $k \perp m$	6. Definition of perpendicular lines

5. $d = 7$

6. $d = \dfrac{5}{\sqrt{2}}$

7. $d = \dfrac{8}{\sqrt{34}}$

8. $d = \dfrac{3}{\sqrt{13}}$

3.4 Puzzle Time

THE ADDER

3.5 Start Thinking

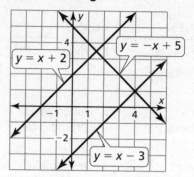

The lines $y = x - 3$ and $y = x + 2$ do not intersect; The line $y = -x + 5$ intersects the line $y = x - 3$ at the point $(4, 1)$ and the line $y = x + 2$ at the point $\left(\dfrac{3}{2}, \dfrac{7}{2}\right)$; The angles are right angles.

3.5 Warm Up

1.

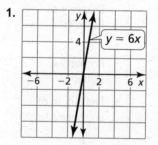

2.

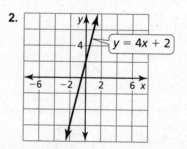

3.

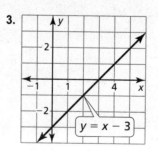

Answers

4.

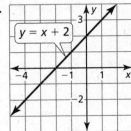

$y = x + 2$

5.

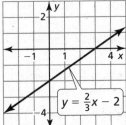

$y = \frac{2}{3}x - 2$

6.

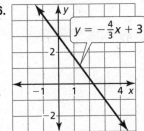

$y = -\frac{4}{3}x + 3$

3.5 Cumulative Review Warm Up

1. Multiplication Property of Equality

2. Subtraction Property of Equality

3. Reflexive Property of Equality for Real Numbers

4. Reflexive Property of Equality for Angle Measures

5. Transitive Property of Equality for Angle Measures

6. Symmetric Property of Segment Lengths

3.5 Practice A

1. $P(3.5, 1)$ **2.** $P(0, 14.2)$

3. perpendicular; Because
$m_1 \bullet m_2 = \left(\frac{9}{2}\right)\left(-\frac{2}{9}\right) = -1$, lines 1 and 2 are
perpendicular by the Slopes of Perpendicular Lines Theorem (Thm. 3.14).

4. neither; Because $m_1 \bullet m_2 = \left(\frac{4}{5}\right)\left(\frac{5}{4}\right) = 1$, lines 1
and 2 are neither parallel nor perpendicular.

5. $y = 4x + 7$ **6.** $y = -6x + 9$

7. $y = \frac{1}{3}x + 8$ **8.** $y = 3x - 8$

9. $2\sqrt{2} \approx 2.83$ **10.** $2\sqrt{26} \approx 10.2$

11. -7.5

12. no; For a line with a slope between 0 and 1, the slope of a line perpendicular to it would be negative.

13. $(5, 4)$

3.5 Practice B

1. $Q = (1.5, 3)$ **2.** $Q = (0, 3)$

3. neither; Because $m_1 \bullet m_2 = (2)\left(-\frac{1}{6}\right) = -\frac{1}{3}$, lines
1 and 2 are neither parallel nor perpendicular.

4. $y = -6x - 10$ **5.** $y = -\frac{1}{4}x + \frac{11}{4}$

6. about 4.5   **7.** about 4.4

8. *Sample answer:* $b = 5, c = 1$

9. a. The slope is m_2, where $-1 \le m_2 < 0$.

  b. The slope is m_3, where $m_3 \ge 1$.

  c. The lines are perpendicular; They are perpendicular by the Perpendicular Transversal Theorem (Thm. 3.11).

10. yes; *Sample answer:* The lines
$y = 2x$ and $y = -\frac{1}{2}x$ have the same y-intercept
and the slopes are negative reciprocals.

11. $\left(-\frac{5}{2}, -2\right)$

3.5 Enrichment and Extension

1. $y = -\frac{4}{3}x - \frac{2}{3}$ **2.** $a = 18, b = 30$

3. a. 3.62   **b.** 2.74

  c. $y = 3.62x - 17.8926$

  d. $y = 0.276x - 1.412$

Answers

4. $-\dfrac{a}{b}$; parallel: $y = -\dfrac{ax}{b}$; perpendicular: $y = \dfrac{b}{a}x$

5. $k = -4$, $y = -\dfrac{1}{2}x + 10$

6. k can have any value, $y = 2x - 5$

7. a. $ae \neq db$

   b. $-\dfrac{a}{b} = -\dfrac{d}{e}$, $b \neq 0$, $e \neq 0$

8. a. *Sample answer:* $(-4, 4), (4, 4), (0, 2)$

   b. *Sample answer:*
   $x = -4, x = 4, x = 0, y = 4, y = 2$

   c. $(-y, y), (y, y), \left(0, \dfrac{y}{2}\right)$

3.5 Puzzle Time

DROP THE S

Cumulative Review

1. 0   **2.** 0   **3.** 13

4. 40   **5.** -5 **6.** 132

7. 25   **8.** 29   **9.** 12

10. -4 **11.** -84 **12.** 3

13. 29   **14.** -58 **15.** -6

16. -20 **17.** -24 **18.** $\dfrac{1}{4}$

19. $-\dfrac{1}{6}$ **20.** $-\dfrac{1}{9}$ **21.** $\dfrac{1}{3}$

22. 4   **23.** -5 **24.** 7

25. -9 **26.** $-\dfrac{7}{4}$ **27.** $\dfrac{5}{2}$

28. $\dfrac{5}{3}$ **29.** $-\dfrac{9}{2}$ **30.** $\dfrac{2}{5}$

31. $\dfrac{7}{8}$ **32.** $-\dfrac{3}{2}$ **33.** $-\dfrac{5}{3}$

34. a. 11 A.M.   **b.** 6.5 in.   **c.** 3 P.M.

35. a. about $42.92
   b. about $9.90
   c. about $1.41

36. $x = 16$ **37.** $x = 8$ **38.** $x = -6$

39. $x = -35$ **40.** $x = -1$ **41.** $x = 8$

42. $x = 9$ **43.** $x = -49$ **44.** $x = -11$

45. $x = -12$ **46.** $x = -11$ **47.** $x = 3$

48. $x = -3$ **49.** $x = -1$ **50.** $x = -6$

51. $x = 5$ **52.** $m = 3, b = -4$

53. $m = -4, b = 5$ **54.** $m = \dfrac{3}{4}, b = -7$

55. $m = -\dfrac{5}{6}, b = 3$ **56.** $m = 1, b = 5$

57. $m = -1, b = 3$ **58.** $m = -1, b = -1$

59. $m = -2, b = 9$ **60.** $m = -3, b = 8$

61. $m = 2, b = -5$ **62.** $m = \dfrac{5}{7}, b = 8$

63. $m = -\dfrac{2}{3}, b = -4$ **64.** $10x$

65. a. $8 - 5 = 3$
   b. $8 - 5.5 = 2.5$
   c. Company A is 3 minutes faster. Company B is 2.5 minutes faster.

66. 9.4   **67.** 7.1   **68.** 20.4

69. 10.2   **70.** 16.4   **71.** 15.8

72. 16.3   **73.** 6.7   **74.** 18.4

75. 12.4   **76.** 7.8   **77.** 9.2

78. $(-2, 5.5)$ **79.** $(8, -1)$ **80.** $(-3.5, -1)$

81. $(2.5, 4)$ **82.** $(-2.5, 9.5)$ **83.** $(-3, 0.5)$

84. $(5.5, -2)$ **85.** $(-0.5, 7)$ **86.** $(-5.5, 1.5)$

87. $(-0.5, -1.5)$ **88.** $(1.5, -0.5)$

89. $(-0.5, 0.5)$

90. a. each individual visit
   b. each individual visit
   c. 5 or more visits

Answers

91. a. $7.80

b. $9.70

c. 7 lb

92. $y = 2x - 3$

93. $y = -3x - 27$

94. $y = \frac{1}{2}x + 5\frac{1}{2}$

95. $y = \frac{1}{5}x + 4$

96. $y = -\frac{1}{4}x + 2$

97. $y = 8x + 93$

98. $y = -4x + 29$

99. $y = -\frac{2}{5}x + \frac{1}{5}$

100. $y = \frac{1}{3}x - 11$

101. $y = -\frac{1}{2}x + 3$

102. $y = \frac{1}{9}x - 10$

103. $y = -2x + 2$

104. $y = 3x + 22$

105. $y = -7$

106. $y = -\frac{1}{3}x + 3$

107. $x = 46$

108. $x = 136$

109. $x = 28$

110. $x = 19$ **111.** $x = 35$ **112.** $x = 21$

Chapter 4

4.1 Start Thinking

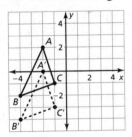

Translate the original triangle 2 units down; Each ordered pair for $\triangle A'B'C'$ contains y-coordinates that are two less than those of $\triangle ABC$; When identifying a translation, you can compare the x- and y-values to determine what happens if the figure is plotted.

4.1 Warm Up

1.

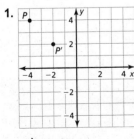

$P'(-2, 2)$

2.

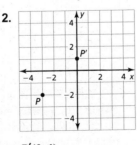

$P'(0, 1)$

3.

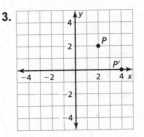

$P'(4, 0)$

4.

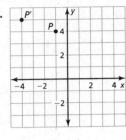

$P'(-4, 5)$

5.

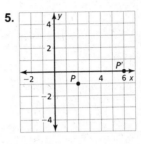

$P'(6, 0)$

6.

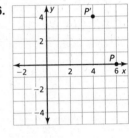

$P'(4, 4)$

4.1 Cumulative Review Warm Up

1.

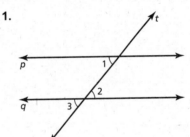

Given $p \parallel q$

Prove $\angle 1 \cong \angle 2$

STATEMENTS	REASONS
1. $p \parallel q$	**1.** Given
2. $\angle 1 \cong \angle 3$	**2.** Corresponding Angles Theorem (Thm. 3.1)
3. $\angle 3 \cong \angle 2$	**3.** Vertical Angles Congruence Theorem (Thm. 2.6)
4. $\angle 1 \cong \angle 2$	**4.** Transitive Property of Angle Congruence (Thm. 2.2)

Answers

2.

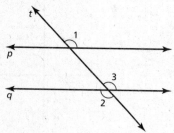

Given $p \parallel q$

Prove $\angle 1 \cong \angle 2$

STATEMENTS	REASONS
1. $p \parallel q$	1. Given
2. $\angle 1 \cong \angle 3$	2. Corresponding Angles Theorem (Thm. 3.1)
3. $\angle 3 \cong \angle 2$	3. Vertical Angles Congruence Theorem (Thm. 2.6)
4. $\angle 1 \cong \angle 2$	4. Transitive Property of Angle Congruence (Thm. 2.2)

4.1 Practice A

1. $\overrightarrow{JK}$; $\langle -3, 2 \rangle$

2. $A'(3, -1)$, $B'(0, -2)$, $C'(1, -3)$

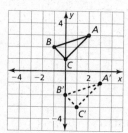

3. $\langle -4, 6 \rangle$

4. $(x, y) \rightarrow (x + 6, y + 4)$

5. $Q'(6, 6)$ **6.** $M'(-2, -11)$

7.

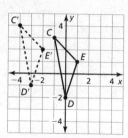

8.

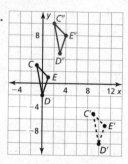

9. no; *Sample answer:* The translation from A to A' could be different than the translation from A' to A''.

10. $(x, y) \rightarrow (x - 2, y - 3)$; 0.25 mi

4.1 Practice B

1. $F'(-4, 1)$, $G'(1, 7)$, $H'(-1, 3)$

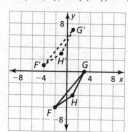

2. $\langle 11, -17 \rangle$

3. $(x, y) \rightarrow (x + 5, y - 6)$

4. $G'(-6, 7)$ **5.** $H'(-14, 8)$

6.

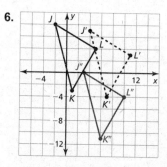

7. no; Multiplying x by 2 does not simply move or translate the object, it stretches the shape.

8. $(x, y) \rightarrow (x + 3, y - 1)$; no

9. *Sample answer:*

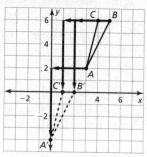

yes; All the vectors are parallel. This makes sense because the vertices are all translated by the same vector, so the segments joining the vertices to their images all have the same slope. Because they have the same slope, they are parallel.

Answers

10. $a = -3, b = 12, P'(7, 1)$

4.1 Enrichment and Extension

1. a. $\sqrt{34}$

  b. 3

  c. $\sqrt{13}$

2. $\langle a + c, b + d \rangle$

3. a. $\langle -4, 1 \rangle$

  b. $\langle 6, -9 \rangle$

  c. $\langle -8, 7 \rangle$

  d. $\langle -2, -2 \rangle$

4. x-y plane   **5.** x-z plane   **6.** y-z plane

7. x-y and y-z planes

8. a. $\sqrt{17}$ **b.** $\sqrt{38}$

4.1 Puzzle Time

AN UMBRELLA

4.2 Start Thinking

yes; Distances are preserved relative to the surface of reflection; no; It appears as though your image in the reflection is holding up its left hand because your image is being reflected as is, so it appears to be backward.

4.2 Warm Up

1.

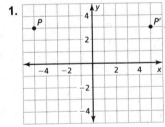

$P'(5, 3)$

2.

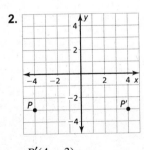

$P'(4, -3)$

3.

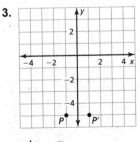

$P'(1, -5)$

4.

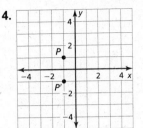

$P'(-1, -1)$

5.

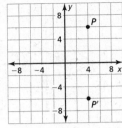

$P'(4, -6)$

6.

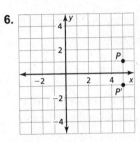

$P'(5, -1)$

4.2 Cumulative Review Warm Up

1. acute   **2.** right   **3.** obtuse

4. obtuse   **5.** acute   **6.** straight

4.2 Practice A

1.

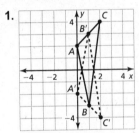

2.

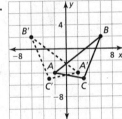

3.

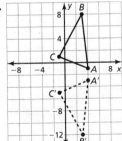

4.

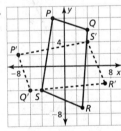

5.

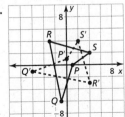

6.

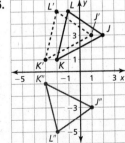

Geometry **A37**
Answers

Answers

7.

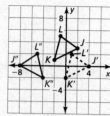

8. *x*-axis, *y*-axis, any line joining opposite outer points or opposite inner points of the star

9. $x = y$, *y*-axis, any line joining an outer point to its opposite inner point of the star

10. $(0, 1)$ **11.** $a = 1$

12. no; Two translations can always be written as a single translation, so the process is the same as a glide reflection.

4.2 Practice B

1.

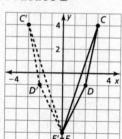

2.

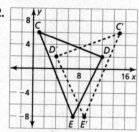

3.

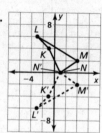

4.

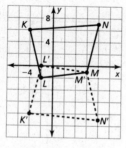

5.

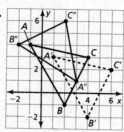

6.

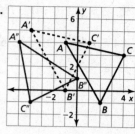

7. *x*-axis, *y*-axis, $y = x$, and $y = -x$

8. $P(1, 0)$

9. yes; *Sample answer:* You can reflect it twice in the same line.

10. no; Angle measures and distances remain constant under any rigid motion.

11. yes; Two reflections do not combine into another reflection, so the motion is not a glide reflection.

4.2 Enrichment and Extension

1. $(-a, c)$ and $(-a, b)$

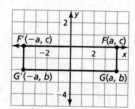

rectangle

2. $(a, -c)$ and $(a, -b)$

3.

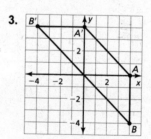

isosceles trapezoid

4.

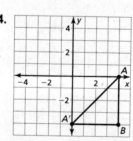

isosceles right triangle

Answers

5.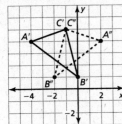

6.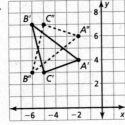

4.2 Puzzle Time

A SQUARE DANCE

4.3 Start Thinking

O; H, I, N, O, S, X, and Z; no

4.3 Warm Up

1.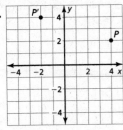

$P'(-2, 4)$

2.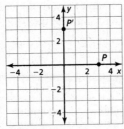

$P'(0, 3)$

3.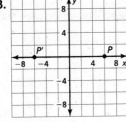

$P'(-6, 0)$

4.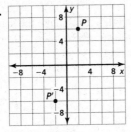

$P'(-2, -6)$

5.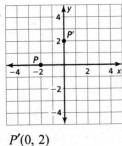

$P'(0, 2)$

6.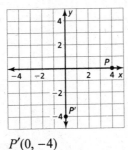

$P'(0, -4)$

4.3 Cumulative Review Warm Up

1. Reflexive Property of Segment Congruence (Thm. 2.1)

2. Symmetric Property of Angle Congruence (Thm. 2.2)

4.3 Practice A

1.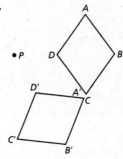

2.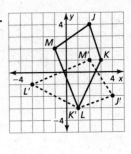

3.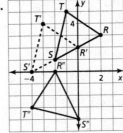

4.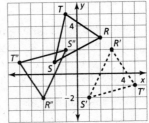

5. yes; $45°, 90°, 135°, 180°$ **6.** yes; $30°, 120°$

7.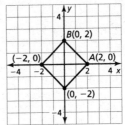

square

8. H, I, N, O, S, X, Z; H: 180°; I: 180°; N: 180°; O: all angles; S: 180°; X: 90°, 180°; Z: 180°

4.3 Practice B

1.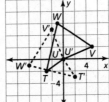

Answers

2.

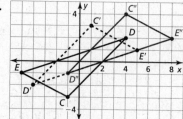

3.

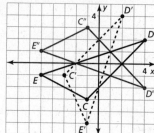

4. yes; 90°, 180°, 270°   **5.** yes; 180°

6. no; A 360° rotation just takes the shape back to the original, so it must be the same.

7. yes; A rotation of 180° maps the figure onto itself; 6 times

8. no   **9.** yes

10. 0, 8; 0:180°; 8:180°; Some students may also include the number 1, depending on how it is written.

4.3 Enrichment Extension

1. $y = -\dfrac{2}{3}x + \dfrac{4}{3}$ **2.** $y = -x + 8$

3. $y = \dfrac{2}{3}x + 3$ **4.** $y = -\dfrac{1}{2}x + 5$

5. a. $(x_0, y_0 + a - x_0)$

   b. $(x_0 - b + y_0, a - x_0 + y_0)$

   c. $(2, -7)$

   d. $(9, 12)$

6. a.

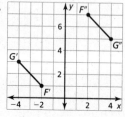

---

b.

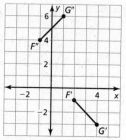

4.3 Puzzle Time

WHAT A SHAME WE WILL NEVER MEET

4.4 Start Thinking

Answers should include two or more shapes from each of the categories listed (circle, square, triangle, and rectangle) and should include a table for each category. An example of one category is shown.

Sample answer: Circle: penny, jar lid

Circle

	Angles	Shape	Size
Penny	no angles	circle	smaller
Jar lid	no angles	circle	larger

Both objects have one continuous curve (360°), but no angles; Both have the same shape; The objects are not the same size.

4.4 Warm Up

1.

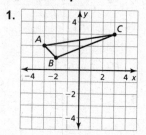

triangle

2.

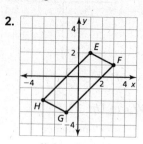

parallelogram

Answers

3.

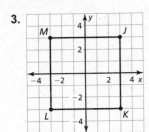

square

4.

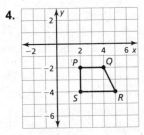

trapezoid

4.4 Cumulative Review Warm Up

1. $P(6, -2.2)$

2. $P(5.4, -1)$

3. $P(1.25, 2.75)$

4. $P(1, -1.25)$

4.4 Practice A

1. Triangle 1, triangle 5, and triangle 8 are all congruent to one another; Square 6 is congruent to square 2; Parallelogram 4 is congruent to parallelogram 7.

2. Triangle 1, triangle 2, and triangle 9 are all congruent to one another; Rectangle 3 is congruent to rectangle 10; Triangle 5 is congruent to triangle 8.

3. translation 8 units right and 2 units up

4. reflection in the x-axis, followed by a translation 2 units right

5. congruent; $\triangle ABC$ can be mapped on to $\triangle STU$ by a reflection in the y-axis, followed by a translation 1 unit right and 7 units down.

6. not congruent; It is not possible to transform polygon $EFGH$ to polygon $WXYZ$ using only rigid transformations.

7. $CD \parallel CD''$, $DE \parallel D''E''$, and $CE \parallel C''E''$; $\overline{EE''} \cong \overline{DD''} \cong \overline{CC''}$

8. $14°$

9. $45°$

4.4 Practice B

1. Squares 1, 3, and 7 are congruent; Triangles 6 and 8 are congruent; Parallelograms 4 and 5 are congruent; Each can be translated to one of the others by a sequence of rigid motions.

2. not congruent; Although three of the four points retain their relative positions, the fourth point changes the shape, so the quadrilaterals are not congruent.

3. 8 units

4. $160°$

5. no; The angle between lines a and b is not $90°$.

6. $45°$

7. sometimes; It depends on the shape of the object undergoing the transformation.

8.

9. yes; It will produce a translation of the same image after any even number of reflections. This is not true for odd numbers of reflections, which will result in a reflection of the original image.

4.4 Enrichment and Extension

1. $\begin{bmatrix} 7 \\ -1 \end{bmatrix}$

2. $\begin{bmatrix} 1 & 5 & 7 & 1 \\ 3 & 3 & -1 & -1 \end{bmatrix}$

3. $\begin{bmatrix} 6 & -1 \\ 9 & -10 \end{bmatrix}$

4. $\begin{bmatrix} 5 & 15 & 5 \\ 0 & 11 & -4 \end{bmatrix}$

5. $\begin{bmatrix} 1 & 5 & 3 \\ 1 & 0 & -1 \end{bmatrix}$

6. $\begin{bmatrix} -1 & -1 & -1 \\ 3 & 3 & 3 \end{bmatrix}$

7. $\begin{bmatrix} -1 & -1 & -1 \\ 3 & 3 & 3 \end{bmatrix} + \begin{bmatrix} 1 & 5 & 3 \\ 1 & 0 & -1 \end{bmatrix} = \begin{bmatrix} 0 & 4 & 2 \\ 4 & 3 & 2 \end{bmatrix}$

8.

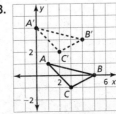

The coordinates of triangle $\triangle A'B'C'$ are the same as the image matrix in Exercise 7.

Answers

4.4 Puzzle Time

A POLYGON

4.5 Start Thinking

yes; The ratio of the distance of the flashlight from the wall and the diameter of the circle remains constant. As the flashlight moves closer to the wall, the circle gets smaller.

4.5 Warm Up

1. 8 units   **2.** 4 units

4.5 Cumulative Review Warm Up

1.
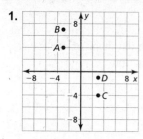

$$\overline{AB} \cong \overline{CD}$$

2.
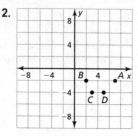

$$\overline{AB} \not\cong \overline{CD}$$

3.
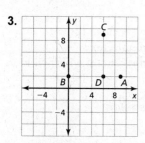

$$\overline{AB} \not\cong \overline{CD}$$

4.
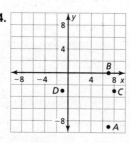

$$\overline{AB} \cong \overline{CD}$$

4.5 Practice A

1. 3; enlargement   **2.** 2.5; reduction

3.
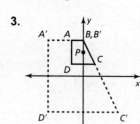

4.
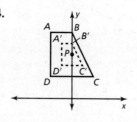

5.
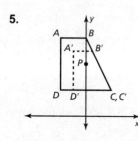

6.
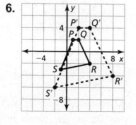

7.
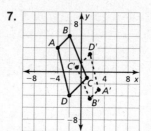

8. 0.77

9. the old film-style camera

10. no; Every dimension would dilate by the same scale factor k, so the area would increase by k^2, one factor of k for each dimension.

11. no; A scale factor of 1 does not dilate the object at all. The object is neither enlarged nor reduced.

4.5 Practice B

1. $\frac{1}{6}$; reduction   **2.** 1.5; enlargement

3.
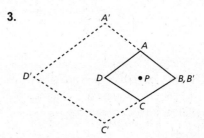

4.
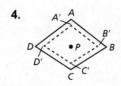

5.
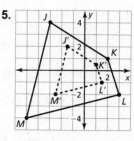

6.
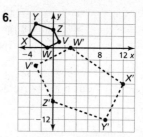

7. It would look like it is 80 millimeters across.

8. A dilation with a scale factor of $k = 0$ would send all the vertices to the center of the dilation, so the object would be reduced to a point.

Answers

9. yes; The perimeter is additive, so it is scaled by the same factor by which the object is dilated.

10. The scale factor is x; $x = 2$

4.5 Enrichment and Extension

1.

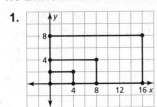

	Length	Width	Perimeter	Area
1. Points A, B, C, and D	2	4	12	8
2. Points A', B' C', and D'	4	8	24	32
3. Points D, E, F, and G	8	16	48	128

2. The length and width double; The perimeter doubles; The area increases by a factor of 4.

3. The perimeter is 4 times as large, and the area is 16 times as large.

4. The perimeter increases by a factor of a, and the area increases by a factor of a^2.

5. $(x, y) \rightarrow (2x, 2y)$ 6. 23.04 mm^2

4.5 Puzzle Time

THE OUTSIDE

4.6 Start Thinking

Sample answer:

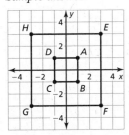

square $ABCD$: $A(1, 1)$, $B(1, -1)$, $C(-1, -1)$, $D(-1, 1)$,
square $EFGH$: $E(3, 3)$, $F(3, -3)$, $G(-3, -3)$, $H(-3, 3)$;
To find square $EFGH$, use a scale factor of 3, with the origin as the center of the dilation.

4.6 Warm Up

1. $n = 9.5$ 2. $w = 18$

3. $x = 4.4$ 4. $y = 123.5$

5. $c = 12$ 6. $n = 34$

4.6 Cumulative Review Warm Up

1. inductive reasoning; A pattern is used to reach the conclusion.

2. deductive reasoning; Facts about numbers and the laws of logic are used to reach the conclusion.

3. deductive reasoning; The laws of logic are used to reach the conclusion.

4.6 Practice A

1. 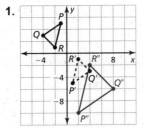   2.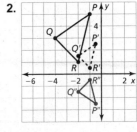

3. reflection in the y-axis, followed by a dilation with a scale factor of 2

4. yes; The triangle is a translation; $(x, y) \rightarrow (x + 5, y - 1)$ followed by a dilation of $(x, y) \rightarrow \left(\frac{2}{3}x, \frac{2}{3}y\right)$; Points C and F do not follow these transformations, so it is not a similarity transformation.

5. yes; The quadrilateral can first be rotated 180° about the origin (or, reflected in the y-axis and then the x-axis). Then the figure can be dilated with a scale factor of $k = 0.5$ and translated to its final position.

6. Rotate $\triangle PQR$ so that side a is parallel to side b. Translate $\triangle GHI$ so that point G maps to point P. Because translations preserve angle measure, and all of the angles of an equilateral triangle are 60°, $\triangle GHI$ lies on $\triangle PQR$. Because, $\overline{GI}$ coincides with $\overline{PR}$ and $\overline{GH}$ coincides with $\overline{PQ}$, $\overline{GI}$ lies on $\overline{PR}$ and $\overline{GH}$ lies on $\overline{PQ}$. Finally, dilate $\triangle PQR$ about point P by a scale factor of $\frac{b}{a}$ so that it is the same size as $\triangle GHI$. Because a similarity transformation maps $\triangle PQR$ onto $\triangle GHI$, the triangles are similar.

Answers

7. no; A square and a rectangle are not similar, so you cannot use a similarity transformation to change the shape of the object.

8. no; For example begin with a unit square centered at the origin. If you perform a dilation centered at the origin with a scale factor 2 and then translate 1 unit right, the result is not the same as if you first translate the square 1 unit right and then perform a dilation centered at the origin with a scale factor of 2.

9. All white triangles are dilations and translations. There are no rotations in the image.

4.6 Practice B

1.

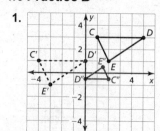

2.

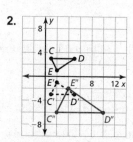

3. a 180° rotation followed by a dilation with a scale factor of 3

4. similar; The transformation is a translation 6 units to the right and 3 units up, followed by a dilation with a scale factor 2.

5. not similar; The transformation is a reflection in the *y*-axis, followed by a translation, however two vertices were translated 2 units up and two vertices were translated 3 units up.

6. Rotate $\triangle ABE$ onto $\triangle DBC$ such that $\angle ABE$ coincides with $\angle DBC$. Because rotations preserve length and measure, $\angle ABE \cong \angle DBC$ and $\overline{AE}$ is still parallel to $\overline{DC}$. So, $\overline{AB}$ coincides with $\overline{BD}$ and $\overline{BE}$ coincides with $\overline{BC}$. Dilate $\triangle ABE$ until $\overline{AE}$ coincides with $\overline{CD}$. Therefore, $\triangle ABE$ is similar to $\triangle DBC$.

7. no; Circles of different size are simply a dilation of each other, so they remain similar.

8. no; The edges are distorted and curved, and are not an exact replica of the original text. So, a magnifying glass does not produce a perfect similarity transformation because the image is distorted.

9. no; Similar triangles do not need to be the same size, so there are more similar triangles than there are congruent triangles.

4.6 Enrichment and Extension

1. 15 square units   **2.** 4

3. 4 square units   **4.** 64 square units

5. The area has increased by a factor of $4^2 = 16$.

6. a. $k = 3, a = \frac{1}{3}, b = -\frac{2}{3}$

   b. Because k is 3, the radius of Circle A is 3 times the radius of Circle B, so $t = 3r$.

4.6 Puzzle Time

THE TEACHER TOLD THEM NOT TO USE TABLES

Cumulative Review

1. $5x - 4$ **2.** $7x + 11$ **3.** $4x + 15$

4. $-9x - 99$ **5.** $4x - 8$ **6.** $-6x + 36$

7. $3x$ **8.** $9x - 6$ **9.** $-3x + 6$

10. $-x + 9$ **11.** $5x - 88$ **12.** $20x - 74$

13. $x = 32$ **14.** $x = -10$ **15.** $x = -12$

16. $x = 23$ **17.** $x = 30$ **18.** $x = -8$

19. $x = -96$ **20.** $x = 8$ **21.** $x = 3$

22. $x = -22$ **23.** $x = -4$ **24.** $x = -3$

25. $x = -20$ **26.** $x = 2$ **27.** $x = -8$

28. $x = -12$

29. a. $9.35

   b. $10.65

30. a. 48 fluid ounces

   b. 6 cups

   c. 3 pints

   d. 1.5 quarts

Answers

31. yes   **32.** no   **33.** yes   **34.** no

35. a. 1.5 ft
   b. $1.60 per ft
   c. $2.40

36. a. 12 in. by 18 in.
   b. 216 in.^{2}
   c. $6.48
   d. $13.52

37. 80°   **38.** 80°   **39.** 80°   **40.** 100°

41. 50°   **42.** 20°   **43.** 70°   **44.** 180°

45. 150°   **46.** 100°   **47.** 71.5 ft^2 **48.** 363 yd^2

49. 717.5 mm^2 **50.** 40 cm^2 **51.** 54 in.^{2}

52. 735 mi^2 **53.** 101.25 in.^{3} **54.** $230\frac{21}{32}$ in.^{3}

55. a. $3.75   **b.** $0.08

56. $y = -3x - 24$ **57.** $y = 4x - 7$

58. $y = \frac{1}{2}x + 17$ **59.** $y = -5x - 11$

60. $y = \frac{1}{4}x - 11$ **61.** $y = -\frac{2}{3}x - 9$

62. $y = \frac{1}{2}x + 2$ **63.** $y = \frac{3}{8}x - 2$

64. $y = \frac{5}{7}x + 7$ **65.** $y = -\frac{1}{4}x - 13$

66. $y = -x + 2$ **67.** $y = \frac{1}{3}x - 3$

68. $y = 3x - 5$ **69.** $y = -\frac{1}{2}x + 7$

70. $y = -\frac{1}{2}x + 4$ **71.** $y = 4x - 8$

72. $y = -\frac{1}{3}x$ **73.** $y = -3x - 20$

74. $y = \frac{1}{4}x + 3$ **75.** $y = -2x - 12$

76. $y = 4x - 19$ **77.** $y = \frac{1}{5}x + 2$

78. $y = -5$ **79.** $y = -\frac{1}{2}x - 5$

80. $A'(5, 0)$, $B'(2, 3)$, $C'(4, -7)$

81. $A'(3, 6)$, $B'(0, 9)$, $C'(2, -1)$

82. $A'(1, 4)$, $B'(-2, 7)$, $C'(0, -3)$

83. $A'(7, 2)$, $B'(4, 5)$, $C'(6, -5)$

84. $A'(2, 3)$, $B'(-1, 6)$, $C'(1, -4)$

85. $A'(4, -2)$, $B'(1, 1)$, $C'(3, -9)$

86. $A'(5, 8)$, $B'(2, 11)$, $C'(4, 1)$

87. $A'(-2, 7)$, $B'(-5, 10)$, $C'(-3, 0)$

Chapter 5

5.1 Start Thinking

If $m\angle A = 120°$, then $m\angle B = 60°$ because together they make a straight angle. If $m\angle D = 40°$, then $m\angle E = 140°$ under the same reasoning. If the sum of $m\angle B$, $m\angle C$, and $m\angle D$ is 180°, then $m\angle C = 80°$.

5.1 Warm Up

1. $m\angle 1 = 31°$ **2.** $m\angle 2 = 59°$

3. $m\angle 3 = 59°$ **4.** $m\angle 4 = 90°$

5.1 Cumulative Review Warm Up

1. $x = 69$ **2.** $x = 6$

3. $x = 60$ **4.** $x = 30$

5.1 Practice A

1. scalene; right   **2.** isosceles; acute

3. scalene; not a right triangle

4. isosceles; right triangle

5. $x = 32$ **6.** $x = 29$ **7.** $x = 30$ **8.** $x = 17$

9. 19.5°, 70.5°

10. no; An exterior angle will be acute when it is adjacent to the obtuse angle of an obtuse triangle.

11. 145°

5.1 Practice B

1. scalene; obtuse   **2.** isosceles; acute

3. $x = 14$ **4.** $x = 9$

5. $x = \frac{116}{9}$ **6.** $x = 7$; $y = 19.5$

Answers

7. The measure of each exterior angle is equal to the sum of the measures of the nonadjacent interior angles. So, $m\angle 1 = A + C$, $m\angle 2 = B + C$, and $m\angle 3 = A + B$.

$$
\begin{aligned}
\text{Sum of exterior angles} &= \angle 1 + \angle 2 + \angle 3 \\
&= A + C + B + C + A + B \\
&= 2(A + B + C) \\
&= 2(180°) \\
&= 360°
\end{aligned}
$$

8. $x = 67$; $y = 124$ **9.** yes; $15°, 60°, 105°$.

10. no; For instance, in a $10°$-$40°$-$130°$ triangle, at the $130°$ angle you have a $50°$ exterior angle which is complementary to the $40°$ angle.

11. $\angle C \cong \angle T$; The sum of the angle measures of each triangle is $180°$, so if two pairs of corresponding angles are congruent, then the third pair of corresponding angles must also be congruent.

5.1 Enrichment and Extension

1. $63°, 36°, 81°$; acute   **2.** $x = 10$; $y = 71$

3. $x = 50$; $y = 33$ **4.** $x = 29$; $y = 64$

5. $x = 12.9$; $y = 51.4$ **6.** $m\angle A = m\angle 1$

5.1 Puzzle Time

THE LETTUCE WAS A "HEAD" AND THE TOMATO WAS TRYING TO "KETCHUP"

5.2 Start Thinking

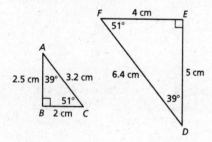

$\overline{AB}$ corresponds to $\overline{DE}$; $\overline{BC}$ corresponds to $\overline{EF}$; $\overline{AC}$ corresponds to $\overline{DF}$.

$\angle A \cong \angle D, \angle B \cong \angle E, \angle C \cong \angle F$

To get $\triangle DEF$, multiply the side lengths of $\triangle ABC$ by a scale factor of 2 and rotate $\triangle ABC$ $180°$.

5.2 Warm Up

1. $x = 9$ **2.** $x = 69$

5.2 Cumulative Review Warm Up

1.

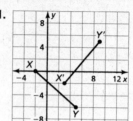

5.2 Practice A

1. $\angle A \cong \angle E, \angle B \cong \angle F, \angle C \cong \angle G, \angle D \cong \angle H$, $\overline{AB} \cong \overline{EF}, \overline{BC} \cong \overline{FG}, \overline{CD} \cong \overline{GH}$, and $\overline{DA} \cong \overline{HE}$; Sample answer: $BCDA \cong FGHE$

2. $x = 8$; $y = 19$

3. From the figure, $\angle J \cong \angle N, \angle K \cong \angle P$, $\angle Q \cong \angle M, \overline{JK} \cong \overline{NP}, \overline{KL} \cong \overline{PL}, \overline{LQ} \cong \overline{LM}$, and $\overline{QJ} \cong \overline{MN}$. Also, $\angle KLQ \cong \angle PLM$ by the Vertical Angles Congruence Theorem (Thm. 2.6). Because all pairs of corresponding angles and all pairs of corresponding sides are congruent, $JKLQ \cong NPLM$.

4. The figure shows that $\angle A \cong \angle R$ and $\angle B \cong \angle S$. So, $\angle C \cong \angle T$ by the Third Angles Theorem (Thm. 5.4). Using the Triangle Sum Theorem (Thm. 5.1), $m\angle T = 65°$.

5. $\triangle ABC$ and $\triangle DEF$ are both equilateral and equiangular.

5.2 Practice B

1. $\angle A \cong \angle H, \angle B \cong \angle I, \angle C \cong \angle J, \angle D \cong \angle F$, $\angle E \cong \angle G, \overline{AB} \cong \overline{HI}, \overline{BC} \cong \overline{IJ}, \overline{CD} \cong \overline{JF}$, $\overline{DE} \cong \overline{FG}, \overline{EA} \cong \overline{GH}$; $ABCDE \cong GFJIH$

2. $x = 65$; $y = 6$; $z = 146$

3. From the figure, $\overline{LP} \cong \overline{ON}, \overline{PM} \cong \overline{NM}$, and $\overline{LM} \cong \overline{OM}$. $\angle P \cong \angle N$ because all right angles are congruent to each other. By the Vertical Angles Congruence Theorem (Thm. 2.6), $\angle LMP \cong \angle OMN$. $\angle L \cong \angle O$ by the Third Angles Theorem (Thm. 5.4). Because corresponding sides and angles are congruent, $\triangle LPM \cong \triangle ONM$.

Answers

4. $x = 14$, $y = 3$, $m\angle RST = 133°$; Because $RSTU \cong UVQR$ and $\angle VUR$ is a right angle, $\angle SRU$ is a right angle. Using vertical angles, $m\angle UPV = 47°$, and by the Triangle Sum Theorem (Thm. 5.1), $2x + 5y = 43$ and $m\angle RSV = 43°$. Because it forms a linear pair with a $47°$ angle, $m\angle UPS = 133°$. Using angle addition and corresponding parts of congruent figures, $\angle VST$ is a right angle. Then

$$m\angle PUT = 360 - (90 + 90 + 133)$$
$$= 47$$
$$= 4x - 3y.$$

Solving the system $2x + 5y = 43$
$$\quad\quad\quad\quad\quad\quad 4x - 3y = 47$$

gives $x = 14$ and $y = 3$. Finally, $m\angle RST = 90 + 43 = 133°$.

5.

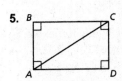

yes; To prove the triangles congruent, use the facts that $AC = CA$ and opposite sides of a rectangle are congruent to show that 3 pairs of corresponding sides are congruent. Then use the Alternate Interior Angles Theorem (Thm. 3.2) to show two pairs of angles congruent. The third pair of corresponding angles are congruent right angles.

5.2 Enrichment and Extension

1.

STATEMENTS	REASONS
1. $\angle ABD \cong \angle CDB$	1. Given
2. $\angle ADB \cong \angle CBD$	2. Given
3. $\overline{AD} \cong \overline{BC}$	3. Given
4. $\overline{AB} \cong \overline{DC}$	4. Given
5. $\overline{BD} \cong \overline{BD}$	5. Reflexive Property of Congruence
6. $\angle BAD \cong \angle BCD$	6. Triangle Sum Theorem
7. $\triangle ABD \cong \triangle CDB$	7. All corresponding parts are congruent.

2.

STATEMENTS	REASONS
1. $\overline{AB} \parallel \overline{DC}$	1. Given
2. $\overline{AB} \cong \overline{DC}$	2. Given
3. E is the midpoint of $\overline{AC}$ and $\overline{BD}$.	3. Given
4. $\overline{AE} \cong \overline{EC}$	4. Definition of midpoint
5. $\overline{BE} \cong \overline{ED}$	5. Definition of midpoint
6. $\angle EAB \cong \angle ECD$	6. Alternate interior angles
7. $\angle ABD \cong \angle BDC$	7. Alternate interior angles
8. $\angle AEB \cong \angle CED$	8. Vertical Angles Theorem
9. $\triangle AEB \cong \triangle CED$	9. All corresponding parts are congruent.

3. a. yes; You are given $\triangle ADB \cong \triangle CDA \cong \triangle CDB$. So, $\overline{AB} \cong \overline{BC} \cong \overline{CA}$. Because all three sides of $\triangle ABC$ are congruent, it is an equilateral triangle.

b. $120°$

c. $30°$, $30°$

d. The angle measures are equal because $\triangle CDB$ is isosceles.

e. The measure of each of the congruent angles of each small triangle is $30°$. By the Angle Addition Postulate (Post. 1.4), the measure of each angle of $\triangle ABC$ is $60°$.

5.2 Puzzle Time

CRAB CAKES

5.3 Start Thinking

Sample answer:

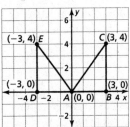

$\triangle ABC \cong \triangle ADE$ because all angles and sides are congruent. There is no further information needed because the given directions make it impossible to construct $\triangle ADE \not\cong \triangle ABC$.

5.3 Warm Up

1. $\overline{AC}$　　　　　　**2.** $\overline{FH}$

Answers

5.3 Cumulative Review Warm Up

1. $\overline{ED}$ 2. $\overline{EC}$

5.3 Practice A

1. yes; You know that two sides and the included angle are congruent, so you can use the SAS Congruence Theorem (Thm. 5.5).

2. no; The congruent vertical angles are not the included angles, so SAS cannot be used.

3. $\triangle ABO \cong \triangle CBO$; $\overline{OB} \cong \overline{OB}$, and because they are radii, $\overline{AO} \cong \overline{CO}$. It is given that $\angle AOB \cong COB$. So, SAS is satisfied.

4. $\triangle ABE \cong \triangle CBE$; Because $\overline{AB} \cong \overline{BC}$, $\angle ABE \cong \angle CBE$, and $\overline{BE} \cong \overline{BE}$, SAS is satisfied.

5. no; The SAS Congruence Theorem (Thm. 5.5) applies after a translation, reflection, or rotation, because those are congruence transformations, but not after a dilation, which changes the size of the figure.

6.

STATEMENTS	REASONS
1. $\angle ABD$ and $\angle CBD$ are right angles.	1. Given
2. $\overline{BD}$ bisects $\overline{AC}$.	2. Given
3. $\overline{AB} \cong \overline{BC}$	3. Definition of a segment bisector
4. $\overline{BD} \cong \overline{BD}$	4. Reflexive Property of Segment Congruence (Thm. 2.1)
5. $\triangle ABD \cong \triangle CBD$	5. SAS Congruence Theorem (Thm. 5.5)

5.3 Practice B

1. yes; You know that two sides are congruent, and using the Third Angles Theorem (Thm. 5.4) you can find that the included angles are congruent, so SAS applies.

2. yes; One pair of sides is marked congruent, you can use segment addition to show a second pair of sides congruent, and you can use the Third Angles Theorem (Thm. 5.4) to show their included angles congruent. So, SAS applies.

3. $\triangle PLM$, $\triangle PMN$, and $\triangle PNL$; The sides $\overline{PL}$, $\overline{PM}$, and $\overline{PN}$ are congruent because they are radii of the same circle. The three angles at P are congruent, so you can use SAS with these angles and the sides including them.

4. $\triangle RVU$, $\triangle SXW$, and $\triangle TZY$; Show that each obtuse angle measures $360 - (60 + 90 + 90)$ and that the sides including these angles are all congruent because they are sides of squares that border an equilateral triangle. So, SAS applies.

5. $x = 7$; $y = 24$

6. $\triangle AED$ is equilateral and equiangular, so $\overline{AE} \cong \overline{DE}$, and $\angle CAD \cong \angle BDA$. $\overline{EB} \cong \overline{EC}$, so $EB + DE = EC + DE$ by the Addition Property of Equality. Substituting AE for DE gives $EB + DE = EC + AE$. Using the Segment Addition Postulate (Post. 1.2), $BD = EB + DE$ and $CA = EC + AE$. So, $BD = CA$ by substitution. Also, $\overline{AD} \cong \overline{DA}$ by the Reflexive Property of Segment Congruence (Thm. 2.1). $\triangle ACD \cong \triangle DBA$ by the SAS Congruence Theorem (Thm. 5.5).

5.3 Enrichment and Extension

1. $\overline{NP} \cong \overline{OP}$ because they have an equal length of 6; $\overline{MP} \cong \overline{MP}$ by the Reflexive Property of Segment Congruence (Thm. 2.1); $\overline{MO} \cong \overline{MN}$ because they have an equal length of $3\sqrt{2}$. So, $\triangle PMO \cong \triangle PMN$ by the SSS Congruence Theorem (Thm. 5.8). It is possible to prove $\triangle PMO \cong \triangle PMN$ by the SAS Congruence Theorem (Thm. 5.5) because you already know that $\overline{MP} \cong \overline{MP}$ and $\overline{MO} \cong \overline{MN}$. You also know that $\overline{NO} \perp \overline{MP}$ because the slopes are opposite reciprocals. So, $\angle OMP \cong \angle NMP$, leading to $\triangle PMO \cong \triangle PMN$ by the SAS Congruence Theorem (Thm. 5.5).

2. yes; HL Congruence Theorem (Thm. 5.9)

Answers

3.

STATEMENTS	REASONS
1. $\overline{AC} \perp \overline{BD}$	1. Given
2. D is the midpoint of $\overline{AC}$.	2. Given
3. $\angle ADB$ is a right angle.	3. Definition of perpendicular lines
4. $m\angle ADB = 90°$	4. Definition of right angle
5. $\angle CDB$ is a right angle.	5. Definition of perpendicular lines
6. $m\angle CDB = 90°$	6. Definition of right angle
7. $m\angle ADB = m\angle CDB$	7. Substitution
8. $\overline{AD} \cong \overline{DC}$	8. Definition of midpoint
9. $\overline{BD} \cong \overline{BD}$	9. Reflexive Property of Segment Congruence (Thm. 2.1)
10. $\triangle ADB \cong \triangle CDB$	10. SAS Congruence Theorem (Thm. 5.5)

4.

STATEMENTS	REASONS
1. $DE = BF$	1. Given
2. $AE = CF$	2. Given
3. $\overline{AE} \perp \overline{DB}$	3. Given
4. $\overline{CF} \perp \overline{BD}$	4. Given
5. $\angle AEB$ is a right angle.	5. Definition of perpendicular lines
6. $\angle CFD$ is a right angle.	6. Definition of perpendicular lines
7. $\angle AEB \cong \angle CFD$	7. Right Angles Congruence Theorem (Thm. 2.3)
8. $BE = BF + FE$	8. Segment Addition Postulate (Post. 1.2)
9. $FD = FE + ED$	9. Segment Addition Postulate (Post. 1.2)
10. $FD = FE + BF$	10. Substitution
11. $FD = BE$	11. Substitution
12. $\overline{AE} \cong \overline{CF}$	12. Definition of congruent segments
13. $\overline{FD} \cong \overline{BE}$	13. Definition of congruent segments
14. $\triangle AEB \cong \triangle CFD$	14. SAS Congruence Theorem (Thm. 5.5)

5. $X(4, 10), Y(15, 3)$

5.3 Puzzle Time

OBTUSE

5.4 Start Thinking

Sample answer:

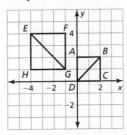

$\triangle ABD \cong \triangle CBD$. The length of $\overline{BD} = \sqrt{8}$.
$\triangle EGH \cong \triangle EGF$ because all side lengths and angles are congruent.

5.4 Warm Up

1. $x = 89$
2. $x = 83$
3. $x = 21$
4. $x = 80$

5.4 Cumulative Review Warm Up

1. A triangle is an isosceles triangle if and only if the legs are of equal length.

2. A Chinese puzzle is a tangram if and only if it is made up of seven pieces.

3. A parallelogram is a rectangle if and only if it has four right angles.

5.4 Practice A

1. $x = 25$
2. $x = 6$
3. $x = 20; y = 30$
4. $x = 30; y = 4$

5. Because they are vertical angles, $\angle DCE \cong \angle BCA$. Because they both measure 70°, $\angle B \cong \angle D$. So, $\angle A \cong \angle E$ by the Third Angles Theorem (Thm 5.4). But $\angle E \cong \angle D$ because they are base angles of an isosceles triangle, so $m\angle A = 70°$. Because they have equal measures, $\angle A$ and $\angle B$ are base angles of an isosceles triangle.

6. yes; An isosceles triangle is obtuse when the vertex angle is obtuse and the base angles are acute.

Answers

5.4 Practice B

1. $x = 36$

2. $x = 90$

3. $x = 14; y = 7$

4. $x = 29; y = 3$

5. It is given that $\angle CBD \cong \angle CDB$ and $\angle CAE \cong \angle CEA$. By the Converse of the Base Angles Theorem (Thm. 5.7), $\overline{BC} \cong \overline{DC}$ and $\overline{AC} \cong \overline{EC}$. By the Reflexive Property of Angle Congruence (Thm. 2.2), $\angle C \cong \angle C$. $\triangle ACD \cong \triangle ECB$ by the SAS Congruence Theorem (Thm. 5.5). Because congruent parts of congruent triangles are congruent, $\overline{AD} \cong \overline{EB}$.

6.

STATEMENTS	REASONS
1. $\angle EBC \cong \angle ECB$, $\overline{AE} \cong \overline{DE}$	1. Given
2. $\overline{EB} \cong \overline{EC}$	2. Converse of the Base Angles Theorem (Thm. 5.7)
3. $\angle AEB \cong \angle DEC$	3. Vertical Angles Congruence Theorem (Thm. 2.6)
4. $\triangle AEB \cong \triangle DEC$	4. SAS Congruence Theorem (Thm. 5.5)
5. $\overline{AB} \cong \overline{DC}$	5. Corresponding parts of congruent triangles are congruent.

5.4 Enrichment and Extension

1. $r = \frac{1}{2}(p + q)$

2.

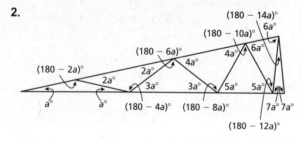

3. $x = 12.9; y = 51.4$

4. $x = 29; y = 64$

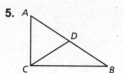

5.

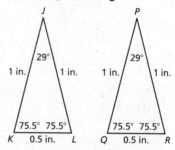

It is possible to partition a right triangle into two isosceles triangles. Suppose $\triangle ABC$ is a right triangle with right angle C. Because $m\angle CAD$ is less than $m\angle ACB$, it is possible to construct D such that $m\angle ACD = m\angle CAD$, as shown above. Because $m\angle ACD + m\angle DCB = 90° = m\angle CAD + m\angle DBC$ and $m\angle CAD = m\angle ACD$, it follows that $m\angle DCB = m\angle DBC$. So, $\triangle DBC$ is an isosceles triangle.

5.4 Puzzle Time

NEITHER IT'S BEST TO WRITE WITH A PEN

5.5 Start Thinking

In $\triangle JKL$, $m\angle J = 29°$, $m\angle K = 75.5°$, $m\angle L = 75.5°$. $\triangle JKL$ is an isosceles triangle. The angles in $\triangle PQR$ are congruent. It is not possible to create two triangles with the same side lengths but different angles. As discussed in Section 5.4, the side lengths and angles are related.

5.5 Warm Up

1. $\angle RUT$

2. $\angle STR$

3. $\angle TRS$

4. $\angle UTR$

5. $\angle SRT$

6. $\angle RST$

5.5 Cumulative Review Warm Up

1. $m\angle 1 = 54°$; straight angle

   $m\angle 2 = 54°$; Corresponding Angles Theorem (Thm. 3.1)

2. $m\angle 2 = 131°$; Corresponding Angles Theorem (Thm. 3.1)

   $m\angle 1 = 49°$; straight angle

5.5 Practice A

1. congruent; Two pairs of sides are marked congruent and the third pair of sides is shared, so the SSS Congruence Theorem (Thm. 5.8) applies.

Answers

2. not congruent; The hypotenuse and a leg of one triangle are congruent to the legs of the other triangle, so the triangles cannot be congruent.

3. congruent; The hypotenuses are shared and a pair of legs is congruent, so the HL Congruence Theorem (Thm. 5.9) applies.

4.

STATEMENTS	REASONS
1. $\overline{AB} \cong \overline{AD}$; $\overline{AC}$ bisects $\overline{BD}$.	1. Given
2. $\overline{AC} \cong \overline{AC}$	2. Reflexive Property of Segment Congruence (Thm. 2.1)
3. $\overline{BC} \cong \overline{DC}$	3. Definition of segment bisector
4. $\triangle ABC \cong \triangle ADC$	4. SSS Congruence Theorem (Thm. 5.8)

5.

STATEMENTS	REASONS
1. $\overline{JL} \cong \overline{GF}$ and $\overline{KL} \cong \overline{HF}$	1. Given
2. $\angle J$ and $\angle G$ are right angles.	2. Given
3. $\triangle JKL$ and $\triangle GHF$ are right triangles.	3. Definition of a right triangle
4. $\triangle JKL \cong \triangle GHF$	4. HL Congruence Theorem (Thm. 5.9)

6. not congruent

7. a. You know the shared sides are congruent, so you need to measure each of the other sides of the two triangular faces to determine whether the SSS Congruence Theorem (Thm. 5.8) applies.

b. a regular hexagon

5.5 Practice B

1. yes; *Sample answer:* SSS Congruence Theorem (Thm. 5.8)

2. yes; HL Congruence Theorem (Thm. 5.9)

3. yes; *Sample answer:* SAS Congruence Theorem (Thm. 5.5)

4.

STATEMENTS	REASONS
1. $\overline{BC} \cong \overline{ED}$, $\overline{AB} \cong \overline{FE}$, $\overline{AD} \cong \overline{FC}$	1. Given
2. $BC = ED$	2. Definition of congruent segments
3. $BD = BC + CD$, $EC = ED + CD$	3. Segment Addition Postulate (Post. 1.2)
4. $BD = ED + CD$	4. Substitution Property of Equality
5. $BD = EC$	5. Substitution Property of Equality
6. $\overline{BD} \cong \overline{EC}$	6. Definition of congruent segments
7. $\triangle ABD \cong \triangle FEC$	7. SSS Congruence Theorem (Thm. 5.8)

5.

STATEMENTS	REASONS
1. $\overline{PS} \cong \overline{RS}$, $\overline{SQ} \perp \overline{PR}$	1. Given
2. $\angle PQS$ and $\angle RQS$ are right angles.	2. Definition of perpendicular lines
3. $\triangle PQS$ and $\triangle RQS$ are right triangles.	3. Definition of right triangles
4. $\overline{QS} \cong \overline{QS}$	4. Reflexive Property of Segment Congruence (Thm. 2.1)
5. $\triangle PSQ \cong \triangle RSQ$	5. HL Congruence Theorem (Thm. 5.9)

6. *Sample answer:* Sketch the lines in a coordinate plane. The slopes of lines a and b show that they form vertical right angles of the triangles. The Distance Formula shows that the hypotenuses have different lengths, so the triangles are not congruent.

Answers

5.5 Enrichment and Extension

1. a. $x = 7$ **b.** $x = 4$ **c.** $x = -4$ or 4

2.

STATEMENTS	REASONS
1. $\overline{WA} \cong \overline{WT}$	1. Given
2. S is the midpoint of $\overline{AT}$.	2. Given
3. $\overline{AS} \cong \overline{ST}$	3. Definition of midpoint
4. $\overline{WS} \cong \overline{WS}$	4. Reflexive Property of Segment Congruence (Thm. 2.1)
5. $\triangle WSA \cong \triangle WST$	5. SSS Congruence Theorem (Thm. 5.8)
6. $m\angle WAS + m\angle 1 = 180°$	6. Definition of perpendicular lines
7. $\angle AEB \cong \angle CFD$	7. Definition of linear pair
8. $m\angle WTS + m\angle 2 = 180°$	8. Definition of linear pair
9. $\angle WAS \cong \angle WTS$	9. Corresponding parts of congruent triangles are congruent.
10. $m\angle WAS = m\angle WTS$	10. Definition of congruence
11. $m\angle WAS + m\angle 1 = m\angle WTS + m\angle 2$	11. Substitution
12. $m\angle WAS + m\angle 1 = m\angle WAS + m\angle 2$	12. Substitution
13. $m\angle 1 = m\angle 2$	13. Subtraction
14. $\angle 1 \cong \angle 2$	14. Definition of congruent angles

3.

STATEMENTS	REASONS
1. $\overline{GR} \cong \overline{GT}$	1. Given
2. $\overline{RS} \cong \overline{ST}$	2. Given
3. $\overline{GS} \cong \overline{GS}$	3. Reflexive Property of Segment Congruence (Thm. 2.1)
4. $\triangle GRS \cong \triangle GST$	4. SSS Congruence Theorem (Thm. 5.8)

4.

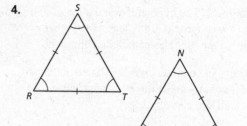

If one side of $\triangle RST$ is congruent to one side of $\triangle DEF$, such that $\overline{RS} \cong \overline{MN}$, then you know that the triangles are congruent because equilateral triangles have three congruent sides. So, all sides in $\triangle RST$ would be equal to all sides in $\triangle MNO$, making them congruent by the SSS Congruence Postulate.

5. $J(2e - c, 2f - d), K(2e - a, 2f - b)$

5.5 Puzzle Time

A TEENAGER

5.6 Start Thinking

Sample answer:

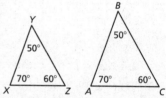

$\triangle XYZ \not\cong \triangle ABC$; Any size triangle can have the angle measures indicated. One example would be to draw the triangle on a coordinate plane and then dilate it with the origin as the center. This example shows that knowing two triangles have the same angle measures is not enough to prove congruence.

5.6 Warm Up

1. SAS Congruence Theorem (Thm. 5.5)

2. none

3. SAS Congruence Theorem (Thm. 5.5)

4. none

5.6 Cumulative Review Warm Up

1.

5.6 Practice A

1. yes; AAS Congruence Theorem (Thm. 5.11)

Answers

2. no

3. yes; ASA Congruence Theorem (Thm. 5.10)

4.

STATEMENTS	REASONS
1. $\overline{PS} \parallel \overline{RT}$, $\overline{PQ} \cong \overline{TQ}$	1. Given
2. $\angle S \cong \angle R$ and $\angle P \cong \angle T$	2. Alternate Interior Angles Theorem (Thm. 3.2)
3. $\triangle PSQ \cong \triangle TRQ$	3. AAS Congruence Theorem (Thm. 5.11)

5.

STATEMENTS	REASONS
1. $\overline{BD}$ bisects $\angle ADC$, $\overline{BD} \perp \overline{AC}$	1. Given
2. $\overline{BD} \cong \overline{BD}$	2. Reflexive Property of Segment Congruence (Thm. 2.1)
3. $\angle ADB \cong \angle CDB$	3. Definition of angle bisector
4. $\angle ABD$ and $\angle CBD$ are right angles.	4. Definition of perpendicular lines
5. $\angle ABD \cong \angle CBD$	5. Right Angles Congruence Theorem (Thm. 2.3)
6. $\triangle ABD \cong \triangle CBD$	6. ASA Congruence Theorem (Thm. 5.10)

6. Given: $\overline{AB} \cong \overline{CD}$, $\angle ABD \cong \angle CDB$; $\overline{BD} \cong \overline{DB}$ by the Reflexive Property of Segment Congruence (Thm. 2.1); So, $\triangle ABD \cong \triangle CDB$ by the SAS Congruence Theorem (Thm. 5.5).

Given: $\overline{AB} \cong \overline{EF}$, $\angle ABD \cong \angle F$; $\angle ADB \cong \angle EDF$ by the Vertical Angles Congruence Theorem (Thm. 2.6); So, $\triangle ABD \cong \triangle EFD$ by the AAS Congruence Theorem (Thm. 5.11).

Given: $\overline{CD} \cong \overline{EF}$, $\angle BDC \cong \angle F$; $\overline{BD} \cong \overline{DF}$ because congruent parts of congruent triangles are congruent; So, $\triangle CDB \cong \triangle EFD$ by the SAS Congruence Theorem (Thm. 5.5).

There is not enough information to show that $\triangle AGD$ is congruent to any other triangle.

5.6 Practice B

1. yes; ASA Congruence Theorem (Thm. 5.10)

2. no

3. yes; AAS Congruence Theorem (Thm. 5.11)

4.

STATEMENTS	REASONS
1. $\overline{BD}$ bisects $\overline{AE}$, $\angle A \cong \angle E$	1. Given
2. $\overline{AC} \cong \overline{CE}$	2. Definition of segment bisector
3. $\angle ACB \cong \angle ECD$	3. Vertical Angles Congruence Theorem (Thm. 2.6)
4. $\triangle ABC \cong \triangle EDC$	4. ASA Congruence Theorem (Thm. 5.10)

5.

STATEMENTS	REASONS
1. $\angle I \cong \angle J$, $IM \parallel JN$, $\overline{KL} \cong \overline{MN}$	1. Given
2. $\angle M \cong \angle N$	2. Corresponding Angles Theorem (Thm. 3.1)
3. $KL = MN$	3. Definition of congruent segments
4. $KL + LM = LM + MN$	4. Addition Property of Equality
5. $KM = KL + LM$ and $LN = LM + MN$	5. Segment Addition Postulate (Post. 1.2)
6. $KM = LN$	6. Substitution Property of Equality
7. $\overline{KM} \cong \overline{LN}$	7. Definition of segment congruence
8. $\triangle IKM \cong \triangle JLN$	8. AAS Congruence Theorem (Thm. 5.11)

Answers

6. Draw $\overline{RT}$. By the definition of a parallelogram, $\overline{RS} \parallel \overline{QT}$ and $\overline{QR} \parallel \overline{TS}$. $\angle QTR \cong \angle SRT$ and $\angle QRT \cong \angle STR$ by the Alternate Interior Angles Theorem (Thm. 3.2). $\overline{RT} \cong \overline{TR}$ by the Reflexive Property of Segment Congruence (Thm. 2.1). $\triangle QRT \cong \triangle STR$ by the ASA Congruence Theorem (Thm. 5.10). So, $\overline{QR} \cong \overline{TS}$ and $\overline{RS} \cong \overline{QT}$ because corresponding parts of congruent triangles are congruent.

5.6 Enrichment and Extension

1. $m =$ any real value except 2; $m = -\frac{1}{2}$ or $m = 0$; The triangles are congruent by AAS or ASA.

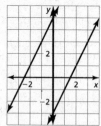

2. *Sample answer I:* Label point $(1, 6)$ as A, point $(5, 4)$ as B, point $(4, 3)$ as C, point $(1, 0)$ as D, and point $(5, 2)$ as E. You can calculate $AB = DE \approx 4.472$, $CE = CB \approx 1.414$, and $AC = CD \approx 4.242$. So, $\triangle ABC \cong \triangle DEC$ by the SSS Congruence Theorem (Thm. 5.8).

Sample answer II:

Label point $(1,6)$ as A, point $(5,4)$ as B, point $(4,3)$ as C, point $(1,0)$ as D, and point $(5,2)$ as E. $CE = CB \approx 1.414$ and $AC = CD \approx 4.242$. Additionally, the slope of $BD \perp AE$, so, $m\angle ACB = m\angle DCE = 90°$. By the SAS Congruence Theorem (Thm. 5.5), $\triangle ABC \cong \triangle DEC$.

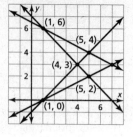

3. $\overline{BC}$ and $\overline{AD}$ are parallel, because their slopes are equal, with $\overline{AC}$ being a transversal. The Alternate Interior Angles Theorem (Thm. 3.2) applies to make $\angle BCA \cong \angle CAD$. $\overline{AB}$ and $\overline{CD}$ are parallel because their slopes are equal, with $\overline{AC}$ being a transversal. The Alternate Interior Angles Theorem (Thm. 3.2) applies to make $\angle BAC \cong \angle ACD$. $\overline{AC} \cong \overline{AC}$ by the Reflexive Property of Segment Congruence (Thm. 2.1). So, $\triangle ABC \cong \triangle CDA$ by the ASA Congruence Theorem (Thm. 5.10).

4.

STATEMENTS	REASONS
1. $\triangle ABC \cong \triangle ABD$ $\angle FCA \cong \angle EDA$	1. Given
2. $\overline{CA} \cong \overline{DA}$	2. Corresponding parts of congruent triangles are congruent.
3. $\angle CAF \cong \angle DAE$	3. Vertical Angles Congruence Theorem (Thm. 2.6)
4. $\triangle CAF \cong \triangle DAE$	4. ASA Congruence Theorem (Thm. 5.10)

5.

STATEMENTS	REASONS
1. $\overline{HB} \cong \overline{EB}$ $\angle BHG \cong \angle BEA$ $\angle HGJ \cong \angle EAD$ $\angle JGB \cong \angle DAB$	1. Given
2. $m\angle BHG = m\angle BEA$ $m\angle HGJ = m\angle EAD$ $m\angle JGB = m\angle DAB$	2. Definition of congruency
3. $m\angle HGJ + m\angle JGB$ $= m\angle HGB$	3. Angle Addition Postulate (Post. 1.4)
4. $m\angle EAD + m\angle DAB$ $= m\angle EAB$	4. Angle Addition Postulate (Post. 1.4)
5. $m\angle EAD + m\angle DAB$ $= m\angle HGB$	5. Substitution
6. $m\angle HGB = m\angle EAB$	6. Substitution
7. $\angle HGB \cong \angle EAB$	7. Definition of congruency
8. $\triangle BHG \cong \triangle BEA$	8. AAS Congruence Theorem (Thm. 5.11)

Answers

6.

STATEMENTS	REASONS
1. $\overline{AE} \parallel \overline{BF}$ $\overline{CE} \parallel \overline{DF}$ $\overline{AB} \cong \overline{CD}$	1. Given
2. $\angle EAC \cong \angle FBD$	2. Corresponding Angles Theorem (Thm. 3.1)
3. $\angle ECA \cong \angle FDB$	3. Corresponding Angles Theorem (Thm. 3.1)
4. $\overline{BC} \cong \overline{BC}$	4. Reflexive Property of Segment Congruence (Thm. 2.1)
5. $\overline{AB} + \overline{BC} = \overline{AC}$	5. Segment Addition Postulate (Post. 1.2)
6. $\overline{CD} + \overline{BC} = \overline{DB}$	6. Segment Addition Postulate (Post. 1.2)
7. $\overline{AB} + \overline{BC}$ $= \overline{CD} + \overline{BC}$	7. Addition Property of Equality
8. $\overline{AC} = \overline{DB}$	8. Substitution
9. $\overline{AC} \cong \overline{DB}$	9. Definition of congruent segments

5.6 Puzzle Time

A WATCH

5.7 Start Thinking

Answer should include, but is not limited to: Any construction of a small triangle (preferably small enough to fit on a notebook page) with labels for side lengths and angle measurements.

5.7 Warm Up

1. Transitive Property of Segment Congruence

2. Reflexive Property of Angle Congruence

3. Symmetric Property of Angle Congruence

4. Reflexive Property of Segment Congruence

5. Symmetric Property of Segment Congruence

6. Transitive Property of Angle Congruence

5.7 Cumulative Review Warm Up

1. $\angle ABC, \angle CBA, \angle B$ 2. $\angle JKL, \angle LKJ, \angle 2$

3. $\angle HMN, \angle NMH, \angle M$ 4. $\angle MPR, \angle RPM, \angle P$

5.7 Practice A

1. The figure shows that $\angle DAC \cong \angle E$, $\angle B \cong \angle C$, and $\overline{AB} \cong \overline{DC}$. So, $\triangle ACD \cong \triangle EBA$ by the AAS Congruence Theorem (Thm. 5.11) and $\overline{EB} \cong \overline{AC}$ because corresponding parts of congruent triangles are congruent.

2. The figure shows that $\angle ACB \cong \angle DCB$ and $\overline{AC} \cong \overline{DC}$. Use the Reflexive Property of Segment Congruence (Thm. 2.1) to show $\overline{BC} \cong \overline{BC}$. Then $\triangle ABC \cong \triangle DBC$ by the SAS Congruence Theorem (Thm. 5.5). So, $\angle A \cong \angle D$ because corresponding parts of congruent triangles are congruent.

3. Show that $PQSR$ is a parallelogram by definition, then show $\angle QPS \cong \angle RSP$ by the Alternate Interior Angles Theorem (Thm. 3.2). Show $\overline{PS} \cong \overline{SP}$ by the Reflexive Property of Segment Congruence (Thm. 2.1). The figure shows $\overline{PQ} \cong \overline{SR}$. So, $\triangle PQS \cong \triangle SRP$ by the SAS Congruence Theorem (Thm. 5.5), and $\overline{PR} \cong \overline{SQ}$ because corresponding parts of congruent triangles are congruent.

4. The figure shows that $\overline{HI} \cong \overline{JI}$ and $\overline{HK} \cong \overline{JK}$. Use the Reflexive Property of Segment Congruence (Thm. 2.1) to show that $\overline{IK} \cong \overline{IK}$. Then $\triangle HIK \cong \triangle JIK$ by the SSS Congruence Theorem (Thm. 5.8), and $\angle H \cong \angle J$ because corresponding parts of congruent triangles are congruent.

5. Place a stake at L so that $\overline{LM} \perp \overline{MN}$. Find K, the midpoint of $\overline{ML}$. Locate the point J so that $\overline{ML} \perp \overline{JL}$, and J, K, and N are collinear. Then find JL; **Given:** $\angle M$ and $\angle L$ are right angles, K is the midpoint of $\overline{ML}$. **Paragraph proof:** Because they are right angles, $\angle M \cong \angle L$. $MK = LK$ by the definition of the midpoint of a segment. $\angle JKL \cong \angle NKM$ by the Vertical Angles Congruence Theorem (Thm. 2.6). $\triangle JKL \cong \triangle NKM$ by the ASA Congruence Theorem (Thm. 5.10). $LJ = MN$ because corresponding parts of congruent triangles are congruent.

6. $DE = 5$; *Sample answer:* $m\angle C = 44°$ by the Triangle Sum Theorem (Thm. 5.1), so you have $\angle A \cong \angle D$, $\angle C \cong \angle F$, and $\overline{AC} \cong \overline{DF}$. $\triangle ABC \cong \triangle DEF$ by the ASA Congruence Theorem (Thm. 5.10). Therefore, $DE = AB$ because corresponding parts of congruent triangles are congruent.

Answers

5.7 Practice B

1. The figure shows that $\angle G \cong \angle J$, and $GI = JH$. Because they are vertical angles, $\angle GKI \cong \angle JKH$. So, $\triangle GKI \cong \triangle JKH$ by the AAS Congruence Theorem (Thm. 5.11) and $\overline{GK} \cong \overline{JK}$ because corresponding parts of congruent triangles are congruent.

2. The figure shows that $BE = CE$ and $\overline{AD} \perp \overline{CB}$. Because they are right angles, $\angle AEB \cong \angle AEC$. $\overline{AE} \cong \overline{AE}$ by the Reflexive Property of Segment Congruence (Thm. 2.1). $\triangle AEB \cong \triangle AEC$ by the SAS Congruence Theorem (Thm. 5.5). Because corresponding parts of congruent triangles are congruent, $BA = CA$.

3. The figure shows that $\overline{BA} \cong \overline{FG}$, $\angle A \cong \angle G$, and $\angle B$ and $\angle F$ are right angles. So, show that $\triangle ABC \cong \triangle GFE$ by the ASA Congruence Theorem (Thm. 5.10). Then $\angle BCA \cong \angle FEG$ because corresponding parts of congruent triangles are congruent, which leads to congruence of their respective vertical angles, $\angle DCH \cong \angle DEH$. Then $\overline{DH} \cong \overline{DH}$ by the Reflexive Property of Segment Congruence (Thm. 2.1) and right angles are formed by $\overline{DH} \perp \overline{CE}$, so $\triangle CDH \cong \triangle EDH$ by the AAS Congruence Theorem (Thm. 5.11). So, $\overline{DC} \cong \overline{DE}$ because corresponding parts of congruent triangles are congruent.

4. Use the Converse of the Base Angles Theorem (Thm. 5.7) to show that $\overline{SV} \cong \overline{SU}$. Show that $\angle RVS \cong \angle TUS$ because they form linear pairs with congruent angles. Then $\triangle RVS \cong \triangle TUS$ by the SAS Congruence Theorem (Thm. 5.5), which leads to $\angle 1 \cong \angle 2$ because corresponding parts of congruent triangles are congruent.

5. a. *Sample answer*: Mark point C along the edge of your roof. Then find the midpoint D of $\overline{AC}$. Locate point E so that $\overline{AC} \perp \overline{CE}$ and E, D, and B are collinear. Measure $\overline{CE}$. This is the same as AB.

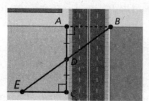

b. *Sample answer*: The method works because you have right angles, congruent segments, and vertical angles which lead to $\triangle ABD \cong \triangle CED$ by the ASA Congruence Theorem (Thm. 5.10), and $\overline{CE}$ corresponds to $\overline{AB}$ in these congruent triangles.

5.7 Enrichment and Extension

1. $x = 2; x = 5$ 2. $x = 0; x = 4$

3. $x = 20, y = 120, z = \pm 6$

4. In $\triangle ABC$ and $\triangle DEF$, you can use the Distance Formula to find that $AB = DE = 5$ units, $BC = EF \approx 5.385$, and $AC = FD = 10$ units. So, you can conclude that $\triangle ABC \cong \triangle DEF$ by the SSS Congruence Theorem (Thm. 5.8). So, $\angle A \cong \angle D$ because corresponding parts of congruent triangles are congruent.

5.

STATEMENTS	REASONS
1. L is the midpoint of $\overline{JN}$. $\overline{PJ} \cong \overline{QN}$ $\overline{PL} \cong \overline{QL}$	1. Given
2. $\overline{JL} \cong \overline{LN}$	2. Definition of midpoint
3. $\triangle PLJ \cong \triangle PLN$	3. SSS Congruence Theorem (Thm. 5.8)
4. $\angle PKJ$ and $\angle QMN$ are right angles.	4. Given
5. $\angle PKJ \cong \angle QMN$	5. Right Angles Congruence Theorem (Thm. 2.3)
6. $\angle KJP \cong \angle MNQ$	6. Corresponding parts of congruent triangles are congruent.
7. $\triangle PKJ \cong \triangle QMN$	7. AAS Congruence Theorem (Thm. 5.11)
8. $\angle MQN \cong \angle KPJ$	8. Corresponding parts of congruent triangles are congruent.

Answers

6.

STATEMENTS	REASONS
1. $\angle R \cong \angle S$ $\angle 2 \cong \angle 3$	1. Given
2. $\overline{TV} \cong \overline{TV}$	2. Reflexive Property of Segment Congruence (Thm. 2.1)
3. $\triangle RTV \cong \triangle SVT$	3. AAS Congruence Theorem (Thm. 5.11)
4. $\overline{RT} \cong \overline{SV}$	4. Corresponding parts of congruent triangles are congruent.
5. $\angle 5 \cong \angle 6$	5. Vertical Angles Congruence Theorem (Thm. 2.6)
6. $\triangle RTU \cong \triangle SVU$	6. AAS Congruence Theorem (Thm. 5.11)
7. $\overline{RU} \cong \overline{SU}$	7. Corresponding parts of congruent triangles are congruent.

5.7 Puzzle Time

TO KEEP THEIR INSIDES IN

5.8 Start Thinking

Answer should include, but is not limited to: Any construction using dynamic geometry software consisting of $\triangle ABC$ with whole-number degree angle measures, centered at the origin. A second triangle, larger or smaller, should also be centered at the origin and contain the same angle measures. The two triangles both have the same angle measures but are not the same size, so that they are not congruent.

5.8 Warm Up

1. 11.7   **2.** 3.2   **3.** 18

4. 7.3   **5.** 12.6   **6.** 21.8

5.8 Cumulative Review Warm Up

1. $30 + EF$ **2.** $4 \cdot GH$ **3.** $AB - JK$

5.8 Practice A

1.

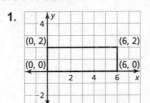

It is easy to find the width and length of the rectangle by placing a vertex at the origin.

2.

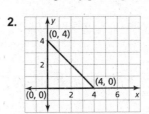

It is easy to see the length of each leg by placing the vertex with the right angle at the origin.

3.

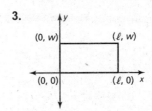

It is easy to see the width and length of the rectangle by placing a vertex at the origin.

4.

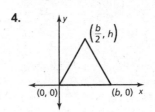

It is easy to see the length of the base and the height, and to determine that the triangle is isosceles by placing one vertex at the origin.

Answers

5.

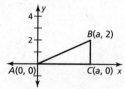

$AB = \sqrt{a^2 + 4}$, slope of $\overline{AB}$: $\dfrac{2}{a}$, midpoint of

$\overline{AB}$: $\left(\dfrac{a}{2}, 1\right)$

$BC = 2$, slope of $\overline{BC}$: undefined, midpoint of

$\overline{BC}$: $(a, 1)$

$AC = a$, slope of $\overline{AC}$: 0, midpoint of $\overline{AC}$: $\left(\dfrac{a}{2}, 0\right)$

$\triangle ABC$ is a right triangle because $\overline{AC}$ is horizontal and $\overline{BC}$ is vertical.

When $a = 2$, $\triangle ABC$ is also isosceles because then $AC = BC = 2$.

6.

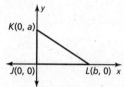

$JK = a$, slope of $\overline{JK}$: undefined, midpoint of $\overline{JK}$:

$\left(0, \dfrac{a}{2}\right)$

$KL = \sqrt{a^2 + b^2}$, slope of $\overline{KL}$: $-\dfrac{a}{b}$, midpoint of

$\overline{KL}$: $\left(\dfrac{b}{2}, \dfrac{a}{2}\right)$

$JL = b$, slope of $\overline{JL}$: 0, midpoint of $\overline{JL}$: $\left(\dfrac{b}{2}, 0\right)$

$\triangle JKL$ is a right triangle because $\overline{JL}$ is horizontal and $\overline{JK}$ is vertical. $\triangle JKL$ is not isosceles because $a \neq b$.

7. $O(0, 0), C(h, 0)$; $OB = \sqrt{h^2 + k^2}$

8. $G(-2h, 0), D(2, 4k)$; $FD = 4\sqrt{4k^2 + 1}$,

$DE = 2\sqrt{4k^2 + h^2 - 2h + 1}$

9. Coordinate proof:

Segments $\overline{CO}$ and $\overline{DO}$ have the same length.

$CO = |0 - (-h)| = h$; $DO = |h - 0| = h$

Segments $\overline{AC}$ and $\overline{BD}$ have the same length.

$AC = |k - 0| = k$; $BD = |k - 0| = k$

Segments $\overline{AO}$ and $\overline{BO}$ have the same length.

$AO = \sqrt{(-h - 0)^2 + (k - 0)^2} = \sqrt{h^2 + k^2}$;

$BO = \sqrt{(h - 0)^2 + (k - 0)^2} = \sqrt{h^2 + k^2}$

$\triangle ACO \cong \triangle BDO$ by the SSS Congruence Theorem (Thm. 5.8).

10. *Sample answer:* yes; In this position, it is relatively easy to find the lengths of the horizontal base and the side adjacent to the base with its vertex at $(0, 0)$.

11. *Sample answer:* $R(0, 0), S(0, 3a), T(4a, 0)$; $5a$

5.8 Practice B

1.

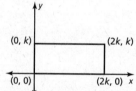

It is easy to find the width and length of the rectangle by placing a vertex at the origin with one side on each axis.

2.

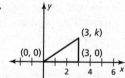

It is easy to see the length of one leg by placing a vertex at the origin with a side on the horizontal axis.

3.

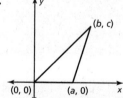

It is easy to see the length of one side by placing a vertex at the origin with a side on the horizontal axis.

Answers

4.

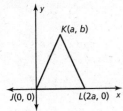

$JL = 2a$, $m\overline{JL} = 0$, midpoint of $\overline{JL}$: $(a, 0)$

$JK = \sqrt{a^2 + b^2}$, $m\overline{JK} = \dfrac{b}{a}$, midpoint of $\overline{JK}$:

$\left(\dfrac{a}{2}, \dfrac{b}{2}\right)$

$KL = \sqrt{a^2 + b^2}$, $m\overline{KL} = -\dfrac{b}{a}$, midpoint of $\overline{KL}$:

$\left(\dfrac{3a}{2}, \dfrac{b}{2}\right)$

$\triangle JKL$ is isosceles, because $\overline{JK} \cong \overline{KL}$.

5.

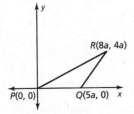

$PQ = 5a$, $m\overline{PQ} = 0$, midpoint of $\overline{PQ}$: $(2.5a, 0)$

$PR = 4a\sqrt{5}$, $m\overline{PR} = \dfrac{1}{2}$, midpoint of $\overline{PR}$: $(4a, 2a)$

$QR = 5a$, $m\overline{QR} = \dfrac{4}{3}$, midpoint of $\overline{QR}$: $(6.5a, 2a)$

$\triangle PQR$ is isosceles, because $\overline{PQ} \cong \overline{QR}$.

6. $F(0, 0)$, $G(0, k)$, $H(2k, -k)$, $J(k, 0)$;
$GH = 2k\sqrt{2}$, $FH = k\sqrt{5}$

7. $A(0, 0)$, $B\left(\dfrac{k}{2}, 2k\right)$, $C\left(\dfrac{3k}{2}, 2k\right)$, $E(k, 0)$; $BC = k$,

$CD = \dfrac{1}{2}k\sqrt{17}$

8. parallelogram; $m\overline{WX} = -\dfrac{5}{2}$, $m\overline{XY} = \dfrac{1}{2}$,

$m\overline{YZ} = -\dfrac{5}{2}$, and $m\overline{ZW} = \dfrac{1}{2}$. Because both pairs of opposite sides are parallel, $WZYZ$ is a parallelogram by definition. It is not a trapezoid because it has two pairs of parallel sides instead of one. It is not a rectangle because the slopes are not negative reciprocals of each other, which indicates that the sides are not perpendicular.

9. **Given:** Vertex C of $\triangle ABC$ is on the line $x = 0$, the perpendicular bisector of $\overline{AB}$.

Prove: $\triangle ABC$ is isosceles.

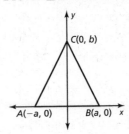

$\overline{AC}$ and $\overline{BC}$ have the lengths

$AC = \sqrt{(-a)^2 + b^2} = \sqrt{a^2 + b^2}$,

$BC = \sqrt{a^2 + b^2}$.

So, $AC = BC$, and by the definition of congruent segments, $\overline{AC} \cong \overline{BC}$. Therefore, $\triangle ABC$ is isosceles by the definition of isosceles triangle.

5.8 Enrichment and Extension

1. Call the point S the midpoint of $\overline{RP}$, with the coordinates $S = \left(\dfrac{-b + a}{2}, \dfrac{a + b}{2}\right)$. The slope of

$\overline{RP} = \dfrac{-(b - a)}{-b - a}$, and the slope of $\overline{SQ} = \dfrac{-a - b}{b - a}$,

making them opposite reciprocals and forming the $90°$ angles RSQ and PSQ. $\overline{SQ} \cong \overline{SQ}$ by the Reflexive Property of Segment Congruence (Thm. 2.1). The length of both $\overline{RS}$ and $\overline{SP}$ is equal

to $\sqrt{\left(\dfrac{a + b}{2}\right)^2 + \left(\dfrac{b - a}{2}\right)^2}$, so $\triangle RSQ \cong \triangle PSQ$

by the SAS Congruence Theorem (Thm. 5.5). The slope of $\overline{RQ} = -\dfrac{a}{b}$ and the slope of $\overline{QP} = \dfrac{b}{a}$.

They are opposite reciprocals and form the right angle PQR.

Answers

2. The slope of $\overline{CD}$ is equal to the slope of $\overline{AB}$, but $AD \neq BC$. So, it is a trapezoid, but not an isosceles trapezoid.

3. a. coordinates of P: $\left(\dfrac{s}{2}, \dfrac{t}{2}\right)$; coordinates of

Q: $\left(\dfrac{s+r}{2}, \dfrac{t}{2}\right)$

b. equation of $\overline{PR} = y = \dfrac{t}{s-2r}(x-r)$;

equation of $\overline{QO} = y = \dfrac{t}{r+s}x$

4. The trapezoid is isosceles because $\overline{TR} \cong \overline{PA}$. The base is on the x-axis, and the y-axis bisects the bases. Label point $E = (0, 2c)$, point $G = (0, 0)$, point $D = (-b - a, c)$, and point $F = (b + a, c)$. You can then show that

$DE = EF = FG = DG = \sqrt{c^2 + (b+a)^2}$.

All sides are equal, making $DEFG$ a rhombus.

5. $(b, -b)$ **6.** $(0, a)$

7. $(a - b, -b)$ or $(a - b, b)$

8. $(b - a, b)$

5.8 Puzzle Time

AIR BAG

Cumulative Review

1. $M\left(-\dfrac{3}{2}, 3\right)$ **2.** $M\left(-\dfrac{5}{2}, \dfrac{3}{2}\right)$ **3.** $M\left(\dfrac{5}{2}, 2\right)$

4. $M(2, 0)$ **5.** $M(5, 4)$ **6.** $M\left(\dfrac{11}{2}, 1\right)$

7. $M\left(\dfrac{7}{2}, -1\right)$ **8.** $M\left(1, -\dfrac{3}{2}\right)$ **9.** $M\left(\dfrac{9}{2}, -1\right)$

10. $M\left(0, -\dfrac{1}{2}\right)$ **11.** $M(-1, 3)$ **12.** $M\left(\dfrac{5}{2}, 2\right)$

13. $M\left(-\dfrac{5}{2}, 0\right)$ **14.** $M\left(\dfrac{15}{2}, -4\right)$ **15.** $M\left(\dfrac{3}{2}, -2\right)$

16. $M\left(\dfrac{15}{2}, \dfrac{9}{2}\right)$ **17.** $M\left(-7, -\dfrac{1}{2}\right)$ **18.** $M(5, 6)$

19. $M(5, -3)$ **20.** $M\left(\dfrac{3}{2}, \dfrac{3}{2}\right)$ **21.** 8.54

22. 12.37   **23.** 10.44   **24.** 13.34

25. 7.21   **26.** 6.32   **27.** 15.03

28. 6.32   **29.** 12.53   **30.** 5

31. 7   **32.** 10   **33.** 8.25

34. 6.40   **35.** 13.60   **36.** 7.62

37. 6.71   **38.** 7.62   **39.** 12.53

40. 15.81   **41.** 24 in.^{3} **42.** 234 in.^{3}

43. 21   **44.** 11   **45.** 18

46. 9   **47.** 10   **48.** 22

49. 8   **50.** 34   **51.** 2750 ft

52. a. 216 ft^2

   b. 2 containers

   c. \$31.98

53. 87°   **54.** 69°   **55.** 74°

56. 61°   **57.** 115°   **58.** 78°

59. $x = 20$ **60.** $x = -6$ **61.** $x = -5$

62. $x = -9$ **63.** $x = 8$ **64.** $x = 4$

65. $x = -2$ **66.** $x = 7$ **67.** $x = 9$

68. $x = 11$ **69.** $x = 6$ **70.** $x = 5$

71. $x = 5$ **72.** $x = 4$ **73.** $x = -3$

74. $x = 14$ **75.** $x = 1$ **76.** $x = 10$

77. $x = 6$ **78.** $x = 4$ **79.** $x = -4$

80. $x = -6$ **81.** $x = -32$ **82.** $x = -8$

83. $y = -3x + 9$ **84.** $y = 7x - 11$

85. $y = 8x - 13$ **86.** $y = 3x - 6$

87. $y = -2x + 6$ **88.** $y = 5x - 7$

89. $y = -0.125x + 3$ **90.** $y = 12x + 8$

91. $y = 0.125x - 8$ **92.** $y = -2x - 24$

Answers

93. $y = \frac{9}{4}x - 24$ **94.** $y = 8x - 2$

95. a. $224\,\text{ft}^2$ **b.** 12 ft by 14 ft   **c.** $168\,\text{ft}^2$

96. a. 10 ft   **b.** 24 ft   **c.** $24\,\text{ft}^2$

Chapter 6

6.1 Start Thinking

The roof lines become steeper; The two top chords will get longer as the king post gets longer, but the two top chords will always be congruent to each other. The angles formed by the top chords and the king post are congruent. The angles formed by the top chords and the bottom chord are congruent.

6.1 Warm Up

1. 5   **2.** 8   **3.** 2   **4.** -1

6.1 Cumulative Review Warm Up

1.

STATEMENTS	REASONS
1. P is the midpoint of $\overline{MN}$ and $\overline{TQ}$.	1. Given
2. $\overline{MP} \cong \overline{NP}$	2. Definition of segment midpoint
3. $\overline{PT} \cong \overline{PQ}$	3. Definition of segment midpoint
4. $\angle MPQ \cong \angle NPT$	4. Vertical Angles Congruence Theorem (Thm. 2.6)
5. $\triangle MQP \cong \triangle NTP$	5. SAS Congruence Theorem (Thm. 5.5)

2.

STATEMENTS	REASONS
1. $\overline{AB} \cong \overline{DC}$, $\overline{AC} \cong \overline{DB}$	1. Given
2. $\overline{BC} \cong \overline{BC}$	2. Reflexive Property of Segment Congruence (Thm. 2.1)
3. $\triangle ABC \cong \triangle DCB$	3. SSS Congruence Theorem (Thm. 5.8)

6.1 Practice A

1. P lies on the perpendicular bisector of $\overline{RS}$; The markings show that $\overrightarrow{TP}$ satisfies the definition of a perpendicular bisector.

2. P lies on the perpendicular bisector of $\overline{RS}$; Because T is equidistant from the endpoints R and S, T lies on the perpendicular bisector of $\overline{RS}$ by the Converse of the Perpendicular Bisector Theorem (Thm. 6.2). Because only one line can be perpendicular to $\overline{RS}$ at U, $\overleftrightarrow{TU}$ must be the perpendicular bisector of $\overline{RS}$, and P is on $\overleftrightarrow{TU}$.

3. P lies on the angle bisector of $\angle DEF$; P is equidistant from sides $\overleftrightarrow{ED}$ and $\overleftrightarrow{EF}$ of angle $\angle DEF$, so P is on the angle bisector of $\angle DEF$ by the Converse of the Angle Bisector Theorem (Thm. 6.4).

4. 20; Because D is on the perpendicular bisector of $\overline{AC}$, D is equidistant from A and C.

5. 17; By the Perpendicular Bisector Theorem (Thm. 6.1), $GJ = GH$. Solving $4x + 5 = 2x + 11$ gives $x = 3$, so $2x + 11 = 17$.

6. 14; Q is on the angle bisector of $\angle PSR$, so Q is equidistant from $\overrightarrow{SP}$ and $\overrightarrow{SR}$.

7. 76°; By the Converse of the Angle Bisector Theorem (Thm. 6.4), $\overrightarrow{GE}$ bisects $\angle DGF$. Solving $3x + 8 = 5x - 12$ gives $x = 10$. So, $m\angle DGF = \left[3(10) + 8 + 5(10) - 12\right]° = 76°$.

8. $y = -4x + 7$

9. Because any point on the perpendicular bisector of a segment is equidistant from the endpoints of the segment, you can draw an isosceles triangle by drawing segments from each endpoint of the segment to the same point on the perpendicular bisector.

10. yes; In a right triangle, the bisector of the right angle is also the perpendicular bisector of the hypotenuse when the right angle is isosceles. The figure shows that when right $\angle C$ of $\triangle ABC$ is bisected by $\overline{CD}$, $\triangle ACD \cong \triangle BCD$ by either the ASA Congruence Theorem (Thm. 5.10) or the SAS Congruence Theorem (Thm. 5.5). Then the corresponding sides $\overline{AC}$ and $\overline{BC}$ must be congruent, so $\triangle ABC$ is isosceles.

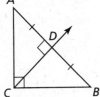

Answers

6.1 Practice B

1. neither; Because $\overrightarrow{PQ}$ is not marked perpendicular to $\overline{RS}$, you cannot be certain that point P is on the perpendicular bisector of $\overline{RS}$.

2. neither; Because there is no indication that $PD = PF$, you cannot be certain that point P is on the angle bisector of $\angle DEF$.

3. P lies on the bisector of $\angle DEF$; Using the HL Congruence Theorem (Thm. 5.9), $\triangle DEQ \cong \triangle FEQ$, so $DQ = FQ$ and $\overrightarrow{EQ}$ bisects $\angle DEF$ by the Converse of the Angle Bisector Theorem (Thm. 6.4). The figure shows that point P is on $\overrightarrow{EQ}$.

4. 36; Point D lies on the perpendicular bisector of $\overline{AC}$ by the Converse of the Perpendicular Bisector Theorem (Thm. 6.2). $m\angle DBC = 90°$ by the Triangle Sum Theorem (Thm. 5.1), so $\overrightarrow{BD}$ is the perpendicular bisector of $\overline{AC}$. Solving $-x + 25 = 3(2x - 8)$, gives $x = 7$, so $AC = 36$.

5. 45°; Because L is $\dfrac{\sqrt{5}}{2}$ units from each side $\overline{NK}$ and $\overline{NM}$, $\overline{NL}$ bisects $\angle KNM$. Because $m\angle KNM = 90°$, $m\angle LNM = \dfrac{1}{2}(90°) = 45°$.

6. 42°; $\overrightarrow{TV}$ bisects $\angle UTW$ because $VU = VW$. Solving $2x + 3 = 5x - 24$ gives $x = 9$, so $m\angle UTW = 2[2(9) + 3]° = 42°$.

7. $y = -\dfrac{1}{3}x + \dfrac{4}{3}$

8. no; yes; Point Q does not lie on line m because Q is not the same distance from P and R. Point S lies on line m, the perpendicular bisector of $\overline{PR}$, because S is the same distance from P and R.

9. Install the fountain at the point where the bisectors of the angles of the triangle intersect. That point is the same distance from each side of each angle, or equivalently, each side of the triangle.

6.1 Enrichment and Extension

1. 73

2. $\sqrt{(x+1)^2 + (y-5)^2} = \sqrt{(x-5)^2 + (y-2)^2}$; $y = 2x - \dfrac{1}{2}$

3. $x = 12$, $y = 8$

4. $x = 3$, $y = 2$

5.

STATEMENTS	REASONS
1. $PQRST$ is a regular polygon. $\overline{SV} \cong \overline{RV}$	1. Given
2. $\overline{TP} \cong \overline{QP}$ $\overline{TS} \cong \overline{QR}$ $\angle S \cong \angle R$	2. Definition of regular polygon
3. Draw $\overline{TV}$ and $\overline{QV}$.	3. Through any points there exists exactly one line.
4. $\triangle TSV \cong \triangle QRV$	4. SAS Congruence Theorem (Thm. 5.5)
5. $\overline{VT} \cong \overline{VQ}$	5. Corresponding parts of congruent triangles are congruent.
6. $VT = VQ$ $PT = PQ$	6. Definition of congruent segments
7. V lies on the perpendicular bisector of $\overline{TQ}$. P lies on the perpendicular bisector of $\overline{TQ}$.	7. Converse of the Perpendicular Bisector Theorem (Thm. 6.2)
8. $\overline{PV}$ lies on the perpendicular bisector of $\overline{TQ}$.	8. Perpendicular Postulate (Post. 3.2)

Answers

6. STATEMENTS	REASONS
1. $\overline{LQ} \cong \overline{NQ}$	1. Given
2. $\angle 2 \cong \angle 3$	2. Base Angles Theorem (Thm. 5.6)
3. $\angle 1 \cong \angle 4$	3. Given
4. $\angle 1 + \angle 2 = \angle MLR$ $\angle 3 + \angle 4 = \angle MNR$	4. Angles Addition Postulate (Post. 1.4)
5. $\angle 4 + \angle 3 = \angle MLR$	5. Substitution
6. $\angle MLR \cong \angle MNR$	6. Substitution
7. $\overline{MN} \cong \overline{MN}$	7. Converse of the Base Angles Theorem (Thm. 5.7)
8. $\overline{MQ}$ is the perpendicular bisector of $\overline{LN}$.	8. Converse of Perpendicular Bisector Theorem (Thm. 6.2)
9. $\overline{LP} \cong \overline{NP}$	9. Converse of Perpendicular Bisector Theorem (Thm. 6.2)

6.1 Puzzle Time

TOOK HIS MEDICINE AND FORGOT TO SHAKE IT

6.2 Start Thinking

They intersect at one point that appears to be the center of the circle. They also appear to be both angle bisectors and perpendicular bisectors.

6.2 Warm Up

1.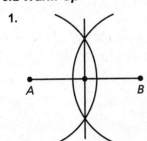

2.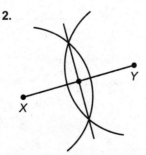

3.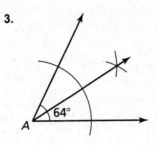

4.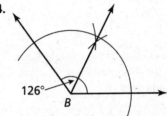

6.2 Cumulative Review Warm Up

1.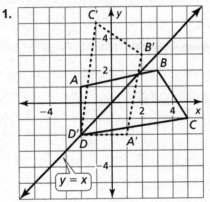

2.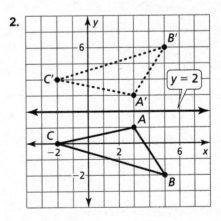

6.2 Practice A

1. 9; Circumcenter Theorem (Thm. 6.5)

2. 10; Circumcenter Theorem (Thm. 6.5)

3. 2; Incenter Theorem (Thm. 6.6)

4. $(3, 2)$　　　　5. $(-2, 4)$

Answers

6. 12   **7.** 50

8. *Sample answer:*

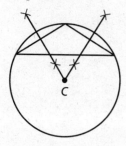

9. Construct the circumcenter of the triangle formed by the locations of the three buildings. The tower is located at the circumcenter.

10. no; The circumcenter of an obtuse triangle lies outside the triangle, and the circumcenter of a right triangle lies on the hypotenuse.

6.2 Practice B

1. 6; Circumcenter Theorem (Thm. 6.5)

2. 15; Circumcenter Theorem (Thm. 6.5)

3. 11; Incenter Theorem (Thm. 6.6)

4. $\left(\frac{9}{2}, \frac{3}{2}\right)$ **5.** $MG = 10, NG = 10$

6. $GJ = 18, GE = 17$

7. a. Find the incenter by finding the intersection of two angle bisectors.

    b. Find the circumcenter by finding the intersection of the perpendicular bisectors of two sides.

    c. the circumcenter; The circumcenter is centered between the three vertices, whereas the incenter is toward the bottom of the triangular lawn in the figure.

8. The circumcenter lies outside the triangle when the triangle is obtuse.

9. 8

6.2 Enrichment and Extension

1. $Q\left(\frac{11}{5}, \frac{23}{5}\right)$ **2.** 13 units

3. $(15.4, 21.2)$ **4.** $(3.2, 11.0)$

5.

STATEMENTS	REASONS
1. $\overline{GJ}$ is the $\perp$ bisector of $\overline{HK}$.	1. Given
2. $\overline{HJ} \cong \overline{JK}$	2. Definition of segment bisector
3. $\overline{MH} \cong \overline{MK}$	3. Perpendicular Bisector Theorem (Thm. 6.1)
4. $\overline{GH} \cong \overline{GK}$	4. Perpendicular Bisector Theorem (Thm. 6.1)
5. $\overline{GM} \cong \overline{GM}$	5. Reflexive Property of Segment Congruence (Thm. 2.1)
6. $\triangle GHM \cong \triangle GKM$	6. SSS Congruence Theorem (Thm. 5.8)
7. $\angle GHM \cong \angle GKM$	7. Corresponding parts of congruent triangles are congruent.

6. Begin by drawing a line segment from point B to point F, as shown. You are given $\overline{FC}$ is the perpendicular bisector of $\overline{AB}$ and $\overline{FE}$ is the perpendicular bisector of $\overline{BD}$. By the Perpendicular Bisector Theorem (Thm. 6.1) you know that $AF = FB$ and $FD = FB$. Using the Transitive Property of Equality, you can conclude that $AF = FD$. By the definition of congruent segments, you know that $\overline{AF} \cong \overline{FD}$.

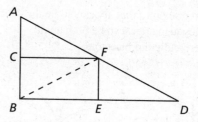

6.2 Puzzle Time

HAD A BYTE

Answers

6.3 Start Thinking

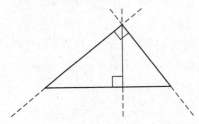

Two of the altitudes coincide with the two legs of the right triangle, and the three altitudes intersect at the vertex of the right angle.

6.3 Warm Up

1.
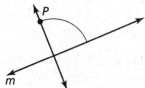

2.
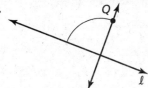

6.3 Cumulative Review Warm Up

1. $y - 4 = \frac{3}{2}(x + 2)$ 2. $x = 5$

3. $y + 9 = -1\left(x - \frac{3}{4}\right)$ 4. $y + 7 = -\frac{1}{2}(x - 1)$

5. $y + 2 = -\frac{5}{3}(x - 3)$ 6. $y = -\frac{3}{2}$

6.3 Practice A

1. $BP = 8, PL = 4$ 2. $PL = 8, CL = 24$

3. $AP = 18, PL = 9$ 4. $PL = 51, BL = 153$

5. $(4, 4)$ 6. $(2, 1)$

7. on; $(0, 0)$ 8. outside; $(1, -5)$

9. orthocenter; When the strings are pulled tight, right angles are formed on opposite sides of each vertex. Three altitudes are formed, which are concurrent at the orthocenter.

10. no; The orthocenter and the centroid are the same point in an isosceles triangles.

6.3 Practice B

1. $QL = 42, AL = 63$ 2. $JQ = 48, QA = 24$

3. $QA = 5, KA = 15$ 4. $(-3, 4)$

5. inside; $(1, 3)$ 6. outside; $\left(-8, \frac{9}{2}\right)$

7. 1; *Sample answer*: The two vertices give one side of the triangle. The centroid and each given vertex can be used to find the exact location of the midpoint of another side. The two midpoints and the two given vertices can be used to find the third vertex of the triangle.

8. 1; *Sample answer*: The two vertices give one side of the triangle. Each vertex and the orthocenter can be used to draw a line containing the altitude from that vertex. The line perpendicular to that line and passing through the other vertex contains another side of the triangle. The third vertex is the intersection of the new sides.

9. $(10, -2)$ 10. $(3, -6)$

11. no; *Sample answer*: A congruent pair of adjacent sides in a triangle have a perpendicular bisector, angle bisector, median, and altitude from the shared vertex that are all the same segment. An equilateral triangle has three pairs of congruent adjacent sides, so the special segments will all be the same, as will their points of concurrency.

12. yes; *Sample answer:* The median is the same as the altitude only when the sides that share the vertex are congruent, so the triangles formed by this median will be congruent by the HL Congruence Theorem (Thm. 5.9).

13. no; The circumcenter of an obtuse triangle is outside the triangle and the incenter of any triangle is inside the triangle.

6.3 Enrichment and Extension

1. $N\left(\dfrac{x_1 + x_2 + x_3}{3}, \dfrac{y_1 + y_2 + y_3}{3}, \dfrac{z_1 + z_2 + z_3}{3}\right)$

2. $N\left(\dfrac{a}{3}, \dfrac{b}{3}, \dfrac{c}{3}\right)$

Answers

3. $T\left(\dfrac{a}{2}, \dfrac{b}{2}, 0\right)$; The distance of

$$FN = \sqrt{\left(\dfrac{a}{3}\right)^2 + \left(\dfrac{b}{3}\right)^2 + \left(\dfrac{2c}{3}\right)^2}$$

$$= \dfrac{\sqrt{a^2 + b^2 + 4c^2}}{3}$$

and the distance of

$$NT = \sqrt{\left(\dfrac{a}{6}\right)^2 + \left(\dfrac{b}{6}\right)^2 + \left(\dfrac{2c}{6}\right)^2}$$

$$= \dfrac{\sqrt{a^2 + b^2 + 4c^2}}{6},$$

so $FN = 2 \bullet NT$.

4. 2   5. 1 or 7   6. -1 or 5.5

7. $\dfrac{8\sqrt{1794}}{3}$ square units

8. about 2.237 square units

9. $\overline{AM} = y = \left(\dfrac{2c}{2b - a}\right)x - \dfrac{6ac}{2b - a}$,

$\overline{BN} = y = \left(\dfrac{c}{a + b}\right)x$,

$\overline{CP} = y = \left(\dfrac{c}{b - 2a}\right)x - \dfrac{6ac}{b - 2a}$;

$(2a + 2b, 2c)$

6.3 Puzzle Time
A BOOKWORM

6.4 Start Thinking

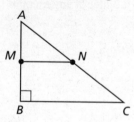

The measure of $\overline{MN}$ is one-half the measure of $\overline{BC}$.

6.4 Warm Up

1. $(-3, 0)$ 2. $\left(1, \dfrac{3}{2}\right)$ 3. $\sqrt{73}$ 4. $\sqrt{65}$

1. $79°$ 2. $48°, 42°$ 3. $88°, 50°, 42°$

6.4 Practice A

1. The slope of $\overline{ED} = \dfrac{1 - 4}{2 - 1} = -3,$ and the slope of

$\overline{BC} = \dfrac{-2 - 4}{5 - 3} = -3.$ So, $\overline{ED} \parallel \overline{BC}.$

$ED = \sqrt{(2 - 1)^2 + (1 - 4)^2} = \sqrt{10},$

$BC = \sqrt{(5 - 3)^2 + (-2 - 4)^2} = 2\sqrt{10},$ so

$ED = \dfrac{1}{2}BC.$

2. $E(1, 4), F(4, 1)$

3. The slope of $\overline{EF} = \dfrac{1 - 4}{4 - 1} = -1,$ and the slope of

$\overline{AC} = \dfrac{-2 - 4}{5 - (-1)} = -1.$ So, $\overline{EF} \parallel \overline{AC}.$

$EF = \sqrt{(4 - 1)^2 + (1 - 4)^2} = 3\sqrt{2},$

$AC = \sqrt{\left[5 - (-1)\right]^2 + (-2 - 4)^2} = 6\sqrt{2},$ so

$EF = \dfrac{1}{2}AC.$

4. $D(2, 1), F(4, 1)$

5. The slope of $\overline{DF} = \dfrac{1 - 1}{4 - 2} = 0,$ and the slope of

$\overline{AB} = \dfrac{4 - 4}{3 - (-1)} = 0.$ So, $\overline{DF} \parallel \overline{AB}.$

$DF = 4 - 2 = 2,$ and $AB = 3 - (-1) = 4,$ so

$DF = \dfrac{1}{2}AB.$

6. 32   7. 34   8. 23

9. 17   10. 12   11. 21

12. yes; Because each midsegment is half as long as the corresponding side, the sum of the lengths of the midsegments (the perimeter of the midsegment triangle) will be half the sum of the lengths of the corresponding sides (the perimeter of the original triangle).

13. 116 ft

Answers

6.4 Practice B

1. $D(-2, 2)$, $E(-1, -2)$, $F(-4, -1)$

2.

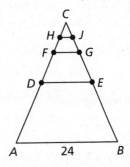

3. The slope of $\overline{FD} = \dfrac{2 - (-1)}{-2 - (-4)} = \dfrac{3}{2}$, and the

slope of $\overline{CB} = \dfrac{1 - (-5)}{1 - (-3)} = \dfrac{3}{2}$. So, $\overline{FD} \parallel \overline{CB}$.

The slope of $\overline{FE} = \dfrac{-2 - (-1)}{-1 - (-4)} = -\dfrac{1}{3}$, and the

slope of $\overline{AB} = \dfrac{1 - 3}{1 - (-5)} = -\dfrac{1}{3}$. So, $\overline{FE} \parallel \overline{AB}$.

The slope of $\overline{DE} = \dfrac{-2 - 2}{-1 - (-2)} = -4$, and the

slope of $\overline{AC} = \dfrac{-5 - 3}{-3 - (-5)} = -4$. So, $\overline{DE} \parallel \overline{AC}$.

4. $FD = \sqrt{(-2 - [-4])^2 + (2 - [-1])^2} = \sqrt{13}$,

$CB = \sqrt{(1 - [-3])^2 + (1 - [-5])^2} = 2\sqrt{13}$, so

$FD = \dfrac{1}{2}CB$.

$FE = \sqrt{(-1 - [-4])^2 + (-2 - [-1])^2} = \sqrt{10}$,

$AB = \sqrt{(1 - [-5])^2 + (1 - 3)^2} = 2\sqrt{10}$, so

$FE = \dfrac{1}{2}AB$.

$DE = \sqrt{(-1 - [-2])^2 + (-2 - 2)^2} = \sqrt{17}$,

$AC = \sqrt{(-3 - [-5])^2 + (-5 - 3)^2} = 2\sqrt{17}$, so

$DE = \dfrac{1}{2}AC$.

5. 9   **6.** 4   **7.** 64   **8.** 8

9. *Sample answer:* The two pairs of equal measures determine the midpoints of two sides of a triangle. The midsegment of the triangle is represented by the surface of the bottom step. So, the bottom step is parallel to the floor, which represents the bottom side of the triangle.

10. no; *Sample answer:* The midsegments of a triangle with side lengths of $2a$, $2b$, and $2c$ divide the triangle into 4 triangles with side lengths of a, b, and c. So, the smaller triangle has only one-fourth the area of the larger triangle.

6.4 Enrichment and Extension

1. a.

b.

Stage n	0	1	2	3	4	5
Midsegment length	24	12	6	3	$\dfrac{3}{2}$	$\dfrac{3}{4}$

c. Midsegments of Triangles

$y = 24 \cdot \left(\dfrac{1}{2}\right)^n$

d. $y = w \cdot \left(\dfrac{1}{2}\right)^n$

2. $G(4, 4)$, $H(0, 2)$, $J(8, 0)$

3. perimeter $= 17.1$ units, area $= 12.5$ units^2

Answers

4. You are given $\triangle ABC \cong \triangle DEF$. Because corresponding parts of congruent triangles are congruent, you can conclude $\overline{AB} \cong \overline{DE}$, $\overline{BC} \cong \overline{EF}$, and $\overline{CA} \cong \overline{FD}$. By the definition of congruent segments, you can also conclude $AB = DE$, $BC = EF$, and $CA = FD$. You are also given that T, U, and V are the midpoints of $\triangle ABC$ and X, Y, and Z are midpoints of $\triangle DEF$. So, $TV = \frac{1}{2}BC$ and $XZ = \frac{1}{2}EF$. By the Substitution Property of Equality, you have $TV = \frac{1}{2}EF$ and $TV = XZ$. You know $UV = \frac{1}{2}AB$ and $YZ = \frac{1}{2}DE$. So, by the Substitution Property of Equality, you have $UV = \frac{1}{2}DE$ and $UV = YZ$. Finally, you know $TU = \frac{1}{2}CA$ and $XY = \frac{1}{2}FD$. So, by the Substitution Property of Equality, you have $TU = \frac{1}{2}FD$ and $TU = XY$. By the definition of congruent segments, you can conclude $\overline{TV} \cong \overline{XZ}$, $\overline{UV} \cong \overline{YZ}$ and $\overline{TU} \cong \overline{XY}$. By the SSS Congruence Theorem (Thm. 5.8), you can conclude $\triangle TUV \cong \triangle XYZ$.

6.4 Puzzle Time

STICK WITH ME AND WE WILL GO PLACES

6.5 Start Thinking

1. $\overline{BC}$ is the longest side and $\angle A$ is the largest angle.

2. $\overline{YZ}$ is the longest side and $\angle X$ is the largest angle.

3. $\overline{NP}$ is the longest side and $\angle M$ is the largest angle.

The largest angle is always opposite the longest side.

6.5 Warm Up

1. If there is no right angle in a triangle, then it is not a right triangle.

2. If two lines do not have the same slope, then they are not parallel.

3. *Sample answer*: If a quadrilateral does not have four right angles, then the quadrilateral is not a rectangle.

4. *Sample answer*: If no two angles of a triangle are congruent, then the triangle is a scalene triangle.

5. If the sum of the measures of the interior angles of a polygon is not 180°, then the polygon is not a triangle.

6. *Sample answer*: If a triangle does not contain three congruent angles, then it is not equiangular.

6.5 Cumulative Review Warm Up

1. 110   **2.** 28   **3.** -2

6.5 Practice A

1. $\angle N, \angle L, \angle M$ **2.** $\angle F, \angle D, \angle E$

3. $\overline{AB}, \overline{CA}, \overline{BC}$ **4.** $\overline{QP}, \overline{PR}, \overline{RQ}$

5. no; The sum of the first two sides is $15 + 37 = 52$, which is not greater than 53.

6. yes; The sum of the lengths of any two sides of the triangle is greater than the length of the third side.

7. Assume that a triangle has more than one obtuse angle. An obtuse angle is an angle that is greater than 90°. This makes the sum of the angles in the triangle greater than 180°. However, the sum of the angles of a triangle must be equal to, not greater than 180°. This is a contradiction, so the assumption that a triangle has more than one obtuse angle must be false, which proves that a triangle has, at most, one obtuse angle.

8. $x > 14$

9. $\angle ACD, \angle D, \angle A$; Using the properties of exterior angles, you can solve for $x = 14$, and then obtain all of the angle measures.

10. *Sample answer*: In terms of the Triangle Inequality Theorem (Thm. 6.11), this can be thought of as a direct route between two points by traveling along one side, or an indirect route between two points by traveling along the other two sides. Because the sum of the lengths of any two sides of a triangle is greater than the length of the third side, the direct route along a single side is the shortest distance between two points.

6.5 Practice B

1. $\angle L, \angle M, \angle N$ **2.** $\angle V, \angle U, \angle W$

3. $\overline{QS}, \overline{RQ}, \overline{SR}$ **4.** $\overline{BC}, \overline{DB}, \overline{CD}$

Answers

5. Assume temporarily that a right triangle has three acute angles. So the measure of each angle is less than 90°, but by the definition of a right triangle, one angle must have a measure of 90°. So, the assumption that a right triangle has three acute angles must be false. Next assume temporarily that a right triangle has exactly one acute angle, which means the triangle has one right angle and one obtuse angle. The measure of an obtuse angle plus 90° is greater than 180°. By the Triangle Sum Theorem (Thm. 5.1), $m\angle A + m\angle B + m\angle C = 180°$. So, the assumption that a triangle has exactly one acute angle must be false, which proves that a right triangle has exactly two acute angles.

6. yes; Substituting the given value of x into the expressions for the measures of the sides gives 60, 107, and 122. Because the sum of any two of these lengths is greater than the third, it is possible to construct such a triangle.

7. $\triangle DEF$, $\triangle FGC$; Use the Triangle Inequality Theorem (Thm. 6.11). For $\triangle DEF$, $DE + DF > EF$, $DE + EF > DF$, and $DF + EF > DE$. For $\triangle FGC$, $FC + CG > FG$, $CG + FG > FC$, and $FG + FC > CG$.

8. yes; If you know all three angles measures, you can use a protractor and a straightedge to construct a triangle with the given angles that obeys the Triangle Inequality Theorem (Thm. 6.11).

6.5 Enrichment and Extension

1. $\overline{CD}, \overline{BC}, \overline{BD}, \overline{AB}, \overline{AD}$

2. $\overline{DE}, \overline{AE}, \overline{AD}, \overline{AB}, \overline{BD}, \overline{BC}, \overline{CD}$

3. *Sample answer:*

STATEMENTS	REASONS
1. $\triangle ABC$ and median $\overline{AM}$	1. Given
2. Extend $\overline{AM}$ to point D such that $\overline{AM} \cong \overline{DM}$. Draw $\triangle CDB$.	2. Construction
3. $\overline{MB} \cong \overline{MC}$	3. Definition of median
4. $\angle AMB \cong \angle DMC$	4. Vertical Angles Congruence Theorem (Thm. 5.5)
5. $\triangle AMB \cong \triangle DMC$	5. SAS Congruence Theorem (Thm. 5.5)
6. $\overline{AB} \cong \overline{DC}$	6. Corresponding parts of congruent triangles are congruent.
7. $AB = DC$, $AM = DM$	7. Definition of congruent segments
8. $AM + MD = AD$	8. Segment Addition Postulate (Post. 1.2)
9. $AM + AM = AD$	9. Substitution Property of Equality
10. $2AM = AD$	10. Simplify.
11. $AD < AC + CD$	11. Triangle Inequality Theorem (Thm. 6.11)
12. $2AM < AC + AB$	12. Substitution
13. $AM < \frac{1}{2}(AC + AB)$	13. Division Property of Equality
14. $\frac{1}{2}(AB + AC) < \frac{1}{2}(AB + AC + BC)$	14. Properties of real numbers
15. $AM < \frac{1}{2}(AB + AC + BC)$	15. Transitive Property of Inequality

Answers

4. *Sample answer:* In $\triangle ABC$, let $\overline{AX}, \overline{BY}$, and $\overline{CZ}$ be medians. By the Centroid Theorem (Thm. 6.7) and the Triangle Inequality Theorem (Thm. 6.11), $\frac{2}{3}AX + \frac{2}{3}BY > AB$, $\frac{2}{3}AX + \frac{2}{3}CZ > AC$, and $\frac{2}{3}BY + \frac{2}{3}CZ > BC$. Adding the left sides and right sides of the three inequalities gives $\frac{4}{3}(AX + BY + CZ) > AB + AC + BC$.

Multiplying each side by $\frac{3}{4}$ gives

$AX + BY + CZ > \frac{3}{4}(AB + AC + BC)$. Finally, $\frac{3}{4} > \frac{1}{2}$ and the Transitive Property of Inequality gives $AX + BY + CZ > \frac{1}{2}(AB + AC + BC)$, as desired.

5. $60° < x < 180; 0° < x < 60°$

6. a. $\frac{3}{4} < x < 8$

  b. $x > 2$

7. If a line segment is perpendicular to a plane, then it is perpendicular to every line segment in the plane. So, $\overline{PC} \perp \overline{DC}$, and $\triangle PCD$ is a right triangle. The largest angle in a right triangle is the right angle, so $m\angle PCD > m\angle PDC$. Finally, you can conclude that $PD > PC$ because if one angle of a triangle is larger than another angle, then the side opposite the larger angle is longer than the side opposite the smaller angle.

6.5 Puzzle Time

A JUMP ROPE

6.6 Start Thinking

The length increases; The angle must be less than 180 degrees; 8

6.6 Warm Up

1. yes; $\triangle ABE$ and $\triangle DCE$ are congruent by the AAS Congruence Theorem (Thm. 5.11).

2. no   **3.** no

4. yes; $\triangle CDB$ and $\triangle CEA$ are congruent by the SAS Congruence Theorem (Thm. 5.5).

6.6 Cumulative Review Warm Up

1. rotation   **2.** dilation   **3.** translation

6.6 Practice A

1. $AC > DF$; By the Hinge Theorem (Thm. 6.12), because $\overline{AC}$ is the third side of the triangle with the larger included angle, it is longer than $\overline{DF}$.

2. $m\angle HGI = m\angle IGJ$; The triangles are congruent by the SSS Congruence Theorem (Thm. 5.8). So, because corresponding parts of congruent triangles are congruent, $m\angle HGI = m\angle IGJ$.

3. $m\angle 1 < m\angle 2$; By the Converse of the Hinge Theorem (Thm. 6.13), because $\angle 1$ is the included angle in the triangle with the shorter third side, its measure is less than that of $\angle 2$.

4. $KL < MN$; By the Hinge Theorem (Thm. 6.12), because $\overline{KL}$ is the third side of the triangle with the smaller included angle, it is shorter than $\overline{MN}$.

5. $x + 7 < 2x - 3, x > 10$

6. $6(x + 1) > 14x - 10, x < 2$

7.

STATEMENTS	REASONS
1. $\overline{TV} \cong \overline{UW}$	1. Given
2. $\overline{UV} \cong \overline{UV}$	2. Reflexive Property of Segment Congruence (Thm. 2.1)
3. $TU > VW$	3. Given
4. $m\angle TVU > m\angle WUV$	4. Converse of the Hinge Theorem (Thm. 6.13)

Answers

8.

STATEMENTS	REASONS
1. $\overline{BD} \cong \overline{BE}$	1. Given
2. $\overline{AB} \cong \overline{BC}$	2. Definition of segment midpoint
3. $m\angle 1 > m\angle 2$	3. Given
4. $AD > CE$	4. Hinge Theorem (Thm. 6.12)
5. $\overline{DF} \cong \overline{EF}$	5. Given
6. $DF = EF$	6. Definition of congruent segments
7. $AD + DF > CE + DF$	7. Addition Property of Inequality
8. $AD + DF > CE + EF$	8. Substitution
9. $AD + DF = AF$, $CE + EF = CF$	9. Segment Addition Postulate (Post 1.2)
10. $AF > CF$	10. Substitution

9. no; You cannot apply either the Hinge Theorem (Thm. 6.12) or the Converse of the Hinge Theorem (Thm. 6.13) in this situation; These theorems require that two sides of one triangle are congruent to two sides of the other triangle. In this case, the ladders are different heights, so you only have one pair of congruent sides.

6.6 Practice B

1. $BC > DE$; By the Hinge Theorem (Thm. 6.12), because $\overline{BC}$ is the third side of the triangle with the larger included angle, it is longer than $\overline{DE}$.

2. $JI > GH$; By the Hinge Theorem (Thm. 6.12), because $\overline{JI}$ is the third side of the triangle with the larger included angle, it is longer than $\overline{GH}$.

3. $m\angle 1 > m\angle 2$; By the Converse of the Hinge Theorem (Thm. 6.13), because $\angle 1$ is the included angle in the triangle with the longer third side, its measure is greater than that of $\angle 2$.

4. $m\angle U < m\angle R$; By the Converse of the Hinge Theorem (Thm. 6.13), because $\angle U$ is the included angle in the triangle with the shorter third side, its measure is less than that of $\angle R$.

5. $2(3x - 8) > x + 14, x > 6$

6. $2(x + 22) > 3x - 18, x < 62$

7.

STATEMENTS	REASONS
1. $\overline{PQ} \cong \overline{SR}$	1. Given
2. $PS + SR > PR$	2. Triangle Inequality Theorem (Thm. 6.11)
3. $PR = PQ + QR$	3. Segment Addition Postulate (Post. 1.2)
4. $PS + SR > PQ + QR$	4. Substitution
5. $PQ = SR$	5. Definition of congruent segments
6. $PS + SR > SR + QR$	6. Substitution
7. $PS > QR$	7. Subtraction Property of Inequality
8. $m\angle PQS > m\angle RSQ$	8. Converse of the Hinge Theorem (Thm. 6.13)

8. Sailboat A; Because $151° > 129°$, the distance Sailboat A traveled is a greater distance than the distance Sailboat B traveled by the Hinge Theorem (Thm. 6.12).

9. Each theorem refers to the included angles of two triangles when two sides of one triangle are congruent to two sides of the other triangle, The Hinge Theorem (Thm. 6.12) refers to the case when the included angle of the first is larger than the included angle of the second. The SAS Congruence Theorem (Thm. 5.5) refers to the case when the included angles are congruent.

6.6 Enrichment and Extension

1. a. never **b.** never **c.** always
d. never **e.** never **f.** sometimes

Answers

2. $\overline{AB} \cong \overline{AD}$ and $\overline{AC} \cong \overline{AE}$ because they are radii of the circles and all radii are congruent. By the Hinge Theorem (Thm. 6.12), because $m\angle BAC > m\angle DAE$, then $BC > DE$.

3. $16.5 < y < 37.5$

4.

STATEMENTS	REASONS
1. $\angle ADB$ and $\angle CDA$ are supplementary.	**1.** Linear Pair Postulate (Post. 2.8)
2. $m\angle ADB + m\angle CDA = 180°$	**2.** Definition of supplementary angles
3. $m\angle CDA = 180° - m\angle ADB$	**3.** Subtraction Property of Equality
4. $m\angle ADB = 100°$	**4.** Given
5. $m\angle CDA = 180° - 100°$	**5.** Substitution
6. $m\angle CDA = 80°$	**6.** Subtraction Property of Equality
7. $m\angle ADB > m\angle CDB$	**7.** Definition of congruent angles
8. D is the midpoint of $\overline{BC}$.	**8.** Given
9. $\overline{BD} \cong \overline{CD}$	**9.** Definition of midpoint
10. $\overline{AD} \cong \overline{AD}$	**10.** Reflexive Property of Segment Congruence (Thm. 2.1)
11. $AB > CA$	**11.** Hinge Theorem (Thm. 6.12)
12. $m\angle C > m\angle A$	**12.** Triangle Longer Side Theorem (Thm. 6.9)

6.6 Puzzle Time

DUCK

Cumulative Review

1. $c > 9$ or $c < -3$ **2.** $2 < s < 11$

3. $-10 < m \leq -7$ **4.** $1 \leq p < 15$

5. $j \leq 6$

6. $8 < v < 13$

7. $-5 \leq r < 12$

8. $b \geq 17$ or $b < 3$

9. $m = -\dfrac{3}{2}$

10. $m = 1$

11. m is undefined.

12. $m = -\dfrac{19}{5}$

13. $m = -\dfrac{2}{13}$

14. $m = -\dfrac{3}{2}$

15. $m = -\dfrac{6}{5}$

16. $m = -\dfrac{15}{4}$

17. m is undefined.

18. $m = -\dfrac{9}{7}$

19. $m = -\dfrac{3}{5}$

20. $m = \dfrac{7}{6}$

21. $m = -\dfrac{2}{3}$

22. $m = -\dfrac{1}{15}$

23. $m = -\dfrac{1}{24}$

24. $y = -2x - 10$

25. $y = x - 2$

26. $y = \dfrac{1}{2}x - \dfrac{5}{2}$

27. $y = -\dfrac{1}{3}x - \dfrac{1}{3}$

28. $x = -6$

29. $x = -3$

30. $y = \dfrac{1}{2}x - 3$

31. $y = -\dfrac{5}{3}x - 1$

32. a. $C = 1.25t + 12.50$
   b. \$16.25
   c. \$18.75

33. $y = -\dfrac{1}{8}x + \dfrac{37}{8}$

34. $y = -\dfrac{3}{2}x - \dfrac{39}{2}$

35. $y = 6$

36. $y = 0$

37. $y = \dfrac{4}{7}x - 7$

38. $y = -x - 4$

Answers

39. $y = \dfrac{1}{4}x - \dfrac{5}{4}$ **40.** $y = -\dfrac{3}{2}x + \dfrac{5}{2}$

41. $x = 152$, $y = 28$ **42.** $x = 77$, $y = 103$

43. $x = 26$, $y = 77$ **44.** $x = 4$, $y = 82$

45. $x = 115$, $y = 13$ **46.** $x = 33$, $y = 103$

47. a. $67°$ **b.** $113°$

48. a. $46°$ **b.** $92°$

49. $A'(3, -3)$ **50.** $B'(-4, 6)$

51. $C(-5, -6)$ **52.** $D(-10, 8)$

53. $A'(-5, 8)$ **54.** $B'(3, 9)$

55. $C(-5, -3)$ **56.** $D(4, -2)$

57.

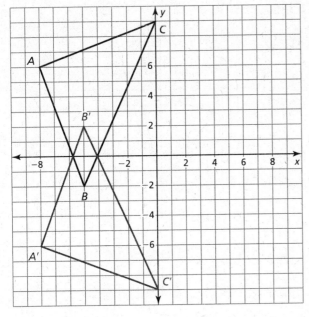

58.

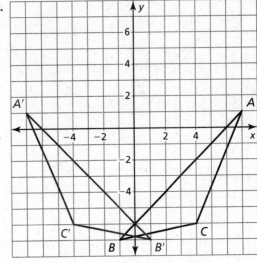

59.

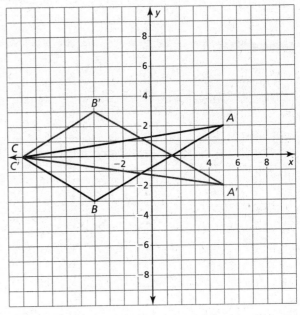

Answers

60.

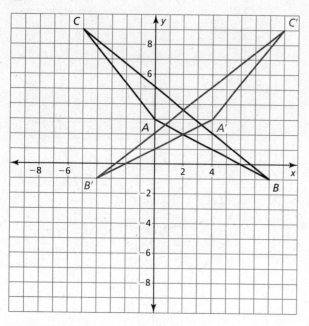

62.

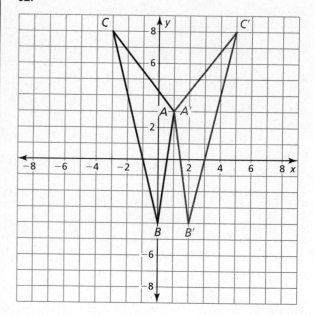

61.

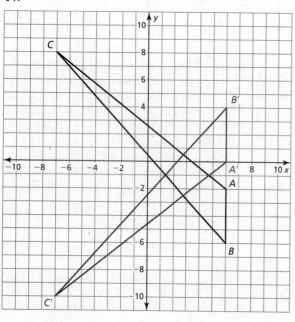

63.

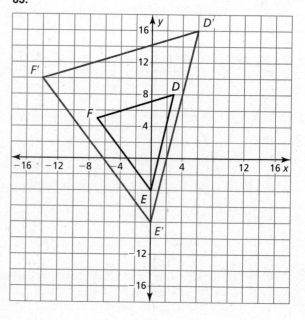

Answers

64.

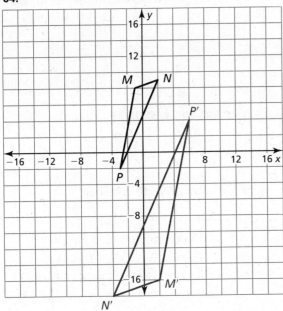

65.

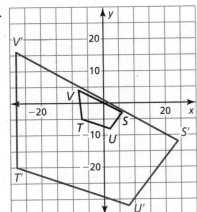

66.

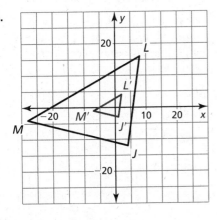

67.

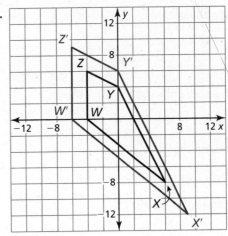

68.

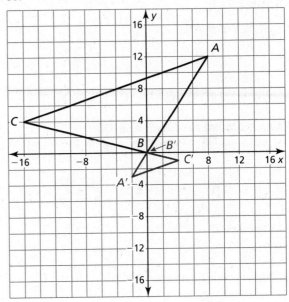

69.

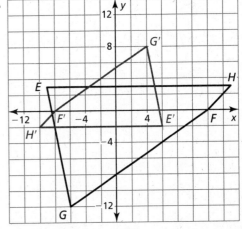

Answers

70. equilateral triangle

71. acute isosceles triangle

72. right scalene triangle

73. obtuse scalene triangle

74. 55°; obtuse scalene triangle

75. 76°; acute isosceles triangle

76. 24°; right scalene triangle

77. 95°; obtuse scalene triangle

78. 33°   79. 52°   80. 76°

Chapter 7

7.1 Start Thinking

1. 540°   2. 720°   3. 900°

7.1 Warm Up

1. 120   2. 70   3. 119

7.1 Cumulative Review Warm Up

1. $x = 1$ 2. $y = -1$

3. $y + 1 = \dfrac{2}{3}(x - 5)$ 4. $y - \dfrac{11}{2} = \dfrac{14}{5}(x + 1)$

7.1 Practice A

1. 900°   2. 19-gon

3. interior: 168°, exterior: 12°

4. 84   5. 125

6. $m\angle X = m\angle Y = 75°$

7. $m\angle X = m\angle Y = 135°$

8. 76   9. 88

10. 120°   11. 144 people

7.1 Practice B

1. 103   2. 68

3. $m\angle X = m\angle Y = 116°$

4. $m\angle X = m\angle Y = 130°$

5. 56   6. 55

7. interior: 165°, exterior: 15°

8. 20

9. 14; The sum of the interior angle measures of the polygon is $2(90°) + 3(180°) + 1440° = 2160°$.

So, the polygon has $\dfrac{2160°}{180°} + 2 = 14$ sides.

10. a. 720°   b. 135

7.1 Enrichment and Extension

1. 61°   2. 130°   3. 58°   4. 50°

5. 84°   6. 85°   7. 146°   8. 145°

9. regular decagon   10. 12 sides

11. You know that $a + b + c = 180°$, $d + e + f = 180°$, and $g + h + i = 180°$ because the sum of the interior angles of a triangle equals 180°. You can add those three equations to obtain $a + b + c + d + e + f + g + h + i = 540°$. $m\angle YZV = f + i$, $m\angle ZVW = h$, $m\angle VWX = g + d + a$, $m\angle WXY = b$, and $m\angle XYZ = c + e$, so $m\angle YZV + m\angle ZVW + m\angle VWX + m\angle WXY + m\angle XYZ = 540°$.

7.1 Puzzle Time

THEY DIDN'T WANT TO WAIT FORTY YEARS FOR A TRAIN

7.2 Start Thinking

yes; *Sample answer*: The scout could use the Pythagorean Theorem to determine the distance that should be between opposite corner posts, the length of the hypotenuse. It should be approximately 15 feet $7\frac{7}{16}$ inches. Or, the scout could make sure that the distances between the two pairs of opposite corners are the same and not be concerned about the exact measure. This method uses the SSS Congruence Theorem (Thm. 5.8).

7.2 Warm Up

1.

STATEMENTS	REASONS
1. $\overline{MN} \cong \overline{PO}$, $\overline{NO} \cong \overline{MP}$	1. Given
2. $\overline{NP} \cong \overline{NP}$	2. Reflexive Property of Segment Congruence (Thm. 2.1)
3. $\triangle PMN \cong \triangle NOP$	3. SSS Congruence Theorem (Thm. 5.8)

Answers

2.

STATEMENTS	REASONS
1. $\overline{AB} \cong \overline{CD}$, $\overline{AB} \perp \overline{BD}$, $\overline{CD} \perp \overline{BD}$	1. Given
2. $\overline{BD} \cong \overline{BD}$	2. Reflexive Property of Segment Congruence (Thm. 2.1)
3. $\angle ABD$ and $\angle CDB$ are right angles.	3. Perpendicular lines form right angles.
4. $\angle ABD \cong \angle CDB$	4. Right Angles Congruence Theorem (Thm. 2.3)
5. $\triangle ABD \cong \triangle CDB$	5. SAS Congruence Theorem (Thm. 5.5)
6. $\overline{AD} \cong \overline{BC}$	6. Corresponding parts of congruent triangles are congruent.

7.2 Cumulative Review Warm Up

1. $x = -\dfrac{13}{2}$;

$2x - 8 = 5 + 4x$	Write the equation.
$-8 = 5 + 2x$	Subtraction Property of Equality
$-13 = 2x$	Subtraction Property of Equality
$-\dfrac{13}{2} = x$	Division Property of Equality

2. $x = 14$;

$\dfrac{1}{2}(3x + 8) = 2x - 3$	Write the equation.
$\dfrac{3}{2}x + 4 = 2x - 3$	Distributive Property
$4 = \dfrac{1}{2}x - 3$	Subtraction Property of Equality
$7 = \dfrac{1}{2}x$	Addition Property of Equality
$14 = x$	Multiplication Property of Equality

3. $x = 1$;

$\dfrac{11 - x}{5} = 9 - 7x$	Write the equation.
$11 - x = 5(9 - 7x)$	Multiplication Property of Equality
$11 - x = 45 - 35x$	Distributive Property
$11 + 34x = 45$	Addition Property of Equality
$34x = 34$	Subtraction Property of Equality
$x = 1$	Division Property of Equality

7.2 Practice A

1. $x = 14, y = 40$ **2.** $a = 10, b = 37$

3. $u = 62, v = 59$ **4.** $s = 9, t = 14$

5. $(2, 1)$ **6.** $C(2, 0)$ **7.** $B(1, 1)$

8. Two angles are $50°$, and two angles are $130°$.

9. no; The side lengths of the parallelograms may not be congruent.

10.

STATEMENTS	REASONS
1. $PQRS$ is a parallelogram.	1. Given
2. $\overline{PQ} \cong \overline{SR}$	2. Parallelogram Opposite Sides Theorem (Thm. 7.3)
3. $\overline{QT} \cong \overline{TS}$	3. Parallelogram Diagonals Theorem (Thm. 7.6)
4. $\overline{PT} \cong \overline{TR}$	4. Parallelogram Diagonals Theorem (Thm. 7.6)
5. $\triangle PQT \cong \triangle RST$	5. SSS Congruence Theorem (Thm. 5.8)

Answers

1. $x = 11, y = 8$

2. $u = 66, v = 38$

3. $a = 7, b = 42$

4. $c = 15, d = 48$

5. $(0, 4)$

6. $C(2, -2)$

7.

STATEMENTS	REASONS
1. *CEHF* is a parallelogram.	**1.** Given
2. $\overline{CE} \cong \overline{FH}$	**2.** Parallelogram Opposite Sides Theorem (Thm. 7.3)
3. $CE = FH$	**3.** Definition of segment congruence
4. *D* bisects $\overline{CE}$. *G* bisects $\overline{FH}$.	**4.** Given
5. $CD = \frac{1}{2}CE$ $GH = \frac{1}{2}FH$	**5.** Definition of segment bisector
6. $CD = GH$	**6.** Substitution
7. $\overline{CD} \cong \overline{GH}$	**7.** Definition of segment congruence
8. $\overline{CF} \cong \overline{EH}$	**8.** Parallelogram Opposite Sides Theorem (Thm. 7.3)
9. $\angle C \cong \angle H$	**9.** Parallelogram Opposite Angles Theorem (Thm. 7.4)
10. $\triangle CDF \cong \triangle HGE$	**10.** SAS Congruence Theorem (Thm. 5.5)

8. a. always; Parallelogram Opposite Sides Theorem (Thm. 7.3)

  b. sometimes; when the parallelogram is a square

  c. sometimes; when the parallelogram is a square

  d. always; Parallelogram Opposite Angles Theorem (Thm. 7.4)

  e. sometimes; when the parallelogram is a square

  f. never; The angles are supplementary by the Consecutive Interior Angles Theorem (Thm. 3.4).

7.2 Enrichment and Extension

1. $(-9, -7)$, $(5, -7)$, $(-1, 5)$

2. $(2, -2)$, $(-4, 6)$, $(8, 4)$

3. $(a + 2, b + 3)$, $(a + 6, b + 3)$, $(a - 2, b - 3)$

4. (a, b^2), $(a, 2b - b^2)$, $(2a^2 - a, b^2)$

5.

Number of sides (n)	Number of diagonals (d)
3	0
4	2
5	5
6	9
7	14

6. $\dfrac{n(n - 3)}{2}$ **7.** 35; 65   **8.** 21 sides

9. a. *Sample answer:*

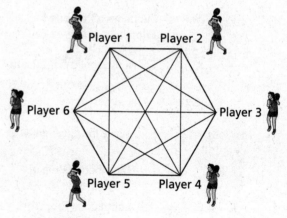

  b. 15 total games

  c. $n + \dfrac{n(n - 3)}{2} = \dfrac{n(n - 1)}{2}$

7.2 Puzzle Time

ON THE BEACH

7.3 Start Thinking

1. no; *Sample answer:* $\overline{AB} \cong \overline{BC} \cong \overline{CD}$

Answers

2. no; *Sample answer:* $\angle E$ or $\angle H$ is a right angle.

3. no; *Sample answer:* $\angle X \cong \angle Z$

7.3 Warm Up

1. $\dfrac{4}{3}$

2. $\sqrt{34}$

3. 2

4. $\sqrt{45} = 3\sqrt{5}$

5. $-\dfrac{3}{5}$

6. 5

7.3 Cumulative Review Warm Up

1. original: If a triangle is right, then it contains two acute angles; converse: If a triangle contains two acute angles, then it is a right triangle; inverse: If a triangle is not right, then it does not contain two acute angles; contrapositive: If a triangle does not contain two acute angles, then it is not a right triangle; The original and contrapositive are true. The converse and inverse are false.

2. original: If two lines have the same slope, then they are parallel; converse: If two lines are parallel, then they have the same slope; inverse: If two lines do not have the same slope, then they are not parallel; contrapositive: If two lines are not parallel, then they do not have the same slope; All statements are true.

3. original: If there is ice on the road, then I will not go shopping; converse: If I do not go shopping, then there is ice on the road; inverse: If there is not ice on the road, then I will go shopping; contrapositive: If I go shopping, then there is not ice on the road; The original and contrapositive are true. The converse and inverse are false.

7.3 Practice A

1. Parallelogram Opposite Angles Converse Theorem (Thm. 7.8)

2. Parallelogram Diagonals Converse Theorem (Thm. 7.10)

3. 12

4. 4

5.

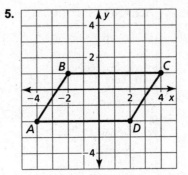

Because $BC = AD = 6$, $\overline{BC} \cong \overline{AD}$. Because both $\overline{BC}$ and $\overline{AD}$ are horizontal line segments, their slope is 0, and they are parallel. $\overline{BC}$ and $\overline{AD}$ are opposite sides that are both congruent and parallel. So, $ABCD$ is a parallelogram by the Opposite Sides Parallel and Congruent Theorem (Thm. 7.9).

6.

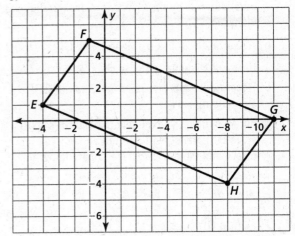

Because $EF = GH = 5$ and $EH = FG = 13$, $\overline{EF} \cong \overline{GH}$ and $\overline{EH} \cong \overline{FG}$. Because both pairs of opposite sides are congruent, quadrilateral $EFGH$ is a parallelogram by the Parallelogram Opposite Sides Converse (Thm. 7.7).

Answers

7. STATEMENTS	REASONS
1. $\angle A \cong \angle ABE$	1. Given
2. $\overline{AE} \cong \overline{BE}$	2. Base Angles Theorem (Thm. 5.6)
3. $\overline{AE} \cong \overline{CD}$	3. Given
4. $\overline{BE} \cong \overline{CD}$	4. Transitive Property of Segment Congruence Theorem (Thm. 2.1)
5. $\overline{BC} \cong \overline{DE}$	5. Given
6. $BCDE$ is a parallelogram.	6. Parallelogram Opposite Sides Converse Theorem (Thm. 7.7)

8. **a.** Because $\overline{AB} \parallel \overline{CD}$ and $\overline{AB} \cong \overline{CD}$, $ABDE$ is a parallelogram by the Opposite Sides Parallel and Congruent Theorem (Thm. 7.9).

  b. Because $ABDC$ is a parallelogram, $\overline{CE} \parallel \overline{DF}$. From the diagram, you can see that $\overline{CD} \parallel \overline{EF}$. Because the opposite sides are parallel, $CDFE$ is a parallelogram.

  c. no; You are only given that one pair of opposite sides are parallel, which is not enough information to prove that it is a parallelogram.

  d. $m\angle ACD = 35°$, $m\angle DCE = 145°$, $m\angle CEF = 35°$, $m\angle EFD = 145°$

7.3 Practice B

1. Opposite Sides Parallel and Congruent Theorem (Thm. 7.9)

2. Parallelogram Opposite Sides Converse Theorem (Thm. 7.7)

3. 11   4. 35

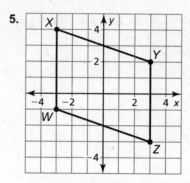

Because $WX = YZ = 5$, $\overline{WX} \cong \overline{YZ}$. Because both $\overline{WX}$ and $\overline{YZ}$ are vertical line segments, their slope is undefined, and they are parallel. $\overline{XW}$ and $\overline{YZ}$ are opposite sides that are both congruent and parallel. So, $WXYZ$ is a parallelogram by the Opposite Sides Parallel and Congruent Theorem (Thm. 7.9).

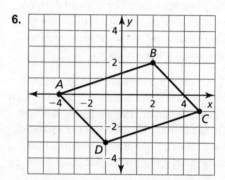

Because $AD = BC = \sqrt{18}$ and $AB = CD = \sqrt{40}$, $\overline{AD} \cong \overline{BC}$ and $\overline{AB} \cong \overline{CD}$. Because both pairs of opposite sides are congruent, quadrilateral $ABCD$ is a parallelogram by the Parallelogram Opposite Sides Converse (Thm. 7.7).

Answers

7.

STATEMENTS	REASONS
1. $\angle A \cong \angle FDE$	1. Given
2. $\overline{AB} \parallel \overline{CD}$	2. Alternate Interior Angles Converse (Thm. 3.6)
3. $\angle AFB \cong \angle DFE$	3. Vertical Angles Congruence Theorem (Thm. 2.6)
4. F is the midpoint of $\overline{AD}$.	4. Given
5. $\overline{AF} \cong \overline{DF}$	5. Definition of midpoint
6. $\triangle ABF \cong \triangle DEF$	6. ASA Congruence Theorem (Thm. 5.10)
7. $\overline{AB} \cong \overline{ED}$	7. Corresponding sides of congruent triangles are congruent.
8. D is the midpoint of $\overline{CE}$.	8. Given
9. $\overline{ED} \cong \overline{CD}$	9. Definition of midpoint
10. $\overline{AB} \cong \overline{CD}$	10. Transitive Property of Segment Congruence (Thm. 2.1)
11. $ABCD$ is a parallelogram.	11. Opposite Sides Parallel and Congruent Theorem (Thm. 7.9)

8. no; You cannot determine if a quadrilateral is a parallelogram by only knowing the values of the angles. You must also know the orientation of the angles, and whether the congruent angles are opposite of each other.

9. a. $m\angle FCG = 135°$, $m\angle BCF = 45°$, $m\angle D = 135°$

b. Parallelogram Opposite Angles Converse Theorem (Thm. 7.8)

c. $8x$

7.3 Enrichment and Extension

1. yes **2.** yes **3.** no **4.** no

5. no **6.** yes **7.** yes **8.** yes

9. $\dfrac{1}{11}$ **10.** $G(-4, 1)$, $H(1, 3)$

11. yes; It is given that $PQRS$ and $QTSU$ are parallelograms. Because the diagonals of a parallelogram bisect each other, $PX = RX$ and $TX = UX$. Because $\overline{PR}$ and $\overline{TU}$ are diagonals of $PTRU$ that bisect each other, $PTRU$ is a parallelogram.

12. You would need to show that one angle is supplementary to each consecutive angle.

7.3 Puzzle Time

FRIENDSHIP

7.4 Start Thinking

Sample answer: For both the square and the rhombus: The diagonals bisect each other, the diagonals form right angles, the diagonals form congruent triangles, and the opposite angles are congruent. For the square only: The diagonals are congruent.

7.4 Warm Up

1. $51°$ **2.** $39°$ **3.** $90°$

4. $33°$ **5.** $33°$ **6.** $22°$

7.4 Cumulative Review Warm Up

1. sometimes; An isosceles triangle could also be an acute or an obtuse triangle.

2. sometimes; A right triangle could also be an isosceles triangle.

3. always; An equilateral triangle will always have three 60° angles.

4. never; A right triangle always has one side that is the longest, so it cannot be equilateral.

7.4 Practice A

1. $90°$ **2.** $23°$ **3.** $67°$ **4.** 5

5. 12 **6.** 19 **7.** 22

8. rectangle; The sides are perpendicular and not congruent.

9. rectangle, rhombus, square; The diagonals are congruent and perpendicular.

Answers

10.

STATEMENTS	REASONS
1. *PSUR* is a rectangle.	1. Given
2. $m\angle U = 90°$ $m\angle P = 90°$	2. Definition of a rectangle
3. $\angle U \cong \angle P$	3. Transitive Property of Angle Congruence (Thm. 2.2)
4. $\overline{PS} \cong \overline{RU}$	4. Definition of a rectangle
5. $\overline{PQ} \cong \overline{TU}$	5. Given
6. $\triangle PQS \cong \triangle UTR$	6. SAS Congruence Theorem (Thm. 5.5)
7. $\overline{QS} \cong \overline{RT}$	7. Corresponding parts of congruent triangles are congruent.

11. a. It is a rectangle; By definition, all four angles are right angles.

b. It is a rhombus; By definition, all four sides are congruent.

c. It is a square; By definition, all four sides are congruent and all four angles are right angles.

d. 90°

e. 45°

7.4 Practice B

1. rhombus; It has four congruent sides, but it does not have four right angles.

2. square, rectangle, rhombus; Any square is also a rectangle and a rhombus.

3. 90°   **4.** 37°   **5.** 53°

6. 16   **7.** 24   **8.** $(2, 5)$

9.

STATEMENTS	REASONS
1. $\angle XWY \cong \angle XYW$	1. Given
2. $\overline{XW} \cong \overline{XY}$	2. Converse of the Base Angles Theorem (Thm. 5.7)
3. *WXYZ* is a parallelogram.	3. Given
4. $\overline{XY} \cong \overline{WZ}$ $\overline{WX} \cong \overline{YZ}$	4. Definition of a parallelogram
5. $\overline{WX} \cong \overline{XY} \cong$ $\overline{YZ} \cong \overline{WZ}$	5. Transitive Property of Segment Congruence (Thm. 2.1)
6. *WXYZ* is a rhombus.	6. Definition of a rhombus

10. no, Because a similarity transformation maintains the shape of an object, the corresponding angles remain congruent. A rhombus may not have all right angles, but a square always will.

11. yes; The quadrilateral is a rectangle or square, which are both parallelograms.

12. no; Because the quadrilateral is not a rectangle, the other two angles are not 90°. So, the opposite angles are not congruent and the quadrilateral is not a parallelogram by the contrapositive of the Parallelogram Opposite Angles Theorem (Thm. 7.4).

13. yes; If the rectangle is a square, the side lengths of the triangle will be congruent. So, the triangles will be isosceles.

7.4 Enrichment and Extension

1. no; *Sample answer:* If the diagonals of a parallelogram are congruent, then it would have to be a rectangle and have a right angle.

2. yes; *Sample answer:* If there are congruent diagonals in a parallelogram, it can be a rectangle or square with two opposite sides 2 centimeters long.

3. no; *Sample answer:* In a parallelogram, consecutive angles must be supplementary, so all angles must be right. This would make it a rectangle.

Answers

4. 9   **5.** $10\sqrt{2}$ **6.** $40\sqrt{2}$

7. $\dfrac{5\sqrt{2}}{7}$ **8.** 16°

9. *Sample answer:* Let parallelogram $DFGH$ have vertices $D\left(a, \sqrt{b^2 - a^2}\right)$, $F(b, 0)$,

$G\left(-a, -\sqrt{b^2 - a^2}\right)$, and $H(-b, 0)$, respectively.

The slope of both $\overline{HG}$ and $\overline{DF}$ is $\dfrac{\sqrt{b^2 - a^2}}{a - b}$, and

the slope of both $\overline{HD}$ and $\overline{GF}$ is $\dfrac{\sqrt{b^2 - a^2}}{a + b}$. The

products of the slopes of the pairs $\overline{HG}$ and $\overline{GF}$, $\overline{GF}$ and $\overline{DF}$, $\overline{DF}$ and $\overline{HD}$, and $\overline{HD}$ and $\overline{HG}$ are all equal to -1, making each pair of consecutive segments perpendicular and each angle a right angle. So, parallelogram $DFGH$ is a rectangle.

7.4 Puzzle Time

ALL THE ANGLES

7.5 Start Thinking

Sample answer: $\overline{BD}$ is a perpendicular bisector of $\overline{AC}$. $\overline{AB} \cong \overline{BC}$, $\overline{AD} \cong \overline{CD}$, $\angle BAD \cong \angle BCD$, and $m\angle ABC > m\angle ADC$.

7.5 Warm Up

1. 120°   **2.** 60°   **3.** 90°

4. 45°   **5.** 135°   **6.** 109°

7.5 Cumulative Review Warm Up

1. $x = 4, y = 5.5$ **2.** $x = 24, y = 10$

3. $x = 9, y = \sqrt{370}$

7.5 Practice A

1. 86   **2.** 70   **3.** 6   **4.** 6

5. isosceles trapezoid; $WXYZ$ has exactly one pair of parallel sides and one pair of congruent base angles.

6. kite; $WXYZ$ has two pairs of consecutive congruent sides, but opposite sides are not congruent.

7. The quadrilateral is not a kite. Because the opposite sides are congruent, the quadrilateral is a rhombus.

8.

STATEMENTS	REASONS
1. $ABCD$ is a parallelogram	**1.** Given
2. $\overline{AB} \parallel \overline{DC}$	**2.** Definition of a parallelogram
3. $\overline{AE} \cong \overline{AD}$	**3.** Given
4. $\angle E \cong \angle ADE$	**4.** Base Angles Theorem (Thm. 5.6)
5. $\angle ADE \cong \angle C$	**5.** Definition of a parallelogram
6. $\angle E \cong \angle C$	**6.** Transitive Property of Angle Congruence (Thm. 2.2)
7. $ABCE$ is an isosceles trapezoid.	**7.** Isosceles Trapezoid Base Angles Converse (Thm. 7.15)

9. a. 90°

    b. 22 in.

    c. $\angle XWZ$

7.5 Practice B

1. Slope of $\overline{TU}$ = slope of $\overline{VW}$ and slope of $\overline{UV} \neq$ slope of $\overline{TW}$; $\overline{TW} \cong \overline{UV}$, so $TUVW$ is an isosceles trapezoid.

2. Slope of $\overline{QR}$ = slope of $\overline{PS}$ and slope of $\overline{PQ} \neq$ slope of $\overline{RS}$; $\overline{PQ} \not\cong \overline{RS}$, so $PQRS$ is not an isosceles trapezoid.

3. 17   **4.** 61

5. rhombus; $ABCD$ is a quadrilateral with four congruent sides.

6. kite; $DEFG$ is a quadrilateral with two pairs of consecutive congruent sides, but opposite sides are not congruent.

Answers

7.

STATEMENTS	REASONS
1. *VXYZ* is a kite.	1. Given
2. $\angle VXY \cong \angle VZY$	2. Kite Opposite Angles Theorem (Thm. 7.19)
3. $\angle WXV \cong \angle UZV$	3. Congruent Supplements Theorem (Thm. 2.4)
4. $\overline{VX} \cong \overline{VZ}$	4. Definition of a kite
5. $\overline{WX} \cong \overline{UZ}$	5. Given
6. $\triangle WXV \cong \triangle UZV$	6. SAS Congruence Theorem (Thm. 5.5)

8. $(6, 0)$

9. no; A kite is a quadrilateral and by definition it is a convex polygon.

10. a. The opposite sides are parallel, and all angles are right angles; $A = ac$

b. $A = \dfrac{bc - ac}{4}$

c. $2\left(\dfrac{bc - ac}{4}\right) + ac = \dfrac{bc + ac}{2}$

7.5 Enrichment and Extension

1. about 56.6 in.; about 418.3 in.

2. $a = 9$

3. $AD = 7.08$ in., $AB = CD = 5.08$ in., $BC = 10.16$ in.

4. $(a + 3, 3b)$ **5.** $(a + c, b + c)$

6. $(x + y, y + z)$

7. any point of the form (a, a), where a is a real number, $a > 3.5$, and $a \neq 7$

7.5 Puzzle Time

INCORRECTLY

Cumulative Review

1. $x = 5$ **2.** $x = -16$ **3.** $x = -5$

4. $x = 0$ **5.** $x = 15$ **6.** $x = -8$

7. $x = 16$ **8.** $x = -1$

9. $x = -2$ **10.** $x = 10$

11. $x = 8$ **12.** $x = 2$

13. $x = -3$ **14.** $x = 3$

15. $x = 4$ **16.** $x = -2$

17. equilateral triangle   **18.** rectangle

19. rhombus   **20.** parallelogram

21. right triangle   **22.** square

23. a. $x = 9$

b. 11 units

24. a. $P = 2(3x + 4) + 2(2x + 7)$

b. 4

c. length $= 16$ units, width $= 15$ units

25. dilation   **26.** rotation

27. reflection   **28.** translation

29. rotation   **30.** dilation

31. $A'(-1, 2)$ **32.** $B'(11, 3)$

33. $C'(6, -11)$ **34.** $A'(4, 0)$

35. $B'(-16, 2)$ **36.** $C(2, 5)$

37. $D(7, 5)$ **38.** $139°$

39. $105°$ **40.** $115°$

41. $143°$ **42.** $x = 3, y = 9$

43. $x = 5, y = 2$

44. a. 8 **b.** $48°$ **c.** $42°$

45. a. 4 **b.** $17°$ **c.** $73°$

46. $\angle DGF$ **47.** $\angle EFG$ **48.** $\angle GDF$

Answers

49. $\angle FED$ **50.** $\angle FDE$ **51.** $\angle DFE$

52. $\angle EDG$ **53.** $\angle DFG$

54. 11.4; Perpendicular Bisector Theorem (Thm. 6.1)

55. 1.9; Converse of the Perpendicular Bisector Theorem (Thm. 6.2)

56. 36; Converse of the Perpendicular Bisector Theorem (Thm. 6.2)

57. 22; Perpendicular Bisector Theorem (Thm. 6.1)

58. a. 3   **b.** 36 units   **c.** 72 units

Chapter 8

8.1 Start Thinking

Sample answer: The three diagrams are the same image, but stretched or shrunk into different sizes or forms; The first resizing is not "similar" to the original in a geometric sense. The proportions of the map were not maintained. The second resizing is "similar" to the original in a geometric sense. It appears to be a dilation of the original in a geometric sense. It appears to be a dilation of the original by a factor less than one and maintains proportionally with the original.

8.1 Warm Up

1. $x = \dfrac{3}{2}$ **2.** $x = 20$

3. $x = \pm 3$ **4.** $x = -\dfrac{9}{5}$

5. $x = \dfrac{64}{7}$ **6.** $x = -\dfrac{3}{2}, x = 4$

8.1 Cumulative Review Warm Up

1. 120°   **2.** 60°   **3.** 60°

4. 60°   **5.** 75°   **6.** 45°

8.1 Practice A

1. 3; $\angle L \cong \angle Q$, $\angle M \cong \angle R$, $\angle N \cong \angle S$,

$$\dfrac{LM}{QR} = \dfrac{MN}{RS} = \dfrac{NL}{SQ}$$

2. $\dfrac{2}{5}$; $\angle A \cong \angle E$, $\angle B \cong \angle F$, $\angle C \cong \angle G$,

$\angle D \cong \angle H$, $\dfrac{AB}{EF} = \dfrac{BC}{FG} = \dfrac{CD}{GH} = \dfrac{DA}{HE}$

3. 3   **4.** 22.5   **5.** 3   **6.** 67°

7. 12   **8.** 60; 540   **9.** 9

10. 13, 39; By the SAS Congruence Theorem (Thm. 5.5), $\triangle ADC \cong \triangle BDC$ and $\triangle XWZ \cong \triangle YWZ$. Because corresponding parts of congruent triangles are congruent, $BC = 13$ and $YZ = 39$.

11. 3   **12.** 336 ft^2

8.1 Practice B

1. $\dfrac{3}{4}$; $\angle A \cong \angle H$, $\angle B \cong \angle I$, $\angle C \cong \angle J$,

$$\dfrac{AB}{HI} = \dfrac{BC}{IJ} = \dfrac{CA}{JH}$$

2. $\dfrac{3}{2}$; $\angle W \cong \angle S$, $\angle X \cong \angle T$, $\angle Y \cong \angle U$,

$\angle Z \cong \angle V$, $\dfrac{WX}{ST} = \dfrac{XY}{TU} = \dfrac{YZ}{UV} = \dfrac{ZW}{VS}$

3. 6   **4.** 9   **5.** 7 in.   **6.** 11 ft

7. a. $\dfrac{7}{4}$

   b. 7.5

   c. 108°

   d. about 74.2 units

   e. about 219.73 square units

   f. yes; Because corresponding angles of similar triangles are congruent, $\angle ABC \cong \angle D$. By the corresponding Angles Converse Theorem (Thm. 3.5), $\overline{BC} \parallel \overline{DE}$.

8.1 Enrichment and Extension

1. *Sample answer*:

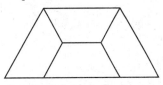

2. *Sample answer*:

Answers

3. *Sample answer:*

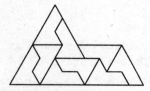

8.1 Puzzle Time

HEY I THINK I AM COMING DOWN WITH SOMETHING

8.2 Start Thinking

Sample answer: If the $m\angle A = 30°$, you can conclude that $m\angle D = 60°$ because $\triangle ADG$ is a right triangle. The parallel lines in the diagram are cut by two transversals creating congruent corresponding angles. $\angle A \cong \angle EBG \cong \angle FCG$, so they all have a measure of 30°. In a similar way, you can conclude that $\angle D \cong \angle BEG \cong \angle CFG$, so they all have a measure of 60°.

8.2 Warm Up

1. 56   **2.** 19   **3.** 122   **4.** 90

8.2 Cumulative Review Warm Up

1. 9   **2.** 7   **3.** 3.5

4. 14.6   **5.** 132°   **6.** 48°

8.2 Practice A

1. yes; $\triangle ABC \sim \triangle MLN$; $\angle A \cong \angle M$, $\angle B \cong \angle L$, and $\angle C \cong \angle N$, so $\triangle ABC \sim \triangle MLN$.

2. no; $m\angle F = 66°$ and $m\angle R = 95°$

3. $\angle ADB \cong \angle E$ and $\angle A \cong \angle A$, so $\triangle ABD \sim \triangle ACE$.

4. $\angle WXZ \cong \angle ZXY$ and $\angle W \cong \angle XZY$, so $\triangle WXZ \sim \triangle ZXY$.

5. a. yes; Because $\triangle ABC \sim \triangle EDC$, $\angle BAC \cong \angle CED$. By the Alternate Interior Angles Converse Theorem (Thm. 3.6), $\overline{AB} \parallel \overline{DE}$.

   b. $\overline{BE} \parallel \overline{AD}$, so $\angle EBD \cong \angle BDA$ by the Alternate Interior Angles Theorem (Thm. 3.2). $\angle BCE \cong \angle DCA$ by the Vertical Angles Congruence Theorem (Thm. 2.6). So, $\triangle ACD \sim \triangle ECB$ by the AA Similarity Theorem (Thm. 8.3).

c. 50°

d. 12

e. 12; Because the diagonals are perpendicular, by the Rhombus Diagonals Theorem (Thm. 7.11), *ABED* is a rhombus. By definition, all sides are congruent. So, $AD = 12$.

6. no; $m\angle X = 45°$ and $m\angle C = 76°$

7. yes; $m\angle A = m\angle X = 90°$, and $m\angle B = m\angle C = m\angle Y = m\angle Z = 45°$

8.

STATEMENTS	REASONS
1. $\angle Q \cong \angle T$	1. Given
2. $\angle PRQ \cong \angle SRT$	2. Vertical Angles Congruence Theorem (Thm. 2.6)
3. $\triangle PQR \sim \triangle STR$	3. AA Similarity Theorem (Thm. 8.3)
4. $\angle P \cong \angle S$	4. Corresponding parts of similar triangles are similar.
5. $\overline{PQ} \parallel \overline{ST}$	5. Alternate Interior Angles Converse (Thm. 3.6)

8.2 Practice B

1. yes; $\triangle WXY \sim \triangle STR$; $\angle W \cong \angle S$, $\angle X \cong \angle T$, and $\angle Y \cong \angle R$, so $\triangle WXY \sim \triangle STR$.

2. no; $m\angle L = 32°$ and $m\angle JKM = 48°$

3. $\angle C \cong \angle FDE$ and $\angle E \cong \angle E$, so $\triangle ECG \sim \triangle EDF$.

4. $\angle X \cong \angle Z$ and $\angle XWY \cong \angle ZYW$, so $\triangle XWY \sim \triangle ZYW$.

5. yes; $m\angle A = m\angle X = 90°$ and $m\angle B = m\angle C = m\angle Y = m\angle Z = 45°$

6. no; $75° + 105° = 180°$

7. no; The corresponding angles may not be congruent to each other.

8. 550 ft

Answers

9. STATEMENTS	REASONS
1. $\angle ABC$ and $\angle BDC$ are right angles.	1. Given
2. $\angle ABC \cong \angle BDC$	2. Right Angles Congruence Theorem (Thm. 2.3)
3. $\angle C \cong \angle C$	3. Reflexive Property of Angle Congruence (Thm. 2.2)
4. $\triangle ABC \sim \triangle BDC$	4. AA Similarity Theorem (Thm. 8.3)
5. $\angle A \cong \angle CBD$	5. Corresponding angles of similar triangles are congruent.

10. STATEMENTS	REASONS
1. $\overline{YZ} \cong \overline{YV}$ $\overline{XY} \cong \overline{WY}$	1. Given
2. $\angle V \cong \angle Z$ $\angle W \cong \angle X$	2. Base Angles Theorem (Thm. 5.6)
3. $\angle XYW \cong \angle VYZ$	3. Vertical Angles Congruence Theorem (Thm. 2.6)
4. $m\angle X + m\angle W + m\angle XYW = 180°$ $m\angle V + m\angle Z + m\angle VYZ = 180°$	4. Triangle Sum Theorem (Thm. 5.1)
5. $m\angle X + m\angle W + m\angle XYW = m\angle V + m\angle Z + m\angle VYZ$	5. Transitive Property of Angle Congruence (Thm. 2.2)
6. $m\angle X + m\angle W + m\angle XYW = m\angle V + m\angle Z + m\angle XYW$	6. Substitution Property of Equality
7. $m\angle X + m\angle W = m\angle V + m\angle Z$	7. Subtraction Property of Equality
8. $m\angle X + m\angle X = m\angle Z + m\angle Z$	8. Substitution Property of Equality
9. $2m\angle X = 2m\angle Z$	9. Simplify.
10. $m\angle X = m\angle Z$	10. Division Property of Equality
11. $\triangle XYW \cong \triangle VYZ$	11. AA Similarity Theorem (Thm. 8.3)

8.2 Enrichment and Extension

1. $(6, 4), (6, -4)$ 2. $(0, 9), (0, -9)$

3. $\left(\dfrac{54}{13}, \dfrac{36}{13}\right), \left(\dfrac{54}{13}, -\dfrac{36}{13}\right)$ 4. $(0, 4), (0, -4)$

5. $(6, 9), (6, -9)$ 6. $\left(\dfrac{24}{13}, \dfrac{36}{13}\right), \left(\dfrac{24}{13}, -\dfrac{36}{13}\right)$

Answers

7. $\dfrac{4}{3}x$; *Sample answer*: Solve the proportion

$$\dfrac{a}{a + \dfrac{8}{3}x} = \dfrac{x}{3x} \text{ where } PS = a.$$

8.

STATEMENTS	REASONS
1. $\angle PQR$ is a right angle $\overline{QS}$ is the altitude of $\triangle PQR$ drawn from the right angle.	1. Given
2. $\overline{QS} \perp \overline{PR}$	2. Definition of altitude
3. $\angle PSQ$ and $\angle QSR$ are right angles.	3. Definition of perpendicular
4. $m\angle PSQ =$ $m\angle QSR =$ $m\angle PQR = 90°$	4. Definition of right angle
5. $\angle PSQ \cong$ $\angle PQR$	5. Definition of congruent angles
6. $\angle QSR \cong$ $\angle PQR$	6. Definition of congruent angles
7. $\angle P \cong \angle P$	7. Reflexive Property of Angle Congruence (Thm. 2.2)
8. $\angle R \cong \angle R$	8. Reflexive Property of Angle Congruence (Thm. 2.2)
9. $\triangle PSQ \sim \triangle PQR$	9. AA Similarity Theorem (Thm. 8.3)
10. $\triangle QSR \sim \triangle PQR$	10. AA Similarity Theorem (Thm. 8.3)
11. $\triangle PSQ \sim \triangle QSR$	11. Transitive Property of Congruency

9.

STATEMENTS	REASONS
1. $\overline{AC} \parallel \overline{GE}$ $\overline{BG} \parallel \overline{CF}$	1. Given
2. $\angle A \cong \angle E$ $\angle EDF \cong$ $\angle EHG$	2. Corresponding Angles Theorem (Thm. 3.1)
3. $\angle EHG \cong$ $\angle AHB$	3. Vertical Angle Congruence Theorem (Thm. 2.6)
4. $\angle EDF \cong$ $\angle AHB$	4. Transitive Property of Angle Congruence (Thm. 2.2)
5. $\triangle ABH \sim \triangle EFD$	5. AA Similarity Theorem (Thm. 8.3)

8.2 Puzzle Time

A TOWEL

8.3 Start Thinking

Sample answer: The four-inch block measurements are $x = 4\dfrac{1}{3}$ inches and $y = 3\dfrac{1}{3}$ inches. The five-inch block measurements are $x = 5\dfrac{5}{12}$ inches and $y = 4\dfrac{1}{6}$ inches.

8.3 Warm Up

1. $\triangle ABC \sim \triangle DEC$ or $\triangle ABC \sim \triangle GEF$

2. $\triangle FEG \sim \triangle CED$ or $\triangle FEG \sim \triangle CBA$

3. $m\angle ACB = 58°$ 4. $m\angle FEG = 32°$

5. $m\angle ACE = 122°$ 6. $\overline{AD} \parallel \overline{FG}$

8.3 Cumulative Review Warm Up

1. $y = \dfrac{1}{5}x - 3$ 2. $y = -\dfrac{1}{9}x + \dfrac{4}{9}$

3. $y = -\dfrac{3}{2}x + 1$ 4. $y = \dfrac{2}{5}x + \dfrac{19}{15}$

8.3 Practice A

1. $\triangle DEF$ 2. 4   3. 9

4. $\dfrac{15}{35} = \dfrac{21}{49} = \dfrac{18}{42} = \dfrac{3}{7}$

Answers

5. $\dfrac{AC}{BC} = \dfrac{EC}{DC}$ and $\angle C \cong \angle C$, so

$\triangle ACE \sim \triangle BCD$; SAS Similarity Theorem
(Thm. 8.5)

6. $\dfrac{18}{27} = \dfrac{14}{21} = \dfrac{10}{15}$, so $\triangle EFG \sim \triangle MNL$; SSS
Similarity Theorem (Thm. 8.4)

7. $\triangle VWZ \sim \triangle XYZ$ **8.** $m\angle VZY = 90°$

9. $m\angle VWY = 54°$ **10.** $m\angle WXY = 91.5°$

11. $XY = \sqrt{185} \approx 13.6$

12. no; The lengths of the legs are not proportional.

13.

STATEMENTS	REASONS
1. $\dfrac{PR}{QR} = \dfrac{TR}{SR}$	1. Given
2. $\angle R \cong \angle R$	2. Reflexive Property of Angle Congruence (Thm. 2.2)
3. $\triangle PRT \sim \triangle QRS$	3. SAS Similarity Theorem (Thm. 8.5)
4. $\angle RQS \cong \angle RPT$	4. Corresponding angles of similar triangles are congruent.
5. $\overline{QS} \parallel \overline{PT}$	5. Corresponding Angles Converse (Thm. 3.5)

8.3 Practice B

1. 8   **2.** 9

3. $\dfrac{15}{12} = \dfrac{30}{24} = \dfrac{25}{20} = \dfrac{5}{4}$

4. $\dfrac{15}{27} = \dfrac{35}{63}$ and $\angle X \cong \angle X$, so $\triangle WXY \sim \triangle VXZ$;
SAS Similarity Theorem (Thm. 8.5)

5. $\dfrac{10.5}{7} = \dfrac{18}{12} = \dfrac{12}{8}$, so $\triangle LMN \sim \triangle RQP$; SSS
Similarity Theorem (Thm. 8.4)

6. 15 units, 18 units

7. $x = 12, y = 16, z = 7$

8.

STATEMENTS	REASONS
1. $\dfrac{AC}{DF} = \dfrac{AB}{DE}$	1. Given
2. $m\angle A = 43°$ $m\angle D = 43°$	2. Given
3. $\angle A \cong \angle D$	3. Transitive Property of Angle Congruence (Thm.2.2)
4. $\triangle ABC \sim \triangle DEF$	4. SAS Similarity Theorem (Thm. 8.5)
5. $\angle B \cong \angle E$	5. Corresponding angles of similar triangles are congruent.

9.

STATEMENTS	REASONS
1. $LN = 2x$ $MN = 2y$ $NP = x$ $NQ = y$	1. Given
2. $\dfrac{LN}{NP} = \dfrac{2x}{x} = 2$ $\dfrac{MN}{NQ} = \dfrac{2y}{y} = 2$	2. Ratio of corresponding sides
3. $\dfrac{LN}{NP} = \dfrac{MN}{NQ}$	3. Transitive Property of Equality
4. $\angle LNM \cong \angle QNP$	4. Vertical Angles Congruence Theorem (Thm. 2.6)
5. $\triangle MLN \sim \triangle PQN$	5. SAS Similarity Theorem (Thm. 8.5)

8.3 Enrichment and Extension

1. a. $\dfrac{3}{2}$ **b.** $\dfrac{9}{4}$

2. 33°   **3.** about 15.4 ft   **4.** 26.7 ft

Answers

5.

STATEMENTS	REASONS
1. $\overline{AH} \parallel \overline{CF}$ $\overline{CA} \parallel \overline{FH}$	1. Given
2. $\angle AHC \cong \angle FCH$	2. Alternate Interior Angles Theorem (Thm. 3.2)
3. $\angle ACH \cong \angle FHC$	3. Alternate Interior Angles Theorem (Thm. 3.2)
4. $\angle DKC \cong \angle JKH$	4. Vertical Angles Congruence Theorem (Thm. 2.6)
5. $\triangle DKC \sim \triangle JKH$	5. AA Similarity Theorem (Thm. 8.3)
6. $\dfrac{DK}{JK} = \dfrac{KC}{KH} = \dfrac{DC}{JH}$	6. All sides of similar triangles are proportional.
7. $\angle CKB \cong \angle HKG$	7. Vertical Angles Congruence Theorem (Thm. 2.6)
8. $\triangle CKB \sim \triangle HKG$	8. AA Similarity Theorem (Thm. 8.3)
9. $\dfrac{CK}{HK} = \dfrac{KB}{KG} = \dfrac{CB}{HG}$	9. All sides of similar triangles are proportional.
10 $\dfrac{DK}{JK} = \dfrac{KB}{KG}$	10. Substitution
11. $\angle BKD \cong \angle GKJ$	11. Vertical Angles Congruence Theorem (Thm. 2.6)
12. $\triangle BKJ \sim \triangle GKD$	12. SAS Similarity Theorem (Thm. 8.5)

8.3 Puzzle Time

AN ECHO

8.4 Start Thinking

Sample answer:

$\angle ABE \cong \angle EBD \cong \angle BDC \cong \angle BCD$, $\overline{CB} \cong \overline{DB}$,

$\triangle ADC \sim \triangle AEB$, $\dfrac{AD}{AE} = \dfrac{DC}{EB}$,

$\dfrac{AD}{AE} = \dfrac{AC}{AB} \therefore \dfrac{AE + ED}{AE} = \dfrac{AB + BC}{AB} \therefore$

$1 + \dfrac{ED}{AE} = 1 + \dfrac{BC}{AB} \therefore \dfrac{ED}{AE} = \dfrac{BC}{AB}$;

By substituting *DB* for *BC*, you have $\dfrac{ED}{AE} = \dfrac{DB}{AB}$.

8.4 Warm Up

1. $x = -5$

2. $x = -\dfrac{9}{2}$

3. $x = 0, x = -15$

4. $x = -1, x = -5$

5. $x = 5, x = 2$

6. $x = 2, x = 6$

8.4 Cumulative Review Warm Up

1.

STATEMENTS	REASONS
1. $\overline{AC} \cong \overline{AB}$, $\overline{AD} \cong \overline{AE}$	1. Given
2. $\angle A \cong \angle A$	2. Reflexive Property of Angle Congruence (Thm. 2.2)
3. $\triangle ADB \cong \triangle AEC$	3. SAS Congruence Theorem (Thm. 5.5)

2.

STATEMENTS	REASONS
1. $\overline{MR} \perp \overline{KP}$, $\overline{KO} \perp \overline{PM}$	1. Given
2. $\angle RKM \cong \angle OMK$	2. Given
3. $\angle MRK$ and $\angle KOM$ are right triangles.	3. Definition of perpendicular
4. $\angle MRK \cong \angle KOM$	4. Right Angles Congruence Theorem (Thm. 2.3)
5. $\overline{KM} \cong \overline{KM}$	5. Reflexive Property of Segment Congruence (Thm. 2.1)
6. $\triangle RKM \cong \triangle OMK$	6. AAS Congruence Theorem (Thm. 5.11)

Answers

8.4 Practice A

1. 6 **2.** 12 **3.** no **4.** yes

5. 7.2 **6.** 2 **7.** 40 **8.** 9

9. 256 ft; If $\overline{BE} \parallel \overline{CF}$, then by the Three Parallel Lines Theorem (Thm. 8.8), $\dfrac{AB}{DE} = \dfrac{BC}{EF}$.

By substitution, $\dfrac{100}{80} = \dfrac{320}{EF}$ and $EF = 256$ feet.

8.4 Practice B

1. 37.5 **2.** 56

3. 45 **4.** $16\dfrac{2}{3}$

5. no; The Three Parallel Lines Theorem (Thm. 8.8) proves that the parallel lines divide the transversals proportionally, so you cannot use it to prove that three lines are parallel.

6. yes; Let x equal the length of PN. You are given enough information to write the equation $x + (2x - 9) = 45$ to solve for x; $LP = 27$, $PN = 18$.

7.

STATEMENTS	REASONS
1. $\overline{WY}$ bisects $\angle XYZ$. $\overline{YW}$ bisects $\angle XWZ$.	**1.** Given
2. $\angle XYV \cong \angle ZYV$ $\angle XWV \cong \angle ZWV$	**2.** Definition of angle bisector
3. $\dfrac{XV}{VZ} = \dfrac{XY}{YZ}$ $\dfrac{XV}{VZ} = \dfrac{XW}{WZ}$	**3.** Triangle Angle Bisector Theorem (Thm. 8.9)
4. $\dfrac{XY}{YZ} = \dfrac{XW}{WZ}$	**4.** Substitution
5. $\overline{YZ} \cong \overline{WZ}$	**5.** Given
6. $XY = WX$	**6.** Substitution
7. $WXYZ$ is a kite.	**7.** Definition of a kite

8.4 Enrichment and Extension

1. $a = 22.8125$, $b = 15.625$, $c = 15$, $d = 8.33$, $e = 4$, $f = 8$

2. $a = 9$, $b = 4$, $c = 3$, $d = 2$

3. 22.1 in

4. a. 4 **b.** 3 **c.** $52\dfrac{4}{9}$ units

5. Because $\overline{BE} \perp \overline{AC}$ and $\overline{HG} \parallel \overline{AC}$, then $\overline{HG} \perp \overline{BG}$ by the Perpendicular Transversal Theorem (Thm. 3.11). Then $\angle GHA \cong \angle CAF$ by the Corresponding Angles Theorem (Thm. 3.1). Because $\angle AFC$ is also a right angle, $\triangle AFC \sim \triangle HGB$ by the AA Similarity Theorem (Thm. 8.3). So, $\dfrac{AC}{FC} = \dfrac{BH}{GB}$. In $\triangle BHG$, $\overline{AE} \parallel \overline{HG}$, so, $\dfrac{AH}{GE} = \dfrac{BH}{GB}$. Using substitution, $\dfrac{AC}{FC} = \dfrac{AH}{GE}$. Because we are given $GE = FC$, it follows that $AC = AH$.

8.4 Puzzle Time

THE WHEELS BECAUSE THEY ARE ALWAYS TIRED

Cumulative Review

1. no **2.** yes **3.** yes **4.** no

5. no **6.** yes **7.** yes **8.** yes

9. no **10.** no **11.** no **12.** no

13. $x = \pm 6$ **14.** $x = \pm 12$

15. $x = \pm 3$ **16.** $x = \pm 4$

17. $x = \pm 8$ **18.** $x = \pm 7$

19. $x = \pm 11$ **20.** $x = \pm 6$

21. $x = \pm 13$ **22.** $x = \pm 5$

23. $x = \pm 8$ **24.** $x = \pm 7$

25. $x = \pm 3$ **26.** $x = \pm 8$

27. $x = \pm 9$ **28.** $M\left(-\dfrac{5}{2}, 2\right)$

Answers

29. $M\left(-\dfrac{9}{2}, -\dfrac{1}{2}\right)$ **30.** $M(9, -4)$

31. $M\left(5, \dfrac{9}{2}\right)$ **32.** $M(4, -1)$

33. $M\left(-\dfrac{1}{2}, -\dfrac{5}{2}\right)$ **34.** $M(9, 3)$

35. $M\left(\dfrac{11}{2}, \dfrac{7}{2}\right)$ **36.** $M\left(\dfrac{3}{2}, \dfrac{5}{2}\right)$

37. $M\left(-\dfrac{13}{2}, -\dfrac{5}{2}\right)$ **38.** $M\left(-\dfrac{5}{2}, \dfrac{17}{2}\right)$

39. $M(5, 1)$ **40.** $M\left(\dfrac{7}{2}, -6\right)$

41. $M\left(\dfrac{7}{2}, \dfrac{13}{2}\right)$ **42.** $M(-5, -3)$

43. $\sqrt{181}$ **44.** $\sqrt{218}$

45. $\sqrt{61}$ **46.** $\sqrt{505}$

47. $\sqrt{97}$ **48.** $\sqrt{149}$

49. $\sqrt{197}$ **50.** $\sqrt{365}$

51. $\sqrt{509}$ **52.** 5

53. $11\sqrt{5}$ **54.** $5\sqrt{17}$

55. $2\sqrt{29}$ **56.** $2\sqrt{85}$

57. $\sqrt{313}$ **58.** $\overline{XV}$

59. $\overline{YW}$ **60.** $\overline{YZ}$

61. $\overline{XZ}$ **62.** $\overline{ZV}, \overline{ZW}, \overline{ZX}, \overline{ZY}$

63. $\overline{ZW}$ and $\overline{ZY}$, or $\overline{ZV}$ and $\overline{ZX}$

64. *Sample answer:* $\overline{ZV}$ and $\overline{ZW}$

65. point M; 26   **66.** line s; 16

67. $\overline{Mk}$; 32   **68.** $\overline{Mm}$; 10

69. line s; 84   **70.** point M; 24

71. $\overline{Mm}$; 90   **72.** $\overline{Mk}$; 110

73. If $\overline{WZ} \cong \overline{XZ}$, then $\angle ZWX \cong \angle ZXW$; Base Angles Theorem (Thm. 5.6)

74. If $\overline{XZ} \cong \overline{XY}$, then $\angle XZY \cong \angle Y$; Base Angles Theorem (Thm. 5.6)

75. If $\angle V \cong \angle WZV$, then $\overline{WV} \cong \overline{WZ}$; Converse of Base Angles Theorem (Thm. 5.7)

76. If $\overline{ZV} \cong \overline{ZY}$, then $\angle V \cong \angle Y$; Base Angles Theorem (Thm. 5.6)

77. If $\angle ZWX \cong \angle ZXW$, then $\overline{ZW} \cong \overline{ZX}$; Converse of Base Angles Theorem (Thm. 5.7)

78. If $\angle XZY \cong \angle Y$, then $\overline{ZX} \cong \overline{YX}$; Converse of Base Angles Theorem (Thm. 5.7)

79. If $\angle V \cong \angle Y$, then $\overline{ZV} \cong \overline{ZY}$; Converse of Base Angles Theorem (Thm. 5.7)

80. 16   **81.** 9   **82.** 10   **83.** 13

84. 2   **85.** 5

86. $\overline{EF}, \overline{FG}, \overline{EG}$ **87.** $\overline{ST}, \overline{RS}, \overline{RT}$

Chapter 9

9.1 Start Thinking

$A = a^2 + b^2$

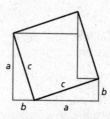

$A = c^2$; Because the area of the original diagram must equal the area of the reassembled diagram, $a^2 + b^2 = c^2$, which is a statement of the Pythagorean Theorem (Thm. 9.1). You have proved the theorem with your construction.

9.1 Warm Up

1. $x = \pm 5$ **2.** $x = \pm 2\sqrt{114}$

3. $x = \pm \dfrac{\sqrt{221}}{6}$ **4.** $x = \pm \sqrt{239}$

Answers

5. $x = \pm\sqrt{139}$ **6.** $x = \pm2\sqrt{62}$

9.1 Cumulative Review Warm Up

1. $P = 11 + \sqrt{61}$ units

2. $P = 10$ units

3. $P = 5 + 2\sqrt{13} + \sqrt{53}$ units

4. $P = 24$ units

9.1 Practice A

1. 5; yes   **2.** $7\sqrt{2}$; no

3. 21; yes   **4.** $\sqrt{133}$; no

5. $2\sqrt{13}$; no   **6.** 34; yes

7. no   **8.** yes

9. yes; right   **10.** yes; acute

11. yes; obtuse   **12.** yes; obtuse

13. 5630 ft

9.1 Practice B

1. $8\sqrt{3}$; no   **2.** 41; yes

3. $\sqrt{205}$; no   **4.** no

5. yes   **6.** yes; $36^2 + 15^2 = 39^2$

7. yes; right   **8.** yes; obtuse

9. yes; acute   **10.** yes; 6 ft $< x <$ 30 ft

11. a. $\sqrt{1152} \approx 33.94$ ft

    b. $\sqrt{288} \approx 16.97$ ft

9.1 Enrichment and Extension

1. $EF = 6, EC = 4, FC = 2\sqrt{5}$

2. $EF = x, EC = 10 - x, FC = \sqrt{x^2 - (10-x)^2}$,

    area of $\triangle EFC = \dfrac{(10 - x)\left(\sqrt{x^2 - (10-x)^2}\right)}{2}$

3. $k = -7, k = -1, k = 8,$ and $k = 23$

4. a. no; *Sample answer:* Let $a = 3, b = 4,$ and $c = 5$. So, $a + 1 = 4, b + 1 = 5,$ and $c + 1 = 6$. So, 3, 4, and 5 form a Pythagorean triple, but 4, 5, and 6 do not because $4^2 + 5^2 \neq 6^2$.

b. yes; *Sample answer:* If a, b, and c form a Pythagorean triple, $a^2 + b^2 = c^2$ is true. Multiply each side by 4 to get the equation $4a^2 + 4b^2 = 4c^2$. This is equivalent to $(2a)^2 + (2b)^2 = (2c)^2$. So by definition, $2a$, $2b$, and $2c$ also form a Pythagorean triple.

c. no; *Sample answer:* Let $a = 3, b = 4,$ and $c = 5$. So $a^2 = 9, b^2 = 16,$ and $c^2 = 25$. So, 3, 4, and 5 form a Pythagorean triple, but 9, 16, and 25 do not because $9^2 + 16^2 \neq 25^2$.

d. no; *Sample answer:* Let $a = 3, b = 4,$ and $c = 5$. So, $\sqrt{a} = \sqrt{3}, \sqrt{b} = 2,$ and $\sqrt{c} = \sqrt{5}$. So, 3, 4, and 5 form a Pythagorean triple, but $\sqrt{3}$, 2, and $\sqrt{5}$ do not because $\left(\sqrt{3}\right)^2 + 2^2 \neq \left(\sqrt{5}\right)^2$.

5. 3   **6.** $4\sqrt{29}$ in.   **7.** 44 beads

9.1 Puzzle Time

A SCREENSAVER

9.2 Start Thinking

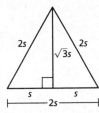

s, $2s$, and $\sqrt{3}s$; no; The side lengths cannot all be integer values that satisfy the equation $a^2 + b^2 = c^2$.

9.2 Warm Up

1. $x = 4\sqrt{2}$ **2.** $x = \dfrac{\sqrt{3}}{2}$

3. $x = 4\sqrt{7}$ **4.** $x = \dfrac{5\sqrt{6}}{3}$

5. $x = \dfrac{3\sqrt{3}}{2}$ **6.** $x = 4.2\sqrt{2} = \dfrac{21\sqrt{2}}{5}$

Answers

9.2 Cumulative Review Warm Up

1. $\dfrac{28}{5}$ 2. 7   3. $\dfrac{11}{5}$ 4. $\dfrac{5}{2}$

9.2 Practice A

1. 4   2. $3\sqrt{2}$ 3. $5\sqrt{2}$

4. $x = \sqrt{3}, y = 2$ 5. $x = 4, y = 8$

6. $x = 5\sqrt{3}, y = 5$ 7. 60.5 m^2

8. 173.2 yd^2 9. 6 ft; 8.5 ft; 10.4 ft

9.2 Practice B

1.

x	5	4	$\sqrt{2}$	$12\sqrt{2}$
y	$5\sqrt{2}$	$4\sqrt{2}$	2	24

2.

a	11	$3\sqrt{3}$	8	5
b	$11\sqrt{3}$	9	$8\sqrt{3}$	$5\sqrt{3}$
c	22	$6\sqrt{3}$	16	10

3. a. 30°-60°-90° triangle
   b. neither
   c. 45°-45°-90° triangle

4. $x = 4\sqrt{3}, y = 2\sqrt{3}$

5. $x = 12\sqrt{2}, y = 24$

6. $x = 8\sqrt{3}, y = 8, z = 8\sqrt{2}$

7. about 101.6 ft^2

9.2 Enrichment and Extension

1. $s = 13, v = 13, w = 13, x = 13, y = 20,$
   $z = 20 + 13\sqrt{3}$

2. about 4.3094 units   3. $7\sqrt{2}$

4. about 28.39 units

5. 4 points; $(1, 1), (1, -1), (-1, 1), (-1, -1)$

6. $VW \approx 2.54, VX \approx 9.80, WX \approx 9.46$

7. $BC = 0.5, CD \approx 1.73, BD \approx 1.80$

9.2 Puzzle Time

A TURTLE

9.3 Start Thinking

1. Both $\triangle ABC$ and $\triangle ACD$ contain $\angle A$, which is congruent to itself by the Reflexive Property of Congruence (Thm. 2.2). Both triangles contain a right angle, and all right angles are congruent. So, the two triangles are similar by the AA Similarity Theorem (Thm. 8.3).

2. Both $\triangle ABC$ and $\triangle CBD$ contain $\angle B$ which is congruent to itself by the Reflexive Property of Congruence (Thm. 2.2). Both triangles contain a right angle, and all right angles are congruent. So, the two triangles are similar by the AA Similarity Theorem (Thm. 8.3).

3. By the Transitive Property of Congruence, you can conclude that $\triangle ACD \sim \triangle CBD$.

9.3 Warm Up

1. $x = 10$ 2. $x = \dfrac{25}{7}$ 3. $x = \dfrac{22}{5}$ 4. $x = 6$

9.3 Cumulative Review Warm Up

1. $m\angle 1 = 32°, m\angle 2 = 148°$

2. $m\angle 1 = 95°, m\angle 2 = 85°$

3. $m\angle 1 = 67°, m\angle 2 = 113°$

9.3 Practice A

1. $\triangle KLM \sim \triangle JLK \sim \triangle JKM$

2. $\triangle YXU \sim \triangle ZXY \sim \triangle ZYU$

3. 4.8   4. about 14.5

5. about 7.1   6. 6

7. $2\sqrt{14}$ 8. $4\sqrt{15}$

9. 40   10. 3

11. 12   12. about 67.8 cm

9.3 Practice B

1. $\triangle CBD \sim \triangle ABC \sim \triangle ACD$

2. $\overline{CB}$

3. $CD = 8, AD = 10\dfrac{2}{3}, AC = 13\dfrac{1}{3}$

Answers

4. 24

5. $\sqrt{10}$

6. $x = \sqrt{15}$

7. $12\sqrt{2}$

8. 20

9. $2\sqrt{5}$

10. $w = 3$

11. $x = 6\sqrt{5}, y = 2\sqrt{55}, z = 3\sqrt{11}$

12. $x = 12\frac{1}{4}, y = 3\frac{3}{4}, z = \dfrac{7\sqrt{15}}{4}$

13. a. 48 in.

   b. 11.6 in.

   c. The support attaches about 3 inches from the top of the plywood; It divides the plywood into pieces measuring approximately 3 inches and 45 inches.

9.3 Enrichment and Extension

1. 16

2. $DC = 7, BD = \sqrt{35}, AB = 2\sqrt{15}$

3. a. 12

   b. 8.4

   c. yes; When you compute the harmonic mean using $4x$ and $12x$, you get an answer of $6x$.

4. $PR = 12.5; QS = 12$ **5.** $D(0,0)$

6. $D\left(-\dfrac{6}{5}, \dfrac{32}{5}\right)$ **7.** $\dfrac{\sqrt{5}}{5}$

9.3 Puzzle Time

BECAUSE HE WANTED TO TURN OVER A NEW LEAF

9.4 Start Thinking

Sample answer: $x_1 \approx 1\frac{1}{2}$ in., $y_1 \approx 2\frac{5}{8}$ in., $x_2 \approx 2$ in.,

$y_2 \approx 3\frac{1}{2}$ in., $x_3 \approx 2\frac{1}{2}$ in., $y_3 \approx 4\frac{3}{8}$ in.

1. $\dfrac{y_1}{x_1} = 1.75$ **2.** $\dfrac{y_2}{x_2} = 1.75$

3. $\dfrac{y_3}{x_3} = 1.75$

It appears that regardless of the size of the $30°$-$60°$-$90°$ triangle, the ratios of corresponding sides are equal or approximately equal.

9.4 Warm Up

1. $x_1 = \sqrt{161}, \dfrac{y_1}{x_1} = \dfrac{8\sqrt{161}}{161}$

2. $y_1 = 8, \dfrac{y_1}{x_1} = \dfrac{4}{3}$

3. $x_1 = \dfrac{\sqrt{115}}{2}, \dfrac{y_1}{x_1} = \dfrac{9\sqrt{115}}{115}$

9.4 Cumulative Review Warm Up

1.

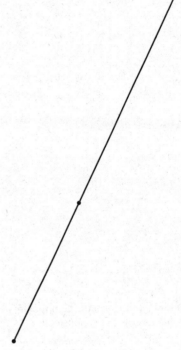

2.

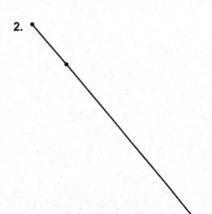

Answers

3.

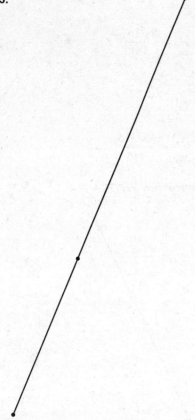

9.4 Practice A

1. $\tan S = \dfrac{5}{12} \approx 0.4167$, $\tan R = 2.4$

2. tangent ratio should be the ratio of the opposite side to the adjacent side, not the adjacent to the opposite; $\tan K = \dfrac{32}{24}$

3. 13.5   **4.** 8.2   **5.** 17.9

6. 64.0   **7.** 9   **8.** 1

9. 13 m

9.4 Practice B

1. $\tan J = \dfrac{7}{24} \approx 0.2917$, $\tan K = \dfrac{24}{7} \approx 3.4286$

2. $\tan D = 2\sqrt{2} \approx 2.8284$, $\tan E = \dfrac{\sqrt{2}}{4} \approx 0.3536$

3. *Sample answer:*

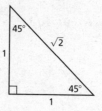

4. 22.5   **5.** 38.6

6. $x = 82$, $y \approx 154.2$ **7.** 64 ft

8. 12.0 units

9.4 Enrichment and Extension

1. $AB = BC = CD = DA = \sqrt{89}$,
$m\angle ABC = \angle ADC \approx 64°$,
$m\angle DAB = \angle BCD \approx 116°$; The diagonals of a rhombus bisect each other and intersect at a right angle to form four congruent right triangles. The Pythagorean Theorem (Thm. 9.1) is used to find the side lengths, and the tangent ratio is used to compute the measures of the angles of the rhombus.

2. $\tan x° = \dfrac{a}{b}$; $\tan(90° - x°) = \dfrac{b}{a}$

3. They are reciprocals of each other.

4. The relationship will be true in all cases except when $x = 90°$ or $x = 0°$; This is because $\tan 0° = 0$ and $\tan 90°$ are undefined.

5. 51.96 in.   **6.** 18.7

7. $\tan 30° = \dfrac{1}{\sqrt{3}}$ and $\tan 60° = \sqrt{3}$;
If $a° = b° = 30°$,
$\tan a° + \tan b° = \dfrac{1}{\sqrt{3}} + \dfrac{1}{\sqrt{3}} = \dfrac{2}{\sqrt{3}}$, but
$\tan(a° + b°) = \tan(30° + 30°) = \tan 60° = \sqrt{3}$.
So, $\tan a° + \tan b° \neq \tan(a° + b°)$.

8. 82.9°

9.4 Puzzle Time

A PEST TEST

Answers

9.5 Start Thinking

Sample answer: Because the hypotenuse of a right triangle is always the longest side, the sine and cosine ratios of an acute angle will always be less than one. Because the length of each leg is always greater than zero, the sine and cosine ratios of an acute angle will always be greater than zero. As the acute angle gets larger, the sine ratio will get closer to one, and the cosine ratio will get closer to zero.

9.5 Warm Up

1. about 24.4   **2.** about 17.8   **3.** about 3.9

9.5 Cumulative Review Warm Up

1. $(6, 3.5)$ **2.** $\left(-\dfrac{43}{16}, \dfrac{11}{32}\right)$

3. $(13.5, 17)$ **4.** $\left(\dfrac{57}{17}, -\dfrac{2}{17}\right)$

9.5 Practice A

1. $\sin J = \dfrac{12}{13} \approx 0.9231$, $\sin K = \dfrac{5}{13} \approx 0.3846$,

$\cos J = \dfrac{5}{13} \approx 0.3846$, $\cos K = \dfrac{12}{13} \approx 0.9231$

2. $\sin J = \dfrac{15}{17} \approx 0.8824$, $\sin K = \dfrac{8}{17} \approx 0.4706$,

$\cos J = \dfrac{8}{17} \approx 0.4706$, $\cos K = \dfrac{15}{17} \approx 0.8824$

3. $\cos 68°$ **4.** $\sin 34°$

5. $\sin 75°$ **6.** $\cos 53°$

7. $a \approx 14.7, b \approx 20.2$ **8.** $x \approx 18.3, y \approx 17.0$

9. $r \approx 124.5, s \approx 42.6$

10. B; Because $\sin A$ is the ratio of the length of the leg opposite $\angle A$ to the length of the hypotenuse, and the hypotenuse is the longest side of a right triangle, the value of $\sin A$ must be less than 1.

11. 629 ft

9.5 Practice B

1. $\sin R = \dfrac{24}{25} = 0.96$, $\sin S = \dfrac{7}{25} = 0.28$,

$\cos R = \dfrac{7}{25} = 0.28$, $\cos S = \dfrac{24}{25} = 0.96$

2. $\sin R = \dfrac{\sqrt{29}}{6} \approx 0.8975$, $\sin S = \dfrac{\sqrt{7}}{6} \approx 0.4410$,

$\cos R = \dfrac{\sqrt{7}}{6} \approx 0.4410$, $\cos S = \dfrac{\sqrt{29}}{6} \approx 0.8975$

3. $\cos 83°$ **4.** $\sin 59°$

5. $\dfrac{\sin 60°}{\cos 60°}$ **6.** $p \approx 11.3, q \approx 4.1$

7. $x \approx 35.6, y \approx 56.6$ **8.** $a \approx 9.1, b \approx 16.7$

9. 14 cm

10. a. 16.5 ft   **b.** 12 ft   **c.** 31 ft

9.5 Enrichment and Extension

1. $x = 2.999$

2. $w = 11.594$ cm, $x = 12.433$ cm, $y = 26.663$ cm, $z = 29.419$ cm

3. 270 units   **4.** 92.3 in.   **5.** $\sqrt{3} : 2$

6. $\left(\sin a°\right)^2 + \left(\cos a°\right)^2 = \left(\dfrac{x}{z}\right)^2 + \left(\dfrac{y}{z}\right)^2$

$= \dfrac{x^2 + y^2}{z^2} = \dfrac{z^2}{z^2} = 1$

7. 0.8

9.5 Puzzle Time

A TERMINAL ILLNESS

9.6 Start Thinking

1. 60°   **2.** 45°   **3.** 30°

4. 30°   **5.** 60°   **6.** 45°

9.6 Warm Up

1. $\sqrt{51}$; $\sin \theta = \dfrac{7}{10}$, $\cos \theta = \dfrac{\sqrt{51}}{10}$, $\tan \theta = \dfrac{7\sqrt{51}}{51}$

2. $\sqrt{709}$; $\sin \theta = \dfrac{22\sqrt{709}}{709}$, $\cos \theta = \dfrac{15\sqrt{709}}{709}$,

$\tan \theta = \dfrac{22}{15}$

3. $\dfrac{3\sqrt{29}}{2}$; $\sin \theta = \dfrac{10}{19}$, $\cos \theta = \dfrac{3\sqrt{29}}{19}$,

$\tan \theta = \dfrac{10\sqrt{29}}{87}$

Answers

9.6 Cumulative Review Warm Up

1. yes; You can prove $\triangle ABC \cong \triangle XYZ$ by the AAS Congruence Theorem (Thm. 5.11).

2. no; You cannot prove $\triangle ABC \cong \triangle XYZ$. However, you could prove that they are similar by the AA Similarity Theorem (Thm 8.3).

3. yes; You can prove $\triangle ABC \cong \triangle XYZ$. Because of the perpendicular segments, you know both triangles are right, so by the HL Congruence Theorem (Thm. 5.9), you can prove they are congruent.

9.6 Practice A

1. $\angle R$ **2.** $\angle R$ **3.** $\angle Q$

4. 39.8°   **5.** 83.1°   **6.** 65.4°

7. $m\angle P = 53°, QR \approx 17.6, PR \approx 13.2$

8. $m\angle D \approx 42.7°, DF \approx 20.6, m\angle E \approx 47.3°$

9. $m\angle A = 39°, BC \approx 11.3, AB \approx 18.0$

10. 499 ft   **11.** 27.4°

9.6 Practice B

1. $\angle W$ **2.** $\angle X$ **3.** 24.2°

4. 87.1°   **5.** 79.1°

6. $m\angle T = 66°, ST \approx 36.1, RT \approx 14.7$

7. $m\angle E \approx 41.4°, EF = 9, m\angle D \approx 48.6°$

8. $m\angle P \approx 17.7°, PQ \approx 21.9, m\angle R \approx 72.3°$

9. a. about 1039 ft

   b. about 1648 ft

   c. about 609 ft

10. a. about 0.1 mi

    b. about 0.8 mi

    c. about 7.1°

9.6 Enrichment and Extension

1. a. 28°

   b. 40°

   c. 112°

2. $\csc \theta = \dfrac{13}{5}$ **3.** $\sec \theta = \dfrac{13}{12}$ **4.** $\cot \theta = \dfrac{12}{5}$

5. 30°   **6.** 44.4°   **7.** 14.9°

8. 20.9°

9.6 Puzzle Time

MISTAKES

9.7 Start Thinking

1. 12   **2.** 12   **3.** 12

All three ratios are the same; *Sample answer:* yes

9.7 Warm Up

1. $a \approx 10.9$ **2.** $c \approx 23.3$ **3.** $b \approx 10.2$

4. $B \approx 57.8°$ **5.** $A \approx 67.8°$ **6.** $C \approx 49.5°$

9.7 Cumulative Review Warm Up

1. $m\angle X = 121°, m\angle Z = 121°$

2. $m\angle X = 112°, m\angle Z = 112°$

3. $m\angle X = 123°, m\angle Z = 143°$

9.7 Practice A

1. -0.4226 **2.** -11.4301 **3.** 0.5299

4. 22.8 m^2 **5.** 143.9 ft^2

6.

Law of Sines	Law of Cosines	Neither
AAS, ASA, SSA	SSS, SAS	AAA

7. $m\angle B = 105°, a \approx 5.9, c \approx 6.7$

8. $m\angle A \approx 40.8°, m\angle B \approx 60.6°, m\angle C \approx 78.6°$

9. $m\angle A \approx 28.6°, b \approx 17.3, m\angle C \approx 20.4°$

10. $a \approx 90.5°, m\angle A \approx 63.1°, m\angle B \approx 36.9°$

11. $m\angle A \approx 48.2°, m\angle B \approx 106.6°, m\angle C \approx 25.2°$

12. $m\angle B = 74°, b \approx 24.5, c \approx 24.0$

13. 127.2°

9.7 Practice B

1. -1.0724 **2.** -0.6157 **3.** 0.9998

4. 60.4 cm^2 **5.** 12.7 in.^{2}

Answers

6. Draw a diagonal to form the SAS case of a triangle, use the area formula $A = \frac{1}{2}ab \sin C$, and then double this area; $A \approx 6578 \text{ m}^2$

7. $m\angle B = 33°, b \approx 8.3, c \approx 15.2$

8. $a \approx 12.0, m\angle B \approx 26.4°, m\angle C \approx 86.6°$

9. $m\angle B \approx 64.5°, c \approx 2.4, m\angle C \approx 37.5°$

10. $m\angle A \approx 36.2°, m\angle B \approx 43.5°, m\angle C \approx 100.3°$

11. $a \approx 12.6, b \approx 5.2, m\angle C = 71°$

12. $m\angle A \approx 29.5°, m\angle B \approx 112.4°, m\angle C \approx 38.0°$

13. **a.** about 19.7 in.
    b. about 83.8°

9.7 Enrichment and Extension

1. $A \approx 69.7°, B \approx 30.3°, c \approx 54.6$

2. $C = 78.9°, B = 39.1°, a = 12.6$

3. $a \approx 18.9, B \approx 38.9°, C \approx 75.1°$

9.7 Puzzle Time

BECAUSE THEN YOU'LL BE A MILE AWAY AND YOU'LL HAVE THEIR SHOES

Cumulative Review

1. $6\sqrt{3}$

2. $12\sqrt{2}$

3. $9\sqrt{3}$

4. $12\sqrt{10}$

5. $9\sqrt{5}$

6. $8\sqrt{7}$

7. $5\sqrt{2}$

8. $4\sqrt{7}$

9. $3\sqrt{5}$

10. $\dfrac{9\sqrt{5}}{5}$

11. $\dfrac{4\sqrt{7}}{7}$

12. $\dfrac{7\sqrt{3}}{3}$

13. $\dfrac{5\sqrt{11}}{11}$

14. $\dfrac{11\sqrt{2}}{2}$

15. $\dfrac{8\sqrt{3}}{3}$

16. $\dfrac{\sqrt{6}}{3}$

17. $3\sqrt{3}$

18. $\dfrac{9\sqrt{11}}{11}$

19. $x = 80$

20. $x = 15$

21. $x = 112$

22. $x = 55$

23. $x = 104$

24. $x = 187$

25. $x = 9$

26. $x = 2$

27. $x = 6$

28. $x = 5$

29. $x = 11.5$

30. $x = 7.25$

31. $x = 32$

32. $x = 121$

33. $x = 21$

34. $x = 8$

35. $x = 66$

36. $x = 195$

37. $x = 6$

38. $x = 126$

39. $x = 12.5$

40. $x = 6$

41. $x = 4$

42. $x = 5$

43. $x = 3$

44. $x = 7$

45. $x = 2$

46. $r = 5$ ft, $d = 10$ ft

47. $r = 3$ ft, $d = 6$ ft

48. $r = 18$ in., $d = 36$ in.

49. $r = 17$ ft, $d = 34$ ft

50. $r = 4$ in., $d = 8$ in.

51. $r = 11$ in., $d = 22$ in.

52. 41°

53. 94°

54. 168°

55. 123°

56. 155°

57. 138°

58. acute isosceles triangle

59. right isosceles triangle

60. equilateral triangle

61. right scalene triangle

62. $x = 13, y = 8$

63. $r = 9, s = 20$

64. $m = 14, x = 15$

65. $a = 68, k = 8$

66. **a.** 5
    b. 2

67. 20

68. 40

69. 10

70. 24

71. 135

72. 65

73. $4\sqrt{2}$

74. 7

75. **a.** $6\sqrt{2}$ in.
    b. $12 + 6\sqrt{2}$ in.
    c. 20.5 in.

Answers

Chapter 10

10.1 Start Thinking

1.
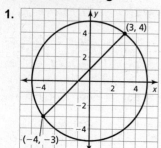

Sample answer: no; It does not pass through the center.

2.
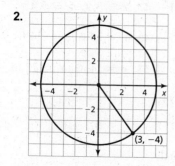

Sample answer: radius; It connects the center of the circle with a point on the circle.

3. *Sample answer*: yes; no

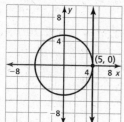

10.1 Warm Up

1. $r = 5$ 2. $r = 9\sqrt{2}$ 3. $r = 6$

10.1 Cumulative Review Warm Up

1. yes; obtuse   2. yes; obtuse

3. yes; right   4. yes; acute

5. yes; obtuse   6. no

10.1 Practice A

1. $\odot A$ 2. $\overline{AB}, \overline{AD}$ 3. $\overline{BD}, \overline{CH}$

4. $\overline{CH}$ 5. $\overrightarrow{EG}$

6. no; $\triangle ABC$ is not a right triangle because the side lengths do not satisfy the Pythagorean Theorem (Thm. 9.1).

7. yes; $\triangle ABC$ is a right triangle because the side lengths satisfy the Pythagorean Theorem (Thm. 9.1).

8. $r = 8$ 9. $r = 20$

10. 5   11. $-\dfrac{3}{2}$ and 4

12. *Sample answer:*

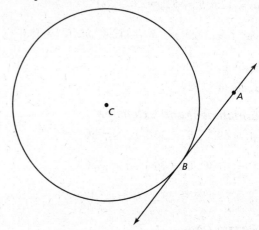

13. a. 40 ft; By the External Tangent Congruence Theorem (Thm. 10.2), the sidewalks are the same length.

   b. 60 ft

10.1 Practice B

1. $\overline{CE}, \overline{EF}$ 2. $\overline{CF}, \overline{BD}$ 3. $\overline{CF}$

4. $\overrightarrow{BD}$ 5. $\overrightarrow{AG}, H$

6. yes; $\triangle ABC$ is a right triangle because the side lengths satisfy the Pythagorean Theorem (Thm. 9.1).

7. no; $\triangle ABC$ is not a right triangle because the side lengths do not satisfy the Pythagorean Theorem (Thm. 9.1).

8. $r = 12$ 9. $r = 1.4$

10. 5   11. $-\dfrac{2}{3}$ and 7

12. when the two circles are concentric; There are no points of intersection and no segment joining the centers of the circles.

Answers

13. a. about 19.2 ft

   b. $AE = BC$ and $DE = CD$, so $BD = AD$ by the SSS Similarity Theorem (Thm. 8.4).

10.1 Enrichment and Extension

1. 9   **2.** $\sqrt{412} \approx 20.3$

3. 19.6

4. It is given that $\overline{IM}$ and $\overline{JL}$ are tangent segments. They intersect at point K. Because tangent segments from a common point to a circle are congruent, $KI = KL$ and $KM = KJ$. By the Addition Property of Equality, $KI + KM = KL + KJ$. The Segment Addition Postulate (Post. 1.2) shows that $IM = KI + KM$ and $JL = KL + KJ$. So, by the Transitive Property of Equality, $IM = JL$ and so $\overline{IM} \cong \overline{JL}$ by the definition of congruent segments.

10.1 Puzzle Time

HE WAS SERVING PI

10.2 Start Thinking

60 min or 1 h

1. 180°   **2.** 270°   **3.** 60°

4. 54°   **5.** 288°   **6.** 312°

10.2 Warm Up

1. 29%   **2.** 119°   **3.** 35°

10.2 Cumulative Review Warm Up

1. $\dfrac{13}{7}$ **2.** 12   **3.** 62   **4.** $\dfrac{8}{3}$

10.2 Practice A

1. minor arc; 55°   **2.** major arc; 245°

3. semicircle; 180°   **4.** minor arc; 120°

5. a. 32°

   b. 208°

   c. 105°

   d. 260°

6. yes; They are arcs of congruent circles and $m\widehat{EF} = m\widehat{GH}$.

7. no; They are arcs of the same circle, but $m\widehat{STV} = 120°$ and $m\widehat{UVT} = 150°$.

8. a. 45°

   b. 14.4°

10.2 Practice B

1. semicircle; 180°   **2.** minor arc; 74°

3. major arc; 286°   **4.** minor arc; 42°

5. yes; They are arcs of the same circle and $m\widehat{AC} = m\widehat{BD}$.

6. no; $\widehat{NM}$ and $\widehat{OP}$ have the same angle measure, but they are arcs of circles that are not congruent.

7. yes; They are arcs of the same circle and $m\widehat{AB} = m\widehat{CD} = 42°$.

8. 22.5°

9. a. 135°

   b. 225°

10. a. 170°

   b. 34 sec

10.2 Enrichment and Extension

1. 18.6 in.   **2.** about 19.1 cm

3. a. 6 times

   b. 60.4%

4.

   a. 72°

   b. about 5.9 in.

   c. about 29.4 in.

   d. about 59.4 in.^{2}

   e. $A = \dfrac{1}{4}nd^2 \left(\cos\left[\dfrac{180}{n}\right]° \right)\left(\sin\left[\dfrac{180}{n}\right]° \right)$

5. 73   **6.** 12   **7.** 126

10.2 Puzzle Time

THE CRAB APPLE

Answers

10.3 Start Thinking

1. sometimes true; If a chord passes through the center of the circle, then it is a diameter.

2. always true; By definition, a chord is a segment whose endpoints are on a circle and a diameter always satisfies this definition.

3. sometimes true; Because a radius is half the measure of the diameter, it is possible to draw infinitely many chords within the circle that have a measure equal to the radius. However, there are also infinitely many chords that do not have the same measure as the radius. For example, all the diameters do not have the same measure.

4. never true; It is possible for a chord to have the same measure as a diameter, but it will never be longer. A diameter is the longest possible chord in a circle.

10.3 Warm Up

1. $6\sqrt{2}$

2. $3\sqrt{3}$

3. 11

10.3 Cumulative Review Warm Up

1. Given B is the midpoint of $\overline{EC}$ and $\overline{DA}$, you can conclude that $\overline{EB} \cong \overline{BC}$ and $\overline{AB} \cong \overline{BD}$. Because $\angle EBA$ and $\angle CBD$ are vertical angles, you can conclude that they are also congruent. Then by the SAS Congruence Theorem (Thm. 5.5), you can conclude that $\triangle AEB \cong \triangle DCB$.

2. You are given $\angle BDE \cong \angle BED$ and $\angle A \cong \angle C$. Then if you conclude $\overline{DE} \cong \overline{DE}$ by the Reflexive Property of Segment Congruence (Thm. 2.1), you have $\triangle AED \cong \triangle CDE$ by the AAS Congruence Theorem (Thm. 5.11).

10.3 Practice A

1. 115°

2. 160°

3. 11

4. 65°

5. 4

6. a. yes; $\overline{AB}$ is a perpendicular bisector of $\overline{MN}$.

   b. no; $\overline{AB}$ is not perpendicular to $\overline{MN}$.

7. 18

8. 6

9. $6\sqrt{10} \approx 19$ units

10. D

10.3 Practice B

1. In a circle, if two chords are congruent, then their corresponding minor arcs are congruent.

2. 10

3. $m\overset{\frown}{AD} = m\overset{\frown}{BE} = 110°$

4. 100°

5. 7

6. 11

7. 3

8. yes; $\overline{AB}$ is a perpendicular bisector of $\overset{\frown}{QR}$.

9. about 12.8 units

10. about 30.4 units

11. Sample answer:

STATEMENTS	REASONS
1. $\overline{PQ}$ is the diameter of $\odot U$. $\overset{\frown}{PT} \cong \overset{\frown}{QS}$	1. Given
2. $\overline{PT} \cong \overline{QS}$	2. Congruent Corresponding Chords Theorem (Thm. 10.6)
3. $\overline{UP} \cong \overline{UQ} \cong \overline{UT} \cong \overline{US}$	3. Definition of radius of circle
4. $\triangle PUT \cong \triangle QUS$	4. SSS Congruence Theorem (Thm. 5.8)

12. Sample answer: You could also use the SAS Congruence Theorem (Thm. 5.5). $\overset{\frown}{PT} \cong \overset{\frown}{QS}$, so $m\angle PUT \cong m\angle QUS$ by the Congruent Central Angles Theorem (Thm. 10.4).

10.3 Enrichment and Extension

1. 60°

2. 19.2°

3. 53.1°

4. 90°

5. 103.5°

6. 180°

7. no; no; Sample answer:

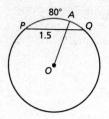

8. 30 units

10.3 Puzzle Time

BECAUSE IT WANTED THE SCHOOL TO HAVE A LITTLE SPIRIT

Answers

10.4 Start Thinking

$m\angle BMC = m\overset{\frown}{BC}$; $m\angle A = m\angle B$; *Sample answer*:
Because $\overline{MB}$ and $\overline{MA}$ are radii of the same circle,
we can conclude that they are congruent. With this
information, we can conclude that $\angle A \cong \angle B$ by the
Base Angles Theorem (Thm. 5.6);
$m\angle BMC = m\angle A + m\angle B$ by the Exterior Angle
Theorem (5.2). Because $\angle A \cong \angle B$, by substitution
$m\angle BMC = m\angle A + m\angle A$ or $m\angle BMC = 2m\angle A$.
Because $m\angle BMC = m\overset{\frown}{BC}$, then $m\angle\overset{\frown}{BC} = 2m\angle A$ or
$\frac{1}{2}m\angle\overset{\frown}{BC} = m\angle A$.

10.4 Warm Up

1. $m\angle C = 100°, m\angle D = 132°$

2. $m\angle X = 97°, m\angle Y = 50°, m\angle Z = 33°$

3. $m\angle P = 115°, m\angle Q = 115°, m\angle R = 65°,$
   $m\angle S = 65°$

10.4 Cumulative Review Warm Up

1. 18 square units

2. about 39.3 square units

3. about 15.9 square units

10.4 Practice A

1. $20°$ 2. $144°$ 3. $58°$

4. B; *Sample answer*: $\angle RQS$ and $\angle RPS$ are inscribed
   angles that intercept the same arc, so the angles are
   congruent by the Inscribed Angles of a Circle
   Theorem (Thm. 10.11).

5. $x = 110, y = 67$ 6. $x = 99, y = 90$

7. $x = 39, y = 29$

8. Opposite angles should be supplementary, not
   congruent; $m\angle B = 95°$

9. a. $62.3°$
   b. $83.1°$
   c. acute, scalene; *Sample answer*: Because
      $m\angle A = 34.6°, m\angle B = 62.3°,$ and
      $m\angle C = 83.1°, \triangle ABC$ has three acute angles
      and no congruent sides.

10.4 Practice B

1. $90°$ 2. $42°$ 3. $58°$ 4. $48°$

5. $58°$ 6. $42°$ 7. $96°$ 8. $180°$

9. $x = 14, y = 38$ 10. $x = 72, y = 90$

11. $x = 16, y = 14$

12. *Sample answer*:

STATEMENTS	REASONS
1. $\odot P$	1. Given
2. $\angle AED \cong \angle BEC$	2. Vertical Angles Congruence Theorem (Thm. 2.6)
3. $\angle CAD \cong \angle DBC$	3. Inscribed Angles of a Circle Theorem (Thm. 10.11).
4. $\triangle AED \sim \triangle BES$	4. AAA Similarity Theorem (Thm. 8.3)

13. yes; *Sample answer*: $\angle ADB$ and $\angle BCA$ intercept
    the same arc, so the angles are congruent by the
    Inscribed Angles of a Circle Theorem
    (Thm. 10.11).

14. yes; *Sample answer*: $m\angle CAB = 60°$ by the
    Measure of an Inscribed Angle Theorem
    (Thm. 10.10) and $m\angle ACB = 90°$ by the Triangle
    Sum Theorem (Thm. 5.1). $\triangle ABC$ is a right triangle
    with hypotenuse $\overline{AB}$. So, $\overline{AB}$ is a diameter of the
    circle by the Inscribed Right Triangle Theorem
    (Thm. 10.12).

10.4 Enrichment and Extension

1. $m\angle 1 = m\angle 4 = 45°, m\angle 2 = 20°, m\angle 3 = 70°$

2. $27.70°$

3. $m\angle 1 = 60°, m\angle 2 = 60°, m\angle 3 = 120°,$
   $m\angle 4 = 30°$

4. $m\angle 1 = 40°, m\angle 2 = 25°, m\angle 3 = 40°$

5. $24°$ 6. $48°$

7. $45°, 135°, 75°, 105°$

10.4 Puzzle Time

IT USED ITS HEAD

Answers

10.5 Start Thinking

Sample answer:

Two chords intersect at the center of the circle.

The circle is divided into four arcs, and opposite arcs are congruent.

Two chords intersect within the circle, but not at the center.

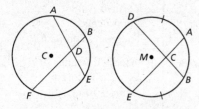

The circle is divided into four arcs. In the diagram of $\odot C$, none of the arcs have the same measure. In the diagram of $\odot M$, $m\widehat{AD} = m\widehat{BE}$ and the chords are congruent.

Two chords intersect at a point on the circle.

The circle is divided into three arcs. Of the three arcs, none may be congruent, two may be congruent, or all three may be congruent.

Two chords do not intersect.

The circle is divided into four arcs. Of the four arcs, you may have none that are congruent, or two, three, or all four congruent.

10.5 Warm Up

1. 120°   2. 74°   3. 84°

10.5 Cumulative Review Warm Up

1. 1   2. 2   3. 4

10.5 Practice A

1. 202°   2. 102°   3. 56°   4. 133

5. 42   6. 35   7. 26

8. *Sample answer*: This finds the supplement of the angle labeled $x°$. The measure of the angle should be one-half the sum of the measures of the arcs intercepted by the angle and its vertical angle; $m\angle x = \frac{1}{2}(66° + 66°)$, so $m\angle x = 66°$.

9. 21°

10.5 Practice B

1. 60°   2. 30°   3. 60°

4. 60°   5. 30°   6. 60°

7. D; The measure of $\angle 4$ is one-half the sum of the measures of the arcs intercepted by the angle and its vertical angle. So, $m\angle 4 = \frac{1}{2}(75° + 125°) = 100° \neq 90°$.

8. 50   9. 7   10. 70

11. a. 120°
    b. 100°
    c. 140°

12. about 6.8°

10.5 Enrichment and Extension

1. a. 164°
   b. 196°
   c. 48°
   d. 32°
   e. 64°
   f. 80°

Answers

2. a. $60°$

  b. $60°$

  c. 2.25

  d. 1.125

  e. $\left(1.125\sqrt{3}\right) \approx 1.95$

  f. $\left(2.25 + 2.25\sqrt{3}\right) \approx 6.1$

3. *Sample answer:* Draw chords $\overline{RU}$ and $\overline{ST}$. It is given that $\overset{\frown}{RU} \cong \overset{\frown}{ST}$. Because congruent arcs have congruent chords, $\overline{RU} \cong \overline{ST}$. It is given that $\overset{\frown}{RS} \cong \overset{\frown}{TU}$. $\angle RUS, \angle URT, \angle TSU,$ and $\angle STR$ are all inscribed angles that intercept either $\overset{\frown}{RS}$ or $\overset{\frown}{TU}$. So, all four angles have the same measure and are congruent. By the SAS Congruence Theorem (Thm. 5.5), $\triangle QRU$ and $\triangle QST$ are congruent triangles. Also, the base angles are all the same, so they are isosceles triangles. So $\overline{RQ}, \overline{UQ}, \overline{SQ},$ and $\overline{TQ}$ are congruent because corresponding parts of congruent triangles are congruent. Congruent segments have equal lengths, so Q is equidistant from points R, U, S and T that lie on the circle. So, Q is the center of the circle.

10.5 Puzzle Time

A PARALLEL

10.6 Start Thinking

1. *Sample answer:* $PX_1 = 7.7, PY_1 = 11.6$

2. *Sample answer:* $PX_2 = 6.8, PY_2 = 13.2$

3. *Sample answer:* $PX_3 = 6.7, PY_3 = 13.3$

4. *Sample answer:* $PX_4 = 8.3, PY_4 = 10.8$

Each pair of segments has approximately the same period.

10.6 Warm Up

1. $x = 16$ **2.** $x = 1$ **3.** $x = \dfrac{3}{2}, 1$

4. $x = -2, 5$ **5.** $x = 6 \pm 2\sqrt{11}$

6. $x = -7, 1$

10.6 Cumulative Review Warm Up

1. $\sqrt{6}$ **2.** $\dfrac{-13 + 5\sqrt{53}}{2}$ **3.** $3\sqrt{10}$

10.6 Practice A

1. 15   **2.** 2   **3.** 12   **4.** 5

5. 6   **6.** 7   **7.** 15   **8.** 12

9. 4   **10.** 4   **11.** 4   **12.** 7

13. about 14.2 ft

10.6 Practice B

1. 10   **2.** 8   **3.** 4   **4.** 4

5. 8   **6.** 15   **7.** 9   **8.** 5

9. 30   **10.** about 20.1 in.

11. about 139.8 in.

10.6 Enrichment and Extension

1. $AC = 16.5, BD = 16.8$

2. 40.5

3. a. $60°$

  b. *Sample answer:* $\angle ACB \cong \angle FCE$ by the Vertical Angles Congruence Theorem (Thm. 2.6). Because $m\angle CAB = 60°$ and $m\angle EFD = 60°$, then $\angle CAB \cong \angle EFD$. Using the AA Similarity Theorem (Thm. 8.3), $\triangle ABC \sim \triangle FEC$.

  c. *Sample answer:* $\dfrac{y}{3} = \dfrac{x + 10}{6}; y = \dfrac{x + 10}{2}$

  d. *Sample answer:* $y^2 = x(x + 16)$

  e. $x = 2, y = 6$

  f. $2\sqrt{30}$; *Sample answer:* Because $\triangle ABC \sim \triangle FEC$ and $\dfrac{CF}{AC} = \dfrac{12}{6} = 2$, then $\dfrac{CE}{CB} = \dfrac{2}{1}$. Let $CE = 2x$ and $CB = x$. So, $2x^2 = 60$ by the Segments of Chords Theorem (Thm. 10.18), which implies $x = \sqrt{30}$ and $CE = 2\sqrt{30}$.

4. $OT^2 = OP \bullet OQ$ and $OT^2 = OR \bullet OS$ by the Segments of Secants and Tangents Theorem (Thm. 10.20). So, $OP \bullet OQ = OR \bullet OS$.

Answers

10.6 Puzzle Time

BECAUSE THE ELLIPSES ARE TOO ECCENTRIC
FOR THE CIRCLES

10.7 Start Thinking

$x^2 + y^2 = 4;$

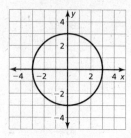

10.7 Warm Up

1. $PQ = 4$, midpoint $= (0, 8)$

2. $PQ = \sqrt{53}$, midpoint $= \left(\dfrac{7}{2}, -6\right)$

3. $PQ = 10\sqrt{2}$, midpoint $= (-5, 4)$

4. $PQ = \dfrac{\sqrt{117}}{2}$, midpoint $= \left(-1, -\dfrac{3}{4}\right)$

10.7 Cumulative Review Warm Up

1. $63°$ 2. $42°$ 3. $138°$

4. $117°$ 5. $180°$

10.7 Practice A

1. $x^2 + y^2 = 49$

2. $(x - 5)^2 + (y - 1)^2 = 25$

3. $x^2 + y^2 = 64$

4. $x^2 + (y + 5)^2 = 4$

5. $x^2 + y^2 = 25$

6. $(x - 3)^2 + (y + 2)^2 = 841$

7. B   8. A   9. C

10. center: $(0, 3)$, radius: 2

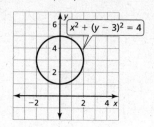

11. *Sample answer*: The distance from point $(-3, 3)$ to the origin is $3\sqrt{2}$, but the radius of the circle is 4, so the point does not lie on the circle.

12. **a.** from left to right, top row:
$(x - 28)^2 + (y - 44)^2 = 169,$
$(x - 57)^2 + (y - 44)^2 = 169,$
$(x - 86)^2 + (y - 44)^2 = 169;$
from left to right, bottom row:
$(x - 42.5)^2 + (y - 31)^2 = 169,$
$(x - 71.5)^2 + (y - 31)^2 = 169$

b. *Sample answer*: Subtract 3 from the radius to obtain 100 on the right side of each equation.

10.7 Practice B

1. $x^2 + y^2 = 9$

2. $(x - 3)^2 + (y - 2)^2 = 4$

3. $(x - 4)^2 + (y + 7)^2 = 16$

4. $(x + 3)^2 + y^2 = 25$

5. $x^2 + y^2 = 1$

6. $(x - 4)^2 + (y + 1)^2 = 25$

7. $(x - 2)^2 + (y - 4)^2 = 169$

8. center: $(0, 0)$, radius: 10

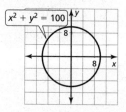

Answers

9. center: $(2, 9)$, radius: 2

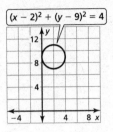

10. center: $(0, -2)$, radius: 6

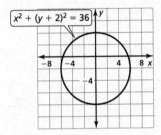

11. center: $(1, 0)$, radius: 2

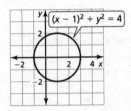

12. *Sample answer*: The statement is true. The distance from point $(-3, 4)$ to the origin is 5, and the radius of the circle is 5, so the point lies on the circle.

13. *Sample answer*: The statement is false. The distance from point $(2, \sqrt{3})$ to the origin is $\sqrt{7}$, but the radius of the circle is 3, so the point does not lie on the circle.

14. a. $(x + 6)^2 + (y - 4)^2 = 16$
$(x - 2)^2 + (y - 1)^2 = 25$
$(x + 2)^2 + (y + 2)^2 = 36$

b. $(-2, 4)$

c. no; The point $(4, -5)$ is about 10.8 miles away from the epicenter.

10.7 Enrichment and Extension

1. *Sample answer:* $(x + 3)^2 + (y + 3)^2 = 9$

2. $(3, -2), (x - 3)^2 + (y + 2)^2 = 26$

3. $x^2 + (y + 9.5)^2 = 56.25$

4. $(x - 12)^2 + (y - 19)^2 = 56.25$

5. a. $h = -14$ and $h = 10$

b. 4

c. $(x + 2)^2 + (y + 4)^2 = 16$ and
$(x + 2)^2 + (y + 4)^2 = 484$

6. a. $(x + 5)^2 + y^2 + (z - 4)^2 = 121$

b. $(x - 10)^2 + (y + 6)^2 + (z - 2)^2 = 169$

c. $(x + 1)^2 + (y - 2)^2 + (z + 4)^2 = 59$

10.7 Puzzle Time

COINCIDE

Cumulative Review

1. $x^2 - 10x + 21$ **2.** $j^2 + 4j + 3$

3. $c^2 + 4c - 96$ **4.** $m^2 - 12m + 20$

5. $y^2 + 21y + 110$ **6.** $s^2 + 11s + 30$

7. $5q^2 - 17q - 12$ **8.** $12p^2 - 40p - 7$

9. $-2f^2 - 17f + 84$ **10.** $54b^2 - 36b + 6$

11. $-15g^2 + 46g - 24$ **12.** $21k^2 + 35k - 56$

13. $x = -8$ and $x = 9$ **14.** $x = 10$ and $x = 12$

15. $x = 6$ and $x = 12$ **16.** $x = -7$ and $x = 6$

17. $x = 1$ and $x = 7$ **18.** $x = -4$ and $x = 8$

19. $x = -10$ and $x = 11$ **20.** $x = 4$ and $x = 9$

21. $x = -9$ and $x = -1$ **22.** $x = -1$ and $x = 8$

23. $x = -4$ and $x = 2$ **24.** $x = -8$ and $x = -5$

25. $x = -6$ and $x = -1$ **26.** $x = -2$ and $x = 8$

Answers

27. $x = -8$ and $x = 7$ **28.** $x = -4$ and $x = 7$

29. $x = 43$ **30.** $x = 102$ **31.** $x = 112$

32. $x = 18$ **33.** $x = 26$ **34.** $x = 84$

35. $x = 133$ **36.** $x = 26$ **37.** $x = 19$

38. $x = 1275$ **39.** 34   **40.** 25

41. 82   **42.** 34   **43.** 8

44. 12   **45.** 9   **46.** 6

47. 18

48. a. $2x + 11$
  b. 6
  c. 11
  d. 17

49. $(-3, -3)$ **50.** $\left(-2, \dfrac{11}{2}\right)$ **51.** $\left(-1, -\dfrac{1}{2}\right)$

52. $\left(-\dfrac{15}{2}, \dfrac{7}{2}\right)$ **53.** $\left(-\dfrac{13}{2}, -\dfrac{7}{2}\right)$ **54.** $\left(\dfrac{11}{2}, -6\right)$

55. $\left(-\dfrac{5}{2}, \dfrac{9}{2}\right)$ **56.** $\left(-\dfrac{5}{2}, -\dfrac{1}{2}\right)$ **57.** $\sqrt{745}$

58. $2\sqrt{29}$ **59.** $\sqrt{233}$ **60.** $2\sqrt{145}$

61. $\sqrt{365}$ **62.** $\sqrt{109}$ **63.** $\sqrt{569}$

64. 8

65. *Sample answer:* $\angle ABC$, $\angle ABD$, and $\angle CBD$

66. *Sample answer:* $\angle GFJ$, $\angle GFH$, and $\angle JFH$

67. $107°$ **68.** $113°$ **69.** $2\sqrt{130}$

70. $\sqrt{218}$ **71.** $3\sqrt{65}$ **72.** $\sqrt{466}$

73. $8\sqrt{2}$ **74.** $2\sqrt{102}$

75. a. 18.4 in.
  b. 44.4 in.

76. a. 7.6 in.
  b. 17.6 in.

Chapter 11

11.1 Start Thinking

$10\pi \approx 31.4$ cm

1. $5\pi \approx 15.7$ cm   **2.** $\dfrac{5\pi}{2} \approx 7.9$ cm

3. $\dfrac{25\pi}{6} \approx 13.1$ cm

11.1 Warm Up

1. $120°, 8\pi$ **2.** $90°, 15\pi$ **3.** $135°, 16\pi$

11.1 Cumulative Review Warm Up

1. $130°$ **2.** 54

3. $\sqrt{164} = 2\sqrt{41}$

11.1 Practice A

1. 21 m   **2.** about 169.6 ft

3. about 47.1 in.   **4.** 12.4 cm

5. Divide the circumference of the tree by π to find the diameter of the tree. Because the diameter is $50 \div \pi \approx 15.9$ inches, which is less than 18 inches, the tree is not suitable for tapping.

6. about 6.28 cm   **7.** about 47.1 in.

8. about 7.33 ft   **9.** about 36.57 mm

10. about 86.85 in.   **11.** $\dfrac{\pi}{3}$

12. $225°$ **13.** 1257 ft

11.1 Practice B

1. $\dfrac{36}{\pi}$ m   **2.** 10.8π ft

3. about 44.0 cm   **4.** $160°$

5. $200°$ **6.** about 19.54 m

7. about 24.43 m   **8.** $280°$

9. about 34.21 m   **10.** about $114°$

11. about 58.03 ft   **12.** about 20.53 cm

13. $\dfrac{7\pi}{12}$ **14.** $150°$

15. a. 35.6 in.   **b.** about 71 teeth

Answers

11.1 Enrichment and Extension

1. a. $18\pi \approx 56.55$ cm   **b.** $6\pi \approx 18.85$ cm

2. 8   **3.** about 30.16 cm

4. about 36.85 cm   **5.** about 28.57 in

11.1 Puzzle Time

SO THAT THE AUDIENCE WOULD BE GLUED TO THEIR SEATS

11.2 Start Thinking

$49\pi \approx 153.9$ in.^{2}

1. $\dfrac{49\pi}{2} \approx 77.0$ in.^{2} **2.** $\dfrac{147\pi}{4} \approx 115.5$ in.^{2}

3. $\dfrac{245\pi}{18} \approx 42.8$ in.^{2}

11.2 Warm Up

1. $81\pi \approx 254.5$ in.^{2} **2.** $4\pi \approx 12.6$ ft^2

3. $\sqrt{\dfrac{100}{\pi}} \approx 5.6$ mi   **4.** $2\sqrt{\dfrac{42}{\pi}} \approx 7.3$ m

5. $36\pi \approx 113.1$ cm^2

11.2 Cumulative Review Warm Up

1. $x = 4\sqrt{3},\ y = 4$ **2.** $x = 7,\ y = 7\sqrt{2}$

3. $x = 22,\ y = 11$

11.2 Practice A

1. 145.27 ft^2 **2.** 289.53 cm^2

3. 18 m   **4.** 30 in.

5. about 10,610 people/mi^2

6. about 883,573 people

7. about 21.38 ft^2, about 132.56 ft^2

8. about 184.35 in.^{2}, about 346.58 in.^{2}

9. about 1.22 m^2, about 1.92 m^2

10. about 25.13 cm^2, about 175.93 cm^2

11. 804.24 yd^2 **12.** about 12.57 m^2

13. about 85.13 ft^2 **14.** about 879.65 mm^2

15. about 21.46 cm^2

16. coverage area is 4 times greater;

$$\frac{\text{new coverage area}}{\text{old coverage area}} \approx \frac{7260.57 \text{ ft}^2}{1815.14 \text{ ft}^2} \approx 4$$

11.2 Practice B

1. about 143.14 in.^{2} **2.** about 0.07 mi^2

3. about 4.5 km   **4.** about 36.4 yd

5. about 5.5 mi   **6.** about 10.5 mi

7. about 0.18 m^2, about 0.33 m^2

8. about 2.86 cm^2, about 23.56 cm^2

9. about 0.39 in.^{2}, about 0.84 in.^{2}

10. about 1.87 yd^2, about 6.86 yd^2

11. about 2.5 cm   **12.** about 0.6 ft

13. about 1099.56 m^2 **14.** about 230.91 ft^2

15. about 32.99 in.^{2} **16.** about 26.18 in.^{3}

11.2 Enrichment and Extension

1. $\dfrac{3}{\pi}$ **2.** $36°$

3. $\dfrac{7\pi}{3}$ m^2 **4.** 8π square units

5. a. $\dfrac{1}{8}$ **b.** $\dfrac{3}{8}$ **c.** $\dfrac{1}{2}$

6. $36\sqrt{3} \approx 62.4$ cm^2

7. a.

Measure of arc, x	30°	60°	90°	120°	150°	180°
Area of sector, y	$\dfrac{3\pi}{4}$	$\dfrac{3\pi}{2}$	$\dfrac{9\pi}{4}$	3π	$\dfrac{15\pi}{4}$	$\dfrac{9\pi}{2}$

b. $y = \dfrac{\pi}{40}x$

11.2 Puzzle Time

A SCREWDRIVER

Answers

11.3 Start Thinking

1. *Sample answer*: To find the area of the triangle, draw an altitude and create two congruent 30°-60°-90° triangles. Using the special right triangle, the altitude would have a measure of $2\sqrt{3}$ units. Using the formula for the area of a triangle, you have
$$A = \frac{1}{2}bh = \frac{1}{2}(4)(2\sqrt{3}) = 4\sqrt{3} \text{ square units.}$$

2. *Sample answer*: To find the area of the regular hexagon, connect two pairs of non-consecutive vertices and create four congruent 30°-60°-90° triangles and a rectangle as shown. Using the special right triangle, you can find the measures needed to calculate the area. The area of the hexagon would be the sum of the areas of the four congruent triangles and the rectangle in the center, or
$$A = 4\left[\frac{1}{2}(2\sqrt{3})(2)\right] + 4(4\sqrt{3})$$
$$= 24\sqrt{3} \text{ square units.}$$

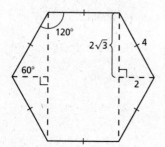

11.3 Warm Up

1. $4\sqrt{5} \approx 8.9$

2. $15 \sin 45° \approx 10.6$

3. $\dfrac{4.6}{\cos 32°} \approx 5.4$

11.3 Cumulative Review Warm Up

1. sometimes
2. always
3. always
4. never
5. always
6. sometimes

11.3 Practice A

1. 202.5 square units
2. 54 square units
3. 126 square units
4. 120 square units
5. 40°
6. 22.5°
7. 18°
8. 12.9°
9. 60°
10. 30°
11. 60°
12. 120°

13. 32.4 square units
14. 554.4 square units
15. 1119.6 square units
16. 178 cm^2
17. 1175.6 m^2
18. a. about 73.9 ft
    b. 3 containers; The area of the floor is about 416.5 square feet. Because $416.5 \div 200 \approx 2.08$ and you cannot buy part of a container, you will need 3 containers of wood sealer.

11.3 Practice B

1. 285.25 square units
2. 110.36 square units
3. 252.5 square units
4. 384 square units
5. 51.4°
6. 25.7°
7. 64.3°
8. 154.3°
9. 27.5 square units
10. 8.7 square units
11. 3.9 square units
12. 16 ft, 48 ft
13. 22 mm, 44 mm
14. a. *Sample answer*:

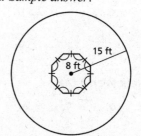

    b. 1481 ft^2

15. yes; One side length of the 11-gon is $\dfrac{16.5}{11} = 1.5$ meters. The length of the apothem a is $a = \dfrac{0.75}{\tan 16.4°}$. So,
$$A = \frac{1}{2}\left(\frac{0.75}{\tan 16.4°}\right)(16.5) \approx 21 \text{ square meters.}$$

11.3 Enrichment and Extension

1. 1.5 ft^2
2. $3 + \dfrac{\pi}{2}$
3. $A_0 = \dfrac{\sqrt{3}}{4}s^2$
4. $\dfrac{\sqrt{3}}{36}s^2$
5. 3; $A_1 = \dfrac{\sqrt{3}}{4}s^2 + \dfrac{\sqrt{3}}{12}s^2$

Answers

6. $A_2 = \dfrac{\sqrt{3}}{4}s^2 + \dfrac{\sqrt{3}}{12}s^2 + \dfrac{\sqrt{3}}{27}s^2$

7. $A_3 = \dfrac{\sqrt{3}}{4}s^2 + \dfrac{\sqrt{3}}{12}s^2 + \dfrac{\sqrt{3}}{27}s^2 + \dfrac{4\sqrt{3}}{243}s^2$

8. $S = \dfrac{9}{5}$

9. $A_n = \dfrac{2\sqrt{3}}{5}s^2$ square units

11.3 Puzzle Time

A WATCH DOG

11.4 Start Thinking

triangular prism: $F = 5$, $V = 6$, $E = 9$, rectangular prism: $F = 6$, $V = 8$, $E = 12$, pentagonal prism: $F = 7$, $V = 10$, $E = 15$, hexagonal prism: $F = 8$, $V = 12$, $E = 18$; $F + V - E = 2$ for each of the prisms; As you increase the number of faces by 1, the numbers of vertices increases by 2, and the number of edges increases by 3.

11.4 Warm Up

1. yes

2. no; The sides are not segments.

3. no; It is not a plane figure.

11.4 Cumulative Review Warm Up

1. 8   **2.** $\sqrt{29}$ **3.** $\dfrac{\sqrt{313}}{6}$

11.4 Practice A

1. yes; rectangular prism   **2.** yes; triangular pyramid

3. no   **4.** circle

5. triangle   **6.** rectangle

7.

cylinder with height 9 and base radius 5

8.

sphere with radius 2

9.

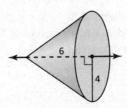

cone with height 6 and base radius 4

10. yes; It is bounded by polygons only.

11.

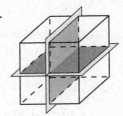

yes; *Sample answer*: parallel to a horizontal face and parallel to a vertical face

12. a. $4 + 4\sqrt{5} \approx 12.94$ in.

   b. $4\sqrt{5} \approx 8.94$ in.^{2}

11.4 Practice B

1. triangle   **2.** trapezoid   **3.** semicircle

4.

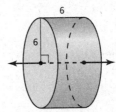

cylinder with height 6 and base radius 6

5.

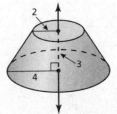

Sample answer: part of a cone with height 3 and two different circular bases with radii 2 and 4

Answers

6.

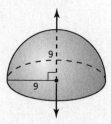

hemisphere with radius 9

7. none of the parts are polyhedrons; *Sample answer*: Two parts contain some faces that are polygons, but all three parts also contain faces that are not polygons.

8.

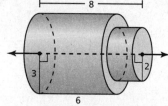

Sample answer: two adjacent cylinders that share the same axis of symmetry

9. a. trapezoid, triangle

  b. trapezoid: perimeter $= 12 + 2\sqrt{13} \approx 19.21$ in., area $= 18$ in.^{2}

  triangle: perimeter $= 4 + 2\sqrt{13} \approx 11.21$ in., area $= 6$ in.^{2}

  c. no; *Sample answer*: It is flatter than a circle, more like an oval.

11.4 Enrichment and Extension

1.

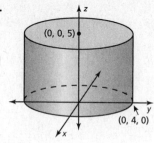

2.

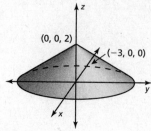

3. circle

4. no; *Sample answer*: An oblique cylinder does not have rotational symmetry, so you cannot draw a shape and an axis of revolution that could form the cylinder.

5.    **6.**

7.

11.4 Puzzle Time

BECAUSE THEY HAD JUST FINISHED A MARCH OF THIRTY-ONE DAYS

11.5 Start Thinking

$\frac{9}{64}\pi$ cubic units; $\frac{9}{64}\pi$ cubic units; no; no; The volume of a right solid and an oblique solid will be the same if the height and cross-sectional area are the same.

11.5 Warm Up

1. 168 cm^3 **2.** 480 in.^{3}

3. $30\pi \approx 94.2$ cm^3

11.5 Cumulative Review Warm Up

1. 0.6561   **2.** 0.9903   **3.** -0.2679

4. -0.5299 **5.** -0.9925 **6.** -4.3315

11.5 Practice A

1. 84 in.^{3} **2.** 864 cm^3

3. about 314.16 ft^3 **4.** about 1130.97 yd^3

Answers

5. about 2497 g **6.** 6 m

7. about 11.00 in.

8. 12 ft^2; *Sample answer*: length: 4 ft, width: 3 ft

9. 24 cm^2; *Sample answer*: length: 4 cm, width 6 cm

10. 337.5 m^3 **11.** 323 cm^3

12. about 3383.87 gallons

11.5 Practice B

1. 288 ft^3 **2.** 17.28 m^3

3. about 10,433.62 in.^{3} **4.** about 1334.55 cm^3

5. 3700 g **6.** 4 ft **7.** about 3.00 m

8. 18 yd^2; *Sample answer*: length: 6 yd, width: 3 yd

9. 32 in.^{2}; *Sample answer*: length: 8 in., width: 4 in.

10. 378π in.^{3} **11.** about 174 ft^3 **12.** 144 in.^{3}

11.5 Enrichment and Extension

1. $V = x^3 + x^2 - 2x$

2. $V = \pi x^3 + 2\pi x^2 + \pi x$

3. $7\sqrt{5}$

4. *Sample answer*: The volume is equal to the surface area, so $\pi r^2 h = 2\pi r^2 + 2\pi rh$. Solve for r to obtain $r = \dfrac{2h}{h - 2}$. If $0 < h < 2$, then $r < 0$, so h must be greater than 2. Similarly, if you solve for h, you get $h = \dfrac{2r}{r - 2}$. If $0 < r < 2$, then $h < 0$, so r must be greater than 2.

5. $1280\sqrt{3} \approx 2217.0$ cm^3

6. $125\pi\sqrt{3} \approx 680.2$ in.^{3}

7. $736\pi \approx 2312.2$ cm^3

8. 5 in. **9.** 5 ft

11.5 Puzzle Time

POST OFFICE

11.6 Start Thinking

Sample answer: The volume of the cube is clearly greater than the volume of the pyramid. You can see that the pyramid would fit inside the cube. The volume of the cube is 125 cubic inches and the volume of the pyramid will be one third of that value.

11.6 Warm Up

1. 210 in.^{2} **2.** 17.5 m^2

3. 45 tan 54° $\approx$ 61.9 cm^2

11.6 Cumulative Review Warm Up

1. $(x - 2)^2 + (y - 5)^2 = 49$

2. $(x + 3)^2 + (y - 9)^2 = 9$

3. $(x - 8)^2 + (y + 4)^2 = 64$

4. $(x + 11)^2 + (y + 3)^2 = 169$

11.6 Practice A

1. 240 m^3 **2.** 845 in.^{3} **3.** 84 ft^3

4. 8 cm **5.** 7.5 ft **6.** 12 m

7. 32 in.^{3} **8.** 1024 mm^3 **9.** 704 yd^3

10. 1155 m^3 **11.** 960 cm^3 **12.** $\dfrac{98}{3}$, or $32\frac{2}{3}$ m

11.6 Practice B

1. about 367.04 cm^3 **2.** about 96.99 ft^3

3. about 643.79 yd^3 **4.** 6.3 m

5. 12.5 in. **6.** 2211.84 cm^3

7. 32.175 yd^3 **8.** 290 cm^3

9. 3840 in.^{3} **10.** 750 m^3 **11.** 8

11.6 Enrichment and Extension

1. 96 cm^3 **2.** $\dfrac{1000\sqrt{2}}{3}$ cm^3

3. 320 cubic units

4. *Sample answer*: $V = \dfrac{1}{3}B(h_1 + h_2)$;

$V \approx 433.3$ units^3

Answers

5. $V = \dfrac{10.91}{3}\left(576 + 196 + \sqrt{576 \cdot 196}\right)$

   $= 4029.43 \text{ cm}^3$

11.6 Puzzle Time

A CAR POOL

11.7 Start Thinking

$\dfrac{50}{3}\pi \approx 52.4 \text{ in.};\ 8\dfrac{1}{3} \text{ in.};\ \dfrac{250}{3}\pi \approx 261.8 \text{ in.}^2$

11.7 Warm Up

1. about 28.3 cm^2 **2.** about 153.3 in.^2

3. about 548.2 m^2

11.7 Cumulative Review Warm Up

1. $y = 2x - 8$ **2.** $y = x + 9$

3. $y = \dfrac{1}{5}x - \dfrac{14}{5}$

11.7 Practice A

1. about 377 ft^2 **2.** 537.2 m^2

3. about 209.44 cm^3 **4.** about 16.76 in.^3

5. $\dfrac{512}{3}\pi \text{ mm}^3$ **6.** $\dfrac{7}{2}\pi \text{ in.}^3$

7. about 871.27 in.^3 **8.** about 47.24 cm^3

9. $3h;\ r\sqrt{3};$ *Sample answer*: The original volume is $V = \dfrac{1}{3}\pi r^2 h$ and the new volume is $V = \pi r^2 h$.

10. cylindrical container; The cost of the cylindrical container is \$4.75 per 96π cubic inches (or about \$0.02 per cubic inch), whereas the cost per cubic inch for the cone-shaped container is \$3.25 per 32π cubic inches (or about \$0.03 per cubic inch).

11.7 Practice B

1. about 593.8 yd^2 **2.** about 379.3 mm^2

3. about 1773.95 in.^3 **4.** about 25.13 cm^3

5. $\dfrac{756}{5}\pi \text{ ft}^3$ **6.** $\dfrac{2744}{9}\pi \text{ m}^3$

7. about 2814.87 in.^3 **8.** about 16.20 cm^3

9. $\dfrac{1}{2}h;\ r\dfrac{\sqrt{2}}{2};$ *Sample answer*: The original volume is $V = \dfrac{1}{3}\pi r^2 h$ and the new volume is $V = \dfrac{1}{6}\pi r^2 h$.

10. about 10.05 sec

11.7 Enrichment and Extension

1. a. $15\pi \approx 47.1 \text{ m}$

   b. $\dfrac{225}{4}\pi \approx 176.7 \text{ m}^2$

   c. about 389.6 m^2

2. $\dfrac{2\pi}{9} \text{ ft}^3$ **3.** $\dfrac{2\pi}{3} \text{ ft}^3$

4. $2\pi \text{ ft}^3$ **5.** about $191.45\pi \text{ m}^3$

6. *Sample answer*: You are increasing the area of the base by a factor of $3^2 = 9,$ so the height of the cone must be $\dfrac{1}{9}$ the original size.

7. $282\pi \approx 885.9 \text{ ft}^2$ **8.** about 634.3 m^2

11.7 Puzzle Time

BECAUSE THEY TAKE TOO LONG TO CHANGE

11.8 Start Thinking

$S_{\text{cube}} = 6(9.55)^2 \approx 547.2 \text{ in.}^2,$

$S_{\text{cyl}} = 2\pi\left(\dfrac{9.55}{2}\right)(9.55) + 2\pi\left(\dfrac{9.55}{2}\right)^2$

$\approx 429.8 \text{ in.}^2;$ no; cylinder

11.8 Warm Up

1. 15 in. **2.** 5 in. **3.** 3 in.

11.8 Cumulative Review Warm Up

1. radius   **2.** tangent   **3.** diameter

4. chord   **5.** secant   **6.** radius

11.8 Practice A

1. about 50.27 in.^2 **2.** about 314.16 mm^2

3. about 201.06 ft^2 **4.** 3 m

5. 9 yd **6.** about 113.10 ft^3

7. about $14,137.17 \text{ cm}^3$ **8.** about 659.58 m^3

Answers

9. about 4.19 in.^{3} **10.** about 9202.8 km^3

11. about 3053.63 cm^3 **12.** about 791.68 ft^3

13. about 100.53 m^2, about 134.04 m^3

14. about 12.57 yd^2; The edge length of the cube, 2 yards, is the diameter of the sphere.

15. surface area of new ball is

$$\left(\frac{40}{38}\right)^2 = \left(\frac{20}{19}\right)^2 = \left(\frac{400}{361}\right)^2 \approx 1.11 \text{ times the}$$

surface area of the old ball (an 11% increase), volume of new ball is

$$\left(\frac{40}{38}\right)^3 = \left(\frac{20}{19}\right)^3 = \frac{8000}{6859} \approx 1.17 \text{ times the}$$

volume of the old ball, (a 17% increase); Use the properties of similar solids;

$$\frac{\text{surface area of new ball}}{\text{surface area of old ball}} = \frac{1600\pi}{1444\pi} = \frac{400}{361},$$

$$\frac{\text{volume of new ball}}{\text{volume of old ball}} = \frac{32,000\pi/3}{27,436\pi/3} = \frac{8000}{6859}$$

11.8 Practice B

1. about 113.10 m^2 **2.** about 76.97 yd^2

3. about 254.47 in.^{2} **4.** 5 cm

5. 2.5 in.   **6.** about 3053.63 ft^3

7. about 575.17 cm^3 **8.** about 4188.79 m^3

9. $288\pi \approx 904.78$ ft^3 **10.** about 0.52 mi^3

11. about 5089.38 yd^3 **12.** about 83.78 in.^{3}

13. surface area shrinks to one-fourth original size, volume shrinks to one-eight original size

14. a. no; You also need to know the radius of one of the cannonballs.

b. 9 lb

11.8 Enrichment and Extension

1. greater than; The volume of the box is 32 cubic inches. The volume of the four balls is less than 17 cubic inches. So, there is more than 15 cubic inches left over inside the box, and the volume of a fifth ball is less than 6 cubic inches, so the volume left over inside the box is greater than a fifth ball.

2. 1,876,578 L   **3.** 1.0 in.

4. a. $r = \dfrac{\sqrt{S\pi}}{2\pi}$

b. $V = \dfrac{S\sqrt{S\pi}}{6\pi}$

c.

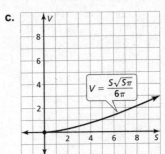

The shape of the graph is similar to half a parabola.

5.

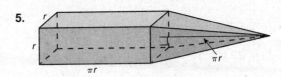

6. $S = 4\pi r^2 + r^2 + r^2\sqrt{4\pi^2 + 1}$

7. $S = r^2 + 2\pi r^2 + \pi r^2\sqrt{2}$

11.8 Puzzle Time

EGG SHELLS

Cumulative Review

1. 9 ft   **2.** 16 cm   **3.** 5 in.

4. 18 km   **5.** 11 m   **6.** 18 mm

7. $M(1, 2)$ **8.** $M(-1, 1)$ **9.** $M(-3, 4)$

10. $M(8, -2)$ **11.** $H(3, 0)$ **12.** $G(-5, 3)$

13. $G(-10, 5)$ **14.** $H(-6, 8)$ **15.** 1

16. $\sqrt{386}$ **17.** $\sqrt{157}$ **18.** $\sqrt{74}$

19. $\sqrt{181}$ **20.** 6

21. $\angle XYZ, \angle ZYX, \angle Y$ **22.** $\angle JKL, \angle LKJ, \angle K$

23. *Sample answer*: consecutive even integers beginning with 2; 12, 14

24. *Sample answer*: consecutive odd integers beginning with -1, alternatively negative and positive; 11, -13

Answers

25. *Sample* answer: skip two letters in the alphabet, beginning with A; P, S

26. *Sample answer*: skip one letter in the alphabet, beginning with B; L, N

27. $x = -1$

28. $x = 1$

29. $x = -6$

30. $x = 1$

31. $x = 2$

32. $x = 3$

33. $x = -7$

34. $x = 1$

35. $y = -4x - 7$

36. $y = 5x + 2$

37. $y = x + 8$

38. $y = -10x + 6$

39. $y = 35x - 50$

40. $y = 9x - 6$

41. $x = 3, y = 4$

42. $x = 15, y = 18$

43. $x = 15, y = 10$

44. $x = 21, y = 26$

45. 54

46. 47

47. 26

48. 7

49. $y = 3x - 39$

50. $y = -8x - 41$

51. $y = 4x + 36$

52. $y = -2x - 1$

53. $y = \dfrac{1}{4}x - 3$

54. $y = x - 11$

55. $y = -\dfrac{2}{3}x - 7$

56. $y = -8x + 26$

57. $A'(-9, 2)$

58. $B'(6, -3)$

59. $C'(-6, 7)$

60. $D(9, 1)$

61. $E(-11, -3)$

62. $P'(-10, 11), Q'(-6, 13), R'(-2, 9)$

63. $P'(5, -4), Q'(9, -2), R'(13, -6)$

64. $P'(-13, -1), Q'(-9, 1), R'(-5, -3)$

65. $P'(-1, -6), Q'(3, -4), R'(7, -8)$

66. $P'(-9, -1), Q'(-5, 1), R'(-1, -3)$

67. $A'(27, -21), B'(21, 0), C'(0, -12)$

68. $X'(-4, -20), Y'(0, 22), Z'(22, -22)$

69. $M'(-2, 0), N'(-4, 3), P'(3, 2)$

70. $Q'(-5, -4), R'(0, -6), S'(4, 5), T'(3, -6)$

71. $D'(32, 8), E'(32, -40), F'(28, 16), G'(24, 4)$

72. a. 50.3 in.

b. 56 in.

c. 54 in.

73. a. 50.3 cm^2

b. 49 cm^2

c. 48 cm^2

d. the circle

Chapter 12

12.1 Start Thinking

Sample answer:

1. *Sample answer*: It is not too likely that you will grab the number that matches your jersey. You have a 1 in 15 chance of choosing a matching pair of shorts.

2. *Sample answer*: Possible Outcomes: Jersey and shorts – 11 and 1, 11 and 2, 11 and 3, 11 and 4, 11 and 5, 11 and 6, 11 and 7, 11 and 8, 11 and 9, 11 and 10, 11 and 11, 11 and 12, 11 and 13, 11 and 14, 11 and 15

12.1 Warm Up

1. "H" for heads, "T" for tails, HHH, HHT, HTH, HTT, THH, THT, TTH, TTT

2. "B" for blue, "Y" for yellow, "G" for green, "R" for red, BB, BY, BG, BR, YY, YB, YG, YR, GG, GB, GY, GR, RR, RB, RY, RG

3. BH, BT, YH, YT, GH, GT, RH, RT

12.1 Cumulative Review Warm Up

1. $\sin \theta = \dfrac{4}{7}$, $\cos \theta = \dfrac{\sqrt{33}}{7}$, $\tan \theta = \dfrac{4\sqrt{33}}{33}$, $\csc \theta = \dfrac{7}{4}$, $\sec \theta = \dfrac{7\sqrt{33}}{33}$, $\cot \theta = \dfrac{\sqrt{33}}{4}$

Answers

2. $\sin \theta = \dfrac{\sqrt{17}}{9}$, $\cos \theta = \dfrac{8}{9}$, $\tan \theta = \dfrac{\sqrt{17}}{8}$,

$\csc \theta = \dfrac{9\sqrt{17}}{17}$, $\sec \theta = \dfrac{9}{8}$, $\cot \theta = \dfrac{8\sqrt{17}}{17}$

3. $\sin \theta = \dfrac{5\sqrt{41}}{41}$, $\cos \theta = \dfrac{4\sqrt{41}}{41}$, $\tan \theta = \dfrac{5}{4}$,

$\csc \theta = \dfrac{\sqrt{41}}{5}$, $\sec \theta = \dfrac{\sqrt{41}}{4}$, $\cot \theta = \dfrac{4}{5}$

4. $\sin \theta = \dfrac{3}{8}$, $\cos \theta = \dfrac{\sqrt{55}}{8}$, $\tan \theta = \dfrac{3\sqrt{55}}{55}$,

$\csc \theta = \dfrac{8}{3}$, $\sec \theta = \dfrac{8\sqrt{55}}{55}$, $\cot \theta = \dfrac{\sqrt{55}}{3}$

5. $\sin \theta = \dfrac{4}{5}$, $\cos \theta = \dfrac{3}{5}$, $\tan \theta = \dfrac{4}{3}$,

$\csc \theta = \dfrac{5}{4}$, $\sec \theta = \dfrac{5}{3}$, $\cot \theta = \dfrac{3}{4}$

6. $\sin \theta = \dfrac{2\sqrt{14}}{9}$, $\cos \theta = \dfrac{5}{9}$, $\tan \theta = \dfrac{2\sqrt{14}}{5}$,

$\csc \theta = \dfrac{9\sqrt{14}}{28}$, $\sec \theta = \dfrac{9}{5}$, $\cot \theta = \dfrac{5\sqrt{14}}{28}$

12.1 Practice A

1. 8 outcomes; HHH, HHT, HTT, HTH, TTT, THH, THT, TTH

2. 9 outcomes; Pa, Pb, Pc, Ya, Yb, Yc, Ta, Tb, Tc, where "Pa" represents a purple balloon labeled *a*

3. $\dfrac{3}{14}$

4. a. 0.44   **b.** 0.50

5. red

12.1 Practice B

1. 4 outcomes; H-P, H-R, T-P, T-R

2. 3 outcomes; BBY, BYY, YYY

3. a. $\dfrac{1}{9}$ **b.** $\dfrac{8}{9}$ **c.** $\dfrac{5}{18}$ **d.** $\dfrac{1}{6}$

4. 0.170

5. always; Equally likely events have the same probability.

6. sometimes; The experimental probability could be greater than or less than the theoretical probability.

7. always; Together, the event and the complement of the event make up the entire sample space.

8. 0.027; about 1 defective dishwasher

12.1 Enrichment and Extension

1. T, T, T, T, T, H, H, T, T, H, H, H

2. 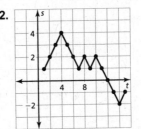   **3.**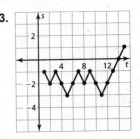

4.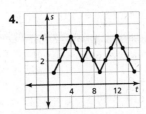

5. $t = 12; 12\,\text{s}$ **6.** $t = 14; 1\,\text{s}$

7. does not exist; 15 s

8. a. *Sample answer:* 80%

b. *Sample answer:* 6 tosses

9. the financial status of a gambler; Graphing several random walks can help you visualize and better understand the random nature of a random process.

12.1 Puzzle Time

TIMES UP

12.2 Start Thinking

Abbey's softball team winning the district and state championships are dependent events because they cannot win the state title without winning the district title. Abbey being accepted at her favorite college is independent of the other two events because winning the championships should not affect whether she is accepted at the college and being accepted at college will not affect her chances of winning.

Answers

12.2 Warm Up

1. $\dfrac{5}{32}$

2. $\dfrac{35}{128}$

3. $\dfrac{73}{128}$

4. $\dfrac{55}{128}$

5. 1

6. 0

12.2 Cumulative Review Warm Up

1. $2(x + 2)(x - 2)$

2. $3(2x - 3)(3x + 4)$

3. $(2 - 3x)(4 + 6x + 9x^2)$

4. $(x^2 + 2)(x + 3)(x - 3)$

5. $5x^4(x + 1)(x^2 - x + 1)$

6. $x(x - 5)(x - 3)(x + 3)$

12.2 Practice A

1. independent; Because the first tool was put back in, it does not affect the occurrence of the second choice.

2. dependent; Because the first juice box is not put back in, it does affect the occurrence of the second choice.

3. yes; What you roll on a die does not affect what is next rolled on that die.

4. no; Selecting the thirty-year-old for the game affects the selection of the second contestant.

5. a. $\dfrac{1}{100}$ b. $\dfrac{1}{90}$

6. 48%

12.2 Practice B

1. dependent; Because the player was not put back in, it does affect the pick of the second player.

2. independent; The pick of a charm does not affect the pick of a piece of leather.

3. yes; The result of flipping the coin first time does not affect the result of flipping the coin the second time.

4. no; The selection of one male does affect the selection of the next male.

5. a. $\dfrac{1}{676}$ b. $\dfrac{1}{650}$

6. 25%

12.2 Enrichment and Extension

1. 0 2. 0.0701 3. 0.1857 4. 0.4264

5. a. 0.25 b. 0.0667

6. 0.3265   7. 0.6232

12.2 Puzzle Time

A HOLE

12.3 Start Thinking

		Owns a Dog		
		Yes	No	Total
Owns a cat	Yes	6	8	14
	No	28	8	36
	Total	34	16	50

Sample answers: Some may prefer the Venn diagram because it is more familiar. The Venn diagram also clearly shows the overlapping circles indicating those who have both a cat and a dog. The number outside the circles clearly shows those students who do not have a dog or cat. Some may prefer the two-way table because it is similar to a binomial product set up, algebra tiles, and games like Battleship. The two-way table also shows totals that are not as clear in the Venn diagram; and with the totals, you can check your work.

12.3 Warm Up

1.

		Age Started Driving		
		≤ 16	> 16	Total
Gender	Male	28	5	33
	Female	14	8	22
	Total	42	13	50

Answers

12.3 Cumulative Review Warm Up

1.
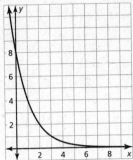

2.
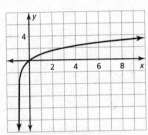

3.
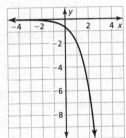

4.
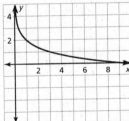

5.
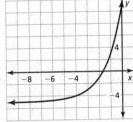

6.
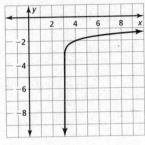

12.3 Practice A

1.

		Ran a Half Marathon		
		Yes	No	Total
Role	Student	12	112	124
	Teacher	7	151	158
	Total	19	263	282

2.

		Owns Dog		
		Yes	No	Total
Owns Cat	Yes	24	61	85
	No	107	34	141
	Total	131	95	226

3. a.

		Amount of Fresh Water Should Be Reduced		
		Yes	No	Total
Fish	Yes	98	12	110
	No	14	75	89
	Total	112	87	199

112 people agree; 87 people do not agree; 110 people fish; 89 people do not fish

b.

		Amount of Fresh Water Should Be Reduced		
		Yes	No	Total
Fish	Yes	0.49	0.06	0.55
	No	0.07	0.38	0.45
	Total	0.56	0.44	1

Answers

c.

		Amount of Fresh Water Should Be Reduced	
		Yes	No
Fish	Yes	0.89	0.11
	No	0.16	0.84

12.3 Practice B

1. 2.

		Surfing Style		
		Regular	Advanced	Total
Gender	Male	0.42	0.12	0.54
	Female	0.38	0.09	0.46
	Total	0.8	0.2	1

3. a.

		Exercise Regularly		
		Yes	No	Total
Feel Tired	Yes	1	1	2
	No	4	20	24
	Total	5	21	26

2 people feel tired; 24 people do not feel tired; 5 people exercise regularly; 21 people do not exercise regularly

b.

		Exercise Regularly		
		Yes	No	Total
Feel Tired	Yes	0.04	0.04	0.08
	No	0.15	0.77	0.92
	Total	0.19	0.81	1

c.

		Exercise Regularly	
		Yes	No
Feel Tired	Yes	0.20	0.05
	No	0.80	0.95

12.3 Enrichment and Extension

1.

	Yes	No	Total
Adults	0.42	0.31	0.73
Students	0.21	0.06	0.27
Total	0.63	0.37	1

2. 22%   **3.** 58%   **4.** 63%   **5.** 583

12.3 Puzzle Time

THEY BOTH DRIBBLE

12.4 Start Thinking

1. {White 1, White 2, White 3, Black 4, Black 5, Black 6}

2. $\dfrac{1}{6}$ **3.** $\dfrac{1}{2}$ **4.** $\dfrac{2}{3}$ **5.** $\dfrac{2}{3}$

12.4 Warm Up

1. $P(\text{green}) = \dfrac{11}{24}$ **2.** $P(\text{blue or green}) = \dfrac{5}{6}$

12.4 Cumulative Review Warm Up

1. $a_n = 3n - 3$ **2.** $a_n = \dfrac{n}{2n + 2}$

3. $a_n = (-2)^n$

12.4 Practice A

1. 0.6   **2.** $\dfrac{5}{6}$ **3.** 0.75

4. $\dfrac{2}{3}$ **5.** $\dfrac{2}{3}$ **6.** 15%

7. a. 0.65

b. 0.70

c. 0.65

d. Door 2; Both the probability of winning the Grand Prize and the probability of winning either the Grand Prize or the Nice Prize are greater for Door 2.

12.4 Practice B

1. 0.575   **2.** $\dfrac{9}{20}$ **3.** 0.675

4. $\dfrac{5}{6}$ **5.** 1   **6.** 65%

Answers

7. $P(A) = 0.96$; $P(\overline{A}) = 0.04$; $P(B|A) = 0.92$;

$P(\overline{B}|A) = 0.08$; $P(B|\overline{A}) = 0.80$; $P(\overline{B}|\overline{A}) = 0.20$;

$P(B) = 91.52\%$

12.4 Enrichment and Extension

1. a. Given: $P(A) = 0.25$, $P(A \text{ or } B) = 0.35$,

$P(A \text{ and } B) = 0.05$. Determine: $P(B)$

b. 15%

2. a. $\dfrac{1}{4} = \dfrac{2s}{5s + 6}$

b. 16 songs

c. $\dfrac{7}{8}$

3. 70%

4. a. 27 marbles

b. 24 marbles

12.4 Puzzle Time

CLOGS

12.5 Start Thinking

24 possible outcomes; Each row represents a different event. Each branch represents a possible outcome; *Sample answer*: To determine the total number of outcomes from the tree diagram, you can count the outcomes (branches) in the bottom row. Another way to determine the total number of outcomes from the tree diagram would be to multiply the different outcomes represented in each row. For example, in this tree diagram you have 6 different outcomes in the first row, 2 in the second, and 2 in the third. Therefore, there are $6 \cdot 2 \cdot 2 = 24$ possible outcomes.

12.5 Warm Up

1. 3; PPO, POP, OPP

2. 6; TAP, TPA, ATP, APT, PAT, PTA

3. 6; NNOO, NOON, NONO, ONNO, ONON, OONN

4. 12; KEEP, KEPE, KPEE, EKEP, EKPE, EEKP, EEPK, EPEK, EPKE, PKEE, PEKE, PEEK

12.5 Cumulative Review Warm Up

1. $A = 30°$, $BC \approx 8.0829$, $AC \approx 16.1658$

2. $B = 40°$, $BC \approx 8.4265$, $AC \approx 7.0707$

3. $C = 53°$, $BC \approx 3.0142$, $AC \approx 5.0085$

12.5 Practice A

1. a. 6   **b.** 6

2. a. 24   **b.** 12

3. a. 120   **b.** 20

4. 24   **5.** 30   **6.** 8   **7.** 120

8. 15,120   **9.** 1   **10.** 2730   **11.** 0.0179

12. 10   **13.** 10   **14.** 6   **15.** 21

16. 1   **17.** 36   **18.** 462   **19.** 66

20. 56

21. combinations; The order in which you visit the stations does not matter; 28

22. permutations; The 7 logos are all distinct and the three chosen are being ranked, so the order matters; 210

12.5 Practice B

1. a. 120   **b.** 20

2. a. 720   **b.** 30

3. a. 362,880   **b.** 72

4. 360   **5.** 12   **6.** 604,800

7. 1   **8.** 600   **9.** 27,907,200

10. 5040   **11.** 0.0083   **12.** 15

13. 15   **14.** 9   **15.** 1

16. 210   **17.** 1716   **18.** 3003

19. 53,130

20. permutations; The order in which the three top athletes finish matters; 830,490

21. combinations; The order in which the 6 seniors are chosen does not matter; 7,059,052

12.5 Enrichment and Extension

1. 2160   **2.** 720   **3.** 2880

4. 1440   **5.** 479,001,600   **6.** 1,437,004,800

7. 48   **8.** 72   **9.** 24

Answers

12.5 Puzzle Time

IT KNEW WHAT WAS IN STORE

12.6 Start Thinking

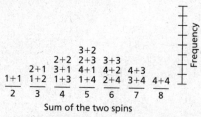

Sum: 2, Frequency: 1; Sum: 3, Frequency: 2; Sum: 4, Frequency: 3; Sum: 5, Frequency: 4; Sum: 6, Frequency: 3; Sum: 7, Frequency: 2; Sum: 8, Frequency: 1; *Sample answer*: It appears that the frequency chart has a vertical line of symmetry. The frequency starts at 1, climbs to 4, and then declines in a similar pattern back down to 1; {1, 2, 3, 4, 3, 2, 1}

12.6 Warm Up

1. 6   **2.** 7   **3.** 1   **4.** 126

5. 1   **6.** 11   **7.** 20   **8.** 45

12.6 Cumulative Review Warm Up

1. amplitude: 2; period: $\dfrac{2\pi}{3}$

2. amplitude: 1; period: 8

3. amplitude: $\dfrac{4}{3}$; period: $\dfrac{2\pi}{3}$

4. amplitude: 1; period: 2π

5. amplitude: $\dfrac{1}{2}$; period: 2π

6. amplitude: 3.8; period: $\dfrac{4\pi}{3}$

12.6 Practice A

1.

X	A	B	C
Outcomes	2	5	1
$P(X)$	$\dfrac{1}{4}$	$\dfrac{5}{8}$	$\dfrac{1}{8}$

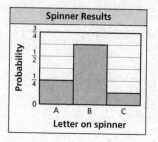

2.

F	Apples	Pears	Oranges
Outcomes	3	4	4
$P(F)$	$\dfrac{3}{11}$	$\dfrac{4}{11}$	$\dfrac{4}{11}$

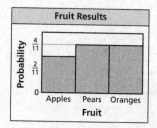

3. a. 2

   b. $\dfrac{5}{8}$

4. a. 6

   b. $\dfrac{1}{2}$

5. 0.0002   **6.** 0.0739   **7.** 0.0370

8. The exponents should sum to 6, the total number or rolls;

$$P(k = 4) = {}_6C_4\left(\dfrac{1}{6}\right)^4\left(\dfrac{5}{6}\right)^{6-4} \approx 0.008$$

Answers

12.6 Practice B

1.

V	1	2
Outcomes	15	11
$P(V)$	$\frac{15}{26}$	$\frac{11}{26}$

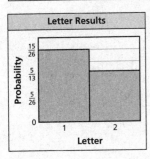

2.

X	1	2	3	4
Outcomes	3	6	22	4
$P(X)$	$\frac{3}{35}$	$\frac{6}{35}$	$\frac{22}{35}$	$\frac{4}{35}$

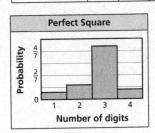

3. 0.0011   **4.** 0.0148   **5.** 0.0002

6. a.

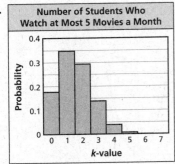

b. 1

c. 0.954

7. The number k is the number of successes (5), not the number showing on the number cube (4);

$$P(k = 5) = {}_6C_5\left(\frac{1}{6}\right)^5\left(\frac{5}{6}\right)^{6-5} \approx 0.006$$

8. a. not valid; The fifth box has the same probability (20%) as any other box of having a prize, and is not affected by the prize status of any previously opened boxes.

b. 0.4096

c. 0.32768

d. 0.00032

12.6 Enrichment and Extension

1. a. 4.8; 0.98

b. 0.34464

c. 0.90112

d. 0.7379

2. 20.28; 4.22   **3.** 2.4; 1.50   **4.** 40; 2.83

12.6 Puzzle Time

GRILLED HIM

Cumulative Review

1. $\frac{14}{80} = \frac{x}{100}$; $x = 17.5\%$

2. $\frac{x}{78} = \frac{74}{100}$; $x = 57.72$

3. $\frac{25.2}{35} = \frac{x}{100}$; $x = 72\%$

4. $\frac{9}{48} = \frac{x}{100}$; $x = 18.75\%$

5. $\frac{x}{63} = \frac{45}{100}$; $x = 28.35$

6. $\frac{15.68}{98} = \frac{x}{100}$; $x = 16\%$

7. $\frac{45}{120} = \frac{x}{100}$; $x = 37.5\%$

8. $\frac{x}{230} = \frac{32}{100}$; $x = 73.6$

9. $\frac{12.1}{55} = \frac{x}{100}$; $x = 22\%$

10. $\frac{57.8}{68} = \frac{x}{100}$; $x = 85\%$

Answers

11.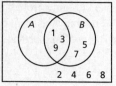

12.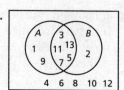

13.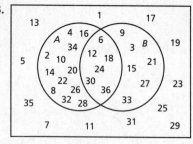

14.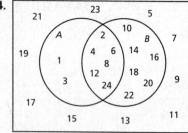

15.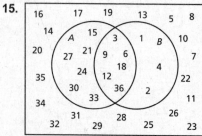

16.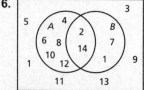

17. 87.3%

18. 8%

19. **a.** 82.9% **b.** 88.6% **c.** 5.7% better

20. translation 1 unit down

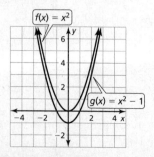

21. translation 9 units up

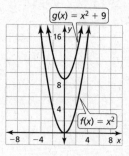

22. translation 5 units down

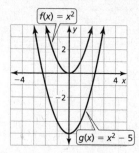

23. translation 3 units right

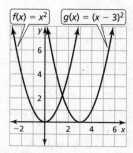

24. translation 6 units left

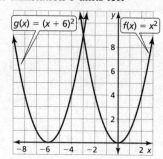

25. translation 4 units right

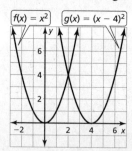

A124 **Geometry**
Answers

Answers

26. translation 9 units left and 3 units down

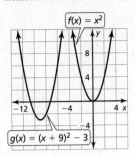

27. translation 2 units right and 6 units down

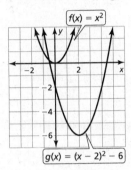

28. translation 5 units left and 8 units up

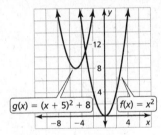

29. reflection in the x-axis

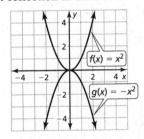

30. vertical stretch by a factor of 4

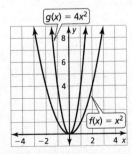

31. vertical stretch by a factor of 3 and a reflection in the x-axis

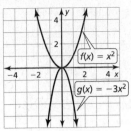

32. vertical shrink by a factor of $\dfrac{1}{4}$

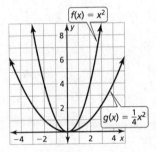

33. vertical shrink by a factor of $\dfrac{1}{2}$ and a reflection in the x-axis

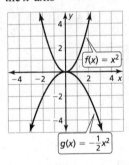

34. vertex: $(-5, 0)$, axis of symmetry: $x = -5$

35. vertex: $(9, 0)$, axis of symmetry: $x = 9$

36. vertex: $(0, 4)$, axis of symmetry: $x = 0$

37. vertex: $(0, -5)$, axis of symmetry: $x = 0$

38. vertex: $(-8, 1)$, axis of symmetry: $x = -8$

39. vertex: $(3, 8)$, axis of symmetry: $x = 3$

40. vertex: $(0, 7)$, axis of symmetry: $x = 0$

41. vertex: $(-1, -1)$, axis of symmetry: $x = -1$

Answers

42. vertex: $(6, -7)$, axis of symmetry: $x = 6$

43. vertex: $(8, -6)$, axis of symmetry: $x = 8$

44. $x = 4$ **45.** $x = 4$ **46.** $x = 5$

47. $x = 16$ **48.** $12i$ **49.** $7i$

50. $50i$ **51.** $-132i$ **52.** $40i\sqrt{5}$

53. $-24i\sqrt{2}$ **54.** $-1 - 9i$ **55.** $-9 - 8i$

56. $6 + 10i$ **57.** $8 - 23i$ **58.** $-2i$

59. $17 + 5i$ **60.** $-150 + 15i$ **61.** $48 - 30i$

62. $-42 - 134i$ **63.** $158 - 189i$ **64.** $-578i$

65. $-44 + 240i$ **66.** 3 **67.** 4

68. 5 **69.** 216 **70.** 36

71. 27 **72.** 2.08 **73.** 0.43

74. 9 **75.** 6.87 **76.** 8

77. 243 **78.** e^{10} **79.** e^8

80. $6e^9$ **81.** $3e^{18}$ **82.** $64e^{36x}$

83. $729e^{-12x}$ **84.** $8, 9, 10, 11, 12, 13$

85. $3, 2, 1, 0, -1, -2$ **86.** $-7, -6, -5, -4, -3, -2$

87. $1, 8, 27, 64, 125, 216$

88. $-1, 6, 25, 62, 123, 214$

89. $-2, 1, 6, 13, 22, 33$ **90.** $36, 25, 16, 9, 4, 1$

91. $4, 9, 16, 25, 36, 49$ **92.** 40

93. 285 **94.** 110 **95.** 123 **96.** -78

97. $\dfrac{208}{105}$ **98.** $\dfrac{565}{252}$ **99.** 12 **100.** 1785

101. **a.** $12.75

      b. 264 days

102. **a.** $a_n = n + 2$

      b. 33 dancers

      c. 42 dancers

      d. 9 dancers